THE TENTH MUSE

THE TENTH MUSE

WRITING ABOUT CINEMA IN THE MODERNIST PERIOD

LAURA MARCUS

OXFORD

UNIVERSITY PRESS

OXFORD

UNIVERSITY PRESS

Great Clarendon Street, Oxford OX2 6DP

Oxford University Press is a department of the University of Oxford.
It furthers the University's objective of excellence in research, scholarship,
and education by publishing worldwide in

Oxford New York

Auckland Cape Town Dar es Salaam Hong Kong Karachi
Kuala Lumpur Madrid Melbourne Mexico City Nairobi
New Delhi Shanghai Taipei Toronto

With offices in

Argentina Austria Brazil Chile Czech Republic France Greece
Guatemala Hungary Italy Japan Poland Portugal Singapore
South Korea Switzerland Thailand Turkey Ukraine Vietnam

Oxford is a registered trade mark of Oxford University Press
in the UK and in certain other countries

Published in the United States
by Oxford University Press Inc., New York

© Laura Marcus, 2007

British Library Cataloguing in Publication Data

Data available

Library of Congress Cataloging in Publication Data

Data available

Typeset by Laserwords Private Limited, Chennai, India
Printed in Great Britain
on acid-free paper by
Biddles Ltd., King's Lynn, Norfolk

ISBN 978–0–19–923027–3

1 3 5 7 9 10 8 6 4 2

For Daniel and William,
with love and gratitude

Acknowledgements

The research for this book has been conducted over a number of years, and I have accumulated many debts. I am very grateful to the British Academy and to the Leverhulme Trust for grants which enabled me to begin work in this field, and to the Arts and Humanities Research Council for a grant which allowed me to complete this book. I am also particularly grateful to the Beinecke Library at Yale University for granting me a Beinecke Visiting Fellowship (the H.D. Fellowship in English and American Literature) which enabled me to do extensive work on the papers of H.D. and Bryher. The Beinecke curators and staff were unfailingly informative and efficient. Janet Moat, in charge of Special Collections at the British Film Institute Library, was also extremely helpful during my visits to the BFI to work on the papers of Ivor Montagu, Thorold Dickinson and the Film Society. I have further benefited from library services at the University of Sussex, the London Library, the British Library, and the British Institute Library in Florence. Collaborative work with James Donald and Anne Friedberg on the film journal *Close Up* sowed the seeds of this book, and I would like to thank them both. I am grateful for research help to Paul Smethurst, Argha Banerjee and the late, and much missed, Chris Willis: it is my great regret that I cannot thank Chris for her generosity and enthusiasm, which contributed a great deal to this project. Anna Bogen gave much needed, and greatly appreciated, help with the manuscript at the eleventh hour. At Oxford University Press, I have had the good fortune to work with Jacqueline Baker, Tom Chandler, Elizabeth Robottom, Fiona Smith, and Andrew McNeillie: Andrew's interest in and support of this project from its early stages onwards has been an inspiration.

Birkbeck College gave research support in the very early stages of this project, and I am very grateful to former friends and colleagues there, including Steve Connor, Tom Healy and Carol Watts. The book was written during my years at the University of Sussex, and I would like to thank friends and colleagues there for advice and help of many kinds. Lindsay Smith was the most thoughtful and supportive of heads of department, making possible a period of research leave which enabled me to focus the project and to shape it into its final form. I am also grateful in this context to Steve Burman, Andrew Crozier, Michèle O'Malley, Alasdair Smith, and Jenny Taylor, and to Andrew Hadfield, for his support and for his encouraging comments on the manuscript. I have indeed had wonderful colleagues and graduate students at Sussex, and it is not possible to name them all: I would, however, like to thank, in particular, Paul Betts, Peter Boxall, Alistair Davies, Margaret Healy, Maurice Howard, David Mellor, Vicky Lebeau, Vincent Quinn, Nicholas Royle, Alan Sinfield, Daniel Steuer, Celine Surprenant, and Sophie Thomas for exemplary collegiality and friendship. Peter Nicholls has been a collaborator on many projects over the last few years, and our co-organization of the Centre for Modernist Studies at the University of Sussex has been immensely interesting and pleasurable. I am extremely grateful to him for intellectual inspiration of many kinds and in many capacities, and for a friendship that means a great deal to me.

I have benefited greatly from responses to parts of the book at seminars and conferences, and would like to thank, for invitations to speak at various events and for stimulating discussions, Sally Alexander, Tim Armstrong, Charles Barr, David Bradshaw, Peter Brooker, Peter Buse, Rod Edmond, Tom Gunning, Michael Hammond, Leslie Kathleen Hankins, Andrew Higson, Antonia Lant, Sally Ledger, Catherine Liu, Leo Mellor, Drew Milne, Julian Murphet, Lydia Rainford, John David Rhodes, Elinor Shaffer, Andrew Thacker, and David Trotter, as well as the organisers of, and participants in, the London Modernism Seminars and the Modernist Studies Association conferences. Deborah Parsons gave invaluable help and advice, and has been a loyal and valued friend, as have Rachel Bowlby, Claire Buck, Helen Carr, James Donald, Stephanie Hemelryk Donald, Paula Krebs, Alison Mark, Peter Middleton, Jo McDonagh, Howard Mills, Jan Montefiore, Lynn Nead, and Sharon Shaloo, who provided extraordinary hospitality during visits to the US. The friendship and advice of Isobel Armstrong has been sustaining throughout. My greatest debt of all is recorded in the dedication.

L.M.

Contents

List of Illustrations

Unless otherwise stated all images are reproduced by kind permission of the British Film Institute © BFI Stills.

Epigraphs

[Robert Sherwood] depicted a lovely muse as a symbol of the new art of the cinema: 'Apollo surveyed her; she was indeed comely, with a little of the Mona Lisa in her enigmatic smile, and a little of the Bella Donna in her baby-blue eyes. Flaxen curls tumbled in semi-permanent waves about her immature shoulders.' In no uncertain terms the tenth muse spoke: ' "I desire to break into the snobbish muse colony" '. Sherwood expressed his sympathy with this appeal, for 'the cinema is the tenth art, allied to the other arts in various degrees, and greater in its appeal than all of them. It embraces the young and the old, the rich and the poor, the strong and the weak—everyone, in fact, who possesses the price of admission, plus war tax.' At the conclusion of his allegory, Sherwood bid his readers to read *Life* weekly to discover how the new muse might substantiate her brave claims.[1]

People are only barely beginning to realise that an unforeseen art has come into being. One that is absolutely new. We must understand what this means. Drawing was on hand to see the mammoths die. Olympus heard the Muses numbered. Since then man has added to their official tally, which is actually a fraud in that it could be reduced to half a dozen, only styles, interpretations and subdivisions. Small minds sank without trace after running after pyroengraving. Books, railways, and automobiles were all amazing, of course, but they had precursors. They were varieties, but now a new species has mysteriously been born.[2]

Not only does a film ignore frontiers like an aeroplane, but it comes nearer the heart of mankind than any of the other arts. If the muses may be suspected of political tendencies, the deity that presides over the cinema is certainly Socialist. As Walt Whitman cried when he had succeeded in enticing the Muse over from empty Parnassus to the New York Exposition, 'She's here, installed amid the kitchen ware!'—he might have added prophetically, 'the Cinderella of the arts'.[3]

A chapter from a story: 'At the end of the Great War an improbable thing happened. The Festive Parnassus of the seven classical muses who were officially in session was invaded by a long-legged man with a rapid, somewhat surprisingly erratic gait, shaking his curly head of hair and the bowler perched on top of it and invariably waving a cane which he did not hesitate to poke under the noses of one of the respected muses. He took a jump and flopped down into the chairman's seat. Then, making

Figure 1. Lotte Reiniger, *The Tenth Muse.*

a very funny face and tugging at the black whiskers above his upper lip, he shouted (with difficulty, because he was obviously unaccustomed to speaking in such brilliant company) a strange phrase that amazed the inhabitants of Parnassus:

"DO YOU LIKE CHARLIE?"

That is how, unnoticed by the inhabitants of the RSFSR, the transformation of the poor old "bioscope" into a powerful art was accomplished and the genius of Charlie Chaplin took the eighth seat in the Council of the Muses'.[4]

Or perhaps some director may desert the arena for the Ivory Tower. He may decide that his art is creative rather than executive. Retaining all his prestige and decisive authority, he may toss his megaphone to some trusted subordinate and quit the hurly-burly of the floor. In his office he will build a sanctuary where he can be vacant and pensive and cultivate that 'inward eye' which turns the thing seen into the imagined thing; where he can woo this foundling, this Tenth Muse, this *Dea ex Machina*, of whom we know, at present, so little.[5]

The film purists insist on the mechanical nature of the process (as though a paintbrush, an engraving-tool, a piano, were not also pieces of mechanism). The true inspiration for the film, they say, is to be found in its technical possibilities. 'Der Apparat ist die Muse' (Béla Balázs). But it is necessary to distinguish between the tool and the material (the medium), between the *Apparat* and that which is operated upon. The sculptor's muse is not his chisel, but the marble; perhaps more accurately it is the impact of these two factors, creative inspiration depending on a sensuous reaction to the feel of the chisel against the marble. There is the same sensuous factor in the application of a charged brush to canvas; and the same factor is obvious in music. The camera is the film-director's tool, his medium is light, or rather the impact of light on solid objects. It might be better still to regard the camera as a chisel of light, cutting into the reality of objects. In any case, light is the muse.[6]

The greatness of the movies does not lie in their originality or creative power. Their mission has not been to discover new contents of the mind, unknown possibilities of beauty. They use quite legitimately the results of other, older forms of art, especially of the epic and dramatic kind. We may compare them to those plants which are not able to draw their sustenance from the soil directly, but must have their nourishment prepared by other organisms. But this new-born tenth Muse is no parasite. If she lays her hand on the possessions of her elder sisters, she does it because she can transmute them into something different. She turns over the wealth of the past to the present generation, she lets the great mass share in the gifts of the genius. She can do all that and more because she speaks the language of dreams better than anyone else ever did before.[7]

Introduction

The cinema has become so much a habit of thought and word and deed
as to make it impossible to visualize modern consciousness without it.[1]

The Tenth Muse explores writings on the cinema in the first decades of the
twentieth century, examining the impact of cinema on early twentieth-
century literary and, more broadly, aesthetic and cultural consciousness,
and bringing together the terms and strategies of early writing about
film with cinema's interactions with literature in the same period. One
of the book's primary concerns is to open up the ways in which early
writers about film—reviewers, critics, theorists—developed aesthetic and
cultural categories to define and accommodate what was called 'the seventh
art' or 'the tenth muse' and found discursive strategies adequate to the
representation of the new art and technology of cinema. The book also
examines the significance of film's newness for its early commentators, a
newness which was, indeed, made and remade in the decades following
cinema's emergence at the close of the nineteenth century. As late as 1931,
the film theorist and aesthetician Rudolf Arnheim was writing: 'For the
first time in history a new art form is developing and we can say that we
were there.' Here the remaking of cinema's birth was inseparable from the
perception that it had become an art form some years after its invention,
and the role of the writer on film was to chart this new birth.

In examining the writings of early film critics and commentators in
tandem with those of more specifically literary figures, *The Tenth Muse*
offers a new account of relationships between cinema and literature.[2]

Intertwining two major strands of research—the exploration of discourse about the cinema and cinema's presence in literary texts—it shows how issues central to an understanding of cinema (including questions of time, repetition, movement, emotion, vision, sound, and silence) are threaded through both kinds of writing, and explores the ways in which discursive and fictional writings overlap. The book also brings an awareness of cinema's change and development in its first decades into an account of the film—literature relationship, in order to show that this relation was itself dependent on time and place.

One of the defining aspects of the film medium is its interplay between the still and the moving image, and the fact that the projected film turns still into moving images. I examine the ways in which this double, or paradoxical, nature of the film medium shaped discussion of all kinds about cinema. Writers sought to do justice to the movement or motion of the film medium in their commentaries. Some used their writing as a way of halting, or attempting to halt, the flow of the film in an effort to capture a cinematic essence or, to borrow the words of the late nineteenth-century Symbolist poet Arthur Symons, 'to fix it fleetingly'.[3] For others, the function of film was less to crystallize or to conquer the fleeting image or instant than to trace the lineaments of motion itself, 'fixing the instant-by-instant movement of beings and things'.[4] And many critics and theorists, often following Futurist credos, celebrated the speed of film and its 'momentary aesthetic', in the term used by the avant-garde writer and film-maker Jean Epstein. Writing in 1921, Epstein argued that in modern literature (poetry as opposed to the classical theatre) and cinema, 'everything moves', in an aesthetic of 'mental rapidity' or 'seeing quickly', in which the very concept of 'the aesthetic' (conventionally identified with enduring forms of 'beauty') was inseparable from changing fashion:

> Within five years people will be writing cinematographic poems: 150 metres and 100 images arranged as a rosary on a string followed by the intelligence ... The film like contemporary literature accelerates unstable metamorphoses. From Autumn to Spring the aesthetic changes. One talks of the eternal canons of beauty when two successive catalogues of the Bon Marché confound this drivel. The fashion of clothing is the call to the most exact and the best modulated pleasure. Film borrows certain charms from it and it is such a faithful image of our fads that, when it is five years old, it is no more suitable than the fairground lantern.[5]

This understanding of the interrelatedness between fashion, film, time, and transience will recur throughout *The Tenth Muse*.

The interplay between stasis and mobility further intersects with that between the mechanical (frequently represented, as I show in Chapter 1, through images of dolls and automata) and the organic or living. The machine aesthetic, and the celebration of the machine, was central to avant-garde and experimental cinema and to film criticism and theory in the first decades of the century. Yet claims made for film as an art form were often dependent on the suppression of cinema's mechanical and technological dimensions and on attempts (discursive and conceptual) to construct for the medium an 'organic' birth and identity, frequently resting on its perceived ability to renew the representation of life itself.[6] The focus on 'rhythm' in much early writing about cinema was an aspect of a vitalism, strongly influenced by Bergsonian philosophy, which served to militate further against the concept of film as mere mechanism.

Bergson in *Creative Evolution* had stressed the limitations of the 'cinematographical' mechanism of our ordinary knowledge: the cinematograph produces only the illusion of movement, being composed in fact of separate and unconnected 'instants'. Yet cinema's 'becoming' an art owed much to the ways in which it could be represented in the Bergsonian terms of flux, mobility, and even creation itself. Bergson's account of 'creative evolution' strongly informed early writing on cinema, including that of the art historian Elie Faure, whose essay on film, translated into English in the early 1920s as 'The Art of Cineplastics', is discussed in later chapters. We could understand such 'Bergsonian' film writing as a reading against the grain of Bergson's own critique of the cinematographic as a model for time and consciousness, and as driven by the demand that cinema be defined in the terms of the 'mobility' of the inner and outer world so powerfully presented in Bergsonian thought. 'Movement is reality itself', Bergson wrote, a claim that echoed throughout early film aesthetics. The Bergsonism of early writing about cinema could, alternatively, be seen as an attempt to show that, while film in its very early manifestations might have been constituted by mere mechanism, it was now (two or three decades later, and as a result of its 'creative evolution') to be conceptualized in vitalist terms. This alternative conception might further have been informed by a suggestion given in Bergson's writings in *The Creative Mind*, in which he appeared to be departing from the position held in *Creative Evolution* (in which he had argued that the only real movement in film was to be located in the projecting apparatus) to one in which it is 'a weakness in our perception' which leads us 'to divide up the film image by image instead of grasping it in the aggregate'.[7] 'The unrolling of a cinemato-graphic film' might still, in this context, be used to analogize 'material systems which time merely glides over', phenomena 'calculable ahead of time'. The possibility remained, however, that such images, if grasped in the aggregate, might become 'an evolution' rather than 'an unfurling': 'If we could grasp [the universe] in its entirety, inorganic but interwoven with organic beings, we should see it ceaselessly taking on forms as new, as original, as unforeseeable as our states of consciousness'.[8] It is these terms that resonate throughout many of the film writings which I subsequently explore.[9]

For the drama and film critic Huntly Carter (who wrote at length on Russian theatre and film in the 1910s and 1920s, and whose commitment was to the social dimensions of film rather than its aesthetic status), the cinema was 'an organic part of human and social life': 'It seems to me that the only form of art expression ... that rightly belongs to the Cinema is that of the natural aesthetic of an object as when a spider weaves a web out of itself, or, as The Secret of Nature picture natural objects unfold and clothe themselves in their own aesthetic, through the exercise of the power of art expression inhering in themselves.'[10] The fascination with films which speeded up natural processes, as in the growth and unfolding of a flower, and with filmic slow-motion—the other side of the celebration of cinematic speed and motion—was also part of this sense that film could show the very workings of nature, opening up entirely new dimensions of the visible, and the invisible, world.

The power of the film to represent organic processes could, however, also be identified with its unique 'mechanical intelligence', its 'mechanical thought', in Jean Epstein's formulations. For Epstein, the cinema produced 'thought' or 'thinking' (independently of a human observer) precisely because it was able to generate new and unprecedented forms and relations of time and space. This understanding of the machine mind of the medium also informed the writings on film of a number of other critics, including Alexander Bakshy and Arnold Hauser, discussed later in this book, and would be taken up in the film theory of Gilles Deleuze.[11] Writing about the cinema thus not only upheld, but also displaced and reworked, cultural and conceptual distinctions between mechanism and organism.

Film's movement presented new challenges to the critic and commentator, whose object was not only mobile but also transient and ephemeral. Just as spectators had to learn how to read and interpret the new relations of time, space, and narrative that cinema brought into being, the critic had to deploy the faculty of judgement on the move. The repeated verbal play on 'moving' as pertaining to both motion and emotion is a crucial reminder that both these terms are connoted by the Greek word *kinema*, an association central to phenomenological understandings of film spectatorship and to concepts of embodied perception and the embodied viewer at the heart of more recent critical approaches to 'haptic' cinema.[12] As I note throughout this study, the writings of many early film critics and commentators revealed an acute awareness not only of the relationships between filmic motion and the modernity that they inhabited, but also of the need to articulate new understandings of vision and identity in a moving world.

A rather different version of the relationship between 'motion' and 'emotion' informed more cautious early commentaries on the cinema. In 1921 the British literary and drama critic A. J. Walkley commented that 'the movies would be all the more moving for moving slower', his remark revealing something of the widespread anxiety over the extent to which the speed and transience of film and, indeed, its 'mechanical' nature, could coexist with emotional and aesthetic affect.[13] This concern was also expressed in an early pamphlet on film, 'The Photodrama: Its Place among the Fine Arts' (1915), in which its author, the US scenario writer William Morgan Hannon, wrote: 'the moving picture play is moving only in a mechanical and physical sense to a great extent. When it is moving drama in the sense that it moves the mind, the will, the heart, the soul of man, then, and then only, does it enjoy its highest evolution'.[14]

Writing in his journal in the first years of the 1920s, Gamaliel Bradford, the early twentieth-century American biographer or, in his term, 'psychographer' (the study of individuals being the study of 'souls'), described his cinema-going, and the ambivalent responses it generated in him, through the frameworks of psychology and aesthetics:

April 2 [1921]—Again my usual Saturday afternoon experience with the movies and again puzzled and deeply interested by the effect upon me personally. The piece of the most utterly commonplace type, melodrama of love and sentiment, a girl brought up by a snobbish mother, converted by love, working as waitress in a restaurant to prove her democracy, and

then, of course, united to her noble and handsome young man. Nothing
of Harold Bell Wright would be more thoroughly ordinary. Yet it held me
in absorbed interest from beginning to end and in the appropriate crises of
sentiment my eyes regularly filled with tears as they would not be likely to
do at anything of a great artistic effect in the regular theatre. Why is it? Why?
Something about the continuous movement of the things, there being no
break whatever in the silence and darkness. The being all alone, as it were,
with such an elementary display of human passion somehow takes hold of
one. But it is exceedingly curious, this reducing the drama to its elements by
the elimination of style and all literary quality.[15]

Absorption was thus followed by analysis, and the 'experience' was recalled
as a form of experiment: 'the old curious psychological study'. Bradford
was, as he represented it, taken over by the movies in ways that ran counter
to his tastes, his sensibilities, and, it is implied, his class and cultural status.
He was drawn in, taken hold of, by the 'continuous movement', the
absence of a break or interval in, or from, the 'silence and darkness', and
the 'being all alone' with, or in the face of, the emotional intensities of the
melodrama.

A few years prior to Bradford's musings on his responses to the movies,
the psychologist and Harvard professor Hugo Münsterberg had published
his account of the 'new art' of the film, *The Photoplay: A Psychological Study*,
a text I discuss in detail in Chapter 3. At the heart of his study was his
discussion of 'Emotions', an invaluable account of the range of positions
on the topic available to him in the early decades of the twentieth century,
and, in its exploration of the relationship between emotions projected by
the actors to the audience, and those projected from the spectator into
the world of the screen, a formative influence on later cognitive film
theories.[16] 'To picture emotion must be the central aim of the photoplay',
Münsterberg wrote: 'More than in the drama, the persons in the photoplay
are to us, first of all, subjects of emotional experience. Their joy and pain,
their hope and fear, their love and hate, their gratitude and envy, their
sympathy and malice, give meaning to the play.'[17]

The expression of the emotions (following Darwin's study *The Expression
of the Emotions in Man and Animals*, one of the first texts to use photographs
to illustrate its arguments) was perceived by Münsterberg as in large
part, and in the absence of words in the silent cinema, physical and
physiognomic: 'gestures, actions, and facial play are so interwoven with
the physical process of an intense emotion that every shade can find its

characteristic delivery.'[18] It was the power of the filmic close-up (the defining device of the film, unavailable to the stage) that it could enlarge 'this emotional action of the face to sharpest relief' or show us 'a play of the hands in which anger and rage or tender love or jealousy speak in unmistakeable language'. There was a danger, as he and other critics perceived it, in the use of exaggerated facial expressions, deriving from actors' flawed attempts at the imitation and performance of involuntary physiological responses. For the German novelist Robert Musil, as for Virginia Woolf in her essay 'The Cinema' (1926), the expression of emotion in the cinema was to be rejected when it became a trivial or clichéd expressivity, 'where anger becomes rolling of eyes, virtue is beauty, and the entire soul is a paved avenue of familiar allegories'.[19] Nonetheless, the concept of the essentially 'physiognomic' basis of filmic expression was powerfully developed in subsequent writing on film, including that of Jean Epstein and Béla Balázs, where it became inseparable from a perception of 'the face of things', in an inversion of habitual views of the relationship between animate and inanimate objects, and expressive and inexpressive forms. As Balázs wrote, in *Der Sichtbare Mensch*, published in the early 1920s:

> In the world of speaking human beings, silent things are far more lifeless and insignificant than the human being. They are allowed only a life of the second and third order, and even that only in rare moments of especially clear-sighted sensitivity in the people who observe them ... But in the shared silence inanimate things become homogeneous with people and gain thereby vitality and significance. This is the riddle of that special film atmosphere, which lies beyond the capacity of literature.[20]

The understanding of the cinema as an essentially silent medium, making its appeal to the eye alone (a view which became such a site of contestation in the 1920s, with the coming of sound to film) was thus substantially predicated on the belief that expressivity was to be located in 'mute' forms of life. It also reinforced the perception that it was the power of the cinema, with its renewal of the sense of sight and the power of the eye, to recapture and transmit 'primary', 'primal' or, in some formulations, 'primitive' emotions, such as Fear, Anger, Sadness, Joy, in a direct and unmediated fashion. Writing in the first issue of the journal *Experimental Cinema* the critic David Platt claimed: 'In Cinema, emotion is caught and fixed at the very moment it is felt, in all its purity. Things are conceived as they are perceived; to think is to act. In that lies the *omnipotence* of the medium. This is the new cinema.'[21]

Critical debates over the need to develop an adequate film criticism and theory were often premised on the view that it was only in this way that enduring works of art could be created in and from the new medium. Such questions informed the studies of film that began to appear in the mid-1910s, but that grew greatly in number in the 1920s. They intersected with that branch of modernist aesthetics which sought to define the essential nature of any given art form. Assertions of the autonomy of film were crucial to the demand that it be recognized as an art, with its own laws and practices, but there were also strong moves to identify film with one or more of the established arts, including theatre, ballet, opera, music and literature. For film's detractors, on the other hand, the medium was seen as merely parasitic upon these 'higher' cultural forms.

While the task of locating a cinematic essence was central to cultural theory in the 1920s, it was nonetheless the case that discursive approaches to, and representations of, the cinematic in this period frequently rendered it as a hybrid form, combining the representational devices of the verbal and the visual, the word and the image. As Michael North has shown, in his recent study *Camera Works*, photography was perceived, at its nineteenth-century beginnings, as 'Words of Light': 'The sense remained strong that photography provided a sort of notation suspended somehow between letters and pictures, a new alphabet, as it were.'[22] North also addresses the paradox that the camera, 'celebrated from the first as objectivity incarnate, also came to serve as one of modernity's most powerful emblems of the subjectivity of perception and knowledge'.[23] He argues that it was this revelation of 'the rich possibilities left to art by the very imperfection of our sensory filters', combined with the fascination of the new association between word and image, that made photography, and cinematography, a central model for modern art and literature to follow.[24]

In the French film criticism and aesthetics that flourished in the early decades of the century, the equation made between cinema and writing was particularly marked. The poet Blaise Cendrars produced his 'alphabet' of cinema, while Ricciotto Canudo, in his 'Reflections on the Seventh Art', claimed that cinema was 'renewing writing', harking

back to the origin of language in images.[25] Anticipating the development of a 'grammar' of the film, and later semiotic approaches to
film language, most fully articulated in the work of Christian Metz,
the early focus on film writing was also closely linked to the modernist fascination with ideographic and hieroglyphic languages, perceived
to lie between, or to conjoin, word and image. Gesture in the silent
film and the appearance of characters as, in Canudo's words, 'light hu-
manized into dramatic symbols',[26] were also versions of the cinematic
alphabet.

A further dimension of film writing lay in the use of script within the
film, as in the use of intertitles and 'leaders', a topic of much debate in
the 1920s. These forms of writing in film were connected, in significant
ways, to writing about film. In the detailed discussions of early twentieth-
century film criticism in the second part of this book (in Chapters 3–5)
I have sought to show that the preoccupation with word and image,
and with concepts of inscription, light-writing, and hieroglyphics, was not
only an aspect of avant-garde discourse, but also permeated writing about
cinema in a variety of contexts, including those of more mainstream film
criticism.

Early film criticism was, also, however, bound up with talking and
commentary. In the late 1920s, the Imagist poet John Gould Fletcher
wrote: 'Although the film is not, essentially, a medium for words, it
by no means follows that we ought not to talk about the film. As a
matter of fact, the more we do talk about it, the better.'[27] For Tom
Conley, early film brought into being a new form of 'civil conversation'—'The spectator could go to the movie in order to learn how to
talk in the imagination, and how, too, to revive dialogue within his or
her own body, in mimesis of a new panoply of silent types, without
the need of interlocutors'—while at the same time conversation or dialogue became affiliated with printed writings (intertitles which became
'instantaneous reprieves from the labor engaged in the decipherment of
images').[28] Other recent critics have pointed up the significance, and
the historical and gendered dimensions, of the spectator's conversational
behaviour (or cultural representations of such behaviour) in the (silent)
cinema. As Shelley Stamp notes, in her study of women and early film
culture: 'the practice of talking through pictures … was replaced by viewing practices that de-emphasized both the theater space and the viewer's
body … a model of silent, absorbed spectatorship became the norm, a

mode of attention more appropriate for viewing longer, multireel films that were themselves less dependent on extratextual information'.[29] One of the topics explored in this book is that of the relationship between representations of the spectator's speech and silence and the development of film criticism: as I suggest in Chapter 3, writing about the silent film, in particular, came to function as a form of 'talking in the cinema', an issue also at the heart of the novelist Dorothy Richardson's writings on film, discussed in Chapter 5. In more general terms, the diverse writings about cinema in its first decades existed in a complex relationship with concepts of 'conversation', 'commentary', 'voice-over', 'voice-off', and 'internal monologue'. 'Silent or talkie', Gilles Deleuze wrote, 'cinema constitutes an immense "internal monologue" which constantly internalizes and externalizes itself.'[30]

Conceptions of film hieroglyphics, discussed throughout this book, were, however, connected not only to representations of speech and of writing but also, as I have suggested, to a language of the body. As the German writer and aesthetician Walter S. Bloem stated in 1924: 'The means at the disposal of the film actor is his body, which admits of unmeasured and unaccounted possibilities in the way of expressing emotions... In the future, mimicry must develop into an intimate and familiar language.'[31] The concept of 'mimicry' is a significant one here, suggestive not only of the belief in the body's ability to interpret inner feeling as movement but also of new understandings of 'mimesis' and film's doubled nature in its (mechanical) reproductions of the world. Such perceptions of the 'speaking' body further intersected, however, with the ideals of the 'elemental' gesture and physical expressiveness developed and developing in symbolist, expressionist and avant-garde theatre, with its return to ritualized and stylized forms and its conceptions of the power of non-verbal drama to recreate 'primal' emotions. As the modernist writer and dramatist John Rodker, whose work I discuss in Chapter 1, asserted:

> The theatre is the staging for emotion; has been, must be.
> Emotion invariably translates itself into action, immediate or deferred.
> Never in words.
> Words are a waste product of emotion and do not concern it.[32]

While many of the claims of early film writing and aesthetics were predicated on a radical separation between stage and screen, there were in fact significant continuities between the two art forms, in some of their manifestations at least, and in the ways in which they were theorized.

A number of recent studies have opened up new dimensions of the significance of cinema for the avant-garde and for modernist writers in the early twentieth century, and to some extent *The Tenth Muse* is a contribution to this field. My concern has also been, however, with the work of those writers who could be categorized as 'modern' but not necessarily 'modernist', including Rudyard Kipling and H. G. Wells, whose relationship to cinema I explore in some detail. My choice of writers in the first part of the book has been substantially guided by the extent to which their work directly commented on the new medium, in both fictional and non-fictional forms, though my discussion of Virginia Woolf is also concerned with the more diffuse impact of the film medium on her writing.

   Bringing Wells and Woolf together as writers whose work was strongly, though in different ways and to different ends, shaped by cinema, must inevitably raise the question of the relationship between 'the modern' and 'the modernist'. Wells was, after all, one of the writers whom Woolf placed at the heart of her critique of literary naturalism in her essays on fiction of the early 1920s and her early criticism of film as a merely 'locomotive' medium was connected to her repudiation of 'the railway line of a sentence' which typified, in her view, the naturalist and realist novels of Galsworthy, Bennett, Wells, and others. A different version of the film medium emerged for Woolf when she saw its potential for forms of intense visualization and for radical transitions in time and in space, which could be translated into the novel form. These were, however, also its appeals for H. G. Wells, and in looking at the work of both writers as responses to the film medium, new relationships emerge between them. *To the Lighthouse* represents, like Wells's early fiction, forms of time-travel and the passage or time-tunnel between past, present, and future; *Mrs Dalloway* is, in its way, as much a celebration of movement in and through city spaces as Wells's technological and futurological city fantasies; *The Waves* explores the origins of life, and of consciousness emerging out of a world of images, in ways that are, at least, connected to Wells's evolutionary imaginings. Despite the radical differences between Wells and Woolf as writers and thinkers, the exploration of the presence and play of the cinematic in their work might give us new terms for configuring their differences and their connections.

The second part of *The Tenth Muse* explores film criticism and film aesthetics in the first decades of the twentieth century. The primary focus is on British contexts, but Chapter 3 discusses US film theory, and Chapter 5, which examines 'the moment' of the film journal *Close Up*, explores the internationalist dimensions of the film writing and film culture of the period. Just as similar arguments are presented by the mainly literary and academic figures who dominate the early chapters and by the emergent cinema critics whose work is more prominent in the later chapters, so we find related discussions in a number of different national contexts, notably what came to be called the Kino-Debatte in Germany[33] and similar debates in France[34] and Russia[35]. The Kino-Debatte involved writers of all kinds and centrally concerned the relation between film and literature and theatre, as well as themes such as the city and mass culture.

Many of the contributions, including one by Georg Lukács, concerned the question of a cinema aesthetic. For Lukács, stage drama and film were to be divided along the axis of presence and absence respectively: 'The lack of this "presence" is the key characteristic of the "cinema". It is not because films are imperfect, nor because their characters can presently only move but not speak. It is precisely because they are not people, but the movements and actions of people. This is not a lack of the "cinema"; it is its limitation, its *principium stilisationis*.'[36] The terms of absence and presence resonate throughout much of the film criticism and theory I discuss in this book, from the writings in the 1910s of Hugo Münsterberg through to the work of Christian Metz and Stanley Cavell. They also informed, as I show in detail in Chapter 2, Virginia Woolf's writing on, and fictional incorporations of, the cinema and the cinematic.

In the poet and Chaplin enthusiast Yvan Goll's dramatic phrase, cited by Anton Kaes at the beginning of his introduction to his edited collection, 'The basis for all new art to come is the cinema.' The film theorist Béla Balázs saw cinema as having turned culture back towards the visual, after an overemphasis on the conceptual following the introduction of printing. Film revived the language of gesture, 'the real mother tongue of humanity'.[37] Cinema was seen variously as a threat to theatre or as its salvation from massification, as it was by Alfred Lichtenstein.[38] As

Sabine Hake writes, in her comprehensive discussion of the German context:

> Early German film criticism fulfilled a double function. It promoted and evaluated films, and it used their narratives to discuss problems relevant to culture and society at large. On a more conceptual level, emerging film theory did the same: theorists analyzed the mechanisms by which film was constituted as a cultural and artistic practice and, on the basis of its formal characteristics, tried to articulate the relationship between narrative, representation, and visual pleasure.[39]

Similar concerns could be found elsewhere across Europe and North America. In France, for instance, Louis Delluc stressed the 'absolute novelty' of the cinema,[40] an art which is 'an advance towards the elimination of art which surpasses art, in that it is life'.[41]

Russian debates were marked by the massive caesura of 1917; thus the English version of Yuri Tsivian's book on the early reception of cinema in Russia ends in 1920, when private film production ended, rather than the original's 1930. His important study reflects the Russian discussion itself in its close creative engagement with technical aspects of film and performance, marked by Sergei Eisenstein's own fusion of theory and practice. Finally, it is important to note that these national debates intersected with one another, as I show in some more detailed aspects in this book. Silent film was, at least by aspiration, quintessentially international, and film theory and criticism tended to reflect this. As Hake argues, the coming of sound brought 'a growing concern with the process of economic concentration and what was perceived as betrayal of the cinema's original mission as a democratic, international art for the masses'.[42] In the final sections of this book I take up the question of the transition to sound, though I focus on its significance for writers on, and for, the cinema. More generally, my focus on British and, though to a lesser extent, US writings on the cinema is intended to complement the exceptional work, such as that of Abel, Kaes, Hake, Tsivian, and Richard Taylor, that has been produced on French, German, and Russian film writings and film contexts.

Chapter 1 looks at a number of texts—literary and discursive—in which early film is represented, and explores the ways in which writers represented the machinery of the early cinema, and its projections. It discusses writers' depictions of cinema at the close of the nineteenth century and the early twentieth century and the processes by which the genres of 'talking in the cinema' were formed and developed. The impact of film on literature was of course place and time specific, demanding a more particularized and less abstract model of the 'cinematographic' than has been offered in many accounts of the film–literature relationship. Fictional representations and literary incorporations of the cinematic, and statements by early writers on film, frequently inscribed a history, and a historiography, of pre-cinematic and cinematic modes and technologies. The chapter reads literary texts in tandem with writings (critical and journalistic) that were attempting to capture the impact of the new medium, exploring the multiplicity of ways in which it was encountered by, and impacted upon, writers.

   This chapter explores relationships between early film technologies, the first commentaries on the cinema (at the close of the nineteenth century and in the first decades of the twentieth) and literary responses to film in this period, including those of Villiers de l'Isle Adam, H. G. Wells, Maxim Gorki, Rudyard Kipling, D. H. Lawrence, H.D., John Rodker, and James Joyce. It discusses the ways in which early commentators and writers represented filmic motion and the mechanical dimensions of the cinematic apparatus, exploring some of the central tropes and images deployed to represent film, including the 'automatic woman' and the 'danse macabre'. The focus of the chapter is also on writings in which film is represented, directly or obliquely, which often functioned as allegories of the birth and evolution of cinema, and on the ways in which writers on the cinema in its first years developed a genre and a language with which to describe the new medium, with its unprecedented powers of movement.

   Chapter 2 situates Virginia Woolf's relationships to cinema in the context of Bloomsbury culture and aesthetics. It explores in detail Woolf's important essay 'The Cinema', and traces, through her fiction, the variety of ways in which the filmic emerges in her writings. It makes the argument that, while many aspects of photography and cinematography were of long-standing significance to her (including the interplay of presence and absence, time and motion, the representation of emotion in art and the relationship between past and present), the ways in which Woolf represented these dimensions altered substantially between her early experimental writing (including *Jacob's Room*) and her fiction of the 1930s, in particular *The Years*, written in the context of sound film.

Chapter 3 is concerned with aesthetics and early film criticism, with a focus on the United States. Writers on the cinema in its first decades took on something of the role of the early 'film lecturer' or 'film explainer' (who, in the early years of cinema, provided a spoken commentary to accompany films as they were projected), pointing to ways of seeing appropriate to the new medium of film. They also had to find discursive strategies adequate to the new art and technology; in particular its powers of motion and the intensity of its appeal to the eye. The chapter looks at the focus on 'the glimpse of beauty' in early discussions of film and, more broadly, the relationships between temporality and aesthetics in film writings, with particular reference to the writings of Vachel Lindsay, Victor O. Freeburg, Hugo Münsterberg, and Gilbert Seldes, authors of the first English-language books of film criticism and theory. The development of an aesthetic for film, as evidenced in these first book-length studies of cinema, demanded a recalibration of the relations between the arts. If film were to be claimed as an art form, should it be allied to one of the established arts, or should a claim be made for its aesthetic autonomy? The various answers given to this question in early film literature had a significant impact on the perception and reception of cinema, and on the development of film criticism and theory.

Chapter 4 extends the exploration of the ways in which film criticism developed in cinema's first decades, examining writing about film in the contexts of 1920s Britain. It discusses a number of the works of film criticism and theory that were published in the 1920s, including books by Iris Barry, Eric Walter White, Eric Elliott, and Ernest Betts. It looks at the emergence of film criticism in periodical literature: before the specialized film critic came into being, the role was taken by, variously, theatre, art, ballet, and literary critics, and this choice significantly affected the ways in which the 'aesthetic' of film was defined. The chapter also examines the film writings of some of the first film critics to establish themselves as experts in the new medium, including Robert Herring (of the *London Mercury* and, as discussed in Chapter 5, the film journal *Close Up*), C. A. (Caroline) Lejeune (*Manchester Guardian*, *Observer*, and author of *Cinema* (1930)), and Iris Barry (*Daily Mail*, *Spectator*, and author of *Let's Go the Pictures* (1926)). I discuss the centrality of women film critics in this period, and the question of the gendered nature of film writings.

Iris Barry was one of the founding members of the Film Society, established in London in 1925 to show 'art' and experimental films, as well as early cinema, and to provide a forum for Soviet film, banned in Britain at this time. Chapter 4 outlines some of the key dimensions of the Film Society's project and history, and the role played by Ivor Montagu, another founder member, who translated the film writings of V. I. Pudovkin, and established essential links between British and Soviet film cultures, campaigning for the exhibition of Soviet cinema in Britain during a period of censorship. It also explores the material conditions of film spectatorship and exhibition in the early decades of the century as a further dimension of film's transience, leading to the desire not only to preserve the fragile film stock, but also to give some kind of permanence and historical contour to the medium in archives and film museums.

Close Up, discussed in Chapter 5, described itself as 'The Only Magazine Devoted to Films as an Art'. Founded by the writer Bryher (Winifred Ellerman) and the Scottish artist Kenneth Macpherson, and with substantial contributions from the writers H.D. and Dorothy Richardson, *Close Up* played a crucial role in developments in film culture and film theory; its contributions included, for example, the first English-language versions of some of Eisenstein's most significant articles. The journal represents a moment in which new theories of psychoanalysis and educational theory met a new critical and analytical awareness of the filmic medium, founding a concern with gender, spectatorship and the cinematic apparatus. The years of *Close Up* were, moreover, those of the transition from silent to sound film, and the journal is a primary resource for cultural perceptions of the 'transition'. This chapter outlines these aspects of the journal, while focusing on the ways in which it attempted to create a discursive medium and forum adequate to the new art, and constructed spectatorship and 'writing about cinema' as a form of 'film-making'. Writings by Bryher, Macpherson, and Robert Herring are of central significance here, as are the films made by the *Close Up* group, in particular *Borderline* (in which Paul Robeson appeared). The chapter also looks at the intersections between H.D.'s and Dorothy Richardson's film writings and their literary work. It addresses the ways in which literary modernism was centrally informed by cinematic consciousness, exploring the relationship between an 'imagist' poetics and film aesthetics, and examining the representation of 'movement' in both the literary and film-writing of the period.

The final section of the book discusses two early sound films, *The Jazz Singer* and Hitchcock's *Blackmail*, and their critical reception. It also addresses the ways in which new relationships between writers and the cinema, and forms of writing about cinema, emerged in the 1930s, substantially shaped by the coming of sound and by a 'documentary' culture in which the uses of commentary and voice-over raised new questions about the relationship between literature and film, including calls such as the film critic Paul Rotha's, in his *Documentary Film* (1936/39) (in the context of a brief reference to W. H. Auden's verses, commissioned and written for documentary films) for the introduction of 'poetry into film speech'. The coming of sound film in the late 1920s changed the ways in which cinema history was understood and narrated, altering both the discursive forms taken by writing about cinema and the understanding of the film–literature relationship.

I

The Things That Move:

Early Film and Literature

[T]he primordial basis of the enjoyment of moving pictures was not an objective interest in a specific subject matter, much less an aesthetic interest in the formal presentation of subject matter, but the sheer delight in the fact that things seemed to move, no matter what things they were.[1]

As regards the content of vision which are placed before us by the motion picture, we are therefore faced here with a peculiar world which is both more restricted and more expanded than the one we are habitually confronting in our daily life. It is as if we were suddenly to lose our sense of hearing while at the same time acquiring a more powerful sense of vision, as well as a new sense of hovering in time in any direction we may wish—in fact of moulding time—rearranging its natural sequences, compressing it into a single moment or expanding it into an infinity. Even Wells's 'time-machine' could not perform such miracles.[2]

Films are 'fabricated' and they remain tied to an apparatus, to a machine in a narrower sense than the products of the other arts. The machine here stands both between the creative subject and his work and between the receptive subject and his enjoyment of art. The motory, the mechanical, the automatically moving, is the basic phenomenon of the film. Running and racing, travelling and flying, escape and pursuit, the overcoming of spatial obstacles is the cinematic theme par excellence. The film never feels so much in its element as when it has to describe movement, speed and pace. The wonders and mischievous tricks of instruments, automata and vehicles are among its oldest and most effective subjects.[3]

Representations of cinema in its early years were inseparable from the cultural and conceptual fascination with questions of motion and movement. These, in turn, were related to an understanding of film motion as, for better or worse, essentially 'locomotive'. Cinema was frequently, as in the quotations above, represented as a form of 'transport'—with its dual connotations, like those of *kinema*, of 'motion' and 'emotion'—and as a machine with the powers to move the spectator through time and space in ways to some extent anticipated in the great machine of the nineteenth century, the railway, but now magically realized in the virtual realm of representation. 'The only real thing in the motion picture', Alexander Bakshy wrote in 1927, 'is *movement* without which all its objects would appear as lifeless shadows ... There are, therefore, clearly defined limits for the illusionist effects of real life and nature in the motion picture: the latter can be realistic only when its shadowy world is set in motion.'[4]

Early cinema came into being with the representation of the moving train, as in the Lumière brothers' 1895 film *Arrivée d'un train en gare à La Ciotat* (*Arrival of a Train at La Ciotat Station*), and extreme motion was in general the filmic motor in the first decades of the medium, with its chase-sequences, representations of city transport, the automobile, and machine-imagery. These dynamics subsequently powered the avant-garde cinema of the 1920s onwards, often blurring the boundaries between narrative cinema and avant-garde film, as experimental film-makers extracted and abstracted machine-movement from the motors of plot and characterization. Writing about cinema—literary and discursive—also took up the question and the representation of motion and locomotion, with the locomotive often appearing as an irruptive force in the fictional text.

In *The Last Machine,* the film historian Ian Christie describes the cinema as 'a laboratory for the twentieth-century imagination'. In accord with a number of recent critics who have argued that the dream of, and demand for, specific technologies tends to precede their actual invention, Christie writes of the nineteenth-century context:

> Space and time were becoming linked in the popular mind, even before science took up the theme. Verne's heroes get ahead of themselves, or travel beyond the end of the map, just as Rider Haggard's explorers in *She* escape from civilisation into the seductive fantasy of eternal youth. What these and many other popular artists created was a cinematic vision before the invention of moving pictures, a space and time machine of the imagination. In this, they joined Zola, Dickens, Tolstoy, Turner, Degas, Wagner and those others who also anticipated the aesthetics of cinema. For they were the first to us the close-up, slow-motion, a moving viewpoint, cross-cutting, the physical sensation of speed and the drama of darkness and light. They, rather than the many local inventors of the camera and the projector, were the pioneers of

cinema as a new kind of experience. All that remained was for reality to catch up with fiction, which it started to do in 1895 as a new industry emerged.[5]

The argument echoes that made by Sergei Eisenstein, in his influential essay 'Dickens, Griffiths and the Film Today', in which he criticized the idea, promoted by so many early writers on film, of

some incredible virgin-birth of this art ... for me personally it is always pleasing to recognize again and again the fact that our cinema is not altogether without parents and without pedigree, without a past, without the traditions and rich cultural heritage of the past epochs. Let Dickens and the whole ancestral array, going back as far as the Greeks and Shakespeare, be superfluous reminders that both Griffith and our cinema prove our origins to be not solely as of Edison and his fellow inventors, but as based on an enormous cultured past; each part of this past in its own moment of world history has moved forward the great art of cinematography. Let this past be a reproach to those thoughtless people who have displayed arrogance in reference to literature, which has contributed so much to this apparently unprecedented art and is, in the first and most important place: the art of viewing—not only the eye, but *viewing*—both meanings being embraced in this term.[6]

The group of 'thoughtless people who have displayed arrogance in reference to literature' might well have included the avant-garde Russian film maker Dziga-Vertov, whose Kino-eye manifestos proclaimed loudly the independence of film from literature and theatre, and whose film *The Man with a Movie Camera* was advertised as a film without intertitles—that is, as free of literary discourse and, by extension, influence. In partially displacing 'Edison and his fellow inventors' as the originators of cinema, Eisenstein was not only granting cinema a longer history, but to some extent substituting the history of 'culture' for that of technology.

The existence of 'a cinematic vision before the invention of cinema' remains a speculative question which, if it were to be adequately explored, would require a detailed analysis of the long history of pre-cinematic visual technologies. My concern is rather with the coexistence of cinema and of the 'cinematic vision' as it emerged in fictional and other writings of the late nineteenth- and early twentieth-centuries, from early accounts of film technology in the writings of Thomas Alva Edison and his collaborator and 'biographer' W. K. L. Dickson, through to the 'filmic' visions of the modernist writers John Rodker and James Joyce. There is a symbiotic relationship, I suggest, between 'culture' and 'technology', and between 'literature' and 'technology', which is particularly marked or, at least, marked in particular ways, in the historical period under discussion: the close of the nineteenth century and the early decades of the twentieth.

This period, and the cultural products and imaginings that emerged from it, were mapped out in Stephen Kern's influential study *The Culture of Time and Space: 1880–1918.* 'From around 1880 to the outbreak of World War 1', Kern wrote, 'a series of sweeping changes in technology and culture created distinctive new modes of thinking about and experiencing time and space'.[7] He argued that the revolutionizing of experiences of time and space arose from 'new energy sources' and 'a crisis of abundance', inseparable from the new experiences of speed and acceleration. Discussion of the cinema is threaded throughout Kern's study, along with accounts of philosophical and literary texts, cultural history, and the visual arts. For Kern, film variously represents 'the technological link' between the 'motion studies' of Marey and Muybridge and the analyses of motion and ergonomics in 'scientific management'; the reproduction of 'the mechanization, jerkiness and rush of modern times';[8] a revolutionizing of the sense of 'distance' and new configurations of time and space; and an argument for 'the persistence of the past and its impact on the present'.[9] There is a strong, though not exclusive, focus in his invocations of the cinema on its avant-garde appropriations, including those of the Futurists.

Kern's book contributed very substantially to a new direction in the study of modernism: an understanding of its inseparability from the exploration of modernity, in which technology played a foundational role. Recent work by Lynne Kirby, Sara Danius, Tim Armstrong, Leo Charney, and many others has both extended and particularized Kern's synoptic study.[10] Danius, for example, has focused on the meanings of 'speed' and 'automobilization' for Proust and, in her *The Senses of Modernism: Technology, Perception and Aesthetics,* analyses the work of Proust, Mann and Joyce through early twentieth-century technologies of perception, including film, the telephone, and the X-ray: 'to chart how the question of perception, notably sight and hearing, is configured in the modernist period is to witness the ever-closer relationship between the sensuous and the technological'.[11] The 'modernist' body thus plays a role that it does not have in Kern's study, connecting to theories of spectatorship informed by phenomenological and 'haptic' understandings of the embodied eye.

These texts and contexts have helped shape my understanding of literature and cinema in the first decades of the twentieth century, but my approach is a little different. I have not focused exclusively in this chapter on the texts of 'high modernism', finding in the more ambiguously situated work (thought of as 'modern' rather than 'modernist') of Kipling and H. G. Wells some of the most powerful responses to the new medium of film. I have also looked in some detail at the earliest accounts of cinema, in order to understand not only the terms of its reception by its first viewers, but also the ways in which this reception, as it was framed discursively, began to shape the new 'genre' of writing about film.

History of the Invention

In 1895, W. K. L. and Antonia Dickson published the first account of the history of the cinema, *History of the Kinetograph, Kinetoscope and Kineto-Phonograph*, a version of which had already appeared in the June 1894 issue of *The Century Magazine*. Dickson, who also co-authored with his sister Antonia *The Life and Inventions of Thomas Alva Edison* (1894), had left England for America and had started work in Edison's laboratories in 1883. In 1888, Edison put him to work on devising 'an instrument which should do for the eye what the phonograph does for the ear, [so] that by a combination of the two all motion and sound could be recorded and reproduced simultaneously'.[12] These terms were repeated throughout early responses to film, as in *The Times* report on the Oxford Street debut of the Kinetoscope on 17 October 1894: 'This instrument is to the eye what Edison's phonograph is to the ear, in that it reproduces living movements of the most complex and rapid character'.[13] Edison's inventions (or, at least, those of his team) were the Kinetograph (a camera which recorded action onto a perforated strip of photo-synthesized celluloid) and the Kinetoscope. Referring to the speed at which the film was mechanically moved forward in the Kinetograph, in an intermittent motion, and the number of 'impressions' taken and subsequently viewed per second, the Dicksons wrote: 'In this connection it is interesting to note that were the spasmodic motions added up by themselves, exclusive of arrests, on the same principle that a train record is computed independently of stoppages, the incredible speed of twenty-six miles an hour would be shown.'[14] The analogical relationship between film motion and locomotion was thus made explicit. The Kinetoscope was a viewer, soon to be superseded by the film projector, which replaced a cylinder-based device. In the Kinetoscope, the perforated film moved continuously, on spools, around the interior of the apparatus (a wooden cabinet with a peephole in the top), powered by an electrically driven motor. The film was lit by an electric lamp, while a shutter device produced intermittent illumination.

The Dicksons' brief book was at once a technical history of the invention, a catalogue of, and advertisement for, the subjects available for viewing, and an imaginatively freighted account of its impact. Scientific description of the ways in which the apparatus worked was in some ways in tension with the attempt to conjure up the marvelous nature of its illusions, though the intricacy and power of the technology also imbued it with a supernatural dimension. The text was illustrated with a variety of images, including some 'self-portraits'—'Photography Extraordinary. W. K. L. Dickson. Taken by Himself'—in which Dickson appeared first as two-headed and then with his head separated from his body. In one image the head is balanced on a tray; in another it is tucked under his arm. These ghost-images looked back to those of the phantasmagoria, but they were also connections to the films that would, soon after, be made by George Méliès, magician turned film-maker.

The Dicksons' discussion was unstable, veering between an evocation of the 'uncanny' dimensions of the new technology and its innocent delights. The 'realism' of the images and accompanying sound was at once on the side of the 'uncanny' and on the other of the 'natural', so that the two terms in fact ceased to be opposed. Describing the projecting room, 'hung with portentous black', and the effects of the 'kineto-phonograph' (which brought sound and image together) the authors wrote:

> The effect of these sombre draperies and the weird accompanying monotone of the electric motor, attached to the projector, are horribly impressive, and one's sense of the supernatural is heightened when a figure suddenly springs into his path, acting and talking with a vigor which leaves him totally unprepared for its mysterious vanishing. Projected stereoscopically, the results are even more realistic, as those acquainted with that class of phenomena may imagine, and a pleasing rotundity is apparent which in ordinary photographic displays is conspicuous by its absence.
>
> Nothing more marvelous or more natural could be imagined than these breathing, audible forms, with their tricks of familiar gesture and speech. The inconceivable swiftness of the photographic successions and the exquisite synchronism of the phonographic attachment have removed the last trace of automatic action and the illusion is complete.[15]

The 'photographic rooms'—the Kinetographic Theatre or the 'Black Maria'—were, in the Dicksons' words, 'the birth-place and nursery of the kinetoscope', the phrase conjuring up both the infancy of the cinematic medium and an image of the laboratory which harked back to Mary Shelley's *Frankenstein*. The remainder of the *History* described the variety of 'kinetographic subjects' whose images the kinetoscope had taken: 'On the platform stand the wrestlers, pantomimists, dancers and jugglers, whose motions it is destined to immortalize ... The *Dramatis Personae* of this stage are recruited from every characteristic section of social, artistic and industrial life, and from every conceivable phase of animal existence within the scope of laboratory enterprise.'[16]

In one photograph in the text a monkey, chained to its keeper, is shown sitting on top of a Kinetoscope cabinet; the caption reads 'Let me look'. The text offered an anecdote in which both master and monkey attempted to see into the peephole of the nickel and slot machine at the same time. In this 'comedy' of colliding heads, it is only the greater size and physical force of the man that differentiates him from the animal, and both seem equally delighted by the observation of their own images, 'the spectacle of these diminutive doubles'. The monkey, it is said, 'laughed, actually laughed, oblivious for a few enchanted seconds of unkind man, of sunless cellars, starvation and chastisement, and the tribute is accepted as one of the most gratifying in all the archives of the sated kinetoscope':

> Monkeydom has an inexhaustible fund of varied emotions, underlying the unfathomable antiquity, the measureless sadness of its exterior ... The most *blasé* and self-contained of the 'four hundred' could hardly have opposed an impassive front to the antics of these prehistoric babies, these prophetic epitomes of man. One tiny Simian fell into ecstasies of delight over his reflected image.[17]

In this representation of 'first contact', the language of evolution plays a complex role, bringing together the figure of the primate with the birth, development and initial reception of cinema, and suggesting (in ways that would become central to the avant-garde film theory of the 1910s and 20s) the 'primitive' dimensions of the medium, which was represented as at one and the same time the absolutely new and as linked to the 'archaic'.[18] Kinetoscope spectacle, in the Dicksons' account, included the representation of the animal world tamed and anthropomorphized—the tricks of the circus—and, in its filming of stranger and more exotic worlds far from the photographic studio, the animal world in the wild, red in tooth and claw: 'All the kingdoms of the world, with their wealth of color, outline and sound, shall be brought into the elastic scope of individual requirement at the wave of a nineteenth-century wand.'[19]

The evolutionary motif continued in the description and illustration of the athletic body as demonstrated in the Kinetograph series: 'In point of classical beauty and as a prophetic exposition of what we may expect in the physical regeneration of the race, Eugen Sandow, the modern Hercules, stands foremost... His normal chest development is forty-seven inches; expanded, it is sixty-one, showing an increase of fourteen inches.'[20] The world, like the body-builder Eugen's chest, appeared to be in every way expanding, as moving picture technology brought to the viewer 'unconventional types of humanity' from across the globe and recorded for posterity vanishing (and vanquished) ways of life: 'Unique in interest also is the Omaha war dance, the Sioux ghost dance and Indian war council, features of aboriginal life which may be historically valuable long after our polished continent has parted with the last traces of her romantic past.'[21]

Enlargement was also present at the microscopic level: the Dicksons described and illustrated scientific films in which the insect world was magnified, 'a class of especial interest as lying outside of the unaided vision of man'. This sphere was at once the product of scientific and technological expertise and gave access to a terrifying new world:

> We will suppose that the operator has at last been successful in imprisoning tricksy water-goblins on the sensitive film, and in developing the positive strip and placing it in the projector. A series of inch-large shapes then springs into view, magnified stereoptically to nearly three feet each, gruesome beyond power of expression, and exhibiting an indescribable celerity and rage... A curious feature of the performances is the passing of these creatures in and out of focus, appearing sometimes as huge and distorted shadows, then springing into the reality of their own size and proportions.[22]

The Kinetoscopic world was, in sum, teeming, with an ability to pass, as numerous writers on the cinema would comment for decades to come, from the infinitely great to the infinitely small. The Dicksons also pointed to the birth of narrative cinema and to a competition with the theatre that would become ever more pronounced: 'Possibly the most exciting scene in our repertoire is a fire rescue with the stage-honored accessories of ladders, a burning house, clouds of steam and smoke, and a lovely female, airily clad, leaping into the extended arms of a gallant hero.'[23] In their account, the final development of the Kinetoscope would, however, be in a perfected technology able to represent a world indistinguishable from material reality:

'The shadowy histrionics of the near future will yield nothing in realistic force and beauty to their material sisters. No imperfections will mar the illusions...It is the crown and flower of nineteenth-century magic, the crystallization of Eons of groping enchantments...It is the earnest of the coming age.'[24]

The text's closing conceit was of film as a *Gesamtkunstwerk*, a total work of art, in which, to the accompaniment of orchestral music, the curtain would rise on 'some one of the innumerable phases of pictorial art' and on a moving landscape:

> The actors will enter singly and in groups, in the graceful interweaving of social life, the swirl of the dance or the changeful kaleidoscope of popular tumult. The tones will be instinct with melody, pathos, mirth, command, every subtle intonation which goes to make up the sum of vocalism; the clang of arms, the sharp discharge of artillery, the roll of thunder, the boom of ocean surges, the chant of the storm wind, the sound of Andalusian serenades and the triumphant burst of martial music,—all these effects of sight and sound will be embraced in the kinetoscopic drama, and yet of that living, breathing, moving throng, not one will be encased in a material frame. A company of ghosts, playing to spectral music.[25]

The closing photographic image of the text is in some ways harder to interpret. It shows a 'Negro' woman, sitting in a rocking chair on a porch outside a wooden house, a rural landscape visible behind her. She has a pipe in her mouth, and is looking towards the camera. The caption is 'Repose'. There is an ethnographic dimension to the photograph, which is presumably intended as an illustration of the book's closing words: 'The kinetograph ... is the earnest of the coming age, when the great potentialities of life shall no longer be in the keeping of cloister and college, sword or money-bag, but shall overflow to the nethermost portions of the earth at the command of the humblest heir of the divine intelligence.'[26]

The photograph of the woman is a quiet image with which to end a work which has reached a crescendo of hyperbole and futuristic fantasy, and it offers a different set of paradoxes from those that have structured the Dicksons' text: the interplay of technology and magic, the gigantic and the miniature, the near and the far. The photograph stills the motion of the rocking chair; the woman looks towards the camera but, unlike almost all the other human subjects pictured in the text, does not seem to 'pose' for it. 'Repose', we might suggest, creates an interval and a rest in the drive of, and towards, movement and spectacle. The woman is, presumably, the subject whose world will be opened up by the Kinetoscope, but in the photograph she looks as if she has little need of it.

The Dicksons' brief study was, at one level, an unabashed advertisement for Edison's new apparatus, but it nonetheless brought into play tropes and images that would remain central to ways of writing about the film medium in its first decades. In his preface to the text, Edison wrote of his vision of a future cinema in which 'grand opera can be given at the Metropolitan Opera House at New York without any material change from the original, and with artists and musicians long since dead'.[27] The Dicksons' model of 'the shadowy histrionics of the near future'[28] also culminated in a total symphony: the plenitude of cinema—analogized or literalized as orchestral performance—coexisted with its spectrality (in Christian Metz's words, the presence of an absence[29]) and its uncanny powers to bring the dead to life. As Noël Burch has written: 'Edison's wish to link to his phonograph an apparatus capable of recording and reproducing pictures…is not just the ambition of an astute captain of industry; it is also the pursuit of the fantasy of a class become the fantasy of a culture: to extend the "conquest of nature" by triumphing over death through an ersatz of Life itself.'[30]

Automatic Woman

Some of the discussion in *History of the Kinetograph, Kinetoscope and Kineto-Phonograph* had already appeared in the Dicksons' biography, *The Life and Inventions of Thomas Alva Edison* (1894). This hagiographic study told Edison's 'rags to riches' story, and recounted each life-stage in relation to his work and 'inventions', from the newspaper he published at the age of 14, through telegraphy, the microphone and megaphone, the phonograph, the electric light, and the kinetoscope. As the prototype of the 'self-made man', Edison could, indeed, be said to have been his own greatest invention.

The Dicksons' biography reveals a marked attraction on its authors' part towards the imaginative and hubristic dimensions of the science and technology they describe. Discussion of the megaphone and aerophone (which used the tympanum also employed in the phonograph to secure an imitation of the human voice which was subsequently magnified and projected) led to speculation, explicitly intended to blend 'the occult wisdom of the past' with 'the progressive science of the present and future', about the possibility of capturing the sounds of history: 'What unsuspected arcana in the kingdom of sound are awaiting our restricted hearing … What symphonies of pent-up fires in the travailing bosom of the earth?'[31]

New technologies were imbued with human, often female, dimensions, and their creation was intertwined with their 'education':

> Aspirants and sibilants were always among the weak points of the phonograph, and Mr. Edison has frequently spent from fifteen to twenty hours daily for six to seven months on a stretch, dinning the word 'Spezia', for instance, into the stubborn surface of the wax. 'Spezia,' roared the inventor—'Pezia' lisped the phonograph in tones of ladylike reserve, and so on through thousands of graded repetitions, until the desired results were attained. The primary education of the phonograph was comical in the extreme.[32]

The introduction of the phonograph into childrens' toys 'gave birth', in the Dicksons' phrase, to the Edison Phonograph Toy Company in 1887. Gaby Wood, in her recent study of the history of automata, *Living Dolls*, discusses Edison's talking dolls and notes that, while studies of Edison tend to give this aspect of his work scant or limited attention, the doll was in fact central to his activities around 1890. Drawing on the fact that the phonograph was first taught to speak the words 'Mary had a little lamb' in Edison's voice, Wood writes: 'It began by speaking the words of a child, and it was not long before a child was invented to give it shape, or to give it life. So the capturing and reproduction of speech were accompanied by a casing for it in human form.'[33] Although the talking doll has been differentiated from the automaton or android in that it did not produce sounds through the replication of the human organs of speech, Edison, Wood suggests, could not resist granting his creation a human shape. In this sense, Edison's talking doll becomes central to the history of automata, and to that of the 'automatic woman' in particular.

In 1887, Edison moved his laboratories from Menlo Park, New Jersey to a new and greatly enlarged site in West Orange, though his nickname—'The Wizard of Menlo Park'—followed him to his new location. In the years that followed, Edison and his team revived and popularized the phonograph. Edison also turned his attentions to the creation of moving images. The Kinetoscope and the Kineto-phonograph (or Kinetophone) were, in the Dicksons' words, 'born amid [the] mysterious surroundings' of the laboratory's darkrooms, and they quote Edison on its origins: 'In the year 1887 the idea occured to me that it was possible to devise an instrument which should do for the eye what the phonograph does for the ear, and that by a combination of the two, all motion and sound could be recorded and reproduced simultaneously.'[34] The Dicksons wrote of the kineto-phonograph and its projections:

> Nothing more vivid or natural could be imagined than these breathing, audible forms with their tricks of familiar gesture and speech. The inconceivable swiftness of the photographic successions, and the exquisite synchronism of the phonographic attachment, have removed the last trace of automatic action, and the illusion is complete.[35]

The sounds described in fact included accompanying music and song, the rhythmic hammer of a blacksmith and the footfalls of a dancer. There was no reference to synchronized speech and, despite the Dicksons' claims for the success of the apparatus and its reproduction of voice and movement, synchronization was imprecise and for the most part limited to musical accompaniments.[36] The Kinetophone was not successful, and popular demand for the peepshow Kinetoscope went into decline. In 1895, W. K. L. Dickson left the Edison laboratory to become one of the founders of the American Mutoscope Company, which would become Edison's major competitor. It was not until the introduction of projected images, with Edison's Vitagraph premiered on April 23, 1896, that his moving picture investments began to revive. The field was, however, becoming increasingly crowded, with new moving-image machines appearing in London and Paris.

One of the many fascinating dimensions of Edison's work, in relation to film history, is his role in the reproduction of sound. Flawed as his Kinetophone might have been, it would be another thirty years before the public would hear fully synchronized sound, though Edison attempted to revive the Kinetophone in the 1910s. In his late nineteenth-century experiments, sight was to be added to sound, not sound to sight. This topic became highly charged in the 'transition' period of the late 1920s, when the defenders of the silent cinema spoke in emphatic terms of the essentially visual nature of the filmic medium.

The Future Eve

The relationship between sight and sound in Edison's universe was strikingly represented in Villiers de l'Isle Adam's *Tomorrow's Eve* (1886), a novel that powerfully allegorized and, arguably, satirized the impact of the

new technologies of the late nineteenth century. In Villiers's novel, a
fictionalized Thomas Alva Edison, 'The father of the Phonograph', 'the
Wizard of Menlo Park', 'the man who made a prisoner of the echo', has
created a female 'Android', Hadaly (whose name is said to mean 'Ideal' in
Arabic). She is, as Raymond Bellour has noted in his reading of the novel,
more than 'just another of Edison's thousand-and-one inventions. She is at
the very source of his capacity to invent'.[37]

In one of the opening chapters of *Tomorrow's Eve*, entitled 'The Lamen-
tations of Edison', Edison is 'murmuring to himself in an undertone':

> What a latecomer I am in the ranks of humanity! Why wasn't I one of the
> first-born of the species?...Plenty of great words would be recorded now,
> *ne varietur*—word for word, that is, on the surface of my cylinders, since
> the prodigious development of the machine now allows us to receive, at the
> present moment, sound waves reaching us from a vast distance. And these
> words would be engraved on my cylinders, with the tone, the phrasing,
> the manner of delivery, and even the mannerisms of pronunciation that the
> speakers possessed...Dead voices, lost sounds, forgotten noises, vibrations
> lockstepping into the abyss, and now too distant ever to be recaptured![38]

To be one of the first-born of the species would imply the being of
Adam and, in his soliloquy, Edison indeed imagines 'lurking behind some
secret thicket in Eden', recording Adam 'just a little after the death of
Lilith' (Adam's first wife). The result of Edison's motivating fantasy has
been the creation of his new Eve, Hadaly, suggesting, in Francette Pacteau's
words, that: 'The creation of a perfect femininity arises out of a desire for
omniscience, which is also a desire for a kind of omnipresence.'[39] Scenarios
of male procreation, as Pacteau and others suggest, are premised on the
exclusion of the reproductive woman; in the lengthy sections of Villiers's
novel in which he exposes and explains Hadaly's interior 'workings', it
is implied that, in her sublimity, she has neither genital parts nor female
reproductive organs. The question of 'reproduction', however, takes on
highly charged meanings in the late nineteenth century, with the emergence
of the new mechanical reproductive technologies of sound and vision.

In *Tomorrow's Eve,* Edison's friend, the English aristocrat Lord Ewald,
is suffering because he has become infatuated with a woman whose
perfection of form coexists with a sensibility that he perceives as entirely
banal, bourgeois and materialistic. Edison undertakes to make Hadaly
(who in the first stages of the narrative appears as a black-veiled spirit)
into an exact physical copy of the unsatisfactory beauty, the singer-actress

Miss Alicia Clary, through a process of 'photosculpting'. Inside Hadaly are a pair of golden 'lungs', from which exquisite song, voice, and sentiment issue forth. 'Below the lungs', Edison explains:

> You see here the Cylinder on which will be coded the gestures, the bearing, the facial expressions, and the attitudes of the adored being. It is the exact analogy of those so-called barrel organs, on the cylinders of which are encrusted...a thousand little metallic points. Each of these points plucks a particular note at a particular time and thus the cylinder plays exactly all the notes of a dozen different dance airs or operatic operas. So here; the cylinder, operating on a complex of electrical contacts leading to the central inductors of the Android, *plays* (and I can tell you exactly how) *all the gestures, the bearing, the facial expressions, and the attitudes of the woman that one incarnates in the Android*. The inductors of this Cylinder are, so to speak, the great sympathetic nervous system of our marvelous phantom.[40]

In this world of artifice, the 'real woman' has no more claim, and in some ways less, to authenticity than Hadaly the Android. The beautiful Alicia Clary is described as having a spirit obscured by a 'layer of sticky wax'.[41] She is a physical double of the Venus de Milo in the Louvre, with the suggestion that she is a 'copy' (though with arms intact) of the sculpture; Hadaly is thus made into a copy of a copy of a copy. In one of the more puzzling dimensions of the text Hadaly is, however, sculpted by, and imbued with, a mysterious spirit, that of one Anny Sowana (who is the transcendent, clairvoyant dimension of Mistress Anderson, the widow of Edison's friend Edward Anderson). Sowana is a part of Hadaly, whose speech and responses are thus not entirely programmed and predictable on the Cylinder of Gestures, and who could be said to have a 'mother' as well as the father, Edison. In the novel, spiritualism, telepathy, and mediumship are strongly linked with the new technologies, and their powers to reach and communicate across time and space.

Edison gifts Hadaly, now made into Alicia Clary's physical image, to Lord Ewald, who, under Edison's instructions, packs her into a satin-lined coffin in preparation for her sea-voyage to his ancestral home in Scotland. We hear, however, at the novel's close, of a fire that broke out on the ship on which Lord Ewald and Hadaly, in her coffin, were travelling; despite his attempts to save her, she was destroyed. Alicia Clary's name appeared on the list of those who did not survive the disaster.

Tomorrow's Eve has generated significant critical commentary in recent decades. Annette Michelson's article 'On the Eve of the Future: The

Reasonable Facsimile and the Philosophical Toy', published in 1984, argued that, while the text 'has not gone without mention within the cinematic context':

> Its place ... and its force as epitomization of the dynamics of representation issuing in the invention of the cinema have been utterly neglected ... I will claim for the text the status of a greatly privileged instance in the formation of our arsenal of mechanical reproduction, initiated, as it were, by photography, extended by telegraphy, phonography, cinematography, holography, television, and the computer. Its fuller understanding will demand, however, that we located its anticipatory instances, embedded and dispersed within the epistemophilic discourse which traverses the art of the Renaissance and of the Enlightenment until the crisis of modernity.[42]

The novel (with its representations of Promethean, and indeed Edisonian, overreaching) seems to have generated, for Michelson as for others, an ambition to write a history of cinema in the context of the *longue durée* of the history of ideas. Michelson's essay, we might say, was an attempt, in the 1980s, to give birth to a new understanding of film's own origins, and to shift the preoccupations of film theory from the dominant psychoanalytic-feminist readings of film narratives to a model of film history in which the female body could be understood as 'the fantasmatic ground of cinema itself'.

Michelson suggested that her essay was a first step in an entire project: the location of cinema's origins in the 'stereoscopic fusion' of (female) body and (cinematic) machine. That this machine was also a 'philosophical toy' opens its history not onto that of technology *per se* but onto the tradition of philosophizing through the figure of the automaton (as in the writings of Descartes, La Mettrie and Condillac), in which were raised the fundamental questions of mind/body, human/machine and human/God. Raymond Bellour's reading of the text also emphasized its philosophical origins and its construction, through the figure of Hadaly, of a 'vision machine':

> Hadaly transfigures the mental image by offering at once the surface on which it is projected and the requisite substantial volume. The Phonograph and the Camera are not only linked within her as twin instruments to reproduce the real; they operate together in such a way as to transform the real.

Bellour suggests that this is significant less because it anticipates the talking film, than because 'it paves the way towards a much wider understanding of the meaning of simulacra'. The centrality of the Android figure to film (from *Metropolis* to *Blade Runner*) pertains, he argues, to the nature of the medium: 'The actual process of substituting a simulacrum for a living being directly replicates the camera's power to reproduce automatically the reality it confronts. Every *mise en scène* of the simulacrum thus refers intrinsically to the fundamental properties of the cinematic apparatus ... in the age of mechanical reproduction the artificial has become a determining condition for modernity.'[43]

More recently, the attempt to balance the history of the vision machine with that of the sound machine has led to an increased emphasis on the role of voice and the auditory in the novel. In her study *The Mechanical Song: Women, Voice, and the Artificial in Nineteenth-Century French Narrative*, Felicia Miller Frank calls attention to the ways in which disembodied voices haunt Villiers's text, and situates the novel in the context of the nineteenth-century desire to make a material record of the voice, which preceded the construction of the phonograph by some decades. A companion text to *Tomorrow's Eve* was George Du Maurier's *Trilby* (1894), in which the sinister Svengali mesmerizes the artist's model Trilby into the production of sublime operatic song, making her into a voice machine. In 1856, the photographer F. Nadar imagined a recording instrument like the phonograph, modelled on photography: an 'ACOUSTIC DAGUERROTYPE, that would reproduce as faithfully as you like any sound submitted to its objectivity'.[44] Hadaly, as Frank notes, *is* a phonograph: 'a machine for recording presence, for canning Alicia's graceful attributes that obsess Ewald, while leaving out her despised subjectivity.'[45]

While it was undoubtedly the case that the technologies imagined or invented in the late nineteenth century split the sensorium, creating conceptual and sensory divisions between eye and ear, this does not imply that the question of vision was entirely absent when sound was foregrounded. In *Tomorrow's Eve*, Edison speaks with pride of the '*expressive correspondences*' between 'the two lungs and the sympathetic nervous system of Hadaly ... the action of the two phonographs, combined with that of the cylinder, must produce a perfect synchronizing of words and gestures as well as of the movement of the lips'.[46] Hadaly would appear to be as much Kinetophone as phonograph. As the concept of 'photosculpting' might suggest, she is also a statue brought to life (hence the repeated references to Alicia Clary's resemblances to the Venus Vitrix), playing on the Pygmalion fantasies, roused in particular ways in the early years of the moving image.

The trope of the animated and moving statue became central to film criticism of the 1910s and early 1920s, as I show in Chapter 3, while the representation of a statue becoming a woman (and then reverting to statuary) was also the subject of numerous films made in cinema's first years by Georges Méliès, Robert Paul and others. The sexual charge of the image would undoubtedly have been recognized by Villiers and his contemporaries. The psychologist and sexologist Iwan Bloch wrote in *The Sexual Life of Our Time*[47] of 'the remarkable "Venus statuaria", the love for and sexual intercourse with statues and other representations of the human person', which he linked to 'necrophilist tendencies', and to 'symbolic necrophilia': 'A prostitute or some other woman must clothe herself in a shroud, lie in a coffin, or on the "bed of death," or in a room draped as a "chamber of death," and during the whole time must pretend to be dead, whilst the necrophilist satisfied himself sexually by various acts'. This is related, Bloch suggests, to 'pygmalionism':

> Naked living women, in such cases, stand as 'statues' upon suitable pedestals, and are watched by the pygmalionist, whereupon they gradually come to life. The whole scene induces sexual enjoyment in the pygmalionist, who is generally an old, outworn debauchee. Canler has desribed such practices as going on in Parisian brothels, on one occasion three prostitutes appearing respectively as the goddesses Venus, Minerva and Juno.[48]

In a footnote, Bloch adds that 'the well-known tableaux vivants of the variety theatre can be regarded as a lesser form of such pygmalionist spectacles'. The emphases on sublimity and spiritualism in Villiers's text might well be seen, in one of their aspects at least, as a teasing repudiation of the ideal Hadaly's connection with the artificial or 'fornicatory' doll, the subject, Bloch reports, of at least one late nineteenth-century 'erotic romance'.[49]

'The process of moving-picture photography' is demonstrated in *Tomorrow's Eve* in a chapter entitled 'Danse Macabre'. One of the novel's interwoven plots is the story of Edward Anderson, whose marriage and, ultimately, life, were brought to ruin by a prostitute, Miss Evelyn Habal. Edison shows Lord Ewald a 'film' of Evelyn dancing:

> A long strip of transparent plastic encrusted with bits of tinted glass moved laterally along two steel tracks before the luminous cone of the astral lamp. Drawn by a clockwork mechanism at one of its ends, this strip began to glide swiftly between the lens and the disk of a powerful reflector. Suddenly on the wide white screen within its frame of ebony flashed the life-size figure of a very pretty and quite youthful blond girl.

The transparent vision, miraculously caught in color photography, wore a spangled costume as she danced a popular Mexican dance. Her movements were as lively as those of life itself, thanks to the procedures of successive photography, which can record on its microscopic glasses ten minutes of action to be projected on the screen by a powerful lampascope, using no more than a few feet of film.

Edison touched a groove in the black frame and lit a little electric light in the center of the gold rose.

Suddenly a voice, rather flat and stiff, a hard, dull voice, was heard; the dancer was singing the *alza* and *ole* of her fandango. The tambourine began to rattle and the castanets to click.

The gestures, glances, and lip movements were reproduced; so were the wrigglings of the hips, the winking of the eyes, the thin suggestions of a smile.

Lord Ewald stared on this vision in silent surprise.[50]

Edison then shows Ewald a second filmstrip:

On the screen appeared a little bloodless creature, vaguely female of gender, with dwarfish limbs, hollow cheeks, toothless jaws with practically no lips, and almost bald skull, with dim and squinting eyes, flabby lids, and wrinkled features, all dark and skinny.

And the whining voice continued to sing an obscene song, and the whole creature continued to dance just like the previous image, with the same tambourine and the same castanets.[51]

He reveals that this is 'the same person; simply, this is the true one'. The woman who first appeared was an entirely artificial product, literally made-up by make-up and by 'falsies' and prostheses of various kinds: 'underneath all her paraphernalia the hybrid creature of [Edward's] passion was as false as his love itself—to the point, in fact, of being nothing but *the Artificial giving an illusion of life*.'[52] The emphasized phrase encapsulates Villiers's model (which drew on Baudelaire's writings in *The Painter of Modern Life*) of (female) artifice as modernity itself, anticipating descriptions of the 'flapper' figure in film writings of the 1920s. Thus the writer on theatre and film Huntly Carter, in *The New Spirit in the Cinema* (1930), quoted a *Daily Express* article (29 November 1927), in which a Professor A. M. Low 'established that the "flapper" was a walking chemical experiment—a parade of substitutes for nature. "Let him who adores a girl reflect that he adores largely a combination of red lead oxide, petroleum greases, henna, cellulose products, paper and wood pulp, nitric acid, and dyes." '[53]

Villiers's phrase—'*the Artificial giving an illusion of life*'—also chimes with cultural perceptions of moving-image technologies in the 1890s. His account of Evelyn Habal's 'danse macabre', though it is only a brief interlude in the text, was prescient, written as it was a number of years before projected film became a reality. Its images were echoed in subsequent literary and cultural representations in which film was epitomized by the mechanical song and dance. In the history of cinema, Villiers's scenario bears a connection to the dances that demonstrated the early medium's powers of movement, including the 'serpentine dances' of early kinetoscope films. More directly, it anticipated the highly sexualized, mechanically agitated robot-dance of the False Maria in Fritz Lang's *Metropolis*, a film on which *Tomorrow's Eve* was an acknowledged influence. As Peter Wollen has noted (in an illuminating discussion of the relationship between Americanism and Fordist social organization in the 1920s, cinema and the figure of the robot) 'technology and sexuality are condensed in the figure of the robot Maria': she is an 'electrical-mechanical spectacle', like the cinema itself.[54]

The 'danse macabre' also became a way of figuring film in literary texts of the early twentieth century. Thomas Mann's *The Magic Mountain* contains a chapter entitled 'The Dance of Death', in which the central characters, the consumptive hero, Hans Castorp and his cousin Joachim, also suffering from tuberculosis, take a young fellow-invalid, Karen Karstedt, 'to the Bioscope Theatre in the Platz':

Life flitted across the screen before their smarting eyes: life chopped into small sections, fleeting, accelerated; a restless, jerky fluctuation of appearing and disappearing, performed to a thin accompaniment of music, which set its actual *tempo* to the phantasmagoria of the past, and with the narrowest of means at its command, yet managed to evoke a whole gamut of pomp and solemnity, passion, abandon, and gurgling sensuality…

They were present at all these scenes; space was annihilated, the clock put back, the then and there played on by music and transformed into a juggling, scurrying now and here…A young Moroccan woman, in a costume of striped silk, with trappings in the shape of chains, bracelets, and rings, her swelling breasts half bared, was suddenly brought so close to the camera as to be life-sized; one could see the dilated nostrils, the eyes full of animal life, the features in play as she showed her white teeth in a laugh, and held one of her hands, with its blanched nails, for a shade to her eyes, while with the other she waved to the audience, who stared, taken aback, into the face of the charming apparition. It seemed to see and saw not, it was not moved by the glances bent upon it, its smile and nod were not of the present but of the past, so that the impulse to respond was baffled, and lost in a feeling of impotence. Then the phantom vanished. The screen glared white and empty, with the one word *Finis* written across it. The entertainment was over, in silence the theatre was emptied, a new audience took the place of that going out, and before their eager eyes the cycle would presently unroll itself again.[55]

The tropes Mann deploys here were repeated throughout representations of the cinema in the first decades of the twentieth century: the 'annihilation' of time and space or (in Marx's formulation) of time by space; the interplay of presence and absence; the haunted dimensions of the shadow-world represented on the screen, with the woman become 'apparition' and 'phantom'; the repetitions of the unrolling cycle of the scenes; the grotesque enlargement of the face, with its 'looming' effect; its merging with, or bleeding into, the whiteness of the screen, and its 'blindness' ('it seemed to see and saw not'); the assault on the spectator's eye; the failure of reciprocity between spectator and spectacle; the abrupt disappearance of the image and the emptiness of the screen. In *The Magic Mountain*, as in many other representations of early film, cinema, for all its conjuring of 'life', was a simulacrum operating on the side of death.

Mann was describing the silent cinema, whose accompanying music provided, in his account, the historical dimensions and the emotions otherwise unavailable to the purely locomotive and fleeting images on the screen, with their 'scurrying now and here'. Representations of cinema's mechanical dance were, however, most prevalent during the period of experiments with sound in the 1920s. The talking film was frequently represented in critical discourse as a mechanical chattering body. 'Here begins something new and interesting', George Bernard Shaw wrote of 'the talkies', though, he added: 'It is not yet free from dry mechanism and it acts in the same manner as one winds the mechanism of a doll.'[56]

For exponents of the silent cinema, sound was a technology too far, a mechanical intrusion into a perfected art which had made its appeal to the eye alone. One example will suffice here: H.D.'s response, in the journal *Close Up* (discussed in detail in Chapter 5), to the 'Movietone'. Her criticisms of the new sound technology were made through an equation between dolls and cinema. (It is perhaps worth noting that H.D., born in 1886, was a young child in America during the period in which the popularity of Edison's talking dolls was at its height.) Are we to discard, she asks, our old dolls 'for another set of boxes, containing such intricate machinery, such suave sophistication of life that we wonder if we really want them?' The question, she suggested, became pressing at a New Gallery demonstration of the Movietone:

> Don't we really want what we know, what we see, what intellectually we can 'aptly' play with? Don't we? Or do we? I mean do we really want to give up curls and painted-in dutch-doll fringe, and beautifully outlined eyes and eyelashes and doll-stuffed bodies (doing for instance trapeze turns just like real circus people) for something perhaps 'better'? Do we really want to discard our little stage sets and all the appliances that we have grown so used to for something more like 'real' life? ...
>
> Here we have our little people. Here comes our heroine. Truly it is not the heroine exactly of our most vapid romances, of our most, most old box of dolls and paper-dolls but it is the sort of toy that we are used to, a doll, a better doll, a more highly specialised evolved creation but for all that a doll (Raquel Meller) steps forward. It bows, it smiles, it is guaranteed to perform tricks that will shame our nursery favourites *but do we want it?*
>
> The doll in question, a Spanish doll this time, done up in Castilian embroidery ... really our old bag of tricks. And then, wonder of wonders, the doll actually lifts its eyes, it breathes it speaks—it *speaks* ... It seemed to me, astonished as I was at both (beauty of face and mellow finish of song) that each in some diabolic fashion was bringing out, was under-stressing mechanical and artificial traits in the other. Each alone would have left us to our dreams. The two together proved too much. The screen image, a mask, a sort of doll or marionette was somehow mechanized and robbed of the thing behind the thing that has grown to matter so much to the picture adept. A doll, a sort of mask or marionette about which one could drape one's devotions ... became a sort of robot. Our old doll became replaced by a wonder-doll, singing, with musical insides, with strings that one may pull, with excellent wired joints. But can we whisper our devotion to this creature?[57]

H.D.'s image of 'the thing behind the thing' (the lure of silent cinema, her 'ghost-love', as she describes it, to its devotees) had connections to the recurrent image in early film criticism of the 'glimpse of beauty', discussed in detail in Chapter 3. It was this 'glimpse', the cinephile's glimpse, that for H.D. was destroyed by the overly-mechanical aspects of the 'movietone', just as, presumably, a walking, talking doll might be said to destroy the child's imaginary, and hence more powerful, animations of its rag or paper doll. There is a suggestion here of both doll, and silent cinema, as fetish objects, whose movements are those of the world of dreams: 'emotion and idea entered fresh as from the primitive beginning. Images, our dolls, our masks, our gods, Love and Hate and Man and Woman.'[58]

The 'primitivism' expressed here, and the model of silent cinema as representing archaic consciousness, with its animations of the inanimate object, chime with the writings of French avant-garde film critics, and in particular Jean Epstein who wrote, in his article 'On Certain Characteristics of Photogénie', of the 'primitive', 'animistic' language of cinema, which attributes 'a semblance of life to the objects it defines'.

> Through the cinema, a revolver in a drawer, a broken bottle on the ground, an eye isolated by an iris, are elevated to the status of characters in the drama. Being dramatic, they seem alive, as though involved in the evolution of an emotion. ... These lives are like the life in charms and amulets, the ominous, tabooed objects of certain primitive religions. If we wish to understand how an animal, a plant, or a stone can inspire respect, fear, or horror, those three most sacred sentiments, I think we must watch them on the screen, living their mysterious, silent lives, alien to the human sensibility ... To things and beings in their most frigid semblance, the cinema thus grants the greatest gift unto death: life.[59]

For H.D., the 'evolution' of doll and cinema (into 'mechanical' form) comes at the expense of the child's and the spectator's imaginary, psychic investments. I will return later to her correlations between cinema and psyche; her linking of the history of consciousness with that of visual technologies; and her distinction (central to accounts of the silent-sound transition) between the mechanical 'welding' of sound and image as opposed to its 'wedding'. My discussion will also come back to H.D.'s model of (silent) cinema as a salvific 'healing' of the wounds inflicted, on bodies and minds, by World War I. Her critique, at the heart of much of the writing in *Close Up*, of the American film industry and its productions was connected to widely shared cultural responses to a new, mechanized industrialism, which contained the image of the worker as robot.

In the context of the present argument, a highly salient detail of her article is indeed its account of a mechanical progression, a form of negative evolution, from 'dolls' to 'robots': '*She* [Raquel Meller] is doing everything. I want to help to add imagination to a mask, a half finished image, not have everything done for me.' If the screen-actor (significantly female) becomes a walking, talking robot-doll, then the spectator, too, denied the possibility of completing 'a half finished image' (through imaginary investments and the production of the 'inner speech' that characterizes both H.D.'s film discourse and her model of silent film spectatorship), also becomes robotic, responding mechanically to the mechanical image.

The concern with tropes and figures of marionettes, puppets, automata, and mechanical figures ran throughout the discussion and representation of film from its inception. It was attached, in more or less direct ways, to a number of arenas; the conceptualization of a medium which was 'life-like' but not life itself; the psychoanalytic theorization of the 'uncanny' through the figure of the automaton; the modernist and avant-gardist preoccupation with automatic life, in turn connected to a questioning of the very nature of human subjectivity. The 'automatic woman' was, for Villiers, an embodiment of technological as well as erotic fantasy. For a number of writers on film in the early decades of the twentieth century, including Rudolf Messel and Huntly Carter, the question of sex and sexual response, both represented in and produced by cinematic spectacle, was never far from the question of the automatic or mechanistic nature of human drives and instincts. The film (or, more specifically, Hollywood film, the 'sex-appeal' film) was a machine for arousing sexual desire, whose enactments were to be understood as a 'sex pantomime'.[60]

The 'stars' of American film were represented as entirely manufactured by the machinery of the film industry, trained, like robots, to act out the mechanics of desire in endlessly recycled sexual plots: 'Take the ordinary young woman ... Train her ... and then ... emplant in her emptied head the idea that she must get, and having, got, must keep her man. Endow this puppet with a name, a simple name for preference, set it in motion, and the film heroine is created ... Take also a young man and ... having removed his brain, fill the gap with sex, and so arrange things that he is in a continual state of desire ... Name the puppet, set it in motion, and the film hero is created ... '.[61] Messel's figure of 'the celluloid man' blurred any distinction between the 'mechanical' plots of popular cinema and the mechanical nature of cinematic representation itself, in which all actors on the screen, however culturally elevated the film drama, could be described as automatic creatures.

A complex and fascinating relationship exists between such representations and those of the puppets (including those of the Japanese Noh and Kabuki theatre) and the 'marionettes' that intrigued so many modernist and avant-garde writers and artists in this period, including Ezra Pound, Wyndham Lewis, and Picasso. 'Marionette theatre' flourished in the late nineteenth and early twentieth centuries: among its most significant creators in England were the theatre director Edward Gordon Craig and the writer John Rodker, whose novel *Adolphe 1920* I discuss at the close of this chapter. Huntly Carter, writing in *The Egoist* (a journal with which H.D. was extensively involved) in 1914 and 1916, in his role as theatre critic, explored, in a 1914 column, 'the impersonal note in drama', whose 'manifestations are believed to be rhythms and silences... For one thing, we want an impersonal actor... Hence, the experiments in England with Space and the marionette'.[62] While Carter suggested in this column that marionettes were in fact insufficiently impersonal—'We need mummers who can so subordinate themselves to the initial flow of Drama as to speak and act by no will of their own. They should manifest the curious hypnotising impression of human beings whose souls are automatically moved by Soul itself'—he later praised marionette performances based on Rodker's work, and more specifically a Japanese dancer, Michio Itow, than whom 'no dancer more resembles a living marionette'.[63] Significant questions open up here about the perception, at this time, of the relationship between theatrical marionettes and the automatic figures represented on the screen and, more broadly, between theatre and film in this period.

For Edward Gordon Craig, writing in 1907 on 'The Actor and the Über-Marionette' in his journal *The Mask*, realist theatre, in which the actor 'impersonates' another being, is merely mimetic: 'The actor looks upon life as a photo-machine looks upon life; and he attempts to make a picture to rival a photograph. He tries to reproduce nature; he seldom thinks to invent with the aid of nature, and he never dreams of *creating*.'[64] In this account, theatrical realism was, paradoxically, identified with photographic (and, by extension, cinematographic) representation. The 'life' of the 'living theatre' (the terms so stressed by the detractors of cinema to defend the vitality and immediacy of theatre, by contrast with the spectrality and the mechanical nature of the screen-world) was, for Craig, antithetical to the purpose of art: 'For its purpose is not to reflect the actual facts of this life, because it is not the custom of the artist to walk behind things, having won it as his privilege to walk in front of them—to lead'.[65] Craig advocated 'a new form of acting, consisting for the main part of symbolical gesture'; 'symbolical movements' and the '*noble artificiality*' whose origins lie in Theban temple-theatre; the actor's creation of 'a new material' ('*if* you could make your body into a machine, or into a dead piece of material such as clay, and *if* it could obey you in every movement for the entire space of time it was before the audience, and *if* you could put aside Shakespeare's Poem, you would be able to make a work of art out

of what you are'[66]); the creation of the 'über-marionette', the actor who
'performed' impersonality (in a context in which the drive of modernist
theatre, like that of poetry, was an escape from 'personality'), 'the body
in Trance [which] will aim to clothe itself with a death-like Beauty while
exhaling a living spirit':

> Do you see, then, what has made me love and learn to value that which
> to-day we call the puppet and to detest that which we call life in art?
> I pray earnestly for the return of the image…the uber-marionette, to
> the Theatre; and when he comes again and is but seen, he will be
> loved so well that once more will it be possible for the people to re-
> turn to their ancient joy in ceremonies…once more will Creation be
> celebrated…homage rendered to existence…and divine and happy inter-
> cession made to Death.[67]

The terms of Craig's writings echo through H.D.'s articles on film for
Close Up, in which she gave heightened accounts of film's classical and
hieratic qualities, its primordial and mythic dimensions, and the bodily
hieroglyphics of the film actor and, in Craig's phrase, 'symbolical gesture'.
In 'The Mask and the Movietone' she drew a clear association between
silent cinema and the marionette theatre. Early film sound (identified with
Hollywood), she suggested, broke this connection between cinema and
theatre, dance, mime and the 'masked' performance, replacing the doll
and the marionette with the robot and the 'musical insides' (like those of
Hadaly) of the 'mechanical' woman. 'I want to help to add imagination',
H.D. wrote, 'to a mask, a half finished image, not have everything done
for me…This screen projection [of the "movietone"] is not a mask, it is
a person, a personality…The mask originally presented life but so crudely
that it became a part of some super-normal or some sub-normal layer of
consciousness.'[68]

There are also strong echoes in H.D.'s film criticism of John Rodker's
writings on experimental theatre from the 1910s, including his espousal
of rhythm and silence in the theatre, and his claim (repeated in H.D.'s
insistence that the 'welding' of image and voice destroyed the power
of both) that 'no two senses may be concentrated without one losing somewhat in intensity'.[69] Her references to 'dutch dolls' (which are
contrasted with Meller's 'Spanish doll') were almost certainly allusions
to Rodker's performance pieces 'Théâtre Muet' and 'Dutch Dolls'. In
his column on 'The Theatre' in *The Egoist*, quoted above, Rodker had
written:

I want to take a theatre in London, using for the plays either human marionettes of the Dutch-doll type or naked humans, or to clothe them in a sort of cylindrical garment. The plays will be the completion of a cycle dealing with the primitive emotions, of which Fear is one, these being I think the simplest for the evocation of race memories.[70]

These contexts suggest that the perception of the (silent) cinema was for H.D. shaped by the aesthetics of the ritualized, non-representational and poetic theatre, including the mime-theatre, of the 1910s, during the years of the London avant-garde whose dissolution, after the war, she never ceased to mourn. She conceptualized the divorce between silent and sound cinema in terms established by Craig and Rodker to define experimental versus conventional theatrical contexts. Silent film, for H.D., equated to anti-naturalism and symbolism: sound film to a merely 'photographic' realism. 'The mask', she wrote of the movietone, 'in other words seems to be ripped off showing us human features, the doll is about to step forward as a mere example of mechanical inventiveness.'[71] The values attached to the terms of the human and inhuman, life and death, were, as in Craig's writings, shifting and often counter-intuitive: photographic mechanism was deplored by Craig, but 'noble artificiality' became the highest value. The debates revolved around the 'machine' but their terms were shifting and multifarious.

The figure of the automaton, and of the 'automatic woman' in particular, further opens out onto psychoanalysis, with Freud's essay on 'The Uncanny' making reference to, while to a significant extent repressing, the identification of 'the uncanny' and the automatic doll in Hoffmann's tale 'The Sandman' (on which 'The Uncanny' is based), which lay at the heart of Wilhelm Jentsch's analysis in his 1906 essay 'On the Psychology of the Uncanny'. Freud was, Laura Mulvey and others have argued, turning his back on the 'technological uncanny' and this was in turn, linked to his apparent repudiation of cinema, which he at one point identified with the figure of 'the flapper', as the embodiment of a feminized modernity, and as a 'newness' radically at odds with psychoanalysis's absorption in the weight of the past and its repetitions in the present.[72] Yet 'newness' on the screen, as Mulvey points out, becomes, with the passing of time, transmuted into the projection of the presence of the past, the presence of an absence, while at the same time the 'uncanny' nature of the cinematic image breaks down the boundaries between organic and inorganic, stasis and motion, life and death.

Motion and Locomotion: H. G. Wells
and the Cinema

Thomas Edison, Portia Dadley has written, 'was keen to develop his mythic powers of creation'.[73] He described his laboratory notebooks, which ran to 3,400 separate volumes by the time of his death in 1931, as his 'novel', and collaborated with George Parsons Lathrop (Nathaniel Hawthorne's son-in-law) on a science-fiction novel whose working title was *Progress*. The story was to explore the possibilities of space travel and of genetic engineering; imaginings very close to the fictions H. G. Wells would begin to write in the 1890s. *Progress* was abandoned before completion, largely because, as Lathrop complained, Edison gave away the details of his inventions to the press, rather than saving them for science fiction. As Wood notes, the episode indicates the inseparability in this period of science-fiction fantasy and technological inventions, such as the creation of moving images.[74]

These imbrications of fantasy and technological advance are also highly telling in the case of a figure such as Wells, another self-made man who became something of a prophet in his time, but whose 'inventions', by contrast with those of Edison, manifested themselves in the laboratory of his fiction rather than taking material form. The moving image in fact blurs the boundaries between fictional imaginings and technological inventions, with the fantastical narrative, the composite figure (human/machine, human/animal), and the perfected machine becoming 'realities' on the screen. Wells was never fully satisfied with the numerous film versions of his work (though he spoke positively of James Whale's 1933 adaptation of *The Invisible Man*) and this may well be connected to the highly complex role played by cinema in his work and thought. The moving image, with its power to make manifest the speculative and the impossible, was such a powerful dimension of Wells's imaginative world that the 'adaptations' of his work could hardly be other than disappointments.

In the writings about film of the first three or so decades of this century, 'cinema history' overlapped with broader models of historical development and histories of consciousness. The view is now widely held that modernist and modernized consciousness was inflected by, and perhaps inseparable from, cinematic consciousness. Early writers on the cinema had to negotiate questions of the 'emergence' of this new form of representation and perception, developing and deploying models and fantasies of time, history and consciousness on the back of the very terms of 'newness', 'emergence', 'coming into being'. The director Abel Gance's comments, written in 1912, can stand here for many such imaginings. Cinema is to be: 'A sixth art where we can evoke in minutes all the great disasters of history and extract from them an immediate objective lesson ... To plumb the depths of each civilization and construct the glorious scenario that sums it up, embracing all the cycles of all the epochs, finally to have ... the cinematographic classic that will guide us into a new era—that is one of my highest dreams.'[75] Here the emergence of and entry into the new is predicated on the gathering up of all that has gone before.

The parallels with H. G. Wells's conception of history writing—and of cinema—are marked, and the echoes emerge particularly strongly in his writings on film of the late 1920s and 1930s. Wells's engagement with film was as complete and as complex as any early twentieth-century writer, and in many ways his writing career ran parallel to the 'evolution' of the cinema. In 1914, *The Times* reported that Wells had entered into a comprehensive contract with the Gaumont Company 'for the right of presenting his works on the cinematograph':

> It applies to all Mr. Wells's library work of the past and to any matter he may write in the future, and it is also hoped that Mr. Wells will construct stories especially for cinematic productions. It has not yet been decided which books will be first employed, though it is obvious that many of them are admirably suited for the purpose, and the Gaumont Company's experts are now endeavouring to make a selection.[76]

As the article noted, the contract marked a particular moment in the relationship between literature and the screen, 'showing that a successful author can hope nowadays for an additional source of revenue beyond literary and dramatic rights'. Wells, Arnold Bennett, and John Galsworthy—'the Edwardians', in Virginia Woolf's somewhat contemptuous phrase—were, of British writers, among those most linked to, and remunerated by, the new medium, with its growing need (in its second decade) for plots and stories.

The 1890s, the decade during which Wells published many of his major scientific and fantasy fictions and short story collections—*The Time Machine* (1895), *The Island of Dr Moreau* (1896), *The Invisible Man* (1897), *The War of the Worlds* (1898), *When the Sleeper Awakes*, and *Tales of Space and Time* (1899)—was the period of greatest ferment and invention in the moving picture world.[77] In 1895, Robert Paul, a scientific instrument-maker turned camera and film-maker, initiated a patent application for a 'Time Machine' based on Wells's novel. The patent was for an arrangement of mobile platforms on which the members of the audience would sit, and which would 'move toward and away from a screen onto which still and motion pictures were to be projected': these would appear to carry the audience into the past and the future. Writing over thirty years later Wells stated that, until reading Terry Ramsaye's film history, *A Million and One Nights*, published in 1926, he had forgotten his involvement with the design which, in his words, 'anticipated most of the stock methods and devices of the screen drama'.[78]

The venture was apparently abandoned because of its cost, and Paul did not complete the necessary formalities for the issuance of the patent. The design was taken up, in a rather different form, Raymond Fielding has argued, in the first permanent, ultrarealistic cinema attraction, *Hale's Tours and Scenes of the World*, which 'took the form of an artificial railway car whose operation combined auditory, tactile, visual, and ambulatory sensations to provide a remarkably convincing illusion of railway travel'.[79] Hale's invention, of course, simulated a known reality (the experience of railway travel, albeit to parts of the world perhaps unknown to the spectator), whereas Paul's design was planned to simulate a fantastical experience—that of time-space travel.

In early 1896, Paul demonstrated his first projector, the Theatrograph (later billed as the Animatographe), described in one scientific journal as 'a new mechanism for throwing on a screen, so as to be visible to an audience, theatrical scenes or events of interest, with their natural motions and in life-size'.[80] Other reports commented on the 'lifelike motions of the figures' projected on the screen, the terms suggesting, even as they celebrate the 'realism' of the new medium, that the movements of the human figure in early film were, to some extent, associated with the simulations of the automaton.[81]

The story of the Wells–Paul 'Time Machine' is a standard element in early histories of film, but the nature of the collaboration remains obscure. In Ramsaye's account, Robert Paul 'wrote to Wells, who went to confer with Paul at his laboratory at 44 Hatton Garden'. 'Out of the author–scientist collaborations in Hatton Garden', Ramsaye states, 'came a screen project to materialize the human wish to live in the Past, Present and Future all at once.'[82] A joint venture with Paul would suggest that Wells was significantly engaged at an early stage with cinematic technology. Yet it seems improbable that Wells would have for so long overlooked the fact that he had narrowly missed being a key figure in the development of early cinema, or have forgotten the work required for the design, and the patent application for, the 'Time Machine'. It is much more likely that Paul, one of the pioneers of early film technology, saw his design as a way of 'producing' Wells's novel *The Time Machine*, which had appeared in its final form, after earlier serial publication, in May 1895 (the patent application is dated 24 October 1895.) This is certainly the version of events suggested by the film historian John Barnes's account of Paul's 'Time Machine', which says nothing about an actual collaboration with Wells, pointing only to his novel as a catalyst for Paul in his thinking about the possibilities of film projection. Barnes quotes from an interview with Paul in *The Era*, in which he recalls that

> that weird romance, 'The Time Machine' had suggested an entertainment to him, of which animated photographs formed an essential part. In a room capable of accommodating some hundred people, he would arrange seats to which a slight motion could be given. He would plunge the apartment into Cimmerian darkness, and introduce a wailing wind. Although the audience actually moved but a few inches, the sensation would be that of traveling through space. From time to time the journey would be stopped, and on the stage a wondrous picture would be revealed—the Animatographe, combined with panoramic effects. Fantastic scenes of future ages would first be shown. Then the audience would set forth upon its homeward journey. The conductor would regretfully intimate that he had over-shot the mark, and traveled into the past—cue for another series of pictures. Mr Paul had for a long time been at work on this scheme, and had discussed it here and there.

As Robert Paul's patent states:

> My invention consists of a novel form of exhibition whereby the spectators have presented to their view scenes which are supposed to occur in the future or past, while they are given the sensation of voyaging upon a machine through time, and means for presenting these scenes simultaneously and in conjunction with the production of the sensations by the mechanism described below, or its equivalent...
>
> After the starting of the mechanism, and a suitable period having elapsed, representing, say, a certain number of centuries, during which the platforms may be in darkness, or in alternations of darkness and dim light, the mechanism may be slowed and a pause made at a given epoch, on which

the scene upon the screen will come gradually into view of the spectators, increasing in size and distinctness from a small vista, until the figures, etc., may appear lifelike if desired ...

The mechanism may be similar to that used in the kinetoscope, but I prefer to arrange the film to travel intermittently instead of continuously ... In order to increase the realistic effect I may arrange that after a certain number of scenes from a hypothetical future have been presented to the spectators, they may be allowed to step from the buildings, and be conducted through grounds or buildings arranged to represent exactly one of those epochs through which the spectator is supposed to be travelling.[83]

Paul visualized the 'time machine' at a crucial transitional moment in the development of cinematic technology: between peepshow and projected film; individual and collective viewing; continuous and intermittent movement of the film strip. Barnes locates the machine's imaginative genesis at the point at which Paul was exhibiting kinetoscopes at the Empire of India Exhibition (held at Earls Court between 27 May and 26 October 1895). As an article in *The Strand Magazine* (August 1896) suggested: 'noticing the rush for these marvellous machines, he wondered if their fascinating pictures could be reproduced on a screen, so that thousands might see them at one time.'[84]

Paul's 'exhibition' or 'time machine' can be understood as, at one level, a fantasy machine in which the apparatus contains its spectators, as if the viewer of the Kinetoscope (itself a form of time machine) were to enter the cabinet, rather than merely looking at the film through its peephole. The spectators are both 'inside' the 'time machine' and collective viewers of projected slides or films, 'representing', in the words of the patent application, 'in successive instantaneous photographs, after the manner of the kinetoscope, the living persons or creatures in their natural motions'. They both watch scenes upon a screen and are put into actual motion by the machinery, as if they too (as in Charlie Chaplin's satire on the machine, *Modern Times)* were mechanical parts of the apparatus, cogs in the wheel. They travel in and through a virtual time continuum which can also be suspended: 'they may be allowed to step from the platforms, and be conducted through grounds or buildings arranged to represent exactly one of the epochs through which the spectator is supposed to be travelling'. 'History' is represented temporally (through movement) and spatially, while the motions of the time machine can be either continuous or intermittent. The movement of the total apparatus thus exists in a complex symbiotic relationship to the movement of its filmic components (slide and film), while the spectator occupies spaces both 'inside' and 'outside' the machine.

Robert Paul clearly saw in Wells's *The Time Machine* powerful 'cinematic' elements that could be translated onto screen and into spectacle. These elements included both the fascination with the time–space continuum and with the 'fourth dimension', expressed in the novel as philosophical/scientific discussion, as well as the time-traveller's journeys into the future. These journeys would have found simulated expression in Paul's 'time machine'. In more precise terms, we could point to those sections of the novel that suggest the direct influence of early cinema, and its play with velocity and with reverse motion. An obvious example is the passage in Chapter 3 in which the time-traveller's housekeeper, walking through the room towards the garden door as the Time-Machine is set in motion, 'seemed to shoot across the room like a rocket'.[85] When the time-traveller returns from the Future, 'I passed again across the minute when she traversed the laboratory. But now every motion appeared to be the direct inverse of her previous one. The door at the lower end opened and she glided quietly up the laboratory, back foremost, and disappeared behind the door by which she had previously entered'.[86] Terry Ramsaye suggested that Wells was taking his inspiration here directly from the motion picture: 'one of the earliest novelty effects sought in the Kinetoscope in the days when it was enjoying scientific attention was in exactly this sort of reversal of commonplace bits of action.'[87]

The Invisible Man, published two years after *The Time Machine*, adds a further dimension, the play of absence and presence and 'the presence of an absence', which became central to theorizations of filmic ontology. The importance of vision and optics to the story is also striking: 'Light fascinated me', Griffin, the 'invisible man', proclaims, recounting his discovery of the means to make matter transparent and then invisible:

> Visibility depends on the action of the visible bodies on light. Either a body absorbs light, or it reflects or refracts it, or does all these things. If it neither reflects nor refracts nor absorbs light, it cannot of itself be visible.[88]

In the novel, Wells exploits the farcical and, indeed, 'slapstick', possibilities of the situation he creates. The proprietors of the rural inn in which the invisible man stays (after giving himself the semblance of a material body with clothes, bandages, a wig and a false nose), enter the stranger's room, believing it to be empty. As the landlady

> [put her hand on the pillow], a most extraordinary thing happened, the bed-clothes gathered themselves together, leapt up suddenly into a sort of peak, and then jumped headlong over the bottom rail. It was exactly as if a hand had clutched them in the centre and flung them aside. Immediately after, the stranger's hat hopped off the bed-post, described a whirling flight in the air through the better part of a circle, and then dashed straight at Mrs Hall's face. Then as swiftly came the sponge from the washstand; and then the chair, flinging the stranger's coat and trousers carelessly aside, and laughing drily in a voice singularly like the stranger's turned itself up with its four legs at Mrs Hall, seemed to take aim at her for a moment, and charged at her. She screamed and turned, and the chair legs came gently but firmly against her back and impelled her and Hall out of the room. The door slammed violently and was locked. The chair and bed seemed to be executing a dance of triumph for a moment, and then abruptly everything was still.[89]

The scene has numerous visual counterparts in early cinema's (and the animated cartoon's) exploitations of the new medium's abilities to animate inanimate objects and to move matter through space without visible agency. *The Invisible Man* inspired *The Invisible Fluid* (1908) and was filmed by Pathé in 1909 as *L'Homme invisible* (1909) (aka *An Invisible Thief*).[90] These films, followed by a Gaumont version in 1910 and a further Pathé film in 1912 (*The Invisible Cyclist*), used stop-motion processes and substitutions, perfected by Georges Méliès, and emphasized bicycle and car chases, bringing together the fascination with invisibility in early film (which allowed for extensive play with trick photography) with the representation of speed and motion.

Wells's speculations on light, vision, time, space, and motion formed part of the broader cultural context in which not only film but also the technology, philosophy, and ontology of cinema developed. The significance of his writings for film is contained in a complex nexus of philosophical abstraction, scientific and technological experiment and design, magic and illusionism, storytelling and narration, and futuristic fantasy. The cross-disciplinary and generic nature of his scientific romances (as of so much of his work) has its corollary in the peculiar placing of film as a technology that becomes an 'art'; one not divorced from machine culture but dependent upon it. When, in 1956, the British Film Institute produced an experimental film employing a new device called 'The Dynamic Frame'—which allowed the screen to be modified to any shape desired, in the course of the shot—they chose as subject, in Ivor Montagu's words, 'a highly obscure piece of *fin-de-siècle* symbolism by H. G. Wells (*The Door in the Wall*) and decorated it with such lavishly Protean quick-changes of "expressive" shape to parade the full capacity of the invention that they made certain every prospective magnate and financier would be utterly bemused. R.I.P a good idea'.[91] It is surely significant, however, that Wells's short story—the narrative of a man who enters another world, an enchanted garden, through the eponymous door in the wall—should have been chosen as the vehicle through which to display the workings of the new device, as if the Wellsian imaginary were still the most appropriate arena for cinematic shape-changing.

In a 1926 article, 'Art and the Cinema: a chance for the British producer', R. E. C. Swann wrote:

> Could anything be more admirably comic or more entirely suitable for projection on the screen than Mr Wells' brilliant essay in the fourth dimension, *The New Accelerator*? We refer to the cinema as the 'moving pictures'. How often does it give us pictures that express motion? The camera-man goes everywhere—he is in the air, on the racing-track, under the sea. He brings back photographs shot in all these spheres, and very dull photographs they are more often than not. Yet the cinema is capable of conveying the actual impressions a man may receive on these trips—the sensations of flight, of speed, of peril—and can see things as the racer and the pilot and the diver see them, and not merely as the spectator who happens to look at the sky or the track or the sea through a pair of field-glasses.[92]

Swann's article was a plea for the use of subjective camera and for a form of 'haptic cinema'. As Swann wrote: 'The art of the cinema is the art of conveying sensation by means of visual movement ... We shall have, for instance, a representation of a village fair, and it will be seen by us not as a series of picture postcard views but as it might be through the eyes of a single visitor to it. We should in fact be put by the camera in his position ... We should go on the swings with him, and the whole fair would turn about our heads; and on the roundabout, we should feel his giddiness. And for a climax there would be the giant racer.'[93]

Whereas Robert Paul, in 1895, had seen the potential for spectacle accompanied by the actual movement of the spectator's body in *The Time Machine*, Swann, writing thirty years later, turned to Wells's early work from which to postulate a future for the cinema, basing it on film's abilities to produce corporeal sensations through camera movement. The 'cinematic' dimensions of Wells' writing were in part connected to those effects which Yuri Tsivian, borrowing the term from experimental psychology, defines as 'proprioceptive'; that is, addressed to the viewer's sense of spatial identity.[94] Such effects would have included, in the early decades of cinema, head-on camera movement in 'phantom rides' and, in travel films in particular, the simulation of rapid and often vertiginous motion. These sensations were then reproduced in many of the avant-garde films of the 1920s, (including *Ballet Mécanique*, *Entr'acte* and *A quoi rêvent les jeunes films*, the viewing of which was the context for Swann's arguments), whose directors were seeking to recreate the shocking novelty of the early filmic experience and to disrupt the conventions of narrative cinema.

In Wells's short story 'The New Accelerator' (1901), the narrator describes the experiences he shared with his friend Professor Gibberne, a physiologist whose research explores 'the action of drugs upon the nervous system' and, in particular, the use of nervous stimulants. At the story's opening, Gibberne tells the narrator about his experiments with a drug that 'stimulates all round ... and makes you go three to everybody else's one'.[95] The narrator comments: 'My own interest in the coming drug certainly did not wane in the time ... I have always been given to paradoxes about space and time, and it seemed to me that Gibberne was really preparing no less than the absolute acceleration of life.'[96] When the distillation is ready for trial, the two men prepare to take it, with Gibberne warning the narrator that he should shut his eyes and open them cautiously: 'there's a kind of shock to the retina, a nasty giddy confusion just at the time if the eyes are open.' The effect of the drug is not to change the way the taker feels, but to make 'everything in the world ... seem to be going every so many thousand times slower than it ever went before'. Thus, as the two men walk out into the street, they see what appears to be a 'frozen edifice':

> There they were, people like ourselves and yet not like ourselves, frozen in careless attitudes, caught in mid-gesture. A girl and a man smiled at one another, a leering smile that threatened to last for evermore ... Frozen people stood erect; strange, silent, self-conscious-looking dummies hung unstably in mid-stride, promenading upon the grass. I passed close to a poodle dog suspended in the act of leaping, and watched the slow movement of his legs as he sank to earth. 'Lord, look *here*', cried Gibberne, and we halted for a moment before a magnificent person in white faint-striped flannels, white shoes and a Panama hat, who turned back to wink at two gaily dressed ladies he had passed. A wink, studied with such leisurely deliberation as we

could afford, is an unattractive thing. It loses any quality of alert gaiety, and one remarks that the winking eye does not completely close, that under its drooping lid appears the lower edge of an eyeball and a line of white. 'Heaven give me memory,' said I, ' and I will never wink again'.

'Or smile,' said Gibberne, with his eye on the lady's answering teeth ...

Consider the wonder of it! All that I had said and thought and done since the stuff had begun to work in my veins had happened, so far as those people, so far as the world in general went, in the twinkling of an eye.[97]

The surprise of the story, perhaps, is that the sensations produced by 'The New Accelerator' (the drug and the short story) entail the observation of life in slow-motion rather than the experience of speed, at least until the effects of the drug wear off: 'The whole world had come alive again, was going as fast as we were, or rather we were going no faster than the rest of the world. It was like slowing down as one comes into a railway station. Everything seemed to spin round for a second or two, I had the most transient feeling of nausea, and that was all.'[98]

While the appeal of the story for Swann would seem to have been its promise of acceleration as sensation, Wells in fact captured other dimensions of temporality and vision that would be addressed, in various ways, in responses to film in the following years. Walter Benjamin's emphasis, in his essay 'The Work of Art in the Age of Mechanical Reproduction' (1936), on film's ability to reveal the minutiae of a gesture, or 'a person's posture during the fractional second of a stride', recalls the motion-studies of the late nineteenth century, in which (as in the stop-motion photography of Jules-Etienne Marey and Eadweard Muybridge) the point was not to construct a continuity out of still images, but to break down motion into its component parts.[99] The paradoxical nature of filmic representation—which creates the illusion of movement in its projection of a series of still images—was displayed in much modernist and avant-garde film of the 1920s, including Dziga-Vertov's *Man with a Movie Camera*. In isolating images as stills, and then reanimating them, Vertov both unveiled the illusion of filmic movement and bodied forth the power of film to make still things move. René Clair's *Paris qui dort*, like *Man with a Movie Camera*, explores the topography of the city and, as Annette Michelson has noted, 'plays upon the relation of still to moving image', with the mad scientist of this 'science-fiction' film, Dr Crase, becoming the film-maker himself: 'Setting a city careening headlong into the dizzying pace of modernity, he can at will arrest the flow of life in the ecstatic suspension of time itself.'[100]

The focus of Wells's story is, in fact, as much on the observation of gesture as on the question of time. The narrative hovers (to borrow Alexander Bakshy's description of motion in film) to observe, as if in close-up, the deformations produced on the human physiognomy by a (man's) winking eye or by a (woman's) smile, with its 'answering teeth'. The suspension of time seems inextricably linked to the enlargement of the image and its proximity to the spectator. There are connections here with the grimacing and 'gurning' faces depicted in early films, but it is also striking that Wells's representations anticipate the responses of numerous other writers to film and, in particular, to gestures or expressions that appeared to be exaggerated and grotesque, like the 'leering smile' described in 'The New Accelerator', developed a little later in the physiognomies of Wyndham Lewis's 'Tyros'. The close-up smile in fact becomes a persistent issue and trope in writing about film. Writers represented the smile, and in particular the woman's smile—that of, in one critic's words, 'the insufferably smirking heroine'—as (along with the close-up 'glycerine tear') one of the cardinal sins of cinema.[101]

Describing the years in which he became a writer in his *Experiment in Autobiography*, Wells wrote of the stories he had contributed to the *Strand* and the *Pall Mall Magazine*, whose steady republication over the years had become highly profitable: 'I became quite dexterous in evolving incidents from little possibilities of a scientific or quasi-scientific sort… many have still undeveloped dramatic and film possibilities'.[102] In 'The Crystal Egg', one of the *Tales of Space and Time*, the eponymous egg, discovered to have curious properties of diffusing light, is subsequently found, when held at a particular angle, to be a lens or window onto 'a wide and peculiar countryside. It was a moving picture: that is to say, certain objects moved in it, but slowly in an orderly manner like real things, and according as the direction of the lighting and vision changed, the picture changed also'.[103] The crystal egg, the narrator of the story goes on to reveal, gives a view of a Martian landscape, the egg in this world being 'in some physical, but at present quite inexplicable, way *en rapport*' with one on Mars.

The story's emphases on light and its refraction and diffusion, on the angle of vision, and on the actuality of the 'moving picture' bring it into a cinematographic arena of representation. Wells' narrative framings also introduce a number of characters entirely irrelevant (in plot terms) to the central vision of the story; the play of light and the view from one world into another. In this way, 'The Crystal Egg' could be read as a curious allegory of the histories of the origins of cinema itself, which almost invariably contain mysterious figures who emerge to pass on information about and to commission new optical technologies: a proliferation of stories ranged or rayed round the central and fundamental desire for the writing of light.[104]

'It moved; it moved.'

At the turn of the century, in cinema's very first years, H. G. Wells's 'prophetic' and utopian imaginings were inextricably intertwined with the representation of speed and locomotion. The first chapter of his *Anticipations (of the Reaction of Mechanical and Scientific Progress Upon Human Life and Thought)* (1901) is a lengthy discussion of 'Locomotion in the Twentieth Century', in which he argued that the symbol of the nineteenth century is 'a steam engine running upon a railway'.[105] The failure of the nineteenth-century imagination in this sphere was, in Wells's account, to tie speed to horse-power and to fix the locomotive on rails: 'Before every engine, as it were, trots the ghost of a superseded horse, refuses most resolutely to trot faster than fifty miles an hour, and shies and threatens catastrophe at every point and curve.'[106] The locomotive future mapped out by Wells included, for towns and cities, a system of moving platforms, underground or elevated, and rotating staircases: 'If the reader is a traveller, and if he will imagine that black and sulphurous tunnel, swept and garnished, lit and sweet, with a train much faster than the existing underground trains perpetually ready to go off with him and never crowded—if he will further imagine this train a platform set with comfortable seats and neat bookstalls and so forth, he will get an inkling in just one detail of what he perhaps misses by living now instead of thirty or forty years ahead.'[107]

Wells had put the transport system he describes in *Anticipations* at the heart of his novel of 1898, *When the Sleeper Wakes*, in which his central character falls into a coma which lasts two hundred years and awakens to a startling new world, and to a London in perpetual machinic motion:

> Then suddenly he discovered the roadway! It was not a roadway at all, as Graham understood such things, for in the nineteenth century the only roads and streets were beaten tracks of motionless earth, jostling rivulets of vehicles between narrow footways. But this roadway was three hundred feet across, and it moved; it moved, all save the middle, the lowest part. For a moment, the motion dazzled his mind. Then he understood.

Under the balcony this extraordinary roadway ran swiftly to Graham's right, an endless flow rushing along as fast as a nineteenth century express train, an endless platform of narrow transverse overlapping slats with little interspaces that permitted it to follow the curvatures of the street. Upon it were seats, and here and there little kiosks, but they swept by too swiftly for him to see what might be therein.[108]

In this new world, Wells also placed inventions based on the 'kinetoscope' of his time. In making Graham a set of new clothes, the tailor 'flicked out a little appliance the size and appearance of a keyless watch, whirled the knob, and behold—a little figure in white appeared kinetoscope fashion on the dial, walking and turning'.[109] Alone in his apartments, Graham sees that one side of the room 'was set with rows of peculiar double cylinders inscribed with green lettering on white … and in the centre of this side projected a little apparatus about a yard square and having a white smooth face to the room. A chair faced this. He had a transitory idea that these cylinders might be books, or a modern substitute for books'.[110] Pressing a button on the square apparatus, Graham

became aware of voices and music, and noticed a play of colour on the smooth front face. He suddenly realized what this might be, and stepped back to regard it. On the flat surface was now a little picture, very vividly coloured, and in this picture were figures that moved. Not only did they move, but they were conversing in clear small voices. It was exactly like reality viewed through an inverted opera glass and heard through a long tube … He forgot everything else and sat down in the chair. Within five minutes he heard himself named, heard 'when the Sleeper wakes', used jestingly as a proverb for remote postponement, and passed himself by, a thing remote and incredible. But in a little while he knew those two people like intimate friends.[111]

The 'kinetescope drama' is a contemporary story, played out between a man and a woman, whose 'intense realism was undeniable' and wholly absorbing, so 'that he awoke to the little white room with more than a touch of the surprise of his first awakening'.[112] Placing a second cylinder in the apparatus, Graham watches 'a musical fantasia', a version of Tannhauser:

He became interested, curious. The story developed with a flavour of strangely twisted sentimentality. Suddenly he did not like it. He liked it less as it proceeded.

He had a revulsion of feeling. These were no pictures, no idealisations, but photographed realities. He wanted no more of the twenty-second century Venusberg. He forgot the part played by the model in nineteenth century art, and gave way to an archaic indignation. He rose, angry and half ashamed at himself for witnessing this thing even in solitude. He pulled forward the apparatus, and with some violence sought for a means of stopping its action. Something snapped. A violet spark stung and convulsed his arm and the thing was still. When he attempted next day to replace these Tannhauser cylinders by another pair, he found the apparatus broken.[113]

The imagined invention may be seen as a prefiguring of sound film, video technology or television, though the references to 'cylinders' and to sound contain a suggestion of Thomas Edison's 'kineto-phonograph', an invention, which, in its first manifestations, used cylindrical shells.

Wells's imaginary viewing apparatus is verbally linked to the transport system by the repetition of modalities of movement. Of the roadway we hear that 'it moved; it moved'; of the first kinetoscope drama Graham watches, Wells writes of 'figures that moved. Not only did they move, but they were conversing in clear small voices'.[114] We have, then, two forms of insistent motion. In one, the metropolis is defined as a moving world, traversed by platforms in perpetual motion, 'the moving ways'. The second is linked to the moving image on the 'kinetoscope', an apparatus which Wells envisages as a 'substitute for a novel' and as either an entirely absorbing dream (characterized by 'intense realism', containing himself, though 'he passed himself by', and continuous with the world outside) or as a pornographic display and a different form of arousal.

In the second half of the novel, Graham encounters a further viewing apparatus: a mirror-like screen which he judged to be 'some modern replacement of the camera obscura' and which shows the city 'passing slowly, panorama fashion, across the oval'.[115] He is told of 'kineto-tele-photographs', by means of which his image will be transmitted across the world, and of an optical contrivance which would throw 'a magnified image of you ... on a screen—so that even the furthest man in the remotest gallery can, if he chooses, count your eyelashes'.[116] The shift is thus made in the novel from accounts of individual to collective viewing and, in the case of the last visual apparatus described, to an account of magnification and a form of 'close up'.

As in Robert Paul's design for 'The Time Machine', 'movement' divides into, firstly, the machine or apparatus of movement (Paul's moving platforms) and, secondly, the projected image itself (which Paul described in terms of slides 'which may be traversed horizontally or vertically' and as slides or films 'representing in successive instantaneous photographs, after the manner of the kinetoscope, the living persons or creatures in their natural motions').[117] Wells's story 'The New Accelerator', too, contains, firstly, movement (fast and slow, or suspended) through time and space, and, secondly, motion (its cessation and 'freeze-framing') in relation to perception, in particular that of gesture and facial expression, viewed as if in close-up and in suspension. In sum, the cinematographic dimensions of Wells's writing are twofold, and open up two primary, interlocking dimensions of the literary response to film: the relationships to (1) film motion (often conceived in physiological, 'haptic' or 'proprioceptive' terms) and (2) the pictorial dimensions of the screen-image, in particular the representation of the human face with its complex connection to the 'face' of the screen.

'A giant of limitless power'

Wells has a particular place in film history because for several decades he was seen as one of its most important prophets. In his Preface to L'Estrange Fawcett's *Films: Facts, and Forecasts* (1927), Charlie Chaplin wrote: 'it has been from the film itself, a device offering constant provocation to the imagination and senses of rhythm and colour that the sheer strength and crude grandeur of the motion picture industry have come. A giant of limitless powers has been reared, so huge that no one quite knows what to do with it. I, for one, am hopeful that Mr. Wells shall settle the question for us in his next novel.'[118] In 1930, the film theorist Paul Rotha commented: 'Mr Wells has written that novel, but the question is no nearer being answered. "The King Who Was a King" (a discursive film scenario, which was never realized as a film) was full of a thousand ideas, gleaned from a scrutiny of the output of Germany and America, but there was precious little in the book that had direct bearing on the position of the film itself. I believe that Mr. Wells saw and realised the greatness of the film, but did not know quite what to do about it.'[119] Wells may thus, for some commentators, have been something of a failed prophet of the cinema, but he retained a significant status in relation to this new art and technology, a status which was substantially based on the admixture in his work and thought of experiments with time and histories of mankind.

The King Who Was a King: The Book of a Film (London: Ernest Benn, 1929) was published in 1929. It is a curious text, which, according to Wells, was the expansion of an early scenario written for a Mr Godal who advertised a title—'The Peace of the World'—as a film ready for booking and then came to Wells (who had written war-time articles under the same title) to write a synopsis for him. This Wells apparently did, but not to his own satisfaction, in part, he claimed, because he came to mistrust the text-books on writing film scenarios that he had consulted. The abandoned synopsis was the embryo of *The King Who Was a King*, in which, Wells stated, 'I am going to tell the reader about a film I have evoked in an imaginary cinema theatre, and having done so, I am going to leave it to my hopeful associates to turn it into a visible reality.'[120] No one rose to the challenge. Wells, interestingly, suggested that he deliberately made the final version of his scenario more 'difficult and expensive' than the first 'practicable scheme'. The grandiosity of his conception was the condition, it would seem, for his satisfaction with it.[121] The film narrative is the story of a royal son, Paul Zelinka, who has gone into exile in America, but is recalled to take up the throne of a small kingdom. Committed to peace and to progress, and hostile to War and tradition, Paul Zelinka averts bloodshed in his kingdom and, through rational economic planning, sets in place the possibility of a World State.

The introductory chapter of the text is concerned with the general possibilities of cinema and with the film treatment more particularly. Wells opened with this account of film and its development:

> It has been interesting to watch the elegant and dignified traditions of the world of literature and cultivated appreciation, under the stresses and thrusts produced by the development of rapid photography during the past half-century. Fifty years ago not the most penetrating of prophets could have detected in the Zoetrope and the dry-plate camera the intimations of a means of expression, exceeding in force, beauty and universality any that have hitherto been available for mankind. Now that advent becomes the most obvious of probabilities.[122]

'By 1890', Wells continued:

> the 'moving picture' was in existence, and the bottling-up and decanting of drama by means of film and record an established possibility. In 1895, it seems—I had completely forgotten about it until I was reminded of it by Mr. Terry Ramsaye's history of the film—Mr. Robert W. Paul and myself had initiated a patent application for a *Time Machine* that anticipated most of the stock methods and devices of the screen drama.[123]

Wells, in his account of Paul's 'Time Machine', focused on its 'story-telling' rather than on its theatrical and spectacular elements, suggesting that the 'theatrical path', or at least, the path of spectacle, would have been a more fruitful one for film to pursue than the development of its 'storytelling' aspects. He also followed the claim that the design anticipated 'most of the stock methods and devices of the screen drama' with a discussion of the dependence of early cinema on 'dramatic scenes' and 'visual story-telling', and on 'the themes, the concepts, the methods that ruled in popular fiction, popular drama and the music-hall.' He made no reference to the transformations of time, space and motion brought into being by the early cinema. Despite his naming of the device as a 'Time Machine', he did not explicitly link the device to his early novel of that title (in which 'the peculiar sensations of time travelling' are likened to the sensations experienced on a switchback) nor to his other scientific romances of the 1890s, whose inventions, as we have seen, seem to bear closely on the very first cinematic experiments.

In the history Wells outlined in *The King Who Was a King* cinema remained dependent upon literature. This, he argued, was undoubtedly of financial benefit to fiction writers, but its result was that the development of film itself was stunted:

> From the first it was evident that a quantity of possible cinema effects were not being utilized at all in the current methods of exploitation, and enquiring spirits sought opportunity to explore this undeveloped hinterland. It is this hinterland of real novelty that is the most interesting aspect of the cinema to-day to people who have outgrown the story-consuming stage.[124]

Established writers like himself, Wells suggests, so well served by the cinema's appetite for stories, had been unwilling to 'hail the advent of a greater and richer artistic process … it was appalling to think of learning over again the conditions of a medium … it was with extraordinary reluctance, if at all, that we could be won to admit that on the screen a greater depth of intimation, a more subtle and delicate fabric of suggestion, a completer beauty and power, might be possible than any our tried and trusted equipment could achieve'.[125]

> Yet lying awake of nights it was possible for some of us to forget the crude, shallow trade 'movies' we had seen, and to realize something of the splendour of the new powers that were coming into the hands of our happy successors. First there is the Spectacle. No limitations remain of scene, stage or arena. It may be the convolutions of a tendril which fill the picture, or the bird's-eye view of a mountain chain, or a great city. We can pass in an instant from the infinitely great to the infinitely little. The picture may be real, realistic

or conventionalized in a thousand ways; it may flow into and out of a play of 'absolute' forms. And colour has become completely detachable from form ... It can be used to pick out and intensify small forms. ... Sound too has become detached for the artist to use as he will ... The effective practical synchronizing of sound with film is plainly possible and close at hand. Then film and music will be composed together.

... The incessant tiresome chatter of the drama sinks out of necessity ... with the film the voice may be flung in here or there, or the word may be made visible and vanish again.

Plainly we have something here that can be raised to parallelism with the greatest musical compositions; we have possibilities of a Spectacle equal to any music that has been or can be written, comprehending indeed the completest music as one of its factors. Behind the first cheap triumphs of the film to-day rises the possibility of a spectacle—music—drama, greater, more beautiful and intellectually deeper and richer than any artistic form humanity has hitherto achieved.[126]

'The problem to which we set ourselves here is this,' Wells continues: 'Can form, story and music be brought together to present the conditions and issues of the abolition of war in a beautiful, vigorous and moving work of art?'[127] Here we have a concept of the *Gesamtkunstwerk* (the total work of art) brought together with a concept of the *Gesamtgeschichtswerk* (total history), in echoes of Thomas Edison's and of Abel Gance's words, quoted earlier, or of Elie Faure's *The Art of Cineplastics* (1920/3), which developed a similar 'aesthetics of synthesis' and defined film as a 'plastic' art in the terms of the Kantian sublime.

One significant dimension of *The King Who Was A King* was its contribution to writing about film in the first decades of the century and to the development of a film aesthetic, allied with its claims for a far-reaching political role for film. Huntly Carter, in his *The New Spirit of the Cinema* of 1930, certainly took Wells seriously in this context: 'Mr H. G. Wells has written a remarkable peace scenario. From what I have read of it, I gather that the author is the one man who is most capable of directing the Cinema peaceward, and who, if there is ever a sane organization of the cinema world, would be best fitted to direct its peace department'.[128]

The King who was a King also became caught up in debates about the relative merits of film and literature, and the question of sound cinema. In relation to the first of these, Wells was quoted on the book's jacket: 'I believe that if I had my life over again, I might devote myself entirely to working for the cinema.' (Wells frequently made such statements at the time of the filming of *Things to Come*). Dorothy Richardson, writing in *Close Up*, levelled some friendly sarcasm at Wells: 'In remarking that it is only at long last that Mr Wells comes forward [to hail the film as the art-form of the future] we do not attempt to suggest the impossible: Wellsian dilatoriness.' He exceeded his brief, she suggests, in prophesying the end of literature. For Richardson, 'The film is skyey apparition, white searchlight. The book remains the intimate, domestic friend, the golden lamp at the elbow.'[129]

The context for Richardson's comments was the intense discussion over the coming of sound cinema, at its height in 1929, when Wells published his film scenario. Although Wells celebrated the possibilities of sound in his introduction to *The King who was a King*, he wrote the scenario using inter-titles, and indeed making great play with the possibilities of lettering:

> The awful words drop one after another upon the screen. The lettering of each is a little larger than that of its predecessor, and the letters of the last four quiver increasingly:
> Yankees
> Dutchmen
> Continental statesmen
> Dagoes
> Chinamen
> Hindoos
> Bolsheviks.[130]

The irony directed at a British Foreign Secretary here is of course embodied in the lettering, a device, and a pun, also used earlier, when Wells has floating over Paul Zelinka, the King who would rather not be a King, 'I hate these titles that cling to me.'[131] Wells was, then, marking a farewell to titles, without yet having fully embraced speech-sound film. The film critics Robert Herring and Kenneth Macpherson, writing in the same issue of *Close Up* (March 1929), were far more approving of *The King who was a King* than Paul Rotha, but wanted him to have taken the further step. Thus Macpherson wrote, in a review of the book:

> But, my word! The next bit is gorgeous! I do like the quill pen dipped in ink and the lines A draws on the map with it in *bright red*. Click, click, there's good cutting—good (for it's the coming word) montage in this. Not unlike *The Spy*, the terse mechanism, and crisp gesture. Not unlike what we've been praising for so long, the *Russian* touch. Perhaps you are helped

to see it that way because none but Mr. Wells and the Russians have dealt with material that matters.

No, Mr. Wells, this is a great thing, and it's about time to show Britain the way it ought to go. You have done that. In many ways you have saved Britain's face, for it is too grim to go on allowing the world to believe that *Confetti* and *Sailors Don't Care* are the ideals of British cinematography.

Now, about all these sub-titles. Here, if ever, is the place for sound. Sound in its logical progression from the basic principle illustrated by Eisenstein, Pudovkin and Alexandroff in a previous *Close Up*. I would not have words passing across the images, I would use voices instead and sounds instead and not even bother to show the face of the man speaking unless it happened simply to be there. In fact, as in the Sound Imagery suggested by Robert Herring in this issue.[132]

Robert Herring also invoked H. G. Wells, in his account, discussed in Chapter 5, of Vsevolod Pudovkin's visit to London, in which he had lectured on the possibilities of sound film. The whole trend of modern art was, Herring argued, towards unifying. Properly deployed, sound was not mere synchronization, but 'sound imagery': 'Wells, I put it to you. This is your next book. After explaining what a good one it is, you lay the scenes. *The Police of the World*. Paul alone in Hyde Park. Noises of champagne corks and money clinking'.[133] For Herring and Macpherson—committed to avant-garde principles and experiment—Wells appeared as a friend rather than a foe, though one to be treated with a degree of irony.

The very close associations drawn by cultural commentators between Wells and the cinema were based not only on his actual involvements with film-making (including the three short comic films he scripted for his son Frank Wells and Ivor Montagu in the 1920s)[134] but on his fascination with, and embrace of, motion and speed and the connections he continued to make between 'anticipation' and 'acceleration'. The imagined future for Wells, as his representation of the 'city ways' in *Things to Come* showed, continued to be both highly mobile and fast moving.

Things to Come

The representations of the metropolis in motion and of the workers' city in *When The Sleeper Wakes* appear to have been a significant influence on Lang's film *Metropolis*, though there are also echoes of *The Time Machine* in Lang's division of his city into upper and lower kingdoms, the realms of pleasure and play and of grinding labour respectively. Wells was deeply dismissive of *Metropolis*, in part because he had, by 1927, the year in which he saw the film, disowned his early novel. In his preface to the 1921 edition, he had written that he no longer believed in the vision of the future delineated in *When the Sleeper Wakes*: 'The great city of this story is no more then than a nightmare of Capitalism triumphant, a nightmare that was dreamt nearly a quarter of a century ago. It is a fantastic possibility no longer possible. Much evil may be in store for mankind, but to this immense grim organization of servitude, our race will never come.'[135]

In his review article on *Metropolis*, first published as 'Mr Wells Reviews a Current Film' in *The New York Times* (17 April 1927) and reprinted as 'The Silliest Film: Will Machinery Make Robots of Men?' in *The Way the World is Going* (1928), Wells wrote:

> I have recently seen the silliest film. I do not believe it would be possible to make one sillier... It gives in one eddying concentration almost every possible foolishness, *cliché*, platitude, and muddlement about mechanical progress and progress in general served up with a sauce of sentimentality that is all its own... Possibly I dislike this soupy whirlpool none the less because I find decaying fragments of my own juvenile work of thirty years ago, 'The Sleeper Awakes', floating about in it... Originality there is none. Independent thought, none. Where nobody has imagined for them, the authors have simply fallen back on contemporary things. The aeroplanes that wander about above the great city show no advance on contemporary types, though all that stuff could have been livened up immensely with a few helicopters and vertical and unexpected movements. The motorcars are 1926 models or earlier... Six million marks! The waste of it![136]

Wells was particularly hostile to the ways in which social organization was represented in the film, arguing that the 'vertical city of the future' might have been an excusable vision in 1897, but was, by the time at which he writes, 'highly improbable', as cities continued to develop centripetally. His contempt for the vertical vision of the future metropolis (a development hardly absent from modern cities) was undoubtedly shaped by his repudiation of his own late nineteenth-century imaginings, which had been inseparable from his earlier understanding of, and reaction against, class hierarchies. He also took strong exception to the dystopian visions of industrial labour as slavery—' "Efficiency" means large scale productions, machinery as fully developed as possible, and *high wages*... The whole aim of mechanical civilization is to eliminate the drudge and the drudge soul'[137]—and to the film's retreat from the values of modernity into 'soul and love and suchlike'.[138]

The 'crowning imbecility of the film' was, however, 'the conversion of the Robot into the likeness of Mary':

> Mary has to be trapped, put into a machine like a translucent cocktail shaker, and undergo all sorts of pyrotechnic treatment in order that her likeness may be transferred to the Robot. The possibility of Rotwang just simply making a Robot like her, evidently never entered the gifted producer's head.[139]

In his review, Wells referred in negative terms to the narrative of Frankenstein and his creation: 'that soulless mechanical monster of Mary Shelley's, who has fathered so many German inventions, breeds once more in this confusion.'[140] The artificial human being, the mechanical woman, the automaton and the robot were, as we have seen, fundamental to the myth of cinema. In Wells's chilling Darwinian fable of 1896, *The Island of Dr Moreau*, the scientist-figure attempts to turn a female puma into the semblance of a woman: 'I have worked hard at her head and brain,' Moreau declares, '... I will make a rational creature of my own.' The puma, 'a great bleeding scarred suffering female monster', in Margaret Atwood's words, finally kills Moreau.[141]

The issue of the connection between the human and the animal was of central significance to Wells in the late nineteenth century, and fundamental to his absorption in questions of evolution and degeneration. The nexus of the human and the machine appears, by contrast, to have been less significant in the fuelling of his imaginings and his writings and perhaps even to have run contrary to them, in ways that chime with Freud's turning away from the 'automatic doll' in *The Sandman* as the key to 'the uncanny' and as the conceptual basis for his essay on the topic. We might speculate here about Wells's (and Freud's) unease about the machine-woman (and the questions it/she raises about the sterile or non-reproductive female body), for it would seem that Wells was, to some extent, prepared to entertain the concept of a fusion between the human form and the apparatus that transports him, in the recurrent figure in his work of the aeronaut or 'airman' and the correlation of his view from the air and the camera's aerial perspectives. The machine aesthetic would appear, in Wells's writing and thought, to have been subordinated to the utopia of the machine.

In 1935, Wells began work with the Hungarian director Alexander Korda on the film *Things to Come*, adapted from his book *The Shape of Things to Come*. In the published version of the film scenario, Wells included a 'Memorandum', which had been circulated to all those involved in the design and costumes for the film and in which he had written: 'All the balderdash one finds in such a film as Fritz Lange's [sic] *Metropolis* about "robot workers" and ultra skyscrapers, etc. etc., should be cleared out of your minds before you work on this film. As a general rule you may take it that whatever Lange did in *Metropolis* is the exact contrary of what we want done here.'[142] 'Machinery', Wells insisted, 'has superseded the subjugation and "mechanisation" of human beings... The workers to be shown are individualised workers doing responsible co-operative team work.'[143]

Wells was very precise about the costumes that his people of the future would wear: 'For reasons that I have given again and again—the fact that in the future various light apparatus such as a portable radio, electric torch, notebook, will have to be carried on the person and that this will probably necessitate a widening of those broadly padded shoulders which are already necessary in the costume of contemporary men because of their wallets and fountain pens—I anticipate a costume, broad on the shoulders and fine about the legs and feet, with a fairly simple coiffure, more reminiscent of "Tudor" (Renaissance) style than anything the world has seen.'[144] In relation to the architecture of his imagined city, Wells was, however, a good deal clearer about what he did not want rather than what he did. Nonetheless, *Things to Come* was, as the many discussions of the film in the design and architectural journals of the period reveal, a crucial film for the interplay between cinema and European modernism, and Wells and Korda approached the painter and experimental film-maker Fernand Léger, the modernist architects Walter Gropius and Le Corbusier, and the Hungarian-born artist and designer László Moholy-Nagy to design sets and sequences for its final, futuristic sections, although only the work of the last was used in the film.[145]

'This is essentially a spectacular film,' Wells wrote.[146] It brought together, as J. P. Delotte has argued, Wells's belief in the great power of technology and Korda's in the elaborate cinematic spectacle, as it set about constructing the technological attitude needed to move society into the new age.[147] As we have seen, one of the aspects of film that fascinated Wells was its ability to 'pass in an instant from the infinitely great to the infinitely little. First there is the Spectacle. No limitations remain of scene, stage or arena. It may be the convolutions of a tendril which fill the picture, or the bird's-eye view of a mountain chain, or a great city'.[148] This interplay between the miniature and the monumental is seen in *Things to Come* in the representation of the toy soldiers and guns at the start of the film which, as Delotte notes, representing a cultural trivialization of the technological, subsequently transmute into life-size versions with the power to destroy society. The total breakdown brought about by war, and the failure to take technology seriously, can only be reversed by a new system of social engineering, overseen by a technical elite who understand the power of technology. The film's apparent utopianism, however, its belief in the construction of a truly technological society, also has disturbing dimensions in the context of 1930s Europe and the rise of the dictators. And while Wells may have insisted in his 'Memorandum' on the individuality of the workers, in the representations of the machine age and the technological utopia in the final parts of the film the human beings almost disappear from view. Yet the film 'acknowledges both the small and the monumental, human and technological nature, and embraces them as inevitable elements that will mark the future—elements with which we shall continually have to struggle'.[149] And cinema, itself, above all else a technology, had the power, as Wells recognized, to dramatize as spectacle the profound impact of technology on culture.

'The Train Effect'

In turning now to other writers and representations of film in its early years, we find an insistent correlation between locomotion and cinema, though in terms often more ambivalent than those suggested in Wells's writings. In chapters to follow, I discuss the ways in which, as in the work of the late nineteenth- and early twentieth-century writer and aesthetician Vernon Lee, writers differentiated between mechanical 'locomotion' and 'movement' as a question of empathy and aesthetics. This distinction is echoed in that drawn between 'motion' and 'emotion' in film writings of the 1920s and in claims such as the writer G. K. Chesterton's (in an essay on the cinema published in 1929) that motion must have 'motive' to be meaningful.[150] In sum, the qualities of 'motion' were often approached equivocally in writings about cinema, and at times seemingly purely negatively, as in John Rodker's experimental novel *Adolphe 1920*, in which cinematographic motion leads to a 'motion sickness' inseparable from the protagonist's queasy responses to the greasy 'skin' of film, with its close-up views of the heroine's glycerine tears. Critical responses to cinema were frequently framed in strongly visceral terms, as if the film were an assault on the senses and the body, in ways that reproduced, or mimicked discursively, the experiences of shock and disorientation ascribed to, and at times described by, film's first spectators.

There is a symbiotic relationship between the train and the film. As Caroline Lejeune wrote, in a 1925 review of John Ford's *The Iron Horse*: 'Of all the machines that have turned and throbbed their way across the kinema screen none is more potent, none has moved to a finer measure, than the railway engine on the track.'[151] The railway and the train were central representations in early cinema, consolidating the connections between the first *actualité* films and the cinema of the avant-garde in which, as Lynne Kirby has argued, the freedom and/or the disruptive force of the train 'fuel the aesthetic experimentation of the films themselves', becoming, as in Dziga-Vertov's *Man with a Movie Camera*, 'the revelation of a new vision'.[152] Kirby notes that critics have represented cinema's interest in the train as that of the double: 'As a machine of vision and an instrument for conquering space and time, the train is a mechanical double for the cinema and for the transport of the spectator into fiction, fantasy and dream.'[153] The railroad, she argues, should be seen as 'an important *protocinematic* phenomenon' which was not only a significant cultural force during the period in which cinema emerged but, as a perceptual paradigm, helped to *train* the cinema-spectator in 'a new, specifically modern mode of perception'.[154] The cultural historian Wolfgang Schivelbusch defined this as 'panoramic perception', drawing on comments such as that of Benjamin Gastineau, who wrote in 1861 of the train traveller 'gazing through the compartment at successive scenes'.[155]

In his study *The Railway Journey*, Schivelbusch called attention to the ways in which railway travel was said to annihilate space and time, in ways that subsequently became identified with the new medium of the film. He argued that the railway effected the most profound of revolutions in the nineteenth century, confronting the bourgeois traveller with the industrial process. The history of such conceptual and perceptual rupture is a history not only of progress but also of shock and trauma, terms which are reinvented, or come into being, to describe the effects of industrialized modernity and the disasters of the industrial 'accident' on the human organism. Psychoanalysis could also be said to have drawn its most fundamental concepts from the supposed effects of railway travel and railway accidents, with the category of 'male hysteria' developing out of the 'traumatic neurosis' associated with 'railway shock'. Such constructs have become central to recent explorations of the relationships between early film performances, cinema spectatorship and nervous pathologies, including and especially 'hysteria'.

For historians of early cinema, the question of audience responses to the spectacle of the moving image has been centrally located in 'the train effect', linked particularly to the Lumière brothers film *Arrival of a Train at the Station* of 1895, and summarized by Stephen Bottomore as follows: 'an audience in the early days of the cinema is seated in a hall when a film of an approaching train is projected on the screen. The spectators are anxious, fearful—some of them panic and even run.'[156] Bottomore's researches suggest that this account was undoubtedly exaggerated, and that 'tales of audience credulity about film shows' may well have functioned as a form of publicity, used to advertise the realism of the films. A 'them' and 'us' distinction also seems to have been in play, with the panicked reaction being associated with those new to the film and, in more general terms, excluded socially or geographically from the world of the new technologies. Hence the frequent appearance, in early films and in writings about the cinema, of the figure of the unsophisticated viewer (called, in America, the 'rube' or the 'hayseed'), typically come up from the country to the city to view the new attraction, and bemused by what he sees. For Christian Metz, the panicking spectator was the credulous 'child' in cinema's own 'infancy'.[157] The significance of the train in this history is not that it has trained the spectator perceptually, but that its 'arrival' on the screen animates those fears attached to the locomotive, and to railway travel with its attendant dangers, which Walter Benjamin termed 'mythic', and which always have the potential to be reawakened.[158]

Bottomore argues that stories of panicking spectators were not wholly apocryphal, and that there appear to have been contexts in which the image of an approaching train (or similar forms of movement, such as charging horses) did cause anxiety, and at times panic. He draws on Yuri Tsivian's work on early film spectatorship in Russia, in particular his concept of 'a viewer with untrained cognitive habits', and on the earliest accounts of film viewing, to suggest that strong physical reactions—often taking the form of 'starting' or flinching—were evoked by films representing movement,

Figure 2. *Arrivée d'un train en gare à La Ciotat* (Lumière, France, 1895).

Figure 3. *Arrivée d'un train en gare à La Ciotat* (Lumière, France, 1895).

particularly towards the camera and most powerfully impacting on those nearest the screen. Spectators frequently reported the effects of 'auditorium invasion', in which they experienced the feeling that the image was about to jump out of the screen. As Rudolf Arnheim wrote, in *Film* (1933):

> Everyone has seen a railway engine rushing on to the scene in a film. It seems to be coming straight at the audience. The effect is most vivid; and for this reason the dynamic power of the forward rushing movement is enhanced by another that has no inherent connection with the object itself, that is, with the locomotive, but depends on the position of the spectator,—or, in other words—of the camera ... The train rushes forward; the whole shot is covered by its mass with tremendous rapidity; and the mass eventually overflows the margins of the screen.[159]

It seems likely, Bottomore suggests, 'that when a new medium is introduced to an 'inexperienced viewer', his senses need to adjust until, through some kind of a learning process, they build up enough experience to reintegrate themselves into a new mode of operation'.[160]

One of the central contexts for Bottomore's research in this area is Tom Gunning's influential work on early cinema and, in particular, the concept of the 'cinema of attractions', which, in Gunning's words, 'directly solicits spectator attention, inciting visual curiosity, and supplying pleasure through an exciting spectacle—a unique event, whether fictional or documentary, that is of interest in itself'.[161] Gunning, in his essay 'An Aesthetic of Astonishment: Early Film and the (In)Credulous Spectator', does not take issue with the idea 'that a reaction of astonishment and even a type of terror accompanied many early projections'. He does, however, question the concept of the naive spectator, whose childlike credulity leads him to confuse image and reality. The contexts in which the earliest film images can be understood to have exerted 'an uncanny and agitating power' on audiences include, Gunning argues, 'the first modes of exhibition, the tradition of turn-of-the-century visual entertainments, and a basic aesthetic of early cinema I have called the cinema of attractions, which envisioned cinema as a series of visual shocks'.

> The on-rushing train did not simply produce the negative experience of fear but the particularly modern entertainment form of the thrill, embodied elsewhere in the recently appearing attractions of the amusement parks (such as the roller coaster) which combine sensations of acceleration with a security guaranteed by modern industrial technology ... Placed within a historical context and tradition, the first spectator's experience reveals not a childlike

belief, but an undisguised awareness [of] (and delight in) film's illusionistic capabilities.[162]

A central plank in Gunning's argument is the 'evidence' of Maxim Gorki's much-quoted newspaper article, published in July 1896, after a showing of the Lumière brothers' first films at the Nizhni-Novgorod fair. Gorki wrote:

Last night I was in the kingdom of the shadows.

If you only knew how strange it is to be there. It is a world without sound, without colour. Everything there—the earth, the trees, the people, the water and the air—is dipped in monotonous grey. Grey rays of the sun across the grey sky, grey eyes in grey faces, and the leaves of the trees are ashen grey. It is not life but its shadow, it is not motion but its soundless spectre.

Here I shall try to explain myself, lest I be suspected of madness or indulgence in symbolism. I was at Aumont's and I saw Lumière's *cinématographe*—moving photography. The extraordinary impression it creates is so unique and complex that I doubt my ability to describe it with all its nuances...

When the lights go out in the room in which Lumière's invention is shown, there suddenly appears on the screen a large grey picture, *A Street in Paris*—shadows of a bad engraving. As you gaze at it, you see carriages, buildings and people in various poses, all frozen into mobility. All this is in grey, and the sky above is also grey—you anticipate nothing new in this all too familiar scene, for you have seen pictures of Paris streets more than once. But suddenly a strange flicker passes through the screen and the picture stirs to life. Carriages coming from somewhere in the perspective of the picture are moving straight at you, into the darkness in which you sit; somewhere from afar people appear and loom larger as they come closer to you; in the foreground children are playing with a dog, bicyclists tear along, and pedestrians cross the street picking their way among the carriages. All this moves, teems with life, and, upon approaching the edge of the screen, vanishes somewhere beyond it.[163]

Gorki thus emphasized the way in which the still image was animated: 'suddenly a strange flicker passes through the screen and the picture stirs to life.' This is particularly significant for Gunning's arguments, because it shifts the debate from that of the early spectators' 'naive experience of realism' to their 'conscious awareness of artifice': 'Rather than mistaking the image for reality, the spectator is astonished by its transformation through the new illusion of projected motion... The audience's sense of shock comes less from a naive belief that they are threatened by an actual locomotive than from an unbelievable visual transformation occurring before their eyes, parallel to the greatest wonders of the magic theatre.'[164]

While Gorki's article offers exceptional insight into the modes of exhibition governing the first films, it is also a highly encoded piece of writing, in which we see a literary figure searching for, and, in the process, creating a new genre in the representation of the new medium. Gorki was engaging with aspects of Russian symbolist writing, in particular its sense of unreality and its preoccupation with a shadowy world of doubles and disguises. The films Gorki was watching and which he described included 'A Paris Street', 'Arrival of a Train at La Ciotat', and 'The Card-Game', of which he wrote: 'It seems as if these people have died and their shadows have been condemned to play cards in silence into eternity.' For cinema's first spectators, the realism or indexicality of these and other early films, combined with their unlifelike absence of sound and colour, seems to have provoked, in Yuri Tsivian's words, 'the uncanny feeling that films somehow belonged to the world of the dead'.[165]

Gorki's response to the Lumières' 'Arrival of a Train', Tsivian argues, like that of many of his contemporaries, was also inextricably intertwined with the cultural reference point of Anna Karenina's suicide—she throws herself under the carriage of a moving train—at the close of Tolstoy's novel. Perceptual 'shock' becomes literary 'shock'. As Gorki describes the effects of the Lumières' film:

> Suddenly something clicks, everything vanishes and a train appears on the screen. It speeds straight at you—watch out! It seems as though it will plunge into the darkness in which you sit, turning you into a ripped sack full of lacerated flesh and splintered bones, and crushing into dust and into broken fragments this hall and this building, so full of women, wine, music and vice.
>
> But this, too, is but a train of shadows.[166]

Gorki's article powerfully evoked the new and unfamiliar spatial relations constructed by the film, including the way in which moving figures and things vanish after reaching 'the edge of the screen'. He repeated this phrase when describing 'Arrival of a Train at La Ciotat': 'Noiselessly, the locomotive disappears beyond the edge of the screen.'[167] This effect of vanishing into empty space, central to cultural perceptions of the unstable world of the film, raises complex questions about the act of framing the work of art, and the role of the frame in guiding and centering perception. The new medium was characterized by its mobile, shifting frame, in which, as Scott McQuire has written, 'painting's "window" became a screen crossed by a multiplicity of transient appearances and rapid disappearances',[168] creating a moving field of perception. For Gorki, such disappearances served to reinforce the perception of the moving image world as the realm of death.

Yet his article has also been read somewhat partially or selectively, with its first half alone often appearing in translations. In this section Gorki indeed represented cinema as a mute realm of movement devoid of life and as a 'grotesque creation'. The soundless laughter of the Lumières' card players is placed on the side of death, and it carries Gorki as spectator into a state of dissociation:

> This mute, grey life finally begins to disturb and depress you. It seems as though it carries a warning, fraught with a vague but sinister meaning that makes your heart grow faint. You are forgetting where you are. Strange imaginings invade your mind and your consciousness begins to wane and grow dim.[169]

At this point, however, the spectator-commentator is recalled to life, and the site of his viewing (a less than respectable café, perhaps a brothel) by 'a gay chatter and a provoking laughter of a woman'. The films suddenly cease to be uncanny and disturbing, becoming first of all described as scientific marvels, demonstrating 'the energy and the curiosity of the human mind', and then as innocent and wholesome delights. The happy scene of 'The Family Breakfast' and the image of women workers leaving the factory are out of place at Aumont's: 'Why remind her of the possibility of a clean, toiling life? This reminder is useless. Under the best of circumstances this picture will only partially sting the woman who sells her kisses.'[170]

The figure of the prostitute, deployed as an emblem for the cinema as a whole, typified the combination of contempt and fascination in literary intellectuals' responses to this new, overtly commercial form.[171] Such a response is clearly present in Gorki's commentary, though the prostitute's laughter is here a complex image. It brings Gorki as spectator back to life and it makes the films he is watching doubly safe: they cease to be deathly and they become marked as sexually pure. Gorki was sufficiently taken with the contrast between filmic innocence and the 'impure' context in which the film is viewed to write a short story at this time, based on the image of the prostitute who watches the film

('The Family Breakfast') and reconsiders the ways in which she is living her life. In his article, by contrast, the disparity between the film's purity and the café (or brothel) in which the films are being projected leads him to postulate an end to cinematic innocence: 'I am convinced that these pictures will soon be replaced by others of a genre suited to the general tone of the Concert Parisien... The bucolic and the idyllic could not possibly find their place in Russia's markets thirsting for the piquant and the extravagant.'[172] Throughout early writing about film we find such moments in which breaks or transitions in film's history and ontology are invoked—once it was this, now it will be that—often linked to technological changes such as sound and colour. It is striking, however, that for Gorki the division occurs at the point of origin: in his first reception of film.

The uncanny and the ghostly seem to slide out of view in Gorki's account. Yet his first, fearful response remains the most powerful. There was 'a phenomenological fear embedded in the early reception of cinema'[173] which was reinvoked in German expressionist cinema of the 1910s and 20s: films such as *The Student of Prague*, *The Cabinet of Dr. Caligari*, and *Nosferatu* did not merely constitute an episode in the history of cinema, but acted as figurations of the materiality and the phenomenology of film *and* of fear. Such films, with their shadows, their mirrors and their doubles, informed—in however oblique and occluded a way—many of the terms and the images of Freud's writings of the period, in particular the essay on 'The Uncanny'. This, like Rank's *The Double*, attempted to negotiate the relationship between the archaic and the modern: the animations and automations of primitive thought and belief, and of the new technologies, with their power to bring still things to life and to represent (though Freud does not make the connection to filmic representations) 'dismembered limbs, a severed head, a hand cut off at the wrist... feet which dance by themselves'.[174] For Gilles Deleuze, 'German cinema summoned up primitive powers, but it was perhaps best placed to announce something new which was to change cinema, horribly to "realize" it and thus to modify its basic themes.'[175]

Gorki's account of the Lumières' films is particularly charged, as a result both of the power of its images and his status as a writer. It was, however, not an unprecedented response and representation. In particular, it echoed a lengthy article, authored by O. Winter (after seeing the February 1896 opening *Cinematographe* show in London) and published in the *New Review*, the first part of which contained strikingly similar imagery to that of Gorki. Winter wrote:

> Imagine a room or a theatre brilliant with electric lights and decorated with an empty back-cloth. Suddenly the lights are extinguished, and to the whirring sound of countless revolutions the back-cloth quivers into being. A moment since it was white and inanimate; now it bustles with the movement and masquerade of tremulous life. Whirr! And a train, running (so to say) out of the cloth, floats upon your vision. It draws up at the platform; guards and porters hustle to their toil; weary passengers lean through the window to unfasten the cumberous door; sentimentalists hasten to intercept their friends; and the whole common drama of luggage and fatigue is enacted before your eyes. The lights leap up, and at their sudden descent you see upon the cloth a factory at noon disgorging its inmates. Men and women jostle and laugh; a swift bicycle seizes the occasion of an empty space; a huge hound crosses the yard in placid content; you can catch the very changing expression of a mob happy in its release; you note the varying speed of the footsteps; not one of the smaller signs of human activity escapes you. And then, again, a sudden light, and recurring darkness.
>
> Then, once more, the sound and flicker of machinery; and you see on the bare cloth a tumbling sea, with a crowd of urchins leaping and scrambling in the waves. The picture varies, but the effect is always the same—the terrifying effect of life, but of life with a difference.
>
> It is life stripped of colour and of sound. Though you are conscious of the sunshine, the picture is subdued to a uniform and baffling grey. Though the waves break upon an imagined shore, they break in a silence which doubles your shrinking from their reality. The boys laugh with eyes and mouth—that you can see at a glance. But they laugh in a stillness which no ripple disturbs.[176]

As in Vachel Lindsay's film writings (discussed in Chapter Three), Winter's account of the film experience, in the first part of his article, was performative, attempting to conjure the images into life. Like Gorki, Winter used the second person 'you', as if the spectating 'I' had itself been turned into its double by the shadowy, mirror-world on the screen. By contrast with Gorki, however (and *pace* Tom Gunning's argument), Winter did not seem to be describing the coming into movement on the screen of an initially still image (Gorki's 'suddenly a strange flicker passes through the screen and the picture stirs to life'), but the transition from the white and empty screen to 'the movement and masquerade of tremulous life'. He also laid stress on the abrupt change from light to darkness, hinting at the paradox that, in this new world, it was in the dark that 'life' and motion came into being, while the brilliant electric lights revealed only the blankness of the screen. Where Gorki and Winter concurred most strongly was in the perception of the mute, grey world of the film, in which the presence of the visual images served to make more pointed and disturbing the absence of sound and colour.

While Gorki connected the cinematic world with the literary context of symbolist writing, Winter's agenda was to show, in highly critical terms, the relationship between cinematic 'realism' and literary naturalism. Where Gorki's article divided between the conjuring up of the filmic ghost world and the proclamation of cinematic innocence (the shift heralded by the prostitute's laughter), Winter moved from description of the 'terrifying effect of life' to a critique of contemporary art and literature which, he argued, failed, as did the cinema, to frame and select from the multiplicity of detail: 'Both the Cinématograph and the Pre-Raphaelite suffer from the same vice. The one and the other are incapable of selection; they grasp at every straw that comes in their way; they see the trivial and important, the near and the distant, with the same fecklessly impartial eye.' In the literary context, Zola was identified as the writer who most markedly shared the flaws of the Cinématograph, 'as keenly convinced that all phenomena are of equal value as is the impersonal lens'. Winter's article constructed a division between human and mechanical eye, and extrapolated from this the essential falsity of the 'life' represented on the screen: 'Man cannot see with the mechanical unintelligence of a plate, exposed forty times in a second.'[177]

In his account of 'Arrival of a Train', Winter said little or nothing of the impact of the locomotive coming towards the spectator: his model of reception was that of unease but not shock. He focused on the railway station rather than the train, in order to make a point about the necessary selectivity of human perception, by contrast with the flattening effects of the photographic lens:

> The dullest eye, the deafest ear, has a personality, generally unconscious, which transforms every scene, and modifies every sound. A railway station, for instance, is a picture with a thousand shifting focuses. The most delicate instrument is forced to render every incident at the same pace and with the same prominence, only reserving to itself the monstrous privilege of enlarging the foreground beyond recognition. If you or I meet an arriving train, we either compose the scattered elements into a simple picture, and with the directness distinguishing the human vision from the photographic lens, reject

the countless details which hamper and confuse our composition, or we stand on the platform eager to recognise a familiar face. The rest of the throng, hastily scanned, falls into a shadowy background. Thus in the moving picture, thrown upon a screen, the crowd is severally and unconsciously choosing or rejecting the objects of sight. But we find the task impossible. The grey photograph unfolds at an equal pace and with a sad deliberation. We cannot follow the shadows in their enthusiasm of recognition; the scene is forced to trickle upon our nerves with an equal effect; it is neither so quick nor so changeful as life. From the point of view of display the spectacle fails, because its personages lack the one quality of entertainment: self-consciousness.[178]

In this argument, the world depicted on the screen existed at a further remove from artistic vision than unmediated human perception, which was capable of selection, focus and composition. In Winter's eyes, the Cinématograph produced that 'movement without motive' which was the basis for Chesterton's criticism of the film.

Winter's selection of the railway station to illustrate his arguments was in line (though his critical attitude to cinematic 'lifelikeness' was not) with numerous other accounts of the first films, in which the representation of passengers alighting from the train and moving about and along the platform was given equal, or more, weight to the arrival of the train itself. As one commentator wrote in 1896 of a film showing: '*The Railway Station* again forms another scene. The station is at first apparently empty when the train is seen approaching, and gradually gets nearer and larger until the engine passes where we are apparently standing, and the train stops, the guard comes along the platform, passengers get out and in, and all is *real.*'[179] For another: 'The third picture, perhaps the most ingenious, represented a train arriving. The locomotive, advancing with lightning rapidity, then slows up, the guard jumps out, opens the doors, out pop the passengers, and go off until the platform is quite empty and the guard slowly inspects each carriage. The illusion was so perfect that one felt like pinching oneself or a neighbour to be sure one was not dreaming, but awake, and actually gazing on a mere photograph.'[180] And for a third: 'The great train appears in the distance, and rushes forward as though to overwhelm the audience, but presently slows down in time, and discharges its living freight amid a scene of bustle and excitement.'[181] As in the structure of Gorki's article, 'Arrival of a Train' was perceived to fall into two parts or scenes (the arrival of the train, the alighting of the passengers), and shock, or the potential for shock, transmuted into a celebration of the motion on the screen.[182]

The representation of complex movement certainly appears to have been the most striking aspect of the cinema to its first spectators, with representations of moving water and, in particular, breaking waves often receiving the most marked attention.[183] Winter's highly critical reception of the Cinematograph was not typical of the first journalistic responses, which were for the most part celebratory of the new medium, with the films' 'realism' becoming a cause for wonder:

> Of all the marvels that have recently been brought to light in the way of photography the 'Cinématographe,' which reproduces photographs of actual scenes and persons from life—moving, breathing, in fact, living pictures—is the most startling and sensational, if not the most original, as in the case of invisible photography ... pictures are thrown on a screen through the medium of the 'Cinématographe' with a realism that baffles description. People move about, enter and disappear, gesticulate, laugh, smoke, eat, drink and perform the most ordinary actions with a fidelity to life that leads one to doubt the evidence of one's senses ...
> Then followed a picture of a card-party. You could almost hear the clink of the money, the rustle of the cards, and the popping of the cork as a waiter opened a bottle of champagne and proceeded to fill the glasses.
> This piece of realism awoke keen applause, but the best was reserved for the last, which was a reproduction of a party of bathers in the surf of the ocean. Nothing could have been more realistic than the breakers rolling in, and a great deal of merriment was evoked by the antics of the bathers as they dived successively from the bathing-pier.[184]

In this response, the absence of sound was remarked on in ways quite different to those noted by Gorki and Winter: the visual scene was so lifelike that it 'almost' had the power to conjure up its appropriate aural accompaniment.

All writers on the cinema in its first years were in search of a genre and a language with which to describe the new medium, with its unprecedented powers of movement. Some commentators stressed the scientific nature of the medium; others produced a highly charged language to describe its 'uncanny' qualities. The very quality of cinematic realism was readily transformed into the unreality of representations with the power to simulate life. 'Arrival of a Train', and similar films, had a particularly significant role in the constructions of this early film writing because it lent itself so readily to the model of an irruption of the new into the discursive and representational arena. As a *Punch* correspondent wrote in August 1898 of the American Biograph:

There's a rattling, and a shattering, and there are sparks, and there are showers of quivering snow-flakes always falling, and amidst these appear children fighting in bed, a house on fire, with inmates saved by the arrival of fire engines, which, at some interval, are followed by warships pitching about at sea, sailors running up riggings and disappearing into space, trains at full speed coming directly at you, and never getting there, but jumping out of the picture into outer darkness where the audience is, and then, the train having vanished, all the country round takes it into its head to follow as hard as it can, rocks, mountains, trees, towns, gateways, castles, rivers, landscapes, bridges, platforms, telegraph-poles, all whirling and squirling and racing against one another, as if to see which will get to the audience first, and then, suddenly ... all disappear into space!! Phew! We breathe again!! But, O heads! O brandies and sodas! O Whiskies and waters! Restoratives, quick! It is wonderful, most wonderful![185]

'The evolution never varied'

Maxim Gorki's article is a striking example of the literary writer's nego-tiations with the new medium of film, but its context was a journalistic one. It is indeed telling that he simultaneously sought to represent the experience, or at least one of its aspects, in a short story whose narrative (that of the prostitute shown the light by the 'good' film of 'The Family Breakfast') suggested the kind of melodrama that would, some years later, become central to narrative cinema.[186]

Film—and, markedly, a 'train' film—arrived most powerfully in the literary arena with Rudyard Kipling's 1904 short story 'Mrs Bathurst'. Kipling's story is a frame tale; the narrator is visiting Simon's Bay in South Africa, when he runs into his friend Inspector Hooper of the Cape Government Railways. As they shelter from the heat inside a railway carriage, they are joined by two marines, Pyecroft and Pritchard. They drink beer and Pyecroft and Pritchard exchange stories about deserters from the Navy they have known, including a man called Vickery, known as Click because of his ill-fitting false teeth. Vickery's desertion seems to have been linked to his feelings for a woman called Mrs Bathurst, who kept a hotel near Auckland and used 'to look after us all'. Pycroft and Pritchard both attest to the extraordinary quality of Mrs Bathurst—of remembering the men who had stayed in her hotel, and of being remembered: 'how she stood an' what she was sayin' an' what she looked like ... Some women'll stay in a man's memory if they once walk down a street.'[187] There is a mystery about the relationship between Mrs Bathurst and Vickery/Click, though there is a repeated insistence that Mrs Bathurst was not to blame, could not have been at fault, whatever had transpired.

At this point the conversation takes a different turn. Pyecroft asks Hooper if he has visited the Circus in Cape Turn where he would have seen the Biograph or Cinematograph: 'London Bridge with the omnibuses—a troopship goin' to the war—marines on parade at Portsmouth, an' the Plymouth Express arrivin' at Paddin'ton.'[188] He continues with his story about the events of the previous year—of shore leave and of Vickery's insistence that he join him to watch the pictures. Pyecroft had hoped for a drink to match the shilling seats, but was told by Vickery that he wanted him sober for the occasion. 'I caught 'is face under a lamp just then, an' the appearance of it quite cured me of my thirst ... It made me anxious.'

> Then the Western Mail came in to Paddin'ton on the big magic-lantern sheet. First we saw the platform empty an' the porters standin' by. Then the engine come in, head on, an' the women in the front row jumped: she headed so straight. Then the doors opened and the passengers came out and the porters got the luggage—just like life. Only—only when any one came down too far towards us that was watchin', they walked right out o' the picture, so to speak. I was 'ighly interested, I can tell you. So were all of us. I watched an old man with a rug 'oo'd dropped a book an' was tryin' to pick it up, when quite slowly, from be'ind two porters—carryin' a little reticule an' looking' from side to side—comes our Mrs Bathurst. There was no mistakin' the walk in a hundred thousand. She come forward—right forward—she looked out straight at us with that blindish look which Pritch alluded to. She walked on and on till she melted out of the picture—like—like a shadow jumpin' over a candle, an' as she went I 'eard Dawson in the tickey seats be'ind sing out: 'Christ! There's Mrs B.!'[189]

Vickery, he continues, 'touched me on the knee again. He was clickin' his four false teeth with his jaw down like an enteric at the last kick'. Leaving the Circus, Vickery dragged him on a joyless bar-crawl round the town, uttering not a single word other than 'Let's have another'.

For the next four evenings, the pattern was repeated: 'The evolution never varied. Two shillings for us two; five minutes o' the pictures, an' perhaps forty-five seconds o' Mrs B. walking down towards us with that blindish look in her eyes an' the reticule in her hand. Then out—walk—and drink till train time'.

It became clear that Vickery was being driven into a state of madness by what he saw: ' "She's looking for me," he says, stoppin' dead under a lamp an' clickin'.' Vickery is sent by the ship's captain alone on a mission to Bloemfontein, after which he apparently deserted. Hooper (the railway inspector who had been listening to this story) reveals that he had recently come across the charred bodies of two men on the railways, burnt to charcoal in a lightning storm. One of the men was tattooed with the letters M.V., and had false teeth—Pritchard and Pyecroft affirm that it must have been Vickery. The story ends with Pyecroft's words, in reference to his picture-going at the Circus with Vickery: ''avin' seen his face for five consecutive nights on end, I'm inclined to finish what's left of the beer an' thank Gawd he's dead'.[190]

The story is an enigmatic one, and the enigma lies very largely with the Cinematograph. As in Gorki's article, film is at one level seen to possess a fundamental innocence, that of a world on the screen at one and the same time magical and mundane: 'I watched an old man with a rug 'oo'd dropped a book an' was tryin' to pick it up.' It is this vision of cinema that the figure of Mrs Bathurst disrupts, as she emerges on the screen. As we have seen, the inaugural 'shock' of the cinema has become tied to the Lumières' 1895 film 'Arrival of a Train', which became the founding myth, or 'primal scene', of cinema: a story of the irruption of the new and of an unprecedented encounter with the force and trajectory of the moving image. Kipling reinscribed this inaugural moment, sidelining the train, or putting it into a siding—'The engine come in, head on, an' the women in the front row jumped: she headed so straight'—and made the true moment of shock that of the recognition of one of its passengers: ' "Christ! There's Mrs B.!"'.' Mrs Bathurst, or at least her screen image, heads as straight as the engine, and might indeed be said to take the place of the train in this differently played out narrative of cinematic shock; one in which the interplay of shock and recognition paralleled that of the simultaneous 'astonishment and knowledge' ascribed by Gunning to the historical spectator of early cinema.

'She come forward—right forward—she looked out straight at us with that blindish look which Pritch alluded to.' In some sense, Mrs Bathurst had always been walking that walk towards the camera: 'Some women'll stay in a man's memory if they once walk down a street.' 'Blindish' is a telling attribute, or defect, in this context. Kipling shifts from the film spectators—'us that was watching'—to Mrs Bathurst, 'looking from side to side' and then looking out 'straight at us'. How do you look, and what do you see, with a blindish look? We could read Mrs Bathurst's 'blindish look' (attributed to her before we hear of her cinematic appearance) as an analogue for early cinema's looking without seeing, as in the passage, quoted earlier, from Thomas Mann's *The Magic Mountain*: 'it seemed to see and saw not.' The muteness of figures in the silent film also seemed to bring with it the implication of blindness.

The technique of the Cinematographe was a continuous shooting of a single event from a single and fixed point of view, before multiple-shot films and editing techniques were developed to create interwoven relations of point of view and spatial relationships, including eyeline matches, outlawing (other than in avant-garde film and other specific cases) the direct look at the camera. Vickery is 'lost' because Mrs Bathurst's look at the camera—which he turns into a look at him—creates a confusion in him between 'looking at' and 'looking for', and it drives him to madness and to death.

Neither Vickery nor Kipling is interested in the other Circus spectacles and shows of which the five minutes of the pictures are only one part—though Pycroft had hoped for a 'swift drink and a speedy return [to the Circus], because I wanted to see the performin' elephants'. We could contrast Kipling's story with D. H. Lawrence's novel *The Lost Girl*, in which the moving pictures appear alongside live acrobatic performances as a way, it would appear, of contrasting the mechanical, lifeless, repetitive nature of the cinema with the marvellous movements of the live human body. The miracles of motion and transformation in *The Lost Girl* are all on the side of the living body, not mechanical reproducibility:

> Mr May had worked hard to get a programme for the first week. His pictures were: 'The Human Bird', which turned out to be a ski-ing film from Norway, purely descriptive; 'The Pancake', a humorous film: and then his Grand Serial: 'The Silent Grip'. And then, for Turns, his first item was Miss Poppy Traherne, a lady in innumerable petticoats, who could whirl herself into anything you like, from an arum lily in green stockings to a rainbow and a catherine wheel and a cup and saucer: marvelous, was Miss Poppy Traherne.[191]

Miss Poppy's Catherine wheel 'brings down the house'. Athough it seems certain that the drive of Lawrence's text was that of the contrast between the life-force of the human body and the deadness of film, there are also clear ironies in Lawrence's presentation of his performers. Miss Poppy is rather disappointed at her 'vulgar' audience's inability to appreciate the qualities of her turning herself into a cup and saucer, and in this cup and saucer is the suggestion of a rather absurd, maidenly and very English gentility in Miss Poppy herself. The Catherine wheel is followed by a film: 'The lamps go out: gurglings and kissings—and then the dither on the screen: "The Human Bird", in awful shivery letters. It's not a very good machine, and Mr May is not a very good operator.'[192]

Here the cinema is represented as appealing to infantile eroticism— 'gurglings and kissings'—'dither'—a word which by the late nineteenth century had become particularly associated with the disturbing vibrations of machinery, including the railway—and finally as bad writing or cultural inscription—'awful shivery letters'. Lawrence was writing about a period in which the cinema was about to displace the live performance; Alma (the English spinster who will become 'the lost girl'), tells Mr May that the collliers prefer the films to the live performances because 'they can spread themselves over a film, and they *can't* over a living performer. They're up against the performer himself. And they hate it … They hate to admire anything that isn't themselves. And that's why they like pictures. It's all themselves to them, all the time.' The distinction here is between the unsettling experience of difference produced by the live performance, and the solipsism—and indeed onanism—of the spectators' identification with the figures on the screen—'they can spread themselves over a film'.[193] This was echoed in Lawrence's essay 'Pornography and Obscenity', in which he wrote of the 'pornographical' nature of 'the close-up kisses on the film, which excite men and women to secret and separate masturbation', an attack which lay at the heart of his repudiation of the new medium and its singular appeal to the eye.[194]

Lawrence, in reinserting film back into the contexts of live performance (and he was writing in 1920, not in the very early years of the cinema, as Kipling was), puts all the emphasis on the question of motion and on the somatic (as in the spreading of the self across the screen) as a cultural 'ooze' through which, here and in other writings, he could represent the contamination of modernity by cinematic vision. Kipling, by extracting the film from the performances that surround it, makes the question much more one of temporality, and of the relentless forward movement and irreversibility of cinematic time and locomotion. Mrs Bathurst just keeps on coming forward. 'The evolution never varied.'

What is the role of repetition in Kipling's story? Vickery's 'clicking' becomes not only increasingly frenetic but increasingly mechanical: ' "'e was clickin' 'is four false teeth like a Marconi ticker".' This is a reference to Marconi's wireless telegraph, which printed out messages in ticker-tape fashion, and, we could say, in the fashion of celluloid moving through a projector. Vickery's clicking is, indeed, as much an accompaniment to the film as the ' "little dynamo like buzzin' " ' of the projector as the pictures are screened, while his mechanical 'clicking' and his capture by the mechanisms of repetition—'the evolution never varied'—puts him in the position of the film projector rather than the spectator, running the frames through himself over and over again. His frenetic walking round the town after the films—his 'desperate round'—is mechanical and mimetic, linked both to the film apparatus and to Mrs B's walking on and on till she melted out of the picture. He dies by burning up—like paper or like nitrate film. After death, his tattoo—his mark—shows up on his charred skin as 'writing shows up white on a burned letter'.[195]

Film, in this story, is on the side of repetition, obsession, and death, though it could be argued that this stems from Vickery's inability to negotiate the particular forms of presence and absence projected in the new art of the film, even as he comes to embody the workings of the cinematic apparatus itself. For Franz Kafka, absorbed in cinema as he was, film, as Stephen Heath has noted, ultimately produced an excess in seeing, a demonic technological element which both challenges our habits of vision and confronts the author's powers of sight and writing with impossible demands. It is interesting, at least, that Kafka calls films *phantasie-prothesen*, 'artificial props', and that he likens these to false teeth.[196]

In a detailed reading of 'Mrs Bathurst', Nicholas Daly has argued that 'Mrs Bathurst' should be seen as one of Kipling's Boer War stories:

> The capacity of the camera to conjure up [Tom] Gunning's 'parallel world of phantasmatic doubles' took on a special role in a Britain that had to simultaneously assimilate the new medium of motion pictures and a particular national trauma, the military catastrophe of the distant Anglo-Boer War (1899–1902). While 'Mrs Bathurst' takes stock of a revolution of the image, then, it is also a story about industrialized warfare.[197]

Vickery, Daly suggests, is petrified not by machine culture *per se*, 'but an encounter with the specific nature of the Boerograph or Wargraph, and his excessive annihilation at the story's end is a symptom of what the story has elided: the war dead'.[198] The question of 'seeing' also evokes the issues of visibility raised by the war: 'for those actually there in South Africa who found that their experience of other wars was no preparation for warfare with an invisible enemy, but also for those at home who longed desperately to "see" the war, and who had to make do with actualités of marching troops, and "photo-faked" battle scenes from Salisbury Plain ... If "Mrs Bathurst" is one of Kipling's most inscrutable tales ... it is in part because we sense in it [as Kipling wrote in his autobiography *Something from Myself*] the "whole pressure of [the] dead of the Boer War flickering and re-forming".'[199]

In Daly's account, the actuality film thus becomes a form of screen for the (Boer) war film. This is a powerful reading, which nonetheless leaves open the question of what Kipling wanted from the cinematic image, as well as the question of the relationship between literary and film form. A significant instance here is Kipling's use of aposiopesis—the rhetorical device of breaking off the sentence or the narrative in order to withhold information or a secret—and its links to the filmic walking out of the frame. Mary Ann Doane has suggested (following Jacques Aumont's discussion of D. W. Griffith) that 'time, death and invisibility are welded together at the edge of the frame and between shots, in the unseen space that makes it possible for the cinema to say anything at all', a comment that chimes with the emphases in early commentaries on the ways in which figures and objects 'vanish' from the edge of the screen.[200] Mrs Bathurst's 'melting out of the picture', the phrase suggesting combustibility, is the counterpart to, and an anticipation of, Vickery's death by burning. The open-endedness of the short story is another kind of vanishing, with the literary frame-tale's borders becoming as unstable as the film frame itself.

While the pictures in 'Mrs Bathurst' are described as 'the real thing—alive an' moving ... taken from the very thing itself—you see', it remains unclear what it was that Kipling believed that you see in the Cinematograph. Elliot Gilbert, in a commentary on the story published in 1970, understood it to be an exploration of the workings of 'blind chance'.[201] These terms can, in the context of the story's filmic preoccupations, be translated into those of 'vision' and 'contingency'. The single-shot actuality film has come to exemplify a contingency which welds together, as Doane has written, 'movement, time and bodies'.[202] While the ascription of a concern with filmic ontology to Kipling can only be speculative, there is certainly a perception of cinema in the story as 'lost presence', or, in Christian Metz's phrase, 'the presence of an absence'. This then comes together with a blurring of the borderline between the living and the dead.[203]

'Flicker, flicker ... flicker, flick': John Rodker and James Joyce

The modernist poet and translator John Rodker's *Adolphe 1920* (1927), first published in Ezra Pound's short-lived magazine *The Exile*, was an experiment in the writing of a single day in a prose, as Andrew Crozier notes, 'which elides distinctions between sensation, affective states and objective consciousness ... [and] which locates time and space in a continuous moment'.[204] During the course of the day, the central protagonist visits a fair, where he looks into mechanical peepshows and then watches projected film. The peepshow apparatus is described as a 'man-eating one-leg ... with dark square eyes staring from its breast, waiting dumbly to be taken to others of its clan sunk like buoys throughout the street':

> He slipped a penny into it. A warm light moistened its eyes, lit up its chest. He put his eyes on its eyes, his heart on its heart, listening deeply, anxiously; forgetting the fair, his fellows reading other hearts around him. But the excitement of beating air thrilled him, and the prospect of some approaching revelation made delay unendurable. It began to mutter. Where its heart was, a woman rose from a chair, smiled, patted her elaborate hair, unhooked a shoulder-of-mutton blouse, a petticoat or two, stood self-consciously for a minute in lace-edged drawers, laced boots and black stockings, smiling a timid 1890 smile. Wondering, fearful of losing it, he thought he could not bear her smile to fade, yet suddenly the eyes were dark, and he was with his thoughts. She too in that darkness, from which for a moment he had called her. A coin called her back: as though gratefully she shyly reappeared, went through all her senseless gestures, smiled and smiled. And darkness again, heavy, inevitable. That room, that sofa, filled his brain with warm shapes and comforting light, and the woman moved amicably through it.
>
> He turned away. Another creature in supplication held tentacles out to him, and when he slipped a coin into a dark hole in its side warbled and whispered. But he thought of Angela, and the heart he had just looked into made him loathe her and himself, and angrily he tore its tentacles from his ears, its lying words of love and bliss; wading from it into the watery flood, now swirling silently like an inundation. He walked on tiptoe, borne up by the tight mass, the corners of his eyes cut by the whirling flapping flags and pallid lights that filled the washed air.
>
> In mid-air the endless band fluttered into the sky with its laughing staggering falling figures; above him flew boats with other figures; and on ostriches, pigs and in chamber-pots, flying wheeling crawling were still

others. And the street was full of them, and the eating places; and their smell, vanilla urine garlic, blended, censing all in a vulgar sabbat.[205]

The passage, for all its estranged and estranging qualities, repeats many of the tropes encountered in the work of the other writers discussed in this chapter. It expresses, in particular, the curious relationship between the machine and its interior show, and between money, prostitution, and cinematic, automated repetition, in which, as in 'Mrs Bathurst', 'the evolution never varied'. The machine has a heart and eyes that match the protagonist's own; the animated figure of the woman exists and moves in an impossible realm that he can, nonetheless, bring into being. There is pathos in that 'timid 1890 smile', which is, at one level, the pathos of superseded technologies; the peepshow exists alongside the projected film, but it has already become a part of cinema's pre-history, and the woman in her Victorian garments, called back by his coin to repeat her routines, is already part of the past.

The space through which Rodker's protagonist wanders, which is continuous with the optical shows and screens, is described as an underwater world, in which the peephole machines are at once tentacled fish and Sirens. Writing in 1925, the German novelist Robert Musil described film as 'an event reduced to moving shadows which nonetheless generates the illusion of life … Silent like a fish and pale like something subterranean, film swims in the pond of the only-visible'.[206] Musil's perception is also at the heart of Rodker's representations:

> Now he vibrated perpetually, tapping the air, all currents puzzling him. His solidity was illusion. Like the squat crayfish he took stock of the world through quivering antennae, but under his carapace shook with emotion …
> It was growing dark, recalling him to himself. The faces round him grew still and white. A pale watery light from the sheet flooded the tent, and a throbbing pole of light turning upon itself pushed at it through the air. Greasy black, dry grey, chocolate sepia moved deliberately on the screen, found shape, took on life. That flicker of shadow on deeper shadow was a substitute for his thoughts, moving in him with strange shapes. Out of the screen, a face swam up to him, at first remote, small, its surface matt; coming closer, growing larger, the skin of a cheek immensely magnified into rough crevices of powder, the corners of the eye vast fields of pulp dribbling a heart-breaking revolting moisture. The eyes moved with effort in sticky sockets, the lips twitched painfully, impossibly, and a glycerine tear crept heavily down the cheek. The face swam nearer; the eyes grew more glassy, expressionless, drifting like clouds over him, sucking him into a white

frozen lake of grief. Like a ghost the face grew larger till it passed through and beyond him, moving onward with blind eyes, groping to some light of which he could not be aware. He saw them come up to him, for a moment lie wonderingly on his own, impalpably vanish.

Outside a barrel organ played, there was a noise of swaying trees in the canvas roof and he was by a river. In pale morning small waves ran past him, their pale crests made a little clapping noise. It was Russia, tardy spring, the buds opening with effort. There was a shed, tables, and he thought perhaps there had just been a party. Yet while he took his ease, forboding of riot chilled his teeth in fear and rage, and in the tortuous alleys of some river port, far far away, Bordeaux perhaps, a dark quivering mass fought and shouted; but louder were the shrill cries and moans of someone they were tearing. And a great noise of lamentation rang on the air, and after silence.[207]

Again, we find the familiar tropes of cinema's phenomenological and sensory disturbances: the 'greasy' skin of the film, in which face and screen bleed into each other; the 'looming' effect of the magnification in the facial close-up; the 'ooze' (tears, semen) which recalls Lawrence's strictures on film and pornography, as well as the attacks on film 'sentiment' (H. L. Mencken wrote in 1927, in a critique of the cinema, of a 'lady co-star squeezing a tear' and of the 'greasy kiss' of hero and heroine[208]); the 'blind' spectral image, whose eyes, like those of the peepshow apparatus, swallow up his own before vanishing.

The nausea and fear suggest a now-familiar repudiation of a feminized mass-culture. Yet the most significant dimension of Rodker's novel is that he does not seek to erect a boundary between film and not-film, interior and exterior realities. The projected images become a 'substitute' for his protagonist's thoughts, which are, in turn, projected onto the world around him. His vision is as 'cut' by the flags and lights of the fairground as it is by the screen images. There is reciprocity of a kind between human and mechanical eyes, in a perceptual arena in which the divide between animate and inanimate worlds can no longer be upheld. The new medium cannot be meaningfully rejected in a context in which there is no 'outside' to its ways of seeing. And while Rodker's, or his narrator's, overwhelming response to film might seem to be that of disgust (his terms are close to those deployed by Mann in the passage from *The Magic Mountain,* quoted earlier), they also echo the images of the avant-garde film-maker and theorist Jean Epstein, who, in a 1921 article on 'Magnification', celebrated the 'anatomical' tragedy embodied in the close-up:

Muscular preambles ripple beneath the skin. Shadows shift, tremble, hesitate. Something is being decided. A breeze of emotion underlines the mouth with clouds. The orography of the face vacillates. Seismic shocks begin. Capillary wrinkles try to split the fault. A wave carries them away. Crescendo. A muscle bridles. The lip is laced with tics like a theater curtain. Everything is movement, imbalance, crisis. Crack. The mouth gives way, like a ripe fruit splitting open. As if split by a scalpel, a keyboard-like smile cuts laterally into the corner of the lips. ... The close-up is an intensifying agent because of its size alone ... The close-up modifies the drama by the impact of proximity. Pain is within reach. If I stretch out my arm I touch you, and that is intimacy. I can count the eyelashes of this suffering. I would be able to taste the tears. Never before has a face turned to mine in that way. Ever closer it presses against me, and I follow it face to face ... This is cyclopean art, a unisensual art, an iconoscopic retina.[209]

In Rodker's text, experience enters through the human senses, reflecting and reinscribing, as Sara Danius writes of James Joyce's *Ulysses*, 'a social history of the sensorium', in which 'each sensory organ now appears to operate independently and for its own sake. In fact, each sensory organ, particularly the eye, tends to perform according to its own autonomous rationality, as though detached from any general epistemic tasks'.[210]

Joyce's work, and *Ulysses* in particular, must enter into any discussion of film–literature relationships. The cinema impacted upon him, and he upon it, in a variety of ways that I can only sketch here. In 1909, Joyce travelled from Trieste, where he had been living since 1904, back to Dublin, in order to establish the first cinema in Ireland. In Trieste (where there were twenty-one permanent cinemas by 1909), Nora Joyce was a regular filmgoer, while Joyce had written to his brother Stanislaus in 1909 of his flight from depression in 'the sixty-miles-an-hour pathos of some cinematograph'.[211] The immediate spur to Joyce's entrepreneurship appears to have been his sister Eva, newly arrived from Dublin, who commented that 'she liked one aspect of Trieste, its cinemas, and remarked one morning how odd it was that Dublin, a larger city, had not even one'.

Joyce and his business partners, proprietors of cinemas in Trieste, called their new cinema, located in Dublin's Mary Street, the Cinematograph Volta; it opened on December 20 1909 with a screening of predominantly French and Italian films. Thereafter the programme changed twice weekly, showing a wide range of films, including melodramas, Film d'Art tragedies, and slapstick comedies. The Volta seems to have been popular and, confident of the success of the enterprise, Joyce returned to Trieste in the

New Year. By April 1910, however, his business partners were writing to tell him that the concern was losing money and would have to be wound up, and the Volta was sold that June.[212]

This was the end of Joyce's connections with film exhibition, but by no means the close of his engagement with cinematic representation. This profoundly shaped his fiction, *Ulysses* in particular, as a number of early commentators on his work observed, though at times in critical terms. Reviewing *Portrait of an Artist as a Young Man*, H. G. Wells focused on Joyce's experiments with 'paragraph and punctuation' and, in particular, the absence of the inverted comma (which Joyce would later call the 'perverted comma'). For Wells: 'One conversation in the book is a superb success, the one in which Mr. Dedalus carves the Christmas turkey ... but most of the talk flickers blindingly with these dashes, one has the same wincing feeling of being flicked at that one used to have in the early cinema shows.'[213] The *New Age* reviewer wrote, in the same context, of Joyce's 'wilful cleverness, his determination to produce Kinematographic effects instead of a literary portrait ... a mere catalogue of unrelated states'.[214] A 1922 review of *Ulysses* in the *Evening News* declared that Joyce's style 'is in the new fashionable kinematographic vein, very jerky and elliptical'.[215]

By the time of Harry Levin's 1944 study of Joyce (revised 1960), such 'effects' had become perceived as part of Joyce's experimental genius rather than mere fashionable novelties. Levin wrote of *Ulysses* that Leopold Bloom's mind is a motion picture, cut and edited 'to emphasize the close-ups and fade-outs of flickering emotion, the angles of observation and the flashbacks of reminiscence'. The organization of the raw material of Joyce's fiction, Levin suggested, entails the operation of *montage*.[216]

For the Soviet director and film theorist Sergei Eisenstein, the importance of *Ulysses*, which he described as the most significant event in the history of *cinema*, lay in substantial part in the ways in which it confirmed the relationship between montage and 'inner monologue'. For Eisenstein, 'montage form as structure is a reconstruction of the laws of the thought process',[217] and in this way it becomes allied to 'that particular penetration of interior vision which marks the description of intimate life in *Ulysses* and in *Portrait of the Artist* with the aid of the astonishing method of the interior monologue'.[218] As I explore in later chapters, it was the coming of sound in the late 1920s, Eisenstein argued, that made possible the 'practical realisation' in film of 'inner monologue', with voice-over representing interior discourse, and in the early 1930s he discussed with Joyce the making of a film of *Ulysses*, although the novel was not in fact filmed until Joseph Strick's version in 1967.

For Joyce, the two possible directors for such a film were Eisenstein himself, and Walter Ruttmann, director of the 1927 *Berlin: Symphony of a Great City*, a 'day-in-the-life-of a-city-film' that has strong affinities with both *Ulysses* and Virginia Woolf's *Mrs Dalloway*.[219] Urban consciousness and cinematic consciousness become intertwined in these city fictions, with the deployment of the fictional equivalent of a fixed camera, which records, as pure contingency, everything that passes by it, and of 'montage' techniques represented by contrast and juxtaposition. As Ezra Pound wrote in 1922: 'The life of a village is a narrative... In the city the visual impressions succeed each other, overlap, overcross, they are cinematographic.'[220] In the 1930s, 'city symphonies' were widely recreated in the work of writers of the British Left, including John Sommerfield, whose *May Day* (1936) was one of many panoramic and cinematic pictures of contemporary urban life influenced by the work of John Dos Passos and Joyce, by film-makers like Dziga-Vertov and Ruttmann, and by montage theories.

In his account of the cinematographic nature of *Ulysses*, Harry Levin added, however, that, while 'montage' is a useful metaphor, 'Joyce's medium is far less vivid and swift, far more blurred and jerky. His projections, to our surprise, tend to slow down and at times to stop altogether, suddenly arresting the action and suspending the characters in mid-air'.[221] In this way, Levin's discussion anticipates recent work on the influence of 'stop-motion' tricks in early films on *Ulysses*. In recent years, the renewed interest in early cinema has led to work on the more precise and specific relationship between early films and modernist literature. Joyce's experiences of film viewing in Trieste in the first decade of the century, and his involvement with films at the *Volta* cinema, are explored in studies of the ways in which early trick and animated films themselves animated *Ulysses*, and in particular the *Circe* chapter of the novel with, in Keith Williams's words, its 'Protean deformation of time, space, body and identity'.[222] The cinematic animism, the endowment of objects with 'intense life', in Jean Epstein's phrase, so celebrated in early film theory (including that of Vachel Lindsay, with his assertion of our 'yearning for personality in furniture' and his claims for the 'Hallowe'en witch-power' of cinema)[223] and in avant-garde and surrealist writings on film, was most fully embodied in early trick films, with their metamorphoses, transformations, and object animations. As David Robinson writes of Georges Méliès's films: 'Nothing in his world is what it seems. In an instant, objects turn into people, butterflies metamorphose into chorus beauties, men become women, anyone may vanish in a puff of smoke. Limbs and heads become detached, and go on about their normal business amiably unconcerned until they eventually find their way back to their rightful locations.'[224] It seems certain that Joyce was drawing upon such cinematic effects for his own animations of the object world in *Ulysses*—Bloom's singing bar of soap ('We're a capital couple are Bloom and I/He brightens the earth, I polish the sky'), the brothel-madam Bella's erotic talking fan—and, as Williams suggests, for the phonetic deformations of the text, linguistic versions of the visual distortions found in early animated cartoons.[225]

'I maintain', the avant-garde artist and film-maker Fernand Léger wrote in 1926, 'that before the invention of the moving-picture no one knew the possibilities latent in a foot—a hand—a hat.'[226] Léger's account of 'the possibilities of the fragment or element' has significant parallels with Joyce's representations in *Ulysses* of part-objects and of human forms in which feet and hands and hats appear independently of the whole. Bloom, standing in front of an advertisement, is described in these terms:

> While his eyes still read blandly he took off his hat quietly inhaling his hairoil and sent his right hand with slow grace over his brow and hair. Very warm morning. Under their dropped lids his eyes found the tiny bow of the leather headband inside his high grade hat. Just there. His right hand came down into the bowl of his hat. His fingers found quickly a card behind the headband and transferred it to his waistcoat pocket.
>
> So warm. His right hand once more slowly went over his brow and hair. Then he put on his hat again.[227]

As Sara Danius notes of this passage: 'the notion of a conscious nucleus is displaced, and a dissociated Bloom stands before the reader, reborn in each new visual frame which presents the physiological makeup of the hero in what could be described as a series of close-ups.'[228] Joyce's focus on the minutiae of the everyday and the breaking down of gesture into its component parts is shaped by the ways in which the camera frames reality, and by the new relation to the object-world, including the animation of the inanimate, and the mechanization of the human, that it brought into being.

The complexity of Joyce's uses of cinema and the cinematic is in part a result of the range of film 'styles' that he seems to appropriate and incorporate. 'Wandering Rocks' is, in John McCourt's words, 'a series of moving pictures, providing a carousel of short clips of Dublin'.[229] Father

John Conmee's tram-ride, in this section of the text, represents a form of movement through the city brought into being at the turn of the city in actuality films, in which street scenes and tram and railway rides structured filmic motion. At the same time, the characters in 'Wandering Rocks', as Thomas Burkdall noted, 'resemble automatons, comprising the moving parts of a Dublin machine', while, in 'Circe', 'Bloom's stiff walk', which seems to imitate that of Charlie Chaplin, 'turns his movements into mechanical ones'.[230]

Like Dorothy Richardson's *Pilgrimage* (discussed in later chapters), *Ulysses* contains an embedded history of pre-cinematic and early cinematic technologies. Bloom, like Richardson's Miriam, appears at moments to take on the aspect of Baudelaire's 'kaleidoscope gifted with consciousness': 'in middle youth he [Bloom] had often sat observing through a rondel of bossed glass of a multicoloured pane the spectacle offered with continual changes of the thoroughfare without, pedestrians, quadrupeds, velocipedes, vehicles, passing slowly, quickly, evenly, round and round and round the rim of a round precipitous globe.'[231] At the heart of the 'Nausicaa' section of *Ulysses* is the mutoscope vision that John Rodker also conjured into being, which, along with Joyce's invocations of early projected films, raises central questions about the experience of pre-cinema and early cinema in relation to solitary and collective viewing experiences, and of the 'voyeurism' inseparable from the act of looking.

The mutoscope (which translates as 'dumbshow') was the coin-operated peephole machine patented by W. K. L. Dickson, who, after leaving Edison's employ in 1895, founded the American Mutoscope Company (which became the American Mutoscope and Biograph Company in 1899). As the *New York Herald* explained, the attraction of the mutoscope for investors was that 'it is operated by hand and requires no motor battery or attendant; so simple is it that a child can operate it'. Its attraction for the viewer was that 'in the operation of the mutoscope the spectator has the performance entirely under his own control by the turning of the crank. He may make the operation as quick or as slow as fancy dictates, or he may maintain the normal speed at which the original performance took place; and if he so elects the entertainment can be stopped by him at any point in the series and each separate picture inspected at leisure'.[232]

In 'Nausicaa', Gerty McDowell, sitting on Sandymount Strand, is watched by Bloom, and observes him watching:

It was getting darker but he could see and he was looking all the time that he was winding the watch or whatever he was doing to it and then he put it back and put his hands back into his pockets ... and she leaned back ever so far to see the fireworks ... And she saw a long Roman candle going up over the trees, up, up, and in the tense hush, they were all breathless with excitement as it went higher and higher and she had to lean back more and more to look up after it, high, high, almost out of sight, and her face was suffused with a divine, an entrancing blush from straining back and he could see her other things too, nainsook knickers, the fabric that caresses the skin, better than those other pettiwidth, the green, four and eleven, on account of being white and she let him and she saw that he saw and then it went so high it went out of sight for a moment and she was trembling in every limb from being bent so far back he had a full view high up above her knee no-one ever not even on the swing or wading and she wasn't ashamed and he wasn't either to look in that immodest way like that because he couldn't resist the sight of the wondrous revealment half offered like those skirtdancers behaving so immodest before gentleman looking and he kept on looking, looking.[233]

After the climaxes, of both the masturbating Bloom and the Roman candle, Bloom sees Gerty, now revealed to be lame, limping away, and thinks about the 'natural craving' of women:

Pity they can't see themselves. A dream of well-filled hose. Where was that? Ah, yes. Mutoscope pictures in Capel street: for men only. Peeping Tom. Willy's hat and what the girls did with it. Do they snapshot those girls or is it all a fake? *Lingerie* does it.[234]

'Willie's Hat' has been identified as a Biograph Mutoscope picture dating from 1897, considered too risqué for the general catalogue and carried only in their special 'Club' list, under the title 'What the Girls Did with Willie's Hat' or 'Kicking Willie's Hat'.[235] This particular mutoscope picture seems, indeed, to have provoked the special ire of campaigners against peepshow entertainments. In July 1897, it was the subject of a ban by the American reformer the Reverend Frederick Bruce Russell, who raided a number of Coney Island locales to halt the showing of mutoscope pictures.[236] In England, the Parliamentarian Samuel Smith, writing to *The Times* in 1899, protested against 'viciously suggestive pictures' in the mutoscope, including 'nude female figures as living and moving', but reserved special condemnation for 'one machine [that] contained a series of pictures of girls in short frocks engaged in kicking at a hat which was held above their heads, there being at each attempt a liberal display of underclothing'.[237]

Figure 4. Viewing Mutoscope machines at the seaside, *c.*1912.

The picture thus described would certainly seem to have been 'Kicking Willie's Hat', the *resumé* of which appeared thus in the Library of Congress catalogue: 'In a drawing room, four young women are frolicking about. There is a silk hat on the table and one of the young women picks it up and holds it high above her head, while the remaining three girls attempt to reach the hat by kicking high over their heads. One of them apparently overextends herself for she falls over, landing flat on her back as the film ends.'[238] Joyce echoes this in Gerty's reflections on her friend Cissy's running: 'It would have served her just right if she had tripped over something accidentally on purpose with her high crooked heels on her to make her look tall and got a fine tumble. *Tableau!* That would have been a very charming exposé for a gentleman to witness.'[239] The 'accidentally on purpose' chimes with Bloom's musings on the 'reality' of the girls' performances in mutoscope pictures, which characteristically posed dramas of 'accidental' revelation:[240] 'Do they snapshot those girls or is it all a fake?'

Austin Briggs has suggested that early projected film was a possible referent for Joyce in 'Nausicaa', and not just the mutoscope machine. 'Peeping Tom' was a 1901 film made by George A. Smith, the Hove film pioneer whose films included 'The Kiss in The Tunnel' (1899) and 'As

Seen Through a Telescope' (1900). Smith used close-ups and point-of-view shots, as did Edwin S. Porter, in his 'Gay Shoe Clerk' of 1903, a film which shows a close-up of a woman's ankle and foot, and, as Briggs notes, echoes Bloom's voyeuristic gaze across the street at a fashionable woman in 'Lotus-Eaters'—'Watch! Watch! Silk flash rich stockings white. Watch!'—cut across by a tramcar, leaving him with 'Flicker, flicker: the laceflare of her hat in the sun: flicker flick'.[241]

Yet the technology of the mutoscope, and the particular kind of vision machine that it represents, possesses specific significance, which argues against its absolute conflation into a more generalized 'cinematic' mode of viewing in *Ulysses*. Joyce's mutoscope—like the other 'time machines' discussed earlier in this chapter—created ambiguities over the placing of spectator and spectacle as inside or outside the box, a blurring of the boundaries between watcher and watched, and a particularly charged relationship between solitary and collective viewing. There was particular moral concern over the 'hand-cranking' mechanism of the mutoscope which was linked to the 'performance' of the aroused male viewer. Gerty is seen by Bloom as a mutoscope girl, raising her skirts higher and higher—'up, up'—but it is his physical and visual activity that produces the sequencing of images. At the same time, Gerty commends to herself the ways 'her wellturned ankle displayed its perfect proportion beneath her skirt and just the proper amount and no more of her shapely limbs encased in finespun hose with high spliced heels and wide garter tops'[242] 'swung her leg more in and out in time' as she sees Bloom 'looking all the time', and makes the connection between 'her wondrous revealment' and that of the 'skirtdancers and highkickers' whose pictures Bertha Supple's gentleman lodger had, so Bertha had told her, 'cut out of papers … and she said he used to do something not very nice that you could imagine sometimes in the bed'.[243]

Here, as Philip Sicker suggests, we see the ways in which still images resemble moving ones, with 'Gertie's gradual exposure of her stockings, garters, and nainsook knickers unfold[ing] for Bloom like the sequential images on a mutoscope reel'.[244] The hand-cranking mechanism of the mutoscope, unlike that of the electrically driven Kinetoscope or, of course, projected film, allowed the spectator to keep the image still, in order, as the *New York Herald* suggested, to inspect it at leisure. The relationship between stasis and motion was thus particular charged, emphasized, as Katherine Mullin notes, by the marketing of stills as postcards and the use of the first photograph in a series of flickercards to be visible through the viewfinder.[245]

'Playing Galatea to Bloom's Pygmalion', Mullin writes, 'Joyce makes his heroine simulate the first frame of a mutoscope reel, perfectly still yet waiting for the penny to drop and the handcrank to turn.'[246] Bloom's earlier musings on Pygmalion and Galatea and on the 'shapely goddesses' in the library museum—'They don't care what man looks'—return in 'Circe': '*The keeper of the Kildare Street Museum appears, dragging a lorry on which are the shaking statues of several naked goddesses, Venus Callipyge, Venus Pandemos, Venus Metempsychosis, and plaster figures, also naked, representing the new nine muses*' of the Bloomusalem.[247] Bloom's is indeed a dream of the moving statue, and *Ulysses* takes us back to the fantasies generated by the vision-machines of cinema at the medium's very inception.

2

The Shadow on the Screen:
Virginia Woolf and the Cinema

Bloomsbury and Film

It is, at first sight, surprising that there is relatively limited written evidence of the Bloomsbury Group's intellectual engagement with film in its first decades. The art critic Clive Bell wrote two brief articles on cinema in the 1920s. The first, published in 1922, was highly critical of the medium, while suggesting that the German expressionist film *The Cabinet of Dr Caligari* had brought about some change in his attitudes; the second, which appeared in 1929, celebrated surrealist films, as anti-commercial projects which could present the unfamiliar and marvellous aspects of everyday reality, and explore the aesthetic possibilities of the unexpected.[1] Some years earlier, Roger Fry had incorporated brief discussion of the 'Cinematograph' in 'An Essay in Aesthetics', reprinted in *Vision and Design* (1920). He also mentioned 'the Cinema' in his 1924 essay 'The Artist and Psycho-analysis' as an example of an art in which 'wish-fulfilment reigns supreme ... appeal[ing] to the desire to realize ideally what reality had denied', contrasting this with 'a peculiar detachment from the instinctive life' that characterized the effects of great literature on the reader.[2] The most substantial essay was Virginia Woolf's 'The Cinema', published in 1926, which I explore in detail in this chapter, along with discussion of Fry's early comments on the new medium. The Woolfs' Hogarth Press also published two pamphlets on film, the music critic Eric Walter White's *Parnassus to Let: An Essay about Rhythm in the Films* (1928) and *Walking Shadows: An Essay on Lotte Reiniger's Silhouette Films* (1931).

A significant commitment to cinema and its cultural 'elevation' is, in fact, suggested by Roger Fry's and Maynard Keynes's roles as founding members of the Film Society, established in London in 1925. Scattered comments suggest that Leonard and Virginia Woolf attended some of the Sunday afternoon screenings, which were reviewed in the *Nation and Athenaeum* while Leonard Woolf was literary editor. Brief notes in Woolf's diaries also indicate visits to the 'Picture Palace', though she rarely, if ever, commented on the contents of the film programmes.[3] A further connection between Bloomsbury and cinema existed through *The Spectator*, edited until 1925 by John St Loe Strachey (Lytton Strachey's uncle). This was one of the first journals to establish a regular film column, written for a number of years by Iris Barry, one of the founder members of the Film Society and film critic for a variety of journals and newspapers in the 1920s, whose writing I explore in detail in Chapter 4.

Given these diverse engagements with the new medium, the absence of sustained published discussion of film aesthetics is tantalizing. The relations between the visual and the verbal, the artist and the writer, were at the heart of Bloomsbury culture, and film played a crucial role in redefinitions of the established arts in the modernist period.[4] Cinema, indeed, was undoubtedly a more active point of reference for Bloomsbury aesthetics than the brief 'bibliography' I have outlined would suggest, shaping, for the art critics Fry and Bell in particular (as photography had before it, and would continue to do), questions of realism and illusion, machine-art and 'personal' or hand-made art. For Woolf, as a writer and not a painter, the issues were not identical, but those of realism and mimesis, and of 'vision' as a question of the eye or of the mind and imagination, were shared concerns, which inflected her responses to the cinema in significant ways.

There is an early example of the connections that flourished in broader European contexts between the visual arts and experimental film in a work by Duncan Grant of 1914, *Abstract Kinetic Collage Painting with Sound* or (*The Scroll*) of 1914. This was a scroll with an abstract motif of rectangles made from painted paper, and Grant's original conception appears to have been that it should be viewed through an opening in a lit box. As the canvas wound through, it would be accompanied by music, probably the 'Adagio' from Bach's *First Brandbenburg Concerto*. There is no record of it ever being displayed in this way: the filmed reconstruction at the Tate Gallery represented the scroll moving horizontally, though Simon Watney has suggested, on the evidence of a sketch made by Grant, that the movement was intended to be vertical.[5] If this were the case, its movement would be closer to that of the film-strip than to that of the panorama.[6] The influences on *The Scroll*, as Ian Christie has suggested, were probably the scrolls produced by artists such as Viking Eggeling and Hans Richter in Germany, who would become central figures in experimental film-making.[7] In this work we see the desire to bring together image and music and a fascination with pure colour combined with the desire for kinesis. A note by Grant indicates the effect he wished to create: 'Black green white yellow to grey to dark grey to black. Begin again solemnly in grey and green ... yellow again gayer to red and yellow accompaniment.'[8] Christie calls Grant's scroll an example of '*graphic proto-cinema*' and further connects it to projects of the European avant-garde (including those of Kandinsky, Survage and Sonia Delaunay, Apollinaire, and Cendrars) in colour and motion and in colour-music. *The Scroll* was a significant anticipation of avant-garde and experimental film effects and, as a 'future' film, bears on Virginia Woolf's imaginings of a film-art yet to emerge at the close of her essay 'The Cinema'. Its context was also that of early twentieth-century experiments in synaesthesia; of particular interest at a point at which the new technologies of sound and vision were seen to be splitting the sensorium, and rendering autonomous the realms of the eye and the ear.

Grant's interest in the representation of movement is apparent in much of his work: for example, the painting *Bathers*, where the diving and swimming bodies could be perceived as a single body in the different stages of motion, as in early film experiments in stop-action cinematography. Nonetheless, *The Scroll* was an isolated instance in Grant's artistic career: he made no further attempts to move his art into the arena of experimental film, perhaps (though this must remain speculative) discouraged by comments such as D. H. Lawrence's, in a letter to Lady Ottoline Morrell: 'Tell him not to make silly experiments in the futuristic line with bits of colour on moving paper.'[9]

It may also be that Diaghilev's Russian Ballet, understood as quintessentially an art of movement and colour, and of colour in movement, overwhelmed Grant's experiment with kinetic art in these years, becoming a more vital and immediate model for the Bloomsbury artists to follow. In 1912, Virginia Stephen had written in a letter of settling in London for the summer, 'which will be absolutely dry, and all awhirl with Wagner and with Russian dancers'.[10] In 1911, Leonard Woolf described the Russian ballet as a revelation, and wrote of the entrancement of 'a new art', a term, as we have seen, often reserved for film.[11] While the silent, monochromatic, spectral world of the early film might at one level seem to have been radically distinct from that of the Russian Ballet's colour, sound and immediacy, critics in the 1920s found strong associations between the rhythms of avant-garde cinema and the ballet.[12] Towards the end of her life, Woolf connected the Ballets Russes with film when she wrote in her notebooks, in the context of a discussion of the Elizabethan theatre and the absence of written commentary from its contemporary audiences:

> That silence is one of the deep gulfs that lies between us and the play. They [audiences] come crowding across the river daily; but they sit there silent. They neither praise nor blame. We can compare this silence with our own silence at the Russian ballet or at the cinema in their early days. A new art comes upon us so surprisingly that we sit silent, recognising before we take the measure.[13]

This comment adds a further dimension to one of the central concerns of this book: the question of writing about film as a form of 'talking in the cinema'. It suggests that the relative 'silence' of Woolf and her Bloomsbury contemporaries on the question of the new art of film is to be understood as a necessary pause—a reticence in the face of the unfamiliar. It by no means connoted indifference. The impact of the Russian ballet resonated throughout Woolf's life and writing, and the same can in fact be said for the cinema.

'A book of cinema'

Woolf's direct commentaries on the art and medium of film were not, however, uniformly celebratory. In 1918, she wrote a review of Compton Mackenzie's novel *The Early Life and Adventures of Sylvia Scarlett* (which would become a film in 1935) entitled 'The Movie Novel'. Woolf compared Mackenzie's heroine with characters in earlier fiction, including Tom Jones and Moll Flanders, who also had 'adventures':

> Compared with Mr Mackenzie's characters they are a slow-moving race— awkward, ungainly and simple-minded. But consider how many things we know about them, how much we guess, what scenes of beauty and romance we set them in, how much of England is their background—without a word of description perhaps, but merely because they are themselves. We can think about them when we are no longer reading the book. But we cannot do this

with Mr Mackenzie's characters; and the reason is, we fancy, that although Mr Mackenzie can see them once he can never see them twice, and, as in a cinema, one picture must follow another without stopping, for if it stopped and we had to look at it we should be bored. Now, it is a strange thing that no one has yet been seen to leave a cinema in tears. The cab horse bolts down Haverstock Hill and we think it a good joke; the cyclist runs over a hen, knocks an old woman into the gutter, and has a hose turned upon him. But we never care whether he is wet or hurt or dead. So it is with Sylvia Scarlett and her troupe. Up they get and off they go, and as for minding what becomes of them, all we hope is that they will, if possible, do something funnier next time. No, it is not a book of adventures; it is a book of cinema.[14]

For Woolf, at this stage, cinema was thus perceived as motion without emotion, and as a surface vision incapable of suggesting interiority. These terms, as I discuss in Chapter 3, were central to Victor O. Freeburg's film aesthetics (drawing on the work of the philosopher of art Vernon Lee), in which 'movement' as mere mechanical motion was disaggregated from 'movement' as connected to sensation and emotion, and they resonated throughout writing about film in the 1920s.[15] As Eric Walter White commented in his *Parnassus to Let*: 'Rhythm appears to be most obviously successful in a film when motional and emotional rhythms alternate, and the appeal to the spectator is at once visual and mental... Although movement is the breath of life to the cinema, yet it is of no use to photograph movement and nothing but movement.'[16]

The distinction White drew between the 'visual' and the 'mental' maps onto to that between the 'eye' and the 'mind' or 'brain', a contrast at the heart of writing about cinema in this period and expressive of the concern, indicated briefly in Woolf's review, that the new medium of the film was able to engage the eye but not the mind, so that its impact was purely retinal. Hence Woolf's suggestion that literary characters such as those of Fielding and Defoe ('slow-moving' as opposed, presumably, to the mechanically agitated figures on the cinematic screen) had an afterlife in the reader's mind (which could indeed be understood as a form of after-image). Moving images, by contrast, were perceived to have only the instantaneous life of their immediate projection and brief retinal reception, each image being replaced by the one that succeeds it.

John Galsworthy wrote of the early cinema in very similar terms in a letter of 1930:

> When the film was silent I came to look on it with tolerance, and once in a way with gratitude as a form of entertainment, and certainly with admiration as a means of education, and with alarm as a means of propaganda. It had a certain power when very ably and restrainedly handled of exciting aesthetic emotion. It had a very real and rather dangerous power of holding the eye even at its worst. It could sway you while you looked on, but when you came away (with the rarest exceptions) you were wholly unmoved. And this, I think, was partly because you were conscious of its enormous faking power, and partly because the eye was held at such a pace that the mind did not stir in concord.[17]

The movement Woolf described is locomotive, and she, like Galsworthy, connected it to a total absence of affect and identification. 'Now it is a strange thing that no one has yet been seen to leave a cinema in tears', she wrote. The 'yet' suggests that such an eventuality might occur in the future, but it is nonetheless curious that Woolf's account of the cinema was so at odds with the habitual criticisms of its sentimentality. The critique was far more likely to be that the representations of feeling in film, and the responses it produced, were wet-eyed rather than dry. Woolf appears to be describing forms of early film comedy, suggesting that she had, at this stage at least, no great familiarity with the narrative cinema of the period in which she was writing.[18]

In 1926, Woolf returned to the analogy between the film and the novel in a review of G. B. Stern's *The Deputy was King*, titled 'Life and the Novelist'. In this essay, Woolf outlines an aesthetic, in which the novelist, by contrast with visual artists or composers, 'is terribly exposed to life ... He can no more cease to receive impressions than a fish in mid-ocean can cease to let the water rush through his gills.' While the world of everyday realities, 'the crowded dance of modern life', is the novelist's element, however, it remains necessary that the writer at some point retreat from the world in order, through the strenuous processes of the creative act, to turn immediate impressions into 'something stark, formidable and enduring'. This, in Woolf's account, was Stern's failure:

> The grudging voice will concede that it is all very brilliant; will admit that a hundred pages have flashed by like a hedge seen from an express train; but will reiterate that for all that something is wrong. A man can elope with a woman without our noticing it. There is a proof that there are no values.

There is no shape to these apparitions. Scene melts into scene; person into person. People arise out of a fog of talk, and sink back into talk again. They are soft and shapeless with words. There is no grasping them.

... We have been letting ourselves bask in appearances. All this representation of the movement of life has sapped our imaginative power. We have sat receptive and watched, with our eyes rather than our minds, as we do at the cinema, what passes on the screen in front of us ... All is fluent and graphic; but no character or situation emerges cleanly. Bits of entraneous [sic] matter are left sticking to the edges. For all their brilliancy the scenes are clouded; the crises are blurred.[19]

Again, the invocation of the cinema serves to suggest speed (analogized through locomotion) and the surface response of the eye and not the depths of the mind. Woolf's critique was directly primarily at Stern's use of descriptors, in which detail is added to detail: 'As if we had not enough to see already, she goes on to add how there were tiny stamens springing from every flower, and circles ringing the eye of each separate stork, until the Chinese coat wobbles before our eyes and merges into one brilliant blur.'[20] The overload is represented in visual terms; the Chinese coat Stern describes in such detail also has too much detail, so that both the coat and its description are to be understood as over-decorated and excessively ornate. The flow of words is represented, indeed, as an assault on the eye, and this is where the question of cinema enters for the second time: not only to signify the passive readerly reception of the realist novel, but a visual overload: 'the Chinese coat wobbles before our eyes and merges into one brilliant blur.'

The failure of Stern's novel, which, Woolf implied, was, like Compton Mackenzie's *Sylvia Scarlett*, a 'movie novel', rested on its failure to select from the welter of details and impressions that fill the world. The criticism recalls those early accounts of film in which the new medium was indeed seen as incapable of 'the tasks of selection and revision', able only to record the life that passes in front of the camera eye.[21] In the words of W. T. Stead,

The attraction of the Cinema is Life ... The Cinema show represents Life as it is lived to-day—Life caught in the act of living, and made to reproduce itself before the Cinema crowd ... The chief fault that can be found with the Cinema is that it is too stimulating. The rapid and constant succession of moving pictures leaves no time for reflection. You see life as from the window of an express train. You have not even opportunity to recollect the impression of the scene.[22]

The cinema, in both 'The Movie Novel' and 'Life and the Novelist', was invoked primarily as a figure for the contemporary novel and its representations of 'the crowded dance of modern life'. The motion of the film—its way of 'passing' in front of the eyes—was connected to 'the froth of the moment' from which the modern novelist concocts his books: 'But his work passes as the year 1921 passes, as foxtrots pass, and in three years time looks as dowdy and dull as any other fashion which has served its turn and gone away.'[23] The analogy of the cinema, on the surface at least, served little more purpose than to represent the lack of substance of a medium—whether film, fiction, or fashion—that existed only in and for the present, merely moving from one frame to another without leaving a trace. The 'passing' of the film image, and its mechanically driven forward motion, became inextricably linked to the ephemeral qualities of the medium as a whole, as well as to 'the railway-line of a sentence' which was Woolf's critique of the realism of the 'Edwardian' novelists.

Yet it is significant that Woolf opened 'Life and the Novelist' with a discussion of the differences between the various arts—music, literature, the visual arts—and suggested that the novelist differs from artists in the other media ('they shut themselves up for weeks alone with a dish of apples and a paint box, or a roll of music paper and a piano') in his or her commitment to 'life': 'Taste, sound, movement, a few words here, a gesture there, a man coming in, a woman going out, even the motor that passes in the street or the beggar that shuffles along the pavement, and all the reds and blues and lights and shades of the scene claim his attention and rouse his curiosity.'[24] This appears to be a 'filmic' vision, predicated upon movement, spatial relations and the play of light, raising central questions about the extent to which Woolf saw a positive alliance between the cinema and the novel. As with Woolf's discussions of the relationships between writing and the other arts more generally, she was in dialogue with the aesthetic theories and practices of the artists around her—Roger Fry, Clive Bell, Vanessa Bell, Duncan Grant—and, in particular, with Clive Bell's and, to an extent, Roger Fry's constructions of the 'aesthetic life' as necessarily remote from practical life and everyday praxis. The novelist, Woolf implied, has the more difficult (and, perhaps, more significant) task of finding a balance between involvement in 'life' and the aesthetic retreat. The question was whether the film had a place in such definitions of, and divisions between, the arts. The novel was also a relative latecomer and the cinema had the potential to become an ally in its newness, rather than a medium from which the novelist, intent on upholding the seriousness of his or her craft, would take a critical distance.

'The Cinema'

Some months before the publication of 'Life and the Novelist', Woolf had published her fullest and most reflective account of the new art and medium of the film in her essay 'The Cinema', which appeared in *Arts* (New York) for June 1926. A variant edition, in which some sentences and emphases were altered, was published in the *Nation and Athenaeum* on 3 July 1926 and (without Woolf's consent) as 'The Movies and Reality' in the *New Republic* of 4 August 1926. The variant edition omitted, in particular, a passage in which Woolf dwelt on the essentially speculative nature of any commentary on the cinema, given that the future development of film could only be surmised. There would be a long journey, she wrote, before the film-maker could persuade 'us' that 'what he shows us, fantastic though it seems, has some relation with the great veins and arteries of our existence ... How slow a process this is bound to be, and attended with what pain and ridicule and indifference can easily be foretold when we remember how painful novelty is'.[25] The words anticipate those that Woolf wrote in her notebooks many years later on the inevitable critical 'silence' in the face of the new art. She may well, however, have omitted the paragraph on the essay's second publication because it seemed too tentative and self-deprecating, in its qualified comments and its reference to her own 'guessing and clumsy turning over of unknown forces'.

In 'The Cinema' Woolf at times appeared to be suggesting that cinema is a lesser art than literature, and certainly more 'primitive'. She opened her article with an account of the cinema as appealing to the cultural 'savage' within: 'We are peering over the edge of a cauldron in which fragments seem to simmer, and now and again some vast shape heaves and seems about to haul itself up out of chaos and the savage in us starts forward in delight'.[26] This could in fact be seen as cinema's second stage, for the films began, for Woolf as, in some part, for Gorki, innocently:

> to begin with, the art of the cinema seems a simple and even a stupid art. That is the King shaking hands with a football team; that is Sir Thomas Lipton's yacht; that is Jack Horner winning the Grand National. The eye licks it all up instantaneously and the brain, agreeably titillated, settles itself

down to watch things happening without bestirring itself to think. For the ordinary English eye, the English unaesthetic eye, is a simple mechanism, which takes care that the body does not fall down coal-holes, provides the brain with toys and sweetmeats and can be trusted to go on behaving like a competent nursemaid until the brain comes to the conclusion that it is time to wake up. What is its surprise then to be roused suddenly in the middle of its agreeable somnolence and asked for help? The eye is in difficulties. The eye says to the brain, 'Something is happening which I do not in the least understand. You are needed.' Together they look at the King, the boat, the horse, and the brain sees at once that they have taken on a quality which does not belong to the simple photograph of real life. They have become not more beautiful, in the sense in which pictures are beautiful, but shall we call it (our vocabulary is miserably insufficient) more real, or real with a different reality from that which we perceive in daily life. We behold them as they are when we are not there. We see life as it is when we have no part in it. As we gaze we seem to be removed from the pettiness of actual existence. The horse will not knock us down. The King will not grasp our hands. The wave will not wet our feet ... Watching the boat sail and the wave break, we have time to open our minds wide to beauty and register on top of it this queer sensation—this beauty will continue, and this beauty will flourish whether we behold it or not. Further, all this happened ten years ago, we are told. We are beholding a world which has gone beneath the waves. Brides are emerging from the abbey—they are now mothers; ushers are ardent—they are now silent; mothers are tearful; guests are joyful; this has been won and that has been lost, and it is over and done with. The war sprung its chasm at the feet of all this innocence and ignorance, but it was thus that we danced and pirouetted, toiled and desired, thus that the sun shone and the clouds scudded up to the very end. The brain adds all this to what the eye sees upon the screen.[27]

The temporalities in the essay are curious ones, with Woolf's discussion of the embryonic new medium moving backwards into an account of documentaries of the pre-war world, so that there is a seeming dislocation of historical reference. Any construction of the history of the medium is, indeed, rendered complex by a number of factors, not least the perception, which I noted in Gorki's article, that cinema was perceived as at one and the same time 'new' and 'archaic', so that points of transition, of something that comes before and something that comes after, were also constructed out of a single present. Moreover, while there was an undoubted shift from early film as the representation and celebration of the visible world to a narrative cinema predicated on plot and action—the transition, as Tom Gunning has outlined it, from the 'cinema of attractions' to narrative cinema—film theorists also postulated a model of viewing which could extract 'pure' vision, pure beauty, from the 'banality' of narrative. It was possible, that is, to read against the grain of the history of the medium. The essence of film, Woolf and other writers seemed to be suggesting, could be perceived or captured in a way that ran counter to its narrative form, and this essence lay both at the origin of cinema and traced the lineaments of its future.

The temporal dislocation also has a more precise context and cause. As David Trotter has suggested, it is very likely that Woolf saw the 1919 film *The Cabinet of Dr Caligari* (which she goes on to discuss in the essay) at the Film Society Screening on Sunday, 14 March 1926, in which it was shown alongside 'Williamson's Animated Gazette', a programme of brief documentary films made between 1910 and 1912 whose topics were indeed those to which Woolf alluded.[28] Hence also the temporal shift in the essay from the description of film in the present to the sentence: 'Further, all this happened ten years ago, we are told.' It was the context of viewing which determined the ways in which Woolf represented the 'evolution' of cinema, at a time in which cinema was beginning to be represented as a medium with a history, not only by the Film Society, with its programmes of early cinema, but, as we have seen, by film critics of the 1920s who were arguing for the preservation of films, against the common perception of film's ephemerality as a medium.

The film-maker René Clair described a similar development in the reception of film in France in his *Reflections on the Cinema*. Clair's study combined reflections from the platform of the present (the early 1950s) with his writings from the 1920s and early 1930s, in a double temporality that echoes the 'archival' programming of films in film forums such as the Film Society, as well as Woolf's narrative and temporal position in 'The Cinema'. Clair wrote:

> It was in 1925...that cinema, for the first time, turned back towards its past. The event took place at the Cinéma des Ursulines, whose opening programme, comprising *The Joyless Street*, *Entr'acte* and 'Five Minutes of Pre-war Films', made Parisians flock to the obscure little cinema hall behind the Panthéon. Those 'five minutes' in the course of which we were shown pre-1914 news-reels and little film plays of the same period, made the majority of the spectators roar with laughter, but a few of us were inspired to sobering thoughts. Did we have the right to laugh at these primitive little

pieces? What if time were to attack our films as well, and gnaw off all their present verisimilitude, to leave only a funny skeleton?

With some melancholy, I wrote:

'Cinema lives under the sign of relativity. Its makers, its actors, the films themselves and the ideas that inspired them, pass quickly. It looks almost as though the cinematograph, that apparatus designed to capture the transient moments of life, has thrown out a challenge to time, and that time is taking a terrible revenge by speeding up its effects on everything pertaining to the cinema.'[29]

Woolf's address, in 'The Cinema', to the turning back of the medium to its past complicated and altered her earlier perceptions of film (in 'The Movie Novel' and 'Life and the Novelist') as the production of unreflective presentness, driven ever forward by its mechanism. The historicizing context in which she viewed the early documentary films, which brought to the forefront the gap between the 'then' and the 'now' of film production, led her to see film anew as a medium with a history and as a medium for the recording of history. It could no longer be divorced from questions of time and memory. The question of the tense and the temporality of cinema was a central one for film aesthetics of the 1920s, and it was addressed in particular ways by those writers exploring the psychology of film, for whom filmic devices (such as the flashback and the close-up) could be mapped onto mental states and, more specifically, the workings of memory.

Woolf's construction of a dialogue between 'eye' and 'brain' shifted the perception, present in her essays 'The Movie Novel' and 'Life and the Novelist', that film's address was to the eye alone. In the passage from Galsworthy, quoted earlier, film is said to make its entry through the 'eye-gate' (to borrow W. T. Stead's term) while failing to stir the mind in concord. The terms of 'eye' and 'mind' were also at the heart of Gerald Buckle's 1926 book *The Mind and the Film*. This study, while conceptually confused and confusing, is of interest for the ways in which it attempted to connect film form and the psychology of spectatorship, drawing on work such as Hugo Münsterberg's (discussed in Chapter 3) on the psychology of attention. Buckle also made explicit an attitude to film spectatorship that was more deeply buried in most other accounts; that of the perceived problems of a mass medium which was addressed to audiences with differential intelligences and which ran at a single and invariable speed in a context in which intelligence was measured by the relative rapidity of reflexive responses. As he explained it: 'the result will be that to the quick witted (people with short reflex) the story will lag, and to the slow minded (long reflex) it will be bewildering... one way to assist in speeding up the reflex is to assist the senses by which the brain is fed.'[30] '[In] the Motion Picture', Buckle continued, 'one is deliberately awakening the brain through the eye':

> The faculty of the human eye to receive an impression on the back of the retina, and to hold it until such time as the impression is replaced, or more accurately, until another impression is superimposed (with a slight alternation in its formation) is the whole secret of motion picture photography, and is known as 'Constancy of Vision'... Here we are, faced with what is undoubtedly the greatest factor in the film, namely, that constancy of vision becomes translated by the human eye in conjunction with the brain into constancy of thought.[31]

One of Buckle's concerns was the 'almost complete elimination of retrospection' in film.[32] He defined the concept as 'the act of considering things from a different angle of view (looking back)—in minor cases reflection, in deeper cases the calling up of the subconscious mind to aid the conscious thought in order to come to a conclusion'.[33] Whereas 'retrospection' is strongly present in the other arts, he argued, it could only exist to a very limited extent in film.

For Woolf, retrospection, or an equivalent term, was a significant concept in her account of the reception of early cinema. The passage from 'The Cinema' quoted above in fact gives us two forms of distancing or displacement: the one aesthetic, and the other temporal. Beauty becomes inseparable from time passing, and it is 'retrospection' that allows beauty to emerge. The issue is, however, not only the ten years that separate the spectator from the time of the spectacle. When the brain, in Woolf's account, bestirs itself to think, it sees that the image on the screen is not a 'simple photograph of real life', but that its existence opens up a different, more complex and elusive relationship to reality and to the relationship between presence and absence: 'We behold them as they are when we are not there. We see life as it is when we have no part in it... beauty will continue to be beautiful whether we behold it or not.' Screen beauty, as in the early writings on film which I discuss in Chapter 3, becomes a way of defining the essence of film, though Woolf also suggested that beauty is intimately connected to the 'different reality' presented in the film, whose lineaments seem to depend on the absolute separation of the spectator from the world depicted on the screen.

This appears to echo Münsterberg's 'aesthetic of isolation' in his 1916 study *The Art of the Photoplay*: 'We annihilate beauty when we link the artistic creation with practical interests and transform the spectator into a selfishly interested bystander.'[34] Woolf's words also seem to be in dialogue with Roger Fry's brief comments on the 'cinematograph', first published in 'An Essay in Aesthetics' (1909) and reprinted in *Vision and Design* (1920). Fry deployed the example of the cinematograph in the service of his 'aesthetic of autonomy', which also shared with Bergsonian thought a distinction between 'practical' and 'speculative' ways of knowing the world, and a desire for a break with both instrumentalism and habitual modes of perception. Fry wrote:

> We can get a curious side glimpse of the nature of this imaginative life from the cinematograph. This resembles actual life in almost every respect, except that what the psychologists call the conative part of our reaction to sensations, that is to say, the appropriate resultant action is cut off. If, in a cinematograph, we see a runaway horse and cart, we do not have to think either of getting out of the way or heroically interposing ourselves. The result is that in the first place we *see* the event much more clearly; see a number of quite interesting but irrelevant things, which in real life could not struggle into our consciousness, bent, as it would be, entirely upon the problem of our appropriate reaction. I remember seeing in a cinematograph the arrival of a train at a foreign station and the people descending from the carriages; there was no platform, and to my intense surprise I saw several people turn right round after reaching the ground, as though to orientate themselves; an almost ridiculous performance, which I had never noticed in all the many hundred occasions on which such a scene had passed before my eyes in real life. The fact being that at a station one is never really a spectator of events, but an actor engaged in the drama of luggage or prospective seats, and one actually sees only so much as may help to the appropriate action.
>
>   In the second place, with regard to the visions of the cinematograph, one notices that whatever emotions are aroused by them, though they are likely to be weaker than those of ordinary life, are presented more clearly to the consciousness. If the scene presented be one of an accident, our pity and horror, though weak, since we cannot know that no one is really hurt, are felt quite purely, since they cannot, as they would in life, pass at once into actions of assistance.
>
>   A somewhat similar effect to that of the cinematograph can be obtained by watching a mirror in which a street scene is reflected. If we look at the street itself we are almost sure to adjust ourselves in some way to its actual existence ... but, in the mirror, it is easier to abstract ourselves completely, and look upon the changing scene as a whole ... The frame of the mirror,

then, does to some extent turn the reflected scene from one that belongs to our actual life into one that belongs rather to the imaginative life. The frame of the mirror makes its surface into a very rudimentary work of art, since it helps us to attain to the artistic vision.[35]

Towards the close of her essay, Woolf seems to have been rewriting Fry's terms and conclusions. Whereas Fry made the early 'cinematograph' analogous to the street-scene observed in a mirror, as distinct from the street-scene itself, Woolf presented 'the chaos of the streets' as the next stage of cinema, beyond its age of innocence, and as modernism itself, which puts into question the model of art as mirror.

> How all this [the future film] is to be attempted, much less achieved, no one at the moment can tell us. We get intimations only in the chaos of the streets, perhaps, when some momentary assembly of colour, sound, movement, suggests that here is a scene waiting a new art to be transfixed.[36]

Whereas Fry's 'true spectator' watches street-life in the mirror, removed from the action, Woolf's spectator, while at present watching and waiting 'in the lazy way in which faculties detached from use watch and wait', is not free from the demand that he or she 'seize' the sights and sounds of the street, the city, and 'convert their energy into art'. Woolf, it would appear, was turning Fry's examples of the cinematograph and the street-scene against his own arguments. The potential of the cinema would be achieved, Woolf suggested, when the spectator's faculties ceased to be 'detached from use' and moved to seize sense-impressions at the moment of their fleeting unity—although the paradox might well have been that the energies of the city and the cinema lay precisely in their chaos and dispersal, their own freedom from a unifying aesthetic.

In one way, then, Woolf might well have been defining her theories of art in 'The Cinema' against Fry's formalism. Yet if we look a little differently at the passage from Fry, we see that it addressed the question of the particular kind of reality represented by the film, and the relationships between frame, memory, screen, and scene, in ways cognate with Woolf's understandings of cinematic 'beauty' and 'reality'. Furthermore, Woolf's discussion can be situated as an early contribution to the development of a realist film theory, whose chief exponents were Siegfried Kracauer and André Bazin and which explored film as the tracing and duplication of the world.[37]

The film writings of the philosopher Stanley Cavell are, to a significant extent, located in this tradition. His work, in *The World Viewed* in particular, may help illuminate Woolf's brief and exploratory comments on the new medium, as well as her explorations of 'life as it is when we have no part in it' and of, as she wrote in her diary soon after completing *To the Lighthouse*, 'the thing that exists when we aren't there'. These ontological questions lie both at the heart of her fiction and of Cavell's film theory. 'Photography', Cavell writes, 'maintains the presentness of the world by accepting our absence from it':

> The reality in a photograph is present to me while I am not present to it; and in a world I know, and see, but to which I am nevertheless not present (through no fault of my subjectivity) is a world past…movies allow the audience to be mechanically absent. The fact that I am invisible and inaudible to the actors, and fixed in position, no longer needs accounting for; it is not part of a convention I have to comply with; the proceedings do not have to make good the fact that I do nothing in the face of tragedy, or that I laugh at the follies of others. In viewing a movie my helplessness is mechanically assured: I am present not at something happening, which I must confirm, but at something that has happened, which I absorb (like a memory). …How do movies reproduce the world magically? Not by literally presenting us with the world, but by permitting us to view it unseen…It is as though the world's projection explains our forms of unknownness and our inability to know. The explanation is not so much that the world is passing us by, as that we are displaced from our natural habitation within it, placed at a distance from it. The screen overcomes our fixed distance; it makes displacement appear as our natural condition.[38]

The central question Cavell poses in *The World Viewed* is: 'What do we wish to view in this way?' For Cavell, the question can only be posed, and the answer sought, in a historically situated understanding of a specularized modernity, to which film, as Garrett Stewart has argued, 'can be both a surrender and a diagnostic rejoinder'.[39] Cinema, Cavell argues, 'entered a world whose ways of looking at itself—its *Weltanschauungen*—had already changed, as if in preparation for the screening and viewing of film…film's presenting of the world by absenting us from it appears as confirmation of something already true of our stage of existence. Its displacement of the world confirms, even explains, our prior estrangement from it'.[40] For Cavell, cinema's *modernism* is defined as any given film's self-reflexive awareness of its essential conditions: 'I was led to consider that what makes the physical medium of film unlike anything else on earth lies in the absence of what it causes to appear to us; that is to say, in the nature of our absence from it; in its fate to reveal reality and fantasy (not by reality as such, but) by projections of reality, projections in which … reality is freed to exhibit itself.'[41]

At points in his discussion, Cavell appears to be producing a diagnosis of our times, in his model of a specularized distance held to be indicative of more general forms of estrangement from the world. This, however, does not represent the totality of his thoughts on film, which are as powerfully represented in his account of reality's freedom 'to exhibit itself'. It is this dimension of *The World Viewed* that comes closest to Woolf's vision of the world perceived without a self, along with his explorations of the interplay of presence and absence or 'the presence of an absence'.

Woolf undoubtedly saw or found in film a relationship to reality that gave visible form to her own world-view, and her fascination with 'the thing that exists when we aren't there', the phrase linked, at one point in her diaries, to the concept of images and ideas 'shoulder[ing] each other out across the screen of my brain'.[42] I have been reading this response in tandem with Cavell's cinema theory, but there are also important connections to that of Gilles Deleuze, for whom the screen is, in Claire Colebrook's words, 'a dehumanization of the image, a scene where the visual can be freed from the local subject, and released to yield its autonomous power'.[43] References to Woolf's fiction (including *Mrs Dalloway*) in Deleuze's writings—though not in the two cinema books—suggest that he saw her work as significant for his concepts of the 'nonhuman becomings of man' and 'the nonhuman becomings of nature'.[44] We could certainly link this back to Woolf's understanding of the 'nonhuman' world which cinema opened up, or unfolded onto.

There is, however, a further aspect to the world represented as if without a perceiving consciousness, which is the fantasy of being there to watch things happen as if one were not there. This too is part of filmic ontology, as Alexander Bakshy noted in 1927:

> The spectator, it must be remembered, observes the motion picture world by proxy, his intermediary being the camera-eye and the film. By employing the camera he acquires the ability to be invisibly present in the very midst of the events he observes, and of following them from place to place.[45]

In this sense, 'absence' is also to be understood as 'invisible presence' (a central concept for Woolf herself, who used it to describe the continuing influences upon her of 'ghosts', and her dead mother in particular, a theme at the very heart of *To the Lighthouse*) as well as, or rather than, the distancing, displacement or even total evacuation of the subject from the world viewed.

'Some scene by the way'

'The Cinema' was also a defence of the novel against filmic adaptation. Woolf was highly critical of film when it attempted to usurp what she perceived as the ground of the other arts, and of the novel in particular. Her hostility to adaptations, motivated as it may have been by a need to defend the terrain of literature and its own image-making powers ('compact of a thousand suggestions, of which the visual is only the most obvious or the uppermost'),[46] was in line with the anti-narrative ethos of avant-garde artists, writers, and film-makers. The artist and cinéaste Fernard Léger wrote, in a 1924 essay, of the 'fundamental mistake' of filming a novel, and of the ways in which such an endeavour represented 'a completely wrong point of departure' for the 'incredible invention' of cinema, 'with its limitless plastic possibilities'. Directors, he argued, 'sacrifice that wonderful thing, "the image that moves", in order to present a story that is so much better in a book ... It is such a field of innovations that it is unbelievable they can neglect it for a sentimental scenario'.[47]

Leaving behind the recording of reality—of 'the actual world' and of 'contemporary life'—film-makers had turned to literary texts as their sources, Woolf argued, in disastrous and vampiric fashion:

> The cinema fell upon its prey with immense rapacity and to this moment largely subsists upon the body of its unfortunate victim. But the results have been disastrous to both. The alliance is unnatural. Eye and brain are torn asunder ruthlessly as they try vainly to work in couples. The eye says, 'Here is Anna Karenina,' and a voluptuous lady in black velvet wearing pearls comes before us. The brain exclaims, 'That is no more Anna Karenina than it is Queen Victoria!' For the brain knows Anna almost entirely by the inside of the mind—her charm, her passion, her despair, whereas all the emphasis is now laid upon her teeth, her pearls and her velvet ... So we lurch and lumber through the most famous novels of the world. So we spell them out in words of one syllable in the scrawl of an illiterate schoolboy. A kiss is love. A smashed chair is jealousy. A grin is happiness. Death is a hearse. None of these has the least connection with the novel that Tolstoy wrote and it is only when we give up trying to connect the pictures with the book that we guess from some scene by the way—a gardener mowing the lawn outside,

for example, or a tree shaking its branches in the sunshine—what the cinema might do if it were left to its own devices.[48]

These last images echo Woolf's account of early cinema and its representation of reality, which is also screen beauty. The potential of the cinema, the possibility of its self-realization as an art, manifests itself in 'some scene by the way'. This is accidental beauty, a concept that had been expressed by O. Winter in his 1896 article in the *New Review*, in which he wrote of the Cinematograph : 'Its results will be beautiful only by accident, until the casual, unconscious life of the street learns to compose itself into rhythmical pictures. And this lesson will never be learned outside the serene and perfect air of heaven.'[49] This was reconceptualized in the contexts of French avant-garde film criticism in particular.

In 'The Cinema', Woolf located the significant aesthetic of the cinema in that which was not in the film, but a 'blemish' upon its surface, and the accidental and the contingent became the 'mark' of cinema's aesthetic autonomy. At a screening of *Dr Caligari*, Woolf wrote:

> A shadow shaped like a tadpole suddenly appeared at one corner of the screen. It swelled to an immense size, quivered, bulged, and sank back again into nonentity. For a moment it seemed to embody some monstrous diseased imagination of the lunatic's brain. For a moment it seemed as if thought could be conveyed by shape more effectively than by words. The monstrous quivering tadpole seemed to be fear itself, and not the statement 'I am afraid'. In fact the shadow was accidental and the effect unintentional. But if a shadow at a certain moment can suggest so much more than the actual gestures, the actual words of men and women in a state of fear, it seems plain that the cinema has within its grasp innumerable symbols for emotions that have so far failed to find expression. Terror has besides its ordinary forms the shape of a tadpole; it burgeons, bulges, quivers, disappears. Anger might writhe like an infuriated worm in black zigzags across a white sheet.[50]

The demand here is for a new mode of symbolization, one not dependent on literature but capable of conveying the emotions in visual terms, and in the form, it is implied, of a hieroglyphics: that mode of representation ('fluttering between word and image') which had become, for early film theorists from Vachel Lindsay to Sergei Eisenstein, the most appropriate way of conceiving the new 'language' of film, and the one that bore the closest relations to a modernist poetics. Such symbols, for Woolf, were, however, to be differentiated from a fixed symbolic lexicon (of the kind indeed mapped out by Lindsay): 'A kiss is love. A smashed chair is jealousy. A grin is happiness. Death is a hearse.'[51]

In her perception of the accidental shadow on the screen, Woolf momentarily transmuted *Caligari* into an abstract film, in terms echoed in the American film critic Gilbert Seldes's response to her essay, in which he wrote of the new French experimental cinema: 'There may be a swelling blot of ink on a pane of glass, a shadow endowed with proper life, mysterious darkness or twilight on the screen.'[52] In his article, titled 'The Abstract Movie', Seldes quoted the following passage from Woolf:

> Something abstract, something which moves with controlled and conscious art, something which calls for the very slightest help from words or music to make itself intelligible, yet justly uses them subserviently—of such movements and abstractions the films may, in time to come, be composed.[53]

Woolf's essay, Seldes suggested, was of particular interest because 'it is apparently written without knowledge of the abstract films which have been made in Paris in the last two or three years, films which already make the conditional future unnecessary'.[54] In fact, if we accept that Woolf saw *Dr Caligari* at the Film Society screening (at which Clive Bell is known to have been present), she would presumably have watched not only the early documentary films in 'Williamson's Animated Gazette' but a D. W. Griffith Western (*The Sheriff's Baby*), a Pathé film on *The Circulation of the Blood* ('a diagram of the blood circulation, the beating of a heart extracted from a dead tortoise, and a number of photographs, made through a microscope, showing the actual passage of individual blood-corpuscles along various tissues') and, most significantly, Fernand Léger and Dudley Murphy's experimental film *Le Ballet Mécanique*. This film, the *London Mercury* film critic wrote in a review of the March 1926 Film Society programme, relied for its interest 'on a number of repeated patterns which included a straw hat, a girl's smile, a triangle, a circle and various pieces of machinery. Its result was equivalent to the writing of Miss Gertrude Stein'. The critic (Milton Waldman) also noted of the film programme that *The Sheriff's Baby* 'was offered for the amusement of the audience because of its elaborately sentimental captions, but the joke partially misfired, because the captions were not widely different from what we now have to suffer in the silent drama'.[55] He thus appears to have been unpersuaded by the Film Society's endeavours to construct a history for the medium.

Seldes discussed *Le Ballet Mécanique* in 'The Abstract Movie' along with Clair's *Entr'acte* and Comte Etienne de Beaumont's 'Of What are the Young Films Dreaming', noting that all three films depict 'objects in motion' and that 'in each of the films the most significant part was that played by the variation of movement and the variation of forms... They have all created images on the screen and proved that these images can call our emotions into being; but none of them has tried to be specific. None of them has tried to use a definite image for the communication of a definite thought. They have proved that symbols can be evocative on the screen; it is enough.'[56]

Seldes argued that 'the movie can be made great by ceasing to be realistic'. Much depends here on the definition of realism; Seldes's argument was that film art inhered in the transposition of objects by means of the camera, which cannot be a 'mere recorder'. Woolf, as I have suggested, found a film aesthetic in the recording of 'physical realities', but imagined a future film in which 'emotion, and thought' would be added to this reality: 'Then as smoke can be seen pouring from Vesuvius, we should be able to see wild and lovely and grotesque thoughts pouring from men in dress suits and woman with shingled heads.'[57] (In the variant version, this was altered to 'pouring from men with their elbows on a table; from women with their little handbags slipping to the floor', the images becoming more gestural, more mobile and more cinematic, though losing some of the focus on film as 'fashion' and, indeed, on the 'shingled' or 'bobbed' female head which Messel and Freud had identified with the cinema and the 'flapper'[58]). In this imagined film, eye and brain would be in concord, with the representation of physical reality combined with that of the interior life—'thought in its wildness, in its beauty, in its oddity'—to be represented, in ways not yet realizable, through a new symbolic system, perhaps like that (though Woolf does not make this explicit) of the psychoanalytic model of the dream-work, with its condensations and displacements.

In her discussion of the medium's potential, Woolf also deployed the view of film most striking to its early commentators, its power to transform, even to 'annihilate', familiar relations of time and space. 'The most fantastic contrasts', she writes, 'could be flashed before us with a speed which the writer can only toil after in vain. The past could be unrolled, distances could be annihilated. And those terrible dislocations which are inevitable when Tolstoy has to pass from the story of Anna to the story of Levin could be bridged by some device of scenery. We should have the continuity of human life kept before us by the repetition of some object common to both lives.'[59] Critical as Woolf was of the filmed novel, it was undoubtedly the case that she found in cinematic devices a way of bridging time and space in her fiction, with the continuity of objects through time and across space becoming particularly important in her work, from *Jacob's Room* through to *The Years*. In this sense, she was not only attempting in her speculations on the cinema to characterize its essential 'devices' (in an aesthetic model in which autonomy and not hybridity was the defining quality), but also working through the different ways in which stories could be told in the literary medium. 'The Cinema' was written as Woolf composed *To the Lighthouse* in which, as I discuss later in this chapter, she was centrally concerned with ways in which to represent the passage of time and the simultaneity of events. More generally, she was throughout her writing preoccupied with the ways in which consciousness encountered the phenomenal world, as in her imagined future film 'thought' and 'emotion' would be connected to objects.

The 'frame' of 'The Cinema' essay was, however, one in which Woolf distanced herself from film, at least in its present form. She opened her discussion with 'the savages of the twentieth century watching the pictures', and closed it with a similar sentiment:

> For the cinema has been born the wrong end first. The mechanical skill is far in advance of the art to be expressed. It is as if the savage tribe instead of finding two bars of iron to play with had found scattering the sea shore fiddles, flutes, saxophones, grand pianos by Erard and Bechstein, and had begun with incredible energy but without knowing a note of music to hammer and thump upon them all at the same time.[60]

This last image was in fact a familiar one in the period. In *Heraclitus, or the Future of Films* (1928), the film critic Ernest Betts wrote: 'In the cinematograph we have had a means of expression presented to us before the desire to express, the orchestration before the music, the telescope before the star, with the result that we have known that uncomfortable experience, victory without a battle.'[61] For Eric Elliott, writing in *Art of the Motion Picture*: 'The cinema medium depends upon a new "sense" in ourselves as well as in its artists. The cinema is not only a new interpretative art form, *it is the only new one mankind has ever known*. The other arts evolved with Man himself, and were ready only when he was ready. With the cinema it is as if all the instruments and resources of music were dropped suddenly into a world where the people had heard hitherto only a tom-tom.'[62]

A decade later, Elizabeth Bowen, whom Woolf came to know well in the 1930s, ended her essay 'Why I Go to the Cinema', with a discussion in terms that seem to echo those deployed by Woolf, Betts, and Elliott:

> In time, the cinema has come last of all the arts; its appeal to the racial child in us is so immediate that it should have come first. Pictures came first in time, and bore a great weight of meaning: 'the pictures' date right back in their command of emotion: they are inherently primitive. A film can put the experience of a race or a person on an almost dreadfully simplified epic plane.
>
> We have promise of great art here but so far few great artists. Films have not caught up with the possibilities of the cinema: we are lucky when we get films that keep these in sight. Mechanics, the immense technical knowledge needed, have kept the art, as an art, unnaturally esoteric; its technical progress … moves counter to its spiritual progress. An issue keeps on being obscured, a problem added to. Yet we have here, almost within our grasp, a means to the most direct communication between man and man. What might be a giant instrument is still a giant toy …
>
> I should like to be changed by more films, as art can change one: I should like something to happen when I go to the cinema.[63]

The shared view would seem to be that film's mechanical skill had militated against its artistic growth. For Betts, the machine 'has enslaved only the commercial film: the thing of beauty, the finer film, is free, notwithstanding the incredible fence of mechanics it must overleap to obtain freedom, fineness and beauty'.[64] Yet there were ambiguities and inconsistencies in the positions taken. Betts and Elliott, writing as participants in the new film industry, at times suggested that cinema's means of expression had run ahead of the human capacity to invent artistic forms adequate to the new medium; the machine would have to wait for human endeavour and expressiveness adequate to it. Woolf and Bowen, novelists first and foremost, represented the medium as technically proficient but nonetheless, in its productions, still inadequate in both aesthetic and human terms.

Bowen, in fact, gave a rather different valuation to the primitive than Woolf, coming closer to Vachel Lindsay's understanding of cinematic picture-language as a primary language, and finding in its 'racial' appeal the promise of a shared humanity that chimed with the utopian models of film's internationalism and universality in the writings of H.D. and Bryher, discussed in Chapter 5. Yet reading Bowen's discussion alongside

Woolf's opens up the possibility that Woolf's was not so much an attack on cinema's remove from aesthetic 'civilisation' (to borrow Clive Bell's term), but an exploration, or trying out, of the evolutionary discourses prevalent in much writing about cinema of the early twentieth-century, with its dominant anthropological trope of 'first contact'. This was further inflected by her understandings of prehistory as persisting into the present (as she explored in much of her fiction) and her ongoing debate with the artists around her over the nature of visual apprehension and the primacy of the eye.[65]

Woolf's and Bowen's discussions also suggest that the film apparatus, the cinematic machine, could appear as at one and the same time the archaic and the absolutely modern, the pre- and post-human. In Woolf's account, the film, at its worst, 'heaves', 'lurches' and 'lumbers', terms that might well have summoned up the image of a First World War tank (another new technology in 'prehistoric' guise). 'An issue keeps on being obscured', Bowen wrote, the sentence (itself obscure about the issue that is obscured) chiming with Woolf's account of the 'glimpse' of meaning: 'At the cinema for a moment through the mists of irrelevant emotions, through the thick counterpane of immense dexterity and enormous efficiency one has glimpses of something vital within. But the kick of life is instantly concealed by more dexterity, further efficiency'.[66] The 'vital', 'the kick of life'—images of a non-mechanical energy—can be related to Bowen's model of emotions and experiences as 'almost dreadfully simplified', and of film's epic dimensions. More generally, such images are aspects of one of the dominant tropes of cinematic discourses: that of organicism or vitalism contrasted with, or placed in relation to, mechanism.

Bowen's essay, unlike Woolf's, was written in the post-sound era, and sound was one of the technologies she named as obscuring the issue or, perhaps, the essence of film. As I discussed in the previous chapter, and as I explore in more detail later, there was a strongly gendered dimension in the resistance to a purely technological 'evolution' of the film-machine and, as in H.D.'s discussions, a perception that technological advances (particularly colour and sound) had destroyed the world of film-dreams. This response was much more prominent in the writings of women literary figures who were exploring film (including H.D., Richardson, and Bryher) than in the work of women film critics (such as Iris Barry and Caroline Lejeune) for whom early film was perceived as contingently and not essentially silent. The divide (though it was not absolute) between the two groups suggests a different relationship to language and vision. The literary writers were, for the most part, in search of a medium that would coexist but not compete with their own words and images, and they frequently framed the competition in the image of a devouring machine.

Caligari's Cabinet

If at one level *Caligari* was discursively displaced in Woolf's essay (and it is certainly possible that the Film Society event was not her first viewing of the film, which had been shown quite widely in London a few years earlier, thus perhaps muting her response to it), at another level the film was central to the emergent aesthetics of cinema. Woolf's representation of the shadow could be equated with a concept of cinematic essence, *photogénie*, conceptualized as a sublime instant: 'For a moment it seemed as if thought could be conveyed by shape more effectively than by words. The monstrous quivering tadpole seemed to be fear itself, and not the statement "I am afraid",' as she wrote of the shadow on the screen.[67] Her words were echoes of Expressionist concepts themselves, as in the writer Kasimir Edschmid's statement of 1917: 'The key component is transformed into the idea: not a thinking person, no: thought itself. Not two people embracing: no, the embrace itself.'[68] In *Caligari*, inner, psychological states are externalized and visualized, and thought is indeed made visible. Woolf's 'accidental' shadow could thus be seen as the truly Expressionist element of a film that has come to define German Expressionist cinema. For Béla Balázs, *Caligari* was 'complete and pure expressionism ... in which the physiognomy and mimicry of things achieved the same democratic animation as the faces and gestures of the human characters', and in which 'it is the author, the film-maker himself who is the madman seeing the world in this strange fashion'.[69]

Woolf looked away from the film only to find herself captured, it would seem, by something that was its very essence, the shadow as the metonym for Expressionist cinema itself, with its shadows, mirrors and doubles—and perhaps for cinema itself. She suggested that 'the art of the cinema is about to be brought to birth', and that it would be

seen with a new eye, one brought into being with the apparent su-
persession of a Kantian aesthetics predicated on vision abstracted from
necessity.

For Woolf, as we have seen, it was the faculty of vision which, currently 'detached from use', would awaken to seize sense impressions at
the moment of their fleeting unity. In her account of the cinema she
sought to reclaim the ideality of sight and to mend the split, produced
by the technologies of perception, between interiority and the mechanical exteriority of the camera-eye.[70] Nonetheless, her 'accidental' shadow
cannot, ultimately, be incorporated fully, either into the film which it
disrupts or into an aesthetic schema, and to this extent Stephen Heath
is correct to read it as an excess in seeing; a *'thing* that sticks out on
the screen, radically *obscene'*.[71] It is an image of 'fear itself' (the affect of
Fear, to borrow Deleuze's terms).[72] The 'monstrous quivering tadpole'
might also be understood, however, as protozoic, or 'protoplasmic' (Sergei
Eisenstein's word for animated drawings), and thus as a life form—the
'vital', 'the kick of life', in Woolf's words—which could engender and
birth a 'new' cinema. This might either be conceived as cinema lib-
erated from its mechanical origins or, in Deleuze's formulation, as a
confounding of the distinction between organic and mechanical. In a
comment on German Expressionist cinema, he argued, in terms that echo
Woolf's in striking ways, that 'it is not the mechanical which is opposed to the organic: it is the vital as potent pre-organic germinality,
common to the animate and the inanimate, to a matter which raises
itself to the point of life, and to a life which spreads itself through all
matter'.[73]

The Cabinet of Dr Caligari had a significant role as the film that 'converted'
many intellectuals to the cinema, elevating it from a mass or popular form
to the status of high culture. The literary critic William Hunter wrote in
his *Scrutiny of Cinema*: 'Criticism everywhere forgets that the cinema has
just been born and is still in its swaddling clothes... Assuming *The Cabinet
of Doctor Caligari* to be the first work of art the cinema produced, this new
art-form has, then, existed for twelve years. It should not be necessary to
point out the greater maturity of the other arts.'[74] The less elitist Gilbert
Seldes, commenting on the film in 1957, in the revised version of *The
Seven Lively Arts*, his influential study of 1924, wrote that *Caligari* would
be the appropriate point of reference for 'a history of taste in America, and
particularly a history of the vexing relationship between highbrows and the

popular arts'. In 1924, he had in fact read the film in relation to popular cinema:

> *The Cabinet of Dr Caligari* ... the only film of high fantasy I have ever seen—is the seeming exception which proves the rule, since it owes its success to the skilfully concealed exploitation of the materials and technique of the spectacle and of the comic film, and not to the dramatic quality of its story. The studio settings in distortion represent the spectacle; they are variations of scenery or 'location'; the chase over the roofs is a psychological parallel to the Keystone cops; and the weak moment of this superb picture is that in which the moving picture always fails, in the double revelation at the end, like that of *Seven Keys to Baldpate*, representing 'drama'.[75]

The Cabinet of Dr Caligari also provided a context for Clive Bell's thoughts on the cinema. In an article published in 1922, 'Art and the Cinema: a prophecy that the motion pictures, in exploiting imitation art, will leave real art to the artists', Bell had asserted that photography and the illustrated papers had dealt a 'knock-out blow' to Victorian realism and its doctrine of 'pure imitation': 'By the general public even it came to be dimly surmised that an art of imitation which in every respect was inferior to an imitating machine was not art at all. Impressionism took its place and held the field.'[76] *Caligari*, he argued, had alerted him to the possibility that film had the capacity to perform a similar function for his own time, though his conclusion was that 'personal art' (by which he meant painting, by contrast with the 'machine art' of photography or cinema) would become increasingly esoteric, and wholly, and not altogether happily, divorced from popular consciousness. The article was, then, a diagnosis, but by no means a celebration, of the cinema and its impact.

Bell came to these arguments after a lengthy disquisition on how he might, had he written his piece before seeing *Caligari*, have merely discussed the 'ridiculous' nature of films, characterized in particular by their representation of mere motion ('vast crowds were continually dashing across the stage') without particularization: 'And I should have gone on to demonstrate that the inability, or unwillingness rather, of the cinema to say anything of interest to the eye was more striking even than its contempt of brain; for it was on the visual side that the possibilities of development seemed boundless ... That is what I should have said a few months ago, but since then we have seen the *Caligari* film, not only in England but all over America':

> Let no one imagine that I am going to call the Caligari film a great work of art: it is a very poor one. Only, in relation to the ordinary melodramas it is much what the pictures of Orpen and Lavery are to those of Collier and Fildes. There is some appeal to the brain and the eye; there is arrangement and accent; there is a rudimentary, aesthetic intention. Caligari, so far as I know, is the first attempt to create an art of the cinema. To begin with, the story is not wholly contemptible; and it is well chosen because there are things in the nightmare of a lunatic that can be perhaps better expressed by the cinema than by any other means.
>
> ...And it is because the Caligari film seems to suggest an invasion of the middle country, of the territory hitherto occupied by those painters and writers who stood between the uncompromising artists and the barbarous horde—painters and writers who while giving the semicivilized public what it wanted inveigled that public into wanting something better than the worst—it is because, in a word, the Caligari film forbodes another victory for the machine on the frontiers of art, for the standardized on the frontiers of the personal, that I am inclined to regard its appearance as an event of some importance.[77]

Seldes and Bell, while close friends in the 1920s, had very different views of the 'popular' arts, but both saw *Caligari* as occupying 'the middle country'. For Jean Cocteau, as quoted by René Clair, the film represented a 'wrong turning' in cinema's development: 'People began to photograph theatre. Gradually that theatre became cinematographic theatre, but never pure cinema... *Caligari* was the first step towards another even more serious mistake which consists in flatly photographing eccentric sets, instead of achieving surprises through camera work.'[78] Cocteau's view of *Caligari* was shared by a number of other modernists, including Blaise Cendrars and Ezra Pound, but for many commentators the film had opened up new dimensions of cinematic space, and a new understanding of the 'plastic' and architectural aspects of film. In Britain, Europe, and the United States, *Caligari* became 'an exemplary film for the early art cinema' and, in its mixture of modernist and conventional realist elements, 'a kind of model of the artistic film, a paradigmatic alternative film for a developing alternative discourse'.[79] The course of Expressionism, Giles Deleuze wrote, 'is that of a perpetually broken line'; its 'Gothic' geometry constructs space instead of describing it.[80] Such spatial and geometrical constructions, as I explore in Chapter 5, on *Close Up* and its creation of an 'alternative discourse' for cinema, were formative in the avant-garde reception of, and commentary on, film in the 1920s.

In 1921, the poet Marianne Moore wrote to Bryher, *Close Up*'s co-editor:

I have seen a wonderful movie. If it should be in London, I hope you and Hilda [H.D.] will be sure to see it—The Cabinet of Dr. Caligari. It is the only movie except the Kid that I have gone to voluntarily in New York ... It is a German film and the settings are modern. All vertical lines slant and the shadows on stairs, on attic floors and through casements, are wonderful; Cesare, the somnambulist on appearing—although standing with legs side by side—looks as if he had but one leg. Later, when [roused?] from a trance in total darkness against the back of his cabinet, wedge-shaped lights slant down from his eyes at Lida, the heroine, the exact shape of a dagger that he uses later when intending to kill her. In a scene in an insane asylum, stripes on the ground in a courtyard, radiate from a central point like the rays painted on King Arthur's table on the wall at Winchester, and before you at the back of the stage, are three Romanesque entrances to the building like the openings from which animals came out, in the Coliseum.[81]

Peter Conrad has recently written, of the scene Moore discussed in her letter, in which the somnambulist Cesare is roused from a sleep which has lasted twenty-three years, that the overwhelming image is the opening of Cesare's eyes, which Conrad suggests, 'gape wide like open wounds'.[82] The attack on the eye occurs in film after film, from Bunuel's surrealist film *Un chien andalou*, in which an eye is slit open, to Hitchcock's *Spellbound* and *Psycho*. The surrealist Antonin Artaud wrote that a film should come as 'a shock to the eye, drawn so to speak from the very substance of the eye', and Conrad extends this argument when he writes that 'Film takes a dangerous delight in challenging the organ from which it derives and to which it is addressed. It exposes the eye's vulnerability, looking back at it in order to look through it.'[83] The mechanical eye and the human eye are locked, as George Bernard Shaw suggested through his image of the 'serpent's eye' of cinema, in a perilous exchange.[84] The 'wakening' of Cesare also alerts us to cinema's own sense of its powers of animation, of its ability to make still things move and to give life to matter.

'Mrs Woolf had discovered the cinema'

The short stories by Virginia Woolf that appeared from the newly founded Hogarth Press in the late 1910s, and the publication of *Jacob's Room* in

1922, led reviewers and critics to search for aesthetic categories with which to account for and define her 'experimental' prose. They frequently invoked the other arts, and in particular the visual arts. For Rebecca West, writing in the *New Statesman*, *Jacob's Room* was to be taken 'not as a novel but as a portfolio ... for not only are Mrs Woolf's contributions to her age loose leaves, but they are also connected closely with the pictorial arts ... She can write supremely well only of what can be painted; best of all, perhaps, or what has been painted.'[85] In a 1925 article published in *The Dial*, Clive Bell wrote of her 'painterly vision', which he connected with Impressionism. He also contrasted her 'vision' with 'the ready-cooked, hot and strong, cinematographical world beloved of modern novelists'.[86]

The photographic or cinematographic technique of Woolf's novels was, however, discussed by a number of early critics and commentators. One review of *Jacob's Room*, entitled 'Dissolving Views', called Woolf's method 'snapshot photography, with a highly sensitive, perfected camera handled by an artist ... *Jacob's Room* has no narrative, no design, above all, no perspective: its dissolving views come before us one by one, each taking the full light for a moment, then vanishing completely'.[87] The analogy with film was at times used pejoratively, as Woolf herself deployed it in her reviews of Compton Mackenzie and G. B. Stern. The *Times Literary Supplement* review of *Mrs Dalloway* referred to 'the cinema-like speed of the picture [which] robs us of a great deal of the delight in Mrs Woolf's style'.[88]

For Winifred Holtby, whose study of Woolf was published in 1932, 'cinematographic technique' was a significant dimension of her early writing, though one ultimately replaced by 'the orchestral effect' of the later novels.[89] Holtby's model of the cinematographic in Woolf's early short stories, and in particular 'Kew Gardens' focused on the close-up and shifts in perspective:

> It is no longer a question of thoughts passing through her mind, but of light, insects, people, sounds, passing through the garden. The dimensions of the objects seen do not remain at the steady human size to which novelists have accompanied us; they suddenly diminish to the consciousness of a snail who sees cliffs and lakes and round boulders of grey stone between the passage from one stalk to another; then suddenly they swing to the vast bird's-eye view from an aeroplane flying above the trees ...

To let the perspective shift from high to low, from huge to microscopic, to let figures of people, insects, aeroplanes, flowers pass across the vision and melt away—these are devices common enough to another form of art. They are the tricks of the cinema. Mrs Woolf had discoverered the cinema. There is no reason why it should monopolise powers of expansion and contraction. In *Kew Gardens* the external figures appear and disappear with such brilliant clarity that we could almost photograph them from the words.[90]

Holtby's terms can be compared with those deployed by Béla Balázs, in his account (which is in turn echoed in Walter Benjamin's model, in his essay 'The Work of Art in the Age of Mechanical Reproduction', of the 'optical unconscious') of the ways in which the film camera, in the early years of cinema, discovered a new world which was 'the hidden life of little things': 'the adventures of beetles in a wilderness of blades of grass, the tragedies of day-old chicks in a corner of the poultry-run, the erotic battles of flowers and the poetry of miniature landscapes ... By means of the close-up the camera in the days of the silent film revealed also the hidden mainsprings of a life which we had thought we already knew so well.'[91] Balázs concentrates here on the microscopic dimensions of the camera, and on microphysiognomy, whereas for Holtby the film camera was characterized by its powers to move from 'huge to microscopic'.

Such terms were close to those used by H. G. Wells in his introduction to *The King who was a King*, in which he wrote of the 'new powers' of the film: 'No limitations remain of scene, stage, or arena. It may be the convolutions of a tendril which fill the picture, or the bird's-eye view of a mountain chain, or a great city. We can pass in an instant from the infinitely great to the infinitely little.' For Wells, these Asphodean powers were invoked in an argument for the film's potential to be greater 'than any artistic form humanity has hitherto achieved'.[92]

Holtby's concern, by contrast, was with the ways in which film's techniques were beginning to shape literature, and with the deployment of a 'cinematographic technique' in Woolf's newly experimental writing, at the point at which she was making an absolute break with 'tradition'. Holtby arrived, indeed, at the filmic analogy after discussion of the poetic dimensions of Woolf's style, and she clearly saw a connection between poetry's mode of expression through symbol and synecdoche and that of film. In Holtby's words:

Poets present sensations, emotions, and processes of thought, with only lightly indicated backgrounds. They reveal, rather than explain. They suggest. They illumine. They flash a torch through the darkness on to a child's green bucket, an aster trembling violently in the wind, or blades of grass bent by the rain, and leave us to imagine the wild storm-swept garden, and the children safely tucked in bed for the night. Poets have immense advantages over novelists.[93]

This account of an essentially visual presentation of part-objects anticipates Holtby's account of *Jacob's Room*, and contains, indeed, direct quotation from the novel, in which Woolf wrote: 'The harsh light fell on the garden; cut straight across the lawn; lit up a child's bucket and a purple aster and reached the hedge'.[94]

Holtby's chapter on *Jacob's Room* is titled 'Cinematograph':

> In *Jacob's Room* Mrs Woolf built for the first time a complete novel with her new tools, and chose for it the cinematograph technique tried out in *Kew Gardens*. Almost any page in the book could be transferred straight on to a film. The story deals mainly with the external evidence of emotions, even thoughts and memories assuming pictorial quality. Sometimes, it is true, the action passes to that confused twilight which dwells within the mind; but for the most part it is indicated by the changing positions and gestures of the characters. Betty Flanders weeps, strokes the cat Topaz, writes letters; Jacob yawns, stretches, reads; Florinda draws her cloak about her to hide the evidence of her pregnancy. It is a picture-maker's novel.
>
> It is not a perfectly easy book to read. Its obscurity puzzled a good many intelligent people when it was published, for Mrs Woolf gives no clue to her intention. There is no preliminary announcement, as on a film, 'Produced by—Scenario by—From the story of—' But the first chapter betrays her method. Its scenario might be summarised, 'Jacob as a small boy at the seaside in Cornwall,' and Mrs. Woolf begins, as any producer might, by photographing a letter, word by word welling out slowly from the gold nib of Betty Flanders' pen. 'So of course there was nothing for it but to leave.' She shows us next the complete figure of the woman pressing her heels deeper in the sand to give her matronly body a firmer seat; then there is a close-up of her face, maternal, tearful, because Scarborough, where Captain Barfoot is, seems so far from Cornwall where she sits writing. The camera swings round then to photograph the entire bay, yacht and lighthouse, quivering through her tears, and flashes back to indicate a blot spreading across the writing paper.[95]

Holtby suggested that the 'obscurity' of the novel could be penetrated by the awareness that Woolf was using a 'cinematographic technique', which took on something of the aspect of a hidden camera. There is an interesting connection here with the novelist Dorothy Richardson's response to Bryher's 1931 review of *Dawn's Left Hand* (the tenth volume of *Pilgrimage*), in which Bryher wrote: 'What a film her books could make. The real English film for which so many are waiting...in each page an aspect of London is created that like an image from a film, substitutes itself for memory, to revolve before the eyes.'[96] Richardson wrote to Bryher to thank her: 'And what can I say about your review in C.U., [*Close Up*] emphasizing the aspect no one else has spotted.'[97] She was, it would be safe to assume, referring to Bryher's comments on the cinematic dimensions of the novel. 'Cinematographic technique' thus appears to have been a method and a way of seeing that writers of this period understood to be both central and hidden or occluded, revealing itself only to those who had learned to 'read' the film image, and the film image in the literary text.

This was certainly implied in Dorothy Brewster's study of Virginia Woolf, published in 1962, in which she commented on the 'cinematic technique' of *Jacob's Room*—'the camera sometimes sweeping over crowds, then focusing on an individual or a group, now giving a close-up of a little scene and again ranging the heavens'—and argued that it was 'no longer an obstacle to comprehension'.[98] Such a perception chimes with the sense that early film spectators had to be trained perceptually in order to watch films.[99] It was as if readers, too, had to learn how to recognize the ways in which film was entering the literary arena.[100]

Holtby's definition of 'cinematographic technique' moved from the play of expansion and contraction that she found in 'Kew Gardens' to the pictorial method of *Jacob's Room*. She identified in the opening passages, which she indeed described as a film 'scenario', specific filmic tropes, including the close-up on the face and the projection onto the screen of written letters (which, along with telegrams and newspaper clippings, were defined by Hugo Münsterberg as 'leaders' between the pictures.) Her reading could be continued further into the opening pages of the novel, in Woolf's suggestion of a subjective camera (as the bay appears to quiver through the tears in Betty Flanders' eyes) and her focus on the shifting relations and proportions of bodies (animate and inanimate) in space and time. As the young Jacob climbs over the rocks on the beach, he sees below him 'stretched entirely rigid, side by side, their faces very red, an enormous man and woman'. Woolf continues:

An enormous man and woman (it was early-closing day) were stretched motionless, with their heads on pocket-handkerchiefs, side by side, within a few feet of the sea, while two or three gulls gracefully skirted the incoming waves, and settled near their boots.

The large red faces lying on the bandanna handkerchief stared up at Jacob. Jacob stared down at them.[101]

The scene (whose cartoon-like focus on the couples' heads and boots renders it as a comic seaside picture-postcard) is predicated on the repetition of phrases as 'frames' ('the enormous man and woman', 'the large red faces'), and on the instability of perception and spatial distortions, as if not only characters but also readers had found themselves in a world whose scale, dimensions and forms of movement (like those represented in Lewis Carroll's *Alice* books) were unfamiliar to them. We could think of this as an experimental film scenario or, perhaps more interestingly, as a reconstruction of early film's impact on its new audience, appropriately figured through the child-eye's view of the world and its anthropomorphous vision. Jacob mistakes the shape of the rock for the form of his nurse. In pursuit of an animal's skull lying on the beach, he is depicted not as running towards it but as 'farther and farther away': Betty Flanders, searching for him, is described as 'coming round the rock and covering the whole beach in a few seconds'. It is, moreover, as if Woolf were 'animating' Vanessa Bell's painting 'Studland Beach', in which two groups of figures, at once huddled and monumental, are situated on a diagonal plane across the beach, and in which maternity is imaged as a rock-like solidity.

A further 'cinematic' dimension of *Jacob's Room* is the play of light in the novel. As in *To the Lighthouse* and *The Waves*, Woolf represented the illumination of objects in a sleeping world and connected it to the question of the world seen both with and without a perceiving subject:

> There was a click in the front sitting-room. Mr Pearce had extinguished the lamp. The garden went out. It was but a dark patch. Every inch was rained upon. Every blade of grass was bent by rain. Eyelids would have been fastened down by the rain. Lying on one's back one would have seen nothing but muddle and confusion—clouds turning and turning, and something yellow-tinted and sulphurous in the darkness.
>
> The little boys in the front bedroom had thrown off their blankets and lay under the sheets. It was hot; rather sticky and steamy. Archer lay spread out, with one arm striking across the pillow. He was flushed; and when the heavy curtain blew out a little he turned and half-opened his eyes. The wind actually stirred the cloth on the chest of drawers, and let in a little light, so that the sharp edge of the chest of drawers was visible, running straight up, until a white shape bulged out; and a silver streak showed in the looking-glass.

In the other bed by the door Jacob lay asleep, fast asleep, profoundly unconscious. The sheep's jaw with the big yellow teeth in it lay at his feet. He had kicked it against the iron bed-rail.[102]

If the chest of drawers and its cloth, stirred by the wind, are to be understood as seen through Archer's half-opened eyes, the issue of who sees the world when his eyes are closed becomes all the more pointed. In *Jacob's Room* Woolf overtly eschewed omniscience; Jacob is an enigma to the novel's narrator who, separated from him by 'ten years' seniority and a difference in sex', is largely excluded from the world he occupies, and the reader views him in glimpses and gleams. Later in the novel, Jacob, now a young man, sees Florinda, his lover, 'upon another man's arm':

> The light from the arc lamp drenched him from head to toe. He stood for a minute motionless beneath it. Shadows chequered the street. Other figures, single and together, poured out, wavered across, and obliterated Florinda and the man.
> The light drenched Jacob from head to toe. You could see the pattern on his trousers; the old thorns on his stick; his shoe laces; bare hands; and face ...
> Whether we know what was in his mind is another question.[103]

The image of Jacob drenched with light creates the effect of a film frame, and this is reinforced by the near-repetition (the same but not quite) of the phrasing and the shadow-effects on the street. Jacob is 'reborn in each new visual frame', to borrow Sara Danius's account of Joyce's Leopold Bloom.[104] The moving figures (contrasted with Jacob's motionlessness) block Jacob's gaze across the street, in ways that echo the intensely cinematographic scene in *Ulysses* in which Bloom's view of an attractive woman is blocked by a passing tram:

> Watch! Watch! Silk flash rich stockings white. Watch!
> A heavy tramcar honking its gong slewed between.
> Lost it. Curse your noisy pugnose ...
> The tram passed. They drove off towards the Loop Linen bridge, her rich gloved hand on the steel grip. Flicker, flicker: the laceflare of her hat in the sun: flicker, flick.[105]

For Holtby, Woolf's 'pictorial' and 'cinematographic' focus was an experimental moment in her writing career, which she subsequently moved beyond:

> The cinematographic style was brilliantly effective, but it was not as subtle as the orchestral effect which she was to use in *To the Lighthouse*; she was

to obtain a surer control over her material in *Mrs Dalloway*. She was to adventure further into obscure realms of human consciousness in *The Waves*. The contrasts, perhaps, in *Jacob's Room* are too violent. There are obscurities which even the most diligent study cannot penetrate. The effect created is very largely visual. Later she would plunge into the nerves, the brain, the senses of her characters, exploring further, yet binding the whole more closely into a unity of mood.[106]

Holtby was, indeed, describing *Jacob's Room* as if it were, to borrow Woolf's terms, 'a movie novel'. While she was far more appreciative of the novel than Woolf was of Compton Mackenzie's and G. B. Stern's fictions, she nonetheless saw the 'pictorial method' and 'cinematographical style' as essentially surface representation, tied to a forward linear movement. Woolf indeed played with such a representation in the novel, and, through structure and typography influenced by *The Waste Land*, with gaps, ellipses, intervals or 'spaces of complete immobility' between sections or 'movements':

> A window tinged yellow about two feet across alone combated the white fields and the black trees … At six o'clock a man's figure carrying a lantern crossed the field … […] A motor car came along the road shoving the dark before it … The dark shut down behind it …
> Spaces of complete immobility separated each of these movements.[107]

'For *Jacob's Room*', Holtby wrote, 'the cinematographic form sufficed. Picture can follow picture when the chronology is comparatively straightforward; but *Mrs Dalloway* demanded the more subtle complexity of orchestration.'[108] As in the review entitled 'Dissolving Views', the assumption was that in cinematographic technique one image simply followed and replaced another. Little concern was thus shown with the complexities of the fact that the still image is perceived as a moving one, or with the ways in which movement occurs within the frame.

Holtby's shift to a musical analogy might seem (and was undoubtedly intended) as a way of moving her critical discussion on from the cinematographic. It was, however, in line with contemporary discussions of the rhythmic basis of film form, most prominent in texts, such as White's *Parnassus to Let* and William Hunter's *Scrutiny of Cinema,* in which music, art, and literary critics sought for an appropriate critical and aesthetic language for film in the terms of rhythm, metre and *caesura*, at a time at which questions of rhythm and repetition, and the relationship between the two, had become central to aesthetic theories, not least those of Roger Fry.

The chronology of *Jacob's Room*, moreover, is far from straightforward, as Holtby's reading of the text itself acknowledged at a number of points. Written in the aftermath of World War I, but set in the years before and leading up to it, the novel creates a highly complex interplay between prospect and retrospect. This is, in turn, mapped on to an issue at the heart of much of Woolf's writing; that of the relationship between presence and absence, and the exploration of 'the thing that exists when we aren't there', an issue, as we have seen, at the heart of filmic ontology. The abiding image of the novel is of an empty room: Jacob's room does not contain him. The calling out of Jacob's name throughout the novel is a powerful image of loss, inseparable from the losses of the war-dead. As Leonard Woolf commented of the novel: 'The people are ghosts.'[109] If film can be understood as 'the presence of an absence', it would appear to be this dimension, on which Woolf was to focus in her 1926 essay, that drew her to the 'cinematographic method' as strongly as its pictorialism and intense visuality.

The question of 'character' and its depiction was also of absorbing interest to Woolf in the early 1920s, and was at the heart of her quarrel with the Edwardian novelists who, she stated, described externals while failing to give any sense of the complexities of selfhood. The argument would seem to return to the divide between the exterior realms of 'the movie novel' and the interior spaces that could be opened up in and by literary texts. Yet film could also take the issue of character into new dimensions. Holtby, whose journalism in the early 1930s included commentary on films, was predominantly interested in the personality of the actor, writing of: 'The moments when a flat shadow on a screen becomes a symbol for some truth about human character, about physical or spiritual beauty, love or hatred, power or passion, or wonder, or revenge, so long as life endures we have one endless source of interest—the diversities and similarities of the human heart.'[110]

Whether Woolf would have concurred is an open question, but it is undoubtedly the case that *Jacob's Room* is caught up with the relationship between flatness and depth in the representation of 'character'.[111] In film, light, movement, and camera-angles give the effect of three dimensions to the two-dimensional world on the screen. The word 'character' is derived from the Greek *kharratein*, 'to engrave'. There is a significant link here with *The Cabinet of Dr Caligari* which, as the film theorist Noël Burch has written, is characterized by a visual style in which each tableau is a flat, stylized rendering of a deep space, achieved by a design of oblique strokes which are so plainly graphic that they recall the surface of the engraver's page. At the same time the movement of the actors is staged in depth (along the axis of the lens and perpendicular to the picture plane).[112] The aesthetic of Woolf's early short stories (including 'Mark on the Wall', 'Kew Gardens', and 'An Unwritten Novel') and of *Jacob's Room* can be understood in an analogous way; an insistent emphasis on imprinting, inscription, and engraving draws attention to tactile and graphic surfaces while the narrative voice simultaneously insists upon a hollowing out of the world and the production of meaning as depth. This extends itself to a model of realism taken up in the earliest theorisations of film: this is and is not reality.

Throughout *Jacob's Room* the reader is reminded that Jacob is both without substance and the most substantial element of all:

> In any case life is but a procession of shadows, and God knows why it is that we embrace them so eagerly, and see them depart with such anguish, being shadows. And why, if this and much more than this is true, why are we yet surprised in the window corner by a sudden vision that the young man in the chair is of all things in the world the most real, the most solid, the best known to us—why indeed? For the moment after we know nothing about him.
> Such is the manner of our seeing. Such the conditions of our love.[113]

At the very close of the novel, Jacob's absence, his death, is presented, when Betty Flanders asks: "What am I to do with these, Mr Bellamy?" She held out a pair of Jacob's old shoes.' This ending is a freeze-frame, which, in the cinema, Garrett Stewart argues, is 'the end and suspension of all movement, the obtruded intervallic origin in itself'.[114]

In her diaries and letters, Woolf repeatedly referred to *Jacob's Room* as an experiment: 'too much of an experiment', 'nothing but an experiment', 'more an experiment than an achievement'.[115] Its function was, she asserted, to break with traditional forms and thus to move the genre of the novel in new directions, though at other times she suggested that its decomposition of character was too radical, writing of the novel in her diary that '[Roger Fry] wishes that a bronze body might somehow solidify beneath the gleams & lights—with which I agree.'[116] The question of 'character' was at the heart of the experiment, as a letter to Gerald Brenan (Christmas Day 1922) suggests. Responding to his argument that 'one must renounce' the novel, Woolf had written that she could not follow the path of 'limit[ing] oneself to one's own sensations... but not set people in motion, and attempt to enter them, and give them impact and volume':

> This generation must break its neck in order that the next may have smooth going... The human soul, it seems to me, orientates itself afresh every now and then. It is doing so now. No one can see it whole, therefore. The best of us catch a glimpse of a nose, a shoulder, something turning away, always in movement. Still, it seems better to me to catch this glimpse, than to sit down with Hugh Walpole, Wells, etc. etc. and make large oil paintings of fleshy monsters complete from top to toe.[117]

At no point does Woolf appear to have commented on her use of filmic techniques nor on the ways in which critics were reading *Jacob's Room* through the lenses of the pictographic and cinematographic, yet it seems highly probable that this was the way in which she had conceived her 'experiment', engaging in a strategic and self-conscious play with film form. It was film that was, at this time, setting people in motion and offering the 'glimpse' of 'something turning away, always in movement'. The novel is indeed fascinated by the ways in which movement can be broken down—'A few moments before a horse jumps it slows, sidles, gathers itself together, goes up like a monster wave, and pitches down on the further side'[118]—and in which it gathers momentum:

> The lamps of London uphold the dark as upon the points of burning bayonets... Such faces as one sees... Shawled women carry babies with purple eyelids; boys stand at street corners; girls look across the road—rude illustrations, pictures in a book whose pages we turn over and over as if we should at last find what we look for. Every face, every shop, bedroom window, public-house, and dark square is a picture feverishly turned—in search of what? It is the same with books. What do we seek through millions of pages? Still hopefully turning the pages—oh, here is Jacob's room.[119]

Woolf's criticism of Compton Mackenzie's 'movie novel', we recall, was that 'one picture must follow another without stopping'. In *Jacob's Room*, she took on, rather than wholly rejecting, this way of proceeding, in her representation of 'a picture feverishly turned'. 'I feel time racing like a film at the Cinema', she wrote in her diary for January 1922: 'I try to stop it. I prod it with my pen. I try to pin it down.'[120] The 'experiment' of *Jacob's Room* was to work with, rather than against, the filmic racing of time, and to explore the very ways (which were intertwined with cinema's difficulties, as her generation of writers tended to perceive it, in representing the 'interior' life) in which a 'character' (the novel's central protagonist, indeed) might be figured as unknown and unknowable or, at least, apprehended only in glimpses. It is striking that the passages Woolf excised from the revised novel were those in which the 'interiority' of her characters was most fully explored.

Yet, as Woolf's letter to Roger Fry suggests, she was ambivalent towards her own excising impulses. *Jacob's Room* stages a debate between 'character-mongers' ('those gossips') and 'the other side—the men in clubs and Cabinets', for whom 'character-drawing is a frivolous fireside art' and who send young men off to die in battle. The machinery of war is, like the cinema, locomotive: 'Like blocks of tin soldiers the army covers the cornfield, moves up the hillside, stops, reels slightly this way and that, and falls flat, save that, through field-glasses, it can be seen that one or two pieces still agitate up and down like fragments of broken match-stick.'[121] This is a war film, or war seen as film, and it is at least implied that 'the strokes which oar the world forward'—'the unseizable force' (the 'force' of historical process, of patriarchal precedence, of the workings of power, of the drive towards death)—move forward as relentlessly and mechanically as the cinematic apparatus itself.

While there is no evidence that Woolf read Bergson's writings on 'the cinematographical method' in *Creative Evolution*, there are some significant echoes of his critique of the cinematographical 'mechanism of our ordinary knowledge' in *Jacob's Room*.[122] The example Bergson gave is of the reconstitution of the marching past of a regiment, to be portrayed on a screen. The method of cutting out jointed figures, giving to each of them 'the movement of marching' and then projecting them, he wrote, would fail to 'reproduce the suppleness and variety of life'. The more effective method would be 'to take a series of snapshots of the passing regiment and to throw these instantaneous views on the screen, so that they replace each other very rapidly. This is what the cinematograph does... In order that the pictures may be animated, there must be movement somewhere. The movement does exist here; it is in the apparatus':

> It is because the film of the cinematograph unrolls, bringing in turn the different photographs of the scene to continue each other, that each actor of the scene recovers his mobility; he strings all his successive attitudes on the invisible movement of the film. The process then consists in extracting from all the movements peculiar to all the figures an impersonal movement abstract and simple, *movement in general*, so to speak: we put this into the

apparatus, and we reconstitute the individuality of each particular movement by combining this nameless movement with the personal attitudes. Such is the contrivance of the cinematograph. And such is also that of our knowledge. Instead of attaching ourselves to the inner becoming of things, we place ourselves outside them in order to recompose their becoming artificially. We take snapshots, as it were, of the passing reality, and, as these are characteristic of the reality, we have only to string them on a becoming, abstract, uniform and invisible, situated at the back of the apparatus of knowledge, in order to imitate what there is that is characteristic in this becoming itself... Whether we would think becoming, or express it, or even perceive it, we hardly do anything else than set going a kind of cinematograph inside us.[123]

There may be no direct link between Woolf's literary 'experiment' and Bergson's concepts, but the terms of his argument appear to have had some form of life in her novel, caught up as it is in the ways in which a writer might 'move' her characters through her narrative, and with that narrative as an 'apparatus' onto which 'successive attitudes' and gestures are strung. She represented—typographically as well as struc-turally—the gaps between consecutive states, which, for Bergson, were the intervals through which movement would in fact slip, 'because every attempt to reconstitute change out of states implies the absurd propo-sition, that movement is made of immobilities'.[124] The parodic use of the bildungsroman in *Jacob's Room* entails a play with questions of form, formation and 'becoming', and with external views of that 'becoming'. To this, Woolf was not, in this novel at least, contrasting a Bergsonian ideal of inner duration, though the question of Woolf's 'Bergsonism' has been a topic for extended critical debate. The issue here is that Woolf appears to have adopted 'the cinematographical method' (characterized in this context by externality, gesture, 'successive attitudes', snapshots, and intervals, all driven forward by the movement of the machine) in or-der to explore how traditional forms of narration might be broken and remade.

Modernity and Montage

In a discussion of the stream-of-consciousness novel and film, Edward Murray noted Woolf's conveyance of 'a sense of simultaneity' through cross-cutting in section thirteen of *Jacob's Room*, and its similarities to 'The

Wandering Rocks' episode in Joyce's *Ulysses*. In Murray's description of part of the section from Woolf:

> As Julia moves out of the park, she glances at her watch, which 'gave her twelve minutes and a half in which to reach Bruton Street. Lady Congreve expected her at five.' Mrs Woolf then cuts to a clock at Verrey's striking five—followed by a second cut to Florinda looking at the clock. Someone appears who reminds Florinda of Jacob—and the novelist switches abruptly to Jacob, who is seated in Hyde Park. The latter reads a letter from Sandra … and almost imperceptibly Virginia Woolf dissolves back to the woman writing the letter … and then back to Jacob again, who is now talking to a ticket collector. Jacob's contemptuous treatment of the man permits the author to cut to Fanny Elmer as she reflects upon Jacob's behaviour to such menials. As Fanny rides past Westminster, Big Ben sounds five o'clock—which again suggests diverse actions occurring simultaneously.[125]

The representation of time in *Mrs Dalloway* extends that in *Jacob's Room*, using clock-faces and the sound of church bells to spatialize and segment time—'Shredding and slicing, dividing and subdividing, the clocks of Harley Street nibbled at the June day'—in ways that further echo Bergson's critique of 'the cinematographical method'. In *Mrs Dalloway*, however, Woolf was concerned to draw the narrative backwards into the past, even as the numerous events of the day drive it forward, and to counter, in Paul Ricoeur's phrase, 'monumental time' ('resulting from all the complicities between clock time and the figures of authority') with alternative temporal measures: the time of memory, Clarissa Dalloway's ability to plunge 'into the very heart of the moment', the bells of St Margaret's, which sound in the wake of the 'great booming voice' of Big Ben.[126]

'Nowadays I'm often overcome by London', Woolf wrote in her diary in June 1920.[127] In 1924, the Woolfs moved back from suburban Richmond into Bloomsbury, and Woolf's private writings celebrate the city and its abilities to transport its inhabitants: 'London is enchanting. I step out upon a tawny coloured magic carpet, it seems, & get carried into beauty without raising a finger.'[128] The words were echoed by those of Dorothy Richardson, in her account of the new form of consciousness brought into being by the cinema: 'the film, by setting the landscape in motion and keeping us still, allows it to walk through us.'[129]

At the time of the move to London, Woolf was working on *The Hours*, which would become *Mrs Dalloway*, and she was explicit about the ways in which the city became caught up in the process of writing the novel: 'I like London for writing it.' Like *Ulysses*, *Mrs Dalloway* is a 'city symphony', a day in the life of the city, with close thematic and structural connections to some of the most significant avant-garde city films of the 1920s, notably Walter Ruttmann's *Berlin: Symphony of a City* and Dziga-Vertov's *Man with a Movie Camera*, which traced the rhythms of urban time and space from daybreak until night-time. Woolf used perambulation and locomotion around the city as narrative routings, and played with the 'new' devices of the cinema, including flashbacks and tracking shots. The 'sky-writing scene' in *Mrs Dalloway* could be understood, for example, as a montage sequence, from the viewpoints of a cross-section of individuals.[130] As a 'cinematic' technique, it bears comparison to that used in a film of 1924, the British director George Pearson's *Reveille*, which represented (in the silent film) the striking of Armistice time (11.00 a.m.) by means of eleven shots showing the film's characters, in their different locations, at that one moment.

James Donald has argued that the attraction of cinema for Woolf in *Mrs Dalloway* was not 'the explosive epistemological power of montage … Rather, it was the ontological precision of the camera that opened up new ways of recording and dramatising London'.[131] Peter Walsh's two walks through London—the first in the late morning, and the second in the evening, as he makes his way to Clarissa's party—render him simultaneously an observer and a voyeur, as his passages through the city streets and squares put the city itself into motion—'it seemed as if the whole of London were embarking in little boats moored to the bank, tossing on the waters, as if the whole place were floating off in carnival'[132]—and in which evening (as in *Berlin* and *Man with a Movie Camera*) is given over to the city's leisure and pleasure. Pleasure-making (like the image of the end of life, in Clarissa's observation through the window, as she removes herself from her party, of the old woman in the house opposite) emerges in *Mrs Dalloway* 'through the uncurtained window, the window left open'; this 'prolonged evening' (a result of 'Mr Willett's summer time' and, it is implied, the end of the war), is new to Peter, recently returned from five years in India, and he observes it in 'the young people', in whom 'joy of a kind … flushed their faces. They dressed well too; pink stockings; pretty shoes. They would now have two hours at the pictures'.[133]

This is the first invocation in Woolf's fiction of film as a medium; it creates a continuum, and blurs the boundaries, between city and cinema, the life on the streets and the spectacle that will be projected onto the screen. At the close of the episode, the energies of the city, 'the chaos of the streets', and their impact upon vision, accumulate to bursting point—'And here a shindy of brawling women, drunken women; here only a policeman and looming houses, high houses, domed houses, churches, parliaments, and the hoot of a steamer on the river, a hollow misty cry'—and Peter finally ceases to be a kino-eye: 'The cold stream of visual impressions failed him now as if the eye were a cup that overflowed and let the rest run down its china walls unrecorded. The brain must wake now.'[134]

As we have seen, Woolf, in 'The Cinema', made explicit the connection between cinema and urban modernity, and rendered the city as cinematic: 'We get intimations only in the chaos of the streets, perhaps, when some momentary assembly of colour, sound, movement, suggests that here is a scene waiting a new art to be transfixed.' It was to *Orlando* that the critic Raymond Williams turned when, in *The Country and the City*, he offered a very brief but suggestive account of the relationships between modernism, urban experience, and cinema. Writing of the passage in which Orlando, now living in the present day, motors out of London and has her identity 'entirely disassembled'—'it is an open question in what sense Orlando can be said to have existed at the present moment'—Williams commented:

> This fragmentary experience—now accelerated by 'motoring fast'—has remained a perceptual condition. It is deeply related to several characteristic forms of modern imagery, most evident in painting and especially in film which as a medium contains much of its intrinsic movement. There is indeed a direct relation between the motion picture, especially in its development in cutting and montage, and the characteristic movement of an observer in the close and miscellaneous environment of the streets … This experience of urban movement has been used … to express a gamut of feelings from despair to delight.[135]

Glossing this passage in his introduction to Williams's posthumously published collection of essays *The Politics of Modernism*, Tony Pinkney commented on the ways in which 'it is the essence of film to have no essence, to be uniquely responsive as a medium to the disorientating ephemerality of the modern city … if film is the definitive Modernist mode, then Modernism can now be located … in the *intermediate zone* of urban experience … in a "structure of feeling" that has not yet assumed the relatively formalized shape of aesthetic doctrine or political act'.[136]

The concept of Modernism's location in the 'intermediate zone' of urban experience chimes with Woolf's complex sense that a future cinema might move to seize the sense-impressions of the city at the moment of their fleeting unity, but in such a way as to capture their energies without thereby petrifying them: 'to catch them', as Woolf wrote in another context, 'before they become "works of art".'[137]

We could also see in *Orlando* (with its rapid transformations through space and in time) a radical interpretation of the characteristics of cinema as they were defined in its first decades by commentators, including Woolf herself in 'The Cinema': the flashing before the spectator of fantastic contrasts; the unrolling of the past; the annihilation of distances. Woolf's fantasy novel summons up the play of surrealist cinema, giving literal form to figurative language—'it was Lust the vulture, not Love, the Bird of Paradise, that flopped, fouly and disgustingly, upon his shoulders'[138]—and effecting a sudden transmutation in Orlando's sexual identity in an extravagantly ocular and specular mode, the baroque scene culminating, or deflating, in these words: 'Orlando looked himself up and down in a long looking-glass, without showing any signs of discomposure, and went, presumably, to his bath.'[139] In *Orlando*, as in the early trick-films of Méliès, a major influence on the Surrealist film-makers, men metamorphose into women, and figures vanish in a puff of smoke.

Arresting Beauty

The novel with which Woolf's essay on 'The Cinema' was most closely connected, temporally and conceptually, was *To the Lighthouse*. As Suzanne Raitt has argued, 'the story of *To the Lighthouse* lies behind Woolf's essay on "The Cinema"': 'the war sprung its chasm at the feet of all this innocence and ignorance.'[140] The ten-year gap or interval observed by Woolf in 'The Cinema' between the early documentary films and the cinema of the present maps onto the 'chasm' at the centre of the novel, the 'passage' of ten years that begins with Mrs Ramsay's death and ends after World War I, with the restoration of the holiday house and the return of those who are left.

In *To the Lighthouse* Woolf transmuted 'point of view' into the observation of perception itself, looking at people looking and being looked at, and creating a complex interplay of eyelines and sightlines within the text. In the first section of the novel, 'The Window', characters are shown 'looking at' Mrs Ramsay. Some twenty pages into the novel we are told that, from its opening, Mrs Ramsay has been sitting for Lily Briscoe's painting, framed in the 'window' of the novel's first section. Towards the novel's close, years after Mrs Ramsay's death, Lily considers again the difficulties of representing her:

> One wanted fifty pairs of eyes to see with, she reflected. Fifty pairs of eyes were not enough to get round that one woman with, she thought. Among them, must be one that was stone blind to her beauty. One wanted most some secret sense, fine as air, with which to steal through keyholes and surround her where she sat knitting, talking, sitting silent in the window alone; which took to itself and treasured up like the air which held the smoke of the streamer, her thoughts, her imaginations, her desires.[141]

The image of a circling, encompassing vision evokes the multiple perspectives of cubist painting, as well as the shifting angles and multiple perspectives open to photography and cinematography. Woolf's invocation of a 'secret sense', moreover, returns us to the image of cinematic perception as observation by proxy, and to Bakshy's account of the film spectator's ability 'to be invisibly present in the very midst of the events he observes, and of following them from place to place'.[142]

In the final section of the text, 'The Lighthouse', Woolf experimented with the representation of two events happening simultaneously—Lily completing her painting, Mr Ramsay's journey to the lighthouse—in ways that were almost certainly influenced by film's ability to represent parallel or 'double' action, either by the use of a split screen or by rapid cutting from one to the other. As the Soviet film theorist V. I. Pudovkin wrote of American cinema: 'the final section is constructed from the simultaneous rapid development of two actions, in which the outcome of one depends on the outcome of the other.'[143] The technique served the ends of filmic suspense, and Woolf plays with the notion of double actions and their simultaneous (and possibly interdependent) completion, while radically disrupting the filmic representation of the race against time, as the movement of the boat in which Mr Ramsay, Cam, and James journey to the lighthouse (and time itself) is suspended with the absence of the tide: 'The sails flapped over their heads. The water chuckled and slapped the sides of the boat, which drowsed motionless in the sun. Now and then the sails rippled with a little breeze in them, but the ripple ran over them and ceased. The boat made no motion at all.'[144] Woolf could also be seen to be playing with, and subverting, popular representations of the wife who looks out to sea as she waits for her lost or shipwrecked sailor-husband—a theme that had become central to narrative cinema of the 1910s, including D. W. Griffith's *Enoch Arden* (1911).

When she was working on this section, Woolf was particularly concerned with the problem of bringing Lily and Mr Ramsay together, writing in her diary:

> Should there be a final page about her & Carmichael looking at the picture & summing up R's character? In that case I lose the intensity of the moment. If this intervenes between R & the lighthouse, there's too much chop and change, I think. Could I do it in a parenthesis? So that one had the sense of reading the two things at the same time?[145]

Woolf's use of parentheses in the central section of the novel, 'Time Passes', and in 'The Lighthouse' is one of the most radical aspects of the narration. In 'Time Passes', she literally brackets off those elements which traditionally form the substance of novels (childbirth, marriage, death) and gives the narrative over to 'unnarratable' events, such as the passing of time and the decay of matter. Yet it could be argued that the words between brackets become more, not less, significant, framed by the brackets as if by a window, or, indeed, as if they were silent film intertitles, placed within square brackets against the background of the screen.

The movement in 'The Lighthouse' between two sets of scenes—Lily painting on the shore, Mr Ramsay sailing with Cam and James to the lighthouse (finally making the trip promised in the novel's opening sentence)—is also presented in ways analogous to shot-reverse shot structure in film, alternating between the view from the boat (to the island shore and then the lighthouse rock) and the view of the boat from the island shore. 'She [Lily] felt curiously divided', Woolf writes, 'as if one part of her were drawn out there—it was a still day, hazy; the Lighthouse looked this morning at an immense distance; the other had fixed itself doggedly, solidly, here on the lawn.'[146] As in *Jacob's Room*, there is a form of 'gesturing' between boat and shore—'The steamer itself had vanished, but the great scroll of smoke still hung in the air and drooped like a flag mournfully in valediction'—with parallels in 1920s cinema, as in Béla Balázs's account of Eisenstein's use of 'metaphors' in *Battleship Potemkin* and the 'gesture' made by small sailing-boats to the battleship.[147] Gesture as a form of bodily hieroglyphics is also central in *To the Lighthouse*, as in this description of Mr Ramsay sitting in the boat: 'He raised his right hand mysteriously high in the air, and let it fall upon his knee again as if he were conducting some secret symphony.'[148] In 'The Lighthouse' (as in Woolf's novel *The Waves*) the breaking of waves on the shore, and their lapping against the boat, becomes not only a marker of repetition and duration, but of the relationship between stasis and motion, and between singular and continuous action: 'a wave incessantly broke and spurted a little column of drops which fell down in a shower.' In 'The Cinema', Woolf instanced the image of the wave breaking as central to early cinema and the rhythm of the waves sounds throughout her fiction.

In the middle section of *To the Lighthouse*, 'Time Passes', we see Woolf exploring the possibilities of a future or potential cinema, as imagined in 'The Cinema', using visual images to express emotions and to animate objects into non-human life. Sound is incorporated or 'folded' into silence (the silence of the cinema), while the unfolding of Mrs Ramsay's shawl (a highly cinematic image, as the fold of the shawl swings too and fro) becomes an image of historical rupture. Mrs Ramsay, whose medium is light, appears after her death as in a film or slide-projection on a wall, and Woolf explores the play of light, the concept of memory as projection, and the corrosive effects of time on matter.

The ten-year passage of time in the central section of *To the Lighthouse* is also the passing of one night, between the days of 'The Window' and 'The Lighthouse', from the midnight hour when the lights are extinguished to the breaking of dawn and of the veil on the sleeper's eyes. During this interlude, the narrative oscillates between absolute stillness and the eruptions of nightmare, in which the world tosses and turns. Time is thus radically condensed (as the ten-year passage was itself a condensation of the period between the Victorian childhood of the 1880s and early 1890s and the return to the house after the end of World War I) or, in cinematic terms, speeded up.

'Time Passes' is also a dream-space, drawing upon the profound conceptual connections between dreams and cinema, and echoing Woolf's reference in 'The Cinema' to the 'dream architecture' of a future film, in which the 'cascades falling and fountains rising, which sometimes visits us in sleep or shapes itself in half-darkened rooms, could be realized before our waking eyes'. As in Vernon Lee's discussions of motion, including her repeated returns in her study *The Beautiful* to the terms of the mountain *rising*, always *rising*, the appropriate tense, or mode, of movement and, in Woolf's writings, of cinema, would appear to be the gerundive—'falling' and 'rising', 'falling' and 'rocking'.[149] Woolf's account of damaged and lost beauty in 'Time Passes' takes this form—'It seemed now as if, touched by human penitence and all its toil, divine goodness had parted the curtain and displayed behind it, single, distinct, the hare erect; the wave falling, the boat rocking, which, did we deserve them, should be ours always.'[150] The image is closely echoed in the variant version of 'The Cinema': 'the curtain parts and we behold, far off, some unknown and unexpected beauty'. In 'The Lighthouse', Lily, sitting on the lawn,

> could not shake herself free from the sense that everything this morning was happening as if for the first time, perhaps for the last time: as a traveller, even though he is fast asleep, knows, looking out of the train window, that he must look now, for he will never see that town, or that mule-cart, or that woman at work in the field, again.[151]

This 'glimpse' provides a very different understanding of the view from the express train, correlated with the locomotion of the film, given in 'Life and the Novelist', in which it represents nothing more than transience.

To the Lighthouse is caught up in the dimension of the scopic; its overt concern is with pictorial representation, but its exploration of the ways in which images of the past function in the present bears a much closer relationship to theories of photography and cinematography. When Lily begins to paint, near the opening of 'The Lighthouse' section: 'She saw her canvas as if it had floated up and placed itself white and uncompromising directly before her. It seemed to rebuke her with its cold stare ... and then, emptiness. She looked blankly at the canvas, with its uncompromising white stare.'[152] The words recall those used by the art critic O. Winter, at the very beginning of film's history, to describe the backcloth on which film would be projected—'white and inanimate'—and Thomas Mann's in *The Magic Mountain*, in which 'the screen glared white and empty'. Lily's canvas is finally filled with shape and colour, but this can only come about when memory and desire have brought back the dead Mrs Ramsay for Lily, backing the empty drawing-room window pane with a 'wave of white', casting 'an odd-shaped triangular shadow over the step', bringing her into the frame: 'There she sat.'

The novel is concerned both with impressions that leave behind the shape where they have been and no longer are, and with the empty centre that retains the power to shape or orchestrate the space around it:

> What people had shed and left—a pair of shoes, a shooting cap, some faded skirts and coats in wardrobes—those alone kept the human shape and in the emptiness indicated how once they were filled and animated; how once hands were busy with hooks and buttons; how once the looking-glass had held a face; had held a world hollowed out in which a figure turned, a hand flashed, the door opened, in came children rushing and tumbling; and went out again. Now, day after day, light turned, like a flower reflected in water, its clear image on the wall opposite. Only the shadows of the trees, flourishing in the wind, made obeisance on the wall, and for a moment darkened the pool in which light reflected itself; or birds, flying, made a soft spot flutter slowly across the bedroom floor.[153]

Woolf's profound interest in Platonic thought—she translated extensively from Plato's writings—is observable in this passage.[154] It is linked to the cinematic elements of light and projection, anticipating the assertion of the classicist Francis Cornford, with whose translations Woolf was familiar, that: 'A modern Plato would compare his cave to an underground cinema, where the audience watch the play of shadows thrown by the film passing before a light at their backs.'[155] Woolf's radical experiment in narration in 'Time Passes', in which reality itself is presented as if in the absence of the perceiving subject (as if in enactment of Andrew Ramsay's explanation to Lily Briscoe of his father's philosophy: 'Think of a kitchen table ... when you're not there') is also, as we have seen, mirrored in 'The Cinema', in which she described the different 'reality' of screen images: 'We behold them as they are when we are not there. We see life as it is when we have no part in it ... beauty will continue to be beautiful whether we behold it or not.'[156] The world in 'Time Passes' is given over to light, 'light reflect[ing] itself'. This ghostly realism suggests something of the threat and the promise of the filmic medium, whose world is, as Stanley Cavell has written, complete without us.

The novel is concerned with traces, footprints, and the mask of beauty— Mrs Ramsay's beauty—which is also a death-mask, with hollowed-out objects and empty objects, containers of what has been and is lost. Mrs Ramsay, whose medium is light, 'appears' after her death as in a film or slide-projection on a wall: 'and faint and flickering, like a yellow beam or the circle at the end of a telescope, a lady in a grey cloak, stooping over her flowers, went wandering over the bedroom wall, up the dressing-table, across the wash-stand'.[157] If in the first part of the novel, scenes are caught, framed, as if in a box-camera—'[Lily] nicked the catch of her paint-box to, more firmly than was necessary, and the nick seemed to surround in a circle for ever the paint-box, the lawn, Mr Bankes, and that wild villain, Cam, dashing past'—in 'Time Passes' and *To the Lighthouse*, Woolf explores the concept of memory as projection. As in the work of H.D. and Dorothy Richardson, whose writings on film are discussed more fully in later chapters, light and projection become two of the key aspects of the cinematographic.

It is striking that for Woolf, H.D., and Richardson, autobiography was closely linked to a history of optical technologies. In *Tribute to Freud*, H.D.'s memoir of her analysis with Freud in the early 1930s, she represented her memories and dreams as moments of vision which were also moments in a history of pre-cinema and cinema: Aristotelian 'after-images', an Archimedean construction of a burning lens, as she recalled her brother using their astronomer father's magnifying glass to make fire and, most strikingly, the 'writing on the wall', a visionary experience in which she saw the inscription of hieroglyphics, images projected onto a wall in light not shadow. The first images were like magic-lantern slides, while the later ones resembled early films. In Richardson's *Pilgrimage*, parts of which were written during her most intense involvement with cinema, but much of which describes a pre-film era, autobiography is intertwined with a history of optics—including the kaleidoscope and the stereoscope—and the past is recalled by means of the technologies of memory.

A history of visual technologies, whose trajectory moves from the tele-scope to the photograph and to the film, can also be traced in *To the Lighthouse*, Woolf's most directly autobiographical novel. In the summer of 1926, when 'The Cinema' essay was appearing in the journals, and during the writing of *To the Lighthouse*, Woolf was composing an introduction to a Hogarth Press volume of her great-aunt Julia Margaret Cameron's pho-tographs, subsequently published as *Victorian Photographs of Famous Men and Fair Women*, with introductory essays by Woolf and Roger Fry. Cameron had taken up photography in 1865, at the age of fifty, and subsequently became one of the most celebrated of Victorian photographers. Woolf's mother, born Julia Jackson, was, as a young unmarried woman and dur-ing the brief years of her first marriage to Herbert Duckworth, one of Cameron's favourite photographic subjects.

Cameron, whose 'circle' at Freshwater, Isle of Wight had included Tennyson and the painter G. F. Watts, was very much part of family legend. The Stephens possessed a number of her photographs, which Vanessa Stephen hung at 46 Gordon Square, the Bloomsbury house to which the Stephen children moved in 1904, after Leslie Stephen's death. Cameron's work, strongly influenced by Pre-Raphaelite art and literature, was characterized by its elements of performance and creation of narrative tableaux, and she frequently clothed and posed her photographic subjects—friends, servants and strangers alike—as figures from the Bible, legend, and literature. As Woolf wrote in her introductory essay: 'The coal-house was turned into a dark room; the fowl-house was turned into a glass-house. Boatmen were turned into King Arthur; village girls into Queen Guenevere. Tennyson was wrapped in rugs; Sir Henry Taylor was crowned with tinsel. The parlour-maid sat for her portrait and the guest had to answer the bell.'[158]

In this essay, Woolf described photography as 'the new born art', an issue also taken up in Roger Fry's contribution to the volume, in which he wrote:

> The position of photography is uncertain and uncomfortable. No one denies its immense service of all kinds, but its status as an independent art has always been disputed. It has never managed to get its Muse or any proper representation on Parnassus, and yet it will not give up its pretensions altogether. Mrs Cameron's photographs posed the question long ago, but it was shelved. The present publication affords perhaps a favourable opportunity to reopen the discussion.[159]

At the close of his essay, Fry turned to the question of photographic aesthetics, arguing that the recognition of photography as an art was dependent on the abandonment of the idea that manual dexterity necessarily equated to artistic power, as well as of the view that 'nervous control of the hand', which lay at the furthest remove from 'mechanism', was alone 'capable of transmitting the artist's feeling to us'. To this extent, he was revising his own, long-held view that the hand-made object was superior to the machine-made because, in his biographer Frances Spalding's words, 'the tremors of movement visible in the end product betrayed the sensibility of the maker'.[160] Composition, he asserted in 'Mrs Cameron's Photographs', was the most significant aspect of the work of art, and it was 'to some extent independent of the exact quality of the texture at each point'. From this perspective, the mechanical aspect of photography would not preclude its claim to artistic status.

Earlier in the essay, however, Fry had suggested that 'the unique record of a period' which Cameron captured was less dependent on 'the fact of the existence of the camera' than on 'the eye of the artist who directed and focussed it'. He argued, furthermore, that it was 'the accidents and conditions of Mrs Cameron's medium', including the imperfections in the lens which she used and the lengthy exposure times which Victorian photography demanded, that ultimately created its effects:

> The slight movements of the sitter gave a certain breadth and envelopment to the form and prevented those too instantaneous expressions which in modern photography so often have an air of caricature. Both expression and form were slightly generalized; they had not that too acute, too positive quality from which modern photography generally suffers.[161]

In this account, duration (the time of photographic exposure) is connected to a softening of focus, and both (as in Walter Benjamin's discussion of the medium in 'A Little History of Photography', in which 'duration' and 'distance' equate to 'aura') are contrasted with an over-sharp instantaneity held to be characteristic of modern photographic representation. 'Accident' and the interval (the duration of exposure) are thus contrasted with the mechanical efficiency which, as we have seen, lay at the heart of Woolf's critique of the cinema, and which only an accidental beauty, or the 'glimpse' of a non-mechanistic energy, could mitigate: 'through the thick counterpane of immense dexterity and enormous efficiency one has glimpses of something vital within.'

In the variant version of 'The Cinema', the 'glimpse', as we have seen, is presented in Platonist terms: 'the curtain parts and we behold, far off, some unknown and unexpected beauty. But it is for a moment only.' The perception chimes with Woolf's writings on the significance of 'the moment' and of 'moments of vision'. As Perry Meisel has written, in his study of the (unacknowledged) influence of Pater on Woolf, at the centre of her work was 'the vision of a universe in constant flux, with an attendant, and once again compensatory, strategy for seizing and arresting the particularly intense and revelatory node of experience known as the privileged moment'.[162] It is striking, however, that in 'The Cinema' essay, the focus is on space as well as on time, with the privileged instant of beauty, glimpsed through the parted curtain or veil, represented as 'far off'.

Distance is the privileged term here, as it is in 'Time Passes'—'solitary like a pool at evening, far distant, seen from a train window, vanishing so quickly that the pool, pale in the evening, is scarcely robbed of its solitude, though once seen'[163]—and in 'The Window' section of *To the Lighthouse*, in which Lily, returned to the house after ten years, attempts to complete her painting of Mrs Ramsay: 'Distance had an extraordinary power... So much depends, then, thought Lily Briscoe... upon distance: whether people are near from us or far from us; for her feeling for Mr. Ramsay changed as he sailed further and further across the bay.'[164] The 'intercutting' between boat and shore creates a sense of spatial separation and of distance spanned, while at the same time temporal distance becomes simultaneity. As she paints, Lily recalls a scene from the past that is not narrated in 'The Window' (it is thus not a repetition, a scene 'remembered' by the narrative itself): 'it survived, after all these years, complete, so that she dipped into it to re-fashion her memory... and it stayed in the mind almost like a work of art.'[165]

The nexus of *To the Lighthouse* (and, in particular, the 'Time Passes' section, which Woolf wrote in the spring of 1926), *Victorian Photographs of Famous Men and Fair Women*, and 'The Cinema' essay created striking connections, and at times distinctions, between visual representations (photography, painting, film), writing and memory. In both the mid-1920s and the late 1930s (when Woolf wrote her memoir 'A Sketch of the Past'), she was absorbed by the past (her own and her mother's), and optics and optical technologies became linked to memory, negotiations with 'distance' and 'focus', the recovery of time passed, and the 'scene-making' at the heart of her writing. Both Woolf and Vanessa Bell were themselves, as Maggie Humm has shown, active photographers from childhood onwards, and Humm locates a 'photographic syntax' in Woolf's writing, which was, she argues, 'shaped by a powerful investment in the capacity of photography to provide memorial and gendered optics'.[166]

In her essay in *Victorian Photographs*, Woolf quoted from Cameron's autobiographical fragment 'Annals of my Glass House' (1874): 'I longed to arrest all the beauty that came before me, and at length the longing was satisfied.'[167] Woolf also cited Mary Watts's comment on Cameron: 'She used to say that in her photography a hundred negatives were destroyed before she achieved one good result; her object being to overcome realism by diminishing just in the least degree the precision of the focus.'[168] The lines echo others from 'Annals of My Glass House', in which Cameron had written:

> I believe that what my youngest boy, Henry Herschel, who is now himself a very remarkable photographer, told me is quite true—that my first successes in my out-of-focus pictures were a fluke. That is to say, that when focusing and coming to something which, to my eye, was very beautiful, I stopped there instead of screwing on the lens to the more definite focus which all other photographers insisted on.[169]

The terms of 'beauty'—arrested beauty, the beauty that appears to the perceiving eye prior to sharp definition and 'focus'—reverberate throughout *To the Lighthouse* and 'The Cinema'. 'Beauty' was, for Woolf, an overdetermined concept and attribute. Julia Margaret Cameron's 'arrested' beauty became Woolf's 'frozen' beauty, in Lily Briscoe's thoughts about Mrs Ramsay: 'Beauty had this penalty—it came too readily, came too completely. It stilled life—froze it. One forgot the little agitations; the flush, the pallor, some queer distortion, some light or shadow, which made the face unrecognisable for a moment and yet added a quality one saw for ever after. It was simpler to smooth that all out under the cover of beauty.'[170] In order to complete her painting, Lily has to find 'her' Mrs Ramsay, behind the mask of beauty.

The connection, in the novel and in Woolf's writings on the past more generally, between the concept and critique of 'beauty' and the Victorian photographic image was profound. In the weeks following Julia Stephen's death, Leslie Stephen wrote the volume which came to be known in the family as *The Mausoleum Book*. In writing the memoir, he turned to Cameron's photographs of his deceased wife as a young woman:

> Most fortunately, the beautiful series of portraits taken by Mrs. Cameron, chiefly, I think from 1866 to 1875, remain to give an impression to her children of what she really was. To us, who remember her distinctly, they recall her like nothing else … Her beauty was of the kind which seems to imply—as it most certainly did accompany—equal beauty of soul, refinement, nobility and tenderness of character, and which yet did not imply, as some beauty called 'spiritual' may seem to do, any lack of 'material' beauty. It was just the perfect balance, the harmony of mind and body which made me feel when I looked at her the kind of pleasure which I suppose a keen artistic sense to derive from a masterpiece of Greek sculpture … It was the complete reconciliation and fulfilment of all conditions of feminine beauty … Her loveliness thrills me to the core, whenever I call up the vision.

May it never grow weaker till my power of mental vision weakens—as it must so soon.[171]

In *To the Lighthouse*, it is this model of the ways in which 'beauty outside mirrored beauty within' that is shattered by death and war: 'the mirror was broken.'

In 'Mrs. Cameron's Photographs', Fry dwelt on the 'extraordinary passion for beauty' obtaining in mid-Victorian Britain, and the absoluteness of the gendered divide that it both produced and upheld. Writing of Cameron's photograph 'Rosebud Garden of Girls'—and he was in general critical of her group compositions—Fry commented: 'We realize something of the solemn ritual which surrounded these beautiful women. How natural it seems to them to make up and pose like this. They have been so fashioned by the art of the day that to be themselves part of a picture is almost an instinctive function ... In that protected garden of culture women grew to strange beauty, and the men—how lush and rank are their growths! How they abound in the sense of their own personalities!' Cameron's male sitters, Fry suggests, either display or are, simply, themselves; by contrast, 'the women, one may surmise, were more interested in the art which moulded and celebrated them'.[172] The implication is that Victorian photography was essentially a feminine medium, and that a symbiotic relationship existed between the beautiful woman and the photograph's arrest of beauty.

Woolf's memoir 'A Sketch of the Past', written in 1939/40, returned to images of Julia Stephen as a young woman:

Little Holland House was her world then [as a child]. But what was that world like? I think of it as a summer afternoon world. To my thinking Little Holland House is an old white country house, standing in a large garden. Long windows open on to the lawn. Through them comes a stream of ladies in crinolines and little straw hats; they are attended by gentlemen in peg-top trousers and whiskers. The date is round about 1860. It is a hot summer day. Tea tables with great bowls of strawberries and cream are scattered about the lawn. They are 'presided over' by some of the six lovely sisters, who do not wear crinolines, but are robed in splendid Venetian draperies; they sit enthroned, and talk with foreign emphatic gestures—my mother too gesticulated, throwing her hands out—to the eminent men (afterwards to be made fun of by Lytton); rulers of India, statesmen, poets, painters. My mother comes out of the window wearing that striped silk dress buttoned at the throat with a flowing skirt that appears in the photograph. She is of course 'a vision' as they used to say; and there she stands, silent, with her plate of strawberries and cream; or perhaps is told to take a party across the garden to Signoir's [G. F. Watts] studio ... How easy it is to fill in the picture with set pieces that I have gathered from memoirs—to bring in Tennyson in his wideawake; Watts in his smock frock; Ellen Terry dressed as a boy; Garibaldi in his red shirt—and Henry Taylor turned from him to my mother—'the face of one fair girl was more to me'—so he says in a poem. But if I turn to my mother, how difficult it is to single her out as she really was; to imagine what she was thinking, to put a single sentence into her mouth! I dream; I make up pictures of a summer's afternoon.[173]

The passage contains echoes of the scene towards the close of *To the Lighthouse* in which Lily tries to single Mrs Ramsay out 'as she really was', and conjures up a picture of the past:

He [Mr Ramsay] stretched out his hand and raised her from her chair. It seemed somehow as if he had done it before; as if he had once bent in the same way and raised her [Mrs Ramsay] from a boat which, lying a few inches off some island, had required that the ladies should thus be helped on shore by the gentleman. An old-fashioned scene that was, which required, very nearly, crinolines and peg-top trousers. Letting herself be helped by him, Mrs Ramsay had thought (Lily supposed) the time has come now; Yes, she would say it now. Yes, she would marry him. And she stepped slowly, quietly on shore. Probably she said one word only, letting her hand rest still in his. I will marry you, she might have said, with her hand in his; but no more. Time after time the same thrill had passed between them—obviously it had, Lily thought, smoothing a way for her ants. She was not inventing; she was only trying to smooth out something she had been given years ago folded up; something she had seen.[174]

The repetition of 'smoothing', 'smooth out' calls attention to the term, which Woolf also uses in the variant edition of 'The Cinema', in which she wrote of the future film: 'The past could be unrolled, distances annihilated, and the gulfs which dislocated novels ... could, by the sameness of the background, by the repetition of some scene, be smoothed away.'[175] The unrolling of the past suggests that it takes the form of a painting or a screen. Repetition (of gesture, attitude, relationship) has caused the past to become furled and folded. Lily is seeking to smooth out the surface on which the first scene played itself out, and it is essentially gestural and cinematic—'He stretched out his hand and raised her from her chair'—by contrast with the passage from 'A Sketch of the Past', in which Woolf's memories of her mother are 'frozen' (despite her imagined gesticulations) in, and by, the arrested beauty of her photographic image.

The cinematographic nature of *To the Lighthouse* is thus bound up with questions of presence and absence, the recording of the past and negotiations with loss and legacy. Both Mr and Mrs Ramsay are, in their different ways, preoccupied with the traces they will leave behind, and with scholarly fame and with family respectively. Throughout 'The Window', we see Mrs Ramsay observing the present becoming the past: 'With her foot on the threshold she waited a moment longer in a scene which was vanishing even as she looked, and then, as she moved and took Minta's arm and left the room, it changed, it shaped itself differently; it had become, she knew, giving one last look at it over her shoulder, already the past.'[176]

In an essay on 'Photography', published in 1927, Siegfried Kracauer contrasted the workings of photography and memory: 'Photography grasps what is given as a spatial (or temporal) continuum; memory images retain what is given only in so far as it has significance. Since what is significant is not reducible to either merely spatial or merely temporal terms, memory images are at odds with photographic representation.'[177] By contrast, Leslie Stephen, recalling his dead wife, placed memory images and photographic images in close proximity, and even a relation of interchangeability, to each other; the photograph recalled the living woman (as a young and beautiful woman) to those who remembered her, and gave an impression of 'what she really was' to her children, who had no access in memory to this past. In *To the Lighthouse*, Virginia Woolf negotiated between the terms of photography and memory images. Like Kracauer and Walter Benjamin, she connected the ways in which photography and 'fashion' are bound to time, as she called into view the 'crinolines and little striped hats', the 'peg-top trousers and whiskers', and 'that striped silk dress' of her mother's. She wrote *To the Lighthouse* as a ghost-story of a kind, and its ghostliness is profoundly connected to the temporalities of the photographic image. As Kracauer wrote:

> Ghosts are simultaneously comical and terrifying. Laugher is not the only response provoked by antiquated photography. It represents what is utterly past, and yet this detritus was once the present. Grandmother was once a person, and to this person belonged the chignon and the corset as well as the high-Renaissance chair with its turned spindles, ballast that did not weigh her down but was just carried along as a matter of course. Now the image wanders ghost-like through the present, like the lady of the haunted castle. Spooky apparitions occur only in places where a terrible deed has

been committed. The photograph becomes a ghost because the costumed mannequin was once alive ... This terrible association which persists in the photograph evokes a shudder. Such a shudder is evoked in drastic fashion by the pre-World War I films screened in the avant-garde 'Studio des Ursulines' in Paris—film images that show how the features stored in the memory image are embedded in a reality which has long since disappeared.[178]

Kracauer's invocation of the early films screened at the 'Studio des Ursulines' echoes that of René Clair, quoted earlier in this chapter, with his 'melancholy' thoughts in 1924 about the ways in which cinema's transience had proven a challenge to time, which had been met by time's revenge in 'speeding up its effects on everything pertaining to the cinema'. As cinema, 'for the first time', turned back towards its past, its spectators (those who were not roaring with laughter) saw that the present of their own films would soon become the past, attacked by time which would 'gnaw off all their present verisimilitude, to leave only a funny skeleton'.

This leads us back to Woolf's thoughts on pre-World War I films in 'The Cinema', to the 'ten years' between the early, innocent films and those of the present in which she was writing, and to the 'ten years' between 'The Window' and 'The Lighthouse', between which lies the corrosive, gnawing passage of time. Woolf's responses, however, to the representations of the past were not confined to the choice, set up by both Clair and Kracauer, between laughter and the shudder. There was 'vision', also to be remade or 're-fashioned', in which the photographic image, the memory image and the play of imagination could be brought into a new synthesis, each animating the other.

Sight and Sound: *The Years*

The Years tells the story of the extended family of the Pargiters between 1880 and 'the present day' (the 1930s) in an irregular movement that breaks up the smooth flow of passing time and generation (the sections are titled 1880, 1891, 1908, 1910, 1911, 1913, 1914, 1917, 1918, Present Day). Within each section, the time span is part of a single day or evening, focusing sometimes on one location, and at others moving between two or more. In the novel Woolf experimented with the bridging of abysses (to borrow a phrase from Theodora Bosanquet's review of the novel in

Time and Tide[179]) in ways that both recall *To the Lighthouse* and return us to Woolf's speculations in 'The Cinema'.

> The past could be unrolled, distances could be annihilated. And those terrible dislocations which are inevitable when Tolstoy has to pass from the story of Anna to the story of Levin could be bridged by some device of scenery. We should have the continuity of human life kept before us by the repetition of some object common to both lives.

Woolf had originally intended *The Years* to be a 'Novel-Essay', a 'novel of fact', in which essays would be interspersed with extracts from 'a novel that will run into many volumes'. In early 1933, she decided not to have separate interchapters (the essays), instead 'compacting them into the text', and turning the passages in between sections into 'interludes', 'spaces of silence and poetry and contrast'.[180] These are comparable to those in *The Waves*, the novel in which the cinematic enters through the breaking of the waves upon the shore, the play of light upon physical forms ('The sun fell in sharp wedges inside the room. Whatever the light touched became dowered with a fantastical existence'),[181] the coming into being of consciousness out of the world of matter, and the Bergsonian understanding (explored most fully in his *Matter and Memory*) of human subjectivity as both mingled with and emerging out of a universe of images.

The design of combining 'realism' and 'poetry' in *The Years* was echoed in the aspirations of writings on film in this period (as documentary cinema was developed and theorized as a genre). Woolfs' 'interludes' both represent the elemental forces of nature—weather and landscape ('some device of scenery')—in an impersonal universe, and depict their impact on the life of the city. At the opening of the 1908 section, for example, Woolf writes of the March wind:

> Triumphing in its wantonness it emptied the streets; swept flesh before it; and coming smack against a dust cart standing outside the Army and Navy stores, scattered along the pavement a litter of old envelopes; twists of hair; papers already blood-smeared, yellow-smeared, smudged with print and sent them scudding to plaster legs, lamp-posts, pillar-boxes, and fold themselves frantically against area railings.[182]

The visual image of litter, or a sheet of newspaper, blowing along a street is a standard trope in city films; it is one of the opening shots of Ruttmann's *Berlin*, in which the motion of the paper is the only movement in the empty streets at the beginning of the day, and it connects the dailiness of the newspaper with the 'day in the life of a city' theme. Eric Walter White's *Parnassus to Let* (published, we recall, by the Woolfs' Hogarth Press in 1928) had included a discussion of *Berlin*, in which he commended certain uses of the 'still photograph', while warning against the use of the 'pictorial shot', which 'is apt to make a film static and to sap its dynamic force':

> One of the most notable moments in *Berlin* was when the rhythmic acceleration, emotional tension, and musical climax of the arrival by train were suddenly succeeded by quiet photographic stills: of the city, lifeless as a picture post-card in the dawn, of the smokeless factories, of the deserted streets, each accompanied by a low chord *pianissimo*. Still followed after still, like so many lantern slides, until down an exhausted street came the first wind of the day, blowing a piece of white paper along the dry pavement, over and over.[183]

White's terms resonate with Woolf's later descriptions of the cityscape in *The Years*, with Charles Davy's reconstructions of a film scenario drawn from the novel (discussed later in this chapter), and with a comment made by Graham Greene in an article published in 1928 on 'A Film Technique: Rhythms of Time and Space'. In the 'rhythm of time and of space', Greene argued, 'there should be an interval, a breathing space'. He wrote in the same context of 'the wave of rhythm' in *Berlin*, and of films in which 'the camera for a moment turns from the restless race of actions to poetry, perhaps, an empty room, sun-drenched, barred with cool shadows. There is the tip of the rhythmic wave, perhaps of photographic art, and it should break, not once when it is too late to revive the battered eyesight, but at regular intervals—like the recurrence of the great ninth wave, which leaves its spray furthest up the shore'.[184] Greene's focus on the interval, on the wave of rhythm and on rhythm as a wave, not only contains strong echoes of the early US film criticism discussed in my next chapter, but also chimes in significant ways with *To the Lighthouse* and with *The Waves*, written, as Woolf noted, to a rhythm and not a plot.

Siegfried Kracauer commented, rather less lyrically than White and Greene, on the 'sights of refuse' in Ruttmann's 'garbage-minded film'— 'Ruttmann's *Berlin* includes a wealth of sewer grates, gutters and streets littered with rubbish'—and referred to the camera as a 'rag-picker'.[185] Blood-smeared and yellow-smeared, Woolf's 'litter' wraps itself around the architecture of 'a polluted city'. There is, in this passage at least, a refusal of the lyricism in the interludes of *The Waves* or the 'Time Passes' section of *To the Lighthouse*; though the passage, with its shades of *The Waste Land*, the text which forged a concept of 'cinematic' poetics, creates a 'poetry' of the underside of the city. Other interludes are closer to those in *The Waves*: 'It was windless and calm. Sounds coming through the veil [of mist]—the bleat of sheep, the croak of rooks—were deadened. The uproar of the traffic merged into one growl. Now and then as if a door opened and shut, or the veil parted and closed, the roar boomed and faded.'[186] To the 'glimpse' linked with the visible has been added that in the realm of sound, with the appearance and disappearance of the aural trace. Sound has been added to sight, as it was to the cinema in this period.

In 1931, Woolf saw a 'very good' French film, which the editor of her letters identifies as René Clair's city-film *Le Million*.[187] This, like Clair's *Sous les toits de Paris*, Clair's first sound film, opened with a panning shot across the roofs of Paris (echoed in the bird's-eye views of the city given in the 'interludes' of *The Years*) and experimented with the relationship between sound and image. The film critic C. A. Lejeune described *Sous les toits de Paris* in the following terms:

> The true material of the sound *montage* is the music; the individual phrases of the theme song, the commentary of traffic, of street sounds, of accordion notes, which amplify without ever duplicating the content of a scene. This splitting up of the melody between a dozen environments—flashing, with the ear and the eye, from the cafe to the prison, to the attic, to the empty street, running through every floor of a tenement building, surcharged and changed by the changing scene—this modulation of a musical idea, phrase by phrase, according to the temperament of the singer, is the stuff of real cinema, the equivalent in embryo of the work done by the Soviet directors for the silent screen.[188]

Lejeune's terms of description—the ear and the eye; the city soundscape; the rhythmic movement between 'environments'—reverberate throughout *The Years*. *The Years* is structured around repetition. Both the change and the continuity of human life are to a striking extent 'kept before us by the repetition of some object common to … lives'. Domestic objects, referred to throughout the novel as 'things' or 'solid objects'—a tea-kettle, a 'walrus brush', a 'crimson chair with gilt claws', an Italian mirror—are constant presences through shifts of time and location, though they are also shaped by their contexts, as the large Victorian family homes give way, in the course of the novel, to flats and lodging houses. In the 1907 section of the novel, one branch of the still prosperous Pargiter family is out at a party:

> All was silent in the house at Browne Street. A ray from the street lamp fell through the fanlight and, rather capriciously, lit up a tray of glasses on the hall table; a top hat; and a chair with gilt paws. The chair, standing empty, as if waiting for someone, had a look of ceremony; as if it stood on the cracked floor of some Italian ante-room. But all was silent.[189]

At the end of the section, the chair is presented again, but this time through the eyes of a character, Maggie Pargiter:

> Maggie went along the passage. Then she saw that there were lights in the hall beneath. She stopped and looked down over the banister. The hall was lit up. She could see the great Italian chair with the gilt claws that stood in the hall. Her mother had thrown her evening cloak over it, so that it fell in soft golden folds over the crimson cover. She could see a tray with whisky and a soda-water syphon on the hall table. Then she heard the voices of her father and mother as they came up the kitchen stairs...
> Maggie went on a few steps upstairs...
> Then there was a pause. Maggie could hear soda-water squirted into a tumbler; the chink of a glass; and then the lights went out.[190]

The chair is neither a 'symbol' nor a realist detail of the kind which Woolf criticized in the work of the Edwardian novelists, as Edwin Muir noted in his review of *The Years*, in which he contrasted the novel with Galsworthy's *The Man of Property*, 'so full of upholstery and exposition'.[191] The chair first appears in the novel to Abel Pargiter, visiting his brother Digby: 'He looked vaguely at a great crimson chair with gilt claws that stood in the hall. He envied Digby his house, his wife, his children.'[192] In the first passage quoted above, in which light enters to illuminate selected objects, the chair is perceived in the absence of a perceiving subject, in accordance, as in *Jacob's Room*, *To the Lighthouse*, and *The Years,* with Woolf's fascination with the world seen without a self, the chair with gilt feet becoming a relative of Jacob's empty chair. Yet in *The Years* the chair, with its 'look of ceremony'—and the play here is on the 'look' as something that is both seen (as an attribute of the object) and itself sees—is represented far more 'physiognomically'.

Such a relationship to the object chimes with Vachel Lindsay's account of film's 'yearning for personality in furniture'.[193] It also has echoes in film writings of the 1920s and 30s, and, in particular, with the theories of Fernand Léger, with his fascination with 'objects' in the cinema, and Béla Balázs, who wrote extensively of 'the face of things' in film and of the ways in which the close-up 'shows the speechless face and fate of the dumb objects that live with you in your room and whose fate is bound up with your own … a good film with its close-ups reveals the most hidden parts in our polyphonous life, and teaches us to see the intricate visual details of life as one reads an orchestral score'.[194]

In the second passage quoted, we see only what Maggie sees through the frame, or, to borrow Balázs's term, the 'sectional picture' of her vision, as she stands looking over the banisters. The hall is now illuminated by artificial lighting (by contrast with the 'capricious' ray from the street-lamp which had earlier lit the space, when there was no one to see it). The chair's appearance has been altered by the cloak thrown over it by Maggie's mother Eugénie (as Mrs Ramsay, in *To the Lighthouse* had flung a shawl over the corner of a picture and, later in the novel, had used it to conceal an animal's skull in the children's bedroom.) On the hall table, a whisky bottle and a soda syphon have been added to the tray of glasses, as if they were props in the *mise en scène*. The two passages encode two different models of the 'cinematographic'. In the first, which dominates *Jacob's Room* and *To the Lighthouse*, the essence of cinematic reality is its independence from a perceiving subject; in the second, which emerges in *Mrs Dalloway* and, in parallel with the first mode, in *To the Lighthouse,* scenes are visually, or cinematically, framed in a character's field of vision.

Sight then gives way to sound. Maggie no longer sees what is in the hall, as she moves further upstairs, but hears 'soda-water squirted into a tumbler; the chink of a glass', before 'the lights went out' and the chapter ends. Whereas the novels discussed so far (*Jacob's Room*, *To the Lighthouse*, *Mrs Dalloway*) were written during the era of silent cinema, *The Years* was composed in the period in which sound film was becoming fully established: there was, as I discuss in later chapters, intense debate in the late 1920s and beyond about the limitations and 'staginess' of synchronized sound (predominantly dialogue) and exploration of the potential for experiment with sound (articulated most extensively in Soviet film theories). In more general terms, the technologies of sound—wireless radio, gramophone, loudspeaker—were central to Woolf at this time. They were dominating forces in the political culture of the 1930s, and played an increasingly significant role in her writings, becoming a central element in her last novel, *Between the Acts*.[195]

In *The Years*, sight and sound, the eye and the ear, are, as in the passage in which Maggie looks down into the hall and then moves upstairs, represented as functioning autonomously. Later in the novel, in the lengthy 'Present Day' section with which it closes, Woolf uses the telephone to represent the division between sight and sound and the articulation of the disembodied voice, in a form of counterpoint of sound and image. Towards the beginning of the section, North, recently returned from Africa, visits his cousin Sara in her lodging-house:

> From across the road came the voice of the singer deliberately ascending the scale, as if the notes were stairs; and here she stopped indolently, languidly, flinging out the voice that was nothing but pure sound. Then he heard somebody inside, laughing.
>
> That's her voice, he said. But there is somebody with her. He was annoyed. He had hoped to find her alone. The voice was speaking and did not answer when he knocked. Very cautiously he opened the door and went in.
>
> 'Yes, yes, yes,' Sara was saying. She was kneeling at the telephone talking; but there was nobody there. She raised her hand when she saw him and smiled at him; but she kept her hand raised as if the noise he had made caused her to lose what she was trying to hear. …
>
> He sat down on the chair she had pushed out for him, and she curled up opposite with her foot under her. He remembered the attitude; she came back in sections; first the voice, then the attitude; but something remained unknown …
>
> 'And you—' she said, looking at him. It was as if she were trying to put two different versions of him together; the one on the telephone perhaps and the one on the chair.[196]

As in a film, the telephone functions to connect one character and location and another, but Woolf's use of the technology works primarily to divide her characters into their verbal and visual aspects, and to explore the ways in which separations, whether the literal separations of distance or those of the boundaries between selves, are to be negotiated. In the passage above, North hears the singer ('flinging out the voice which was nothing but pure sound') without seeing her, and hears Sara (talking on the phone, though he initially thinks that she is not alone) before he sees her.

The phone transmits the voice; the visual image of the person must be constructed. A little later in the same episode, the telephone rings again, and is answered by North:

'Hullo,' he said, answering the telephone. But there was a pause. He looked at her [Sara] sitting on the edge of the chair, swinging her foot up and down. Then a voice spoke.

'I'm North,' he answered the telephone. 'I'm dining with Sara ... Yes, I'll tell her ...' He looked at her again. 'She is sitting on the edge of her chair,' he said, 'with a smudge on her face, swinging her foot up and down.'

Eleanor was holding the telephone. She smiled, and for a moment after she had put the receiver back stood there, still smiling, before she turned to her niece Peggy who had been dining with her.

'North is dining with Sara,' she said, smiling at the little telephone picture of two people at the other end of London, one of whom was sitting on the edge of her chair with a smudge on her face.

'He's dining with Sara,' she said again. But her niece did not smile, for she had not seen the picture, and she was slightly irritated because, in the middle of what they were saying, Eleanor suddenly got up and said, 'I'll just remind Sara.'

'Oh, is he?' she said casually.

Eleanor came and sat down.

'We were saying—' she began.

'You've had it cleaned,' said Peggy simultaneously. While Eleanor telephoned, she had been looking at the picture of her grandmother over the writing-table.[197]

Fragmentations are operating at a number of levels in this passage. As in the first telephone passage, contrasts and comparisons are being drawn between the ways in which sight and sound operate through the senses and through technologies. Soon after this exchange, Peggy uses the telephone to call a cab to take Eleanor and herself to the party where the family will meet up, and as she waits to be connected: 'she looked at her hands holding the telephone ... Again she waited. As she sat where Eleanor had sat she saw the telephone picture that Eleanor had seen—Sally sitting on the edge of her chair with a smudge on her face ... "One of these days d'you think you'll be able to see things at the end of the telephone?" Peggy said, getting up.'

Such passages emphasize an issue at the heart of the novel; the failure of individuals, like histories, to coalesce, an absence of fixity which brings with it both fear and freedom. *The Years* breaks up patterns as, or before, they are formed, a thematics echoed at the level of the sentence, and in Woolf's extensive use of the trope of aposiopesis (discussed in the previous chapter in relation to Kipling's 'Mrs Bathurst') throughout the novel. In the 'Present Day' section in particular, Woolf appears to have been returning to passages from *To the Lighthouse,* emphasizing the ways in which the human eye attempts to make meaningful patterns out of objects and shapes, but, rather than showing the present becoming the past, she constructs complex temporalities in which the past, like the present, becomes open to the future, and in which that which comes after takes the place of that which has preceded it, leaving us with serially passing moments: 'thing followed thing, scene obliterated scene.'[198] This model of time and experience as a series of passing objects, events and 'scenes' has a filmic dimension, recalling the images of mere locomotion and depthless seriality invoked in Woolf's essays 'The Movie Novel' and 'Life and the Novelist', but it takes on new depths and complexities in *The Years*, in which it is intertwined with questions of identity and consciousness. At the party, North is given a visiting card by a young woman to whom he is attracted: 'And where shall I spend tomorrow night? he added, for the card in his waistcoat pocket rayed out of its own accord without regard for the context scenes which obliterated the present moment.'[199]

At the party with which *The Years* comes to a close, a game of 'Consequences' is played, creating a 'monster' in sections. Characters, too, see themselves and others in sections, as in North's earlier perceptions of Sara ('she came back in sections'), in the recurrent images of seemingly disembodied heads ('Then curtains in the house opposite parted, three heads appeared at the window. They looked at the heads outlined on the window opposite them')[200] and in Peggy's observation of 'her hands holding the telephone'. At the party, Peggy's view, as she sits on the floor, is of people's feet: 'feet pointing this way, feet pointing that way; patent leather pumps; satin slippers; silk stockings and socks. They were dancing rhythmically, insistently, to the tune of the fox-trot... And voices went on over her head... And a pair of pumps crossed Peggy's field of vision and stopped in front of her.'[201]

Such images of part-objects (which at one level serve to indicate the partial and incomplete perspectives available to characters, even as they seek some vision of the whole) also come to us as if framed in and through the technologies of sound and sight. In *Sous les toits de Paris*, for example, Clair used shots of feet and shoes to represent the developing relationship between the film's central characters. It is also as if Woolf chose to depict those images of 'modern life' in contemporary fiction to whose transience she had pointed in her essay 'Life and the Novelist'—'his [the modern novelist's] work passes as the year 1921 passes, as foxtrots pass, and in three years' time looks as dowdy and dull as any other fashion which has served its turn and gone its way'—and sought to show that they took on a different interest and significance when relayed through new understandings of temporality ('passing' now becomes the complexity of modern time), and of perception and motion specific to modernity (the camera eye, the radio ear, montages of sound and vision).

Woolf drew attention to this aspect of the text when she moved from the imaginary 'telephone picture' of Sara (transmitted to Eleanor by North in his description and received, again in imagination, by Peggy after a delay, and as she waits for her call to be connected) to Peggy's imagining of a future technology (a form of video phone). This would reconnect sound and sight, the voice and the 'little snapshot picture' of a person (with its close connections to the use of the 'inset' in the cinema, often used, as the writer on film Eric Elliott noted in 1928, 'to picture a person supposedly conversing at "the other end" of a telephone'),[202] by means of a machine rather than the mind. The question remained as to whether such a technology were necessary, when the mind could, as if telepathically, already 'see things at the end of a telephone'. Yet it may be that Woolf was not so much opposing human vision and the mechanical eye as, in the intensely 'filmic' context of the 1930s, granting to human perception a cinematic dimension:

> But North was not attending. He was looking at a couple at the farther end of the room. They were standing by the fireplace. Both were young; both were silent; they seemed held still in that position by some powerful emotion. As he looked at them, some emotion about himself, about his own life, came over him, and he arranged another background for them or for himself—not the mantelpiece and the bookcase, but cataracts roaring, clouds racing, and they stood on a cliff above a torrent...
> 'Marriage isn't for everyone,' Eleanor interrupted.[203]

The imagined reintegration of sound and sight, and of the voice and the individual, has a markedly political and utopian dimension in the text. The voice cut off, as on the telephone or the radio, from the person is connected in the novel to the politics of the 1930s: 'halls and reverberating megaphones... marching in steps after leaders, in herds, groups, societies, caparisoned.' At the party, North listens to young public-school educated men talking politics: 'People met, he thought, pretending to read, in hired halls. And one of them stood on a platform. There was the pump-handle gesture; the wringing wet-clothes gesture; and then the voice, oddly detached from the little figure and tremendously magnified by the loudspeaker, went booming and bawling round the hall.'[204]

The passage was echoed in a number of Woolf's essays written during the 1930s. In 'The Leaning Tower', she described the way in which war was relayed to the public via wireless voices: 'To-day we hear the gunfire in the Channel. We turn on the wireless; we hear an airman telling us how this afternoon he shot down a raider ... Scott never saw the sailors drowning at Trafalgar; Jane Austen never heard the cannon roar at Waterloo. Neither of them heard Napoleon's voice as we hear Hitler's voice as we sit at home of an evening.'[205] The essay, addressed primarily to that group of young male writers associated with W. H. Auden, describes the distorting effects of two world wars, which have resulted in 'the pedagogic, the didactic, the loud-speaker strain that dominates their poetry. They must teach; they must preach'. It is as if the private life were continually cut across by a form of public and collective 'voice-over', as in the documentary films of the 1930s, with their sound-montages of voices.

In 'The Artist and Politics' (as in Woolf's anti-war work *Three Guineas*), the artist is 'besieged by voices, all disturbing, some for one reason, some for another' and the call to politics and the call to art are in conflict.[206] There were to be no easy solutions or resolutions to these questions, which *The Years*, begun at the beginning at the decade and completed towards its end, started to address. In the novel Woolf allowed her characters to express a degree of ambivalence in the direct invocation of the new media of the period, and in particular the cinema. At no point does the narrative enter the space of the 'picture palace' to explore the world of the screen and its impact upon spectators. At several junctures, however, Woolf implied, as in *Mrs Dalloway*, a continuity between the arena of film-dreams and the spaces of the modern city and modern life. The frequently deployed image, in the first decades of the century, of the audience congregated outside the cinema suggests the extent to which the city had become perceived as a cinematic space. As Emmanuel Beskin wrote in 1916: '[people] form something like a foyer or a club outside the cinema. They stroll up and down, joking and flirting, listening to what the people coming out are saying and so on. The bright lights illuminate the crowd; the smart commissionaire and the

"vulgar extravagant decor" lure them in.'[207] In the 'Present Day' section of
The Years:

> They [Eleanor and Peggy] were driving along a bright crowded street;
> here stained ruby with the light from picture palaces; here yellow from shop
> windows gay with summer dresses, for the shops, though shut, were still lit
> up, and people were still looking at dresses, at flights of hats on little rods, at
> jewels…
>
> 'Where's he taking us?' she said, looking out. They had reached the
> public part of London; the illuminated. The light fell on broad pavements;
> in white brilliantly lit-up public offices, on a pallid, hoary-looking church.
> Advertisements popped in and out. Here was a bottle of beer: it poured: then
> stopped: then poured again. They had reached the theatre quarter. There was
> the usual garish confusion. Men and women in evening dress were walking
> in the middle of the road. Cabs were wheeling and stopping. Their own taxi
> was held up. It stopped dead under a statue: the lights shone on its cadaverous
> pallor.
>
> 'Always reminds me of an advertisement of sanitary towels,' said Peggy,
> glancing at the figure of a woman in nurse's uniform holding out her hand.[208]

The statue is that of Nurse Edith Cavell (which stands in St Martin's
Lane), shot at dawn during the First World War for helping Allied
soldiers to escape, her 'sacrifice' more bitter as the outbreak of a second
world war became increasingly probable. The statue exists alongside the
picture palaces, the shop windows, the offices and the advertisements:
a corpse at the feast. Woolf's vision of London in 'Present Day' is
as a light-show, echoing numerous city films of the 1920s and 30s in
which a continuity is constructed between the light-show that is cinema
and the advertising 'hieroglyphics' which light up the city. The passage
also contains echoes of Siegfried Kracauer's 1927 essay 'Lichtreklame'
('Neon Advertising'), in which Kracauer wrote of the modern metropolis:

> The juxtaposition of the stores produces a storm of light whose sliding
> disorder is not purely terrestrial. In this swarm one can still perceive signs and
> characters, but here these have been detached from their practical purposes;
> their entry into a multi-coloured state has broken them up into fragments of
> brightness which combine according to unfamiliar rules. The drizzle poured
> out by economic life becomes images of stars in a strange sky.[209]

The images of the city later return to Peggy: 'Again she saw the ruby-
splashed pavement, and faces mobbed at the door of a picture palace;

apathetic, passive faces; the faces of people drugged with cheap pleasures; who had not even the courage to be themselves, but must dress up, imitate, pretend.'[210]

These preoccupations of the novel were intensified in the sections—the 'two enormous chunks'—which Woolf omitted from the final version of the novel, as she struggled to revise it. In one part of the first, Miriam Parrish is on her way to meet Eleanor at the theatre: 'For a moment she was bewildered, for she had lost her sense of direction. The streets were glaring with light. Advertisements were popping in and out. The names of the theatres were framed in blue and red lines; there was a bottle of beer that poured and stopped, then poured again. The sky glared as if a red and yellow canopy hung over it.'[211]

Towards the close of the second section, Eleanor dines alone in a restaurant, eating one of the many meals taken in the novel. Again, the scene has numerous counterparts in the films of the period, in which the restaurant meal (a significant dimension of the 'city symphony', most markedly in Ruttmann's *Berlin*, but also central to narrative cinema) punctuates the day in the life of the city and provides the occasion for spectacle, the representation of movement and the observation of people, particularly couples, who may be either central or peripheral to the plot. As Woolf wrote:

> There was the usual music; somewhere behind a column they were playing the usual waltz. But it was distant—a pulse of sound merely that surged up and down beneath the clatter. She [Eleanor] sat there listening and looking about her, amused, distracted by the many voices, by the many movements all around her. They were very busy; people were coming in and going out. She waited. Gradually she became aware of a thudding sound in the background. She identified it. From where she sat, rather at the back, rather at one side, she could see a swing door opening and shutting. A file of waitresses went in; came out; they went in with dirty plates; they came out with the clean ones. She caught a glimpse of them snatching their dishes from a counter in the kitchens beyond. The machine at this hour of the evening was working smoothly but at full pressure. All the time new diners kept arriving; passing between the tables; coming in; going out. She waited.
>
> She looked about her. At the next table was a couple dining together; a young man and a girl. They had finished one course; and they were waiting too. The girl had opened her bag and was carefully and deliberately powdering her face; then she took out a little stick and reddened her lips. The

young man hitched up his trousers and nonchalantly, as if half-consciously, ran his hand through his hair as he caught sight of himself in the glass. He might be a salesman in a motor-car business, she thought, and she a girl in a manicure establishment, for they were both rather lustrous and shiny. And they were both on their best behaviour. 'Preening', Eleanor said to herself with a smile. That is, she added, showing off; acting a part, naturally, she thought, after their day's work in a shop.[212]

The first paragraph of this passage represents a complex soundscape (the 'usual waltz' played by an unseen orchestra underlying the clatter of the restaurant and overlaid by the thudding of the swing door) and the rhythmic integration of visual 'shots' in a montage sequence. Eleanor catches a 'glimpse' (not, in this context, of beauty) of the waitresses through the opening and shutting door; their movements are mechanical routines in the restaurant 'machine'. It is Eleanor's waiting that opens up the temporal space in which the initial confusions of sound and movement can be analysed and resolved into their separate components, and the young couple at the next table with, pace The Waste Land, their 'automatic' gestures, observed. (1937, the year of the novel's publication, was also the year in which the Mass Observation movement was founded, as a project to record everyday life and the 'anthropology of ourselves'.)

The young, lower-middle class man and woman epitomize modern life for Eleanor (and, perhaps, for Woolf) in their self-conscious shininess, at one with the glittering reflective surfaces of the modern city (and here The Years echoes Mrs Dalloway, with Peter Walsh stepping down the street, 'this fortunate man, himself, reflected in the plate-glass window of a motor-car manufacturer in Victoria Street', and pursuing the young woman onto whose lips he projects the colour of the red carnation she wears, 'burning again in his eyes and making her lips red').[213] In the arena of the restaurant, the young couple are performing a part; Woolf invokes the 'illustrated papers' (perhaps as a shorthand for the depiction of movie 'stars') as the model on which they base their enactments of self; the movies would certainly seem to be the relevant cultural influence, in their performances of gesture and attitude. The young man and woman are (or, at least, appear to Eleanor to be) the embodiments of newness; they are, like a screen, without depth. Yet the novel also suggests that depth (of time, memory, subjectivity) may be created by repetition and the formation of patterns across the years; the unknown young man's gesture in front of the glass is anticipated at the very opening of the novel, when Eleanor as a young woman conjures up a picture of her brother Edward as she writes to him: 'His eyes were too close together, he brushed up his crest before the looking-glass in the lobby in a way that irritated her.'[214]

The 'cinematographic' dimensions of Woolf's writings in the 1930s are thus multilayered. They incorporate the cinema as the representation of a world seen without a self; the filmic framing of vision; the representation of sight as separable from sound, in a division of the sensorium into the realms of eye and ear; the cinema as continuous with the life of the city; film as a powerful, and possibly negative, influence on human behaviour and attitude, as in Peggy's passing thoughts on mass culture and its narcotic effects. Woolf extended her thoughts in her essay 'The Cinema' on the ways in which film would capture the energies and 'the chaos of the streets', and rendered significantly more complex the images of film locomotion and the transience of modern life that governed 'The Movie Novel' and 'Life and the Novelist'. The conception of film images merely passing in front of the eyes, one after another, without leaving a trace, no longer pertains; they are brought into interrelationship through rhythm, repetition, juxtaposition, angle of vision, the play of light and dark, and the counterpoint of sound and image.[215] In Woolf's last novel, *Between the Acts*, the interplay and interweaving of voices, murmured and cacophonous, functions as a form of cinematic voice-over, at times ironic, as a sound-montage of noises and voices, or as a type of the 'disembodied voice' that had become central to 1930s documentary film.

Poetry and Cinema

In 1937, the literary editor and film critic Charles Davy concluded his edited volume *Footnotes to the Film* with an article entitled 'Are Films Worth While?' The article is particularly concerned with the combination of 'the realistic and the poetic' in film and with the use of sound in cinema. In the first part of the article, Davy argues that poetry, and not drama, is 'the art most nearly related to the cinema':

> All arts reveal harmonies in nature, but their methods of doing so are conditioned obviously by their respective tools. At one extreme is sculpture, whose harmonies are revealed purely in space and stand there, visible and

changeless, as long as stone endures. At the other extreme is music, whose harmonies are revealed purely in time and cease to exist perceptibly as soon as the time occupied by a performance is over. Cinema, the art of *moving pictures*, expresses itself in time and in space, uniting both on equal terms. There is a sense in which poetry does this also, for the content of its time-patterns consists of images which may be of scenes or objects extended in space.[216]

Disputing the widely held view that drama is film's closest aesthetic associate, Davy asserts: 'In the theatre there is no way of presenting motion speeded up or slowed down; no way of weaving past, present and future events together in a single dramatic sequence.'[217]

In illustrating his contention that poetry and cinema are connected, Davy turned to *The Years*, using one of the 'interludes' in *The Years*—the passage which opens the section titled 1891—in his consideration of 'the relationship of cinema to poetry':

> The autumn wind blew over England. It twitched the leaves off the trees, and down they fluttered, spotted red and yellow, or sent them floating, flaunting in wide curves before they settled. In towns coming in gusts round the corners, the wind blew here a hat off; there lifted a veil high above a woman's head. Money was in brisk circulation. The streets were crowded. Upon the sloping desks of the offices near St Paul's, clerks paused with their pens on the ruled page. It was difficult to work after the holidays. Margate, Eastbourne and Brighton had bronzed them and tanned them. The sparrows and starlings, making their discordant chatter round the eaves of St Martin's, whitened the heads of the sleek statues holding rods or rolls of paper in Parliament Square. Blowing behind the boat train, the wind ruffled the channel, tossed the grapes in Provence, and made the lazy fisher boy, who was lying on his back in his boat in the Mediterranean, roll over and snatch a rope.

Davy comments that the passage 'could be used without much change as the shooting script of a film—though a film we should be lucky to see made'. 'What', Davy asks, 'is Mrs Woolf's method?'

> The scenes she evokes are scattered through space and time: her total picture is of something which does not and cannot exist as an entity in the physical world. It is a picture of something created by herself, which comes into being for the first time as she writes. And in order to create it she has first to break down the given unity of the physical world and choose from it certain elements which are brought together into a new unity designed to convey a particular experience—an experience which could not be had from directly observing the physical world itself.

It is from a precisely similar selective approach to nature—an approach which breaks down and chooses and rebuilds—that the cinema derives its own creative power. Imagine this passage from Mrs Woolf put on the screen... First, a windy landscape: the floating leaves dissolving into hats blowing along city streets. The view widens to show the crowds passing the shop windows: people stopping to look at the windows and going in to buy. A view of money crossing the counter, of the writing of bills, and so of a pen writing in a ledger, and of the pen pausing while a clerk looks up through a window at St. Paul's and sees waves breaking on a beach. But in the wind is a sound of the chattering of sparrows in London; and now, chattering discordantly round the eaves of St Martin's, they are blown away to cast their droppings on the statues in Parliament Square. Following them, the view rises; smoke is blowing off chimney-tops, blowing from the engine of the boat train over fields, from the Channel steamer over the sea, whose waves are the waves of grapes tossed by the wind in Provence and are again the sunlit waves of the Mediterranean, here the lazy fisher boy feels his boat heave and rolls over snatching at a rope.[218]

The 'translation' is substantially from the past tense to the gerundial infinitive, with its implications of continuous action, as if this were indeed the mode of cinema. The word 'waves', which is not mentioned in the passage from Woolf (though it is indicated in the phrase 'the wind ruffled the channel'), is used four times in Davy's 'translation'. This then becomes a question of the ways in which film would represent the scene; the appropriate tense/mood would appear to be the gerundive; there is an explicit reference to dislocations or relocations in time and space and to their traversal; we would see what the clerk imagines as he looks through his office window and remembers the waves on the beach; the ellipses in Woolf's description (the shifts in location) are traversed by the movement of a camera. The brevity and terseness of much of the writing in Woolf's passage, and the relative absence of connectives, is transmuted into a much more fluid and interconnecting movement.

The 'translation' from novel to film-scenario (still of course couched in the medium of words) would thus seem to entail a shift from verbal to visual; a fluidity of movement capable of connecting disparate times and spaces; the deployment of familiar film imagery, and in particular the waves breaking on the shore (at the heart of Woolf's fiction) and the view from the air; the uses of synecdoche (the close-up of the clerk's pen) and of metonymy (the smoke that issues first from the London chimney-tops, then from the boat train and finally from the Channel steamer; the waves that are first grapes blown in the wind, then the waves of the Mediterranean). Cinematic form would, in summary, appear to consist in motion and metonymy.[219] Curiously, Davy does not comment on the play of sound in *The Years*, 'translating' the text into an apparently silent film-scenario, though the greater part of his essay is concerned with the coming of sound to film and the potential for experiment with the relationship between sound and image.

Davy's article could be read as an extension of Winifred Holtby's discussion of Woolf and the cinema, moving from her account of film motion into a more developed account of montage and its ability to remake physical reality by means of editing. There is no way of knowing whether Holtby (who died in 1935) would have found in *The Years* a return on the part of Woolf to filmic techniques: her book, published in 1932, concluded with *The Waves*, and she had in any case suggested that Woolf had left behind the 'cinematographic method' with *Jacob's Room*. Both Holtby and Davy were, however, particularly interested in the correlations between poetry and cinema, a topic that had been addressed by film theorists in the 1910s and 1920s (including Vachel Lindsay, Jean Epstein, and Iris Barry), but that returned in a particular guise in the 1930s, when the rise of documentary culture suggested new questions, as Davy's article indicates, about the 'poetry' within documentary film and its capture of realities, as well as the possibilities for poetry in the film voice-over. Whereas for Holtby, however, poetry was to be differentiated from fiction, Davy was concerned with the poetic dimensions of the novel, in an echo of the distinction Woolf herself drew between the 'poetry of language' and the 'poetry of situation'. It is not altogether clear whether Davy was suggesting, in line with Holtby's discussion, that Woolf's was a cinematic prose (independent of any life it might have on the screen) or, more narrowly, that it had the potential to be 'translated' into the medium of film. He described his reinscription of her words as 'a sorry business; its sole purpose is to suggest how this passage could be translated into *images* on a cinema screen'.[220] Film, in Davy's account, was a lens rather than a mirror, capable of reorganizing the elements of the physical world, and bringing them into a new unity. As he wrote, in a comparison of the novel and the film medium: 'It is from a precisely similar selective approach to nature—an approach which breaks down and chooses and rebuilds—that the cinema derives its own creative power.'

There are echoes here of Elie Faure's Bergsonian account of 'cineplastics', and its assertion that the new and unprecedented dimensions of cinema, distinguishing it from all the other arts, reside in its 'continuous movement' and 'mobile composition': 'ceaselessly renewed, ceaselessly broken and remade, fading away and reviving and breaking down, monumental for one flashing instant, impressionistic the second following'.[221] Davy's arguments also seem to follow the writings on film of the art critic and aesthetician Herbert Read, who had published two significant essays—'Towards a Film Aesthetic' and 'The Poet and the Film'—in the journal *Cinema Quarterly* in the early 1930s. 'Sculpture', Read argued, 'is the art of space, as music is of time. The film is the art of space-time: it is a space-time continuum'. 'Montage' was, for Read as for Davy, the 'justification of the film as an art form ... Montage is mechanised imagination. The producer deliberately interferes with the anonymity, the impersonality of the camera'. No film can survive, Read argued, 'on a purely mechanical inspiration ... finally the public will demand the film of imagination, of vision. And then will come the day of the poet, the scenario-writer, or whatever we are to call him':

> For actually this artist will be a new type of artist—an artist with the visual sensibility of the painter, the vision of the poet, and the time-sense of the musician. Instead of doubting the possibilities of the film as a medium, we should rather doubt the artistic capability of man to rise to the high opportunities of this new medium.[222]

Read's arguments run counter to those film-makers and theorists for whom the development of cinema was dependent upon its liberation from literature. His model of 'the ideal film', however, assumed a particular definition of 'good writing' which was that it should be essentially visual, its aim 'to *convey images*. To make the mind see. To project onto the inner screen of the brain a moving picture of objects and events, events and objects moving towards a balance and reconciliation of a more than usual state of emotion with a more than usual order'. This definition of 'good literature', he argued, 'is also a definition of the ideal film'.[223]

A number of Read's arguments were endorsed in Erwin Panofsky's influential discussion 'Time and Medium in the Motion Picture' (first published in 1934 as the written version of a talk given to enlist support for the new Film Library of the Museum of Modern Art, printed in the avant-garde magazine *transition* and revised in 1947 for *Critique* magazine), which defined the 'unique and specific possibilities' of the film as *'dynamization of space* and, accordingly, *spatialization of time'*.[224] Literary critics' concerns with the workings and representation of time and space in the novel found influential precedents and support in the writings of these art critics and aestheticians who had turned their attention to the cinema; in addition to Panofsky and Read, Arnold Hauser and Rudolf Arnheim took up many of the terms central to earlier studies such as Hugo Münsterberg's. Gottfried Lessing's classification, in *Laocoön*, of the arts as defined by time *or* space, was redefined to accommodate film as the art of time *and* space.

Writing in the early 1950s, the Marxist critic and art historian Arnold Hauser came to his discussion of film through an account of the fiction of Proust and Joyce. In *Ulysses*, Hauser wrote: 'The emphasis lies everywhere on the uninterruptedness of the movement, the "heterogeneous continuum", the kaleidoscopic picture of a disintegrated world…one has the feeling that the time categories of modern art altogether must have arisen from the spirit of cinematic form.' Through the close-up, flash-backs and flash-forwards, double-exposure and alternation, 'time here loses, on the one hand, its uninterrupted continuity, on the other, its irreversible direction'.[225]

Time in the cinema is thus, and in contrast to Bergson's account of the 'cinematographical' method in *Creative Evolution*, represented as radically other to a continuous, progressive order. Hauser's emphases on the simultaneity of parallel plots and 'the simultaneous nearness and remoteness of things—their nearness to one another in time and their distance from one another in space—lead him back to the modernist novels of Proust and Joyce, Dos Passos and Virginia Woolf, in whose work the 'discontinuity of the plot and the scenic development, the sudden emersion of the thoughts and moods, the relativity and the inconsistency of the time-standards' are reminders of 'the cuttings, dissolves and interpolations of the film'.[226] Implicit in Hauser's discussion was the suggestion that the symbiosis between cinema and literature, while it may have found formal representation in the modern novel, had not been matched in the sphere of the film itself: 'the film is not finding its writers or, to put it more accurately, the writers are not finding their way to the film.'[227]

The issues for Hauser were the conflict between the writer's individualism and the collective sphere of film production, and the increasing divorce between film form and subject matter: 'the process of estrangement already makes itself felt in the present-day director's forgoing of most of the so-called "cinematic" means of expression' (camera-angles, changing distances and speeds, cut-ins and flashbacks, close-ups and panoramas) in favour of 'the clear, smooth and exciting narration of a story'.[228] Film movement of many kinds—the radical play with temporal and spatial relations; the sensory mobility of the spectator, so emphasized by Panofsky—has, in this account, been smoothed and tamed. Nonetheless, Hauser suggested, the forms of montage created by the Russian cinema of Eisenstein and Pudovkin (in which 'the doctrine of historical materialism becomes the formal principle of the art'[229]) remained models for films produced in quite different social conditions.

In the 1950s, when Hauser was writing, and in the spate of texts on the film–literature relationship that appeared in the 1960s and 1970s, modernist writers, including Woolf, became central figures for the exploration of past and potential relationships between the novel and the cinema. As Hauser's argument suggests, it was as if modernist fictional experiments with the representation of time and space could serve as models for a cinema that had, it was suggested, lost sight of its own radical and experimental possibilities, embedded and embodied in its very medium, and was seeking out forms of representation and narration that might be characterized as 'realist'. Modernist literature, it was suggested, thus had the potential to re-animate the film medium, and to bring it back to an awareness of its extraordinary capacities, arising out of its machinic nature, 'to describe', in Hauser's words, 'movement, speed and pace.'

Woolf (alongside writers including Joyce, Proust, Stein, and Romains) thus had a crucial role to play in the conceptualization of film–literature relationships at a particular juncture in literary and cultural history. In the middle and later decades of the twentieth century, narrative theory was preoccupied with the representation of time and space; visual-verbal relationships became central to structuralist approaches to narrative; and the anti-metaphysical tenets underlying the *nouveau roman* were concentrated in a fascination with the world of objects and material presences, with movement and gesture, and with the realization of a new clarity in vision and perception, untrammelled by anthropomorphism, sentiment, and habit.

This chapter has, however, traced a longer history, in which Woolf's earliest critics were highly attentive to the role of the cinema in her writing, but were defining the 'cinematographic' in different ways, including those in which 'montage' was not a central category. To focus exclusively on literary 'montage' would be to overlook those other dimensions of the filmic world to which Woolf was drawn and, indeed, by which she was alienated. The fascination of Woolf's writing on the cinema, its brevity notwithstanding, and of the play of the cinematic in her fiction, is its address to and engagement with some of the central dimensions of the film medium and its conceptualization: questions of beauty and aesthetics; absence and presence; film historiography and the 'evolution' of cinema; stasis and movement; motion and emotion; space and time; the realms of eye and ear; private consciousness and the 'voice-over' of public discourses. The return, in this book and in other studies, to the subject of Woolf and the cinema is a recognition of the intensity and complexity of her engagement with the medium, which nonetheless coexisted with her sense that she, and her generation, had sat silent before the new medium, 'recognising before we take the measure'.

3

'A new form of true beauty':
Aesthetics and Early Film Criticism

Talking in the Cinema

The German novelist Gert Hofmann's *The Film Explainer* (1990) is a semi-autobiographical account of Hofmann's grandfather, who was a film 'lecturer' or 'explainer' (and cinema pianist) in provincial Germany throughout the silent era and beyond. Finally made redundant in the early 1930s by the triumph of sound film, he defends his role to the cinema proprietor until the last: 'I'm not superfluous. An audience needs someone to explain a film to them, at least its finer points. They have no idea what is contained in a film if you look at it closely, in every single shot. No, no, said Grandfather, that must be explained. Otherwise, it would be lost.'[1] He is finally routed by a screening of *The Jazz Singer* (which arrives in the village some years after its US premiere): 'After a while, the film started talking again. It explained itself... Ridiculous, all that talking! Who does that in real life, whispered Grandfather, I certainly don't, and everyone shouted: Quiet! You're being a nuisance, Hindenburg!... Anyway, instead of sitting and listening quietly, Grandfather talked and commented his way through the first sound-film ever shown at the Apollo in Limbach.'[2]

As an increasing number of films start to talk, the grandfather retreats into silence. His 'silent period' is broken by his attendance at local Nazi party meetings: 'when the sound-film era began, I suddenly couldn't talk any more. I thought: There is no one left who is interested in your ideas. But now I'm talking again!'[3] In fact, what he wants to talk about are film scenarios and a proposal for 'the re-introduction of silent films in the context of national renewal'.[4] In 1939, the old man is taken to Berlin with a local group to attend a Nazi rally, but, leaving his party and his veteran's flag behind, he slips into Berlin's empty Gloria Palais. 'Then, before the film began—my first and last film in Berlin—said Grandfather—I played my life as a cinemagoer to my inner eye, beginning with my very first picture. Some went by quickly, some slowly, some completely stopped.'[5] The film he saw 'and was to rave about until his death was of course *Gone with the Wind*'; returning to the rally, he listens to Hitler, while thinking about Scarlett O'Hara. Not long after this, he is killed in an explosion in the cinema in his home town.

The novel-memoir ends with these words:

> Grandfather at seventy said: In the beginning was the light. The light was switched off. I stood in front of the screen, all alone. I looked into the audience. There weren't many of them there. I gave the signal *Go!* He said: In all the films of that time, even if they played indoors, it rained. That was because the films had been damaged by the fingers of the projectionists. We lined the gate with black velvet to slow the film. Even that damaged it. Also, they got old and worn. Grandfather took me by the hand. He said it wasn't the shaking projection that made everything tremble. Nor was it people's breathing. It was the heartbeat of the man who was supervising everything, the film explainer's, mine.[6]

The writer on cinema, in its first decades, was a 'film explainer' of a very particular kind. 'Discourse about the cinema' was the phrase Christian Metz used in his account of cinema's 'third machine', the sphere, additional to those of the industry and the spectator, of the *cinematic writer* (critic, historian, theoretician.)[7] Such discourse, inflected in very particular ways in the silent period, can, I would argue, be understood as a form of 'talking in the cinema'.

This is nicely literalized in the first English-language book of film theory, the American poet Vachel Lindsay's *The Art of the Moving Picture*, first published in 1915, and revised in 1922. In the revised version, Lindsay referred to a passage of his original text in which

> I suggest suppressing the orchestra entirely and encouraging the audience to talk about the film. No photoplay people have risen to contradict this theory, but it is a chapter that once caused me great embarrassment. With Christopher Morley, the well-known author of *Shandygaff* and other temperance literature, I was trying to prove out this chapter. As soon as the orchestra stopped, while the show rolled on in glory, I talked about the main points in this book, illustrating it by the film before us. Almost everything that happened was a happy illustration of my ideas. But there were two

shop girls in front of us awfully in love with a certain second-rate actor who insisted on kissing the heroine every so often, and with her apparent approval. Every time we talked about that those shop girls glared at us as though we were robbing them of their time and money. Finally one of them dragged the other out into the aisle, and dashed out of the house with her dear chum, saying, so all could hear: 'Well, come on, Terasa, we might as well go, if these two talking *pests* are going to keep this up behind us.' The poor girl's voice trembled. She was in tears. She was gone before we could apologize or offer flowers. So I say in applying this chapter, in our present state of civilization, sit on the front seat, where no one can hear your whispering but Mary Pickford on the screen. She is but a shadow there, and will not mind.[8]

The story's gendered divide (the absorbed shop-girls and the running commentary of the men) bears an interesting relationship to the narratives of 'talking in the cinema', in which a demotic *feminine* speech tends to operate as a model of distracted viewing.[9] My present focus is on the ways in which the scene in Lindsay's text, too, is shadowed by the film lecturer or film explainer, who, in the early years of cinema, provided a spoken commentary to accompany films as they were projected. Film historians have discussed the continuities between the magic-lantern lecturer of the late nineteenth century and the moving picture commentator of the first years of cinema; early 'film lectures' would indeed have included both lantern slides and moving pictures. In the US, film lecturing appears to have died out in the early 1910s with functions previously filled by lectures now folded into narrative technique and an increasing use of intertitles, as critics including Tom Gunning and Rick Altman have argued.[10] There would also have been a greater use of accompanying written material, including printed synopses, so that spectators would ideally be familiar with the outlines of the film narrative before the film; they would come to the theatre, 'with the facts predigested as it were and … ready for the silent running of the reel'.[11]

Writers about cinema in its first decades inherited something of the role of the commentator on the unfolding action of the film. While narrative and explanatory functions relating to a specific film may have been transmuted into broader formal and aesthetic questions, early writers on film nonetheless retained a significant didactic role, pointing to ways of seeing appropriate to the new medium of film, and, as Altman has argued of early film lecturing, not so much *explaining* the visual as *redefining* the images according to an alternate set of rules.[12] If, moreover, film required from spectators new visual and interpretative skills, it also seemed to demand that writers on the cinema find discursive strategies adequate to the new art and technology—in particular, its powers of motion, its abilities to create a total (virtual) world in which, as Virginia Woolf was to write in her 1926 essay 'The Cinema', '[w]e see life as it is when we have no part in it'—and the intensity of its appeal to the eye.[13]

From the writings of Henri Bergson onwards, the philosophy of film has been focused on the paradoxical relationship between the immobile image and the mobility of the projected film, in part as a way of theorizing consciousness, and time consciousness in particular. One of my concerns is with the ways in which this paradox—of stasis and mobility—was negotiated in the 'talking about the cinema' of critics and theorists. *Photogénie* was a key term for French film theorists of the 1910s and 1920s; it was variously described as a form of defamiliarization, as a seeing of ordinary things as for the first time, and as a temporal category, a sublime instant. The French avant-garde film-maker and theorist Jean Epstein wrote that 'the value of the photogenic is measured in seconds', though what it flashes up also exists in an impossible or illusory time, that of the present:[14] 'The future "I" is shed as "I" past: the present is merely this instantaneous and perpetual sloughing. The present is merely an encounter. The cinema is the only art capable of depicting the present as it is.'[15] *Photogénie* also became synonymous with screen or cinematic 'beauty', a beauty of 'the moment' or 'the interval', glimpsed rather than held. As Louis Delluc wrote, in an article on 'Beauty in the Cinema' (1917): 'For a long time, I have realized that the cinema was destined to provide us with impressions of evanescent eternal beauty, since it alone offers us the spectacle of nature and sometimes even the spectacle of real human activity.'[16] Issues of time, duration, and movement were thus inextricably intertwined with aesthetic questions, and with attempts to define the specific aesthetic of the cinema, which was at times, as for Delluc, differentiated from the properties of the artwork, since its proclaimed abilities to capture reality were held to put it on the side of nature and life rather than that of art.

For the French art historian Elie Faure, writing on the art of cinema in the early 1920s, *photogénie* was both shock or 'commotion' and recognition: 'The revelation of what the cinema of the future can be came to me one day: I retain an exact memory of it, of the commotion that I experienced when I observed, in a flash, the magnificence there was in the relationship of a piece of black clothing to the grey wall of an inn.'[17] Here the aesthetic of film is rendered as a form of visuality quite distinct from plot and narrative: the essence of film is pure image, and it inheres in the instant, 'in a flash.' Faure's account, however, produces a complex model of cinematic time and duration; the image is retained as an 'exact memory', thus becoming, in effect, an 'after-image'. There are echoes here of Goethe's *Theory of Colour*, in which after-images are represented as 'physiological colours':

> I had entered an inn towards evening, and, as a well-favoured girl, with a brilliantly fair complexion, black hair, and a scarlet bodice, came into the room, I looked attentively at her as she stood before me at some distance in half shadow. As she presently afterwards turned away, I saw on the white wall, which was now before me, a black face surrounded with a bright light, while the dress of the perfectly distinct figure appeared of a beautiful sea-green.[18]

Faure's account transmuted Goethe's colour theory into the monochromatic field of the film, and his eroticized vision into the metonymic purity of cloth and wall. Nonetheless, there is for both writers the perception that, in Mary Ann Doane's words, 'the afterimage is accessible only through an experience of intensity, of dazzlement'.[19]

If on the one hand the model of *photogénie* served to isolate a cinematic essence as a sublime instant, to extract the image from the flow, on the other 'talking about the cinema' seemed to demand adequation to the 'movement' or 'motion' that also served to define the qualities of the new art of the film. The film critic Robert Herring's *Films of the Year 1927–1928* (which appears strongly indebted to the pictorial criticism of Vachel Lindsay and Victor Freeburg, discussed later in this chapter) was a collection of stills aimed at providing 'a permanent record' of those 'striking scenes [that] flash across the screen for an instant and then remain only as a memory': 'Movement is life,' he writes, 'and the cinema is the only art that can preserve this quality in its expression. Yet, for doing this, it suffers … A film is projected at the rate of twenty-two pictures a second; much must be unnoticed, much must flash by before we have grasped its essence.'[20] The movement that defines cinema (as it comes so often to define modernity itself) is also a more fragile and unstable ephemerality that inheres at every level, from the fleeting nature of the projected images to the vagaries of cinematic exhibition. In Herring's words: 'A movie is perhaps pre-released. It is then shown everywhere, at once, for a week. Then it is nowhere any more. If you are a day too late you may never see it again, unless you track it down to some village hall or find it by the seaside, drearily.'[21] It was in substantial part the anxiety over the ephemerality of the medium and its exhibition which, from the 1920s onwards, led to the establishment of such institutional spaces for cinema as the film societies, the new film journals, and, in the 1930s, the first film archives. There are significant connections between these sites of cinematic culture, the conceptual, literary, and philosophical understandings of the filmic medium, and theories of modernity more broadly.

Such connections were made explicit in a number of works on film art in the first decades of the twentieth century, as was the concern with the ways in which critical discourse could provide an adequate account of filmic movement and representation. Eric Elliott's 1928 study *Anatomy of Motion Picture Art* addressed directly the problems attendant upon writing about film. In Elliott's words, 'the experience of one observer is necessarily limited. He may read a book at his convenience but a film, like time and tide, waits for no man, and passes out of existence even while he is dutifully engaged in making observation of another.'[22] A correlation, present in many other studies written in this period, existed between the ephemeral screen-image and the ephemeral film as a whole, linked in complex ways to the illusion of screen-motion itself, whereby still photographic images appear as moving ones. For Robert Herring, writing, like Elliott, about attempts to commit films to memory: 'it is unsatisfying, and it does not tend towards critical balance, to sit in a state of suspense, waiting for one scene, trying to carry it away intact and probably being impressed by a new group and another pattern.'[23]

'Coming to the fluent expressions possible in screen continuity,' Elliott wrote, 'one is at a loss how to explain in words the appeal they make.' Verbal description, he argued, might not be 'fully adequate to interpret the appeal of a painting', but 'where there are accepted terms relating to the initiated a sense of the original impressions, there is none at all relating to the screen … Again, the film is not merely a succession of scenes that can be described separately and consecutively; it is not so much the individual expression as the expression of all combined that results in the cinematic effect'.[24] Herring concurs: 'The cinema places before us not a series of patterns one after the other, but a moving, flowing design.'[25]

The problems, it would seem, were manifold and self-perpetuating. The absence of established terms for this new art meant that it eluded the critical grasp and gaze. As Herring wrote of the cinema: 'The transience of its creation makes serious consideration difficult and demands a quickness of apprehension not always forthcoming from those used to more static forms.'[26] At the same time, aesthetic categories deriving from, and addressed to, the static and the verbal arts were, for many commentators, perceived to be inadequate to the mobile, visual representations of film. At a different level of cultural life, the absence of an archive or cinemathèque meant that there was often difficulty in seeing films more than once. Thus viewing became a form of erasure, and the film, once seen, 'passes out of existence.' It could not even be recalled adequately in memory, because, Elliott asserted, 'scientific tests have shown that not more than sixty percent of a film is seen by the spectator'; attention is 'diverted from its material elements and the technique of its scenes' and towards the 'values of story, character and personality'.[27] The attractions of narrative, Elliott suggested, occluded the visual qualities of the film. At yet another level, there was instability and variation in the exhibition of films, which could be edited differently according to localities and at the behest of censorship. The imperative critical task, then, was to establish forms of persistence and permanence—aesthetic and archival—that would nonetheless do justice to film's mobility and the fleeting quality of its medium.

One way of capturing the 'essence' of the mobile medium was to focus on the film still. For Robert Herring, the isolation of the still from the moving whole was justified by the perception that film's significance lies in its patterning of images. 'What one remembers', he wrote, 'of [Chaplin's] *A Woman of Paris* is not the story, but the treatment, and the treatment gave rise to a string of such symbols as Menjou's handkerchief. We remember the lit windows of the train, a dress collar, a necklace flung out of a window, some chocolates and a serviette full of holes.'[28] The film still, in this account, would seem to be an appropriate way of seeing, or a mnemonic for, the objects, or part-objects, in which the film's 'themes' are contained. Moreover, focusing attention on the pictorial or, more precisely, photogenic qualities of the 'scene' was a way of diverting attention away from narrative, character and story, and hence of training the spectator in specifically visual modes of apprehension. Herring's brief comments on each of the stills he selected (from films including Murnau's *Faust*, Galison's *The Student of Prague*, Hitchcock's *The Lodger*, Borzage's *Seventh Heaven*, and Man Ray's *Emak Bakia*) emphasized chiaroscuro effects and the interplay of vertical and horizontal planes. The focus on the film still was, nonetheless, framed in strategic terms; movement, for Herring as for so many other writers on film, continued to define the art of the cinema.

For Charles Davy film was to be situated 'between painting and writing': while painting is an art that exists in space and writing exists in time, 'the cinema exists in both space and time'. Like writing, Davy argued, cinema 'presents itself in the form of movement, of continuous flow', but its language is spatial, 'consisting of images thrown on to a rectangular screen'. Davy's conclusion was

> that the film spectator's attention must be riveted to a single stream of logically related images, and that these images must be so chosen and arranged that they bear within them the distilled essence of the film's narrative purpose. The gesture of a hand, the recurrent focusing of the camera on some familiar object—a handkerchief, a key, a pair of shoes—the perspective of a room or the grouping of a crowd—such visual details as these must speak to the spectator: and as one image flows into the next, their speech must form itself into a sentence, into a chapter, into a complete story.[29]

Other critics pointed up the connections between cinematic motion, including the arrangement of the sequence of impressions in the film, and literary impressionism (James Joyce's writing being a frequently cited instance). The emergence of a film aesthetic had significant conceptual connections with the Impressionist movement in literature in the first decades of the century, on which Walter Pater's writings were such a crucial influence, and which was defined by its preoccupations with the processes of perception and with 'visual' sensation, its evocation of superimposition and multiple perspectives, its concern with 'beauty', and its understanding of 'enduring and essential forms' underlying the visible world.[30] The question of vision and cinema's singular appeal to the eye persisted into the transition period of the late 1920s and beyond, even in discussion of those late silent films possessing a significant aural dimension. Walther Ruttmann's *Berlin*, is, as its subtitle indicates, the 'symphony of a city', expressing, as Steven Connor has argued, 'the sense of visuality passing across into aural form'.[31] F. W. Murnau's *Sunrise*, subtitled 'A Song of Two Humans', clearly revealed that a film's pictorial qualities could coexist with both the representation of movement and engagement with the auditory. Yet, for the majority of commentators in the period, 'beauty' was identified with 'silence', drawing on a long-standing aesthetic credo in which silence is equated with universal and enduring values. The 'silent forms' of Keats's '*Grecian Urn*' (whose lineaments were traced in early accounts of film as a return to Graeco-Egyptian art) lead us back to the question of the 'moment' captured in the work of art, which both represents all time, and takes us out of contingency, time and history.

In the context of French avant-garde criticism, as I have noted, 'beauty' became near-synonymous with *photogénie*, in which concept was also to be found the aspiration, 'to remove the moment from the flow and flux of time and, like the frame of the painting, declare: This is the present moment, right here, right now'.[32] In this sense, concepts of eternal value and of the moment independent of time and change could coexist with the 'modernist' focus on the isolated moment. Baudelaire's much-quoted assertion in his essay 'The Painter of Modern Life' is apposite here: 'By "modernity" I mean the ephemeral, the fugitive, the contingent, the half of art whose other half is the eternal and the immutable.'[33]

'Beauty' in the cinema also has this dual or paradoxical dimension. Writing in the *Fortnightly Review*, the critic Martha Kinross asserted: 'Architecture, sculpture, painting are static arts. Even in literature "our flying minds," as George Meredith says, cannot contain protracted description. But moments of fleeting beauty too transient to be caught by any means less swift than light itself are registered on the screen.'[34] The concept of 'fleeting beauty' can be identified with the modernist effort, in Charney's words, 'to seize a moment on the terms of its evanescence'.[35] It contains an echo of Walter Pater's account, in the conclusion to *The Renaissance*, of 'that continual vanishing away, that strange, perpetual, weaving and unweaving of ourselves'.[36] Yet behind Pater there is Plato, and, in particular, Plato's *Phaedrus* with its allegory of an earthly beauty (the beauty of the human body) which acts as a reminder to the beholder of Beauty, 'true beauty', in the heavenly realm from which he has fallen. Film, too, is a doubled world, and, in the idealizing language of much early film writing, it is as if the film world offers 'glimpses' of pure forms through the lifted veil or screen. This is then linked to the fleeting or evanescent qualities of such 'glimpses' as an effect of filmic movement. 'Platonist beauty' and 'modern beauty' are intertwined.[37]

American Beauty

In turning now to the ways in which cinematic 'beauty' is taken up in early American film criticism, my focus will be a group of texts written and published in the US in the 1910s and 1920s: Vachel Lindsay's *The Art of the Moving Picture* (1915, extended edition 1922) and *Progress and Poetry in the Movies* (written in 1925, but unpublished in Lindsay's lifetime); Hugo Münsterberg's *The Art of the Photoplay* (1916) and Victor O. Freeburg's *The Art of Photoplay Making* (1918) and *Pictorial Beauty on the Screen* (1923). The founding of 'film studies' as a discipline can also be located here: Victor Freeburg taught the first courses on Photoplay Composition at the Columbia University School of Journalism in the mid-1910s, and founded the Columbia Composers Club in 1916. (The term 'photoplay' had been arrived at after the Essanay film production company sponsored a contest in 1910 to select the most appropriate name for the new medium.) Lindsay, Münsterberg, and Freeburg were very much aware of their status as pioneers in the field and of each other's work, so that an internal dialogue or 'conversation' often developed within and between their respective studies. While there were some significant differences between their approaches to film, they were also linked by the perception that the pursuit and the apprehension of beauty in the photoplay was a crucial dimension in the development of the mass art of cinema.

Lindsay, born in Springfield, Illinois, the mid-Western town which remained the centre of his communitarian and localist politics, had studied at the Chicago Institute of Art (1901–3) and subsequently at the New York School of Art (1903–8). One of his teachers in New York was Robert Henri, a central figure in the 'Ashcan School' of art, and his fellow students included George Bellows, Rockwell Kent, and Edward Hopper. Lindsay achieved no great success as an art student—Henri encouraged him to pursue his poetry rather than his drawing. But the terms of 'beauty' in his writings undoubtedly had as one of their contexts the claims, in the first years of the century, for the new forms of beauty awaiting discovery by artists in modern American cities, translated in Lindsay's conceptual schema into 'democratic beauty'.[38]

If Vachel Lindsay is known today, it is most often as a populist poet, who, by the time he was working on *The Art of the Moving Picture*, had published two collections: *The Congo and Other Poems* and *Adventures while Preaching the Gospel of Beauty*. His writing had been taken up by Harriet Monroe and published in *Poetry* magazine in 1913; aligned, for a period, with the Imagists, Lindsay would propose an 'Imagist photoplay' in *The Art of the Moving Picture*, which would, in his words, bring 'Doric restraint' (a term that echoes throughout H.D.'s film articles for *Close Up*) into the 'overstrained' and 'overloaded' world of even the finest photoplays. Calling attention to the significance of the Imagists—Lindsay named Ezra Pound, Richard Aldington, John Gould Fletcher, Amy Lowell, F. S. Flint, and D. H. Lawrence—Lindsay wrote that

> the Imagist impulse need not be confined to verse...There is a clear parallelism between their point of view in verse and the Intimate-and-friendly photoplay, especially when it is developed...from the standpoint of *space measured without sound plus time measured without sound*...Read some of the poems of the people listed above, then imagine the same moods in the films. Imagist photoplays would be Japanese prints taking on life, animated Japanese paintings, Pompeian mosaics in kaleidoscopic but logical succession, Beardsley drawings made into actors and scenery, Greek vase-paintings in motion...Scarcely a photoplay but hints at the Imagists in one scene.[39]

'The imagists are colorists', Lindsay added, suggesting that the use of varying shades of 'photographic black, white, and gray' might be aspects of Imagist film-making, though 'to use these colors with definite steps from one to the other does not militate against an artistic mystery of edge and softness in the flow of line'. In literary terms, the qualifying phrase might suggest the desire for more fluid versions of the chiselled images of Imagism (at work in H.D.'s poetic revisions of Imagist tenets). It also suggests an Impressionist aesthetic ('an artistic mystery of edge and softness in the flow of line') running parallel to the pictorial poetics and intense visualizations of Imagist aesthetics, in art, literature, and the discourses of the cinema.

Lindsay called his most successful poetry the 'Higher Vaudeville', and he was in effect a performance poet, who, at the height of his popularity, travelled the length and breadth of America giving readings. As Edgar Holt observed in his obituary notice in *The Bookman*, Lindsay 'did not view poetry from a purely literary standpoint, but was anxious to bring it into close touch with communal life'.[40]

When the director of the Denver Art Association, George Eggers, wrote his foreword to the 1922 edition of *The Art of the Moving Picture*, he stated that in Lindsay's book, 'the nature and domain of a new Muse is defined. She is the first legitimate addition to the family since classic times'. The appropriate places to house, or, in his words, to 'provide a shrine' for 'the new Muse', Eggers suggested, were art schools and museums, because they, and not 'literary-minded institutions', can meet the needs of a 'visual-minded public', 'a long, long line of picture-readers trailing from the dawn of history'. 'This new pictorial art' of the photoplay, Eggers wrote, represented 'a new renaissance' and 'a new universal instrument'.[41]

In Lindsay's words: 'Edison is the new Gutenberg. He has invented the new printing. The state that realizes this may lead the soul of America, day after tomorrow.'[42]

In a letter written at the beginning of 1915 to Brett, then editor-in-chief at Macmillan's, Lindsay outlined his new book, whose working title was 'The Higher Criticism of the Movies':

> My particular equipment for writing this book is ten years of Art Ed-
> ucation the last three of which were spent (winters) in lecturing in the
> Metropolitan Museum. My fundamental proposition is that the highest type
> of movie is a *picture* not a drama—the movie-theatre is at best an Art-Gallery
> not a play-house. I am proving it out a hundred ways. I have read an
> article in the January Atlantic on the movies which may suggest to you
> some of the possibilities of the subject that I hope to develop. I agree
> with the writer Eaton—precisely in his general feeling as to the dramatic
> possibilities of the Movies. But he does not see their counter possibilities
> pictorially. They are as revolutionary in our age as the invention of Hi-
> eroglyphics was to the cave-man. And they can be built up into a great
> pictorial art. The Egyptian Tomb-painting was literally nothing but en-
> larged Hieroglyphics. We now have Hieroglyphics in motion—and they
> can be made as lovely as the Egyptian if we once understand what we are
> doing.[43]

The article to which Lindsay referred was Walter Prichard Eaton's 'Class-Consciousness and the Movies', published in the January 1915 issue of *The Atlantic Monthly*. Eaton, a journalist and teacher who subsequently became professor of playwriting at Yale, argued that the advent of the movies had brought about an increasingly sharper division between 'the proletariat [and] the *bourgeoisie* and capitalist class'. Whereas theatre had the potential to bridge the gulf between the classes, the vast expansion of movie theatres had led theatre owners to build new spaces without galleries or balconies, which would formerly have housed the cheaper seats, to decorate them like 'gilded drawing-rooms', and to make theatre increasingly more expensive. In this context, '[w]hat chance is there of a democratic audience?' Yet stage-drama, Eaton asserted, was 'the most universal, the most vividly appealing, the most direct and potent of the arts'. The absence of the working class from the theatres, he argued, would mean that drama would increasingly fail 'to achieve the universality and power demanded of any truly national expression in the arts. A theatre without a gallery means a drama without a soul.' At the same time, the 'entire wage-earning population' were being deflected away from the spoken drama to a form of entertainment in which 'the soul is not reached', and in which 'to our personality there is no call whatever'. Movies, Eaton argued:

> have a cruel realism which at once dulls the imagination and destroys the illusive romance of art. They are utterly incapable of intellectual content ... All poetry, all music, all flash of wit, all dignity of spoken eloquence, they can never know .... Impersonal—that is the word which perhaps describes the motion picture better than mechanical. You view the dumb actions of human beings as through a glass.[44]

Eaton's article, in its address to the relationship between aesthetics and democracy or, at least, class-integration, seems to have made its mark on the ways in which Lindsay shaped his arguments in the book that would become *The Art of the Moving Picture*. It was, for example, in Lindsay's account, precisely 'the soul of America' that was reached by the moving pictures. With the advent of cinema, 'the possibility of showing the entire American population its own face in the Mirror Screen has at last come'; Eaton's glass/class barrier had become, in Lindsay's reformulation, reflective, unifying, and, to the extent that it showed the populace its 'natural face in the glass', salutary.[45] 'Personality' and 'vitality' were to be located in 'non-human tones, textures, lines and spaces': 'I have said that it is a quality, not a defect of the photoplays that while the actors tend to become types and hieroglyphics and dolls, on the other hand, dolls and hieroglyphics and mechanisms tend to become human.'[46] In this sense, and as in Béla Balázs's 'physiognomic' model of cinematic representation and Jean Epstein's writings on the close-up, the realms of 'personality' and 'the face of things' were perceived as extended rather than reduced on the film screen. Above all, Lindsay sought to redefine the terms of the relationship between stage and screen, and to show that it was the art gallery, rather than the theatre, which was the true point of comparison for the 'photoplay house'.

Lindsay's 'hieroglyphic' model of film language is perhaps the best-known aspect of his film writings.[47] Reaching back to the American Transcendentalist fascination with hieroglyphics (as in the writings of Poe, Emerson, and (later) Whitman), both as a unity of pictures and words and as a form of occulted knowledge, and forward to Ezra Pound's fascination with the hieroglyphics of Oriental languages, Lindsay's 'hieroglyphs' would also seem to echo or to anticipate a whole gamut of accounts of cinematic representation. These accounts combined, or created a space between, word and image, and included Jean Epstein's references to film as Egyptian hieroglyphics, Ricciotto Canudo's explorations of the cinema 'alphabet' and Eisenstein's writings on the filmic ideogram, extending also to writers of the Frankfurt School, notably Kracauer and Adorno with their interest in 'mass-cultural hieroglyphics'. There were also the gestural, bodily hieroglyphics of the dramaturgical which, as in Artaud's models of theatre, and, from different perspectives, in the 'gestic' theories of Brecht, sought a reconnection with 'primitive' emotions and responses lying before or beyond linguistic systems.

In *The Art of the Moving Picture*, as in his subsequent writings on cinema, particularly *The Progress and Poetry of the Movies* (unpublished in his lifetime),[48] and in his poetry, Lindsay spelled out his vision of modern America (with its advertisements, bill-boards, newspaper photographs, sign-writings) as 'a hieroglyphic civilization far nearer to Egypt than to England'.[49] He analysed a set of Egyptian hieroglyphs, their Roman letter equivalents, and their equivalents in 'the moving-picture alphabet', and wrote that 'It is sometimes out of the oldest dream that the youngest vision is born.' The photoplay audience that uses 'the hieroglyphic hypothesis in analyzing the film before it, will .... find a promise of beauty in what have been properly classed as mediocre and stereotyped productions.'[50]

Lindsay's concept of the 'hieroglyph' often appears to be interchangeable with that of 'symbol', and *The Art of the Moving Picture* attempted to produce a fixed and universal lexicon. The most interesting result of Lindsay's hieroglyphic preoccupations was, perhaps, his reading (in *The Progress and Poetry of the Movies*) of *The Thief of Bagdad*, a 1924 film starring Douglas Fairbanks, which reworked the tales of the *Arabian Nights*. He found there, in Michael North's words, 'a self-reflexive parable of the hieroglyphic ancestry of the movies. The three treasures on which the drama turns—a magic crystal, a flying carpet, and a golden apple—are self-reflexive representations of the powers added to human experience by photography: the power of the crystal to see far away, of the carpet to travel to distant places, of the apple to revive the dead.'[51] This conjoining of myth and medium can also be found in Lindsay's preoccupation with an 'originary' transformative power of the film, continued into narrative cinema, as in his fascination with fairy-tales in which inanimate objects come to life and stasis becomes motion. At points in his texts, Lindsay sought to conjure, through his discourse, the still images of the art gallery into cinematic movement and life. At such moments, he seemed to be emulating, in his narrative, the powers of those late nineteenth- and early twentieth-century presenters of projected images, whose shows would depict the interplay between stasis and motion, the sudden animation of the still image, and the metamorphoses (of objects and spatial relations) that movement, or the appearance of movement, could effect.

I quoted earlier Lindsay's model of 'conversation' in the cinema, as a way of illustrating the claim that early film critics were film explainers of a kind: 'And so my commentary, New Years' Day, 1922, proceeds, using for points of more and more extensive departure the refrains and old catch-phrases of books two and three.'[52] After the publication of *The Art of the Moving Picture*, he began to give film lectures as well as poetry readings, and on occasions the two modes would be combined. He referred repeatedly to 'proving' his theoretical arguments on a film as it was screened. In *The Progress and Poetry of the Movies* he gave an exhaustive reading of *The Thief of Baghdad*, writing: 'If Douglas Fairbanks will not consider it presumption, I would say that his film proves my book [*The Art of the Moving Picture*] and my book proves his film.'[53] His review of Münsterberg's *The Photoplay: A Psychological Study* asserted that in its claims for the 'motion qualities' of the films, its author 'unintentionally wrote the guide book to the newest photoplay experiment, [D. W. Griffith's] *Intolerance*'; he recommended to his readers two screenings of *Intolerance* between two readings of Münsterberg's book.[54] 'Conversation', for Lindsay, was thus a reference to the running commentary of the film spectator as explainer and the explanatory discourse of the film critic and theoretician. It was also connected to the 'hieroglyphic' language of the film. As Lindsay wrote: 'Moving objects, not moving lips, make the words of the photoplay.'[55]

Lindsay's emphasis on discoursing about the cinema gave his study a strongly performative dimension, connecting it to his poetry, with its frequent use of 'call and response'. This link was reinforced when Lindsay began to give readings in which he would combine his lectures on the art of film with performances of his poetry, in an echo of the mixed educational and entertainment modes of the first film exhibitions.[56] Chapter II of the 1915 version of *The Art of the Moving Picture*, 'The Photoplay of Action', opens with these words: 'Let us assume, friendly reader, that it is eight o'clock in the evening when you make yourself comfortable in your den, to peruse this chapter. I want to tell you about the Action Film, the simplest, the type most often seen.'[57] The chapter closes with this address to the reader: 'Having read thus far, why not close the book and go round the corner to a photoplay theatre. Give the preference to the cheapest one. The Action Picture will be inevitable.'[58] Lindsay thus suggested an identity between his written discussion and the kind of film synopsis that had replaced the spoken film lecture, although in this case the explanatory narrative was generic rather than specific. His book functioned in part as a verbal accompaniment to the pictorial art of 'the photoplay', becoming another version of the 'conversation' amongst the audience about the film that he sought to promote. The conceit of opening each chapter by giving a context for its reading, and closing it with the advice to 'prove' its contents at 'some photoplay emporium'[59] continued until the opening of Chapter V, when Lindsay wrote: 'Henceforth the reader will use his discretion as to when he will read the chapter and when he will go to the picture show to verify it.'[60]

'This book is primarily for photoplay audiences' are the opening words of the 1915 edition, a statement Lindsay revised in 1922, when he acknowledged that 'its appeal is to those who spend the best part of their student life in classifying, and judging, and producing works of sculpture, painting, and architecture. I find the eyes of all others wandering when I make talks upon the plastic artist's point of view'.[61] In both versions of the text, Lindsay had, however, a shifting, and at times exclusionary, model of his audience. In Chapter XV, 'The Substitute for the Saloon', Lindsay, refers repeatedly to the 'masses', 'the slum', and 'the mob'.[62] His earlier analysis of 'The Picture of Crowd Splendour', formerly identified with architecture and the epic, was now brought into the social and political arena: 'the masses have an extraordinary affinity for the Crowd Photoplay ... the mob comes nightly to behold its natural face in the glass ... The slums are an astonishing assembly of cave-men crawling out of their shelters to exhibit for the first time in history a common interest on a tremendous scale in an art form.'[63]

Lindsay's model of a beneficent shift from saloon to moving picture house, in which 'the light is as strong in the eye as whiskey in the throat',[64] included a change in the nature of conversation as well as a new form of literacy. 'Immigrants', Lindsay wrote, 'are prodded at by these swords of darkness and light to guess at the meaning of the catch-phrases and headlines that punctuate the play. They strain to hear their neighbors whisper or spell them out.'[65] The equation was thus made between a 'universal' response to the new art of film, and that of the immigrant attempting to learn a new language by listening to his or her neighbours articulating or voicing the intertitles. Images penetrated the eye and stimulated the ear.

For 'the lower classes' in general, Lindsay argued, cinema provided new dreams and new forms of words:

> The things they drank to see, and saw but grotesquely, and paid for terribly, now roll before them with no after pain or punishment. The mumbled conversation, the sociability for which they leaned over the tables, they have here in the same manner with far more to talk about. They come, they go home, men and women together, as casually and impulsively as the men alone ever entered a drinking-place, but discoursing now of far-off mountains and star-crossed lovers.[66]

Instead of the bartender, with his 'cynical and hardened soul', through whose 'dead-fish eye and dead-fish brain the group of tired men look upon all the statesman and wise ones of the land', and whose 'furry tongue, by endless reiteration, is the American slum-oracle', comes the 'moving picture man as a local social force': 'In many cases he stands under his arch in the sheltered lobby and is on conversing terms with his habitual customers, the length of the afternoon and evening.'[67] The photoplay might have been, in Lindsay's account, an art whose address was to the eye, but its aesthetic, political, and social import were also represented through the terms of discourse, conversation, and, at times, soap-box oratory or, in Lindsay's phrase, 'great battle cries'.

In his chapter 'The Orchestra, Conversation, and the Censorship', Lindsay, as I noted earlier, argued for the suppression of accompanying music: 'The perfect photoplay gathering-place would have no sound but the hum of the conversing audience. If this is too ruthless a theory, let the music be played at the intervals between programmes.'[68] Discussion of musical accompaniment led on to that of the 'talking moving picture,' which, Lindsay asserted, 'if it becomes a reliable mirror of the human voice and frame', will be 'such a separate art that none of the photoplay precedents will apply. It will be the *phonoplay* not the photoplay'.[69] Lindsay's arguments against the talking pictures anticipated many of those written in the following decade in which the coming of sound was seen as a mechanization too far. He dwelled on the impossibility of storing the 'human magnetism' of the voice in the phonograph machine: 'That device is as good in the morning as at noon. It ticks like a clock.'[70] The perfected talking moving picture, in which 'human magnetism must be put into the mirror-screen and into the clock', would, Lindsay argues, subordinate the image to the voice: 'then the pictures will be brought in as comment and ornament to the speech.'[71]

In the current state of affairs, as Lindsay represented them, the 'human quality' comes not through the 'actual physical storage-battery of the actor', who is absent from the film as it is screened, but 'in the marks of the presence of the producer. The entire painting must have his brush-work. If we compare it to a love-letter it must be in his handwriting rather than worked on a typewriter. If he puts his autograph into the film, it is after a fierce struggle with the uncanny scientific quality of the camera's work.'[72] The aesthetic of the film, in this argument, ran counter to the workings of the apparatus. The use of an accompanying orchestra was a doomed attempt to imbue the film lacking the marks of individual authorship with significance and 'the human-magnetic element':

> But there is a much more economic and magnetic accompaniment, the before-mentioned buzzing commentary of the audience. There will be some people who disturb the neighbours in front, but the average crowd has developed its manners in this particular, and while the orchestra is silent, murmurs like a pleasant brook.
>
> Local manager, why not an advertising campaign in your town that says: 'Beginning Monday and henceforth, ours shall be known as the Conversational Theatre'?[73]

Discussion of 'the picture with the friend who accompanies you to this place' would lead to a voting system—'approved or disapproved'—and the introduction of a ballot-box into the picture theatre. The democratic art of the photoplay should be open to other forms of democratic process, including control over selection, questions of censorship, and critical responses. The photoplay fan, 'neither a low-brow or a high-brow', was compared to the baseball fan, who also 'has the privilege of comment while the game goes on'. Building on these responses, 'the photoplay reporters can then take the enthusiasts in hand and lead them to a realization of the finer points in awarding praise and blame':

> Out of the work of the photoplay reporters let a super-structure of art criticism be reared in periodicals ... They should reproduce the most exquisite tableaus, and be as fastidious in their selection of them as they are in the current examples of the other arts ... have the power to influence an enormous democracy.[74]

As we have seen, Lindsay was prepared in the revised edition of the text to tell, against himself, the anecdote of the furious shop-girls' response to his loquaciousness. Otherwise, Lindsay stood by many of his 1915 arguments, though, as he suggested, the intervention of war had changed much in the world, leaving some, at least, of his chapters, as 'monuments' to a past time rather than as current debates. By 1922, Lindsay could no longer claim to be a pioneer in film theory, though he was always to insist on the influence of the 1915 version on subsequent film writings, including those of Victor Freeburg. Lindsay maintained his focus on the analogies between film and the visual arts, while now being prepared to put them into a more relative critical framework: 'some of the happiest passages in [Freeburg's] work relate the photoplay to the musical theory of the world, as my book relates it to the general Art Museum point of view of the world.'[75]

In *The Art of the Moving Picture* (which Lindsay called 'an open letter to Griffith and the producers and actors he has trained')[76] photoplays were divided into three kinds. The Photoplay of Action (the simplest example of which would be the chase-film) is defined as sculpture-in-motion. The Intimate Photoplay (Griffith's *Enoch Arden* is the example here) is painting-in-motion. The Photoplay of Splendour (fairy splendour, crowd splendour—as in D. W. Griffith's *The Birth of a Nation*—patriotic splendour, religious splendour) is architecture-in-motion. The three types (Action, Intimacy, Splendour) were further correlated with pantomime, personal gesture, and the total gestures of crowds respectively. If a literary analogue were required, Lindsay suggested, his readers might think in terms of the dramatic, the lyric and the epic, but the overarching schema mapped the moving picture onto the visual and plastic arts. 'This book', he wrote, 'tries to find that fourth dimension of architecture, painting, and sculpture, which is the human soul in action, that arrow with wings which is the flash of fire from the film, or the heart of man, or Pygmalion's image, when it becomes a woman.'[77]

As in the art criticism and aesthetic theories of the eighteenth-century aestheticians Joachim Winckelmann and Gotthold Lessing (whose *Laocoön* (1766) was repeatedly invoked in early writing about film, primarily in discussions of film's relationship to the other arts) sculpture was represented as arrested movement. Lindsay wrote: 'An occasional hint of a Michelangelo figure or gesture appears for a flash in the films ... Suppose the seated majesty of Moses should rise, what would be the quality of the action? ... Is it not possible to have a Michelangelo of photoplay sculpture?'[78] The relationship between stasis and movement translated into the desire to put (or the fantasy of putting) into motion the still, or stilled, tableau or sculpture and the momentary stilling of the moving picture into beautiful scenes:

'Action Picture romance', Lindsay wrote, 'comes when each hurdle is a tableau, when there is indeed an art-gallery-beauty in each one of these swift glimpses: when it is a race, but with a proper and golden-linked grace from action to action, and the goal is the most beautiful glimpse in the whole reel.'[79]

What was the relationship of the 'glimpse' of beauty and the 'flash' of fire to the question of the still and the moving image? Lindsay's concept of Beauty, as in his 'Gospel of Beauty', was central to his understanding of democracy and religion, part of his 'subscription to the remedial impact of visual beauty'.[80] It was also inseparable from, and complicated by, his desire for female beauty. 'I am the one poet', he wrote in the opening pages of the 1922 edition of *The Art of the Moving Picture*, 'who has a right to claim for his muses Blanche Sweet, Mary Pickford and Mae Marsh' (all of whom were early Biograph actresses).[81] These 'muses', then, come to figure or embody the new Muse, the Tenth Muse, the Muse of film.

'Why do the people love Mary [Pickford]?', asked Lindsay:

> Because of a certain aspect of her face in her highest mood. Botticelli painted her portrait many centuries ago when by some necromancy she appeared to him in this phase of herself... The people are hungry for this fine and sacred thing that Botticelli painted in the faces of his muses and heavenly creatures. Because the mob catch the very glimpse of it in Mary's face, they follow her night after night into the films.[82]

'Glimpse' is an interesting word. We can say that something 'glimpses': it shines faintly or intermittently, it glimmers or glitters—thus the moon 'glimpses' between the trees. Or we can say that we catch a 'glimpse' of the moon between the trees. In fact, we tend to abbreviate this and say that we 'glimpse' the moon between the trees, though it is in fact the moon doing the glimpsing, not us. In the context of early writing about film, ambiguities in subject–object relations and in the hierarchy of the various 'looks' of the film (of the camera, actor, spectator), in addition to the anthropomorphizing of the object-world effected by the film, were connected to the representation of the cinematic image as a revelation, as in Elie Faure's 'Cineplastics' essay or Virginia Woolf's 'The Cinema', in which, as I discussed in the previous chapter, she wrote that: 'Sometimes at the cinema, in the midst of its immense dexterity and enormous technical proficiency, the curtain parts and we behold, far off, some unknown and unexpected beauty. But it is for a moment only.'[83] Beauty, like *photogénie* (and, as I have suggested, *photogénie* is in a sense 'Beauty'), thus appears to have a temporal dimension, defined, as it was for Epstein, as a value on the order of the second. It could be found, as it would often seem to be for Lindsay, in the cinematic image as a composition, a tableau, or as an interval.

In *The Progress and Poetry of the Movies*, Lindsay wrote of American modernity, with its 'extreme fanaticism in the worship of raw light and raw action':

> I would venture upon another proverb: 'Time must alternate with Eternity.' Let me go farther into the parable, and say: 'The sun makes time, makes machinery'; by it we regulate every watch and every newspaper, every railway schedule, every factory time-clock—all those things that cut our nerves up into bits, $^1/_{16}$ of an inch, no shorter, no longer... Action and speed and blazing light must alternate with moments of mellowness and rest. Even between each heart-beat, there is a split-second of absolute rest, which the American spirit would deny. It is the American idea to destroy that split-second of rest, which is between every heart-beat... No one to whom the moon is sufficiently dear will permit his nerves to be chopped into little pieces $^1/_{16}$ of an inch long, and no longer, nor his time chopped into little pieces $^1/_{16}$ of a second long, and no longer.[84]

This image was taken up later in Lindsay's manuscript in a brief discussion of Chaplin's artistry, located in his films' 'intimate passages, some of them not longer than the split second between every heartbeat, but long enough to give the touch of eternity in time, the hint of moonlight interrupting broad sunlight'.[85] The heartbeat was a way of giving human measure to mechanized modern time, including the factory-time of a society dominated by Taylorist and Fordist models of 'scientific management', with its automatization of the human body and its energies, and to cinematic time (projection at $^1/_{16}$ of a second). For Lindsay, film was both continuous with the world of 'action and speed and blazing light' and resistant to it, in its imagined creation of 'rests' or intervals, whose identity overlapped with that of the passages through which 'beauty' could be 'glimpsed'.

His account finds an echo in the writings on photography of Walter Benjamin and Roland Barthes, in which the medium's 'aura' was perceived to diminish as the duration of exposure time decreased and photography became increasingly instantaneous. There are also connections to the late twentieth-century writings of Paul Virilio, in which the contrast between modernity and postmodernity is often predicated on the idea that the greater the speed of the image, the more absolute the loss of a contextualized time, and in which we find a nostalgia for a slower speed of projection/representation. Charting the shift from 'truth 16 times a second' in the chronophotography of the nineteenth-century pioneer Jules-Etienne Marey to film's 'truth 24 times a second' (as proclaimed in one of Jean-Luc Godard's films), Virilio writes: 'the development of high technical speeds would result in the disappearance of consciousness as the direct perception of phenomena that inform us of our own existence.' The destruction of human consciousness, Virilio suggests, comes with the closure of the interval, temporal and spatial, between the representation and what it records.[86]

Writing of the 'beautiful picture' in the first decades of film history, in the context of a discussion of documentary cinema, the avant-garde film-maker and theorist Hans Richter argued that its advent 'marked the cinema's first direct overtures to the artistic climate of the period—to the tradition of the bourgeois arts ... The cinema took over painting—and the poetry of the painted image took over the cinema'. The creation of the 'beautiful' image, Richter suggested, came at the expense of 'a closeness to reality,' producing a 'contradiction between beautiful image and social task'.[87] The claims for 'beauty' in Lindsay's writings (as in Freeburg's and Münsterberg's) were clearly linked to the granting of a high art status to film, in the ways in which Richter critiques. Nonetheless, it would seem that for Lindsay, in particular, 'beauty' was also credited with the 'social task' of giving human measure to modern time, and of penetrating the seductive surfaces of modernity. In Lindsay's *The Progress and Poetry of the Movies*, the 'glimpse' (of beauty) was contrasted, though the distinction was not absolute, with the 'magical glitter' that created a continuum between the film, the plate glass windows of commodity culture and the glass architecture of the modern city:

> Now this impression of looking into a crystal, which gives a magical glitter to everything within it, is the impression a true movie should convey ... The first story of the principal streets is becoming all glass. It is not the glass itself that is desirable in the eyes of the American. It is the film of light upon the surface of the glass which has become his luxury ... We have come to a time when we are slaves indeed to this glamor. There is many a gigantic shop which owes its influence to the elimination of all but the transfiguring glassy surface between the customer and the goods displayed ... This madness of the crystalline is getting to be more and more a habit of the American eye.[88]

While 'the glimpse' and 'glitter' are both forms of 'beauty', the former was not held to be collusive with a commodified modern time and modern vision. In this sense the 'glimpse of beauty' in the film could be said to anticipate some of the perceived functions of a montage aesthetic, which disrupts surfaces (through fragmentation, collision or the creation of new conceptual relationships) and 'awakens' the spectator.

Training the Modern Eye: Psychology and Aesthetics

Nobody can foresee the ways in which the new art of the photoplay will open, but everybody ought to recognize, even today, that it is worthwhile to help this advance, and to make the art of the film a medium for an original creative expression of our time, and to mold by it the aesthetic instincts of the millions. Yes, it is a new art—and this is why it has such fascination for the psychologist who in a world of ready-made arts, each with a history of many centuries, suddenly finds a new form still undeveloped and hardly understood. For the first time the psychologist can observe the starting of an entirely new aesthetic development, a new form of true beauty in the turmoil of a technical age, created by its very technique and yet more than any other art destined to overcome outer nature by the free and joyful play of the mind.[89]

In early 1917, Lindsay reviewed a new book of film entitled *The Photoplay: A Psychological Study*. Its author, the Harvard psychologist Hugo Münsterberg, had died, suddenly and unexpectedly, at the end of 1916, and Lindsay noted his regret in his review: 'it was with the feeling of the sudden loss of a comrade in a new quest that I read of his death':

Like most readers of *The New Republic* I could not have conversed with him long at a time on international matters. But I had had a most gratifying correspondence with the professor about the films. I had anticipated a glorious evening with him in some photoplay theatre this spring, where we would have been absolutely at one in our joy in the hopeful young art.[90]

Münsterberg had published his account of the 'new art' of the film, *The Photoplay: A Psychological Study*, in the year of his death. It was written during the summer of 1915, when his personal and professional situation, as a patriotic German living in the US, was becoming increasingly untenable. In 1916, he died of heart failure at the age of 53. As his daughter and biographer Margaret Münsterberg wrote of *The Photoplay*: 'In this new study Münsterberg sought distraction for himself from the wearing anxieties caused by the international stress, and at the same time hoped to make the imagination of the public link his name with a more serene interest.'[91]

In December 1915, *The Cosmopolitan* published an article by Münsterberg entitled 'Why We Go to the Movies'. The inclusive 'we' of the title is significant; he was, he wrote, a recent convert to the film:

> I may confess frankly that I was one of those snobbish late-comers. Until a year ago I had never seen a real photoplay. Although I was always a passionate lover of the theatre, I should have felt it as undignified for a Harvard Professor to attend a moving-picture show, just as I should not have gone to a vaudeville performance or to a museum of wax figures or to a phonograph concert. Last year, while I was travelling a thousand miles from Boston, I and a friend risked seeing *Neptune's Daughter*, and my conversion was rapid. I recognized at once that here marvelous possibilities were open, and I began to explore with eagerness the world which was new to me. Reel after reel moved along before my eyes—all styles, all makes. I went with the crowd to Anita Stewart and Mary Pickford and Charles Chaplin; I saw Pathé and Vitagraph, Lubin and Essanay, Paramount and Majestic, Universal and Knickerbocker. I read the books on how to write scenarios; I visited the manufacturing companies, and, finally, I began to experiment myself. Surely I am now under the spell of the 'movies' and, while my case may be worse than the average, all the world is somewhat under this spell.[92]

Münsterberg may have represented his 'conversion' to the moving pictures as of recent date, but the preoccupations he brought to his writings about film were not.[93] He had left Germany for the US in 1892 when William James invited him to take charge of the psychological laboratory at Harvard (where his students included the young Gertrude Stein) and was centrally concerned with the psychology of vision and perception, though his extensive publications also included work on aesthetics, American culture, the 'applied psychology' of law, advertising, industry, and 'scientific management'. *The Photoplay* drew on a number of his long-standing interests; optical technologies and the physiology and psychology of perception; the philosophy of attention; the relationship between 'inner' and 'outer' realities; a neo-Kantian 'aesthetic of isolation' and an affirmation of eternal and absolute values in art. These were all areas on which he had written extensively. He brought them to his analysis of an art which was defined on the basis of its newness, and whose departure, as he presented it, from existing aesthetic and, in particular, theatrical conventions (a focus his text shared with Lindsay's *The Art of the Moving Picture*) became the essence of its independence: 'We want to study the right of the photoplay, hitherto ignored by aesthetics, to be classed as an art in itself under entirely new mental life conditions.'[94]

Opening with a history of nineteenth-century technologies, and with the question 'what invention marked the beginning?', Münsterberg suggested that the account of cinema's development would vary according to whether the focus were placed on the moving picture as entertainment and art, or as science. A combined history of 'the scientific and the artistic efforts of the new and the old world' produces a set of 'dates and achievements' from the early nineteenth century onwards, centred on experiments with movement and vision, the creation of such 'philosophical toys' as the phenakistoscope, the stereoscope, and the zootrope (a development from the more purely scientific 'daedelum'), the motion studies of Muybridge, Marey, and Anschütz and, finally, the machines of Edison, Lumière, and Robert Paul. In locating film's origins in nineteenth-century optical devices (which, it is emphasized, were aids to scientific experiment before they become entertainments), and not the longer history of the *camera obscura*, the magic lantern, the phantasmagoria, the panorama, and the diorama, Münsterberg focused on the study of movement rather than on the play of light, shadow, and projection, and on scientific exploration rather than illusionism.

In the second chapter of *The Photoplay*, 'The Inner Development of the Moving Pictures', Münsterberg charted the stages and types of early cinema: actuality films, showing current events; war films; nature films; 'the magazine on the screen', including the genre of scientific films with which he was briefly involved, which were able to provide 'food for serious thought' to 'the masses of today [who] prefer to be taught by pictures rather than by words'; and, finally, narrative cinema, from 'little playlets' to 'great dramas'.[95] The significant evolution and aim of the cinema would thus seem to be, he suggested, towards the provision of 'a real substitute for the stage', its democratized version, and the reproduction of 'the theatre performance without end'. 'Of course', he wrote, 'the substitute could not be equal to the original'; the photoplay is without colour, 'real depth', and the 'spoken word'.[96]

As Münsterberg's argument continues, it transpires that what may seem a limitation may not in fact be one at all: 'while this movement to reproduce stage performances went on, elements were superadded, which the technique of the camera allowed, but which would hardly be possible in a theatre. Hence the development led slowly to a certain deviation from the path of the drama.'[97] The difference that might first strike an observer in fact resides in, perhaps surprisingly, the superior realism achieved by the film; the 'color' of the theatre is in fact that of painted cloth, which 'appears thoroughly unreal compared with the throbbing life of the street scenes and of the foreign crowds in which the cameraman finds his local color'.[98]

It becomes increasingly apparent, however, that he perceived the true development of the photoplay as a departure from both the theatre and the reproduction of reality. The moving pictures can produce a 'rapid change of scenes' impossible, he argued, on the stage; the possibility of 'allowing the eye to follow the hero and heroine continuously from place to place'; the ability to be 'simultaneously here and there'; 'a rapidity of motion which leaves actual men behind'.[99] As readers, we are gradually led from the valuation of realism to that of illusionism: 'Every dream becomes real, uncanny ghosts appear from nothing and disappear into nothing, mermaids swim through the waves, and little elves climb out of the Easter lilies.'[100]

Yet even while 'unheard of effects' were reached, the photoplay still 'showed a performance ... as it would go on in the outer world'.[101] An entirely new perspective was reached, Münsterberg argued, with the introduction of the close-up, which 'leaves all stagecraft behind'. It is at this juncture that the photoplay becomes 'a new art which long since left behind the mere film reproduction of the theatre and which ought to be acknowledged in its own aesthetic independence ... A new aesthetic cocoon is broken; where will the butterfly's wings carry him?'[102] In his account of the evolution of the moving picture, then, the photoplay emerged into newness, after an embryonic period in which it was still to an extent in thrall to drama on the stage. It was, he suggested, 'an independent art, controlled by aesthetic laws of its own, working with mental appeals which are fundamentally different from those of the theatre'.[103] Newness thus became synonymous with aesthetic autonomy.

The Photoplay provides an exemplary instance of the ways in which the new art of the film—'the seventh art', 'the tenth muse'—brought about a rearrangement of existing categories and hierarchies in the field of aesthetics. This was an area in which Münsterberg had written extensively. His views on the nature and value of art were succinctly expressed in an essay of 1909, 'The Problem of Beauty', the transcript of a lecture delivered to the American Philosophical Association at the end of 1908. Here he reaffirmed his position on aesthetic experience and value (both in the domains of art and nature) as inseparable from the 'eternal values' of unity, harmony and the transcendence of 'the chaos of experience' through the affirmation of a non-individualistic 'will'. The work of art was defined as 'cut off from the chain of practical events' and as 'disconnected from the remainder of the world; in short, it must be entirely isolated'.[104] Beauty of nature

> is possible only when nature suggests to us its own will... and that again can be realized only when those outer impressions do not come in question for us as starting points for action and as material for the satisfaction of our personal demands. If we fight with the waves of the ocean, they are to us only a dangerous object; they have no meaning to us because our personal interest demands from us that we treat those impressions in their causal connectiveness and thus as non-living physical objects. But if we stand on the safe rock, each wave and the foam of the surf suggests to us impulse and energy and we feel the perfect symphony and the mutual agreement of the acts of the excited ocean.[105]

There is an insistent splashing and plashing of waves in early writings about film, as there is in early cinema itself, from its first years through to Griffith's use of seascapes and beyond. The image (connected to the perception of the filmic medium as at once static/repetitive and dynamic) transmuted in Münsterberg's writings as he accommodated film into his aesthetic scheme. In the 'pre-cinematic' essay 'The Problem of Beauty', the ocean waves were deployed both as an example of nature's will (as in the passage quoted above) and of aesthetic 'unreality':

> To be unreal in the aesthetical sense means that the object of this experience does not transcend itself, does not awake any expectations for future changes or any reminiscences of previous stages. The waves in the painted ocean are not expected ever to move; the hero in the marble monument is not expected ever to speak. No artistic experience points away from itself.[106]

By the time of *The Photoplay*, however, Münsterberg was arguing that, while, the theatre stage manager 'can paint the ocean... his effect [is far] surpassed by the superb ocean pictures when the scene is played on the real cliffs, and the waves are thundering at their foot, and the surf is foaming about the actors'.[107] This apparent valuation of cinematic realism was bypassed in the ultimate claim for its illusionism. Yet this image of the natural sublime—the ocean, the crashing waves—was redeployed in the filmic context as a way of newly evaluating the 'movement' which, in 'The Perception of Beauty', was disallowed to the work of art: 'The waves in the painted ocean are not expected ever to move.'[108]

In his section on 'The Psychology of the Photoplay,' Münsterberg devoted separate chapters to 'Depth and Movement', 'Attention', 'Memory and Imagination', and 'Emotions', categories that echoed the chapter topics of William James's *The Principles of Psychology* and which were also central to Münsterberg's work on 'psychotechnical knowledge' in his 1913 study *Psychology and Industrial Efficiency*. In *The Art of the Photoplay*, Münsterberg's interest lay in 'the mental processes which this specific form of artistic endeavour produces in us'.[109] He claimed that 'We have no right whatever to say that the scenes which we see on the screen appear to us as flat pictures.' As he wrote:

> *Depth and movement alike come to us in the moving picture world, not as hard facts but as a mixture of fact and symbol. They are present and yet they are not in the things. We invest the impressions with them.* The theater has both depth and motion, without any subjective help; the screen has them and yet lacks them. We see things distant and moving, but we furnish to them more than we receive; we create the depth and the continuity through our mental mechanism.[110]

In his discussion of depth in the moving pictures, he drew a sharp distinction between our 'knowledge' that the objects on the screen have only two dimensions, and our 'immediate impression' that they have depth: 'We have no right whatever to say that the scenes which we see on the screen have only two dimensions.'[111] Drawing upon the example of the stereoscope (which 'illustrates clearly that the knowledge of the flat character of pictures by no means excludes the actual perception of depth') and the mirror (in which we see two localizations of our reflection which produce a 'conflict of perception', though one we have all learned to ignore) he argued that the photoplay 'brings our mind into a peculiar complex state': '*We have reality with all its true dimensions; and yet it keeps the fleeting, passing surface suggestion without true depth and fullness, as different from a mere picture as from a mere stage performance.*'[112]

An even greater complexity lay in the problem of movement and in the relationship between the motionless picture which 'objectively reaches our eye',[113] and the 'continuous movement' that we perceive. Münsterberg described at some length experiments with the perception of movement, and concluded that the postulation of 'after-images' and of the perception of successive stages of movement are inadequate to the impression of movement, which involves 'a complex mental process by which the various pictures are held together in the unity of a higher act'[114] an 'inner mental activity'. The postulation of a 'positive after-image' (sometimes defined as 'persistence of vision') is insufficient explanation, he suggested, for the fact that the film spectator sees not the 'objective reality' of a 'succession of instantaneous impressions' but 'continuous movement'.[115]

For a number of recent commentators, Münsterberg's questioning of the widely held belief in 'persistence of vision' as an explanation for the impression of film's continuous motion earns him at least a mention in the history of film theory. Joseph and Barbara Anderson write that Münsterberg 'shows the direct influence of Wertheimer's short-circuit theory and other current hypotheses of movement perception', and that he proposed, as an alternative explanation to 'persistence of vision', and with reference to a two-element display, a 'central "filling-in" or impletion process', whereby the observer's mind fills in the gap between two stimuli perceived at different locations and at different times.[116] In fact, Münsterberg offered no very fully developed alternative to the model of the 'after-image', which he at one point in *The Photoplay* deployed quite uncritically:[117] his argument rested on the premise that the impression of continuous movement 'is a product of our own mind which binds the pictures together'.[118] Despite the extended discussion in *The Photoplay* of experiments in the psychology of vision (and Münsterberg detailed the postulated workings of the after-image in relation to pre-cinematic optical technologies), he thus allowed the question of movement in the cinema to remain as a non-particularized issue of consciousness or 'mental mechanism':

> *Depth and movement alike come to us in the moving picture world, not as hard facts but as a mixture of fact and symbol. They are present and yet they are not in the things. We invest the impressions with them.* The theater has both depth and motion, without any subjective help; the screen has them and yet lacks them. We see things distant and moving, but we furnish to them more than we receive; we create the depth and the continuity through our mental mechanism.[119]

'*They are present and yet they are not in the things.*' In Münsterberg's argument, we give more than we receive, and film spectatorship entails an encounter between an abundance of inner processes and 'the world of impressions'. 'The best', he wrote, 'does not come from without.' This view contrasts strikingly with those early detractors of cinema for whom moving-image consumption was perceived as purely passive. It also gives support to recent discussions of the new form of illusionism brought into being by nineteenth-century optical devices. As Tom Gunning has written: 'the illusion of motion was no longer based on credulity: the viewer actually *saw* the images superimposed or the succession of motions or the illusion of three-dimensionality.'[120] Münsterberg's model of perception in the cinema might also be construed, however, as a compensatory response to the absence of spatial and temporal dimensions in the cinema. Depth and movement became the gift consciousness made to a screen-world that lacked them, while at the same time there was a closing of the gap between the films of the present and the initial, utopian imaginings of a cinema which had never in fact existed: 'The flickering black and white images that appeared on theater screens of the twentieth-century were a far cry from the "myth of total cinema" that Edison and others had foreseen'.[121]

A key issue in *The Photoplay* is that of 'attention', an internal function which, Münsterberg argues, is the most central of all the internal functions that create the meaning of the world around us.[122] The world of impressions is a 'chaos' given order and meaning by our acts of attention, 'voluntary' and 'involuntary': 'Our life is a great compromise between that which our voluntary attention aims at and that which the aims of the surrounding world force on our involuntary attention.'[123] In his *Psychology: General and Applied*, Münsterberg had rejected the idea that involuntary attention was any less an 'inner activity' than voluntary attention; in both cases, he argued, it is our own activity that directs the attention. In *The Photoplay*, Münsterberg produced a version of this argument to support a fundamental tenet of his text; that the cinematic close-up can be identified with the mental act of attention:

> *The close-up has objectified in our world of perception our mental act of attention and by it has furnished art with a means which far transcends the power of any theater stage* ... Wherever our attention becomes focused on a special feature, the surrounding adjusts itself, eliminates everything in which we are not interested, and by the close-up heightens the vividness of that on which our mind is concentrated. It is as if that outer world were woven into our mind and were shaped not through its own laws but by the acts of our attention.[124]

If the 'close-up' is the 'projection' or 'objectivation' of the 'mental act of attention', in the 'cut-back' (or, in more familiar terms, the flashback) 'we must recognize the mental act of remembering':

In both cases, the act which in the ordinary theater would go on in our mind alone is here in the photography projected into the pictures themselves. It is as if reality has lost its own continuous connection and become shaped by the demands of our soul. It is as if the outer world itself became molded in accordance with our fleeting turns of attention or with our passing memory ideas.[125]

The statement looked forward to arguments in the third and final part of *The Photoplay*, which explore the aesthetics of film. The combination of aesthetic analysis and psychological research were said to produce a unified principle: '*the photoplay tells us the human story by overcoming the forms of the outer world, namely, space, time, and causality, and by adjusting the events to the forms of the inner world, namely, attention, memory, imagination, and emotion.*'[126] While strongly rejecting the view that it was the role of art to imitate reality, Münsterberg appears to have been claiming that film images and movement were projections, perhaps reflections, of consciousness.

The last chapter in the section on psychology focused on emotions, an aspect of the text I discussed in the Introduction. In the structure of Münsterberg's text, the chapter on the 'Emotions' in fact divided and connected the sections of the book on 'psychology' and 'aesthetics', bringing together the terms 'motion' and 'emotion'. Münsterberg hypothesized a future for film in which, for example (and along the model of a psychological experiment), a rocking camera would give to every motion 'an uncanny whirling character', creating in 'the mind of the spectator unusual sensations which produce a new shading of the emotional background'.[127] He thus sent, for a moment, an embodied, corporealized perception into whirling, vertiginous space before returning to the 'laws' of aesthetics—'isolation' and 'detachment'.[128]

The final section of *The Photoplay* was an argument for aesthetic value as the overcoming of reality. Münsterberg, as Michael Pressler has noted, shared with Clive Bell and Roger Fry a view of the aesthetic experience 'as essentially autotelic and transcendental, a mode of formal contemplation freed from all practical context'.[129] As Münsterberg wrote: '*The work of art shows the things and events perfectly complete in themselves, freed from all connections which lead beyond their own limits, that is, in perfect isolation*';[130] 'We annihilate beauty when we link the artistic creation with practical interests and transform the spectator into a selfishly interested bystander'.[131] The connection to Fry's writings, and the 1909 'An Essay on Aesthetics' in particular, returns us to the ways, discussed in Chapter 2, in which Fry deployed the example of the cinematograph in the service of his autonomy aesthetic, and the complexity of its implications for a theory of cinematic ontology.

Münsterberg's study of film was concentrated more on questions of editing (and, by implication, on the issue of the spectator's engagement with filmic *narrative*) in the photoplay than Freeburg's writings, though both writers were concerned with models of spectatorial absorption and 'attention'. He shared with Lindsay a fascination with film's ability to produce the most rapid of alternations and alterations in space and time, through such devices as close-ups, parallel editing, and dissolves; for both writers the film-making of D. W. Griffith (with its extensive use of close-ups as inserts, deployed to clarify the plot, close-ups of the human face, objectifying 'attention', parallel action, and iris shots) was central.[132] Lindsay, in his 1925 study, *The Progress and Poetry of the Movies*, quoted Münsterberg extensively, and the film hieroglyph took on the aspect of the close-up. Münsterberg also wrote far more positively than Freeburg of filmic speed and motion: 'Not more than one sixteenth of a second is needed to carry us from one corner of the globe to the other, from a jubilant setting to a mourning scene. The whole keyboard of the imagination may be used to serve this emotionalizing of nature.'[133]

'Beauty' was not, as it was for Lindsay and Freeburg, 'glimpsed' in those intervals which were, in Lindsay's words, 'a pulse of the rhythm in the silence-of-time that we call the motion picture'.[134] For Münsterberg, unlike Freeburg, the 'unnatural rapidity' of the photoplay was represented as energizing, 'heighten[ing] the feeling of vitality in the spectator'.[135] The film, in his account, moved to the measure of our own 'fluttering and fleeting' mental states,[136] and beauty would seem to inhere in this symbiosis, and not in the attempt to arrest time and motion.

While the writers I have discussed do not mention the work of Henri Bergson in their film writings, his account of the 'cinematographic mechanism of thought' in *Creative Evolution* would appear to be a highly significant conceptual context. As we have seen, Bergson argued that the cinematographic model spatializes and segments time, rather than understanding time as a vital flow into which human subjectivity could be inserted. Lindsay and Freeburg's counters to the 'mechanical' movement of the cinematic frame were the pictorial image or tableau that could momentarily arrest time and the interval as the glimpse of beauty, while Münsterberg postulated a mode of perception inextricably intertwined with our 'mental mechanism'. Moreover, his account of the filmic 'cut-back', and its counterpart in the work of the mind, is suggestive of the concept of 'thinking backwards' for which Bergson argued, claiming, in *Creative Evolution*, that such a process ran entirely counter to the relentless forward motion of the cinematic apparatus and that it reversed 'the bent of our intellectual habits'.[137]

Were Münsterberg's psychophysical preoccupations—central to his engagement with the new forms of mental and physical life demanded by modern industrial society—merely appearing in tandem with his idealist aesthetics, without the two finding reconciliation, or was cinema perceived, and embraced, as the means by which the tensions between the two could finally be resolved? In the closing paragraph of his text he engaged with the question of 'modern beauty,' in his assertion that film 'is a new form of true beauty in the turmoil of a modern age, created by its very technique and yet more than any other art destined to overcome outer nature by the free and joyful play of the mind'.[138] Underlying his analysis of film was undoubtedly an interest in the ways in which film motion and cinematic spectatorship might aid the eye of the viewer in the organization—spatial and perceptual—of 'the chaos of experience' and help to improve reaction times, 'training' the eye and the mind to deal with the rapid, visually orientated tasks demanded by modern industry and commerce. These required, as he phrased it in *Psychology and Industrial Efficiency* (1913): 'the closest attention and concentration ... [and] a quick power of perception accompanied by quick responsive action.'[139] The act of 'attention' was thus inextricably intertwined with the training of eye and brain, perceived to be essential for the successful management of modern life, with its unprecedented speed and motion. Thus, in *Psychology and Industrial Efficiency*, he described laboratory experiments, designed to reduce the number of accidents on the electric railway by testing the motormen's responsive speeds and the quality of their 'attention', in markedly cinematic terms, bringing together film and the urban scene, 'the quickly changing panorama of the street':

> I found this to be a particular complicated act of attention by which the manifoldness of objects, the pedestrians, the carriages, and the automobiles, are continuously observed with reference to their rapidity and direction in the quickly changing panorama of the street. Moving figures come from the right and from the left toward and across the track, and are embedded in a stream of men and vehicles which moves parallel to the track. In the fact of such manifoldness ... we have a great variety of mental types of this characteristic unified activity, which may be understood as a particular combination of attention and imagination.[140]

His discussion of the close-up in the cinema in *The Photoplay* used advertising and the lure of the shop-window as direct analogies, showing how 'attraction' could shape 'attention': 'As we are passing along the street we see something in the shop window and as soon as it stirs up our interest, our body adjusts itself, we stop, we fixate it, we get more of the detail in it, the lines become sharper, and while it impresses us more vividly than before, the street around us has lost its vividness and clearness.'[141] Here he deployed one of the three nineteenth-century positions on 'attention' identified by Jonathan Crary—the production of an attentive subject through 'the knowledge and control of external procedures of stimulation as well as a wide-ranging technology of "attraction"'—though this was always to be combined in Münsterberg's thought with the concept of attention as, in Crary's words, 'an expression of the conscious will of an autonomous subject for whom the very activity of attention, as choice, was part of that subject's self-constituting freedom'.[142] 'The best', as Münsterberg would remind us, 'does not come from without.'

It would certainly be possible to read Münsterberg's study of film as continuous with, and indeed an extension of, his work in the psychological laboratory, where much of his research served the needs of industrial psychology, and as an evaluation of cinema on the basis of its effectiveness in training the modern eye. His plans for Paramount Pictographs, developing in the months before his death, included the making of films which would serve as 'mental tests ... so that motion picture audiences may learn what characteristics equip one for special kinds of work, so that each individual may find his proper setting... There need be no limits practically to the influence of the motion picture as an educator, although there is no subject which can be more clearly presented through the camera than psychology'.[143]

An 'aesthetic of isolation', however, continued to lie at the heart of Münsterberg's theories. The apparent contradiction can to some extent be resolved if we understand his 'aesthetic' valuation of 'the forms of the inner world' over those of the 'outer world' as commensurate with, and implicated in, his 'psychotechnical' concern with 'mental attitude'[144] and psychological 'fitness' for industrial and commercial tasks, understood as inner qualities of the mind. 'The best does not come from without' was as applicable to his arguments in the sphere of psychology and industrial efficiency as in the context of film spectatorship. Yet he also wished to preserve the concept of 'pure beauty' for a realm untouched by the visual displays of modernity—he insisted, for example, that an advertisement, if it were to fulfil its function, should not aim for beauty: 'The very meaning of beauty lies in its self-completeness.'[145] While his interest in film was almost certainly a dimension of his work in 'psychotechnics', *The Art of the Photoplay* was nonetheless written to claim an aesthetic status for film, and to find a way of allying 'pure beauty' with 'modern life'.

'An ever originating series of ever vanishing aspects'

In his foreword to *The Art of Photoplay Making* (1918), Victor Freeburg wrote that his study was based on lectures delivered at Columbia University between 1915 and 1917 and on the newspaper articles he wrote for the *New York Times* and other publications. He suggested that his readers have three books to hand: Epes Winthrop Sargent's *Techniques of the Photoplay* (1913), Hugo Münsterberg's *The Photoplay* and Vachel Lindsay's *The Art of the Moving Picture*, 'which makes it perfectly clear that a motion picture, if properly thought out and manufactured, will contain the kind of beauty which we used to look for only in paintings and sculpture'.[146] The preface to *Pictorial Beauty on the Screen* (1923) pursued the theme: 'If I look upon a motion picture as a kind of substitute for some stage play or novel, it seems to me a poor thing, only a substitute for something better; but if I look upon it as something real in itself, a new form of pictorial art in which things have somehow been conjured into significant motion, then I get many a glimpse of touching beauty, and I always see a great range of possibilities for richer beauties in future examples of this new art. Then I see the motion picture as the equal of any of the elder arts.'[147]

Though less idiosyncratic and less overtly polemical than Lindsay's film writings, Freeburg's two books were also attempts to both describe and prescribe for an aesthetics of cinema, taking a classical and formalist approach to the nature of art and the question of beauty, and giving unity the highest aesthetic value. 'What the photoplay world needs at present,' Freeburg wrote, 'is more definite canons of criticism.'[148] Such canons, he implied, were particularly to be desired given that 'the momentary, flashing nature of exhibition and the psychology of the crowd give the spectator little opportunity or desire to exercise his intellectual faculties'.[149] Moreover, they would help to secure for film its enduring qualities: 'Let us constantly remember that if our photoplay is to become a classic it must possess beneath the attractive surface which appeals to the crowd the permanent values of illuminating truth, universal meaning, and unfading beauty.'[150] Freeburg's account of film and its significance was intended to produce a counter-discourse to that of popular and commercial cinematic attractions, particularly as they were constructed in the movie and fan magazines. Thus his theories dissolved, often in the language of Paterianism and of literary Impressionism, actors and 'stars' into shape and shadow: 'We are merely thinking of [actors] as moving shapes upon a screen';[151] 'We cannot thank them for the poignant beauty of glowing lights and falling shadows, of flowing lines, and melting forms, and all that strange evanescence that makes up the lure of cinematic forms.'[152] Freeburg insisted that the film director was 'the legitimate master in movie making',[153] as creator and artist or, in his preferred term, 'cinema composer'.[154]

The interplay between mobility and fixity, 'movement' and 'moment', stasis and fluency, underlies *The Art of Photoplay Making*. The arts, Freeburg argued, can be divided into two categories: the static forms of the painter, sculptor, and architect, which depend upon simultaneity and coexistence, and the 'fluent' arts of the dancer, the orator and the musician, in which movement is 'consecutive'. Cinema, in his account, was concerned with both static and fluent forms, and his evocations of its fluency—its 'evanescence', 'flowing', and 'melting'—were essentially Impressionist.

In his chapter on 'Pictorial Composition in Fluent Forms', Freeburg argued that, while 'in a great many pictured actions certain pictorial instants, or moments, are more impressive and longer remembered than the pictorial movement', it is also the case that 'many subjects in nature and in mobile arts are more beautiful and memorable in motion than in repose'.[155] The cinema composer has a particular responsibility, because 'for the first time in history it has become possible to capture and mobilize in art any movement which the human eye can perceive, and movements even which the unaided eye cannot perceive'.[156] Examples of movement given by Freeburg include the moving pattern on the surface of a pool; 'circles contracting about a common centre, a phenomenon which may be observed by a passenger on the rear platform of a tube-train as he gazes into the receding tunnel';[157] the vortex of water; the movement of the railway-train. Freeburg's descriptions thus created a continuum and synergy between nature and technology; the tube-train and the railway-train, their movements perceived in formal terms, reproduced the physical motions of the natural world, the movement of water as wave or as 'vortex'.

In this sense, technological modernity (in which category cinema would be included) did not represent a break with nature or *physis*. Yet there was a quality of movement in film which was radically different to that of the other visual and plastic arts. 'The visible stimuli' in painting, photography, sculpture or architecture 'do not vanish while you look at them. They are there as long as you look, will be there tomorrow, and will remain constantly present to the eye as long as the art object endures'.

> But the motion picture is an ever originating series of ever vanishing aspects. And the composition of the photoplay is a combination of no-longer-seen pictures with being-seen-pictures with not-yet-seen pictures. In other words, the cinematic composition appeals simultaneously to the memory, the perception and the expectation of the beholder.[158]

In this account, film produced the coexistence of past, present, and future, in contrast with a model of the enduring present tense of the older visual and plastic arts. Like Münsterberg's writing on cinema, Freeburg's work appears strongly indebted to the time philosophies and philosophies of consciousness of his time. These included those of William James, who, in a discussion of temporal 'vanishing', wrote: 'The specious present has, in addition, a vaguely vanishing backward and forward fringe; but its nucleus is probably the dozen seconds or less that have just elapsed.'[159] Edmund Husserl's philosophy of time was also centrally concerned with, as Michael Levenson notes, the 'flickering' instant of our encounter with the world, and the problems with making this a basis for experience, which Husserl resolved through the concept of 'retention', a 'just-having-been', defined, in Levenson's words, as 'the duration inherent in so-called immediate experience … the penumbral quality of a perpetually fading present'.[160] 'Protention', by contrast, was understood as anticipation, a bearing towards the future, or, in the term used by Freeburg, 'expectation'. These time concepts found their echoes not only in literary impressionism, but also in the modernist aesthetics, more broadly conceived, of writers including Proust, Joyce, and Woolf.

Freeburg also drew extensively in his film writings on contemporary research in physiological aesthetics and 'the psychology of beauty', in which aesthetic preferences, for shape, colour, and form, were the subject of scientific and psychological experiment. The work of Ethel Puffer (author of *The Psychology of Beauty* (1907) and a student and, subsequently colleague, of Münsterberg's) was a strong influence on both Freeburg's and Münsterberg's film writing. For Puffer, 'the beauty of an object lies in its permanent possibility of creating the perfect moment. The experience of this moment, the union of stimulation and repose, constitutes the unique aesthetic emotion.'[161] She explored the extent to which perceptions of balance and symmetry in pictures were determined by acts of 'attention', the concept that was central to late nineteenth- and twentieth-century psychology and was also, as we have seen, at the heart of Münsterberg's theories of film and aligned by him with the filmic device of the close-up. Research in these areas, as explored in C. W. Valentine's *Experimental Psychology of Beauty* (referred to by Freeburg), was extended to the question of 'suggested movement': 'It seems possible', Valentine wrote, 'that pleasure may be found in the *suggestion* of movement by a line, if that suggestion is of the right kind.'[162] This was echoed in Freeburg's formulation 'that movement in a photo-play may come from other things besides motions'.[163]

In discussing the question 'what is beauty?' in *The Art of Photoplay Making*, Freeburg referred his reader to the work of the writer, art historian and aesthetician Vernon Lee (the pseudonym of Violet Paget). Lee was engaged closely, though at times critically, with Hugo Münsterberg's research and writing, highly approving his 'physiological aesthetics' but rejecting his 'autonomy aesthetic': the meaning of art, she wrote, is not its separation from but its connection with us. In *The Beautiful* (1913), the text which Freeburg cited, Lee made one brief reference to the 'cinematographic' in tandem with the 'kaleidoscopic,' as a way of describing a succession of aspects connected to non-aesthetic (practical, scientific) responses, as in a landscape 'which is swished over by the mental eye as by an express train, only just enough seen to know what it was, or perhaps nothing seen at all, mere words filling up gaps in the train of thought'.[164] Film itself, it would seem, did not figure on her conceptual horizon.

She was, however, substantially concerned with the question of 'movement,' and with the contrast between 'the locomotion of things' and 'the empathetic movement of lines' which, in her account, lay at the heart of the aesthetic experience. While she opposed the 'reiteration' and hence 'stability' on which the 'healing quality of aesthetic contemplation' depended to 'the perpetual flux of action and thought',[165] she did not represent the aesthetic experience as a static one: in linguistic terms, as Lee defined it, it could be represented in the infinitive of the verb—more accurately a gerundial infinitive—in a perception of the mountain (used in Lee's text, as in John Ruskin's work[166] and in the long history of writing on the 'dynamic sublime', to explore and analogize aesthetic response) rising, 'always rising without ever beginning to sink or adding a single cubit to its stature, "the general idea of *rising*" the thought and emotion, *the idea of rising as such*'.[167]

In *The Beautiful*, Lee outlined a theory of aesthetics and empathy (drawing on the work of Theodor Lipps, and in particular his book *Spatial Aesthetics and Optical Illusions*). 'Dramas', she wrote, 'enacted by lines and curves and angles, take place not in the marble or pigment embodying those contemplated shapes, but solely in ourselves, in what we call our memory, imagination and feeling.'[168]

> The movements of the eye, slight and sketchy in themselves, awakening the composite dynamic memory of all our experience of the impetus gained by switch-back descent. Moreover this sequence, being a sequence, will awaken expectation of repetition, hence sense of rythm [*sic*]; the long chain of peaks will seem to perform a dance, they will furl and unfurl like waves.[169]

The Beautiful thus presented a moving world without the felt necessity of the moving image.

In Lee's definition, which Freeburg quoted: 'Beautiful means satisfactory for contemplative, i.e. *for reiterated perception*.'[170] 'The very essence of contemplative satisfaction', Lee continued, 'is its desire for such reiteration.'[171] There were strong echoes here, too, of *Laocoön*, in which Lessing wrote of the 'single moment in ever-changing nature' to which the painter and sculpture are restricted; the moment must therefore be as suggestive as possible, while avoiding gestural excess. It is not, Lessing specified, 'merely to be given a glance but to be ... contemplated repeatedly and at length'.[172] Freeburg, borrowing Lee's (and Lessing's) definitions, attempted to redefine the cinematographic in the terms of satisfied contemplation, reiterated perception, and thus beauty. He sought out 'repetition' through formal, spatial relations, repeated within individual shots and across the span of the film, and connected repetition in the photoplay with the use of the theme or motif in musical composition. 'The photoplay,' Freeburg wrote in *Pictorial Beauty on the Screen*, 'needs repetition, especially because of the fact that any pictorial motion or moment must by its very nature vanish while we look ... from our minds as well as from the screen.' Repetition with difference was a way of 'fix[ing] these fleeting values' without risk of monotony.[173]

'Repetition,' for Freeburg as for Lindsay, also became a question of repeated viewings of a single film. Lindsay wrote in *The Progress and Poetry of the Movies* of watching *The Thief of Bagdad* twenty times, while Freeburg asked rhetorically (in a coded reference, perhaps, to Vachel Lindsay's figure for the most beautiful cinematic tableau, 'the breaking of the tenth wave upon the sand'):[174]

> Has any reader of this book gone to see the same photoplay ten times? And if so, why? Was it because of some irresistible, undying lure in the content of that photoplay or in the pictorial form of that content? Did you go of your own free will? Did you ever make a sacrifice to see it the tenth time? If so, then you have known the calm joy of a reserve power in the newest of the arts.[175]

'Reserve' was a central and multiply determined term, signifying decorative simplicity and 'restraint', a containment, rather than an expenditure, of the spectator's psychical and physiological 'energy', and 'the emotion which comes over us at the overwhelming discovery that a given masterpiece of art has a wealth of beauty that we can never hope to exhaust'. 'Reserve', in Freeburg's arguments, also functioned as a counter to the 'speed' that defined filmic movement and the 'jazz' of the screen: 'The hysterical extravagance of the movies is further illustrated in the breathless speed which so often characterizes every moving thing on the screen ... It has nothing of that abiding joy which comes from the consciousness of restrained energy in art.'[176]

Rhythm, pictorial values, restraint, slowness of movement, 'dynamic repose',[177] reserve and repetition were all represented as ways of holding back the speed and inexorable forward movement of the projected film, which came to stand for the relentless drive and 'shock' effects of modernity itself. Speed, quick close-ups, 'large violent movements on the screen',[178] and stark contrasts between black and white tones 'hurt the eyes', producing 'pictorial hysterics'.[179] Acts of 'attention', the work (or play) of 'our eyes and minds',[180] could, to an extent, Freeburg suggested, fix the fleeting instant, arresting the moment, arresting beauty: 'At such times the whole pattern on the screen becomes as static as a painting, and its power or weakness, its beauty or lack of beauty, may be appreciated much as one would appreciate a design in a painting.'[181] Freeburg lamented, however, the impossibility of 'rests', 'blank periods', and 'intervals' in cinematic projection and the absence in the film of visual equivalents to those silences, of varying lengths, which he held to be the most powerful aspects of musical rhythm and composition.[182]

'One would get a sense of movement,' Freeburg wrote, 'even if every scene in a photoplay were itself a fixed picture held for a few seconds on the screen.'[183] The relationship between 'moment' and 'movement' was at the heart of his film theories: 'Try to recall the pictorial aspects of the action in a play you saw years ago. What do you recall? Moments or movements? Rarely a movement, more often a moment. The psychology of this emphasis is usually simple enough. There was a momentary pause of the object just after completing, or just before beginning a movement.'[184]

The 'pause of the object' was in no way to be identified with the cut or the interval between film frames. To a significant extent, Freeburg sought in his film aesthetics an alternative line of development in moving picture technology, based on the pictorial tradition of the tableau, and running counter to contemporary celebrations of mechanization and speed.[185] He also attempted to disaggregate 'movement' as mere mechanical motion from 'movement' as connected to sensation and emotion, contributing to the contrast and connection between motion and emotion that, as we have seen, became a recurrent trope in the writing about cinema of the 1920s.[186]

In his introduction to *Pictorial Art in the Movies*, Freeburg outlined an account of film's progress and development, in the spheres of production and reception. He noted developments in film reviewing and criticism, to be found both in the film magazines and in daily newspapers, and commended the observation of 'the pictorial art in motion pictures'. He also commented on the growth of 'public discussion' of the cinema, to which his book was a contribution: 'men and women are trying to find words and phrases to express the cinematic beauty which they have sensed. And by that discussion they are sharpening their senses for the discovery of richer beauty in the films that are to come.'[187] The terms of the discussion would need to be predicated, however, on the understanding that cinema was 'a new language', which audiences were only beginning to learn to read.[188] 'Words', Freeburg insisted, 'are not proper to the screen. The language of the screen should be in proper terms of the screen; and these terms may be found if we look long enough.'[189]

The approach to 'beauty', a concept celebrated in the film writings discussed in this chapter, was made in more ambivalent terms in subsequent film aesthetics. Indeed, as for Hans Richter, quoted earlier, it was often perceived to be at odds with cinematic realism, or, as in the case of Béla

Balázs, with the motion that defined film. Writing of 'Dangerous Beauty', Balázs asserted:

> Over-beautiful, picturesque shots are sometimes dangerous even if they are the result of good camera work alone. Their over-perfect composition, their self-sufficient closed harmony may lend them a static, painting-like character and thereby lift them out of the dynamic stream of the action. Such beauty has its own centre of gravity, its own frame and does not reach beyond itself to the preceding and the subsequent. *'Je hais le mouvement qui déplace les lignes,'* wrote Baudelaire in his sonnet on beauty. But the film is art in motion.[190]

The pictorial tradition in film and in film criticism, central to Lindsay's and Freeburg's film writings, has been largely written out of the debates and the histories, and the work of the critics discussed in this article was overlooked for many decades, though it resonated throughout the film criticism of the 1920s, often without acknowledgement. Recent modernist studies, with their tendency to equate film and montage aesthetics, have found little place for the writing of these early critics and theorists. Yet among the many interesting aspects of this early work is that, *contra* Balázs, it was precisely an attempt to bring the terms of 'beauty' together with those of 'motion', temporality ('the preceding and the subsequent', in Balázs's phrase) and the mass or democratic art of the cinema.

From *Caligari* to Chaplin

Robert Wiene's 'expressionist' film of 1920, *The Cabinet of Dr Caligari*, which premiered in New York on 3 April 1921, was as significant a film for American as for British critics and cultural commentators. While it had many detractors, it acted, as I discussed in Chapter 2, as an exemplary instance of cinema's status as a new art. The critic John Hutchens suggested in 1929 that the film started 'the little cinema movement' in the US,[191] while it was Gilbert Seldes's claim that it 'created motion-picture criticism in England and America'.[192] *Caligari* was discussed in some detail by Freeburg, in *Pictorial Beauty on the Screen*, and in the 1922 edition of Lindsay's *The Art of the Moving Picture*. For Freeburg, the film was an example of 'the perfect blending of dramatic theme, actors and setting'. While the 'movie fan' might initially be startled by the film's strange and alarming shapes and characters, he will begin to be absorbed by 'the remarkable fitness of these crazy people in crazy places'. The 'sympathy' between setting and

Figure 5. *The Cabinet of Dr Caligari* (Robert Wiene, Germany, 1920).

action was matched, Freeburg argued, by the ways in which 'the various factors are skilfully organized into an excellent pictorial composition',[193] and he enjoined his readers to look closely at the 'still' included in his text (of Cesare the somnambulist 'slinking along an alley of weird lights and shadows'):

> Study the plan of the pictorial design and you will see that as soon as the man has emerged from the shadows in the background he becomes the strongest accent in an area of white. The end of the alley from which he comes is accented by the jagged white shape above the shadows, and the doorway through which he goes is similarly accented by irregular shapes. These two accents keep the composition in balance, and when our glance passes from one to the other the path of attention must cross the area of central interest. There is rhythm in the composition, too, thought one would scarcely realise it at first glance. Note the swinging curves in the white patch on the street and in the corresponding patch of the wall, and note also how some of these curves harmonize with the lines of the actor's body and with his shadow upon the wall.[194]

Freeburg's discourse thus transmuted the jagged shapes of *Caligari* into a harmonious and rhythmic composition, finding, in accord with his

Figure 6. *The Cabinet of Dr Caligari.*

film theory as a whole, 'movement'—'the swinging curves'—within the
pictorial frame of the still.

In his preface to the 1922 edition of *The Art of the Moving Picture*, Lindsay
wrote: 'I have just returned this very afternoon from a special showing of
the famous imported film, *The Cabinet of Dr Caligari*. Some of the earnest
spirits of the Denver Art Association, finding it was in storage in the town,
had it privately brought forth to study it with reference to its bearing on
their new policies.'[195] *Caligari* was thus framed from the start as an 'art' film,
which took on the role in Lindsay' second edition that the 1914 Italian
epic *Cabiria* had occupied in the first. He also compared it to Griffith's
Intolerance—a touchstone of the most significant kind for Lindsay, and
an exemplification of his category of 'architecture-in-motion'. Whereas
Caligari, Lindsay wrote, was 'drawing in motion' and 'a devil's mouse-trap',
confined in its cabinet, *Intolerance* was monumental. 'But', Lindsay argued,
'for technical study for Art Schools, *The Cabinet of Dr Caligari* is more
profitable. It shows how masterpieces can be made, with the second-hand
furniture of any attic. But I hope fairy-tales, not diabolical stories, will come

Figure 7. *The Cabinet of Dr Caligari.*

from these attics.'[196] The film also 'proves', he wrote, 'in a hundred new ways the resources of the film in making all the inanimate things which, on the spoken stage, cannot act at all, the leading actor in the film'.[197]

Like Freeburg, Lindsay found no 'crazy geometry' in the film: 'There is nothing experimental about any of the setting, nothing unconsidered or strained or over-considered. It seems experimental because it is thrown into contrast with extreme commercial formulas in the regular line of the "movie trade"'. The comparison Lindsay drew was between the film and the drawings of Rackham, Dürer, and Rembrandt: '*Dr Caligari* is more realistic.'[198] At no point did Lindsay invoke the stage in connection with *Caligari*, though this was an obvious connection for many commentators on the film, with its theatrical sets. Lindsay's analogies were entirely with drawing and painting—though not 'Expressionist' painting *per se*—and the film became gathered up into the new dimensions of 'film study' within the art schools and (as in the reference to the Denver Art Association's 'storage' of the film) the beginnings of the 'film archive' movement. To this extent, *Caligari* came to embody the shift, between 1915 and 1922, in Lindsay's own aspirations for the new medium and his discourse upon it, and his acknowledgement that his approach would be of interest to a more limited and specialized art student audience rather than to the 'movie audience' at large.

References to Charlie Chaplin, by contrast with the discussion of *Caligari*, appeared only in passing in Lindsay's text (though Lindsay was an admirer of Chaplin) and not at all in Freeburg's. Yet reflections on, and celebrations of, Chaplin dominated much of the writing about cinema of this period, and opened up new dimensions in the relationship between American and European culture. Elie Faure's *The Art of Cineplastics*, published by the Four Seas Company, Boston, in 1923, had originally run as a series in English in the New York journal *The Freeman* in 1920. The essay began with a lament for the theatre and drama of the past as 'collective spectacle', and a celebration of 'the art of the moving picture' as 'the nucleus of the common spectacle',[199] though Faure (like Lindsay, Freeburg, and Münsterberg) insisted on film's radical difference from theatre. Film, he argued, was closest to the plastic arts ('plastics is the art of expressing form in repose or in movement by all the means that man commands') in the unchanging nature of its composition—'once fixed it does not change again'[200]—though it emerges that Faure wished it to be understood as an entirely new, 'unknown art'.

Indeed, the essay described and enacted an 'evolution' of aesthetic responses to the cinema. The first encounters with the new medium entailed comparisons with the other arts and with works of art, which seemed to come to life on the screen: 'a descent into that host of personages whom I had already seen—motionless on the canvases of Greco, Frans Hals, Rembrandt, Velazquez, Vermeer, Courbet, Manet. I do not set down these names at random, the last two especially. They are those the cinema suggested to me from the first.'[201] The connection was thus made between film and Impressionism. Yet, Faure continued,

> as my eye became accustomed to these strange works, other memories associated themselves with the early ones, till I no longer needed to appeal to my memory and invoke familiar paintings in order to justify the new plastic impressions that I got at the cinema. Their elements, their complexity which varies, and winds in a continuous movement, the constantly unexpected things imposed on the work by its mobile composition, ceaselessly renewed, ceaselessly broken and remade, fading away and reviving and breaking down, monumental for one flashing instant, impressionistic the second following—all this constitutes a phenomenon too radically new for us even

to dream of classing it with painting, or with sculpture, or with the dance, least of all with the modern theatre.[202]

Faure's words near-directly repeated those of Bergson in *Creative Evolution*—'evolution is creation unceasingly renewed'[203]—suggesting, as I noted in the Introduction, the extent to which followers of Bergson wished to comprehend cinema through the terms of flux, mobility and, most markedly in Faure's case, 'creative evolution'.

For Faure, cinematography and film spectatorship reconstituted 'memory', remaking the mind's image-repertoire with new elements. Recognition of the newness of the medium—its freedom from association with other art forms—became linked to 'intuition', and the increased familiarity of the eye with cinematic form and movement created the cinema mind. The utopian dimensions of Faure's arguments (to some extent undercut in a footnote in the 1923 version of the text which voiced strong disapproval of the cinema's more recent embrace of 'the novel of episode' and melodrama) found their expression in his model of the cinematic capture of time and history as process and duration, in images of the dynamic and the mathematical sublime ('I would point out, too, the profound universe of the microscopic infinite, and perhaps—tomorrow—of the telescopic infinite, the un-dreamed of dance of atoms and stars, the shadows under the sea as they begin to be shot with light')[204] and in metaphors of origin and evolution. It is indeed striking that so many studies of the cinema from the 1920s offered accounts of a future film written in language as rhetorical and utopian as that of the Dicksons in the 1890s, as if to gather up the first aspirations for, and dreams of, cinema and project them forward into a new future, not yet begun.

The genesis of the film work, Faure suggested, lay in the individual creative genius, and in the ideal film author, producer, photographer and actor (or 'cinemimic', in Faure's preferred term) would be one and the same. It was here that Chaplin first enters the discursive frame: 'a new art presupposes a new artist'. The figure of Chaplin also allowed Faure to draw comparisons between the American and the French film. The latter, Faure argued, is a 'bastard form of a degenerate theatre', while the American film

is a new art, full of immense perspectives, full of the promise of a great future. For the Americans are primitive and at the same time barbarous, which accounts for the strength and vitality which they infuse into the cinema. It is among them that the cinema will, I believe, assume its full significance as plastic drama in action, occupying time through its own movement and carrying with it its own space, of a kind that places it, balances it, and gives it the social and psychological value it has for us. It is natural that when a new art appears in the world it should choose a new people which has hitherto no really personal art. Especially when this new art is bound up, though the medium of human gesture, with the power, definiteness and firmness of action. Especially, too, when this new people is accustomed to introduce into every department of life an increasingly complicated mechanical system, one that more and more hastens to produce, associate and precipitate movements; and especially when this art could not exist without the most accurate scientific apparatus of a kind that has behind it no traditions, and is organized, as it were, physiologically, with the race that employs it.[205]

European 'degeneration' was thus contrasted with American 'primitivism'. The terms of barbarism would be employed in entirely derogatory terms in film writings towards the end of the decade, when the 'transatlantic domination' of cinema by America had become a significant cause for concern in Europe. For the critic Rudolf Messel, whose *This Film Business* was published in 1928, Americans were either money-obsessed immigrants, or sex-obsessed cowboys, 'not very far removed', in Messel's words, 'from the primordial ape ... And here in this purely animal and absolutely primitive instinct we have the keynote of ninety per cent of American films'.[206] The fantasies projected on the screens of the movie houses and picture palaces, whether of Egypt or Old England, were held to indicate a desire for the depth, cultural and historical, otherwise lacking in the new nation: the irony being, of course, that the screen itself provided only the mere illusion of depth. For Faure, writing a decade earlier, American primitivism, which was also American modernity, was primordial. It found its form in cinema's 'protoplasmic' energy, to borrow Eisenstein's term, in which animation and animism became one and the same, and in which entirely new forces were born and new time–space relations came into being.

The second part of *The Art of Cineplastics* is entitled *The Art of Charlie Chaplin*. Here Faure argued:

So far only one man, and only one, has shown that he entirely understands the new art of the cinema. Only one man has shown that he knows how to use this art as if it were a keyboard where all the elements of sense and feeling that determined the attitude and form of things merge and convey in one cineographic expression the complex revelation of their inner life and quality ... Charlie Chaplin is the first man to create a drama that is purely cineplastic, in which the action does not illustrate a sentimental fiction or a moralistic intention but creates a monumental whole.[207]

In Faure's account, Chaplin was Everyman, expressing the extremes of the mind—knowledge and desire—in his movement and gesture, the dance of his two poorly shod feet. He thinks, Faure asserted, 'cinematographically; therefore he can not express his thought except by giving it the tangible shape of which chance has given him the symbol'.[208] Faure ascribed to Chaplin the power of creation that he had earlier attributed to the cinematic medium: in this logic, Chaplin thus becomes the cinema itself.

This conceit runs through French avant-garde film criticism of the late 1910s and 1920s, in work by Louis Delluc, Louis Aragon, and others, and in much of the writing about cinema of the period a syllogism emerges which could be expressed as 'cinema = movement, Chaplin = movement, therefore Chaplin = cinema'. The representation of Chaplin and his cinema as autotelic (a version, indeed, of the 'fitness' which Freeburg located in the relationship between setting and action in *Caligari*) emerged in articles such as Delluc's 'On Decor' (1918), in which Delluc wrote of the 'inversion' of values between the animate and inanimate in Chaplin's films, a dimension of his cinema which also became a focus in Walter Benjamin's writings on film. In 1923, Eisenstein noted: 'The lyrical effects of a whole series of Chaplin scenes is inseparable from the attractional quality of the specific mechanics of his movement': motion and emotion are equivalent.[209] For Gilbert Seldes, 'The little figure...is always a complete creation; it is not Chaplin and it is not a new combination of characteristics Chaplin has seen in other comedies; it is a whole, separate thing, living by its own energies.'[210] The Russian formalist critic Victor Shklovsky observed: 'Chaplin's movements and all his films are not conceived in words or sketches but in the flashing of black and white shadows. He has broken finally and completely with theatre and for that reasons he does of course have the right to the title of the first film actor.'[211]

For the French poet and novelist Philippe Soupault, one of the founders of the Surrealist movement and co-editor with André Breton and Louis Aragon of the avant-garde journal *Littérature*, 'the cinema has brought us a new desire'. Soupault wrote this in a 1930 essay entitled 'The American Influence in France', in which he extended arguments he had made in an article on 'The "U.S.A. Cinema"', published in the little magazine *Broom: An International Magazine of the Arts* in September 1923. *Broom* was edited by two Americans, Harold Loeb and Matthew Josephson; Josephson, also a contributing editor to the magazine *transition*, was introduced to the Parisian Dadaists by Man Ray and used the pages of *Broom* to proclaim an American Dada and 'the Age of the Machine'. The journal also drew its energies from the Parisian Dadaists' and, subsequently, the Surrealists' passion for all things American, and it was here that film played a central role, becoming a reflecting and refracting mirror-screen for each country's perceptions of itself and of the other nation and culture.

Broom, like *transition*, published a number of articles exploring the cultural interactions between France and America, and opening up the question of which way the influence was working—from America to Paris, or from Paris (and Europe more generally) to America. The first issue of the journal contained an article (by Emmy Veronica Sanders) entitled 'America Invades Europe' which was in fact highly critical of the tendency to equate Europe with the Parisian avant-garde and modern America 'with one or two small coteries', and expressed the hope that *Broom* would look beyond it. Her article also opened up a debate about American machine-culture that ran throughout the issues of *Broom* in its two years, as it did throughout *The Little Review*. The intellect of the American elite, Sanders described as 'panting, tonguelolling, movie-movie, electrically lighted braininess; true offspring of its parent, the Machine': 'If an ingeniously constructed, intricate little piece of machinery, a dainty little thing with cogs and wheels and flashes of iron and steel, should suddenly be given a human voice to pour its "soul" into song—to transmute itself into a "poem"—it would stand revealed as a bit of writing by Miss [Marianne] Moore.'[212]

Matthew Josephson's article 'Made in America'—a response to Harold Loeb's article 'Foreign Exchange'—rejected the homogenous view of American artists abroad given by Loeb and was critical of much contemporary French literature. It was in the writings of Aragon, Breton, Eluard, Soupault, and Tzara that Josephson found 'a mood of humour instead of pathos, aggression instead of doubt, and complete freedom of method for [*sic*: from] the restrictions of the previous age': 'To be at least as daring as the mechanical geniuses of the age which has attained the veritable realization of the miracles forecast in primitive fables. To be the prophets alike, the fable-makers for the incredible ages to come! The machine is not "flattening us out" nor "crushing us". [He was referring here to a claim Edmund Wilson had recently made in an article in *Vanity Fair*.] The machine is our magnificent slave, our fraternal genius. We are a new and hardier race, friend to the sky-scraper and the subterranean railway as well.'[213]

The references to the mechanical genius and the prophet were surely intended to invoke Thomas Edison, whose biographer Josephson would become some three decades later (1959), and whose 'realization' of those primitive miracles—the creation of light by means of electricity, the reproduction of reality in the moving image—was part of the fantasy of the technological recreation of life itself. Josephson appears to have been suggesting that literary daring, of a kind equivalent to, but not parasitic upon, the Edisonian miracle, lay in the formal and linguistic experiments of Breton, Aragon, Eluard *et al.*, and not, as he described it, in Jean Cocteau's 'unmusical and irritating verses which refer to expresses, steam-boats, aeroplanes, the unconscious, the rubber heel, etcetera, thereby bringing his writings squarely up to 1922'.[214]

Moreover, Josephson found in the French writers he admired a 'fundamental attitude of aggression, humor, unequivocal affirmation which ... comes most naturally from America, with its high speed and tension'. 'Our preposterous naive profound film', he stated, 'will never be surpassed by artistic or literary German cinemas. No cities will quite equal what New York or Chicago or Tulsa have ... Reacting to purely American sources, to the at once bewildering and astounding American panorama, which only Chaplin and a few earnest unsung film-directors have mirrored, we may yet amass a new folk-lore out of the domesticated miracles of our time.'[215]

The brief reference to Chaplin opens up further the relationship between the European avant-garde and American popular culture. *Broom* included in one of its issues Léger's drawings of Chaplin as a fragmented, mechanical body with which he would open and close his film Ballet Mécanique; he also illustrated Iwan Goll's cinema poem of 1920, *Die Chapliniade* (*Chaplinade*). Léger, Goll, and Gertrude Stein found in the early Chaplin films forms of rhythm, repetition, and automatization which they saw as performances of the essence of the cinematic machine and of modernity itself, and as profoundly at odds with the movements of plot and story. The special film issue of *Broom* included Soupault's 'The "U.S.A Cinema"', and Robert Alden Sanborn on 'Motion Picture Dynamics', in both of which Chaplin stood for the film medium itself. 'With a stroke of his cane', Soupault wrote, 'such a smiling magician was he, Charlie Chaplin was able to give an extraordinary vigor, an incredible superiority, to the American movies ... The "U.S.A." cinema has thrown light on all the beauty of our time, all the mystery of modern mechanics...Everything was revivified with a single stroke.'[216] The pun on the 'stroke' of Chaplin's cane as the magician's wand conjures up the figure of Edison—Josephson's hero—as 'The Wizard of Menlo Park'.

For Soupault, the 'new power' of the cinema—exemplified by Chaplin—had tranformed French poetry and the theatre—while 'painting, which is always a little behind poetry, will yet learn to know the conditions imposed by the cinema'. He ended his article, however, with a warning 'not to go back on one's tracks and look at things the wrong way'.[217] This reverse tendency was represented, for Soupault, by *The Cabinet of Dr Caligari*—'a decisive move backwards', an 'antiquated novelty'—a view recalling Josephson's reference to the literary and artistic cinema of Germany which could not compete with the American movies. Blaise Cendrars, in an essay in *Broom*,[218] described *Caligari* as 'hysterical' and 'sentimental', contrasting it with US cinema—'Hurray for the cowboys'—opening up the question of a gendered response to, and a gendering of, cinematic styles. In contrast to Lindsay, Freeburg and Seldes, Cendrars found *Caligari* 'theatrical' and 'not cinematic', and criticized the disunity between 'real characters' and the 'unreal set': 'It heaps discredit on all modern art because the subject of modern painters (Cubism) is not the hypersensibility of a madman, but rather equilibrium, tension and mental geometry.'[219]

American–European cultural relations in this period, as well as competing definitions of modernism and counter-modernism, and, as Gilbert Seldes pointed out, 'a history of taste in America, and particularly a history of the vexing relationship between highbrows and the popular arts',[220] could indeed be traced through responses to Chaplin and *The Cabinet of Dr Caligari* respectively. In 1924, the periodical *Disque vert* proclaimed 'Charlie est dadaiste';[221] for Léger, on his first viewing of a Chaplin film, he was 'Charlot cubiste', and he made a marionette figure in his image. For the artists at the Bauhaus, Chaplin represented, as Peter Conrad has noted, man's merger with the machine; for the painter and experimental film-maker Hans Richter, his 'technological acting' demonstrated that the body consists of 'levers, weights and pivots' (like the camera).[222] Chaplin again, and as for Faure, became identical with the cinematic apparatus. Yet Chaplin's films were to a significant extent protests against the rule of the machine and the mechanization of man. To this extent, he figured the very ambivalence towards machine culture which lay at the heart of modernism.

The cinema of Chaplin was also central to Gilbert Seldes's early, highly influential study *The Seven Lively Arts,* a defence and celebration of popular culture, including film, jazz, comic-strips, musical comedy, and vaudeville, written while Seldes was living in Paris during 1923. Elie Faure's *The Art of Cineplastics*, as well as Alexander Bakshy's articles on film (many of them published in the journal *Theatre Arts Monthly*, which gave significant space to discussion of cinema and film aesthetics throughout the 1920s) were a strong influence on Seldes's approach to the cinema, disseminated in his articles for *The Dial, The New Republic*, and *Scribner's* as well as in his books on the subject. As Michael Kammen has written, Seldes also shared with his contemporaries Matthew Josephson and George Jean Nathan 'an unabashed enthusiasm ... for popular culture [which] stimulated the genesis of a transformation that required a generation to complete'.[223] For Seldes, there was 'no opposition between the great and the lively arts', and they were united in their opposition 'to the middle or bogus arts'.[224]

Seldes's title—*The Seven Lively Arts*—referred back to the short-lived magazine *The Seven Arts*, begun in 1916, as well, as Kammen points out, to late nineteenth- and early twentieth-century writings and commentaries on the 'seven arts', including those by avant-garde writers in Paris towards the close of the nineteenth century, which were often explorations of the relationships between, and possible syntheses of, the arts of painting, sculpture, music, and so on. The emergence of cinema, as we have seen, produced a new desire on the part of writers and critics to enumerate and define the various arts, with film becoming 'the seventh art'. Seldes, however, was not greatly in thrall to the Muses, and he suggested that his numbering of the popular or 'lively' arts was a convenient fiction.[225] While film played a significant role in his study, it did not serve to reorganize the other forms of artistic expression and entertainment alongside which it sat.

Seldes devoted three chapters of *The Seven Lively Arts* to film: 'The Keystone the Builders Rejected', ' "I Am Here to-Day": Charlie Chaplin' and, towards the book's close, 'An Open Letter to the Movie Magnates'. In his discussion of 'Keystone' (the production company for comedy films founded by the actor and director Mack Sennett in 1912, the year in which he left Griffith's Biograph studio) in the mid-1910s, Seldes called the films to come from this stable 'the most despised, and by all odds the most interesting, films produced in America'. Sennett was, Seldes argues, by contrast with Griffith and Thomas Ince, 'doing with the instruments of the moving picture precisely those things which could not be done with any instrument but the camera, and could appear nowhere if not on the screen. This does not mean that nothing but slap-stick comedy is proper to the cinema; it means only that everything in slap-stick *is* cinematographic … The drama film is almost always wrong, the slap-stick almost always right; and it is divinely just that the one great figure of the screen should have risen out of the Keystone studios.'[226] This was of course Chaplin, who became a Keystone comic in late 1913, though the developing style of his comedy sat at odds with the split-second cutting and chaotic performances that characterized Sennett's films. While Seldes was concerned to chart the changing nature of Chaplin's films, and the birth of the iconic 'tramp', the point of his chapter was to defend Keystone slap-stick comedy and its actors. He also noted the popularity of Chaplin's early films in Paris at the time of his writing, by contrast with the situation in New York: 'you have to go to squalid streets and disreputable neighborhoods if you want to see Chaplin.'[227]

In the chapter devoted to Chaplin, Seldes wrote: 'It is a miracle that there should arise in our time a figure wholly in the tradition of the great clowns.'[228] The French name for Chaplin—'Charlot'—'which is and is not Charlie will serve for that figure on the screen, the created image which is, and at the same time is more than, Charlie Chaplin, and is less':

> Like every great artist in whatever medium, Charlie has created the mask of himself—many masks, in fact—and the first of these, the wanderer, came in the Keystone comedies. It was there that he first detached himself from life and began to live in another world, with a specific rhythm of his own, as if the pulse-beat in him changed and was twice or half as fast as that of those who surrounded him. He created then that trajectory across the screen which is absolutely his own line of movement. No matter what the actual facts are, the curve he plots is always the same. It is of one who seems to enter from a corner of the screen, becomes entangled or involved in a force greater than himself as he advances upward and to the centre; there he spins like a marionette in a whirlpool, is flung from side to side, always in a parabola which seems centripetal until the madness of the action hurls him to refuge or compels him to flight at the opposite end of the screen. He wanders in, a stranger, an impostor, an anarchist; and passes again, buffeted, but unchanged.[229]

In Seldes's representations of 'line', suggestions are connected between Chaplin's films, the animated cartoon, and the 'abstract films' of the avant-garde. As Esther Leslie and others have shown, animation—emblematic of 'popular culture'—fascinated modernist theorists and artists, shaping their theories and their art in its own shifting and subversive forms. For Seldes, the 'line of movement'—which becomes, in his open letter to the movie magnates, a line of beauty—transmuted into a vortex—Chaplin 'spins like a marionette in a whirlpool'—as if Seldes were himself drawing and animating the trajectory of a line across the page or the screen.

If his discourse was intended to render Chaplin as an abstract line and force, however, his approach was also one that he differentiated from that of the 'intellectuals who so reduced Charlie to angles that the angles no longer made them laugh'.[230] The 'line' is also the line of the drama, and, in his recounting of every detail of plot and character in *The Pawnshop*, Seldes showed his commitment to the 'action' of the film. Yet it was 'movement' with which he was primarily concerned, and he prefaced his discussion of the film with T. S. Eliot's comment: 'The egregious merit of Chaplin is that he has escaped in his own way from the realism of the cinema and invented a *rhythm*. Of course the unexplored opportunities of the cinema for eluding realism must be very great.'[231] There are also strong echoes, in the passage quoted above, of Faure's writings on 'cineplastics' and on Chaplin, and of Alexander Bakshy's insistence that 'the only real thing in the motion picture is movement without which all its objects would appear as lifeless shadows': 'By a quick succession of scenes the film makes the whole world dance to its tune—mountains, rivers, buildings, human beings.'[232] As Seldes wrote to the 'movie magnates', the cinema is '*movement governed by light*' and (with more than a glance, perhaps, to Faure) 'the imagination of mankind in action'.[233]

4

'The cinema mind':

Film Criticism and Film Culture in 1920s Britain

'The Critic in Film History', an article by the writer, film critic, and cultural commentator Alistair Cooke, was published in Charles Davy's 1938 collection *Footnotes to the Film*. By the late 1930s, film in Britain was extensively integrated into intellectual and cultural life, and film criticism was to a significant extent an established form of writing. Nonetheless, Cooke argued that the film critic (by which he meant 'not a writer on the theory of film, but a practising reviewer')[1] continued to be confronted by difficulties particular to the nature of the medium.

> No art, entertainment, or whatnot, is more direct than the film. It may be that whatever reserve a critic wishes to keep for himself, he involuntarily yields more of it than he knows. For the movies do not represent emotion, they communicate it almost irresistibly by magnifying and quickening the way emotion comes to us in real life, that is, through optics and dynamics. We cannot say at the moment where film criticism ends and literary or political criticism begins because ideas come at us in the movies with all the beautiful confusion of life itself—we may be moved one moment by a line of dialogue, at the next by the look of the veins on somebody's hands, by the sound of a train's siren fading as the countryside fades. Whether we like it or not, we are *in* a movie all the time, we're not seeing, as we do in the theatre, a level picture grouped at a given distance. We are on trains and falling down cliffs, we are watching with a quick turn of the head a whip hurtling towards a man's ankle, we are staring face downward in a pool, we are at one second watching from the gallery, at the next we are in the stalls, the wings, or the flies. It is we that lean back in chairs and see sympathetic faces come to *us* for pity's sake, and a dreaded door opens suddenly in *our* face. But then, by the snipping of a pair of shears, we are outside looking imperturbably on at

a conversation between two people up there, a conversation that is private from every other person in the plot. We are at once audience, confidant, and victim. If a critic is an assessor of something that is presented to him, then we shall have no film critics until the psychologists and the eye specialists get together and tell us when and how and why we react to such things as double-exposure, to a magnified tear, to dissolves, wipes, movement across the screen and movement into your face; for these are the mechanised units with which the movies attack your nervous system and leave you battered and bedraggled and a willing sucker for a piece that as a literary product, or an example of the best that is known and thought, is pathetic besides the play at the local repertory theatre which leaves you, behind a yawning hand, laughing softly at its naïve conventions, at the archness of its movement, at the engrossed naïveté of its motives.

To practise film criticism honestly but without pain, it is necessary to grasp this dilemma, that we do not yet know the social or artistic power of the movies.[2]

Cooke's polemical article, with its strong echoes of Gilbert Seldes's arguments in *Movies for the Millions* (1937) was (like the introduction to Cooke's 1937 anthology of British and American film criticism, *Garbo and the Night Watchmen*) pitted against 'pretentious' film theorizing, written by those with little sense of 'the vital processes of film construction, about the actual moments in a film that give it speed, fluency or what else'.[3] Cooke followed Seldes in his insistence on cinematic movement—'the pictures have to move ... America has always been *on the* move and has *kept moving*', in Seldes's words—and his sense of the as yet unknown nature of the desire for the cinema. As Seldes wrote: '*we do not know why we go to the movies.* The minute we do know, we will be able to get more out of the movies.'[4]

Posing the question of the critic's relationship to the culture on which he comments, Cooke contrasted the detachment of T. S. Eliot's critical stance with H. L. Mencken's 'complete surrender' to the material, 'in the hope that you will reflect some of its contemporary *tempo* and flavour'. Mencken's approach, Cooke suggested, risked rapid obsolescence, though in its best form it had the potential to represent its age. The alternatives he constructed took on a new coloration when applied to film, precisely because, as the quotation above suggests, the medium refused the position of Olympian detachment to the critic, in that it acted through the impact of 'optics and dynamics' on the sensory system to confound all impersonal critical judgement; 'the work does not come to them primarily as a concept; it comes directly as a sensation'.[5] Nor, he argued, should the critic seek to detach him or herself from the spectacle, because film was above all a democratic medium and, indeed, a 'folk art' akin to jazz music.

There are echoes in Cooke's account of Hugo Münsterberg's physiological model of cinema's effects on the spectator, and of I. A. Richards's literary studies of the 1920s (in particular *Principles of Literary Criticism* (1924) and *Science and Poetry* (1926)), which explored the ways in which the text impacted on the 'nervous system' of the reader, and his project to measure aesthetic responses, as Vernon Lee had attempted to do in the arena of the visual arts. Cooke's suggestion that worthwhile film criticism would not develop until 'the psychologists and the eye specialists get together' to explore the nature of cinematic desire also drew upon the now familiar theme of the relationship between retinal and mental reception in film spectatorship, and of the ways in which the mind or brain would process the images entering through the eye.

Cooke's article was a relatively late contribution to the question of what film criticism should be and do, and of the ways in which film—the 'new art'—would require new forms of language and expression particular to the unprecedented qualities of its medium. In the previous chapter, I touched on the writings of a number of British film critics and commentators—including Robert Herring, Eric Elliott, and Ernest Betts—whose writings exhibited a particular concern with the question of filmic stasis and motion. This chapter takes a broader look at the development of writing about cinema in the Britain of the 1920s, including discussions of the cinema in literary and cultural periodicals and regular newspaper film columns. It examines the work of the Film Society, founded in 1925, and its cultural significance for a range of writers on the cinema and for the reception of film in Britain as a whole. Further topics include an exploration of the ways in which the phenomena of the drama turned film critic shaped writing about cinema in this period, and the writing of women film critics, who played a substantial role in the early years of film criticism. The contributions in this field of Iris Barry and C. A. Lejeune are explored in detail, with the discussion also raising broader questions about the gendering of cinema spectatorship and critical responses to the new medium.

Film writing of many kinds—from brief newspaper columns to substantial historical and critical studies—proliferated in the 1920s. As Rachael

Low notes, the 1920s was the decade in which 'people started treating the film seriously in Britain':

Important papers with regular film correspondents in 1919 were the *Daily News*, which later became the *News Chronicle*, with E. A. Baughan; the *Evening News* with W. G. Faulkner, who left and went into the film trade in November 1921 and was succeeded by Jympson Harmon; and the *Westminster Gazette*, with Macer Wright. Other papers began to include reviews and information, at first often as a side line to dramatic criticism. Iris Barry, previously critic on the *Spectator*, joined the *Daily Mail* in 1925. The *Daily Express*, *The Times*, and G. A. Atkinson on the *Daily Telegraph*, frequently gave news and criticism. Walter Mycroft wrote for the *Evening Standard* and the *Illustrated Sunday Herald*. Ivor Montagu, after writing for *The Observer*, where he followed Angus Macphail, joined *The Sunday Times* at the end of 1927 and was followed on *The Observer* by C. A. Lejeune in 1928. Both McPhail and Montagu had written for *Granta* when at Cambridge. Lejeune, having started as critic on the *Manchester Guardian* in 1922, wrote for a wide, educated and liberal public, and with Iris Barry was one of the first real film critics. Most of the weeklies were slower to take regular notice of the cinema, although the *Bystander* had a feature called 'Picture Plays as seen from the Stalls' in 1923. Such papers as the *English Review*, *Fortnightly Review*, *London Mercury*, *Drawing and Design*, *Illustrated London News* and *New Statesman* noted the phenomenon from time to time with varying degrees of friendliness.[6]

A large number of film magazines had become established in Britain, as in other countries, by this time. The late 1910s and early 1920s saw the creation in France of a number of journals and 'little magazines' devoted to 'film as an art', including *Le Film* (1914–19), Pierre Henri's *Ciné pour Tous* (1919–23), *Cinémagazine* (1921-) and Louis Delluc's *Cinéa* (1921–23). These were not matched in the British context until the emergence in 1927 of the film journal *Close Up*, the topic of my next chapter. Prior to this, there were, in Britain (in addition to the technical and trade journals, the most significant of which were *Kinematograph Weekly*, *The Cinema* and *The Bioscope*) numerous fan magazines, contributing and responsive to the cultural fascination with 'film stars'. *Moving Picture World* was first published in 1910 and, as D. L. Mahieu has noted, 'spawned a number of imitators'.[7] These included, in Britain, *The Pictures*, founded in 1911, which began with a focus on film plots but increasingly moved to discussion of actors and film gossip, *The Picturegoer*, first published in 1913, which merged with *The Pictures* in 1914, and the *Picture Show*, which started in 1919 and continued until 1960, and which provided interviews with Hollywood stars. 'By

1920', LeMahieu writes, 'fan magazines attracted an audience substantial enough for the popular press to adopt some of their features, including gossip columns such as "Cinema Notes" in the *Daily Express*.'[8]

The development of these magazines in relation to popular culture, the 'star' system and the early twentieth-century cult of celebrity raises questions which are, for the most part, beyond the remit of this study. The popular film and fan magazines did, however, play an important role in relation to the film literature with which this chapter is concerned. They were, to a large extent, the medium against which those critics and commentators committed to film as an art form, and often writing in the more culturally elite or intellectual press were, implicitly or explicitly, reacting. If the question of technology (central to the technical and many of the trade journals) had to be suppressed in order for film's 'mechanical' and 'reproductive' dimensions to be overcome in the name of culture and aesthetics, the rejection of the 'star', 'gossip', and 'film-plot' bases of the popular press and the film magazines was also a significant aspect of the attempt to construct more general principles for the new art of film. This was, furthermore, an attempt to divorce the question of the medium's vast potential from its demotic products, often identified with Hollywood and with the 'Americanization' of culture. The borders and boundaries between popular and elite were never entirely sealed, however, either in the new medium of the film or in the discourses that accompanied it. Iris Barry, for example, wrote film columns for journals and newspapers with very different readerships, including *The Spectator, Adelphi, Vogue*, and *The Daily Mail*: she was also a founding member of the Film Society, an organization committed to cinema as an art.[9]

An historian of the press in Britain, writing in 1934, noted the importance of photography in English newspapers: '*The Sketch* and *The Mirror* are daily organs whose *raison d'être* are their illustrations, and the success which these two papers have had shows to what extent the modern mind has become a cinema mind.'[10] The 'cinema mind' took on a further dimension at the point at which film reviews, criticism and listings started to become a standard feature in newspapers, with stills illustrating the films under discussion. The film column served to 'animate', through its description, the still photograph, which in turn functioned as a form of advertisement for the film.

The surge in writing about cinema in Britain in the 1920s operated within important changes in the production and reception of film, not least the steady decrease in the number of British films made and exhibited. This was to some extent a result of the fact that the British industry, like the French, had not recovered from the years of World War I and its immediate aftermath. During this period the American film industry had gained dominance abroad, with companies making the blind (sight unseen) and block booking of their films advantageous to British distributors or 'renters', though the decline had in fact preceded the war years. By 1923 only 10 per cent of films shown in Britain were made in the country, a figure that fell to 5 per cent by 1926. In 1927, the Government, at the urging of the industry, imposed the Cinematograph Films Act, the intention of which was to promote and encourage the British film industry in order to increase the number of films made. At the same time the blind booking of foreign films and block booking were respectively banned and restricted, and a quota (the percentage of British films to be shown, which rose to 20 per cent by 1933) was imposed on renters and exhibitors.[11]

The perceived need to improve the quality of British films was at the heart of much of the writing on cinema in the 1920s, accompanied by the view that a major factor in achieving this goal would be the education of those in the industry through familiarity with the best of foreign (especially European) cinema. Critics who held such aspirations often found themselves writing in opposition to film censorship, and the late 1920s, in particular, saw numerous campaigns against the banning of films, including Soviet ones. Towards the end of the decade, it was the coming of sound and 'the talkies' that dominated discussions of film in every forum, demanding a re-evaluation of tenets that had come to define the medium.

This, then, is a background to the writing on film explored in this chapter, in which I focus on some of the institutions of cinema in the period (the Film Society in particular) as well as on the forms taken by early film criticism, including the search by writers on cinema for new modes of expression adequate to the new medium. The film critics whose writings I examine were acutely aware of the need to forge a new critical language of film and cinema and often described their task as an experimental one, in the process of formation, and as necessar- ily provisional. The film critic C. A. (Caroline) Lejeune, in her 1931 study *Cinema: A Review of Thirty Years' Achievement*, in the context of an apology to readers who had complained of the use of 'jargon' in her newspaper columns, (instanced by 'constructive cutting' and 'three-dimensional movie'), wrote:

> If any such phrases have found their way into this book, I apologise, and offer as an excuse the rather curious and belated position of the cinema among the other arts. Every other form of expression, music, drama, painting, poetry, sculpture, drawing, has its own critical language shaped and understood by usage through the ages; the movie alone is subject to a criticism that has neither established measure nor technical currency. We are treating of movie in a medium that is, in its very essence, intractable; we are faced with the still unresolved problem of conveying, in the sequence of placed word and phrase, the ubiquity and simultaneity of our subject. In this case we must always be, I am afraid, a little slow in expression for those people who feel and live and think movie, a little precious for those others who find in movie nothing but a mass of entertainment to be applauded, presented and dismissed with the usual directness of the good newspaper correspondent. We stumble along, doing the best we can with the old terms while we try to rough out a new vocabulary, borrowing from this art and from that, compromising, slipping in a tentative technicality here and there; without quite the courage to invent, as the movie actually demands, a new vernacular, we invest stock words with strange meanings and combinations of phrase with new connotations, relying on the reader's patience to carry us through this period of transition and experiment in the chronicles of the screen.[12]

For Lejeune, as for so many other critics of the period, it was not only that film was, in Rudolf Arnheim's phrase, 'entirely new'—'For the first time in history a new art form is developing and we can say that we were there'—but that it demanded a new critical language, 'a new vernacular'.[13] As Iris Barry wrote, in her 1926 study *Let's Go to the Pictures*: 'I ask then: critics arise, invent terms, lay down canons, derive from your categories, heap up nonsense with sense, and, when you have done, the cinemas will still be open and we can all flock in as proudly as we do now to the theatre and the opera, which indeed it is regarded as meritorious and noble to support.'[14] My discussion, necessarily selective, examines the discursive dimensions of film criticism in the Britain of the 1920s, written at a point at which, as so many critics noted, the terms of description and evaluation were still in the process of formation and had, moreover, to be applied to a medium not only defined by its movement but one in the process of rapid technological change and development.

Writing about Cinema in the British Periodical Press

In 1934, the Irish playwright and theatre critic St John Ervine delivered 'an oration' to the Union Society of University College London on the topic of 'The Alleged Art of the Cinema'.[15] A decade earlier, the *Spectator*'s film critic Bertram Higgins had taken Ervine to task for his attack on the cinema in an address to the Stoll Club. 'Even if he so mistrusts the mechanism of the Cinema', Higgins wrote, 'that he denies it any aesthetic possibilities, he must recognize that its aims, as well as its actual effects, are more than merely photographic.'[16] Ervine was a cinephobe *après la lettre*, and his later address to the Union Society suggests that no conversion to the new medium, or to its claims to artistic status, had taken place. 'The Alleged Art of the Cinema' rehearsed debates that had become very familiar by the 1930s. Ervine attacked both the medium and its audiences, asserting that while the 'mechanical efficiency' of cinema is great, 'its spiritual and intellectual character is beneath contempt'.[17] 'Its themes', he wrote, 'are concerned with evanescent and fleeting things, things of the moment, matters of detail, actual events.' Its vaunted 'continuous performance' is merely a matter of going 'on and on and on' and, in any case, 'the unreeling of a film is subject to continual interruption … The picture is as intelligible whether it is seen straight through, or middle or end first'. The rapid disappearance of films from the circuit (a matter of regret for so many of the critics I have discussed, and a prime mover in the creation of film clubs) was taken as an indication that the ephemeral nature of the film did not bear revival. The only way in which cinema could be understood as an art, Ervine concluded, was that: 'It does to a large degree express the spirit of our time: that quick, impulsive, unreflecting spirit which must always be doing something, as if mere action were enough.'[18]

Ervine had found a cinephobic ally in the French poet Georges Duhamel, whose rejection of the medium was also an attack on American society, and of whom Walter Benjamin wrote, in his essay 'The Work of Art in the Age of Mechanical Reproduction': 'Duhamel, who detests the film and knows nothing of its significance, though something of its structure, notes [of cinematic spectatorship]: "I can no longer think what I want to think. My thoughts have been replaced by moving images".'[19] Ervine quoted at some length from Duhamel's *America, the Menace*, noting, in particular, Duhamel's rejection of the 'dynamism' of the cinema, which, in Duhamel's words, 'snatches away from us the images over which we should like to linger and dream ... it offers itself at once, like a harlot. It tells us at once all that it knows ... In its essence it is motion, but it leaves us dull and motionless, as if paralysed'.[20] The difference between theatre and film spectatorship was at the heart of Ervine's critique; a theatre audience, he claimed, 'is lively and animated. Between the acts it talks very gaily ... It is alive. But an audience at a cinema sits in a lethargic state, scarcely daring to whisper between pictures, and looking for the most part as if something had hit it. It definitely looks doped'.[21] The image of the narcotic effect of the film on the spectator is a familiar one, but it is nonetheless significant that it was intertwined, in Ervine's account, with the question of speech and silence, represented, in his account, by the animated talk of the audience in the theatre, contrasted with the barest of whispers in the cinema.

The greater part of 'The Alleged Art of the Cinema' was given over to discussion of the current state of film criticism, proceeding from the view that an art (or a medium with pretensions to being an art) receives the criticism it deserves: 'To read about the cinema is almost as boring as to go to it. There is some vulgarity in the moving pictures which easily communicates itself to those whose business it is to criticise them. It robs them of any ability to write English which they may have possessed, and leaves their mind as shallow as their subject.'[22] The exceptions, Ervine suggested, were drama critics who had turned to cinema criticism, and women.

Drama critics were, indeed, very often the authors of the articles on the cinema. The history of the relationship between film and theatre is both complex and contested, and while some critics have seen the identity between stage and screen as closest in the early years of cinema in which film had, like theatre, 'presented a flowing tableau in a fixed space to a spectator (the camera and, of course, the viewer) who was also set in a fixed place',[23] others have argued that, with the rise of the feature film in the 1910s, 'films became much more like plays in the kind of narratives they related'.[24] The articles that began to appear in periodical literature in the 1910s were predominantly attempts to define the 'new art', and to find suitable aesthetic and critical categories, the suggestion being that effective film criticism was dependent upon the existence of 'aesthetic standards'.[25] Underlying many of the discussions was also the uncertainty about the identity of film as a medium and an art in relation to the theatre.

Comparisons were frequently drawn between drama, fiction, and film, although the triumphalist, holistic model of film as gathering up all the other arts in its recreation of life itself had, for the most part, transmuted into a more differentiated model of artistic essences and, in the era of silent film, into a conception of the specificities of conceptual categories and sensory responses, including the separation of the realms of eye and ear. These preoccupations—the status of film as art and its specific aesthetic identity—continued throughout the 1920s, though more specific issues also arose: the hegemony of American cinema and the relative weakness of the British film industry; the Quota Act; film censorship. There was also a consistent concern with the need to differentiate the possibilities of cinema as a medium from commercial films themselves, though the rise of an 'art' cinema—particularly French, German, and Soviet—increasingly gave the critics examples in which the medium and specific films could be discussed in tandem rather than in opposition to each other. In the late 1920s, as I have noted, the coming of sound dominated the approach to cinema, often linked to a sense that the relationship between stage and screen needed to be addressed in new terms. It was significantly harder for critics to define the 'essential' qualities of film once the medium started to talk, and the need to construct an aesthetic divide between dialogue films and stage-plays became at one and the same time more difficult and more imperative.

The established monthlies and reviews such as *The English Review, The Fortnightly Review, The Quarterly Review* and *The Nineteenth Century* (which became *The Nineteenth Century and After*) covered the topic of the cinema no more than half a dozen or so times each between the late 1910s and the 1920s, but each contribution pointed to the urgent necessity of considering the new medium, either aesthetically or in its social dimensions. The latter aspect included questions of morality, regulation, censorship, and the effect of film-viewing upon the child spectator, all topics of some moment in the broader social and political sphere, at a time of widespread concern with the impact of cinema on society.

From the perspective of culture and aesthetics, and by contrast with those journals which included regular film reviews (like the *London Mercury* and the *Spectator*, discussed later in this and in the following chapter) the coverage of cinema was directed towards discussion of film art and the phenomenon of film rather than specific films, though, as I have suggested, this changed quite markedly from the mid-1920s onwards, when 'art' and avant-garde films of the kind shown at the Film Society screenings and cinemas such as the Oxford Street Academy began to provide material for discussion and exemplification. The writings on film in journals and periodicals such as the *Fortnightly* and *The Nineteenth Century* are of some significance, in their revelation of the ways in which the alliances and competitions between the arts were understood and represented, and in their situating of cinema alongside other cultural forms. Practitioners and critics within particular artistic fields divided up the aesthetic territory in ways that at times appeared quite arbitrary, or operated as a trade-off ('Let the stage leave [biographical constructions] alone and the cinema respond by leaving stage-plays alone, and instead take over the department of biography', one periodical critic wrote),[26] while at the same time upholding the generic purity of the individual media.

For a critic writing in the journal *Drama* in 1919, 'there were possibilities of real beauty lying latent in the cinema', and he located these in 'gesture':

> Through gesture the whole story of the play is revealed. Gesture, in a word, is the one form of expression proper to cinema art. Raise the dignity and meaning of the gesture and you raise the dignity and meaning of the film play. Gesture should be studied by the writer of film plays just as the poet studies prosody, the musician harmony, the painter perspective. Dramatic material which is really suitable to this form of expression must be more frequently selected than it is at present. Then when, on the one hand, we see gesture used so that it yields its fullest significance, and when, on the other hand, the material given to it to express is really suited to it, the cinema will take its acknowledged place as a separate art, with its own distinct medium, as an art that has brought a new form of beauty into being.[27]

Bertram Clayton, writing in 1920 in *The Quarterly Review* (the most consistently dismissive towards the cinema of the group of journals under discussion), had been prepared to entertain the possibilities of an art based on a combination of music and pictures, '[which] may result in a new and delightful variation of opera, by which the ear, eye, and intellect may be equally charmed'. His account of film's relation to theatre and drama was nonetheless vexed: 'Though it borrows from the Drama, and sucks much of its life-blood from the Library' (a widespread image of the new medium as both parasite and vampire in relation to the established arts), its only essential connection is with musical accompaniment; 'the eye absolutely refuses to be strained for long while the ear is starved.'[28] Clayton repeated the last phrase in an article for the *Fortnightly Review* published in the following year, arguing that 'the music at these shows is really creating the only atmosphere in which the "silent drama" could be tolerated. The eye absolutely refuses to be strained for long while the ear is starved, but if that organ is well catered for, the other can be more easily coaxed into putting up with a mass of irrelevancies'.[29]

In much of the discussion in the periodicals, the concern with protecting the theatre (and the literature from which narrative cinema took its stories) from incursion by the new medium was paramount. Tensions were undoubtedly fuelled by the fact that drama and theatre critics were, as we have seen, taking on the role of film critics. Opposition to this trend was expressed by, among others, the film actress Betty Balfour, who, writing in 1923 on 'The Art of the Cinema' in the *English Review*, took up cudgels against St John Ervine and argued:

> To appreciate or try to understand Cinema Art one must dispossess oneself of all thoughts of the theatre in particular and of literature and other forms of art in general. Critics whose only knowledge is of the theatre, or of literature or other arts, have no right or qualification to criticise an art of which they are entirely ignorant, and which frequently they do not even attempt to study. Too much damage has been done by these people; they prejudice appreciation of the cinema as an art, and even mislead film artists, both producers and players, into trying to adapt stage technique to the requirements of the film, between which there is little connection. They are, in fact, widely different.[30]

Bryher, co-editor of *Close Up*, also defending the cinema and arguing for the necessity of an improved film criticism, discussed this situation in her *Film Problems of Soviet Russia*:

> Most of the film critics of the various daily, weekly or monthly journals have come to cinematography via dramatic criticism. And if ever there was a gulf between two arts it is between the theatre and the cinema. The cinema depends upon reality; the theatre upon exaggeration…Words are not much good to describe a film. For it is not a play, it is rhythm, and movement, and photography, and cinema-acting, which is utterly removed from theatre-acting, and it needs to be seen, not described. Yet many critics make no effort to see pictures that could give them a standard of criticism.[31]

Bryher's claims are, of course, contentious ones: it could equally be argued that if ever there was a connection between two arts it is between the theatre and the cinema. Her words form a continuum with those of numerous early film aestheticians and modernist and avant-garde film-makers, for whom theatre was 'the contaminating art', from whose tutelage cinema had to emancipate itself in order to become autonomous.[32] Yet the connections between theatre and film inhered not only in such spheres as melodrama and popular spectacle, but also in avant-garde and modernist contexts themselves. As I have suggested, the symbolist theatre and poetic drama of the early twentieth century, often committed to a cult of the ritual and the 'primitive', existed in a strongly symbiotic relationship with the silent, gestural world of early film. Expressionism found its forms in both drama and cinema, as did the political dramaturgy of Bertold Brecht. For the avant-garde writer and playwright Antonin Artaud, film and theatre were profoundly interlinked, and Artaud was intensely involved with cinema during the 1920s and early 1930s, as film actor, scenarist, and theorist. As Christopher Innes has noted, Artaud's theatrical devices corresponded to film techniques: the spotlighting of objects, rhythmic movements, the use of 'single words as the catalyst for extended movement, cries as an accompaniment for action' in a correspondence with the use of subtitles in early silent cinema.[33] One of the tasks of Artaud's 'Theatre of Cruelty' was 'to develop a ritual language by rediscovering universal physical signs, or "hieroglyphs" ':[34] the impulse combines with that of a number of the writers on film whose ideas I discuss, including Vachel Lindsay and H.D. It was with the coming of sound, which he identified with commercialism, that Artaud largely turned against the cinema, rejecting its substitution of words for images, although his last film scenario, *The Butcher's Revolt* (1930), was an experiment with sound, deploying shocking juxtapositions between sound and image.

For the most part, the periodical critics of the period held a rather more conventional view of the nature of the theatre with which they were comparing and contrasting the new medium of film. One drama critic unusually sympathetic towards the popular dimensions of cinema-going, while revealing an awareness of the aesthetic claims of the film medium, was E. A. Baughan, who subsequently became the *Daily News* film critic. 'The cinema is comfortable and restful and you may smoke' Baughan wrote in an article in the *Fortnightly Review* in 1919:

> The whole entertainment, taking place in semi-darkness, has a curious, hypnotic effect. It engages the mind agreeably. Without demanding any special effort for their appreciation, the music and the pictures keep the brain in a state of gentle stimulation ... But that hypnotic calm, produced by the music and the bewildering rapidity of the pictures, is not the chief reason for

the popularity of the cinematograph. It has opened a new world to those who do not read or who cannot afford to go to a theatre except in discomfort, and it has opened a different world.[35]

Absorption in the cinematic space and spectacle was explored by another *Fortnightly Review* critic:

> One goes to the cinema palace in a spirit of inquiry, to find out its secret; one goes again to make sure there is nothing in the pictures, and one comes away a film 'fan'. It is not because of the friendly gloom, that permits young people to hold hands, but because of the never relaxed grip on our thoughts—no tedious waits, little mental effort with complete absorption of mind, forgetfulness of worries: in a word, Nirvana … The appeal is wide, for the servant girl and the scientist respond to it alike.[36]

For Baughan, however, such surrender to the film-world was ultimately inadequate to the critical task of aesthetic definition and evaluation. *Pace* Cooke's terms, absorption would need to be balanced by detachment. The role of the critic, Baughan suggested, was to fill the gap between the commercial producers and the indifferent intellectuals:

> What is not yet generally recognised, especially by those of us who have given our lives to literature, drama, music and the plastic arts, is that the cinematograph is itself an art, with its own aesthetic could we but formulate it. The producers of films are very clever and able men, but they have not had the leisure or the desire to think theoretically of the art they practise. Cultivated men who might have helped them have stood aside in the easy attitude of scorn … the artistic side of the cinematograph is in a state of chaos … The intellectual rulers of mankind cannot afford to ignore an art which appeals to millions and speaks a universal language to all the peoples of the world.[37]

In his account of the genealogy of the cinematic medium, from the early discovery that photography could record action and that the public 'was interested in seeing these moving pictures', Baughan argued that the lack of attention hitherto paid to the definition of film as an art form in its own right was due at least in part to the increasing concentration on narrative in cinema: 'Gradually the pictures were connected by a story. Then the story became the chief thing.'[38] Films became longer, and 'the producer of films looked to drama and to the novel as his inspiration. He could not be expected suddenly to formulate a new art.'[39] The result was, he suggested, that producers 'padded' their film stories in ways that ran counter to the swiftness of the medium:

The telling of stories by moving pictures has been based on the telling of stories by words and action combined, *i.e.*, by drama. The cinematograph has nothing to do with words. It is possible to tell a complete and elaborate story on the screen without using a single word in explanation of it ... The real aim of the cinematograph is not to *tell* a tale, but to *show* one. Pictures in action are its medium of expression. They may and do suggest words, but the spectator must make them for himself. A novel, on the other hand, may suggest pictures by means of words—just the opposite of the cinematograph—but that depends on the imagination of the reader. Drama gives you both pictures and words, but then it lacks the power of explanation of the novel and cinematograph, and is fenced around by all kinds of difficulties of time and space ... The cinematograph must not rely, as it does, on actuality if it means to enter the realm of art. It must select and combine, and to do this it must adopt some kind of artistic convention.[40]

What, then, were these conventions? Baughan states: 'I would boldly begin by casting out the semblance of speech. The cinematograph gives us silent drama. It is practically a wordless play.' Indeed, although he was intent on arguing that moving pictures must develop their own aesthetic conventions, to be differentiated from those of the novel and the theatre in particular, his model of film seems closest to mime or ballet, with its focus on facial expression and gesture, as well, perhaps, as the experimental poetic drama of the 1910s and 1920s, in which Edward Gordon Craig's productions were central. Invoking the Aristotelian distinction between 'telling and showing'—'A novel describes; the camera depicts'—Baughan was particularly cautious about the 'realism' of the cinema: its ability to give the illusion of depicting 'actual photographs of actual characters and events' was a power 'that must be carefully kept in its place'. 'As soon', he argued, 'as the camera seeks to depict a drama of human emotion it must, if it is to be an art, select and combine its action so that the drama is told with the greatest amount of effect. To throw on the screen the action of the story in the crude, as if it were a transcription from life, is an artistic mistake.'[41]

As in earlier discussions of photography, arguments about the aesthetic dimensions of the cinema had to negotiate the 'photographic' dimensions of cinema, its 'reproduction' of a real world, and the extent to which it could be an art form if it were entirely the product of the machine. The emphasis in the article was primarily on the techniques of stage-acting, and on the possibilities for 'an action of feeling and thought brought to a fuller expression than in real life'. Intertwined with, and guiding, these somewhat abstract prescriptions was the invocation of 'beauty' as film's potential and its future: 'Some of the photographs I have seen on the screen have intrinsic beauty, and they can be given a greater and stranger beauty by imaginative selection and lighting.'[42] 'As to the actual future of the art, when it has painfully won its way to recognition, there can be no doubt... Many of the pictures I have seen were quite beautiful in conception and selection.'[43] Despite the emphasis on the swiftness of the camera and the eye, there was little discussion here of movement and no real insistence, such as we find elsewhere, on film as the art of motion.

The pronouncements on film and theatre made by George Bernard Shaw in the first decades of the century appear to have had a significant influence on such critical writings. Shaw, perhaps the most eminent and influential figure in the theatre of his long day, became interested in film at an early stage, writing in 1912: 'I, who go to an ordinary theatre with effort and reluctance, cannot keep away from the cinema.'[44] 'The cinema', he wrote, 'is a much more momentous invention than printing was':

> Ask any man who has done eight or ten hours heavy manual labor what happens to him when he takes up a book. He will tell you that he falls asleep in less than two minutes. Now, the cinema tells its story to the illiterate as well as to the literate; and it keeps his victim (if you like to call him so) not only awake but fascinated as if by a serpent's eye. And that is why the cinema is going to produce effects that all the cheap books in the world could never produce.[45]

This is in many ways a familiar account of the cinema as a drug of popular entertainment: it is not so much that the spectator looks at the cinema, as that the cinema looks at him with its 'fascinating' and deadly 'serpent's eye'. In an article written a year later, however, Shaw wrote of the ways in which theatre would be overtaken by the cinema, which could show aspects of the world unavailable to the stage, and could change scene instantly: 'literally in the twinkling of an eye, sixty times in an hour.'[46] The focus on vision, on seeing, as the condition of modernity was all-encompassing. Reading, Shaw suggested, was largely irrelevant to this modernity but 'all except the blind and deaf can see and hear; and when they begin to see farther than their own noses and their own nurseries, people will begin to have some notion of the world they are living in; and then we, too, shall see: what we shall see'.[47] Modernity created a new perceptual field, and cinema, as Shaw implied, a new form of literacy.

It was also, he argued, a social leveller, opening up a more intimate and less demanding form of public space than the theatre; 'the cinema relieves the spectator of all preoccupying and worrying self-consciousness—about his dress, for instance—whereas the ordinary theatre, the moment it takes its glaring lights off the actors, turns them full on to the blushing spectators.'[48]

Much of the focus of Shaw's discussion of the cinema, in articles and interviews, was on the relationship between film and theatre. In the silent period, he largely rejected the view, implicit or explicit in so much other writing of the time, that the cinema represented a dangerous threat to the stage. When asked if he considered 'that the kinema is a serious rival to the theatre', he responded: 'Yes and No. The kinema will kill the theatres which are doing what the film does better, and bring to life the dying theatre which does what the film cannot do at all.'[49] The conventions and attributes of the film medium would, he argued, release drama from the demands of realism and the concentration on plot at the expense of dialogue: 'the theatre will find itself cut out by the picture palace as regards the very sort of play—the so-called "well-made" or "constructed" play of the French school—on which it has been for so long almost wholly dependent.'[50] The 'elaborate art of scenic illusion' would be so 'hopelessly beaten and exposed' by the film's ability to change scenes instantly, and to take the spectator 'over the hills and far away', that the theatre would be released from the need to fake illusion through the creation of 'elaborate stage pictures'. Dramatists would be given 'a way of escape from the eternal realistic modern interior and enabled … to indulge their imagination with a rapid succession of scenes in the open air, on the sea, in the heavens above, in the earth beneath, and in the waters under the earth, thereby relieving them of intolerable restrictions and of a frowsty, unhealthy atmosphere, far more demoralizing to the theatre than its supposed natural tendency to licentiousness'.[51]

For Shaw, however, the coming of sound effaced many of the differences between film and theatre. 'Now that you have got the talkie', he wrote in 1936, 'and can have real drama you must not cling to the old dissolving views, the old diorama. You must get rid of it … When you get the talkie you are in for drama and you must make up your mind to it.'[52] He was dismissive of the view that it was of the essence of the cinema to be in perpetual motion, concurring with the view of the director Anthony Asquith that 'the ebb and flow of the dialogue' was capable of providing all the movement a film scene might require.[53] When the cinema performed plays, he insisted, 'its function is the function of the theatre'.[54] Even during the silent period, Shaw had on occasions suggested that film could no longer make its appeal to the eye alone. As he asserted in an interview published in the *Fortnightly Review* in 1924:

> The silent drama is producing such a glut of spectacle that people are actually listening to invisible plays by wireless. The silent drama is exhausting the resources of silence. Charlie Chaplin and his very clever colleague Edna Purviance, Bill Hart and Alla Nazimova, Douglas Fairbanks and Mary Pickford and Harold Lloyd, have done everything that can be done in dramatic dumb show and athletic stunting, and played all the possible variations on it. The man who will play them off the screen will not be their superior at their own game, but an Oscar Wilde of the movies who will flash epigram after epigram at the spectators, and thus realize [J. M.] Barrie's anticipation of more subtitles than pictures.[55]

'The silent film was no use to me … When movies became talkies my turn came', Shaw declared in 1936.[56] He refused to have his plays filmed in the silent years, but welcomed their screen adaptations in the sound era, and the wide audiences he was able to reach.[57] From the outset, his interests in film had been very largely in their mass educational potential. As he wrote in 1914: 'The cinematograph begins educating people when the projection lantern begins clicking, and does not stop until it leaves off.'[58] He strongly rejected the activities of those moral reformers protesting the dangers of the cinema to children: 'The people who are agitating to have children excluded from these theatres (they have actually succeeded in some towns in Germany) should be executed without pity.'[59] He fully acknowlededged their claims for the importance of the morality inculcated by the cinema, while turning such attitudes on their heads in arguing that 'the danger of the cinemas is not the danger of immorality, but of morality', of conventionality and platitude, and of a moral, as opposed to a social, levelling. The issue was, for Shaw, crucial for one reason alone: 'The cinema is going to form the mind of England.'[60]

This view, though it was rarely accompanied by Shaw's iconoclasm, pervaded much of the commentary on film in the first years of the century. Articles on the cinema were for the most part written as if middle-class readers had remained aloof from the new medium, so that there was a greater felt necessity to define what film was, or, more frequently, what it might become. In this sense, however strongly critical the discussions of cinema, there was often an element of persuasion. Readers, it was suggested, needed to take an interest in the cinema precisely because it was such a powerful popular form—one critic, writing in 1925, put cinema attendance at some twenty million a week—and one over which, through an indifference born of a 'proper' intellectual elitism, they had lost any control.[61] Thus Alec Waugh's 'The Film and the Future', while rejecting the idea that there were writers who remained wholly ignorant of the cinema, conceded

that a great number of very intelligent persons have never entered a cinema except under extreme pressure, have never sat in one without extreme boredom, have never come out of one without extreme relief. For the film is the parvenu, the *nouveau riche*; that has yet to be accepted socially. It is in too many minds associated with the flickering projections of absurd vulgarities in the stuffy booths of provincial fairs. Too many people can remember its early struggles. The bad photography, the bad acting, the alternating spasms of sentiment and sensation, the rowdy travesty of humour, the maudlin parody of life and there are still people who think and talk and write of films in terms of the cinema as it was in 1907, who will complain of the wild gesticulation and the grimacing close-ups that have been out of fashion for a dozen years; people in plenty who obstinately refuse to recognise the film as a legitimate means of self-expression, and remarkably few who will attempt a definition of the capacities and limitations of a medium that may well prove to be the main art form of the twentieth century.[62]

An article on 'The Cinema', published in *The Nineteenth Century* in 1923, made no greater claims for the standard of 'the pictures', but expressed an interest in the fact that

in spite of everything, there has been an uneasy suspicion growing of late years that there is something in the idea of 'the film' after all. Some of our best daily newspapers, impressed, no doubt, by the enormous circulation commanded by a popular film, have attempted to take the better-class pictures seriously by reviewing them and developing canons of criticism on Crocean lines. A few years ago a small coterie at Oxford (and, no doubt, at Chelsea too) professed to discover in the cinematographic art an aesthetic importance hidden from the Philistine.[63]

The tone was sceptical, but the author of the article, J. Ecclestone, made his own substantial claims for the film:

there may be latent in it a new form of aesthetic expression so vital and important that children of the future will have to be taught appreciation of the great film productions as they are now taught appreciation of Shakespeare. This belief in the future of the film lays no claim to startling originality, nor does it demand adherence to any modern impressionistic theory of art; in fact, the principles on which it is based are derived from no less orthodox a work than Lessing's *Laocoön* ... it attempts to define the limits of the 'artist' (painter or sculptor) on the one hand and of the 'poet' on the other; and if any function of aesthetic value can be attached to the moving picture, it must lie in some sort of union between the idea of the picture and the idea of the poem.[64]

Critics writing in the periodical literature frequently invoked Lessing in their attempts either to provide a definition of film as an autonomous art, or to represent it as a partial combination (rather than a holistic synthesis) of other, established forms. In the 1930s, Sergei Eisenstein wrote at length arguing that, through montage, cinema could overcome the dichotomy established by Lessing between the spatial sphere of painting (and, more particularly, sculpture) and the temporal sphere of poetry. Lessing's *Laocoön* was also used extensively by Eisenstein to suggest that film combines the essential elements of the two arts on whose absolute distinctiveness Lessing, in his critique of *'ut pictura poesis'* ('every picture tells a story') had insisted.[65] In Ecclestone's words:

This, then, is the ground on which it is claimed that, theoretically at least, the cinema can provide a new and vital form of aesthetic expression, distinct from both poetry and painting, though comparable to both. The poet is debarred from presenting a spaced picture in one given moment, and this the film can do; the painter cannot produce the illusion of a developing movement in time, and this, too, the film can accomplish with ease. It seems to follow, then, that the moving picture has all the advantages of poetry and painting combined without their obvious shortcomings.[66]

There was, moreover, recognition of the importance of editing in this article; a photograph, it was argued, would, in its realism, still fall foul of Lessing's strictures (constructed long before him by the norms of Greek 'beauty') against the representation of the extremes of emotion in the work of art. The cinematographer, on the other hand, 'by allying time with space ... has altered the whole problem':

Just as we saw that Virgil could reproduce Laocoön's cry of anguish without losing any power through his realism, so in the same way the cinematographer can welcome realism and yet, at the same time, control and marshal his details in a way impossible to the mere photographer, producing a genuine artistic unity in the shifting sequence of events.[67]

Discussion of Lessing's *Laocoön* enabled the arts in the modernist period, including film, to draw, in Anthony Vidler's words, 'precise theoretical boundaries around the centres of their conceptually different practices ... as if the arts were so many different nations ... each with characteristics of their own to be asserted before any treaties might be negotiated'.[68] It also brought to the fore the question of stasis and movement in aesthetic representation. In Lessing's account, as Ecclestone paraphrased it, the artist, in presenting his picture, 'has to select aright one "moment", and on a true selection depends his whole power to illustrate the eternal in terms of the evanescent, to achieve that triumphant paradox of artistic creation which consists in seizing and fixing a universal idea for ever by the pregnant portrayal of some casual happening or changing accident'.[69] For other commentators on film, the issue was more explicitly that of the power of film to liberate the static pictorial or plastic image into movement. Goethe, writing of the Laocoön sculpture in 1798, had described an exercise whereby the viewer could make the sculpture come alive: standing back from the sculpture, opening and then shutting our eyes, 'we shall see all the marble in motion; we shall be afraid to find the group changed when we open our eyes again'.[70] This magical motion was now something the cinema could engender. Writing of Dovjenko's film *Earth*, and describing an image of a frieze of white horses, the critic Martha Kinross wrote: 'it is but a glimpse, but the mind is haunted by that marmoreal beauty, as if suddenly released from the pediment of some temple where it has been immobilised for centuries—by that frieze of flying horses; is haunted, too, by the final symbol of the series, the apple-orchard seen through strands of disastrous rain.'[71]

For Alexander Bakshy, writing in the New York-based magazine *Theatre Arts Monthly* in the 1920s, time and movement defined the art of the film: 'time is the very soul of the motion picture: it is the governing condition of movement—of changes in the visual aspects of things. Accordingly, from the standpoint of art, the world of images which is created by the motion picture must function in movement, i.e., through movement it must reveal its form and significance.'[72] Echoing Münsterberg, Bakshy suggested that it was 'the power over space and time' that defined the medium. Film movement, in Bakshy's account, took a number of different forms, including 'the change in the position of objects' or the lighting of objects in relation to one another; the quick succession of scenes by means of which 'the film makes the whole world dance to its tune'; and movement as recorded on a film by a camera and thrown on to the screen by means of a projector. Finally, 'there is the movement which is the result of the joint functioning of the projector and the screen—the movement of a small picture growing large, or of a picture traversing the screen from one end to another'.[73]

Bakshy extended these arguments in an article entitled 'The Road to Art in the Motion Picture':

> The only real thing in the motion picture is movement without which all its objects would appear as lifeless shadows. The sea, for example, would look utterly dead and unreal on the screen if there was no light playing on its surface, or if it had no ripples or waves. Mountains, trees and buildings would loom phantom-like if we could not see them continuously changing their shapes. And living creatures, if denied movement, would look scarcely better than masks of wax figures. There are, therefore, clearly defined limits for the illusionist effects of real life and nature in the motion picture: the latter can be realistic only when its shadowy world is set in motion.[74]

The discussion, at this point, strongly recalls the terms of Gorki's 1896 article on the first films—'It is not life but its shadow, it is not motion but its soundless spectre'—though for Bakshy the illusion of motion succeeded in overcoming the deathly dimensions of a filmic ghost-world. Bakshy's article also increasingly echoed Münsterberg's *Art of the Photoplay*, including his claims that the devices which engender movement, such as camera angles, cutting between scenes, and, in particular, the close-up, leave 'all stagecraft' and realism behind. 'Life and nature', Bakshy wrote, 'are not reproduced faithfully, but are shown in a new aspect determined by the peculiar properties of the medium in their relation to the spectator.' The substantial difference between Münsterberg's theories and those of Bakshy, written a little over a decade later, is that Münsterberg's focus was on the part played by the spectator's consciousness and acts of attention, whereas for Bakshy the interest resided almost entirely in the 'nature' of the medium, and in the potential of any given film to embody or realize that 'nature'. His was a characteristically modernist stance, a 'mystique of purity', in Renato Poggioli's term, which produced the desire 'to reduce every work to the intimate laws of its own expressive essence or to the given absolutes of its own genres or means'.[75] For Evelyn Gerstein, writing in *Theatre Arts Monthly* in the same year as Bakshy, the cinema, having begun by aping 'an outmoded stage ... began to grow wise':

> It set out to evolve its own aesthetic. And it was only when it realized that it was its own excuse for being, a medium utterly independent of the theatre, of painting, of sculpture, or of literature, that the cinema began to take on the proportions of an art.[76]

Bakshy's representation of film was as 'a dynamic pattern': 'To enter as an element into a mobile form the static picture has first of all to break down its equilibrium.'[77] Citing *The Cabinet of Dr Caligari*, *Waxworks*, *The Last Laugh*, and *Metropolis*, Bakshy argued that 'the dynamic nature of the motion picture has escaped the notice of the German producers'.[78] By contrast, in Eisenstein's *Potemkin* 'one sees a deliberate attempt to base the emotional appeal of the picture on the variations in the tempo of its moving objects ... A dynamic pattern is obtained by relating and contrasting scenes of varying speeds of movement, the momentum of the whole scene rather than the movement of single figures providing the element of the structural form.'[79] Bakshy's concern here was with the effects of rhythm, and it followed the shift from a focus on *photogénie* in French film criticism of the 1920s as, in Richard Abel's words, 'the singularly transformative nature of the film image', to '*cinégraphie*' as 'the rhythmic principles governing the placement of film images', often analogized as orchestral accompaniment.[80]

Extending his explorations of the potential for freedom from linear sequence, Bakshy further advocated the simultaneous treatment of subjects within the same frame with an enlarged projection: 'The subject would grow large or small, sometimes dwindling into nothingness, and it would move from one end of the screen to the other, while other subjects would be passing through similar evolutions ... as a means for a balanced interweaving of several dynamic motives the total effect of which would be to create a pictorial and dramatic progression governed by the principles of counterpoint and orchestral harmonization.'[81] Thus the 'abstract' nature of musical composition and, though less explicitly, kinetic art and sculpture, became the models for film to follow, even as Bakshy and his contemporaries called for the realization of an autonomous film aesthetic.

Bakshy's articles on cinema, and others published on the topic in *Theatre Arts Monthly* in the same period, were clearly engaged with experimental and avant-garde theatre and art, and their contexts were closer to those of British journals such as *Drawing and Design* and *The Architectural Review*, both of which regularly covered the topic of the cinema, than to mainstream cultural journals such as the *Fortnightly* and the *Nineteenth Century*. Yet similar preoccupations began to appear in these more conservative periodicals, shaped substantially, I would argue, by the emergence of the new sites and institutions of film culture in the mid-1920s.

Bakshy suggested that the essential feature of film art was its power to produce an 'aesthetic thrill',[82] so that movement, and its impact upon the spectator, there at the very beginnings of cinema as 'the thing that moves', was now transmuted into the aesthetic realm. R. E. C. Swann's 'Art and the Cinema: A Chance for the British Producer' which appeared in *The Nineteenth Century* in August 1926, also insisted that it was the function of film to 'express motion'. His article was written with the benefit of the newly founded Film Society's programmes, as references to Ruttmann's experimental films suggest:

> So far, except in the ballet, with which the cinema has much in common, art has only been able to suggest the beauty of movement by depicting objects in motion. The Ruttmann films *are* movement, and it is the sensation of movement that is dominant in them, and the design subsidiary. Here, then, we have something that belongs exclusively to the cinema.[83]

The article, like so many accounts of cinema in this period, offered a condensed history of the medium, arguing that it had been 'born' the wrong way round, charting its wrong turns, and locating its salvation in the undoing of its development. For Ivor Brown, writing in the *Saturday Review* in 1924, film was 'an art in search of its youth … The cinema was born old; or rather it was not born at all, but manufactured. Its art could never spring in the fresh majesty of youth from any people's heart. It was no sooner discovered than exploited; no sooner exploited than corrupted.' The image of cinema is ambiguously gendered: it is both a monstrous, manufactured Caliban and a starlet, harlot or whore, 'swaddled in the trappings of Wardour Street and hand-fed with liqueurs and caviare … the twin of the chattery-smattery photo-press'. Then, 'under occasional wise guidance, the cinema began to go in search of its youth, and by that way it may now find salvation'. Chaplin, who 'sloughed away the mechanical, simplified the narrative, slaughtered sub-titles and close-ups, and brought to the comic film a complete rejuvenation', represented cinema's 'inventive and irrepressible youth'.[84] For Swann:

> The cinema ... is often said to be in its infancy. It is hardly so. It has, it is true, the undeveloped mind of a child, but it has also the strength and ingenuity (and incidentally the lusts) of a grown man. It could be forced to reveal all the wealth and mystery of visible life. Actually it is made only to peep through bedroom keyholes, to push for a place in the crowd round a street accident or to applaud the antics of a drunken tramp; and because the master it serves has not the wit to demand more than these humiliating services, it is neglected by artists and all men with creative minds as too obdurate or banal for their attention.
>
> What has happened?[85]

Swann gave a brief account (with some marked similarities to the trajectory outlined in Virginia Woolf's 'The Cinema') of the early years of cinema and its origins in the circus. At first, in the days of cinematic innocence, 'the world flocked to little tin sheds where it paid its penny and sat enthralled' by the spectacle of 'action and movement'. 'The trouble began' when people began to act, felt they must 'ape the theatre', and 'forgot in their excitement that to keep things moving was the one and only fundamental necessity' of film. Then came war, the increasing hegemony of the American film industry and the commercialism of the industry. The way of the future, Swann suggested, and the potential for originality in film, lay in 'an escape from the bondage of words, from all literary association'; an imaginative use of film space, which would learn (as had *The Cabinet of Dr Caligari*) from non-naturalistic theatrical production, instanced by Gordon Craig's designs for *King Lear*,[86] and from the artist's canvas; a return to the 'art of conveying sensation' which was cinema's legacy from its origins in the circus, and which would take the place of the 'emotional situations' that governed popular cinema.

The 'true aesthetic function' of the cinema, in Swann's account, inhered in its representation of sensation and movement through a subjective camera that would put the spectator into motion. He referred to a recent film (almost certainly Henri de Chomette's *A quoi rêvent les jeunes films?*, produced by Comte Etienne de Beaumont, and shown at the Film Society's third performance on 20 December 1925), writing of its reception: 'The spectators were mildly interested in the play of light on a revolving crystal, but only actively excited to applause when the producer put them in the front of a train and sent them whirling round the roofs of the city, and later in the bows of a Seine steamer and let them fly under bridges and through the river traffic with the speed and relentlessness of an arrow.'[87]

Swann thus drew his aesthetic model from an experimental film dedicated to the reproduction of motion, light, and speed—Comte de Beaumont referred in *The Little Review* to 'working with the living lines which arise in such profusion from the objects about us ... imagining things in motion'—in which the viewer was fully absorbed.[88] Swann substituted for the voyeuristic 'peep through keyholes', condemned at the opening of his article, a different form of corporealized spectatorship, a 'kinaesthetics' in which (as in Hugo Münsterberg's study of cinema) the spectator was transported into whirling, vertiginous space. In this position, he experienced a 'giddiness' that recalled both the origins of the cinema as part of circus spectacle, and the power of the cinematic machine to put the film spectator in the position of the camera eye, and to move him where it would. Film thus represented a radical departure from the 'picture postcard views' usually associated with the magic-lantern show. The article both inscribed the longer history of cinema, from its pre-cinematic technological origins, and, through the concept of the 'aesthetic thrill', not only located the cinema's innocence, its 'chance to be natural, youthful, or spontaneous' in Ivor Brown's words, but wrote film into cultural modernity.

The 'cinema of attractions' and 'astonishment' of the turn of the century was thus repeated and reformed through the concept of the 'aesthetic thrill' in the 1920s. Film's 'becoming' an art, its aesthetic autonomy, its powers to do what no other art form could do, were now being displayed as 'attractions'. Yet this was often perceived as an undoing of the cinema's 'mechanical', commercial being, and as its 'vital' birth (or rebirth), and as the recapturing, or even invention, of its youth and its youthful dreams. For those on whose horizons film had only recently begun to emerge as a legitimate art form, this was cinema's true birth, and they frequently dated its beginnings from the point of their own engagement with it.

The Film Society

The Film Society, founded in London in 1925, was the institution that played the most substantial role in giving cinema intellectual and aesthetic credibility in the Britain of the 1920s, and that brought the broadest range of international cinema to critical attention, including the Soviet films that censorship was preventing from being screened elsewhere. Although the Society continued until 1939, its greatest period of growth and influence was the mid to late 1920s, and it played a central though complex role in relation to international avant-gardism as it appeared in the British context in this period. It was also a major influence on the spread of the film society movement more generally, with the emergence and development of film groups, including workers' and political film societies, across Britain.

The mid-1920s was a period of intense activity in the arena of alternative, non-commercial cinema. In America the Film Arts Guild in New York became an important ally and source of films for the Film Society. A number of film societies already existed in France: *Le Ciné-Club de France* was a merger of three film societies founded in the early 1920s (Ricciotto Canudo's Club des Amis du Septième Art (1921), Delluc's Ciné-Club (1923) and Poirier's Club Français du Cinéma) and out of this forum developed the cinemas devoted to the revival of early films and the exhibition of new and avant-garde work. *Le Vieux Colombier*, opened by Jean Tedesco in the Autumn of 1924, was a theatre turned cinema, which showed American films of the 1910s as well as avant-garde cinema, and screened documentary and scientific as well as narrative films.[89] In 1925, *Le Vieux Colombier* ran a lecture series on 'the creation of the world by the cinema'. The *Studio des Ursulines*, which opened with a screening of Pabst's *Joyless Street* on 21 January 1926, tended to show early films in the first part of its programme, though it too was committed to new and experimental work. Its initial publicity material included a quotation from the film theorist Léon Moussinac: 'An art is being born, developing, discovering its own laws, an art which will be the very expression, robust, powerful and original, of the ideal of modern times.'[90] For Fernand Léger, making the association between avant-garde film and avant-garde painting, the *Ursulines* was 'the cinéaste's studio'.[91] *Le Studio 28*, founded in early 1928, showed predominantly experimental films, and films that had come up against the censor.

The significance of early film revivals in relation to the new avant-garde cinema was noted in a review published in the *Criterion*. Its author, Walter Hanks Shaw, linked the ballet, specifically the Russian Ballet, to 'that so alternately maligned and eulogized youngest daughter of Apollo, the cinema' and discussed the season of classic films shown at the *Colombier* in early 1926:

> Beginning with the nursery days of the old Biograph and Vitagraph one-reel thrillers, the entire history and development of the cinema was exhibited in

chronological sequence; the Wild West cow-boy adventure films, the Key-stone Comedies, the first Griffith spectacles, the latest German productions.

This unique opportunity of reviewing the cinema as a whole, of watching its inceptions and evolution, formed a splendid background and criterion in judging the three latest developments in the cinema; which placed the film at the apex of the Paris theatrical season; the Beaumont film; the l'Herbier film, and the Picabia film. [*A Quoi rêvent les jeunes films?*, *L'Inhumain*, and *Entr'acte*][92]

Accompanying such activities in film production and exhibition was a strong commitment to developing a new film criticism. *Le Ciné-Club de France* passed a resolution in 1926 that newspaper proprietors should be required to include signed comments and reviews, written by independent critics, on all advertised films: 'to bring about the reform of the cinema press which is indispensable to the progress of the French cinema... today more than ever the creation of cinema criticism is indispensable to the artistic existence of cinema.'[93]

On 10 June 1925, Ivor Montagu published, in the Oxford student maga-zine *The Isis*, a statement on 'The New Film Society', announcing the start of its first season in the October of that year, and giving details of the nature of the society.[94] The Paris and New York film societies were clearly a sig-nificant influence, but the model for the Film Society in London was also that of 'the Sunday play-producing societies', in particular the Stage Society of London, founded in 1899, which, as Don Macpherson has written, 'had been set up to produce plays which either for reasons of censorship or of commerce stood little chance of being performed in a West End theatre', and which established the precedent of Sunday performances, still illegal under the Sunday Entertainment act.[95] The Stage Society introduced to London audiences the work of new foreign dramatists, including Ibsen, Strindberg, Gorki, Wedekind, Pirandello, Cocteau, as well as the theatre of Shaw (one of the Film Society's 'original members' or sponsors) and other naturalist playwrights.

In describing the new Film Society, Montagu emphasized the 'private' nature of the film screenings, over which the censor should have had no ju-risdiction, though initially the Society had to overcome the controls exerted by the London County Council. The 'private' nature of the proceedings, as first imagined, also related, however, to the new Society's model of minority film culture. At each of the performances, Montagu wrote:

We shall show some special interesting picture, and complete the programme with old, forgotten Sennett comedies, short British interest pictures, and a remarkably interesting series of short French films, called Etudes de Rhythmes Rapides, that are utterly unsuited for ordinary commercial showing, but have recently been exhibited at the Vieux Colombier in Paris.[96]

As Montagu would later recall, the idea for the Film Society came about in discussion with the actor Hugh Miller, on a train returning from Germany, and German cinema was to the fore in the planning of the Society's early programmes. Nonetheless, Montagu noted of the films named in his article for *The Isis* (which included *Nju*, *Cinderella*, *Waxworks*, *Dracula* (*Nosferatu*), and *Raskolnikoff*) that 'there are others, and the predominance of Germany in this list is due to the fact that we are young and that we have only so far had time to consider those films which one or other of our members has seen and admired. But we are, of course, especially anxious to get films from any sources whatever'.[97]

Increasingly, into the late 1920s, Soviet cinema would become a central dimension of the Society's programmes and policies, but it also showed films from countries including France, India, America, Belgium, Sweden, and Japan. British cinema was not excluded, but the policy of showing films that would not have commercial exhibition tended to limited the British films shown to scientific and experimental cinema and, subsequently, documentary film. In the minutes of 1926, the omission of English films from the Film Society programmes was noted (as Montagu was later to write, 'few British films were made without hopes of or even concrete prearrangements for commercial showing').[98] The Society did, however, screen the comedies of the British editor and director Adrian Brunel, with whom Montagu had formed a film company in 1927. Much of the business of Brunel and Montagu Ltd was post-production work, including the preparation (titling, editing, cutting) of silent and foreign films for British exhibition, including the Film Society performances. In 1928, Brunel and Montagu worked with Frank Wells to produce three short comedy films, *Bluebottles*, *Daydreams*, and *The Tonic*, starring Elsa Lanchester and scripted by H. G. Wells.

It is clear from Montagu's early formulation of the Society's aims that its founders, while emphasizing the 'private' nature of the screenings, had seen themselves, at least initially, as the conduit through which their chosen films could enter into broader exhibition circuits:

After our choice has been endorsed by the members of our society and the press, there will be enough interest generally aroused among this postulated art public to make it worth the while of at least a few exhibitors to show the pictures. After a season or so has justified us, confirmed our position, and got the faith of the small, discriminating public, we shall open a repertory theatre in London. The films, such others as may become available, and revivals of re-edited films will then be shown. The necessity of this re-issue or revival of old, brilliant films is scarcely realised.[99]

The 'archival' emphasis (in line with the programming policies of the Parisian repertory cinemas Studio des Ursulines and Le Vieux Colombier) was a significant one, indicating that the establishing of film as an art was bound up with a commitment to film history and with the beginnings of the archive and film museum movement. Montagu also 'pledged' that the society would never show, nor 'give cachet, to any picture that has not been prepared by us, cut and titled with regard solely to its artistic rightness and integrity, and without the slightest attention to the wishes of the trade or its opinion of the intelligences of its foolish audiences'. There was thus a strong focus on the preservation or restoration of the film's 'integrity' and wholeness, to be protected from the demands, and the scissors, of both commerce and censorship.

The leaflet for members of the new Society gave details of subscription rates and of the films planned for its first series. It also spelled out the Society's aims.

> The Film Society has been founded in the belief that there are in this country a large number of people who regard the cinema with the liveliest interest, and who would welcome an opportunity seldom afforded by the general public of witnessing films of intrinsic merit, whether new or old.
>
> At the moment, although it is possible in the course of a year, for a member of the ordinary cinema-going public to see such remarkable films as: *Warning Shadows, Greed, The Last Laugh* and *The Marriage Circle*, at long intervals and after considerable difficulty in discovering where and when they may be found, it is not possible for such a person to go during any week in the year into any picture house in England and be sure of finding one film of abiding merit.
>
> The Film Society proposes to remedy this condition by showing films which reach a certain aesthetic standard, to a limited membership on Sundays, in the same way that plays are shown by the Phoenix and Stage Societies…
>
> It is felt to be of the utmost importance that films of the type proposed should be available to the Press, and to the Film Trade itself, including present and (what is far more important) future British film-producers, editors, cameramen, titling experts and actors. For although such intelligent films as *Nju* or *The Last Laugh* may not be what is desired by the greatest number of people, yet there can be no question but that they embody certain

improvements in technique that are as essential to commercial as they are to experimental cinematography.

It is important that films of this type should not only be shown under the best conditions to the most actively-minded people both inside and outside the film-world, but that they should from time to time be revived. This will be done. In this way standards of taste and of executive ability may be raised and a critical standard established. This cannot but affect future production, by founding a clearing-house for all films having pretensions to sincerity, irrespective of origin or immediate mercantile interest.[100]

As I have suggested, the selection of films played a very substantial role in shaping critical discussion of the cinema in this period. The years in which the Film Society was most influential—the 1920s and the early 1930s—saw key transitions and developments in film culture, with which it was fully engaged: the construction of a 'film history' and the beginnings of the film archive movement; avant-garde and experimental cinema; the battle against censorship and the spread of a political film culture; the rise of Soviet cinema and film theory; the coming of sound; the significance of scientific films and the birth of 'documentary' cinema.

Montagu's assertion, in his notice in *The Isis*, of the youth of the Film Society's founders (Montagu himself, who was indeed only 21 in 1925, Hugh Miller, the film critics Iris Barry and Walter Mycroft, Sidney Bernstein, running at this time a small chain of cinemas, which would later become the Granada empire, the director Adrian Brunel)—'we are young'—was undoubtedly intended to draw a university audience, and it would seem that Oxbridge undergraduates were well represented at the Sunday afternoon programmes, when they commenced in October 1925. The Society's 'original members' (sometimes described as 'prominent members') were, however, a less youthful and more august group of intellectuals and artists, including David Cecil, Roger Fry, J. B. S. Haldane, Julian Huxley, Augustus John, John Maynard Keynes, George Pearson, George Bernard Shaw, J. C. Squire, J. St Loe Strachey, Lord Swaythling [Montagu's father], Dame Ellen Terry, and H. G. Wells.

A full history of the Film Society has not yet been published.[101] The Society's founding members partially reconstructed it over the years, though with some degree of inconsistency, at times, ambivalence, and frequent later assertions of the large part which self-interest had played in their cause: 'we liked pictures, and ... without the subscriptions of the like-minded enthusiasts who joined the society, we should ourselves never have been able to afford to see them with a big audience and the right music—both essentials for proper appreciation—or maybe even entice their owners to send them to England at all.'[102]

On the occasion of the Film Society's fiftieth anniversary in 1975, Montagu and Sidney Bernstein, in recorded conversation, emphasized that their motivation for founding the Society had been, in Montagu's words, 'to introduce films to intellectual circles—literary and artistic people',[103] and, by extension, to convince the sceptical and the uninitiated that film was indeed an art form. This mission ran throughout much of Iris Barry's film writing in this period, as in her celebration in 1925 of a 'magnificent new picture palace', the Tivoli in the Strand, which 'indicates not only the new type of patron that exists but also the dignity and powers to which this novel but not longer despised art of the cinema is rising'.[104] Bernstein expanded on a similar theme, in the 1975 interview,[105] and in an article written around this time for the British Federation of Film Societies (BFFS) house magazine *Film*:

> Our first programme was on Sunday afternoon the 25th October 1925. We had estimated a membership of 500 but opened with 900 and, with guest tickets, filled the New Gallery—the most comfortable cinema in London at that time. We found we had many supporters among eminent people in politics, art and literature. Our guarantors included H. G. Wells, G. B. Shaw, Maynard Keyes, Roger Fry, H. F. Rubinstein, J. B. S. Haldane, Lord Ashfield and Lord Swaythling (Ivor's father). Judging from press reports we made quite a splash. The gossip columnists took us up; later they dropped us. They commented on the big cars, the women in striking hats, the well-known Bloomsbury figures making themselves conspicuous in the audience with their unconventional dress and loud conversation. The social aspect had nothing to do with our more serious aims, but undoubtedly helped us when we ran into difficulties with the LCC licensing authorities whom we had omitted to consult... Our impressive list of guarantors stood us in good stead. We won our freedom by a narrow majority.
>
> Unfortunately, neither the press nor the film world itself welcomed us as we had expected. Our privileges were resented and we were labelled as 'snobs' and 'intellectuals'. The trade viewed our separatism as a form of criticism of themselves (which it was); the press accused us of subversion and of using our freedom for political ends.

In the minutes of a 1926 Film Society council meeting it was indeed noted with regret that 'very few of those engaged in production, directors, cameramen, and others in this country were among the members of the

Society', while there was hostility among those renters who were not members or did not regularly attend.[106] The Film Society's plan to attract British film technicians to the performances, in the hope that they would learn new techniques from foreign films, to be incorporated into British film production, was never satisfactorily realized.

However, the impact of the Film Society was far-reaching in broader cultural spheres, and the screening of films unavailable elsewhere began to shape the very concept of a film culture. The 'performances', usually composed of four or five films, with a main feature accompanied by a number of shorter films, were, as Jamie Sexton notes, eclectic, and tended to include an abstract film, a revival, sometimes in the 'Resurrection' series, a burlesque, and a feature-length film.[107] As I discussed in Chapter 2 in the context of Virginia Woolf's likely viewing of the *Cabinet of Dr Caligari* at a Film Society screening, the programmes exhibited both the evolutionary dimensions of film and its history and a continuum of cinematic representations, past and present.

There was also a strong emphasis on scientific and nature films—the early 'Bionomics Series', which undoubtedly reflected the particular interests of Ivor Montagu, who had read zoology at Cambridge, included films of plant and animal life, often using slow-motion or microscopic camera-work—as well as a significant focus on the demonstration of new cinematic techniques. Over the years, Film Society performances included short films that explored developments in colour and sound, and techniques such as 'kaleidoscopic cinematography' and the Schufftan process, which used mirrors for the enlargement of models and photographs. Shown alongside experimental and avant-garde films (the Film Society, as noted in the programme written to mark its 100th performance in 1938, had been 'proud to show ... Abstract Films such as those by Walter Ruttmann, Moholy-Nagy, Léger and Murphy, Man Ray, Eggeling, Richter, Nalpas, Cavalcanti, Deslaw and other members of the Avant Garde'), these different modes of filmic experiment and spectacle—scientific, technical, avant-garde—all became key dimensions of 'cinematic specificity' and exhibitions of the powers of the film medium in this period.

The Film Society programme notes were in themselves significant documents in the history of film criticism and in the creation of a critical discourse. Resembling theatre or concert programmes, detailing the Sunday 'performances', which often had orchestral accompaniment, they also contained a substantial amount of information on the history and techniques of the films shown. The lengthy material given on the major film in each programme returns us to the question of 'film explanation', and there was debate over the years among the members of the Society about the ways in which descriptive and explanatory text could best accompany the audience's viewing of the film. The director and critic Thorold Dickinson's experiments in the 1930s included, for example, a short-lived experiment (for foreign language versions of sound texts) with accompanying material printed on transparent paper, to be held up to the light of the screen during the course of the film.

Ivor Montagu was responsible for the programme notes in the Society's first four years (a function subsequently taken over by Dickinson), and there was some overlap between these and the columns he wrote as film critic for *The Observer* in 1925 and 1926. Montagu provided material on the history of individual films, including their provenance, and on details such as intertitles (a topic which much absorbed him, and an area in which he had professional expertise, having worked with the designer E. McKnight Kauffer on the titles for Hitchcock's 1927 film *The Lodger*), 'personal notes' (predominantly information on actors' previous or other roles), and critical or technical 'notes' or 'remarks', which drew attention, for example, to the use of specific camera and editing techniques.

The first programmes, in particular, included references to the work of early film critics, such as Vachel Lindsay and Gilbert Seldes ('For further discussion of Mr Chaplin's methods the student is referred to Mr Gilbert Seldes' brilliant essay in *The Seven Lively Arts*').[108] As Jerry Turvey has noted, both Lindsay's *The Art of the Moving Picture* (reissued in 1922 for Montagu's generation) and Seldes's *The Seven Lively Arts* 'not only helped form [Montagu's] early film-reviewing practice', in which he tended to focus on film's capacity to create new dimensions of space and movement, 'but also stimulated the cinephilia of his friends and gave direction to the Society's early programming strategies'.[109] The 'Resurrection' series, which was intended to revive and preserve early silent film (predominantly films from the 1910s), was undoubtedly influenced by the focus on the films of D. W. Griffith and on slapstick and comic films (including those of Mack Sennett and Chaplin) in the writings of Lindsay and Seldes respectively. When, in 1931, the Society was able to include films from the very beginnings of cinema, the programme notes (now written by Thorold Dickinson) emphasized that the films, 'mainly about 1900, are shown for the precocity of their technical gifts rather than for any shortcomings by present-day standards'.[110]

Programme notes on the first full-length films shown in the Society's performances confirm the extent to which German cinema of the period, including and especially *Caligari*, had come to define an 'alternative' film culture and an art of the film. A note on the programme for the first performance stated:

> The Society is under no illusions. It is well aware that *Caligari*'s do not grow on raspberry bushes, and that it cannot, in a season, expect to provide its members with an unbroken succession of masterpieces. It will be sufficient if it can show a group of films which are in some degree interesting and which represent the work which has been done, or is being done experimentally, in various parts of the world. It is in the nature of such films that they are (it is said) commercially unsuitable for this country; and that is why they become the especial province of the Film Society.[111]

It was, nonetheless, the case that, wherever *Caligari*s did grow, Montagu's notes on *Caligari* itself exhibited a degree of critical distance: 'It has been shown in many countries and gained in no place popular favour, but everywhere a success of esteem greater perhaps than that accorded to any other picture. Though its technique is in some respects old-fashioned (example, the continual use of iris in and iris-out of scenes) in many respects it breaks new ground which is no farther explored to this day.'[112] The comment indicates the rapidity with which films became part of the past—it was, after all, only six years since *Caligari* had first been released in Germany—and, indeed, its showing was advertised as a 'revival'.

A similar critical and temporal distance was exhibited in other programme notes on German cinema, and in particular German Expressionist film. *Doctor Mabuse*, shown in the 10th performance, on 28 November 1926, was described as 'quite different from the other work of Mr. Lang, which tends to be static; indeed the action is characteristically un-German in the rapidity of its development'.[113] Murnau's 1921–2 film *Dracula* (*Nosferatu*), shown at the 27th performance, on 16 December 1928, was described as 'noteworthy for the now discarded trick effects attempted. The use of irises instead of fades and the clumsy seekings after eeriness in the use of strips of negatives and shots taken "one turn one picture" will be especially noted'.[114] By this point, the Film Society had begun to screen the Soviet films that had been advertised from its inception, but which had proved extremely difficult to bring into the country. As Montagu was to write of the first years of the Film Society in this context: 'Despite the fact that two members of the council made in all three journeys to Moscow and four to Berlin, we could not obtain delivery of a single foot of film.'

In October 1928, for its 25th performance, however, the Film Society was able to show Pudovkin's *Mother*, and the programme note celebrated the dynamism of its montage techniques, by implied contrast with the 'static' dimensions of the German Expressionist cinema that had governed the early performances. Montagu went into some detail about the censorship of the film, and the scenes that had been cut before its submission to the British Board of Film Censors. He also drew attention to Pudovkin's film writings, with whose translation he was involved, and to his cinematic technique:

> Unlike that of Mr. Eisenstein, the force of whose impressions derives mainly from beauty of composition, Mr Pudovkin...makes special use of alternation of rhythm by long and short cutting; of groups of successive very short shots, each a few inches only in length, to express violent movements; and peculiar to him, of scenes only remotely connected in external logic with his subject, cut in with others to express the essential significance of the latter... In *The End of St. Petersburg* he uses these methods with a subtler, but surer and yet more effective touch. The extraordinary vigour and sincerity of Russian films, which lead to the depiction of scenes of conflict and violence with a stark brutality repugnant to occidental taste, is rigorously exemplified in the present film, which is shown by courtesy of Brunel and Montagu.[115]

The history of the Film Society, and Montagu's career during this period, were to become profoundly linked to Soviet cinema and its directors, in particular Eisenstein and Pudovkin, though programmes also included films by Dovzenko (*Earth*), Kozintsev and Trauberg (*New Babylon, The Blue Express*), and Dziga-Vertov (*Man with a Movie Camera* and *Enthusiasm*). Soviet film was central to the Society's presentation of the new sound cinema: *Enthusiasm* played a now legendary role in this context, as Vertov sought to overwhelm his Film Society audience with the force and volume of the film's auditory dimensions. As the programme note to *The End of St. Petersburg* indicates, the Society was also having to play a very careful game with the censors, at a point at which Soviet cinema was banned for general distribution, with particular difficulties arising over *Battleship Potemkin* and Pudovkin's *Storm over Asia*. In 1929, Montagu wrote and published his pamphlet *The Political Censorship of Films*,[116] a powerful attack on British censorship laws; in the same year he joined the Communist Party, and became actively involved in the London Workers' Film Society, though he retained a seat on the Film Society council.

In November 1929, Eisenstein gave a series of lectures under the Film Society auspices, an engagement secured by Montagu during his attendance at the La Sarraz Congress of International Independent Cinema, held in September of that year, which brought together avant-garde film-makers, representatives of film clubs, and film theorists. The topics of Eisenstein's London lectures included 'technique of perception', the 'montage of attractions', and 'theory of conflict': he also delivered a lecture on the 'ideological' use of montage (described as 'cutting to affect intellectual processes').[117] Reconstructing the lectures for a BBC radio broadcast in 1949, the documentary film-maker Basil Wright and the academic Jack Isaacs, one of the early members of the Film Society, spoke of their profound impact: 'here was someone laying down (and we must remember laying down for the first time), the laws and principles of the youngest of the arts, an art no older than most of us in the audience'.[118]

During the month in which he gave his lectures, the Film Society's 33rd performance (10 November 1929) showed, for the first time, Eisenstein's *Battleship Potemkin* (1925), Montagu having obtained a print from the Soviet trade delegation in Berlin via Brunel and Montagu Limited after Scotland Yard and the Home Office, under William Joynson-Hicks, had intervened to prevent exhibition of the film in the UK. The Film Society programme notes on *Potemkin* discussed the effects of censorship and subsequent cuts and excisions on the print, but noted that it was, at least, complete. Of the film's techniques it was stated: ' "Potemkin" was the first Russian film in which those remarkable methods of expression—the use of non-acting material and the incitement to hysteria by means of rhythmic cutting—were attempted,'[119] the term 'hysteria' curiously echoing the words of the film's detractors and those opposing its exhibition.

The programme also included an experimental film from the US (Melville Webber's *The Fall of the House of Usher*), Walt Disney's *The Barn Dance* (1929) and, most significantly, the Scottish documentary film-maker John Grierson's *Drifters*, made in 1929 under the aegis of the Empire Marketing Board. '*Drifters*', Grierson wrote, 'is about the sea and about fishermen, and there is not a Piccadilly actor in the piece':

> The life of Natural cinema is in this massing of detail, in this massing of all the rhythmic energies that contribute to the blazing fact of the matter. Men and the energies of men, things and the functions of things, horizons and the poetics of horizons: these are the essential materials. And one must never grow so drunk with the energies and the functions as to forget the poetics.[120]

Heavily influenced by *Battleship Potemkin*, which Grierson had helped prepare for its US exhibition, *Drifters* was shown first in the programme, leading a disgruntled Eisenstein to assert that this act of homage had functioned rather more as a theft of his thunder. The programme was, in fact, highly significant in the future development of the Film Society's activities, with the Griersonian documentary movement gaining the ascendancy, not only in the Society's programmes but also in 1930s British film culture more generally.[121]

While Eisenstein's lectures with discussion (described as on the topic of 'The Theory of Film Direction and Scenario Reconstruction') were in progress, the experimental film-maker Hans Richter was giving a practical course on the making of an abstract film.[122] Earlier that same year, on 3 February, V. I. Pudovkin had delivered an address to the Film Society on the topic of 'Types as Opposed to Actors' translated from the Russian by Montagu. Copies of the address were sent out to members, and it was deployed as a critical frame in the programme notes at this time: Robert Florey's 'The Life and Death of a Hollywood Extra' (1928) was described as an amateur experimental film which 'provides perhaps a comment upon Mr Pudovkin's theory of the use of types as opposed to actors'.[123] Pudovkin's lecture was also published in the journal *Cinema* (6 February 1929), and in the enlarged edition of Pudovkin's 1929 book *Film Technique*, translated and annotated by Montagu and published in 1933, which contained additional essays on the uses of sound and the transcript of a lecture, initially written as an address for the Worker's Film Federation, on 'Close-ups in Time'.

'Types Instead of Actors' was an explication of 'montage' principles, with a description of the Kuleshov–Pudovkin experiments with cutting between static, inexpressive close-ups of an actor's face—'quiet close-ups'—and various shots; of a plate of soup, a dead woman in a coffin, a little girl playing with a toy bear. Audiences, it was said, found in the actor's blank expression the intense emotions of hunger, grief, and joy respectively. Pudovkin linked this to his preferred use of non-actors in films: the Mongols in *Storm over Asia* 'can easily compete, as far as acting honours are concerned, with the best actors'.[124] The final section of the talk discussed the use of sound in films, and the potential for non-synchronous and contrapuntal sound; the most influential account of this had come in the joint statement written by Eisenstein, Pudovkin, and Alexandrov, published for the first time in the October 1928 issue of *Close Up*, and discussed in my next chapter. In 'Types Instead of Actors', Pudovkin wrote of the 'real future' of sound films:

> All the sounds of the whole world, beginning with the whisper of a man or the cry of a child and rising to the roar of an explosion. The expressionism of a film can reach unthought-of heights.
>
> It can combine the fury of a man with the roar of a lion. The language of the cinema will achieve the power of the language of literature.[125]

The programme note for Pudovkin's *The End of St. Petersburg*, alongside which the forthcoming lecture 'Types as opposed to Actors' was promoted, read: 'Note should be made of the frequency in this film of a method with which Mr. Pudovkin experimented in *Mother*, the insertion of spoken titles at the moment of utterance but not in conjunction with the image of the speaker.'[126]

The substance of Pudovkin's lecture was taken up in the national and regional press, with Robert Herring using 'The Week on the Screen' in the *Manchester Guardian* to discuss 'A Russian on Films', as well as his article for *Close Up*, 'Storm over London', to discuss 'sound imagery': 'Pudovkin gets right down, not to the literal thing, but to the common thing between sight and sound, and the common thing they share is not the matching of what we see and hear. Pudovkin would combine the fury of an angry man with the roar of a lion. Think about what that means.'[127] Charles Davy, literary editor and film critic for the *Yorkshire Post*, devoted more than one column to quotation from, and discussion of, Pudovkin's talk and to the question of sound 'used not realistically but as a kind of expressive commentary on visual action'.[128] Davy expressed puzzlement in the article about one aspect of 'contrapuntal sound'; 'Shall we be able to watch comfortably films incorporating sound effects, but in which the observed conversation of the characters is unaccompanied by audible dialogue? Would not this require the acceptance of a rather strained convention?' He put this question to Montagu in a letter, who replied that conversation in film should in any case be avoided, and made the argument for non-naturalistic sound. Drafts of articles written by Montagu on this topic reveal that he was never a true convert to sound film; his physiological, and curiously passive, model of film spectatorship included the perception that apprehension occurs through the eye not the ear—'we do not understand through the ear'—and he argued against 'the assumption that the effect of a visual impulse plus an auditory impulse must be potentially stronger than a visual impulse alone'.[129]

The issue of passive versus active spectatorship, a topic at the heart of the project of *Close Up*, in which it became a way of defining the radical divorce between commercial cinema and 'film as an art', arose in curious ways in the Film Society context. Repeated written enjoinders to the Society's members to refrain from conversation during the films, including sound films, suggests less than rapt audiences, though it is of course conceivable that they were, *pace* Vachel Lindsay, acting as 'film explainers' and producing their own critical commentaries on the spectacle before them. Writing in the first issue of the journal *Cinema Quarterly* in 1932, Montagu produced a retrospective account of the Society's activities (though they would in fact continue for another seven years):

> Times have changed, and it is not easy to recapture some of the highspots of those early days. *Raskolnikov*, when we tried a two-hour show with no music but a battery of coughs; *The End of St. Petersburg*, when a naughty journalist, writing over three different names in about twenty different papers, tried to pretend there was a riot, and only the happy accident of the presence in our audience of a Conservative M.P. saved us from a knuckle-rapping in the Commons; Léger and Murphy's *Ballet Mécanique*, when there really was a riot, but not about politics, and Clive Bell said 'Marvellous,' and Dobson, overhearing, confessed ruefully: 'Begins to make one wonder what they say about one's own work, doesn't it?' There were fights and quarrels a-plenty, and I do not think it is conceit to claim that, in the midst certainly of plenty of dull drivel, we did introduce to England new techniques, new workmen, and new films that have not always been infertile.[130]

In his autobiography, Ivor Montagu again recalled 'the riot', but attached it this time to the occasion on which René Clair's *Entr'acte* (1924) was shown at the New Gallery, with the audience booing, screaming, and cheering, and Clive Bell 'denouncing those who had had the temerity to boo [as] blasphemers of artistic experiment'. The anecdote suggests something of the Society's founders' ironic distance from Bloomsbury culture (in the person of Clive Bell), as well as a refusal to take too seriously what was perceived as Clair's jeu d'esprit rather than a 'serious surrealist' work.[131]

The description of the occasion also relates to accounts of the first Paris showing of *Entr'acte* as part of Francis Picabia's ballet *Relâche*, performed at the Théâtre de Champs-Elysées on 4 December 1924, which has come to emblematize the avant-garde event as 'riot', the audience responding with 'boos, whistles, howls of disgust, and scattered applause', though other accounts have suggested that it was something of a damp squib, with Picabia desperately urging the silent audience to make a noise.[132] Whatever the truth of the matter, there would seem to have been a desire on the part of the Film Society audience to respond in the uproarious fashion of Paris, the heartland of avant-garde art. The Théâtre de Champs-Elysées was, moreover, the arena for the first performance of Stravinsky's *The Rite of Spring* (one of Diaghilev's productions for the Russian Ballet) on 29 May 1913, the violent audience response to which has become a matter of legend. The uproar connoted a resistance to the avant-garde work while at the same time appearing as an avant-garde act in itself.

Montagu's bringing together, in his article for the *Cinema Quarterly*, of the absence of any riot during the showing of *The End of St. Petersburg*, despite the journalist's attempt to whip up a political storm, and the real riot ('but not about politics') accompanying the surrealist film, can be understood as, at one level, a figuration of the 'two avant-gardes' with which the Film Society was involved. In an essay entitled 'The Two Avant-Gardes', Peter Wollen looked back, from the perspectives of the mid-1970s, and the debates about realism and avant-gardism central to that decade, to the situation in the 1920s. He identified one group in film culture—Léger–Murphy, Picabia–Clair, Eggeling, Richter, Man Ray, Moholy-Nagy and others—whose work was associated with painting (we recall Léger's description of the Ursulines as 'the cinéaste's studio'), and another in the Russian directors, 'whose films were clearly avant-garde but in a different sense', and who, coming from the worlds of theatre and poetry rather than Cubist painting, did not break with a realist aesthetic.[133] The division does not, of course, hold fast; Dziga-Vertov's anti-realist experiments, for example, position him in both camps. In any case, it was the crossing of the divide in the 1920s that produced some of the most significant affiliations and configurations. This might prove most fruitful in thinking through the relationship between the Film Society's commitments, not only to both 'the avant-guerre' and the 'avant-garde', but also to both avant-garde film and Left politics. As Annette Michelson has written: 'a certain euphoria enveloped the early film-making and theory. For there was, ultimately, a real sense in which the revolutionary aspirations of the modernist movement in literature and the arts, on the one hand, and of a Marxist or Utopian tradition, on the other, could converge in the hopes and promises, as yet undefined, of the new medium.'[134]

Let's Go to the Pictures

From its inception, the Film Society spurred a number of journals to begin covering the cinema for the first time, or in new ways. In *The Nation and Atheneum*, for which Leonard Woolf acted as literary editor from 1923 onwards (at which point it was still *The Nation*), a film column, 'From Alpha to Omega', appeared on October 31 1925, and discussed the opening programme of the Film Society. The reviewer expressed 'some disappointment': Ruttmann's abstract 'Absolute Films' 'left me cold'; 'the resurrection of a cowboy film of 1912' was less amusing than it might have been; Adrian Brunel's burlesques were 'crude and thin'. The main film, Paul Leni's *Waxworks*, was 'extremely patchy', and only 'Champion Charlie', 'a very early Chaplin film', received unalloyed praise: 'there can be no doubt about the genius of the Anglo-Saxon for the knock-about or about the high place which it takes in the art of humour.' The review concludes thus: 'I hope the Film Society will live and prosper, but it is clear that the selection of a programme will not be easy'.[135]

Later columns gave attention to the screening of *Raskolnikov*, with its 'monotony of horror'. The accompanying film *A quoi rêvent les jeunes films* was, the *Nation and Atheneum* journalist wrote, 'full of suggestions of cinematic possibilities... [with] a giddy journey by water and by land round Paris, which reproduces many of the thrills of the Sensation Park at Wembley'.[136] The fifth performance featured Paul Czinner's *Nju* ('the question of criticizing such a film is a difficult one, for it has never yet been resolved upon what characteristics "a good film" depends')[137] and, on 20 March 1926, there was *Caligari* ('a remarkable film', but with 'great weaknesses', in particular its decor, 'which tries to get its effect... by mere distortion'.)[138] Thereafter the column began to review, in brief, films at other London cinemas (including the New Gallery, the Plaza, and the Tivoli). In May 1926 'From Alpha to Omega' became 'Plays and Pictures', as if to signal that cinema would receive equal attention to theatre, but in fact discussions of film became more perfunctory in the column.

In *Vogue*, Bonamy Dobrée's regular article on London theatre productions, 'Seen on the Stage', first incorporated a review of a Film Society performance in the issue for late December 1925, at once blurring the boundaries between theatre and film, and suggesting the differences between their respective aesthetics. After reviewing productions of a number of plays and revues (including Ibsen's *A Doll's House*, Congreve's *A Mourning Bride*, Cochran's *Still Dancing*, Granville Barker's *The Madras House*, and Frederick Reynolds' *The Dramatist*), both West End and at smaller, independent venues, Dobrée turned to the Film Society and Lotte Reiniger's *Cinderella*. Making no mention of the other films in the programme, which included two from the 'Resurrection' series, one a Sennett Keystone comedy with Chaplin, Dobrée wrote of the silhouette film *Cinderella*, in an echo of Vachel Lindsay's celebration of 'fairy splendour': 'A prettier film could not be imagined... The cinema is made for fairy tales.' Yet he also implied that the film, though charming, was to some extent anodyne, perhaps failing to meet the expectations of the Film Society's self-declared 'forward policy', or 'to do for the cinema', in Dobrée's words, 'what the Stage Society has done for plays': 'It is for its most enterprising productions that the Film Society will receive most unfavourable criticism. But we hope—and are confident—that it will continue undisturbed to base its policy on "de l'audace, de l'audace et toujours de l'audace."'[139]

Towards the end of 1926, Dobrée reviewed, in 'Seen on the Stage', both the Russian Ballet and the Film Society performance of Robert Wiene's *The Hands of Orlac*, shown on 24 October 1926. On this occasion, he discussed the entire programme, rather than the full-length film in isolation, noting the interest of 'the rapid-movement plant pictures, the mating-dances of birds, and some abstract patterns, once more reinforcing the lesson that the film should concentrate on what the stage cannot do'. An early Griffiths film, *Beyond All Law* (1912), 'full of the most naif good sentiments and startlingly unmistakeable "registering" of emotions, filled the house with cynical laughter, while a middle period Chaplin film, [*One A.M.* (1917)], was amusing, but too long. A joke too often repeated becomes an agony'.

Dobrée was critical of *The Hands of Orlac* and of the fact that 'so much technical skill and ingenuity, so much artistry in acting, should be applied to such a foolish play and such a horrible theme... For speech being absent to transform the horror, the thing is too appalling, and subserves neither the purposes of daily life nor those of art. For art is not mere sensation.'[140] Here we see the drama critic finding the horror of the Expressionist cinematic spectacle unredeemed and unredeemable in the absence of words. Reviewing the Film Society's 10th performance, which included Walter Ruttmann's *Kriemhild's Dream of Hawks* from *Siegfried* (1923), and Fritz Lang's *Dr Mabuse* (1922), Dobrée commented that Lang's film failed to stay within the bounds of its chosen genre, the detective tale: 'it is a sad pity that film producers have not defined the confines of their art as clearly to themselves as a writer of a good detective novel must.' He highly commended Ruttmann's film, however, which, with its accompanying organ note, 'gave the mind that feeling of contraction and dilation one experiences with an anaesthetic before one goes under; that painful catching of the conscious on the unconscious; that feeling of some utterly unexplored part of one trying to escape the inevitable. It almost made the captions unnecessary, except that here one very nearly found perfect balance between silence and the spoken word.'[141]

It would be another project, and an interesting one, to explore the ways in which the emergence of 'film as an art' on the cultural scene began to shape the drama critics' responses to theatre as well as to the new medium of film. Of the stage production of Andreyev's *Katerina*, for example, Dobrée wrote that the amount which the director Komisarjevsky's 'manages to make his actors convey by the slightest of gestures, or the movement of an eyelid, is an object-lesson': his critical plaudit was shaped to the scale and dimensions of the cinematic close-up.[142]

Iris Barry's first articles on the cinema for *Vogue* had appeared in August 1924, prior to the Film Society's foundation. 'Seen on the Screen' was a series of captioned stills and publicity shots, of stars and sets, while in 'The Scope of Cinema' Barry began to explore the tenets that would characterize her film criticism throughout the 1920s. The tone differed markedly from the dismissive and defensive attitudes adopted by most of the writers in the periodical press, discussed earlier in this chapter. Barry began with the assertion that 'numbers of well-known writers, and artists too, go frequently to the cinema', and that this was unsurprising, given its powers of 'mental distraction' and the wealth of the imagery and 'experience' that it allowed them to store up 'in their sub-conscious minds for use in the future'. This enrichment of the inner life was, she argued, matched by the knowledge cinema provided of other peoples and places, and its insights into 'the psychological necessities of modern humanity (for it is obvious that the cinema would not have been established itself as it has but for the fact that it does in some way solve the complexes of our age)'.[143] Piling up examples, Barry was concerned to illustrate precisely the 'scope' of film (from travel and nature films to picture-plays in various genres, to Westerns and animated films), before she moved to the question of a cinematic art:

But here and there on the screen in any of these films may flash a fugitive beauty; for a film is not simply photography, it is a story told in motion. In the various rhythms of speed as well as in the more obvious 'artistic' staging the film-producer can now and again capture for us both psychological and visible loveliness. At the moment it is from Germany that the most interesting films are coming... But there are delights for the eye in almost all films... stimulat[ing] vivid flashes of imagination in the spectator.[144]

Barry thus derived the 'aesthetic' of the cinema—its 'fugitive beauty'—from the films themselves, and not as a quality abstracted from or running counter to them. In 'The Cinema in Three Moods', in which she discussed Lubitsch's *The Marriage Circle* (social satire), Fairbank's *The Thief of Baghdad* (fantasy), and *Abraham Lincoln* (biographical film), Barry wrote: 'We shall have to stop generalising about "films".'[145]

For her two articles on 'Paris Screens and Footlights', Barry discussed both theatre and avant-garde films, as a central part of the Parisian film scene. She described (with no mention of a riot) the 1924 performance of the Picabia–Satie ballet *Relâche*, its interval 'gloriously filled with a film by M. M. Picabia and René Clair [*Entr'acte*]. A film which has all the charm and inconsequence of a dream; *avant garde* and *arrière garde* could meet on a common Freudian basis here',[146] and the showing of Marcel L'Herbier's *L'Inhumaine* and Fernand Léger and Dudley Murphy's *Ballet Mécanique*. This 'Dada' film she described as a 'percussion of pictures' in which 'the motion is in the picture rather than in the object, the rhythm is controlled and the effect thereby gained by using static objects instead of moving ones':

> Really moving effects in both senses of the word are accomplished with egg-beaters and cake dishes, whose shapes and surfaces are reflected and repeated not only with mirrors but with special lenses, to the confused delight of the beholder... This is, I believe, an entirely new idea in moving pictures, but the directors do not stop there. They give one rather a study in comparative motion, for the artificial motion achieved by camera treatment is varied from time to time with pictures of the very actual and terrific motion to be found on scenic railways, 'shoot the chutes', and other devices; with the more circumscribed movement of a roulette wheel, or the monstrous movement of a real machine.[147]

Yet, in a 1926 *Vogue* article on 'The Future of Films', which described the Film Society's role in 'giving us all the most admired high-brow films', and discussed a number of the films in the Society's early programmes (including *Crime and Punishment*, *Nju*, and *Entr'acte*), Barry reiterated her scepticism over the possibility of 'abstract' films playing 'a principal part in the development of the art. They are based largely on an analogy with music which is of doubtful validity. Certain movements of form are employed at intervals like the themes in a symphony, but we have not, at least at present, the faculty to appreciate such rhythms with any precision. We can *see* intervals in space, and we can *hear* intervals in time.' The issue here—and the open question—is whether it would take a 'new' human faculty—a new imbrication of eye/ear and space/time—before 'abstract' and 'experimental' films could become part of cinema's central development. Barry ended her article not with an answer to this question, but with a celebration of Chaplin, 'the one certain genius' the cinema has produced, whose 'improbable' behaviour represented the future of film in 'its use of the unexpected': 'Films are photographic in method; they need not be photographic in spirit.'[148] The claims for 'the unexpected' and the endorsement of Jean Cocteau's category of 'accidental beauty' as the highest cinematic values militated against the construction of filmic prototypes: *Caligari* was, for Barry, a great film, but 'le Caligarisme' was pointless imitation.

'At its very lowest, the moving picture brings every week both happiness and a definite nervous and mental relaxation to many millions of jaded human units in our less than ideal industrial civilizations' Barry wrote in 1925, in her regular film column, 'The Cinema', in *The Spectator*:

> Its social value is great: the cinema plays no small part in broadening the common horizon; its ubiquitous Pathé Gazette and travel films alone deserve credit for supplying a vicarious experience of contemporary events and foreign places which quite certainly is evolving, gradually, countless men and women who are 'citizens of the world.' But, beyond all this, though the moving picture has affinities with the respectable muses, it is a substitute for none of them, but one of the phenomena for which our age will be remembered: a new art born painfully and ingloriously, as no doubt the other arts too were born in unremembered days—a new art more than we realize, for though it tells a story it is not a literary form; though it is a pictorial medium it is also a dramatic one; yet its concerns are not those of the theatre and its problems the very opposite of those that confront painters.[149]

At the beginning of her book *Let's Go to the Pictures* (1926), she repeated: 'I should like to discuss why we do slink into the cinema and what happens to us there.'[150] 'The cinema', she argued, 'helps us to live complete lives, in imagination if not in fact.'[151] Writing in 1926, before sound film became more than an experiment (though she did not hold out against sound, seeing it as a 'composite form': for Barry, the conceptual 'transition to sound' was a relatively smooth one)[152], she continued to define the aesthetic of film in more or less entirely visual terms. 'To be a habitué' (of the cinema), Barry wrote, 'makes one easily suggestible through the eye, quick at observing manners, gestures and tricks of expression.'[153] In her *Vogue* articles, as we have seen, she had written of the 'fugitive beauty' that may 'flash' on the screen, and she repeated this in *Let's Go to the Pictures*: 'the finest films are as lovely to the eye as they are moving to the emotions. Their beauties, like those of music and the ballet, are fugitive, it is true: it is the accumulated succession of diverse images which gives aesthetic delight. Yet, because the moving picture speaks direct to the eye, it is a powerful form of communication.'[154] As in so much film writing of the period, eye and ear were polarized, the coming of cinema seeming to fragment the sensorium: 'The eye can take in more and more definite impressions in a given time, and can associate ideas more quickly than the ear'; 'Visual imagery is less primitive and more sophisticated than auditory imagery.'[155]

Barry's long career in film had started in the early 1920s, when she became film correspondent for the *Daily Mail* (from 1923) and began her regular column for the *Spectator*, at the same time writing for a number of other journals, including *The Adelphi* and *Vogue*. She became a founder member of the Film Society in 1925, largely on the basis of her role as the *Spectator*'s film critic.[156] Her other writings of this period included a satirical novel called *Splashing into Society*, published in 1923, and a biography of Lady Mary Wortley Montagu, published in 1928, a work of the 'new biography' which reveals one aspect of the ways in which film and literature were coming together in this period, with biography now focusing on vivid scenes and representing character through gesture, and film (as in *Abraham Lincoln*, much admired by Barry) borrowing the narrative trajectories of the individual life. In 1930 Barry moved to New York, helping to form a New York Film Society in that year, and by 1935 had become the curator of the newly founded Film Library of the Museum of Modern Art. She became its director in 1946, and one of the most significant figures in the history of film studies and the film archive movement.[157]

Prior to her professional involvement with cinema, Iris Barry's artistic aspirations were directed towards literature, and poetry in particular, though she had developed a strong interest in film at an early age. Educated at a convent school in Belgium, she returned to her native Birmingham in 1914 and, while working as a clerk, sought to enter the literary world. Her poetry was published in Harold Monro's magazine *Poetry and Drama* in 1914, and in Harriet Monroe's *Poetry* magazine in 1916 and 1922. In 1916, she was represented by eight poems (poems by Ezra Pound and T. S. Eliot were published in the same issue). Imagist inspired, written in *vers libre*, Barry's poetry revolved around the desire for escape: 'I am here, unhappy,/Longing to escape the hearth/longing to escape from the home.' In the poem 'Double', she wrote: 'Through the day, meekly, I am my mother's child. Through the night riotously I ride great horses.'[158]

Barry came to London in 1916, encouraged by Ezra Pound, with whom she had been in correspondence about her writing.[159] Through Pound she met Wyndham Lewis: two children were born during the brief few years of their relationship.[160] In 1931, Barry published an essay in the New York *Bookman* entitled 'The Ezra Pound Period' in which she recalled literary life in London during the war years, describing with some irony the aspiring young poets of that time, followers of Pound, who ended up producing 'an avoidance in prose rather than in poetry of the use of "seven words where three will do"'. Of her attempt to capture this period, embodied in the extraordinary, 'inflammable', energies of Pound, and representing a preservation of 'creative desire and passionate execution' in the face of war, when 'so much else was being scattered, smashed up, killed, imprisoned or forgotten', Barry wrote: 'by the time what was once the present begins to take on the more shapely form of the past it is possible to distinguish what was really and not merely temporarily interesting, it is already too late to listen, ask questions, get things straight and seize the moment on the wing'.[161] Like a film, the Ezra Pound years had passed into the past.

Peter Brooker, in a reading of 'The Ezra Pound Period' which opens up questions of artistic identity, gender and sexuality 'in the vortex of Pound's Kensington', notes that Barry did not extend this sketch of her London life into the years of the 1920s, the film years, and that this is 'symptomatic of the difficulty, then and since, of making an argument for a different kind of popular or 'vernacular modernism'. While there was an accord, 'The Ezra Pound Years' suggested, between Pound's and Barry's rejections of conventional morality and of 'Mrs Grundy', 'a significant difference had emerged between them outside the frame of her essay. Pound's case for the arts was linked with an unambiguous elitism while [Barry's] work as a curator at MOMA matched a broad conception of art'.[162]

There were, nonetheless, important connections between Barry's 'lit-erary' years of the mid- and late-1910s and her involvement with the cinema.[163] In her early verse are glimpses of the cinematic shadow-play that would allow her to connect poetry and film, as in 'Enough has been said of sunset': 'Mysterious; threatening: Dawn over housetops silhouetted / Like crenelated battlements / Against light of a stage scene.' This is strongly marked in the three poems that appeared in *Poetry* in 1922, with their representation of shadows trailing across dream-screens.[164] In *Nocturne* she wrote of 'Shadows of boughs / Lattice-wise falling / On white walls / Of my home / Beneath the moon', and the echo of this resounds in the open-ing pages of *Let's Go to the Pictures*, in which she defended cinematography as an art, and represented it in terms closely allied to Imagist aesthetics:

> It is already a visual as well as a dramatic art: the finest films are as lovely to the eye as they are moving to the emotions. Their beauties, like those of music and the ballet, are fugitive, it is true: it is the accumulated succession of diverse images which gives aesthetic delight. Yet, because the moving picture speaks direct to the eye, it is a powerful form of communication. Scenes of which we can read or even see with pleasurable excitement played on the stage would be intolerable when given with all the silent and intimate reality of the screen. So it comes about that even in the crudest films something is provided for the imagination, and emotion is stirred by the simplest things—moonlight playing in a bare room, the flicker of a hand against a window. Is this not a virtue, dramatically, and for its enhancement of what, apart from the films, would be common and pointless?[165]

Later in the text, Barry made an explicit link between poetry and film, in a chapter devoted to subtitles, a topic which much absorbed her attention.

> The making of sub-titles might well be held to be a new form of literary style. The sub-title must be crystalline, packed with meaning, allusive, condensed—a work of art and elegance and simplicity, in fact. I think the *vers-librists* would make good title writers: they write fresh active pictorial phrases, they avoid redundancies, elaborations, cliches. Producers in America will have no trouble in discovering the best people in this school of poetry and in harnessing them. I myself have taken past exercise in *vers libre*, and for fear of seeming artful or impertinent, I frankly offer myself as an apprentice sub-titler for a period of six months to any film company that cares to have me. Brevity would be my motto and eloquence (not flowery eloquence but the small sweet voice) my ambition.[166]

Here again we see the close association drawn between an Imagist aesthetic and the literary 'signature' in the film text—one made by a number of writers and critics in the early decades of the century, including Vachel Lindsay. Barry's discussion can, in broader terms, be situated in the context of the Imagist focus on the visual dimensions of literary representation, insisted upon by Herbert Read, early associated with the Imagist movement, who turned his attentions to film in the early 1930s. In Chapter 2, I quoted from 'The Poet and the Film', published in *Cinema Quarterly*, in which Read wrote:

> If you ask me to give you the most distinctive quality of good writing, I would give it to you in this one word: VISUAL. Reduce the art of writing to its fundamentals and you come to this single aim: to convey images by means of words. But to *convey images*. To make the mind see. To project on to that inner screen of the brain a moving picture of objects and events, events and objects moving towards a balance and reconciliation of a more than usual state of emotion with more than usual order. That is a definition of good literature—of the achievement of every good poet—from Homer and Shakespeare to James Joyce or Ernest Hemingway. It is also a definition of the ideal film.[167]

For the most part, Barry argued that film was an autonomous art, independent in its aesthetic of literature, theatre and painting. In her first columns for *The Spectator*, in particular, she explored the question of stage versus screen, arguing that 'the visual beauty of a film should be an aesthetic alternative to the stage's poetry', appealing for 'films throughout which pictures of ineffable loveliness should melt into each other', and rejecting the view that the cinema was inferior to the stage. It had, she declared, 'its peculiar advantages': the intimacy between spectator and spectacle; the representation of a 'fuller world' than could be realised on the stage, and the ability (and here she was echoing Vachel Lindsay) to bring out the significance in 'natural objects': 'Chairs and tables, collar-studs, kitchenware and flowers take on a function which they have lost, except for young children, since animism was abandoned in the accumulating sophistications of "progress". The dramatic advantage of having Desdemona's handkerchief a protagonist, not a property, is obvious.'[168] Arthur Robison's *Warning Shadows* was, she wrote: 'Peculiarly cinematographic, the very inanimate objects speak undeniably.'[169]

For Barry, cinema extended the static visual arts and their aesthetic and conceptual concerns. Here the terms of a debate with Wyndham Lewis could be constructed. Film and cinematic representation undoubtedly penetrated Lewis's writing of the 1920s: its influence can be seen in the broad physical comedy of *Tarr* and of *Childermass*, with its overt references to 'Keystone' comedy (the Keystone giants) and its graphic representations of intertitling. In more complex ways, Lewis's work also exhibited a fascination with 'mechanical' man and with the radical reinscriptions of surface and depth in his constructions—literary and visual—of human subjects. Yet his direct commentary on cinema in this period was, for the most part, derogatory. *Filibusters in Barbary* contains a biting account (with strong echoes of the critiques of mechanical life discussed in Chapter 1) of 'film people' on location in Morocco: 'The whispering masses in the film palaces—it is for them that this description of filibuster filibusts—throwing up shoddy mirages, with his photographic sausage-machine, of the desert life—so falsely selected as to astonish into suspicion sometimes even the tamest robot.'[170] The male film-actors are characterized by their exaggerated physical gestures, and their artificiality (which Lewis contrasted with that of the stage actor); the actresses by their diminutive stature:

> They were all undersized, almost like another species, and their intense artificiality took the form of an odd degenerescence. In *forcing* the normal everyday reality, as it were—in compelling it to conform to what was certainly a vulgar average, but a particularly odd variety of the vulgarest commonplace—they suggested the exact opposite of the *heightening* said to characterize the finest art. Theirs was a *lowering*: but it was a descent so much below the average level as to be eccentric and extraordinary.[171]

In *Time and Western Man*, Lewis both invoked and occluded questions of cinema, with chapters on Chaplin, Gertrude Stein, and Anita Loos and the 'time mind', in which he linked the 'naïf' writing of Stein, and its compulsive repetitions, with that of the Hollywood screenplay writer, and popular novelist, Anita Loos. The diminutive Loos's *Gentleman Prefer Blondes*, with its 'naïf illiterate jargon', achieved, Lewis wrote, 'a similar success to that of the *Young Visiters*', Daisy Ashford's best-seller (which had provided the prototype for Barry's *Splashing into Society*). Lewis further linked the 'child-factor' in Stein—'a huge, lowering, dogmatic Child'—with the *doll* like quality of Picasso's colossal figures, and Loos's 'child-factor' with (in an echo of Léger's use of a Chaplin doll in *Ballet Mécanique*) Chaplin's 'little doll-like face, his stuck on toy moustache, his tiny wrists, his small body' whose appeal, 'as far as the popular audience is concerned, is maternal'.[172] Barry, in strong contrast, argued against an image of cinema as a diminished or diminutive mechanical or doll's house world (attaching this criticism to theatre) and represented cinematic animism as modernity's renewed attentiveness to the visual and object world, giving a positive twist to any imputation of film's infantilism.

Film, Barry argued, animated the world of the object: 'It shows us the object behaving.'

> The objects, seen in the round in a sense, move not only on their own axes but also in free orbit, and the line of their motion describes the depth of the scene ... It may be objected that the objects are not seen in the round because the screen is flat. But in order to reassure oneself that the Venus de Milo is not hollow behind, it is not necessary to walk round her. It is sufficient if she is revolved for us. And that is what happens on the screen: the objects are revolved for us ... I wonder sometimes why the Montmartre cubists go on cubing when the cinema exists.[173]

There are echoes here of Münsterberg's discussion of the impression of depth and motion produced on the screen, as well as of Joyce's Leopold Bloom's meditations on what the female statues—Juno, Venus—in the library museum look like behind.[174] The dream of the moving statue is given a new dimension in cinema's cubistic context. The question of movement governed all aspects of Barry's discussion of cinema: 'Space as a limitation is banished: it becomes not a convention but a factor. Time as a limitation is destroyed too. In a flash we can be seven thousand years back, a century forward, in a thousand ages and areas. And all the while there is something to look at. It moves.' 'A cinema audience is not a corporate body, like a theatre audience, but a flowing and inconstant mass.'[175]

Cinema, it is implied, extends Wyndham Lewis's kind of machine art: 'the cinema, because it is not static, can take up that part of the modern artist's problems where he is forced to leave off.'[176] In Barry's film writings, we find the conjunction of the discursive and the material, brought together in the object-relation to this medium which was, as she defined it in the 1920s, the realm of the object. Here her understanding of the mass medium also connected her to the cinematic avant-garde, including Fernand Léger's writings in the 1920s on the cinematic transformation of the object: 'It becomes an independent personality.' There were, moreover, echoes in her film writing, despite its directness, of the experimental prose-poetry of her contemporaries, such as that of the artist Jessie Dismorr, one of the few women associated with the Vorticist movement, whose 'Matinee' was published in *The Little Review* (as were translations of Léger's articles on the cinema) in 1918:

I treat with respect the sparkling and gesticulating dust that confronts me: of it are compounded fruits and diamonds, superb adolescents, fine manners.

This pigment, disposed by the ultimate vibrations of force, paints the universe in contemporary mode.

I am glad it is up-to-date and ephemeral; that I am to be diverted by a succession of fantasies.

The static cannot claim my approval. I live in the act of departure.

Eternity is for those who can dispose of an amplitude of time.

Pattern is enough. I do not mention the soul.

Give me detail and the ardent ceremonial of commonplaces that means nothing.

...

I spell happiness out of dots and dashes; a ray, a tone, the insignificance of a dangling leaf.

Provided it has a factual existence, the least atom will suffice my need.

But I cannot stomach shadows. It is certain that the physical round world would fit my mouth like a lolly-pop.[177]

Dismorr's poem, like Gertrude Stein's contributions to *Close Up*, made an abstraction of the cinema itself—dust, pigment, movement, pattern, dots and dashes, detail—while giving it embodiment as 'the physical round world'. For Dismorr, as for Barry, cinema would seem to show 'the object behaving'.

Nonetheless, as we have seen, Barry was critical of avant-garde cinema, writing, in *Let's Go to the Pictures*, of "arty" little films', and suggesting that films like *Entr'acte* and *A quoi rêvent les jeunes films* represented a dead end in cinema's development:

'Amusing' in the slang sense as these pictures may be, original as they are, I am confident that there is no future whatsoever for films of this kind. That is to say, for films which merely aim at a rhythmical succession of either static objects or of objects in motion. It is true that the eye is forced to look at what moves, but unless something is going to happen through the motion, unless in fact there is a story value, the eye very quickly tires.[178]

The commitment Barry expressed in this context to 'story' in the film may have been in part strategic; an aspect of her intention to write a popular book on the cinema. Bryher, in her somewhat patronizing review of *Let's Go to the Pictures*—'Miss Barry has probably not seen one of the finest films made, "Joyless Street", which has only been privately shown in England'—was critical of Barry's 'estimate of modern experimental film. There is something imaginative about the abstract picture that is not found in the mere story-telling picture. And, contrary to her statement, there is no limit to what might be achieved.'[179] It was, however, more than mere populism that led to Barry's strictures on avant-garde cinema. Like Robert Herring, whose film criticism is discussed in more detail in the next chapter, Barry held to the view that all films, and not merely the cinema of abstraction, were studies in light and motion. It may also have been that Barry found avant-garde films too painterly, or too inspired by concepts of musical composition, linking the new art of film too firmly to 'the respectable muses', even if they were in their experimental guises.

In more complex ways, her comments also contain echoes of the distinction between 'abstract' and 'empathetic' art theorized by the art historian Wilhelm Worringer, which were mediated to the artists and writers associated with the Imagist and Vorticist movements in the 1910s by T. E. Hulme. For Hulme, 'abstraction' (which Worringer identified with the art of Africa, Egypt and China) was exemplified in the geometric art of his avant-garde contemporaries, and contrasted with an 'empathetic', humanist art, associated with the Renaissance, which Hulme believed had been superseded. In Wyndham Lewis's paintings, Hulme found 'the idea of machinery' relevant to the modern age.[180] Barry, in her account of *Ballet Mécanique* (the Léger-Murphy 'pure' film, in whose making Ezra Pound had been involved) was, in her article for *Vogue* discussed earlier, critical of the film's inclusion of 'a close up of a human eye or ... mouth, looking somewhat ineffectual and oversentimental amid this glittering array of metallic objects'. The use of letterpress in the film—the repeated flashing up of the sentence 'On a volé un collier de cinq millions' [5 million franc pearl necklace stolen]—'is upsetting because one's mind, hampered by literature, concludes that there must be a meaning in it, whereas there isn't':

> It proves, like the close-up of the languishing eye and the alluring mouth, a trap for one's preconceived notions, the art of the 'movie' having hitherto been devoted to merely human affairs and their accompanying emotions. It was a holiday to get among the pots and pans, the revolving crystal balls and dynamos, and the introduction of girls and letter-press constituted almost an intrusion.

At first sight, it would seem that Barry was celebrating the 'abstract', geometric, mechanical dimensions of the film, and rejecting the 'empathetic' elements of the human form which it introduced, in ways commensurate

Figure 8. Katherine Hawley Murphy swinging: *Ballet Mécanique* (Fernand Léger, France, 1924).

Figure 9. *Ballet Mécanique.*

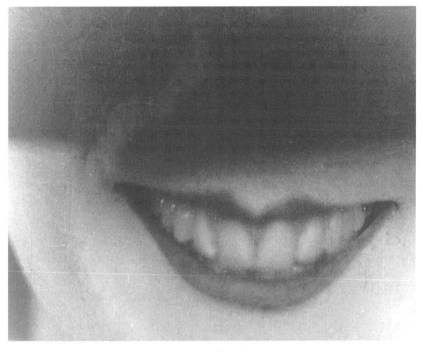

Figure 10. *Ballet Mécanique.*

Figure 11. *Ballet Mécanique.*

with Hulme's theories of art and culture. Yet it would in fact appear that Barry's objection to the close-ups of 'the languishing eye and the alluring mouth' amidst the pots and pans derived from her unease at the ways in which Dadaist and Surrealist film-makers were using the female body as part of their repertoire of images, 'sentimentally', as in the shots of a woman on a swing in *Ballet Mécanique*, or as part-objects. Barry was, it would seem, implicitly criticizing the ways in which the female form, either whole or fragmented, was (like the letter-press standing in for literature and 'the literary') made to bear the weight of an ultimately empty symbolization in the film. The defence of 'story' in the film made in *Let's Go to the Pictures*—at one level a defence of 'empathy' over and against 'abstraction'—also operated as a demand for a non-reified way of representing women in the cinema. Barry's critique of experimental film—her sense of its limitations—was, in ways that Bryher certainly did not seem to recognize, inseparable from her feminism.

While she was critical of the use of the letter-press in *Ballet Mécanique*, Barry was in fact absorbed by the question of the ways in which writing entered the visual world of the cinema, and with the visuality of writing, an issue which was also connected to the ideal of a pictorial poetry central to Imagism, and to its fascination with hieroglyphics. The function and nature of captions and intertitles were, as we have seen, a topic of much debate in film criticism, though particularly in the 1910s and 1920s. In her film criticism for *The Spectator* Barry almost unfailingly made some comment on the subtitling and intertitling, as in her review of Lang's *Der Niebelung*, in which she commended its visual beauty but complained about the horrible subtitling: 'One is forced to close one's eyes while the lettering is displayed in order to enjoy the film fairly at all.'[181] The issue of the subtitle, however, went beyond that of lettering, raising fundamental questions about the nature of film language and, indeed, the extent to which cinematic images could be understood as elements of a language. Did captions and intertitles represent the intrusion of the literary into what should be an essentially pictorial realm (Barry wrote of the absence of subtitles in *The Last Laugh* that 'it is a progress; it is not parasitic on any novel or play, does not resemble any literary form at all'[182]) or were they a valuable authorial signature in a medium otherwise lacking the markers of the individual creative consciousness? Were they to be understood as speech or as writing?

In the late 1920s, with sound film becoming a reality, the defenders of the silent film located audibility in the seeming silence of the cinema—a speaking silence. For Barry the subtitle was at one point defined in ways that both anticipated the function of the voice-over in sound film (akin to the Greek chorus) and as a form of expression or articulation outside, or beyond, the terms of formal language:

> In employing a chorus (among other things) to bridge space and time the Greek and the Japanese dramatists alike found a valuable convention. And the sub-title is really to the film what the chorus was to those dramas. ... This function is not, however, the only one that the sub-title has. As in dreams, there are, in these so real shadows of life, emotional situations which culminate in a cry. At a flash-point of the emotions, the sub-title is needed, unless the actors can let us, by their bearing or by lip-reading, get what their words must inevitably be ... this cry is ... an illumination, an amplification, a secret disgorged—and sometimes when that cry does not break out in lettering on the screen, one feels something missing, and the silence of the screen seems for a moment an empty not an eloquent silence.[183]

Barry was also emphatic, in her articles for *The Spectator* in particular, that writers should become more fully engaged with the new medium of the film, as scenarists in particular. Reviewing Ernst Lubitsch's *The Marriage Circle*, in a column entitled 'Hope Fulfilled' Barry noted: 'Everything is visualized, all the comedy is in what the characters are seen or imagined to be thinking or feeling, in the interplay, never expressed in words, of wills and personalities. There is a minimum of subtitling, and the progress of the plot is not dependent on the letterpress ... any attempt at verbal description at once demonstrates the superiority of the pictorial over the verbal method of telling such a story.'[184] Visual images were thus deemed greatly superior to words.

Barry suggested, in the same column, that playwrights and novelists extend their engagement with the new medium (beyond the granting of permission for 'adaptations' of their work, almost invariably unsatisfactory) and apprentice themselves to the 'seven producers of genius' (Lang, Grüne, Wiene, Lubitsch, Chaplin, Griffiths, and Seastrom) in order to 'learn the business of writing for the screen'. Writers should become 'visualisers'. Running throughout her column, and *Let's Go the Pictures*, was the endeavour to promote a new relationship between literature and film, and to redefine the terms in which word and image, writers and film-makers, would encounter each other. 'It is high time', she wrote, 'that writers sought to interest themselves actively and at first hand in cinematography, the newest and (I personally believe) at the moment the liveliest of the arts. It is by some such liaison that future progress will be assured.'[185] Writers, she reiterated in 'Of British Films' 'should write for the cinema. It is worth writing for'.[186] In an article entitled 'On Writing for Films', she noted 'a prejudice among most men of letters, usually unconscious, against the film as an art form'. Barry's critical task, as she represented it, was to draw attention to the false premises on which such prejudices were founded, and, in particular, to the widely held view of film among writers that 'it is necessary to write, and to think, down to it':

> A new form of artistic expression has arisen since the first picture flickered across the screen. It is the art of creating and 'scenarising' a story for the motion picture: ideally the two operations should be performed by the same person. Involved because it attempts to bridge the gap between one visual conception (that of the story-teller) and another (that of the director who actually makes the film), intricate because the medium is a complex one, yet it is immensely attractive. Lucrative beyond expectation, this game of telling tales in pictures to millions, it is also the work of a high order of imagination, of infinite craft, and of an altogether inspiring power.[187]

The 'progress' of the cinema, to which Barry's film writing was committed, was made substantially dependent on 'film writing' of various kinds, including an increased engagement of literary writers with the medium and the productive discourses of the new film criticism.

In a chapter entitled 'Difficulties' in *Let's Go to the Pictures*, however, she wrote of her increasing feeling that 'established writers of fiction and plays are too much wedded to their own medium to be able successfully to adapt themselves to writing for the films'.[188] The future, in this context, lay, she argued, with women rather than men because: '(a) women are more visually-minded than men on the whole, and (b) because the cinema is more for women than men. They would be persons of education, not necessarily with any kinds of diplomas or degrees, but persons such as now swarm the journalist and art sections of the community—lively-minded, curious, inventive creatures: above all able to project a picture in their own imagination, and to transfer it to paper by means of very non-literary words, very graphic words, and also by means of intelligible sketches.'[189] These 'new women'—like Barry herself—are represented as figures of the new media, working outside literary traditions, and their modernity is closely linked to the visual nature of their intelligence and imagination.

Her writing on this topic echoes articles in the US film magazines of this period (Barry first visited Hollywood in the late 1920s, was appreciative of the film culture she found there, and rarely colluded with the disparagement of American cinema characteristic of much of the British cinema commentary in this period[190]) as well as the numerous guides to scenario writing. An article in a 1923 issue of *Photoplay* described the careers of twelve successful screenwriters: 'women of good education and adaptability who have caught the trick of writing and understand the picture mind. These twelve women are essentially the feminine brains of the motion picture, making good equally with men.'[191] As Lizzie Francke writes, in her study of women screenwriters in Hollywood: 'A pattern was thus established in which screenwriting became the predominant outlet for women wanting to shape the substance of the images on the screen.'[192]

In Barry's film criticism as a whole there was the strong perception that cinema is a female sphere. As she put it: 'Now one thing never to be lost sight of in considering the cinema is that it exists for the purpose of pleasing women. Three out of four or all cinema audiences are women.'[193] Barry's representations and negotiations with this 'feminization' were, however, complex, shaping her writing in marked ways and, on occasions, resulting in a form of demotic, unpunctuated speech intended to represent a feminized, mass cultural reception. As she wrote:

> You do ask for *pictures* ... You only ask that something shall take place on the screen: it is restful and dark and you can talk or not as you like (at least while the music is one) and it is cheap. If you happen to be engaged or walking out, it is the best place in the world in which to sit and lean on each other with clasped hands. If you are married it often keeps your husband out of the club or the pub, and he may even learn some valuable lessons there (as pictures are made to please women).[194]

The second-person pronoun ('you do ask for pictures') could act either inclusively or as a distancing device. Barry was at junctures critical of the forms of 'day-dream' offered by the cinema (and we find here echoes of Siegfried Kracauer's 'The Little Shop-Girls Go to the Movies'). 'Pleasing women' turns out to be a dubious value: 'I suppose all successful novels and plays are also designed to please the female sex too. At any rate the overwhelming, apparently meaningless, and immensely conventional love interest in the bulk of films is certainly made for them.'[195] 'We might as well, then, do something about persuading the film producers not to drop treacle into our mouths any more. It is bad for us.'[196] While celebrating the dream and daydream aspects of film, she also expresses a wish (echoed in Dorothy Richardson's article for *Close Up*, 'This Spoon-Fed Generation') that 'the public could, in the midst of its pleasures, see how blatantly it is being spoon-fed, and ask for slightly better dreams'.[197] In many ways Barry's authorial position was unstable—alternately that of critic and of 'the public', populist and elite, moving between celebration and critique, in the search for a place and a voice for cinematic aesthetics.

'Every habitual cinema-goer', Barry wrote, 'must have been struck at some time or another by the comparative slowness of perception and understanding of a person not accustomed to the pictures... To be a habitué makes one easily suggestible through the eye, quick at observing manners, gestures and tricks of expression.'[198] Cinema was at once the realm of distraction, a 'sedative', and an awakening and attentiveness: a new alertness demanded by, and responsive to, the conditions of modernity.

The Unwilling Calligraphy of Revelation

The voices of women film critics in the first decades of the twentieth century were, indeed, powerful ones. Both Barry and C. A. Lejeune were highly influential figures in the history of film criticism and reception and, as we have seen in the case of Barry, the new institutions of cinema, including film societies and film archives. The newness of the cinematic medium, and, to some extent, its lower artistic status created openings for women journalists and critics less readily available to them in the established arts. For St John Ervine, it was certainly the lowly status of the cinema that made it a suitable medium for the attentions of the woman critic. 'The ablest critics of the cinema in this country, meaning by critics of the cinema those who have never been anything else, are Miss Iris Barry, who formerly wrote in the *Spectator* and the *Daily Mail*, and Miss C. A. Lejeune, who writes about pictures in *The Observer*' he admitted in his address to the Union Society, continuing however:

> The moving picture, indeed, has been called a woman's entertainment, and is primarily intended to appeal to their emotions. 'One thing never to be lost sight of in considering the cinema,' says Miss Iris Barry in her book, *Let's Go to the Pictures*, 'is that it exists for the purpose of pleasing women.

Three out of four of all cinema audiences are women,' and later on, in suggesting who are the right people to make movies, she says that the persons to be employed should be women rather than men, because (a) women are more visually-minded on the whole, and (b) because the cinema is more for women than men. We need not, therefore, feel astonished at the fact that the ablest critics of the cinema are women. But the cinema has not yet produced a great critic, a fact which in itself is sufficient to disqualify its claim to be considered an art; for art almost automatically creates a great body of critical opinion.[199]

Ervine thus used Barry's claim that the cinema 'exists for the purpose of pleasing women' to support his view of the mediocrity, or worse, of the medium and its commentators, while allowing that Barry and Lejeune were the best of their kind. In his view, film, its female audiences and its women critics were well, even symbiotically, matched to each other. This perception, born of his belittling of both women and the cinema, can in fact be turned to critical advantage. The questions raised by women film critics' approaches to the cinema, including their representations of the female audience for cinema, are addressed both in this chapter and the next in discussion of the writings on film of Barry, Lejeune, Richardson, and H.D.

In her memoir *Thank You For Having Me*, written after she had retired from journalism, Caroline Lejeune described her entry into the profession:

A young person has the capacity to live in a great many worlds at once; and about the same time that L.C. was reviewing Gilbert and Sullivan opera in the *Manchester Guardian*, and Miss Lejeune, English Honours student at the University, was exploring the mysteries of ballad opera in the eighteenth century, a 'back-pager' appeared in the *Guardian* over the initials C.L., entitled 'The Undiscovered Aesthetic'.

This was an impasssioned plea, running to a full column, for recognition by 'discriminating persons' of the new art form, the kinematograph.

'That it remains undiscovered as yet is no shame, for kinematography has barely grown beyond childhood, and her powers are not fully developed. Shame however it is, and black shame, that the finer intelligences, the more perceptive critics, should ignore the need for discovery and allow the young art to mature unworthily for lack of sympathetic guidance ... '

'What realms of experience can the new materials of kinematography more perfectly express? The instruments of the scenario-maker are borrowed on the one hand from drama and on the other from painting; here is the one art which can represent actions successive through time and objects adjacent in space; thereby confusing, more completely than the rhythmical school in painting or the descriptive school in music, Lessing's famous distinction of the arts.'

I shall never know why C. P. Scott [Editor of the *Manchester Guardian*] agreed to print this article ... But I know exactly how I came to write it.[200]

Watching Douglas Fairbanks in *The Mark of Zorro* in the summer of her final year at the University of Manchester, when 'the problem of my future had become acute' Lejeune recalled, 'my goal in life suddenly dawned on me. I was going to be a film critic'. 'The profession of film criticism had not yet come into being', she notes, but in 1921 James Bone, the London editor of the *Manchester Guardian* (to whom C. P. Scott, a family friend, had sent her) told her that she was the twenty-seventh person who had come to him with the idea that the newspaper was in need of a film critic. The moment had clearly arrived, and Lejeune was given a regular film column at the start of 1922: 'It was to be called "The Week on the Screen" and signed with the initials C.A.L.'[201] Lejeune produced her weekly column for the *Manchester Guardian* until 1928, when she left the newspaper to become film critic for *The Observer*, a position she held until 1960.

One of the striking aspects of 'The Week on the Screen' is the diversity of its approach to cinema (or 'kinema', as Lejeune, and other *Manchester Guardian* contributors, termed it at this stage), in which discussions of specific films were often mingled with, or subordinated to, broader reflections on technology, spectatorship, exhibition, the star system, and national cinemas. Lejeune did not, however, return to the terms deployed in her very first contribution to cinema criticism, 'The Undiscovered Aesthetic', in which she had attempted to define the essence of cinema by comparison with the other arts (and through the reference to Lessing which, as we have seen, became near obligatory in the meditations on film in the periodical press). 'Kinema', in 'The Week on the Screen', did not have to compete with the established arts for cultural status, though she did not believe it to be isolated from them. Cinema was, for Lejeune, in essence a popular medium; despite her high praise for many films and her life-long commitment to film criticism, she felt that the term 'art' should be used 'sparingly'.[202] She was resistant to the Film Society on its foundation in 1925, and to what she perceived as its exclusionary policies. She declared, in the words of Ivor Montagu, who described her as 'one of the first serious, non-gossip-monger film writers', for whose backing they had hoped, 'with red-hot obstinacy that nothing could be of any use that was not open to the public'.[203]

Lejeune's first column, on 7 January 1922, opened with a brief comment on the 'then and now' of film exhibition, noting the difference between the 'confused feeding' of early multiple programmes—'If we did not like it—well, it was quickly over, and we could try again'—and the double-billing of the present, one aspect of which was the 'use and abuse of the single-star habit'. Thus, at the outset, Lejeune took up her position against the star-system and for recognition of the director's importance; this approach became increasingly marked in her 'auteurist' responses to cinema. The Swedish cinema of Victor Seastrom was particularly commended for its abolition of 'the single star system', but Lejeune also noted that it was a habit to which British cinema 'has not fallen victim'.[204] Here her column echoed and contributed to the debates about the star system running in the trade press (whose most significant context was the perception that the absence of a British star system was responsible for British cinema's failure to compete with the American film) which as Christine Gledhill notes, were profoundly ambivalent: 'So we find in articles and letters by actors, producers and fans a contradictory mix of opinion. This includes outright resistance to stars for economic and high cultural reasons, equally vocal laments at the lack of investment in stars and reliance on the draw of West End stage names, combined with advice on how to produce and nurture stars'.[205]

'Thrills, Contests, and Conflicts' (14 January 1922), in which Lejeune called American cinema 'the film of yesterday', and British 'the film of tomorrow'—'the thrill of its best moments is the thrill of hope for the future, the joy of the immature but growing'—continued discussion of the film trade show world. Lejeune also started to use the gently satirical voice that became a feature of her later film columns:

> On Tuesday we shot a convict through a cupboard door and murdered a villain his own garden gate: on Friday we fought Russia for the possession of the Suez canal and blackmailed the Governor of the Bank of England: on Monday we helped Solomon against the armies of Sheba, poniarded a king, and threw whole dynasties out of gear; on Tuesday we came to earth and won a steeplechase. And the only thrill worthy of the name was the steeplechase—which, to our honour, was of British manufacture—an incident in the Granger Davidson film 'The Sport of Kings'.[206]

The use of the collective pronoun 'we' is significant in the context of early film criticism, in which it marked a range of subject positions. 'And here we all are as never before', Dorothy Richardson would write in one of her articles for *Close Up*, contrasting the collective experience of cinema-going with the more exclusionist and hierarchical theatre.[207] For H.D., in her first film article for the same journal: 'The word cinema (or movies) would bring to nine out of ten of us a memory of crowds and saccharine music and longdrawn out embraces ... and (if 'we' the editorial 'us' is an American) peanut shells and grit and perhaps a sudden collapse of jerry-built scaffolding.' 'I speak here', H.D. continued, 'when I would appear ironical, of the fair-to-middling intellectual, not of the fortunately vast-increasing, valiant, little army of the advance guard of the franc-tireur of the arts, in whose hands mercifully since the days of the stone-writers, the arts really rested.'[208]

'We', in this context, could then be the editorial 'we' of this avant-garde journal, or the ironical 'we' that ventriloquized the middle-brow point of view, or the 'we' that sought a communal experience with the group H.D. rather gracelessly termed 'the lump' (by contrast with the avant-gardist 'leaven'). Film, then, as a 'mass' art and entertainment, appeared to be a cultural leveller that had brought into being a new collective subject, but the cinema's uncertain cultural status, and the diverse nature of its cultural products, meant that the commentating voice ended up adopting a variety of vantage points and perspectives, inclusionist and exclusionist, ironic and otherwise. Thus 'talking in the cinema' was very much a question, though it was often confused or occluded, of who was talking, or appeared to be talking, to whom, and in what mode of address.

In her third film column Lejeune turned to the question of monochrome and colour film, and argued that monochrome film was a more appropriate medium for cinema's innate realism than colour film in its early, and crude, stages of development. Her assertion that cinema's general development was towards realism, and that film was 'rooted in the realism of photography', was lightly stated, but such comments raise questions which would later be very fully engaged by film theorists, as would Lejeune's thoughts on the different demands made, on film technique and film stock, by representations of the human face and form and the world of inanimate objects. It is, however, significant that Lejeune always saw technological developments—including colour and sound—as inevitable dimensions of film's development as a medium; her judgements were rarely predicated on an 'essence' of cinema or on a concept of 'pure' cinema. Thus she wrote, in this early column on 'Monochrome and Colour': 'Ultimately [colour photography] is inevitable; you can only show a coloured world faithfully through a coloured picture, but a clear black-and-white copy seems better to-day than a blurred reflection of pinks and blues, like a landscape seen in the water.'[209]

The realist imperative (to some extent put into question by Lejeune's own attraction to animated films) might, of course, imply some belief in a cinematic essence, but the issue is rather that Lejeune perceived cinema as an evolving medium, the stages of whose evolution were determined by the state of its technology. At the close of her study of 1931, *Cinema: A Review of Thirty Years' Achievement*, she wrote: 'The materials of the movie have been shaped, not by man, nor by nature, but by the conditions of technical competence ... It is this uncertainty, this changing quality of condition, that gives to the criticism of moving pictures its excitement and its difficulty.'[210] To this extent, her sense of film's mobility, and of the need to write a criticism adequate to this, was rooted much less in the perception of the fleeting and ephemeral nature of the film image (as it was for Eric Elliott, Robert Herring and many others), than in a concept of cinema's technological development, 'this changing quality of condition'.

A further early column was entitled 'Qualities of the Good Lay Critic'. Here Lejeune took up an article from the *Kinematograph Weekly* on 'Showmanship and the Lay Press', 'which tackles the subject very fairly, admitting the tremendous power of the daily newspaper, confessing the past mistakes of the kinema trade, but pointing out the utter uselessness of press attacks upon films already booked for the next two years'. The column reveals, very tellingly, that the trade and the trade press were feeling the threat of this new phenomenon, the 'lay' film critic, who had started writing in 'the daily and weekly lay papers'. The trade complaint, Lejeune wrote, was 'not without justice':

Against the half-dozen film critics who are specialists in their work one must set the dozens who, their only qualification being a facile pen, are proving themselves the worst enemies of art in the service of which they are nominally employed. There is the critic who despises the kinema. He has no sympathy with it, sees no value in it, and produces a very readable article by exploiting his own wit at its expense. Then there is the critic who treats the kinema as an inferior branch of the stage play, applying the same tests to both, and blaming the film because it does not answer them. There is the critic who has not troubled to study the technical side of his job, and the critic who has learnt everything a layman can learn about construction but has formed no clear ideas of a film aesthetic and has never considered its relationship to the other arts. These are the men against who showman and producer alike bear a righteous grudge.

The good lay critic, however, is a very different proposition, and the day is coming when the trade may well find him a friend in need. Artistic progress in the film world is threatened from two sides—by the 'intellectual' who sees no beauty anywhere in the output of the motion-picture camera, and by the film fanatic who sees beauty everywhere: by judgement without appreciation on one hand, and appreciation without judgement on the other. This is where the lay critic can be of immense service, acting as interpreter between producer and public, guiding the taste of the impartial, and bringing to the notice of the cynic beauties of acting and production which left to himself, he would wilfully ignore. A producer who is proud of his work should welcome the good lay critic, and it is a fact that the firms who treat him with the greatest courtesy and friendliness are those which are turning out the best screen material to-day.

To pass judgement on the kinema without a knowledge of its technique and a clear understanding of its aims is mere impertinence. And since no art stands or falls by itself, the critic should have experience of the other arts, certainly of painting, literature and the ballet, should know the limitations of each and its relation to the art of the silent stage. The film producer himself is too near his work to see it in proportion. The good lay critic must be a man with faith in the kinema but no prejudice: he must be patient, and not expect too much as yet from a very young industry; he must have a quickly adjustable mind which can flit rapidly from a boxing match to a scene from the Old Testament, from the life of a bee to the exploits of a detective, from Dumas to Ella Wheeler Wilcox, without putting his critical machinery out of gear. He must, above all, have a sliding scale of values, and judge according to the pretensions of a film. There are pictures on which it would be as ridiculous to waste serious criticism as on a Lyceum melodrama: they are intended merely as intoxicants, and the only question is whether they have succeeded in that aim. More often than not they are as flat as stale soda–water. There are other pictures which make great pretensions, and offer themselves for comparison with famous plays or novels, or aim at quality through quantity. They demand serious criticism and should have it. Lastly, there are films which claim very little, but have unwittingly touched greatness, and on these the good critic will fasten joyfully, analyse and annotate them, and hand them to the public with the seal of quality attached.[211]

In this column Lejeune appeared, one month into her new role, to have been writing her own job description or, more accurately, prescription. The writing has a performative dimension (Lejeune went on to discuss, more briefly, the films of the week), which, if rather different from that of Vachel Lindsay, shared something of the same desire to bring into being the new discourses of film criticism. Lejeune also made an implicit warning to the producers of films—respect for the lay critic would be met with respect. She situated the critic, deploying a spatialized language, as a mediator (between wholesale rejection and uncritical celebration, between producer and public) and interpreter. Where Alastair Cooke, writing in the 1930s, would see the film medium as disallowing to the critic any position outside its own overwhelming sensory and mobile qualities, Lejeune sought to balance critical detachment with swiftness, in the image of the critic's 'quickly adjustable mind' which could 'flit rapidly' (like a bee watching 'the life of a bee') from one type of film to another, pollinating each and every one. Here again the question of cinema's movement and motility functioned in the terms of film's diversity, the 'sliding scale' of value, and the nature of film exhibition, rather than in those of the properties of the moving image *per se*.

In many respects, Lejeune's 'The Week on the Screen' could, like Dorothy Richardson's writing on film, be defined as 'cinema' criticism rather than 'film' criticism. While Lejeune looked much more closely at individual films than Richardson, and had a strong sense of the significance of film genres (writing on Westerns, melodramas, romances, serial, historical, and nature films) as well as national cinemas, she was also fully engaged with the broader dimensions of cinema culture, including the different identities of the studios and film exhibition practices. In 'The Summer—and After', for example, she wrote of the deplorable level of film posters, which she related to the 'slump' in film-going:

> Nobody thought of blaming the poster. Now I don't suggest that the poster caused the slump, but I do believe that the poster has been instrumental in causing a spirit of revolt against the things of the screen and that it supplies an answer to that often-repeated question of the indignant showman: 'When we provide good pictures why don't the high-brows come?' The slump is upon us, and showmen know it, because the film-going public is suffering from mental indigestion now that the mad novelty rush of the war days is over. Even enthusiasts are gorged with the crudity and sentiment of which the film poster is the visible sign...The time is a transitional one in the history of the screen; the old order is changing, and nothing yet has come to take its place.[212]

The column prophesied a 'revolution' to come, though not from the West. Lejeune saw it 'foreshadowed in the growing interest of men of science and learning', in the increasing involvement of musicians, architects and authors in the new medium, and in the work of 'dramatic visionaries' like Victor Seastrom. Above all, however, Lejeune was criticizing, in this column as elsewhere, the exhibitors' practice of block-booking films 'blindly' and for months and years ahead. The film trade, in other words, was failing to keep up with (and indeed retarding) developments in the industry, art, and technology of the cinema. In November of the same year, Lejeune wrote that there had been a change in policy in response to the crisis: 'If the public insist upon newer and better pictures the magnates of Wardour Street have decided that there is no use in opposing or cajoling them any longer.'[213] Lejeune repeated the call for 'the public' to demand better films in her final column for 1922, 'The End of a Chapter': 'It is for the kinema public to speak out boldly and to prove in the coming year, that the renters have been completely wrong [in asserting that 'the public does not want art']. For the public alone is a free agent. Let it ask persistently, and nothing can be denied to it. Let it make its own new year.'[214]

In summary, the preoccupations of Lejeune's first year of film criticism included the nature of the relationship between British and American cinema, and the differences between the films their respective studios were producing; praise for the films of the British directors Cecil Hepworth and George Pearson; appreciation of Swedish cinema, and in particular the films of Seastrom; strong criticism of the 'star system' and of the fan magazines: 'You can have not the faintest conception, until you have read a few of these papers, of the torrent of hero-worship which is pouring out daily, and of how vitally it must affect the nature and fortune of films.'[215] She made a plea for a distinction to be drawn between the 'actor' and the 'star' and for recognition of the centrality of the director or 'producer' (her preferred term). She drew attention to the cinema of Erich von Stroheim, in whose work, as in Seastrom's, 'the players have no entity apart from the play'.[216]

During her years as the *Manchester Guardian*'s film critic Lejeune wrote on the new European cinemas of Germany, France, Russia and elsewhere (with columns devoted to films including *The Student of Prague* and *Potemkin*) and their contributions to the art of the film. She drew her readers' attention to film technique, as in her discussion of the significance of 'cutting and assembling' in a British film, Maurice Elvey's *Hindle Wakes* which she placed in the new 'school of jostled vision' (along with *Souls*

Aflame and Hitchcock's *The Lodger*): 'so cunning is the expression, so deft the juxtaposition of ideas, that we come to the crux of the matter with a complete *penetration* of knowledge such as only a subjective experience can induce.'[217]

Much of Lejeune's film writing had a didactic purpose, but she also sought to communicate the non-analytic pleasures of cinema. In a column entitled 'On Enjoyment' she wrote of a recent experience of film-going:

Last Saturday afternoon—it is always on a Saturday afternoon, towards tea and lamplight, that these pleasant things seem to happen—I paid sixpence for an incredibly uncomfortable seat next to an incredibly fat woman just under the screen of an incredibly soiled picture-house, watched an incredibly bad film, and was happy ... If you would look for reasons—though it is ill work analysing enjoyment—I can give you two. It was partly the set of the heroine's nose and partly the hands of the assistant hero ... Foolish? Yes. But enjoyment always is. Those of you who really find pleasure in moving pictures as moving pictures, who have been on good terms with them as an entertainment before anyone thought of discovering them as an art, will understand me when I say that the things in the kinema I have most enjoyed have been the trivial things, the personal things, that react straight upon the fancy and let intelligence go by ... I feel joy in watching the extreme productions of the kinema (though are they not really one and the same?)—Wiene and Mack Sennett, Cubism and the custard pie. I feel a fierce joy in studying the canvases of a Lang, swinging along on the rhythms of a Mosjoukine. I feel an exuberant joy in watching Charlie Chaplin hit another man on the head. But I do not enjoy it in the pure sense. The sense of comfort is not there.

Enjoyment is the middle way, the effortless way that judgement despises and keen brains overlook; a self-coloured, emotional middle way, leading a drab world to romance. The songs and paintings, the stories and films of enjoyment have rarely the qualities of art, but, themselves uncreative, they make creative life in thousands who hear or see them. Enjoyment stirs up fancy. Enjoyment is the father of 'Let's pretend'. Only the fool and the too clever man will be ashamed of it in himself.[218]

Lejeune went on to give a metaphorical 'lunch of homage', within the lines of her column, to 'the personalities from all over the world of film production who have brought me enjoyment'. These she counted not as 'stars' but as companions, 'who give us pleasure, whom we are glad to meet again and again, and weave into mighty films of our own imagining'. The term 'personal' (with its cognate in 'personalities') was a significant one for Lejeune. She took it up again in a column entitled 'The Women' in which she argued for the strangeness of the fact that 'few people in the motion-picture industry know anything about the minds of women'. The 'showman of pictures ... still blunders on in the face of woman's prejudices'.

> He still grounds his appeals to woman on a misconception of her tastes. He still brings her titbits that she despises, and protects her from the pleasures that she loves ... Instead of the romance that tickles every homebound fancy, he expects womanly things to please the woman most. For adventure, domesticity; for the gun, a Paris gown; for the boarhound, a Pekingese; in every way the showman provides his woman patrons with the things that have for the men the least appeal.[219]

The discovery, if it ever came, by 'the men inside the kinema' of 'the tastes and inhibitions of the women outside it' would produce, Lejeune wrote,

> such a turmoil, such a scuffling to and fro to revise the kinema as that complacent industry has never known before. For the kinema must please the women or die. The vast majority of picture-goers are women and always will be. The time of day is in their favour, to steal an odd hour from the afternoon; and woman, whose work lies at home, is just as glad of the opportunity to escape from home as man, whose work lies outside it, is glad of the opportunity to be in it ... The small cushioned seats are women's seats; they have no masculine build. The warmth in winter, the coolness in summer, the darkness, the sleepy music, the chance to relax unseen are all women's pleasures which no man, however tired he may be, can every quite appreciate or understand.
>
> But the main attraction of the kinema for women rises out of a common factor in their natures. Woman is fiercely, desperately personal, and the kinema the most personal of the arts ... Let no one mock at this personal loyalty in women. It is full of a shrewd pity that a shrewder wisdom hides. It is incorruptible and the source of endless power. And if, because of it, no art has ever yet been woman born, through it, and out of it, and by the grace of it each and every art has come to be born of man.[220]

The position Lejeune took up in relation to 'The Women' was at once one of engagement and detachment. Elizabeth Bowen, in her essay 'Why I Go to the Cinema', was insistent that: 'Where the cinema is concerned I am a fan, not a critic.'[221] She explored, almost as a form of self-analysis, her responses to a medium in which spectatorship was at one and the same time a collective experience—'What falls short as aesthetic experience may do as human experience: the film rings no bells in oneself but one hears a bell ring elsewhere'—and a deeply individual one—'when I sit opposite a film the audience is *me*'.[222] Bowen's concern was with the nature of the 'pleasure' afforded by the cinema, as was Lejeune's in her discussion of 'enjoyment'. Lejeune, too, in the first column for the new year of 1926—'Alive and Vigorous'—took up the question of individual and collective dreaming, or day-dreaming, in the cinema, defending the nature of cinematic dreams, if only implicitly, against the moralists and the reformers, and arguing that:

> In the kinema there is no common vision. Each one sees there the dream of his own heart, tricked out in acting clothes and wearing a star's mask. Each one makes of the kinema's kinema a little kinema of his own…The kinema's way to dreaming is perhaps a child's way, but then we are, most of us, children. As the world grows up, so will the kinema, quite naturally and without any conscious reforming, grow up too.[223]

Lejeune was writing as a critic as well as a fan, and class and professional identity separated her from 'the women'. It is significant that the representation of the female audience produced in film criticism by women critics and writers of this period was so often predicated on the imagined experiences of the working-class woman, so that the exploration of film-going often became a form of cultural ethnography, with the writer on film becoming a 'participant observer', watching the audience as much as, or to a greater extent than, the images on the screen. Thus Dorothy Richardson, in her first 'Continuous Performance' article for *Close Up*, wrote of visiting a picture palace:

> one of those whose plaster frontages and garish placards broke a row of shops in a strident, north London street. It was a Monday and therefore a new picture. But it was also washday, and yet the scattered audience was composed almost entirely of mothers. Their children, apart from the infants accompanying them, were at school and their husbands were at work. It was a new audience, born within the last few months. Tired women, their faces sheened with toil, and small children, penned in semi-darkness and foul air on a sunny afternoon. There was almost no talk. Many of the women sat alone, figures of weariness at rest. Watching these I took comfort. At last the world of entertainment had provided for a few pence, tea thrown in, a sanctuary for mothers, an escape from the everlasting qui vive into eternity on a Monday afternoon.
>
> The first scene was a tide, frothing in over the small beach of a sandy cove, and for some time we were allowed to watch the coming and going of those foamy waves, to the sound of a slow waltz, without the disturbance of incident. Presently from the fisherman's hut emerged the fisherman's daughter, moss-haired. The rest of the scenes, all of which

sparked continually, I have forgotten. But I do not forget the balm of that tide, and that simple music, nor the shining eyes and rested faces of those women.[224]

Film, like the moving tide, is 'balm' to the tired women. Bowen, Richardson, and Lejeune laid stress on the cinema as a resting-place, providing, in Lejeune's words, 'the chance to relax unseen', and on the particular quality of women's fatigue, ameliorated by the cinema as it could not be for a man, 'however tired he may be'. Richardson and Lejeune described the weariness of female bodies (Bowen, representing her own experience of cinema-going, referred to the mental exhaustion of the writer seeking a different kind of refreshment in the film), finding rest, and escape, on the 'small cushioned seats' that are so closely matched to their bodies. (Bowen refers to fumbling her way in the cinema's darkness to the 'sticky velvet seat', the image more ambiguously gendered and recalling, though without any of his disgust, D. H. Lawrence's image of the cinema as cultural and bodily ooze: 'they like to spread themselves across the screen'.)

Lejeune also, on occasion, defended 'sentiment' and 'sentimentality', as in her discussion of Henry King's melodrama *Stella Dallas* (1925). This was the original, silent version of the film remade by King Vidor in 1937, in which form it became a central film for the feminist and psychoanalytic film criticism of the 1970s and beyond, in explorations of 'identification' and the nature of gendered spectatorship. 'Sentiment', Lejeune wrote in her 1926 review, 'is the warmth that keeps us happy, the response that brings us friends':

> To admit that *Stella Dallas* moved us is not in the least to admit our critical faculties at fault...We are merely confessing that there is something, a sequence of something, in the film that set our own emotional imaginings free to create. Confessing to a purely physical contraction of the muscles of the throat, a curious physical sense of leap and poise. Confessing that we have lived the ordinary lives of ordinary men and women, and caught a reflection of it here ... These are all real people whose every move rings true; real people, moving in circumstances just unreal enough to give their own reality romance ... the film that, like *Stella Dallas*, can persuade us by cunning emotional experience that we have gone through fire and come out finer, can persuade us that we have gone through fire for someone else's sake, is the film that makes us happiest of all.[225]

The 'moral' Lejeune drew might appear to be an extremely conventional one, but her discussion began to develop a more complex account of the paradoxes and complexities of identification with the world depicted on the screen, which were themselves strikingly at play in *Stella Dallas*, with its depictions of the world of the screen and of film-going within the film itself. There is a striking contrast between her account of film sentiment and Ivor Montagu's review of *Stella Dallas* in *The Observer*. While admiring the film, Montagu deplored the sentimental responses of the (female) audience: 'Two thousand noses will be swallowed in two thousand throats. Two thousand noses will dip, snivelling, into a nearly equal number of pocket-handkerchiefs (tie-up with great white sale next door). And, after the performance, the air will be heavy with the powdery evidence of recent facial repairs…Even if the spectator is one who enjoys a good cry by himself from time to time as much as anybody, he is bound to be rendered a little resistant by the vulgarity of the preliminary publicity and the voluptuous misery of his fellows.'[226] The tears are as drenching as the face-powder is cloying; it is not a space Montagu wishes to find himself in.

In 'The Women', Lejeune's use of the singular collective noun 'woman', also deployed extensively by Dorothy Richardson, is revealing of the ways in which the cinema audience was understood as a female community, and, as Lejeune suggested, of the fact that 'the main attraction of the kinema for women rises out of a common factor in their natures'. This is the attraction to the personal, and from that to the screen personality. The complication here is that Lejeune had written so extensively, from her very first column onwards, of the damaging effects of the star system on cinema's development. To a certain extent, as we have seen, she separated the identity of the screen 'personality' from that of the star, but, in 'The Women', she appeared to be making no such differentiation: 'For women and because of women the "star" system has grown up in the kinema. It is nothing more or less than a commercial means of giving women the most of what they want—personality.' The star system, Lejeune appears to have been suggesting, was the industry's exploitation of women's 'innate' attraction to personality, which she depicted in more positive terms in this context as a connection with the world of others and as an absorption in all that is human.

In her column 'Alive and Vigorous', Lejeune did not appear to be working with the distinction between the appeal of 'personality' and that of 'the star'. The article addressed a reader immune to the appeals of cinematic dreaming:

Don't grudge these folk their dream, you children of the older arts. Let them sit in the tuneful darkness, splendidly alone, yet with every feeling intensified by the consciousness of mass support, and extract from that white oblong of screen all the romance and adventure that their own lives have missed. Let them see countries they will never know, waters they will never sail. Let them walk with strange peoples and trick their fancy in strange clothes. Let them laugh and cry. Let them forget themselves and their weekly bills, their cooking and their office worries, in the, happily, unreal troubles of the people on the screen. Let them gather spurious courage behind the hero's gun. Let them identify their own faces with the heroine's beauty and be content. Let them even worship, if they choose, their bright particular star. The impetus of it will make them live the more fully... You must have lived with milk-jugs and wash-tubs, account-books and carpet-sweepers, shopping-lists and shoe-cleaning, and cold mutton for dinner before you can really appreciate the kinema, fully understand.[227]

There were, in the women critics' representations of spectatorial identification, multiple layers to their identifications with the mass, and predominantly female, film audience. They spoke for the significance and value of women's fantasies and dreams, and defended their attachments to the screen-world, while at the same time critiquing the film industry's cynical manipulations of those fantasies or, in another version of this, its overindulgence of them. One repeated refrain was that women deserved better dreams. Lejeune, as we have seen, was highly critical of the 'star system', but she reserved her fullest attacks upon it for columns in which she discussed the nature of film criticism or the significance of the director's role. When the issue arose in the context of discussion of women's film spectatorship or the question of cinematic pleasure, she softened and relativized the critique.

A chapter on 'Slapstick' in her 1931 book *Cinema* suggested, however, that women's dislike of slapstick comedy, 'their more complicated sense of pleasure, with imagination reaching into the past and the future and finding for every incident a personal application',[228] may have killed off the most valuable aspects of cinema, including 'its movement, its cunning and its fun':

It is we—the public, the critics, the picturegoers—who have lost our simplicity of vision. The modern cinema, with its finicky little problems of social behaviour, its refined argument and high technical polish, has spoilt the primitive joke for us, just as it has obscured our pleasure in movement, and our wonder at the camera's powers.[229]

There are some echoes here, though with little or none of the animus, of the critics quoted earlier in this chapter, for whom cinema's 'development' was the path of its corruption and the loss of a 'youth' which, it was paradoxically held, the mechanized medium, born old, had never in fact experienced.

Women critics often wrote both as insiders and outsiders to the popular cinema's attractions, while at the same time insisting on the importance of that cinema and of its representation in critical writing. They were at once allied with 'the women', part of the collective female audience, and detached observers. This positioning, in which they used the representation of a physical relationship in and to the cinema space, and of the spectator to the screen, to define and depict cultural relationships, was taken up in particularly interesting ways in Richardson's 'Continuous Performance' articles, discussed in more detail in the next chapter.

Lejeune's article 'Alive and Vigorous' was, as I have suggested, addressed to cinema's detractors and, perhaps, to those with the power to legislate against the film. The argument that the filmgoer's dream is an individual one—'In the kinema there is no common vision'—was thus a strategic one; the intention of the censors to control the dreams of the people became entirely hubristic if each and every individual were dreaming his or her own dream in the cinema. This was then an argument against an account of film as narcotic; cinema did not impose its visions and dreams, but opened up a space for dreams and dreamers.

Lejeune's style in this column, and in 'The Women', deployed a rhetoric more heightened, and closer to the language that would characterise Richardson's film writing, than was usual in her criticism, which tended to be of a brisker kind. The subject matter—the women gathered in the cinema, the escape from mundane and often harsh realities into the world of dreams—created a genre of writing about film that was very fully developed in *Close Up*. It was most apparent when the context was the shadowy realm of the dreams, myths, fantasies, and forms of identification surrounding film spectatorship. These preoccupations were taken up, for example, in Huntly Carter's *The New Spirit of the Cinema* (1930):

> Regression is the path to phantasy. There is no doubt that a very large number of Cinema-goers regress to a primitive state, and to childhood in sight of their favourite 'stars'. They put themselves unconsciously into star parts. They are carried back to their earliest days to find their old mythological heroes and

heroines clothed in flesh and blood and no longer dreams but actualities representing desires projected into living symbols.

Human beings have a habit of regressing as a means of progression. In the quaint words of a philosopher they like to look into, unto the unto for material for a fresh start whenever they come to a dead wall. When the famous Professor Patrick Geddes planned his new sociological world he said, 'there shall be little chapels of meditation everywhere to which human beings may retire for rest and meditation and so escape for a time the hard realities of the material world and meditate upon the past, and so enter a world of phantasy to re-emerge with their ideas remodelled.' Thus back, unconsciously it may be, to scratch, returning laden with the new phantasies or re-vitalised inner desires to be consciously projected in fresh symbols of a new form of human life.[230]

The concept of the cinema as a sanctuary and haven was also at the heart of Dorothy Richardson's writing on film. Like Huntly Carter, she combined the image of the cinema as a retreat from the pressures of the modern world with a powerful, paradoxical insistence that it was film that was educating and fitting humanity for modernity: 'And here we all are, as never before. What will it do with us?'

For Lejeune, cinematic modernity was profoundly imbricated with the representation of the machine, in terms that not only echo, if only from a distance, the modernist distinction drawn between 'abstraction' and 'empathy', but also raise the troubled issue of the gendering of the distinction ('abstraction', impersonality, masculinity versus 'empathy', personality, femininity). The value of 'experimental cinema', she wrote in *Cinema*, was that it succeeded 'above all in freeing the movies from their one great obsession—that the human figure should be the director's first concern ... The machine and all the aspects of the machine lie ready for its use—modern stuff for the modern expression of our civilisation. And yet the cinema has obstinately clung to men—not even to mankind in the mass—and their passions and cares and disappointments, as its main preoccupation'.[231] She referred here to 'the fallacy of the narrative idea',[232] and argued that it was the focus on 'man' that had led to the film 'turning, more and more directly, towards the field of the novel and the play ... into the literary convention' and linear time, and away from the 'simultaneous composition of image' which film shared with painting.

In 1925, Lejeune wrote an account of John Ford's *The Iron Horse*, in which she argued that there was a symbiotic relationship between train and film: 'the road to adventure lies along the track of those gleaming rails ... to that goal where dreams are, where we are very young again, and anything may come true':

> The kinema—why should it be forgotten?—is a mechanical thing. It was born of science out of industry, and its whole life runs on wheels. This, the modern medium of expression, fulfils itself most completely in the presentation of modern forms in the shaping of things industrial, the service of the machine. Wheels, piston-rods, screws of steamers, turning lathes, the glow of blastfurnaces, the polished bellies of guns, are all materials of splendour to the motion-picture camera. They and the kinema are of the same stuff and time. In expressing accurately these mechanical things, conveying into flat image their build and texture and power, the kinema is most itself, most forceful and, because most mechanical, most nearly an art.
>
> Of all the machines that have turned and throbbed their way across the kinema screen none is more potent, none has moved to a finer measure, than the railway engine of the track ... the kinema draws magic from science and shapes an art between the wheels of the machine.[233]

Lejeune incorporated this material into *Cinema*. In a chapter entitled 'Films Without a Hero', she discussed *The Iron Horse* in conjunction with *The Covered Wagon* and Turin's *Turksib* (the Russian film representing the building of the railway connecting Siberia and Turkestan) which Lejeune saw as 'a vindication of the theory that the impersonal theme, the story without a hero, provides in mature hands the best matter for movie'.[234] The escape from personality, the star system and the 'human figure' opened up, for Lejeune, the possibility of representing both the world in the broadest, realist sense (the worlds of 'the soil' and of the city) and the pure lines of animation and experimental cinema. In both realms, the 'impersonal' cinematic machine was not occluded but figured and foregrounded, as it had been in early cinema. Underlying Lejeune's film writing was a deep belief in the power of this machine, and she wrote film history as technological evolution. Hence her embrace of sound cinema:

> The movie will go on, sure of ultimate popular backing, adding one new device after another to its equipment of realism, until the machine becomes so complicated that it is hardly distinguishable from life itself, and the age of Robotism will have its complete satisfaction.
>
> And after all, why should the cinema stop short in its mechanical development? Who is to say with any right of jurisdiction that movies should stop here, or put a *ne plus ultra* to the limits of the screen? There seems to be a false

impression abroad that every technical virtuosity of the cinema beyond the ultimate virtuosity of the Russians is betraying an art of silence. But actually the cinema is unlike any other art in that its materials have never been fixed. Its limits have been set in the past by the exigencies of auto-development; it has done what it has done because it could do just so much and no more. If the first film could have talked, there would have been no question of a silent cinema.[235]

There is one further aspect of Lejeune's film criticism to be considered here: her concern with the forms of 'writing' and 'talking' surrounding the film itself. Like Iris Barry and Dorothy Richardson, Lejeune wrote about the importance of subtitles, captions, and lettering in the silent film; the question of 'writing' within the film was, as we have seen, a key concern in the 1920s, and central to the perception of the relationship between literature and film, and to the ways in which films were drawing upon literary texts. For Lejeune, the avoidance of the subtitle in the name of cinematic visuality was an absurdity when it led only to a form of wordless film in which there was 'much hunting for symbols, much play with clocks and calendars, a great deal of gesture as frenzied as a child's secret sign ... It is as far removed from the true wordless kinema, which needs no words to express what has never been verbally conceived, as a game of dumb-crambo is from a harlequinade'.[236] She expressed her admiration for the use of titles in *Turksib* (itself 'a drama of silence, and of sound so tremendous that all individual voice is lost in it, and it has the effect of silence on the mind'), which 'came to us as something profoundly exciting, a bit of real visual rhetoric magnificently used', by contrast with those captions in the cinema which 'had always been static, had more or less held up the action, jerked back the eye, duplicated image and broken design'.[237] Here the discussion of the title was drawn into Lejeune's habitual contrast between regression (in this instance that which holds back the action, jerks back the eye) and progression (the titles in *Turksib* 'played a definite part in the visual and emotional progress of idea') in the medium of the film.

Questions of sound and silence, talking and writing, also emerged more obliquely in Lejeune's discussions of the publicity machines surrounding the film. A column entitled 'The Talkers' (30 January 1926) referred not to the talking films, which Lejeune would start to discuss in 1928, the year in which she left the *Manchester Guardian* to become film critic for the *Observer*, but to film-talk as hype or puffery, the words of managing directors, stars, and producers which were deployed to in-flate the film as product. This is the negative version of 'talking in the cinema':

> Sometimes we complain that the kinema seems to bawl at us from every poster and hoarding, to shout at us from the gilded domes of its palaces and cry from every column of the press. Sometimes we feel that modern life groans under its clamour, under its terrible insistence of sound. But the truth is that the kinema itself is mute. It has nothing to say, and could not say it if it would. The trumpet voice is our own; we have made ourselves the slaves of talk and have not the courage to shake off our chain.[238]

In 'Spotting Winners' (27 January 1927), Lejeune returned to the issue of the film poster, and the impossibility, for the picturegoer, of 'estimating in advance the quality of a film':

> How can he guess, from the bare line of advertisement, from the banner over the door, or the splashed poster on the wall, whether he will be so bored, irritated or amused by the film so confidently offered him?...It is just as well, if he contemplates an evening at the kinema every once in a while, to learn how to read the kinema posters aright...the only safe rule for the poster-beginner is to disregard everything else and make straight for the name of the firm. It may appear at the top of the bill—such-and-such Films present; or at the bottom corner—A such-and-such produc-tion; of in the middle, jammed among the letterpress—A such-and-such masterpiece; or sprawled large across the picture's very face. Somewhere it can be found, and should be found, for it is the unwilling caligraphy of revelation.[239]

There are curious echoes here of Edgar Allan Poe's philosopher-detective Dupin's explanation, in the short story 'The Purloined Letter', of his methods of discovery of a stolen document, which was not in fact hidden by its purloiner but displayed in such an obvious place that it could not, paradoxically, be seen. Dupin uses the analogy of a game of puzzles played upon a map, in which one party requires another to find a given word 'upon the motley and perplexed surface of the chart':

> A novice in the game generally seeks to embarrass his opponents by giving them the most minutely lettered names; but the adept selects such words as stretch, in large characters, from one end of the chart to the other. These, like the over-largely lettered signs and placards of the street, escape observation by dint of being excessively obvious; and here the physical oversight is precisely analogous with the moral inapprehension by which the intellect suffers to pass

unnoticed those considerations which are too obtrusively and too palpably self-evident.[240]

Lejeune's 'unwilling caligraphy of revelation' chimes not only with Poe's hieroglyphic and cryptographic preoccupations, but with the concept of a filmic hieroglyphic language at the heart of Vachel Lindsay's writings, and, more broadly, with that of a modern hieroglyphics of bill-boards and advertisements, the urban scrawl or drizzle to which Poe alluded—'the over-largely lettered signs and placards of the street'—also referred to by commentators from John Ruskin to Walter Benjamin and Siegfried Kracauer. Terry Ramsaye, in his 1926 film history *A Million and One Nights*, wrote of the task of 'indicat[ing] the evolution of narrative styles and technique by the picture makers and the parallel education of the screen audience in the hieroglyphs and vernacular of screen narration'.[241] Lejeune saw the educational task a little differently. Reading the poster correctly, she suggested, meant learning to pick out its mark or seal of quality; the name of the production company. Beyond this, however, was a perception of 'film writing' as having spread or 'splashed' itself—in letters both compressed and enlarged—across the surfaces of an essentially urban modernity. The role of the critic was, then, to guide the picture-goer towards a way of 'reading aright' the plethora of material—much of it mystifactory and hyperbolic—and towards a true recognition of 'the unwilling caligraphy of revelation'.

Glimpses of the Past

Both Barry's and Lejeune's writings reveal a persistent anxiety over the ephemerality of the medium and its exhibition, about the question not only of cinema's future but its past. In Barry's desire to give this art of the modern, the absolutely new, a history and a future, we see the birth of the work she would go on to do at the Museum of Modern Art Film Library, restoring, preserving, and archiving films of the past and present, and establishing the curatorial apparatus for the medium of film. The work of the Film Library would be, 'to create a consciousness of history and tradition within the new art of the motion picture'.[242] In 1935, she travelled to Hollywood, to persuade producers to donate prints of their films to the Film Library, arguing that 'unless something is done to restore and preserve outstanding films of the past, the motion picture from 1914 onwards will be as irrevocably lost as the Commedia dell'Arte or the dancing of Nijinksy'.[243]

Lejeune was also, though to a lesser extent, concerned with the preservation of the films of the past, including the early work of D. W. Griffith, on whom Barry was to publish a significant monograph (to accompany a major retrospective of Griffith's films at MOMA) in 1940. Lejeune took issue with Hilaire Belloc who, in an address to the Stoll Picture Club on 'The Value of Historical Films', had claimed that, for film to fulfil an educational role: 'Each picture must be a precise and accurate record of the past, and should represent the quality of a period rather than any definite episode in that period, manners and customs rather than events.' For Lejeune, the question of historical truth was necessary a relative one, mediated through the perspectives of the present. As she argued:

> The real historical film must be a contemporaneous record, and those who have at heart the future education of the race would do better to concentrate their energies on ways of lengthening the life of a film, thus creating a permanent library of truthful pictures for ages to come, than to delve among the records of the past, trying to recapture their savour through an instrument of modern science.[244]

Here, as in the writings of Barry, we see an early appeal for a film archive, and a redefinition of historical witness, away from Belloc's static conception of the past, and towards a model of preserving an unfolding and developing history. Lejeune took this question up again in *Cinema*, in the context of a discussion of *Caligari*, the scarcity of copies of which, she argued, 'has always seemed to me an argument for that rather dead-sounding thing, a cinema museum, in which any student of the cinema could trace in practical detail the development of the bioscope, pageant, movie, talkie, *montage* film, from its earliest days'.[245] Many of the studies of cinema which appeared in the mid- to late-1920s were structured on this very basis, so that critical histories were themselves ordered and arranged as a form of 'cinema museum': they were, moreover, attempts to give a degree of stability to the flux and ephemerality of the film medium and to encapsulate a state of affairs during, to borrow Lejeune's phrase, a period of transition and experiment. This was particularly charged during the period leading up to, and immediately following, the transition to sound, as Paul Rotha's significant study *The Film Till Now* (discussed in the next chapter) reveals particularly clearly.

For Lejeune, writing in her study *Cinema*:

The revival and re-issue of old moving pictures is in most cases a thankless job; the best of them suffer from the effects of changing camera-work, from the march of technical invention, and we are inclined to spoil, rather than to enhance, pleasant memories by seeing them with modern eyes. What we remember is the spirit of the film; what we see is the crude, jerky photography, the old-fashioned make-up, the flat lighting, the smug captions, the technical devices that have long since been superseded in film practice. The Film Society has shown us, in its 'resurrections,' how much the old stuff of sensation has become the modern stuff of laughter; we feel the energy of the roughing, but the line is comic, the quality of thought in these old films has not been strong enough to stand up to the changes in the reproductive machine.[246]

She made an exception, however, for *Caligari*: 'It does not matter how often *Caligari* is revived, nor how far we may travel in years from its starting-point; the film is still momentous today, and five, ten, twenty years hence—if the projectors of the fifties will run the films of the teens—will still be valuable as a document of cinema progress.' It is at this point that she also envisages a 'cinema museum ... I should like to feel confident that a print of each of the screen's eventful productions—and there are not many of them—has been secured and stored for reference, so that we could put a practical check on our generalities, and the next generation could learn something of the cinema that evolved their own'.[247] The phrase 'cinema museum' echoes writings by Gilbert Seldes in the mid-1920s, in which he envisaged the little cinemas showing both artistic and pre-war popular films: 'While you are creating an audience for new and unpopular things, try to create one also for the old and the popular.'[248]

In a slightly different vein (and with reference to cinemas which showed revivals in London (the Avenue Pavilion and the Plaza), Paris, Munich, and Berlin, Robert Herring, who took over Lejeune's *Manchester Guardian* column 'The Week on the Screen' in July 1928, wrote a piece entitled 'Twenty Years Ago'. Faced with 'an appalling future' (by which he presumably meant 'the talkies'), the kinema has become 'aware of its past'. Herring turned first to the programme at the Avenue Pavilion of pre-war films:

It provides a welcome change in the ordinary programme, and has created something of a sensation. Composed of old news gazettes, it shows us buildings, since demolished, in streets so empty of traffic that we can see across them, old fashions, including a bathing-dress display, and finally King Edward and even Queen Victoria at her Diamond Jubilee. We laugh at the clothes, but there is genuine interest in these glimpses of the past, and something a little mysterious in seeing these figures moving, crossing streets, living their lives, twenty years ago. It is even more strange when the figures are those of people still alive, people who have moved with the times, held here dimensionally in another time. Ten minutes of kinema d'avant-guerre has long afforded a pleasant verbal as well as visual contrast to Parisians in the salles d'avant garde, and they have a kinema, the Ciné Latin, which exists solely for revivals.[249]

For Rudolph Messel, mention of the Film Society was also the occasion for ruminations on 'film history':

There is as yet no reverence for the cinema; no clique of intense persons who study it, live for and in it, and make its discussion their business. This has not happened yet, but it is in the process of happening. Already in London we have the Film Society and its intensely bespectacled Sunday crowd. This Society shows all sorts of films without any sense of discrimination whatsoever. Films good, bad, and indifferent, chase each other across the screen, while the members of the society watch. They crane their necks, grind out cigarette-ends, pass remarks on the purity of the photographic art, and are generally intense. It is the nucleus, I think, of a pre-Raphaelite movement for the films. It has all the ingredients necessary for such a movement; a strong university flavour, a tinge of communism, and a great deal more than a tinge of intensity. Already this infant organisation is showing a marked tendency for a return to the primitive. At each Film Society show one is regaled with two or three 'curiosities', or early films. To-day these films are treated as a laughing matter, but given another fifty years and we shall see Edwin S. Porter enthroned and the intelligentsia bowing before him as once they bowed before Cimabue. Porter, Vidor, and Griffith, and the greatest of these three will be Griffith.[250]

It is striking that the 'Resurrection' series, which formed a relatively small part of the Film Society programmes, should have become such an intense focus of critical attention, as it was in Woolf's 'The Cinema', which Herring's article closely echoes. It suggests that the very concept of 'film history' was in the process of active formation, and reinforces the view that an evolutionary understanding of film was dominant in this period. Lejeune was to write that she was born with the cinema; her lifetime was also that of the medium's. The sense of the strangeness of films which were often little more than a decade old, of the distance between 'now' and 'then' (intensified with the coming of sound), indicates not only the rapidly changing technologies of film, but, in more complex ways, a relationship to the passing of time and the vanishing of the present into the past, definitional of the photographic and cinematic image, as not only novel and remarkable but also as profoundly imbricated with the duration of personal time and the concept of 'lost time'.

5

The Moment of *Close Up*

I was very glad to learn *Close-Up* is still remembered. There has never been anything like it since, alas, but I suppose that's because it flowered at a time when the cinema itself was flowering, & that can happen (like first love) only once.[1]

'The admirable monthly publication *Close Up*'

In November 1930, *The Architectural Review*, a monthly journal which frequently included articles on film, ran a column entitled 'Film Structure and the work of *Close Up*'. Its author wrote under the name of 'Mercurius', producing a regular film column at the end of the 1920s and into the early 1930s. This particular article consisted primarily of a long quotation from the editor of 'the admirable monthly publication *Close Up*' which began:

> Nearly three and a half years ago *Close Up* came into circulation as 'the only magazine devoted to films as an art'. Films as an art. That meant more than looking for beauty, more than analysis and criticism. It involved, immediately, a probing down to source—the expression of life in photographed movement.
>
> Was art unearthed in this probing? Probably not, but principles for artistic construction were soon enough discovered. But think of that—the expression of life in photographed movement. Think of it simply as that, and 'film as art' must take on new meaning.
>
> Not that it was, or is, our purpose to state what constitutes cinema, or what films should be: what we were able to discover was more simple and quickly evident, namely—that certain elements were essential to the structural determination of the film.[2]

These elements were defined as moments, units, details, movements, and projection. The *Close Up* editor called upon a range of theoretical ideas to expand these categories; the psychoanalytic concepts of 'transference' and of the detail as a 'trifle [which] which may hold the key to a situation'; accounts of the relationship between stasis and movement, which at points recall the writings of Victor Freeburg: 'It must be stated that the *pause* and suspended action are of the greatest importance, not to emphasize movement only, but to create it.' The 'uniform speed of the projector' turns 'the film of moments' into a unity, and creates 'a new cinema-time'. There was also a reference to Sergei Eisenstein's concept of 'overtonal montage' (explored in his *Fourth Dimension in the Kino*, published for the first time in English in *Close Up*[3]), used in this piece to explore the workings of continuity in the film (from unit to unit) and of 'the inferential' or 'the *nuance*' which functioned to produce both dramatic continuity and visual intensity. The term employed here was 'repercussion'. Superimposition—'moment placed on top of moment'—achieves 'an X-ray of the simultaneous consciousness of the universe, of which Jung says the artist is the interpreter'. Movement is 'always the "carrier" of something by reason of which it is made, and it is the *intention* to act which gives movement its poignancy'; it is found, in its profoundest form, 'in the content of the film itself, rather than in the movement of the camera turning on a swivel or travelling on a wagon'. The citation closed with a claim for the significance of 'the theorists' of cinema, who are also the artists, and 'Mercurius' stepped back in: 'A magazine working along such lines as these is living in the act of high achievement.'

In this passage it was made apparent that *Close Up*, as a 'theoretical' journal which was nonetheless fully involved with film production, drew its discursive and intellectual energies from a combination of psychoanalytic theories, Eisenstein's montage theories, and models of space-time, 'movement' and 'moment', 'motion' and 'emotion', that had become the currency of early film aesthetics and theories. The question remains, however, of the relationship between 'Mercurius' and *Close Up*, to whose editor's words this column was more or less entirely given over, apart from the 'frame' of Mercurius's admiration. In the following year 'Mercurius' disappeared, and a film column for *The Architectural Review* began to appear under the name of cameraman, photographer, and writer Oswell Blakeston,[4] a major figure in the composition of *Close Up*. Blakeston contributed the greatest number of articles to the journal over its six years, many of them on abstract film and photography, becoming its 'assistant editor' in 1931: he was centrally involved in the journal's project and in the film culture that sustained it, and which it helped sustain, in the London and Berlin of the late 1920s and early 1930s.

The question opens out onto the 'biographical' dimensions of *Close Up*'s moment, and, more broadly, onto the complexities of private, *coterie* and public intellectual life in the modernist period. The letters (a substantial number of which have survived into the archives) that passed between *Close Up*'s editor Kenneth Macpherson, his co-editor Bryher, and H.D., as well as, extending the circle, Blakeston and the film critic Robert Herring, reveal something of the ways in which 'the group' was constructed and sustained. The films Macpherson, Bryher, and H.D. made, of which only one, *Borderline*, exists in complete form, were also 'projections', to borrow a favourite term of Macpherson's and H.D.'s, of their inner and outer worlds. Yet the significance of their fictions, films, and the journal *Close Up* itself was not bounded by the *coterie*. *Close Up* was an international journal and it had an incalculable impact on the developing film culture of this period; the importance and radicalism of *Borderline* was recognized in its time and it has subsequently taken its place in cinema history as a significant avant-garde film.

Publicity material for *Close Up* described it as a magazine 'devoted to the art of the screen' and 'entirely independent of any commercial interests'. Accepting no advertisements from film companies, 'it is able to enjoy a freedom in the expression of its opinions which has made it known as the most candid and outspoken review of the screen yet published'. An advertisement in *transition* (another avant-garde journal which took up the cinema in significant ways[5]), described *Close Up* as 'a monthly magazine to begin battle for film art':

> The first periodical to appoach film from any angle but the commonplace. To encourage experimental workers, and amateurs. Will keep in touch with every country, and watch everything. Contributions on Japanese, Negro viewpoints and problems, etc. Some of the most interesting personages of the day will write.[6]

In *The Dial* it was announced as 'a new European magazine to approach films from the angles of art, experiment and development. A searchlight on all progressive and experimental forms': in *The Nation* and the *London Mercury* as 'a British review', 'the *first* magazine (all British) to approach films from the artistic, psychological and educational points of view'.[7] The representation of the journal's national and international identity—'all British' versus 'European'—thus altered according to context and place. The editorial policy of the journal rarely varied, however, in its dismissive attitude towards English films (Hitchcock's *Blackmail* was a rare exception), the concept of 'an English film revival', and the Quota system, which, Macpherson wrote in his first 'As Is', 'will mean only a needless loss for theatres'.[8]

Marianne Moore, who contributed two articles to *Close Up*[9], wrote a brief account of the first issue of the journal in *The Dial*, the New York 'little magazine' with which she was centrally involved:

> Those who are displeased by an unduly academic literary mechanics may consider the advantages of verbal unfearfulness, in the recently inaugurated little cinema review, *Close Up*. To burst into feeling so to speak, and praise an art through a medium other than its own, without having mastered the terms of the auxiliary art is surely an experiment; but zeal, liberty, and beauty are allied phenomena and apart from oddity there are in *Close Up* to reward us, besides certain other items, a poem about light by H.D.; a report of 'Kopf Hoch Charley' that holds the attention; a contribution entitled 'Mrs Emerson' by Miss Stein; and a letter to the editor: '*About cinema. I do not care for them, but I do not know why I don't ... I think my prejudice is hardly justified. But I couldn't write about it. I've nothing to say. I'm so sorry.*' We like the letter and we like the movies.[10]

Moore's account of the first issue of *Close Up* suggests that she saw the journal as the production of passionate amateurs. 'Prais[ing] an art through a medium other than its own' raises central questions about the ways in which the art of the film was to be explored, and about the role played by literature in *Close Up*'s first issues. It has been suggested that the editors initially sought to gain a status for the journal by inviting significant literary figures to contribute, including Gertrude Stein, who wrote three pieces and Virginia Woolf, who declined the invitation: this desire for literary status soon ceased to govern the journal's editorial policy. There was certainly an interest in the journal's early stages in what literary writers, novelists in particular, were making of film and it was undoubtedly the case that the group's contacts at the start came from the world of literature rather than from cinema. The novelist Dorothy Richardson, who contributed a regular column to the journal, suggested to Bryher that D. H. Lawrence be approached: 'You know Lawrence loathes films? *Foams* about them. I'm sure he'd foam for you.'[11] Lawrence never wrote for the journal, but a number of other writers made contributions, though those by H. G. Wells and Arnold Bennett were brief, and Osbert Sitwell's failed to materialize.[12]

Marianne Moore's suggestion that the language of literature was being deployed in the journal to talk about film, and her perception of the lack of mastery of 'the terms of the auxiliary art', raises important questions about the relationship between the two art forms in the formative period of film criticism. One of the most significant dimensions of *Close Up* was precisely its 'experiment', to borrow Moore's phrase, in finding a form of writing and language adequate to the cinema and its particular modes of representation and movement. While *Close Up* became much more confidently a 'film' journal than Moore's initial impressions suggested, focusing as much on the industry and technology as on the reception of 'art' film, it nonetheless maintained its 'writerly' dimensions, rarely, if ever, to assert the primacy of literature, but because so much of its project was to do with creating a discursive medium and forum commensurate with the new art, and constructing spectatorship and 'writing about cinema' as a form of 'film-making'.[13]

Increasingly, *Close Up* ran articles from film critics and professionals in the film industry. Robert Herring was a film critic and assistant editor of the *London Mercury*; Oswell Blakeston a cameraman in the London commercial studios as well as a writer and a maker of experimental films, stills from which were published in *Close Up*.[14] Other contributors included Ernest Betts, who would go on to become a significant writer on the cinema, and the New York critic Harry Alan Potamkin, also connected to the journals *Experimental Cinema* and the Harvard journal *Hound and Horn*. Marc Allégret, the director, in collaboration with André Gide, of *Voyage au Congo*, became *Close Up*'s Paris correspondent in 1927; French cinema was also covered by Jean Lenauer and Freddy Chevalley, the latter corresponding from Geneva. In 1928, Andor Krasna-Krausz, editor of the journals *Film für Alle* and *Film Technik*, became their Berlin correspondent. Pera Attasheva, Eisenstein's close companion, joined the journal as Moscow correspondent in 1929, and Clifford Howard contributed film news from Hollywood. The journal stressed its internationalism, and devoted special issues to Russian, Japanese, and 'Afro-American cinema', the last a crucial context for *Borderline*, in which Paul and Eslanda Robeson played central roles.

The Austrian director G. W. Pabst, based in Berlin at this time, and the psychoanalyst Hanns Sachs became involved in the journal's project, and the *Close Up* group's reception of film, from an early stage. *Close Up* also ran numerous articles from Soviet Russia, including the first English translations of a number of Eisenstein's most influential writings, articles by Pudovkin, and, in the October 1928 issue, 'The Sound Film: A Statement from U.S.S.R.', written by Eisenstein, Pudovkin, and Alexandrov, perhaps the most significant single document in the shaping of attitudes towards the coming of sound. The years of *Close Up* were the years of the transition from silent to sound cinema, and the journal is a highly significant resource for cultural perceptions of the 'transition'.[15] It also, as we have seen, emerged in the context of film censorship in Britain, and the campaigns against it. The numerous stills in the journal from Soviet films were a way of showing images that British and French filmgoers were for the most part unable to see until the loosening of censorship rules in 1929. The stills also became significant images for the photography of the period and for the new conceptual and experimental work on the relationship between photography and film.

By the time *Close Up* commenced publication in July 1927, the Film Society had completed its second season. Robert Herring reviewed the Film Society screenings in the *London Mercury* and was later to join the Film Society council, and *Close Up* often used its programmes as occasions for discussion of specific films. An account of the season's films written by Montagu was published in an early issue of the journal.[16] The two groups were joined in their commitments to the exhibition of Soviet cinema and the campaigns against its censorship. Yet there were also rivalries between the society and the journal, with Macpherson, on occasion, using his column to criticize the Society's activities and its 'framing' of cinema. Infuriated by what he perceived as a wilfully misleading description of Ernst Metzner's contentious 'Freudian' film *Überfall* in the programme,[17] Macpherson suggested that the Society was promoting a dilettantism and outmoded aestheticism—a 'fin-de-siècle snigger'—in which 'hair-tidies, samplers, tortoise-shell inlay and early Chaplin comedies became in the twinkling of an eye rare objets d'art ... Perhaps it's peculiar, perhaps it's just English, that a society whose one reason for existence, presumably, was in protest against plagiarism and vulgarity, false representation and iconoclasm, should have been either consciously or unconsciously a champion for these forms of original tastelessness.'[18] The 'fin-de-siècle snigger' returns us to the question of the forms of laughter provoked by the showing of early films (as discussed by Clair, Kracauer, and others), and suggests a tension between the archival drive towards 'resurrection' and *Close Up*'s avowed commitment to 'films of the future'. Nonetheless, the Film Society continued to be a

crucial context for *Close Up*'s discussions of how and where experimental
and European cinema could be seen in England.

Bryher in Berlin

> If I say Berlin
> I do not see
> war, hunger or misery
> but all the sharp, white
> overreaching promise
> we call life.
> Others, reading your signs
> have made you home.
> I would rather love you than know you,
> see you once, twice and
> remember you,
> seeded from strife, a new flower
> failing the second year.
>
> Never be anchorage
> never be safety
> only be the kino
> where the truant boy
> and the old knitting cook
> watched shadows
> with carrots in her basket
> and a cabbage.
> And I, between them
> knowing ...[19]

The *ménage à trois* between the young Scottish artist Kenneth Macpherson,
H.D., and Bryher had started in 1926 when Macpherson and H.D. met and
began an affair. H.D.'s long-term companion Bryher married Macpherson
in 1927, soon after her divorce from the American writer Robert McAlmon.
McAlmon's Contact Press (the publishers of many of the major modernist
writers, including Joyce and Stein) was largely funded by the immense
wealth of Bryher's father, the shipping magnate Sir John Ellerman: she
almost certainly made a greater practical and intellectual contribution to
the Press than she has been credited with.[20] Bryher, who was for the most
part open about her lesbianism, married to gain, and then to maintain, her

independence from her family; her marriage to Macpherson was ostensibly motivated by the need to provide a front for H.D.'s liaison, but it also ensured that she was not excluded from the relationship. Bryher and Macpherson legally adopted H.D.'s daughter Perdita at this time.

From the early 1920s, Bryher and H.D. had been living for part of the year in Switzerland and they returned there with Macpherson in 1927. Macpherson's interest in films and film-making was growing, and he and Bryher decided to start a film journal and to take a studio in which Macpherson could make films. They founded POOL, the publishing and production company which included POOL books, POOL films, and *Close Up* itself. Bryher's finances, contacts, and labours undoubtedly kept the journal going for the six years—1927 to 1933—in which it ran and she wrote extensively for it, but Macpherson's words 'fronted' the journal in its first four years, and he used his editorial, 'As If', to declaim his views on the new art of the film.

Macpherson, like many of his contributors, was committed to the establishment of an independent production and distribution sector, distinct from the mainstream of commercial cinema, and the journal enthusiastically reported the setting up of avant-garde production groups. But *Close Up* was, as Anne Friedberg has noted, equally concerned with an avant-garde of cinematic reception: of viewing, criticism, and theory.[21] Underlying the emphasis on activity in the journal—on amateur production, on local exhibition, on participation in anti-censorship campaigns—was an absolute commitment to the concept of 'active' spectatorship, contrasted with the 'passive' consumption of commercial cinema. As an unsigned editorial entitled 'Dope or Stimulus' (perhaps written by Bryher) proclaimed:

> To watch may be a vital way to life. But to watch hypnotically something which has become a habit and which is not recorded as it happens by the brain, differs little from the drug taker's point of view, and is destructive because it is used as a cover to prevent real consideration of problems, artistic, or sociological, and the creation of intelligent English films.[22]

Macpherson, Bryher, and H.D. were all committed to psychoanalytic ideas before they founded the journal, and their interests in film were strongly guided by their particular approaches to psychoanalysis. Macpherson's two early novels, *Poolreflection* and *Gaunt Island* (both published by POOL in 1927) were studies of 'abnormal' family relationships and incestuous desires, their techniques finding their echoes in H.D.'s prose writing, with its explorations of mirroring relationships and its palimpsestic 'superimpositions' of different times and spaces. These forms had their cinematic counterpart in Macpherson's POOL films. As a critic in the *Manchester Guardian* noted, in a review of Bryher's war novel *Civilians* and Macpherson's *Gaunt Island*, and with reference to POOL publications more generally, 'these adventurous writers ... fashion themselves into the likeness of a three-guinea camera. They put into the picture not only all that the eye sees, but all they know to be there ... (It is worth noting that, among arts, the Pool group are deeply interested in the kinema.)'[23]

Where H.D. found in psychoanalyis and film a means of access to hidden realities, Bryher was more concerned with psychoanalysis, cinema and education or, in her terms, 'development'. In her writings, psychoanalysis was presented as a way of liberating individuals and cultures from habit and tradition and educating them for the modern world. A trip at the end of 1927 to Berlin resulted in an invitation to Pabst's house, where Bryher met the 'quiet, almost Eastern-looking figure sitting in one corner who was afterwards to be my analyst, Dr. Hanns Sachs', who 'had recently been acting as adviser on the first attempt to make a psychoanalytic film, *Secrets of a Soul*'. The encounter with the analyst took place in the context of film and, moreover, in the context of a film about psychoanalysis.[24]

Pabst's *Secrets of a Soul* was itself a key moment in the relationship between cinema and psychoanalysis. In 1925 the Freudian analyst Karl Abraham was approached by Eric Neumann of Ufa about the possibility of a film exploring psychoanalytic concepts. Letters between Abraham and Freud chart Abraham's growing enthusiasm for the project and Freud's continuing resistance: 'My chief objection is still that I do not believe that satisfactory plastic representation of our abstractions is at all possible.'[25] By mid-1925, Hanns Sachs had, along with Abraham, become centrally involved in the making of the film, a cinematic case-study exploring the origins of a phobia (in this instance a knife-phobia) and the workings of the psychoanalytic method of understanding and curing the neurosis. Sachs wrote the pamphlet which accompanied the film, in which he described at length and in detail the action of the film as an illustration of central Freudian concepts: repression, sublimation, displacement, condensation.[26] The production of an accompanying, explanatory monograph was taken up by the POOL group in 1930, when H.D. wrote the pamphlet intended to both publicize and explain *Borderline*, defined by

Macpherson as an attempt at something which 'had not been done ... had not been touched, except in Pabst's frankly psychoanalytic film, *Secrets of a Soul*'.[27]

A great deal of the editorial comment in *Close Up* was directed against cinema spectatorship as passive dreaming, and against the use of cinema as a palliative, where people go to 'get out of themselves into the strangely potent drug of dark and light and music', in Macpherson's words.[28] The intense involvement of the *Close Up* group with psychoanalytic thought, and their publication of a number of articles on psychoanalysis and the cinema, in which the equation between film and dream was strongly made, however, complicates the model in which the watching of 'the great films' represented an awakening from the consolatory dreams of commercial cinema. Practioners and theorists of psychoanalysis have found the cinema–dream relationship *tout court* (regardless of the 'value' of the film) a compelling one for their understanding of unconscious processes, and it has indeed been said that we can watch films, with their 'fantastical' transitions in time and through space, precisely because we are dreamers. For Hugo von Hofmannsthal, writing in the early 1920s, 'a secret instinct is appeased' in film-spectatorship, 'an instinct familiar to the dreamers of dreams'.[29] Elsewhere we find the implication that the film has in some sense replaced the dream in and for the twentieth century: the argument might then run that we know how to watch films because we have in the past been dreamers.

Hanns Sachs, a close member of Freud's immediate professional circle, fascinated by the application of psychoanalysis to the creative process and the reception of works of art, and by the concept of the work of art as a 'collective day-dream', explored the idea of 'day-dreams in common', a concept which became central to his articles for *Close Up*. In an article on 'Film Psychology', Sachs also opened up the relationship between conscious and unconscious knowledge in relation to dream and film, suggesting that the film-work functions not only by analogy but by contrast with the dream-work. Whereas the dream disguises unconscious wishes and desires, as a way of eluding 'the censor', the film reveals them.[30] In this sense, the film could be said to be closer to dream-interpretation, with its emancipatory potential, than to the dream itself. The conceptual relationship between film and dream could thus be both sustained and made commensurate with the ideal of active spectatorship at the heart of *Close Up*'s project.

Bryher's preoccupations and passions during Berlin's Weimar years were a mirror-image of its cultural face, as she dashed between film, psychoanalysis, and the Berlin Zoo, and appointed a Berlin architect—Hermann Henselmann—to build a Bauhaus dwelling in Switzerland, which she called 'Kenwin' (a marriage of a kind between Macpherson (Kenneth) and herself (Winifred)), complete with a film studio that was never actually used. Some of the passion that Macpherson had put into film and film-making was transferred in the early 1930s into modernist decor: for some months his letters to Bryher contained little but discussion of paint and linoleum, with the linoleum for the 'cocktail stairs' a recurrent theme. Bryher, it should perhaps be noted, did not go in for cocktails; her tastes were Spartan, and she demanded that Henselmann, the architect, replace the carpets and silk hangings he had planned for her bedroom with reed matting, canvas curtains, and a filing cabinet instead of a mirror.[31] The filing cabinet is an appropriate image; Bryher was a scrupulous historian and archivist of her own life and times.

In unpublished notes on Berlin, made some years after these events, Bryher attempted to define the relationship between cinema and psychoanalysis:

> It is possible that some instinct tells an artist where to go to develop his capacity to the fullest extent. The Berlin of the early Thirties was never as creative as the Paris of the Twenties as far as literature was concerned but it saw the flowering and almost annihilation of the new art of the film. I had rarely been to a cinema in my life, the idea of film seemed alien to me. I thought in 1927 only in terms of literature, of books but when Kenneth Macpherson said that he saw in imagination a new world of pictures that not only moved but moved as if they were reflexions of intellectual thoughts, I was perfectly willing to go to Berlin where apparently the 'movement' had its heart.
>
> It was one of the most exciting moments that I have ever experienced. The people we met said that they had no paper in which to express their views and this was where my Paris training was valuable. 'If you want to write about the film', I said to Kenneth with my background of what used to be called 'the little magazines that die to make verse live' there must be a magazine. I wrote to a printer in France who had printed most of the small experimental papers and in 1927 the first issue of Close Up appeared. We went to Berlin, armed possibly with two issues. I had myself seen perhaps six films in my life, Kenneth had gone to any film available since early boyhood. It was a strange world to me, I did not understand it in the least at first but I made up for my ignorance by being extremely useful. In those days I spoke

German fluently. We were usually there two or three times a year between 1927 and 1932, to see the new films and to meet the friends that Kenneth soon made in the world of the cinema. I had a different interest, I had not been brought up with films but with books, I was intensely interested in the workings of the mind and I had already discovered Freud. I forget who gave me the introduction, but I had met Dr Hanns Sachs, told him that psychology meant far more to me as a would be writer than pictures and within a few days found myself on the analytic couch, having, unlike most analysands, 'the time of my life' because it interested me so much.

I find myself unable to describe the atmosphere of that time. It was violent and strange and I felt more drawn into it than I had been into the literary world of Paris. Chance or destiny who knew, some people fitted into movies like a piece into a puzzle, they soared to the top for a few days or weeks, suddenly to make a fresh start, perhaps never to be heard of again. Work of any kind was hard to get, people in the early Thirties were literally starving. Yet because a camera caught not so much an expression as a thought beneath as if for the first time a lens could record an emotion or thought, we all seemed to be living in a world above ourselves, really something that was utterly new with no reflexions of other ages or thoughts about it.

It was also linked for me with psycho-analysis. I felt that the analysis of that period had been invented just for my own pleasure, I loved it. I had asked 'why' ever since I could remember and now I was getting answers to my 'why' for the first time. It stirred my sense of history and eventually, I was allowed to attend the formal meetings, a carrot being tendered to me in the hope that I would forget the outside world and present myself as a candidate for training. I am sorry for the world today, now it has become a medical preserve and everything is standardized but in those days it was experimental...I used to go to Dr Sachs, he lived in the Mommsenstrasse then, for my hour and in time was promoted to be allowed to go to the evening lectures, on theory and with examples...Films and psychoanalysis, in those experimental days they were twins, some directors were trying to 'make thoughts visible' and this was to some extent visible with the photographic techniques they had. Film was far more interesting in those days, it was flexible, sometimes a little blurred. To-day it is merely a set of colored postcards that move, it is a replica of humanity if you will but not a comment on it. I went five or six times a week in the Berlin of the Thirties, now I doubt if I go once in a year, it is mecanical [sic] now and as far as I am concerned, totally without interest.

Berlin was different.[32]

These were also the 'Berlin years' of W. H. Auden, Stephen Spender, and Christopher Isherwood, for whom the experience of the city was not only highly sexualized ('To Christopher, Berlin meant Boys', Isherwood wrote) but also cinematic: the question of censorship and repression, and the freedom from their constraints represented by Weimar Berlin, prevailed in both arenas.[33] Stephen Spender later described living in Germany at the close of the 1920s and the beginning of the 1930s, and of the significance of the Russian films he and Isherwood saw at this time, including *Earth*, *The General Line*, *The Mother*, *Potemkin*, *Ten Days that Shook the World*, and *The Way into Life*:

> These films, which form a curiously isolated episode in the aesthetic history of this century, excited us because they had the modernism, the poetic sensibility, the satire, the visual beauty, all those qualities we found most exciting in other forms of modern art, but they also conveyed a message of hope like an answer to *The Waste Land*. They extolled a heroic attitude which had not yet become officialized; in this they foreshadowed the defiant individualism of the Spanish Republicans. We used to go on long journeys to little cinemas in the outer suburbs of Berlin, and there among the grimy tenements we saw the images of the New Life of the workers building with machine tools and tractors their socially just world under the shadows of baroque statues reflected in ruffled waters of Leningrad, or against waving, shadow-pencilled plains of corn.[34]

Soviet films, Spender suggested, played a central role in their 'restless and awakening mood', projecting images of a different kind of landscape and a different organization of society in, and onto, the decaying facades of Berlin. In his memoir, Spender also described a party at which an amateur film 'was shown of another party just like the one at which I was now present and with some of the same people':

> Then there were pictures of sun-bathing, swimming. It was as though this Germany were a series of boxes fitting into one another, and all of them the same … Now on the screen there was a party here in this very room, and people dancing. The camera passed through moving figures, surveying the room, occasionally pausing as it were to examine someone's dress or figure. Boys and girls were lying on the ground embracing and then rolling away from one another to turn their faces towards the camera's lens. Willi lay stroking the head of a girl beside him. He turned, his face white in the light, and then he kissed her, the shadow first, and then his head, covering the light on her lips. I heard Willi laugh beside me.[35]

The inherently doubled world of the screen becomes a hall of mirrors as the partygoers watch the film images which, in part, replicate their current reality. The passage encodes the tropes of the cinematic in a number of ways: it describes the impersonal eye of the camera, passing, surveying, and pausing as if by its own agency; the look at the camera of those caught in its lens or eye; the shadow and its shadow, as in Henrik Galeen's 1926 Expressionist film *The Student of Prague*, a film to which Isherwood and Auden, in particular, were drawn. For Spender, as, to a significant extent, for the *Close Up* group, film in these years was predominantly represented by both the Soviet cinema, which conjoined politics and aesthetics, and amateur film, in which spectators were also actors, in which the world on the screen was a mirror-image of the reality they were living through, and in which their own desires could be projected and acted out. The cinema was the 'world within world' which Spender took as the title for his autobiography, and Germany 'a series of boxes fitting into one another', the image echoing Bryher's 'people fitt[ing] into movies like a piece into a puzzle'.

Bryher's discussion, in her Berlin notes, of film and psychoanalysis—and her account in related notes of film as the 'technique of the sudden shock'—also have their echoes in one of the most significant essays on film of the period, Walter Benjamin's 'The Work of Art in the Age of Mechanical Reproduction', in which he outlined a model of the 'optical unconscious':

> The film has enriched our field of perception with methods which can be illustrated by those of Freudian theory. Fifty years ago, a slip of the tongue passed more or less unnoticed. Only exceptionally may such a slip have revealed dimensions of depth in a conversation which had seemed to be taking its course on the surface. Since the *Psychopathology of Everyday Life* things have changed. This book isolated and made analyzable things which had heretofore floated along unnoticed in the broad stream of perception. For the entire spectrum of optical, and now also acoustical, perception the film has brought about a similar deepening of apperception. It is only an obverse of this fact that behaviour items shown in a movie can be analyzed much more precisely and from more points of view than those presented on paintings or on the stage …
>
> By close-ups of the things around us, by focusing on hidden details of familiar objects, by exploring commonplace milieus under the ingenious guidance of the camera, the film, on the one hand, extends our comprehension of the necessities which rule our lives; on the other hand, it manages to assure us of an immense and unexpected field of action. Our taverns and our metropolitan streets, our offices and our furnished rooms, our railroad stations and our factories appeared to have us locked up hopelessly. Then came the film and burst this prison-world asunder by the dynamite of a tenth

of a second, so that now, in the midst of its far-flung ruins and debris, we calmly and adventurously go traveling. With the close-up, space expands; with slow motion, movement is extended...Evidently a different nature opens itself to the camera than opens to the naked eye—if only because an unconsciously penetrated space is substituted for a space consciously explored by man...The camera introduces us to unconscious optics as does psychoanalysis to unconscious impulses.[36]

Benjamin reveals the influence here of Béla Balázs's physiognomic aesthetics, with its focus on the cinematic detail: 'The camera close-up aims at the uncontrolled small areas of the face; thus it is able to photograph the unconscious.'[37] Both were strongly echoed in Hanns Sachs's film writings in *Close Up,* with, in the article 'Film Psychology', his account of film (and he was referring in particular to Eisenstein's *Battleship Potemkin*) as 'a kind of time microscope, that is to say, it shows us clearly and unmistakably things that are to be found in life but that ordinarily escape our notice.'[38] A psychoanalytic emphasis on the revelation of the habitually concealed or occluded was thus combined with a political focus, developed in Russian Formalist and Brechtian theories, on the role of art in 'making strange' the familiar word and world, and on art's 'alienation' effects.

The 'traveling', the 'movement', which Walter Benjamin describes in 'The Work of Art in the Age of Mechanical Reproduction' is everywhere present in Bryher's and Macpherson's accounts of Berlin in the late 1920s. They viewed the city as a cinematic spectacle. Towards the end of 1927 Bryher wrote to H.D.: 'Cinemas open at five on Sundays so we went to the five o'clock show and coming out there was a crowd to fill the whole vast place but arranged circular wise and in perfect grouping as if for a movie. You cant [sic] get the German movies till you've been here.'[39] Macpherson also extolled the virtues of Berlin and marvelled at its cinemas: 'The Ufa palast about the size of Regents Park another gold beehive, with *red* plush walls and red carpets. And miles and miles of entrances and exits and disappearances and cabinets...Berlin is one big movie, like an impossible dream.'[40] Their letters to H.D., Bryher's in particular, recounted Berlin film 'dirt' or gossip which would then be used in the pages of the journal. The film 'group' in Berlin—Pabst, Sachs, and the architect, cameraman, and director Ernst Metzner—was extended to the silhouette film-maker Lotte Reiniger and her husband Paul Koch, whom Bryher met in April 1931, Eric Walter White, English author of the two pamphlets on film published by the Hogarth Press, the photographer Hans Casparius, Andor Krasna-Kraus, and the actress Elizabeth Bergner, with whom Bryher became infatuated, describing her as 'the Colette of the screen'.[41]

Yet Bryher found Berlin too 'American' at the start: 'It appears that Lang is Austrian, Pabst no doubt as well, and almost all the film people. They come from Austria but can't work there. Interesting. Sort of emigration to Berlin in place of New York.'[42] Her love affair with the city began when she met Pabst, who, she wrote to H.D., had told her on their first encounter that *Close Up* was 'the thing we all desire, the paper that expresses our inmost psychological thoughts', and observed the incongruity and humour of the fact that 'an English man should have written it'.[43]

Pabst's *Joyless Street*, starring Greta Garbo, remained a cinematic touch-stone for Bryher and for H.D., who had written about the film in her first article for *Close Up*, contrasting the Garbo of Pabst's film, 'trailing with frail, very young feet through perhaps the most consistently lovely film I have ever seen', and Garbo, 'deflowered, deracinated, devitalized' in the guise of a Hollywood 'vamp' (in *The Torrent*).[44] The transformation epitomized, for H.D., the difference between all that *Close Up* stood for in the way of 'true beauty' and the 'mechanical efficiency and saccharine dra-matic mediocrity' of commercial cinema, with which 'the Censor', whose hostility towards Pabst's cinema was being felt in the late 1920s, had formed an unholy alliance. *Close Up*'s mission, as H.D. represented it, and that 'of every sincere intellectual', was 'to work for the better understanding of the cinema ... to rescue this captured Innocent (for the moment embodied in this Greta Garbo)'. Pabst, she wrote in 1929, 'holds, as it were, the clue, must hold his position almost as the keystone to the vast aesthetic structure we call now unquestionably the Art of the Film': his characters, she added, were 'created, not made', and each and every one of the women in his films was 'shown as a "being", a creature of consummate life and power and vitality. G. W. Pabst brings out the vital and vivid forces in women as the sun in flowers'.[45] The distinction between 'creation' and 'making' becomes an aspect of the critical opposition between the organic 'birth' and the vitalism of the cinema as art form and its mechanical, 'made' origins.

The terms were intended to produce the strongest contrast to the image of the 'mechanical', 'automatic' women represented in commercial film, and even to the 'technically perfected image' of a film such as Dreyer's *Jeanne d'Arc*, towards which H.D. expressed considerable ambivalence, commenting on the cruelty of its relentless representation of Jeanne's agonies: 'Do I *have* to be cut in slices by this inevitable pan-movement of the camera, these suave lines to left, up, to the right, back, all rhythmical with the remorseless rhythm of a scimitar?'[46] Dreyer's technical alternatives to montage were, H.D. suggested, more of an assault, more of a knife-attack, on the spectator than 'Russian cutting': 'We are numb and beaten', she wrote of her experience of watching *Jeanne d'Arc*.[47]

Recalling her first viewing of *Joyless Street*, in a cinema in Montreux, H.D. wrote:

> This is beauty, and this is a beautiful and young woman not exaggerated in any particular, stepping, frail yet secure across a wasted city. Post-war Vienna really wrung our hearts that time … Before our eyes, the city was unfolded, like some blighted flower … War and war and war … La Petite Rue Sans Joie [Joyless Street] was a real, little street. It was a little war-street, a little, post-war street, therefore our little picture palace in our comparatively broad-minded Lake Geneva town, is empty. People won't, they dare not face reality.[48]

Joyless Street explored the interplay of desire and hunger in post-war Vienna.[49] While Lotte Eisner, in her influential study *The Haunted Screen*, found the film melodramatic and overly 'picturesque' in its stylization,[50] for the *Close Up* group it represented reality, the 'real, little street', just as, for Macpherson, in Pabst's *Die Liebe der Jeanne Ney*: 'Paris suddenly became real, Paris suddenly *was* Paris. It was almost a shock to realise *Paris could exist on the films*.'[51] This appeal to the value of cinematic realism might seem to sit oddly with the self-declared avant-gardism of the journal, but a strong driving impulse of *Close Up* was, as we have seen, directed against the false dreaming, as its writers perceived it, of commercial cinema and towards a psychological and phenomenal realism, in which 'reality' was imbued with cinematic dimensions. 'Life and the film must not be separated', H.D. wrote in her article 'Russian Films': 'people and things must pass across the screen naturally like shadows of trees on grass or passing reflections in a crowded city window'.[52] While *Close Up* included significant discussions of, and numerous stills from, abstract, Dadaist and surrealist cinema, these were not by and large the film forms that drove the journal's project, and the group by no means shared the passion of French and American cinéastes for 'Charlot'/Chaplin.[53]

For Bryher and H.D., in particular, psychological realism, also a crucial aspect of the complex representations of women and female sexuality in Pabst's films, was inseparable from a sense of film's importance in representing the realities and depredations of war, and the necessity of countering sentimental and deceptive cinematic representations of heroism and patriotism. Bryher's first and last articles for the journal were on World War I films and the growing threat of a second world war respectively, and she wrote throughout the years of the journal on the topic of war in cinema: 'By all means let us have war films. Only let us have war straight and as it is; mainly disease and discomfort, almost always destructive (even in after civil life) in its effects.'[54] She particularly commended the American director King Vidor's *The Big Parade*, which showed how the American public was, in Paul Rotha's words, 'howled into war'.[55]

The 'internationalism' of silent cinema, both Bryher and H.D. suggested in a number of their articles, opened up the possibility of communication between nations. For Kenneth Macpherson, introducing the 'Russian number' of *Close Up*, Soviet films 'can and will end degradation, and wars and hate'.[56] There was thus a strongly utopian dimension to their film-writing. In H.D.'s words: 'the world of the film today ... is no longer the world of the film, it is *the* world ... There has never been, perhaps since the days of the Italian Renaissance, so great a "stirring" in the mind and soul of the world consciousness.'[57] At the same time, film—'the technique of the sudden shock'—was also imbued with a unique power to represent the violence of war. The war-machine and cinema have been profoundly connected, from the late nineteenth century onwards, and it is the argument of Paul Virilio and others that modern warfare, with its transformations of the conditions of seeing and being seen, its explosion of 'the old homogeneity of vision' and its replacement with 'the heterogeneity of perceptual fields', is an essentially 'cinematic disruption of the space continuum'.[58] Eisenstein's claim that the methods of filmic montage had been revealed to him during the exchanges of gunfire in 1917 was a highly significant one, linking form and thematic in crucial ways, and Macpherson took it up in his account of Eisenstein's *Ten Days* (*October*), writing that the effect achieved 'by cutting alternately from a close up of the soldier's head to the spitting gun' was 'as vivid as if someone had actually turned a Maxim on the auditorium'.[59]

Russian Cutting

Like the Film Society, *Close Up* began with a focus on German cinema. The 'cutting' of Pabst's *Die Liebe Der Jeanne Ney*, about which Macpherson wrote at length in an early issue of *Close Up*, quoting Pabst in interview on the invisible cuts in the film, 'made on some movement', was contrasted with the chopping of censors and renters: 'The principle will be like trimming the edge off rose petals with scissors to improve the shape.'[60] The detailed accounts of Pabst's films on the pages of the journal, as I noted earlier, became a way, analogous to the inclusion of film stills, of defeating censorship by representing, albeit in words rather than images, the narratives that had been suppressed. As Pabst 'moves' his female characters, in particular, through his films, the *Close Up* writers followed in their footsteps, walking through the films as they described them. Macpherson wrote of Edith Jehanne's performance in Pabst's *Die Liebe der Jeanne Ney*: 'Here she goes through the film like an arrow, unblurred and definite and admirable. Her power is in her eyes which give the dual impression of defencelessness and courage. Pabst moves her through his film bringing out both these qualities until the power of it is almost stunning.'[61] Film criticism was to be writing on the move, while the image of filmic motion as a traversal of city streets (encapsulated thematically and structurally in the 'street films' of Weimar cinema) was central to the journal, particularly in its early issues.

A year into the journal's publication, articles on Russin cinema began to appear with more frequency. The September 1928 issue was described as 'a Russian number', a response, as Macpherson wrote in his editorial, to 'a rush of new films from Russia into Germany ... Russia has imposed—without knowing it—a difficult task on *Close Up*':

> For we cannot begin where Russia begins. The ground is not yet ready. Before critical discussions can be made, an impartially critical attitude must be established, and before we can begin to cope with the films as films, we have to cope with the public which has been carefully nurtured to believe that all Russian films are veiled digs at Europe's dwindling thrones.[62]

To illustrate the central role played by cinema in the Soviet Union, Macpherson wrote: 'the Russian populace does not assume merely the role of spectator, but is frequently active in participation, and always carries the right to vote its approval of a film subject before the film is made'.[63] Thus *Close Up*'s ideal of active spectatorship became associated with the greatness of Russian films, and 'Russian cutting'—montage—was identified with 'realism and the reaction of an actual participant'. 'One often reads', Macpherson wrote, 'of the camera being used as an eye. The Russian method uses it not as an eye, but as a *brain*. It darts surely and exactly from one vital thing to another vital thing'.[64] The relationship between 'eye' and 'brain' in film spectatorship was thus redefined, with the camera itself understood to be performing mental operations. Macpherson, in this article at least, bypassed Dziga-Vertov's influential model of the 'Kino-Eye' ('Kinoki'), at the heart of his 1925 film of that title, as well as of his *Man with a Movie Camera*, and appears instead to allude to Pudovkin's 1926 film *Mechanics of the Brain*, an exploration of Pavlov's 'conditioned reflexes' made in collaboration with Pavlov himself.[65]

'Politics are not my world', Macpherson wrote in his introduction to 'the Russian number', and this was echoed by H.D. in her article in the issue on 'Russian Films': 'the greatness of the Moscow art productions that it was my unique privilege to see last month in Berlin, puts the question of the Russian film … on a plane transcending politics. These films do not say to the British or the American workman, go and do likewise. They say look, we are your brothers, and this is how we suffered.'[66] In *Film Problems of Soviet Russia*, published in 1929, Bryher attempted to steer a middle line politically, arguing for Russian films as 'art' and as 'truth', charting the ways in which the bridge from the destruction of war to the construction of peace came through the cinema in Russia, and focusing on questions of 'education': 'The soul of the world can be changed only by attacking conditions from a psychological point of view, not a conventional one, whether it be the convention of the Left or the convention of the Right.'[67] At points, she insisted on the universality, and at times a more specifically national relevance, of the themes explored in Soviet cinema: 'Forget about Russia and remember that [Pudovkin's] *Mother* fundamentally is the story of many English homes, with disease or stagnation, or the Colonies as a substitute for the ending.'[68] The book in its entirety, like so much of the material in *Close Up*, was written as a protest against British censorship regulations, a detailed account of which appeared in Macpherson's 'As Is' in the February 1929 'censorship protest' issue. 'It is to be hoped', Bryher wrote, that united protest by English desirous of liberty will remove the barrier to our cinematographic development and that we shall be able to study the new Russian films as they appear.'[69] Her book was also intended as a spur to the reader-spectator: 'It is really the question of what you, the spectator, are willing to do for the screen, for the cinema is an active, not a passive, art.'[70]

Like Macpherson (who may well have contributed to the writing of *Film Problems of Soviet Russia*), Bryher explored the ways in which the Soviet cinema showed 'mind' on the screen. She discussed Kuleshov's

Sühne (*Expiation*) at some length, as did H.D. in an article for *Close Up*, both Bryher and H.D. focusing on the performance of the actress playing Edith, A. Chocklova: 'this creature that has madness and greatness in her face and movements', in Bryher's words.[71] For H.D., *Expiation* was as much of a revelation as *Joyless Street*, with the realism of the Russian film taking 'the human spirit … further than it can go'. Edith, H.D. wrote, 'has a way of standing against a sky line that makes a hieroglyph, that spells almost visibly some message of cryptic symbolism'.[72] As in her discussion of *The Student of Prague* (the 1926 version, with Conrad Veidt), H.D. gestured towards a secret language of film, encoded in film hieroglyphics, at once 'universal' and revealing their meanings only to the initiated. She was also undoubtedly influenced by Eisenstein's writings on the 'hieroglyphic' nature of cinematographic language, with their appeal to an Imagist poetics, as in his essay 'The Cinematographic Principle and Japanese Culture', also published in *transition*.

For Bryher, Eisenstein's *Ten Days that Shook the World* was the 'greatest' of films, and the one that revealed to her most clearly the nature of cine-matography: 'Perhaps it is because its entire appeal is to the intellect—not to the emotions solely, but to the brain, which is beyond emotion—the super or over-conscious, that is habitually so starved. There is not a shot in the picture that has not been created by mind alone.'[73] Alexander Room's *Bed and Sofa* 'gives to the spectator rather than taking from him: a novel sensation to those used to the ordinarily projected films. Room has obtained his effects by using the correct psychological basis for all actions, however minute, and by his capacity to set symbols of the brain processes, in pictures.'[74] The valorization of active spectatorship was thus combined with an increasing use of a criticism deriving from Eisenstein's theories of 'intellectual montage'.

Eisenstein himself had moved from a focus, in the early to mid 1920s, on the arousal of the viewer's senses and emotions through the arrangement of shots (with, as an early commentator wrote, 'Montage not only on the screen of the movie theatre, but also on the screen of the brain'[75]) to an exploration of the ways in which cinema could generate ideas and the construction of an 'intellectual cinema'. This would be achieved, as Eisenstein suggested in his essays of the late 1920s, a number of which were published in *Close Up,* through a 'language' of the screen heavily dependent upon metaphors and a use of montage as conflict and collision, constructed to provoke the spectator into thought. In 'The New Language of Cinematography', published in *Close Up* in May 1929, Eisenstein contrasted the cinematography of 'the first phase', in which 'we were striving for a quick emotional *discharge*', and 'the new cinema [which] must *include deep reflective processes*, the result of which will find expression neither immediately nor directly'.[76]

Bryher's *Film Problems of Soviet Russia* was widely and well reviewed. The commentaries on the book, almost all of which mentioned the stills of Russian films contained in the book, reveal the intense interest in Russian cinema at this time and the level of frustration generated by censorship. As Anthony Gishford wrote of *Close Up* in the Oxford student paper *The Isis*: 'The "stills" it publishes from contemporary work by Einstein [*sic*] or Pudovkin fill one with impotent rage against the system of censorship under which we suffer.'[77] 'The importance of Bryher's book', a *Saturday Review* critic noted, 'is that it describes for the first time a conscious effort on the part of disinterested persons to use the kinema as a free means of expression.' It was discussed by Robert Herring in the *Manchester Guardian* in a column which also commented on the news that, after the years of censorship, British Instructional Films were to become the distributors of Russian films in Britain: 'Anyone who has followed the kinema with intelligence and discrimination knows that the Russian kinema is the most important in the world, and the reason for this importance is that Russian films deal directly with the problems of daily life.' Bryher's *Film Problems of Soviet Russia*, Herring continued, made something of this daily life known: 'The author sees each one of them as a constructive attempt to deal with some problem arising from the Russian experience, and the various films fall into place in the book rather like the images in the film itself, each one expressing the main theme that people must be taught to think for themselves.'[78] He concluded the column with the hope of the possibilities of Russian directors making sound-films and of an English-German-Russian alliance as 'an answer to the question of Hollywood aggression'.

Film Problems was also reviewed favourably in the journal *Workers' Life*, though the reviewer observed that 'the author is by no means a Communist',[79] and by the film critic Ralph Bond: 'At last somebody has written a book about Russian films, and every man and woman who has faith in the future of the cinema should be grateful.' Bond, who contributed articles to *Close Up* on the topic of censorship and on film and politics, noted the 'enormous importance' attached to 'cutting' in Russian films—'the Russian directors stand alone in the art of short cutting, and cross-cutting, by means of which the spectator is gripped with an almost unbelievable intensity. Cutting is the poetry of the film. Without it, it is understood, rhythmic motion and beauty is impossible'—and the general seriousness with which film-making was taken in Russia.[80] Henry Dobb, writing for the *Sunday Worker*, contrasted Bryher's 'fine study' with H. G. Wells's 'film scenario' *The King Who Was a King*: 'Remote from reality or life it has less aesthetic interest and philosophical importance than a dog fight ... Wells has suddenly uncurled from a hermitage to which has seemingly never reached the fame of the Russian Workers' Cinema.' Bryher's book would open up 'this dazzle of greatness, this gallery of beauty', and while Bryher 'is not a Communist', she has written 'the first detailed study of the Russian film, and a book for every right-minded worker'.[81]

Harry Alan Potamkin reviewed *Film Problems of Soviet Russia* in *Experimental Cinema*, the journal edited by the American Marxist Seymour Stern from 1930 to 1934, which argued for the absolute superiority of Soviet cinema on both artistic and political grounds, and which published articles by Eisenstein and Pudovkin. Potamkin was critical of Bryher's study on the grounds that: 'The sole "problem" of the Russian film considered here is the non-cinematic problem of the British antagonism':

> Bryher's book is a plea for the recognition of the Russian cinema by England. She stresses not only the artistic merit of the Soviet kino, but urges that vital cinema upon the British intelligence as quite in accord ideologically with the social sentiments of the free Briton. This would seem to characterize Russian ideology as reformative in its outlook, a quite acceptable middleman's social philosophy. This sums up the Russian social attack as entirely harmless. If that were so, the Russian film, informed by this assertive ideology, would lack the essential vigor which is its physical health. But the Russian idea is dangerous, decidedly dangerous to the prevailing acceptations. The dangerous idea creates the dangerous, or heroic structure—ultimately.[82]

While Potamkin may have seen Bryher's perspective as that of the political 'middleman', *Close Up* was, by 1929, becoming increasingly identified with Soviet film, and, for the right-wing press and establishment, was certainly becoming 'dangerous'. In January 1915, the *Daily Express* cinema correspondent reported, under the byline 'Storm Over Asia': 'Efforts are being made by a pro-Russia propagandist organisation operating from Territet, in Switzerland, to remove the ban imposed by the Government and the British Board of Film Censors on about forty Russian propagandist films now in cold storage in this country. Circulars demanding the release of these films in the name of "intellectual liberty" have been sent to many people, with a petition which they and their friends are asked to sign.' Russian films, it was claimed, 'are violently propagandistic', and *Storm over Asia* was described as 'an attack on British prestige in China and the East'.[83]

One of the strongest links between the projects of the Film Society and of *Close Up* was their respective campaigns against censorship in the 1920s, with a *Close Up* petition organized by Dorothy Richardson, and extensive activity by Montagu, including the publication of his 1929 pamphlet on *The Political Censorship of Films*. Eisenstein had links both to the *Close Up* group and, as I discussed in the previous chapter, to Montagu, with whom he travelled to Hollywood in 1930, before his troubled trip to Mexico and the failure of his film project there.[84] Letters exchanged in 1927 between Montagu and Kenneth Macpherson reveal something of a territorial battle over insider knowledge of the Soviet Union and its films: Montagu had made his first trip to Russia in 1925, whereas neither Macpherson nor Bryher were to visit the country. But from the perspectives of the censors, and government bodies wary of the ways in which Soviet cinema might impact on British politics, *Close Up* and the Film Society were very much connected.[85] A Memorandum, issued by the Conservative Party Headquarters, 'on revolutionary film propaganda, carried out in England by direction of the Soviet government, 1927–May 1930', linked their activities (along with Ralph Bond's Atlas Films Ltd and the London Workers' Film Society, with which Montagu was by this time actively involved) to those of 'the Communist Party of Great Britain supported by the Komintern'. A reference to 'this accelerated "tempo" of propaganda', instanced by addresses to the Film Society from V. I. Pudovkin and Eisenstein, suggests that the activity (including anti-censorship campaigns) around Soviet cinema was itself perceived as if it were a Soviet film: a *Potemkin*, perhaps, whose banning by Sir William Joynson-Hicks had outraged writers and intellectuals on the Left.

The Conservative Party Memorandum quoted *The Times* (12 November 1929) on the Film Society's 'private' screening of 'the Soviet propaganda film of native mutiny, "The Battleship Potemkin". Potemkin exhibits the Soviet film propaganda method of "alternating rhythm", i.e. first the confused mass, then the individual as spokesman of the mass; then reversion to the mass—the individual on the mass'.[86] It also cited a comment allegedly made in *Close Up* on the film: 'it must have been seen by every worker of every nationality ... by every sailor ashore ... Socialist and Communist societies made a speciality of it … it was amusing to hear the unanimous applause as officer after officer on the good ship Potemkin was set upon and hurled overboard'.[87] The March issue of the journal, the Memorandum added, 'contains an interview with S. M. Eisenstein, Professor of the Soviet Institute of Cinematography, Moscow and producer of the principal Soviet propaganda film, in which he advocates the establishment of an English Film Academy, with lectures, studio work, etc.'[88]

Attack and defence at this time moved back and forth between the question of Soviet cinema and politics, and Soviet cinema and film technique, though for Eisenstein the two were not of course separable. The articles containing the substance of the 1929 lectures were 'The Principles of Film Form', 'The Filmic Fourth Dimension', and 'Methods of Montage', which were later published in *Film Form*, but made their first appearance in the pages of *Close Up* (with 'The Principles of Film Form' also appearing in *Experimental Cinema*). Robert Herring had attended the lecture course, writing to H.D. of Eisenstein's 'putting into new, crystal terms all one knew (nothing else); but surprising one that what one knew was so complicated, & surprising one by his scope & relating of film as it should be to all we all care for.'[89]

Dynamic Discourse on the Film

One of the determining contexts for *Close Up*, the transition from silent to sound film, raised central issues about representation, including the kinds of 'language' articulated by the silent film. It is striking that the early issues of the journal were extremely word-intensive, while the later ones—when sound film was clearly there to stay—were for the most part composed of uncaptioned film stills and photographs, often given an 'ethnographic' or 'anthropological' cast, as if their native subjects were themselves outside, or prior to, the terms of language. There were undoubtedly practical reasons for the increased volume of photographs and stills—the fading of Macpherson's interest in the journal and the difficulty of getting copy—but it may also have been that the later emphasis was a way of returning (talking) film to visuality and to 'silent' imagery, and away from words.

Silent film was, by contrast, highly discursively productive, and a favoured mode of much *Close Up* writing in the early period was a form of stream-of-consciousness or interior monologue. Such fluid techniques were also attempts to represent cinema's movement as modernity itself, and movement was represented as one of the senses. Robert Herring wrote that 'the cinema alone can answer our growing need to be fully articulate', the term 'articulate' operating as a compound word for articulacy and articulation, and suggesting that movement was itself to be defined as a linguistic as well as an experiential and bodily mode.[90]

In the second issue of *Close Up*, published in August 1927, Kenneth Macpherson's editorial, 'As Is', opened with a diatribe against an unnamed 'distinguished author' who had refused his invitation, claiming ignorance and indifference, to 'dynamically discourse on the film.'[91] 'Dynamic discourse' on cinema was central to the journal's ideals of commentary and reception as active and interventionist, shaping the development of film texts and film culture.[92] The phrase also encodes the 'essence' of cinema as motion and the concept that film 'discourse' should be adequate to its object. The core contributors to *Close Up*—Macpherson, Bryher, H.D., Dorothy Richardson, Robert Herring, Oswell Blakeston—all produced articles in its first issues in which the creation of 'dynamic discourse' appears to have been a major aspiration.

Macpherson liked to open his editorials as if they were part of an ongoing conversation. 'Well you are right enough', begins one, 'who says how much the screen must falsify true values.'[93] Dorothy Richardson's *Continuous Performance* articles were also narrative enactments of the entry *in medias res* experienced in 'continuous performance' cinemas; 'So I gave up going to the theatre' is the opening of her first *Close Up* article.[94] The ellipsis (and Richardson was in general much exercised by the question of punctuation) became the graphic equivalent of this particular film experience, although her concern was predominantly with the charting of the everyday experience of cinema-going rather than with an avant-garde of film spectatorship.

Robert Herring's first written contribution to *Close Up* was a lengthy review of Victor Fleming's *The Way of All Flesh*, in which he focused on the performance of the German actor Emil Jannings. Taking the reader through the film scene by scene, Herring appeared to be taking up the role of 'film explainer'. But his commentary was an ironic one, and the ironies were largely levelled at the attempts of an American director to make a 'German' film: 'That is why the film is taking so long, why we are watching so much.'[95] The details of shot and plot that Herring described were laborious because the film, it was suggested, laboured over them, and

Herring, deploying the familiar trope of the eye and retinal reception in its relation to brain or mind in cinematic spectatorship, played with the representation of the 'explainer' holding back the impatient viewer, who had already anticipated the moves the film is slowly making: 'You must not go thinking ahead like this. Watch Jannings. It's all very slow, but there's plenty of it. Why isn't your mind occupied. It finds it easy to disconnect from the eye, does it? Yes, I know; but Watch Jannings.'[96]

In the issues published in the last quarter of 1927, 'dynamic discourse' proliferated. In 'Comment and Review', a *Close Up* writer, possibly Bryher, wrote of the noise of chocolate wrappers in the cinema and 'the breaking of a female voice across drama… "Ices?… Chocolates?… Cigarettes?"… Making a kind of market-place of the gangways, her progress rung by the chink of coins, and long confabulations raucously whispered, and voices hailing from five rows back'.[97] Macpherson's editorial for October was followed, in November, by his extended piece 'Matinee'. Both articles were attempts to emulate or ventriloquize the experience of the 'ordinary' filmgoer, from a position both inside and outside it. 'I am going to peep', Macpherson wrote in the October 'As Is', 'at an average programme of one of the ordinary, larger cinema theatres. Corner sites are popular, so it is on a corner we stop.'[98] 'You', as the pronoun then becomes, buy a ticket from 'a pile of blond curls' with a 'robot voice', and are guided to a seat, entering the cinema in the middle of an American comedy, whose plot and conventions are entirely familiar. 'You', or 'we', runs or run through some ideas about American film, and its comparative virtues and weaknesses, 'think[ing] all this quite leisurely while looking at what is turning out to be quite a dreary little comedy'.[99] The brain and the eye are operating independently, and the film in no way engages the mind, which is free for broader speculations.[100]

This 'thinking' through the film continues throughout the rest of the film programme, which includes newsreel shorts. Here the narrative voice begins to observe the rest of the audience, as they prepare themselves for the 'Big Film'. Speculation then follows on the popular attractions of 'Big Films', which, it is decided, are based on identification not with characters but with stars, and bring about 'a kind of hypnotic daze… Mind in some way neatly obliterates itself'. Here, Macpherson as narrator argues, lies the reason for dismissal of the art of the film. The antidote lies in seeing the best:

See *Kopf Hoch Charley*, see *The Student of Prague*, see *Potemkin, Out of the Mist, Chang, Prince Achmed*, and then begin to judge! … Think of what all these films, considered as different specimens of one medium, amount to in the aggregate! Shuffle them up, make one force of them, and isn't it a mighty force? Think what you have. First of all pure form, every single attribute of photographic art, miracles to work in tones and tone depths, light, geometry, design, sculpture … pure abstraction all of it. Then this not static but with all the resources of movement, change, rhythm, space, completely fluid to the will of the artist. Then miracles to work again with trick photography, infinite possibilities of suggestion, contrast, merging, dissociation; whole realms of fantasy, states of mind, of emotion, psychic things, to symbolise not in the limit of one special moment of time, but in all the ebb and flow of their course, their beginning and their end. Not only have you mastery over the outward manifestion, but over the inner and inmost working too …

But the Big Film comes to its end, and we are still sitting here. We don't want to move. It has been a good show or it has been a bad show, it doesn't greatly matter. We feel that we will sit on and see the comedy round again to the point where we came in.[101]

The avant-garde of viewing, as in Elie Faure's *Cineplastics*, consisted in a form of spectatorship working against the grain of the commercial film, either to extract 'essence' or 'beauty' from the narrative flow or to construct in imagination an entirely different film. 'We remember films damaged by their captions', Dorothy Richardson wrote: 'Not fatally. For we can substitute our own, just as within limits we can remake a bad film as we go. With half a chance we are making all the time. Just a hint of *any* kind of beauty and if we are on the track, not waiting for everything to be done for us, not driven back by rouged pulp and fixed frown, we can manage very well.'[102]

In Macpherson's editorial, the alternative film was composed, in this instance, from an aggregate of those films most highly valued by the *Close Up* group (many of them already discussed in the journal), in a form of compound cinema. This last phrase was that of Harry A. Potamkin, who used it in an article published in *Close Up* in January 1929 to describe the ways in which sound film could and should develop, based on Eisenstein, Alexandrov, and Pudovkin's model of 'contrapuntral' sound.[103] Macpherson did not discuss the coming of sound in this editorial, but (as in other *Close Up* articles in this period) the function of criticism or commentary as film speech, whether it was represented as a form of talking aloud or as interior monologue, was both heightened and loaded.

Macpherson's 'Matinee' essay extended these representations, 'making strange' the cinema space by means of visual or retinal impressions:

> Where is that light? An empty row of plush extends before its ray, arm rests and the bright gleam of a cigarette tray for a fractional space, my left eye perceives cones waving down darkness, pallid elongations sliced by updrifting cigarette smoke. Beside my right eye are splashes, faces, I get photographic semblances of lives, people's thoughts brush consciousness, I get the different sense of different minds seeing things differently, and two in the row were annoyed because I got across their vision.[104]

Like H.D.'s, Macpherson's was a form of film criticism or commentary as film-making, with vision often represented as a form of diagonal slicing or cutting, and sometimes as an assault or attack on the eye. In 'Matinee', he wrote of a photograph of Garbo in the cinema foyer: 'the light broken across my eyes by glass, by the glass of her frame on the stairs the fuschia coloured stairs, that was interesting'.[105] In the cinema's interior, the usherette's torch, whose beam is a smaller version of the film projector, makes the architectural space filmic. Whereas Macpherson, in his editorial, imagined an aggregated 'art' cinema as a counter to the commercial film, in 'Matinee' he 'produces' his own film as a way of correcting and, indeed, erasing the projected spectacle.

> I am not seeing Lya de Putti nor the others with her ... I would somehow contrive my close up differently, along the corridor, dark sliced with triangles of half dark and cubes and oblongs and parallelograms of half dark and half light cutting and criss-crossing to fall and slant across the face, keep the face moving, move the camera with the face. ... there is something quite different you get in the meaning of geometry and plastic tone depths. Films should begin in the middle, end in the middle ...[106]

This is literally 'alternative' cinema, as well as a cinema of the mind. 'Remember', Macpherson wrote in his editorial for December 1929, 'the only real kino-eye is your eye. What it sees is your cinema. Build cinema as vision, your own vision, and you will build something worthwhile.'[107] He took up H.D.'s charged and intense models of telepathic communication and thought-projection, while translating the images of the screen into modernist and, more specifically, cubist geometries. To begin and to end in the middle was not only a rejection of conventional narratives (with their beginnings, middles and endings) but also a way of cutting across the boundaries between film and reality, inside and outside. Modernity, and more specifically urban modernity, was imagined or written as film, producing a synthesis of city and cinema, as in many of H.D.'s letters from London in this period: 'Streets full of wet leaves and much slither of red lights and yellow lights on Picadilly [*sic*] wet pavements'.[108]

This was also a central aspect of Herring's film articles, not only for *Close Up*, but also for the *London Mercury* (for which he acted as assistant editor from 1925 to 1927). The types of film Herring reviewed for *The London Mercury* were not distinct from those he discussed in *Close Up*; his focus in both journals was on European cinema, viewed in Paris, Berlin, and Switzerland as well as London, though with no particular draw towards avant-garde and experimental film. His article for the *London Mercury* 'Film Thoughts from Abroad' opened with a description of Brussels which contained striking echoes of Joris Ivens's documentary film *Rain*. Ivens's film was described by Balázs (in an account developed further by Gilles Deleuze[109]) as capturing 'visual impressions ... not bound into unity by any conception of time and space ... not what rain really is, but what it looks like when a soft spring rain drips off leaves, the surface of a pond gets goose-flesh from the rain, a solitary raindrop hesitatingly gropes its way down a window-pane, or the wet pavement reflects the life of a city ... Not the things but these their pictures constitute our experience and we do not think of any objects outside the impression'.[110] Herring wrote of his experience:

> The rain was falling in Brussels, dripping with deliberation off the Metropole's awning and falling in swift threads beyond, where the fountain played in the square. ... From the other side of the Place de Brouckère, the leaves, as metallic in their wetness as the fountain, shook off the rain-drops—which brought one back to the awning, the circuit completed, one's eye satisfied and as bright as the rain on the lighted windows (or the light in the puddles of rain).
>
> It was movement, in all its rich relationship—arrested, deterred, diagonal, curving, propelled and straight. All of it was movement: and the fountain focussed the picture that the leaves closed in. Here is a poem, I thought, for the films! Not a play, for once, but a poem. This is what I should see on the screen, I thought; and because I was going to Berlin, I thought also that I might.[111]

Here the rain is situated, *contra* Balázs, as 'one particular rain, which fell somewhere, some time'—it drips 'with deliberation' from the Brussels Metropole's awning—but there is also a sense that this is a world composed entirely of 'visual impressions' and that the optical effects of the

Figure 12. *Regen (Rain)* (Joris Ivens, Holland, 1929).

Figure 13. *Regen (Rain).*

rain in the Brussels city square and the images that might be projected on the Berlin city screen are indeed one and the same feast for the eye.

Reviewing Cavalcanti's *Rien que les heures* and Walter Ruttmann's *Berlin* (shown at a Film Society screening) in the same volume of *London Mercury*, Herring defined the camera in Cavalcanti's film as an eye, 'your eye, through which you look at Paris...How can you explain what you have seen? How can anyone explain how he has expressed that fleetest of things, the hopeless drift of time as it drifts? *As* it drifts—not when it has stopped and been broken into sections. It is too indefinite to explain, you have seen something you did not know anyone could let you see. O, the cinema!'[112] With *Berlin*, by contrast, 'you are rushed on': 'It takes possession of one, one is caught up, whirled in the rush of the day, as part of the machinery, whereas in Cavalcanti's film the emotion comes out of the screen, so to speak, and the figures exist solely for the picture they recreate in one's own mind.'

An Audible Running Commentary

Dorothy Richardson, unlike Herring and Blakeston, had no contacts with the professional world of film, and was not drawn, as many other modernist writers were, to experimental and avant-garde cinema. While her initial response to Bryher's invitation to write for *Close Up* was tentative, Richardson became one of the journal's most consistent contributors, with her regular column, 'Continuous Performance', appearing in the journal's first issue and in its last. Bryher's invitation was, in one way, in line with the journal's policy, in its very early issues, of asking literary writers to contribute. Richardson rarely took up, at least in any overt way, the stance of the literary figure considering the new, possibly rival art of the film, but the relationship between her film writing and her fiction is one of the most telling and compelling examples of the film-literature nexus in twentieth-century literature.[113]

As Susan Gevirtz has written, Richardson's 'Continuous Performance' columns 'exist in the interstices where the novel and early film overlap... Richardson invents film as an extra-literary object that provokes her into a continuous writing performance about the desire to write'.[114] Richardson's life's work, a sequence of novels written between 1915 and the 1940s, to which she gave the overall title *Pilgrimage*, created a new space between autobiography and fiction, moving between first and third person narration, in a recapturing of a woman's life between the 1880s and 1912. We see nothing that is not refracted through the consciousness of Richardson's protagonist and *alter ego* Miriam Henderson, as it moves in and out of engagement with scenes, events and people, and with space, movement, light, and reflection. Light and motion are at the heart of *Pilgrimage*'s vision, in the earlier volumes as a form of pre-cinematic consciousness. The tenth volume in the sequence, *Dawn's Left Hand*, which Richardson began writing in 1927, opened with Miriam's return from Switzerland, where she found light at its most radiant, to London: 'The memories accumulated since she landed were like a transparent film through which clearly she saw all she had left behind; and felt the spirit of it waiting within her to project itself upon things just ahead, things waiting in this room as she came up the stairs.'[115] Consciousness has become a 'screen' rather than a 'stream', the latter a metaphor Richardson had resisted from the point at which May Sinclair had written of *Pilgrimage*: 'It is just life going on and on. It is Miriam Henderson's stream of consciousness going on and on.'[116]

On hearing about the plans to start *Close Up*, Richardson wrote to Bryher:

> We are thrilled by the prospect of the Film paper. High time there was something of the sort. I can't however see myself contributing, with my penchant for Wild West Drama & simple sentiment. Now Alan [Richardson's husband, the artist Alan Odle] has *Ideas*. However: I know I have some notes somewhere & will look them up. But I fancy they are simply about seeing movies, regardless of what is seen.[117]

The focus of most of her film articles was indeed on 'seeing movies' and much of the fascination and significance of her accounts lies in her charting of responses to the new medium, its techniques and exhibition—she wrote about captions, slow motion, musical accompaniment, the ideal shape of the cinema auditorium—and the spectator's changing and developing relationship to the cinema.

One of the central elements of her 'cinema theory' was a continuously re-transcribed model of film history which both produced and resisted accounts of the entry of newness into the world, and which sought to construct a history of consciousness neither wholly determined by nor distinct from a history of technologies. Her embedded history of cinematic emergence began not with the image of the volcanic eruption, as it did for Faure, but with the tide or wave. In the previous chapter I quoted from Richardson's first 'Continous Performance' article, in which she described a visit to a North London picture palace:

> It was a Monday and therefore a new picture. But it was also washday, and yet the scattered audience was composed almost entirely of mothers ... It was a new audience, born within the last few months ... Watching these I took comfort. At last the world of entertainment had provided for a few pence, tea thrown in, a sanctuary for mothers, an escape from the everlasting qui vive into eternity on a Monday afternoon. The first scene was a tide, frothing in over the small beach of a sandy cove, and for some time we were allowed to watch the coming and going of those foamy waves, to the sound of a slow waltz, without the disturbance of incident.[118]

The significance of the wave breaking on the shore for early cinema has arisen in a number of critical contexts throughout this study. Contemporary descriptions show that it was the subject of early Vitascope performances in the mid-1890s: 'Next came a picture of a tumbling surf on the Jersey shore. The waves were high and boisterous as they dashed one after the other in their rush for the sandy beach over which they ebbed and flowed. The white crests of the waves and the huge volume of water were true to life. Only the roar of the surf was needed to make the illusion perfect.'[119] Whereas for nineteenth-century photographers the sea and horizon were central subjects, for early film-makers, the wave breaking on the shore became, as we have seen, a way of figuring both the static or repetitive and the dynamic aspects of the cinematic medium. Richardson deployed the image of the wave—a moving threshold, the edge that never stops—to figure transitions in the filmic medium: from spectacle to narrative film in the passage quoted above, and from silent to sound film in a later article. Whereas the commentator on the Vitaphone film of waves breaking on the shore suggested that sound—'the roar of the surf'—would make the illusion perfect, Richardson wrote that: 'Life's "great moments" are silent. Related to them, the soundful moments may be compared to the falling of the crest of a wave that has stood poised in light, translucent, for its great moment before the crash and dispersal. To this peculiar intensity of being, to each man's individual intensity of being, the silent film, with musical accompaniment, can translate him.'[120] One aspect of Richardson's film writing was thus a deployment of the image to figure a kind of film history: one particularly attentive to transitions, while also seeking to complicate linear narrative, to break up sequence, and to make memory—in which film now played a crucial role—a central aspect of historicity.

In her 'Continuous Performance' articles Richardson mapped London through the different cites of cinema spectatorship; the West End, the slums, where she represented it as a more effective 'civilizing agent' than philanthropy, the suburbs, where it was seen as a haven for women burdened by domestic labour, offering the weary the opportunity of contemplative distance and 'perfect rest'. She rarely addressed specific films: 'we are for THE FILM as well as for FILMS', she wrote, alluding both to her fascination with the medium, rather than its specific products, while at the same time suggesting a model of an idealized or essential 'film'.[121] In this same article she implicitly refused the position of the film critic, who must venture forth to see new films, rather than waiting for what comes to the local cinema: 'these films coming soon or late find us ready to give our best here where we have served our apprenticeship and the screen has made in us its deepest furrows'.[122] She laid great emphasis on place: on the 'local' aspect of 'locality' and on the value of staying loyal to the cinema in which one's filmic apprenticeship was served, in literal support of her claim that, 'The film, by setting the landscape in motion and keeping us still, allows it to walk through us.'[123] Cinema thus brings into being a form of '(im)mobile travel'[124] and despite Richardson's distance from Macpherson's avant-gardism, in her celebrations of popular film and popular spectatorship, her constructions of film viewing as a new mode of travelling and transport, and her representations of embodied spectatorship, were at the heart of *Close Up*'s project.

Adopting the position of one both observing and participating in the emergence of a new form of consciousness, she also produced a complex model of development in which cognition was also recognition. In discussing, for example, the use of 'slow motion', she wrote that:

> We may take courage to assume that from the first, behind the laughter, recognition was there and has grown. If now it is present, it was there from the first, for without its work there would be no second seeing. Each seeing would have been a first and the laughter would have continued.[125]

This complication of the question of origins re-emerged in her discussions of the question of the silent to sound 'transition', in which the silent film was presented as the gift of the move to sound. Once 'speech-films' had taken over the cinemas, she wrote, there was 'one grand compensation: we came fully into our heritage of silent films ... beginning its rich, cumulative life as memory'.[126]

The imbrication of film spectatorship with questions of speech and silence, writing and talking, was at the heart of Richardson's film articles. She echoed Iris Barry's conceit of the 'voice' of the silent film as articulated in and by the sub-title and, in her discussion of 'Captions', wrote in terms that also resonated with C. A. Lejeune's models of the encrypted cultural scripts of the cinematic. In Richardson's account, 'we' enter the cinema with no prior knowledge of the programme—'Experience has taught us to disregard placards'—until, at last, after the 'preliminary entertainments ... we are confronted with a title, set, like a greeting in a valentine, in an expressive device. We peer for clues. Sometimes there is no clue but the title, appearing alone in tall letters that fill the screen, fill the hall with a stentorian voice. Thrilling us.'[127] Richardson's discussion of captions led her, as it led Barry, to the question of the film–literature relationship, to a model of film writing as a form of hieroglyphics, and to a rebuttal of Lessing's dicta on the absolute distinctiveness of the written and pictorial arts and the fallaciousness of Horace's 'ut pictura poesis' ('every picture tells a story'):

> Perhaps the truth about captions is just here: that somewhere, if not in any given place then all over the picture, is a hint. The artist can no more eliminate the caption than he can eliminate himself. Art and literature, Siamese twins making their first curtsey to the public in a script that was a series of pictures, have never yet been separated. In its utmost abstraction art is still a word about life and literature never ceases to be pictorial.[128]

In a further *Close Up* article, Richardson, writing critically about the early sound film *Hearts in Dixie*, asserted that 'the right caption at the right moment is invisible. It flows unnoticed into visual continuity. It is, moreover, audible, more intimately audible than the spoken word. It is the swift voice within the mind'.[129] Here it is writing that 'speaks', and 'the swift voice within the mind' becomes linked to a concept of 'inner speech'.

The concept of 'inner speech', defined by the philosopher Peirce as an 'internal dialogue', entered debates in film theory primarily through writings by Eisenstein and by Boris Eikhenbaum, whose 'Problems of Film Stylistics' was published in 1927. Eisenstein addressed the question of 'inner speech' and 'inner monologue' in a number of his essays, including 'Film Form: New Problems', in which he drew the distinction between 'the syntax of inner speech as opposed to that of uttered speech': 'Inner speech, the flow and sequence of thinking unformulated into the logical constructions in which uttered, formulated thoughts are expressed, has a special structure of its own.'[130] Eikhenbaum argued that it is 'inner speech' which allows the spectator to make the connections between separate shots, verbal discourse being the ground upon which the filmic is figured: 'Those who defend cinema from the imitation of literature often forget that though the audible word is eliminated from film, the thought, i.e. internal speech, is nevertheless present.'[131] Silent film was not mute, Eikhenbaum asserted, but nor were its particular forms of language dependent on literary representations. Other thinkers, including the linguist Lev Vygotsky, emphasized the differentially discursive aspects of 'inner speech': 'Inner speech is to a large extent thinking in pure meanings. It is a dynamic, shifting, unstable, thing, fluttering between word and image.'[132]

For a number of early commentators on film, including Eikhenbaum, it was the written elements within the film—captions, sub-titles, legends—which were linked to 'inner speech', in that they also, in Eikhenbaum's phrase, 'introduce mental accent'. Narrative, literary and explanatory intertitles were, however, to be deplored: 'Such intertitles interrupt not only the movement of the film on the screen, but also the flow of internal speech, not thus forcing the viewer to turn into a temporary reader and *remember* what the "author" informs him in words. Quite another thing are *dialogic* intertitles composed with regard to the particularities of cinema and inserted at the proper time.'[133]

It was 'movement' and 'flow' as continuity and, indeed, 'continuous performance', which preoccupied Richardson, as in her writing on musical accompaniment, in which she described the move in a local cinema from the single pianist, whose playing 'was a continuous improvisation varying in tone and tempo according to what was going forward on the screen... As long as he remained with us music and picture were one', to the introduction of a 'miniature orchestra':

> At each change of scene one tune would give place to another, in a different key, usually by means of a tangle of discords. The total result of these efforts towards improvement was a destruction of the relationship between onlookers and film. With the old unity gone the audience grew disorderly. Talking increased. Prosperity waned.[134]

Yet, Richardson wrote, she learned that any kind of musical noise is better than none '... Our orchestra failed to appear and the pictures moved silently by, lifeless and colourless, to the sound of intermittent talking and the continuous faint hiss and creak of the apparatus.' Music 'helps [the spectator] to create the film and gives the film both colour and sound ... And since the necessary stillness and concentration depend in part upon the undisturbed continuity of surrounding conditions, the musical accompaniment should be both continuous and flexible. By whatever means, the aim is to unify. If film and music proceed at cross purposes the audience is distracted by a half-conscious effort to unite them.'[135] Her article was echoed by Erwin Panofsky in the 1930s, when he wrote: 'All of us, if we are old enough to remember the period prior to 1928, recall the old-time pianist who, with his eyes glued on the screen, would accompany the events with music adapted to their mood and rhythm; and we also recall the weird and spectral feeling overtaking us when this pianist left his post for a few minutes and the film was allowed to run by itself, the darkness haunted by the monotonous rattle of the machinery. Even the silent film, then, was never mute'.[136] The cinematic apparatus, without musical accompaniment, becomes a ghostly automata, running by itself, as if the pianist were its now absent creator.

The model of 'distraction' deployed by Richardson and, by extension, its opposite term, 'attention' (which in her lexicon appeared most often as 'concentration'), brings her film writing into the arena of German film theory of the same period, and in particular the commentaries on film of Siegfried Kracauer and Walter Benjamin. Kracauer's writing on cinema in the 1920s and 1930s focused on issues of production, reception (the study of the architecture of Berlin cinema palaces), regulation (attacks on government censorship), and, in Tom Levin's words, 'the development of a critical public sphere through the practice of a responsible film criticism. As such it was among the earliest to make what has since come to be called the important transition from film theory to cinema theory, the latter understood as a practice that is both more historically reflexive and more sensitive to larger institutional factors'.[137]

Richardson's preoccupations—which include reception, regulation (we recall her work for the anti-censorship petition), and the education of the spectator, in particular the female spectator, for modernity and the public sphere—have significant affinities with those of Kracauer. There are also obvious and crucial differences between these two writers: of cultural context, gendered responses, and political affiliation. The reading of Richardson's cinema writing alongside and through Kracauer's cultural theory, including his writing on film, does allow, however, for a heightened apprehension of both thinkers' understanding of the new forms of experience and representation brought into being by modernity and by modern technologies.

The best-known aspect of Kracauer's early writings on film is his account of 'the cult of distraction' in modern culture, later taken up by Walter Benjamin in 'The Work of Art in the Age of Mechanical Reproduction'. Originally a negative attribute (opposed to contemplative concentration), the concept of 'distraction' took on, in the writings of Kracauer and other theorists in the 1920s, a more positive aspect as it becomes anchored in a non-bourgeois mode of visual and sensorial experience. For Kracauer, 'distraction' was the mode of attention or inattention proper to the fragmentary, discontinuous nature of the modern visual media and 'the surface glamor of the stars, films, revues, and spectacular shows. Here, in pure externality, the audience encounters itself; its own reality is revealed in the fragmented sequence of splendid sense impressions. Were this reality to remain hidden from the viewers, they could neither attack nor change it; its disclosure in distraction is therefore of *moral* significance'.[138] For Benjamin, distracted attention became linked to the radically dispersed subjectivities of the cinematic audience.

Richardson's models of cinematic reception were, at one level, at odds with the neo-Marxist theories of Kracauer and Benjamin. Her aesthetic ideal and goal would appear to be precisely the contemplative concentration to which 'the cult of distraction' opposed itself. She celebrated 'distance' (in a complex negotiation with the journal's identification with the aesthetic of the 'close-up', including the regular column by Jean Prévost, 'La Face Humaine a L'Écran' ['The Human Face on the Screen'][139]) as a way of 'focussing the habitual', so that 'what had grown too near and too familiar to be visible is seen with a ready-made detachment that restores its lost quality'.[140] The terms in fact find their echo in those of Benjamin, for whom the photographic 'aura' was: 'A strange weave of space and time: the unique appearance or semblance of distance, no matter how close it may be'.[141] She argued for the kinds of unifying devices—including musical accompaniment to the silent film—which prevented the intrusive knowledge of the heterogeneity of the cinematic apparatus. She described the cinema's role in 'the preparation of vast new audiences', in particular women audiences, in terms of an accommodation to the conditions of modernity, not as a prelude to their overturning.

Yet we might also find in Richardson ways of thinking about cinematic reception, and about culture more generally, which were as ambivalent and in a sense anarchic as they were idealist. This emerges most strongly in the 'Continuous Performance' articles in which she focused most fully on conditions of spectatorship. The terms of speech and silence were, as we have seen, central to Richardson's writings on cinema, and the 'audible running commentary' of the spectators she described was elided with her own 'continuous performances' as spectator and commentator. In 'The Front Rows', she described the responses of the small boys sitting in the front row of the stalls, and argued against those anti-cinema campaigners who decried their presence there. Her interest was in part in the perspective gained from the vantage point of the front row, which indeed provided a kind of distracted attention:

> There was indeed no possibility of focusing a scene so immense that one could only move about in it from point to point and realise that the business of the expert front-rower is to find the centre of action and follow it as best he can. Of the whole as something to hold in the eye he can have no more idea than has the proverbial fly on the statue over which he crawls ... what I wanted if possible to discover was just what it was these three boys got from the discreet immensity so closely confronting us ... Crew, deeds, drama, a centre of action moving from point to point.[142]

From her starting point as a cultural and urban ethnographer, Richardson took up the subjective position of the front-rower, literally and discursively. This scene, in Richardson's article, was a form of flashback, as she turned to the question of 'the development of the front rowers, their growth in critical grace':

> Their audible running commentary is one of the many incidental interests in a poor film ... They come level-headed and serenely talking through drama that a year ago would have held them dizzy and breathless ... They are there in their millions, the front rowers, a vast audience born and made in the last few years, initiated, disciplined, and waiting.[143]

Richardson again addressed the 'audible running commentary' of the spectator in a piece on the young woman who talks in the cinema. Such a woman, in refusing a position of identification with the 'silent, stellar radiance' of the female star shining from the 'surface' of the screen, also refuses the position of the passive spectator. (The article indeed functions as a counter to Kracauer's 'The Little Shop Girls Go to the Movies'.) As in other 'Continuous Performance' articles, Richardson implied a distinction between the progressive dimensions of female spectatorship and the retrogressive images of femininity projected on the screen. While the woman who talked in the cinema destroys 'the possibility of which any film is so delightfully prodigal; the possibility of escape via incidentals into the world of meditation or of thought', Richardson was not altogether mourning the loss of aura in modernity. 'The dreadful woman asserting herself in the presence of no matter what grandeurs, 'unconsciously testifies that life goes on, art or no art, and that the onlooker is part of the spectacle.'[144]

In this article, as in many others, Richardson portrayed women's film spectatorship as a negotiation of speech and silence, a depiction inseparable from her representations of the relationship between silent and sound/speech films and one centrally linked to the question of writing about film in the early decades of this century as a kind of 'audible running commentary', a 'talking in the cinema'. In Richardson's case, the 'audible running commentary' of the spectators she described was, in a sense, elided with her own 'continuous performances' as spectator and commentator. It was not the spectacle that produced continuity, nor spectatorship. Writing about cinema—'talking in the cinema'—was the continuous performance, and the performance of continuity.

In Richardson's film writing, as that of many of her contemporaries, commentary was transmuted into monologue of three primary kinds. Firstly, a simulacrum, via a form of stream-of-consciousness, of the 'inner speech' which silent film, in particular, was held to enable; secondly, the ventriloquizing of a form of demotic, unpunctuated speech intended to represent a feminized, mass cultural reception; and finally, a free associative form of writing which, in its production of perceptual and cognitive connection and dissociation, became a way of acting out, and of thinking through, the forms of attention and of distraction brought into being by the cinema.

'I myself have learned to use the small projector': H.D. and Film Writing

In response to a questionnaire to authors in *The Little Review*, H.D. wrote:

> Just at the moment I am involved with pictures. We have almost finished a slight lyrical four reel little drama [*Foothills*], done in and about the villages here with some of the village people and English friends. The work has been enchanting, never anything such fun and I myself have learned to use the small projector ... All the light within light fascinates me, 'satisfies' me, I feel like a cat playing with webs and webs of silver.[145]

Letters written during the *Close Up* period reveal the intensity with which H.D. followed film, in London as well as Berlin and Switzerland, and her fascination with the ways in which life outside the cinema became film-like. She described leaving the Film Society's screening of Pabst's *Beggar's Opera*: 'We barged out into a driving rain, it made all London unreal (or real). I waited in an alcove and back of me, through an iron railing was complete "set", old boxes, building material, street lamps, half demolished walls and some new going up, and across it the blight of the cold and rain and mist.'[146] She also engaged in her own creative experiments with alternative forms of film-making, writing to Bryher in 1928:

> You will laugh to hear that last night I had two hours solid camera-vision. I worked my little lantern which by the way, has a very nice lense [*sic*]. I paid not quite a pound for it, as I thought one of those toy ones would be only a temp. thing. This has a lovely lense and projects a clear round square of bright light. The screen is bigger than ours at Territet. It looks lovely on my wall, better than a sheet. Then I pushed and poked in bits of the film ... only the light ones came up well, so I went over the 100000 tiny stamp-sized scraps I had and picked all the best ones of those and the bigger slips to show when people come. Some of the shots make the most exquisite stills that way. Then I have time to 'study' them properly ... I know what gets me, what I get a kick from ... but as Pabst said 'I do not often look at stills ... but I would have stopped to look at these whever [*sic*] I had seen them.' There is some lovely quality of vision and a very king-projection of light. I was quite stupefied and staggered into bed about 10 for a change, and tossed through the night ... I had a lot of visual sensation ... and for the first time, I let the full reality of BEEEEErlin sweep and swoop over me and drown me.[147]

In her writings on film, including her *Projector* poems, first published in *Close Up*, H.D. celebrated the power of light: 'Light speaks, is pliant, is malleable. Light is our friend our god. Let us be worthy of it.' 'Projection' was the central concept in H.D.'s vision and aesthetic: Adalaide Morris describes it as 'the master metaphor of H.D.'s technique' and, pursuing the etymology of the word from the verb '*to throw forward*', argues that, in H.D's work and thought, 'projection is the thrust that bridges two worlds. It is the movement across a borderline: between the mind and the wall, between the brain and the page, between inner and outer, between me and you, between states of being, across dimensions of time and space'.[148] H.D.'s engagement with film in the late 1920s—which encompassed film-acting, film-making and writing about the cinema—was both a dimension and a consolidation of her absorption in, to borrow her own terms, 'thought and vision'.[149]

In her autobiographical novel *Bid Me to Live*, which she began writing during the years of World War I, though it was not published until 1958, H.D.'s fictional persona, Julia, visits a cinema packed with soldiers on leave, or waiting to go to the Front. Her surroundings, and the film that is running, seem dangerous, part of the 'frantic maelstrom' of the war years. On the screen, however, there comes 'the answer to everything... for surprisingly, a goddess-woman stepped forward. She released from the screen the first (to Julia) intimation of screen-beauty. Screen? This was a veil, curiously embroidered, the veil before the temple ... Here was Beauty, a ghost but Beauty. Beauty was not dead.'[150] Cinema, and in particular its representations of women's beauty and power, becomes a salvific force against the depredations of (masculine) war, the opposition caught up in H.D.'s habitual polarization of the culture of Ancient Greece and militaristic Rome.

The same terms and representations were at the heart of H.D.'s film articles for *Close Up*, written and published between 1927 and 1929. The Hellenism that characterized H.D.'s Imagist aesthetics, and that she continued to develop in her later long poems, *Helen in Egypt* in particular, was also central to her perceptions of film, linked, as I suggested in Chapter 1, to early twentieth-century experimental and poetic drama and its concept of the 'temple-theatre'. In Chapter 1, I discussed the probable impact of modernist theatre, instanced by the work of Edward Gordon Craig and John Rodker, on H.D.'s representations and idealizations of the cinema, and this influence is particularly apparent in her first film articles, in which she wrote of line, plane, light and design, and of gesture, hieroglyph, tableau, and mask. In 'Restraint', the second of her three articles on 'Cinema and the Classics', which were 'manifestos' for her vision of 'film art', she contrasted the unnecessary 'paste-board palaces' of the film *Helen of Troy*, and 'elaborate stage scenery' in general, with a portrayal of the 'classic' using 'the simplest of expedients': 'A pointed trireme prow nosing side ways into empty space, the edge of a quay, blocks of solid masonry, squares and geometric design would simplify at the same time emphasize the pure *classic* note.'[151]

The terms strikingly echo those of Roger Fry, in an article, published in 1911, on 'Mr. Gordon Craig's Stage Designs', in which he pointed to Gordon Craig's realization of 'abstraction and generalisation' on the stage, and his recognition 'that any particularisation of forms tends to a lowering of the emotional pitch'. In Fry's words:

> The appeal of the picturesque is based upon the notion that certain things—say a palace at Verona, moonlight on a rocky shore, or an old English homestead—have an inalienable imaginative charm which will be evoked by any reminiscence of them, and that the more photographic the likeness of these things the more powerfully will the charm work. The idea of all great art is, on the contrary, that these things have charm because they possess in various degrees certain fundamental qualities which may be traced not only in them but in all objects … and that it is his work to distil from these things these emotion-compelling qualities. We have for so long been dominated by the tyranny of the imitative picturesque view that we are at present merely children spelling out the alphabet of this rational and fundamental method of appeal. But Mr. Gordon Craig has already managed to spell out a few words of it, and these have an almost magical effect upon the imagination … [he] shows that a few elementary rectangular masses, placed in certain relations to one another and illuminated by a diagonal light, will stir the mind to the highest pitch of anticipation, will inspire already the mood of high tragedy. Such a scene clears the mind of all accidental and irrelevant notions, and leaves it free to be filled with the tragic theme.[152]

The implicit task for many of the writers for *Close Up*, H.D. and Macpherson foremost amongst them, was the creation of the dramatic aesthetic to which Fry pointed—the pure forms of mass and light used to create emotional responses—through photography, cinematography and, indeed, writing about the cinema. For Fry, photography, in this article at least, was associated with the picturesque and with excessive detail, accident, and irrelevance; for the exponents of film, the representation of mass and light were the medium's primary means and ends. To an extent, the aesthetic of drama critic and film critic converged, but the perceived (rather than actual) divide between stage and screen remained no less absolute.

'True modernity', H.D. wrote, 'approaches more and more to classic standards'.[153] In describing the 'Beauty' of Greta Garbo in *The Joyless Street*, she defined the medium of cinema itself as a 'goddess'. As she wrote in 'Restraint': 'here is the thing that the Elusinians would have been glad of; a subtle device for portraying of the miraculous... The screen is the medium par excellence of movement—of trees, of people, of bird wings. Flowers open by magic and magic spreads cloud forms, all in themselves "classic"'.[154]

'The film is the art of dream portrayal and perhaps when we say that we have achieved the definition, the synthesis toward which we have been striving', H.D. wrote in her pamphlet on *Borderline*.[155] The importance of 'the borderline' and of transitional states also emerged in the film writings of H.D. in which she described the processes of an initial resistance to film which we could link to the resistance to sleep, understood as a fear of the loss of identity and even of death. As Freud stated in 'A Metapsychological Supplement to the Theory of Dreams' (1917), the ego, in extreme cases, 'renounces sleep because of its fear of its dreams'.[156] H.D., in her article on *Expiation*, wrote of the ways in which, about to enter the cinema to watch the film, she found herself impelled to create a form of pre-filmic experience from the vision of the street, which also recalled the 'real, little street' of *Joyless Street*:

> I plunged down this little street somewhat reeling, making jig-jag to find just how those shadows cut just that block (and that block) into perfect design of cobbled square and square little doorway... I so poignantly wanted to re-visualize those squares of doors and shutters and another and another bit of detail that of necessity was lost at first that I did illogically (I was already late) climb back.[157]

She entered the cinema when the film was a third over: 'Rain poured over a slab of earth and I felt all my preparation of the extravagantly contrasting out of doors gay little street, was almost an ironical intention, someone, something "intended" that I should grasp this, that some mind should receive this series of uncanny and almost psychic sensations in order to transmute them elsewhere; in order to translate them.'[158] Film and pre-film (the 'dimensional dream-tunnel' of the street) are brought into an 'uncanny' relationship, allowing H.D. as spectator to 'translate' the 'remote and symbolical' dimensions of the film. *Expiation*'s destructive beauty was perceived by H.D. as an 'excess' which had echoes of the Romantic sublime: it was something beyond the limit, 'the word after the last word is spoken', 'taking the human mind and *spirit* further than it can go'. Her film aesthetics and her model of vision were predicated on symbol, gesture, 'hieroglyph', and her film writing tended to provide not retrospective judgement on a film, but a performative running commentary on the processes of spectating which became a form of 'inner speech', acting as a screen onto which the film images could be projected.

Her article on *The Student of Prague* described or enacted a spectatorial procedure similar to that in *Expiation*, an initial resistance to film, an irritated awareness of her surroundings, a disorder: 'Something has been touched before I realise it, some hidden spring; there is something wrong with this film, with me, with the weather, with something', and then a moment of understanding and an increasing absorption in the film, until its close, when she 'awakens' to the discordant voices of her fellow spectators: 'A small voice ... will whisper there within me, "You see I was right, you see it will come. In spite of 'Gee' and 'Doug Fairbanks' " and "we must have something cheerful", it must come soon: a universal language, a universal art open alike to the pleb and the inititate.'[159] The promise of the film as 'universal language'—which did not survive the transition to film sound for H.D.—becomes increasingly inseparable from a model of the 'universal language' of the dream, and both were closely connected for H.D. with the 'hieroglyph'.

As I have discussed elsewhere, H.D.'s fascination with hieroglyphics, shared with Ezra Pound, with whom she was for a time closely linked, emerged out of the writings of both Freud and Eisenstein, a conjuncture of poetics, politics, psychoanalysis (particularly Freud's theories of symbolization and of the 'dream-work'), and film aesthetics. These areas were themselves conjoined by a 'modernist' fascination with the varying relations and interactions between different entities, temporalities, images, and concepts, and the exploration of an art and a politics of juxtaposition, palimpsestic superimposition, simultaneity, collision, and dialectic. H.D.'s focus on inscriptions and hieroglyphs could thus be understood as a form of cultural theorizing, whose roots might well lie in the Transcendentalist tradition of 'American hieroglyphs' and its conceptualization of hieroglyphics as both esoteric script and populist communication.[160]

Sergei Eisenstein had found in Japanese hieroglyphs 'the acme of *montage thinking*'. The combination of two hieroglyphs 'corresponds to a *concept*. From separate hieroglyphs has been fused—the ideogram. By the combination of two "depictables" is achieved the representation of something that is graphically undepictable. ... It is exactly what we do in cinema, combining shots that are *depictive*, single in meaning, neutral in content—into *intellectual* contexts and series'.[161] Eisenstein's account of 'intellectual montage' as thought made visible was clearly a crucial influence on H.D.'s film-writings and on her concept of 'thought projection' more generally. His model of the ideogram, and of the film-frame as a 'multiple-meaning *ideogram*' in his 'The Fourth Dimension of the Kino' (published in *Close Up* in March and April 1930) further recalls Freud's accounts, in *The Interpretation of Dreams*, of the workings of picture-language in the dream and of the 'rebus' composed of multiple scripts and image-systems.

In the spring of 1933, as *Close Up* entered its final year, H.D. travelled to Vienna for psychoanalysis with Freud, bearing Sachs's recommendation. She did not refer to her work in and on film in her accounts of the analysis—'Writing on the Wall' (1945/6) and 'Advent' (1933/48), published together as *Tribute to Freud*—but it seems likely that she saw her sessions with Freud as a way of continuing, or perhaps replacing, the work of film, finding in dream and symbolic interpretation an equivalent to, and extension of, the 'language' of the silent cinema, which she invested with both individual and 'universal' meaning.

The 'shapes, lines, graphs' of dreams are, H.D. wrote, 'the *hieroglyph of the unconscious*'.[162] In an echo of Freud's repeated references in *The Interpretation of Dreams* to the popular newspaper *Fliegende Blätter*—in one of which he compares the work of 'secondary revision' with 'the enigmatic inscriptions with which *Fliegende Blätter* has for so long entertained its readers'[163]—H.D. discusses 'the newspaper class' of dreams, implicitly suggesting the ways in which the diurnal newspaper itself provides the materials for the 'day's residues':

> The printed page varies, cheap-news-print, good print, bad print, smudged and uneven print—there are the great letter words of an advertisement or the almost invisible pin-print; there are the huge capitals of a child's alphabet

chart or building blocks; letters or ideas may run askew on the page, as it were; they may be purposeless; they may be stereotyped and not meant for 'reading' but as a test.[164]

The passage strongly recalls the debates about film captions and intertitles in the 1920s, and their indeterminate nature as speech or writing, as in Béla Balázs's account of the ways in which emotions in the silent film were 'made visible in the form of lettering ... It was an accepted convention, for instance, that alerting alarm-signals rushed at us from the screen with tousled letters rapidly increasing in space ... At other times a slowly darkening title signified a pause full of meaning or a melancholy musing'.[165] The 'enigmatic inscriptions' to which Freud refers are also the alphabets or hieroglyphs of film and dream.

In *Tribute to Freud*, as in other of her autobiographical writings, H.D. represented her childhood memories and dreams as moments of vision that were also moments in a history of pre-cinema and cinema, and, as in Richardson's *Pilgrimage,* autobiography was intertwined with a history of optics (lenses, daguerrotypes, transparencies). Most strikingly, there was the 'writing on the wall', her 'visionary' experience in Corfu in the early 1920s, which Freud saw as 'the most dangerous symptom' and H.D. viewed as her most significant life-experience. She recounted, frame by frame, the inscription of hieroglyphs, images projected on a wall in light not shadow. The first were like magic-lantern slides, the later images resembled the earliest films. 'For myself', she writes, differentiating her position from that of Freud, 'I consider this sort of dream or projected picture of vision as a sort of halfway state between ordinary dream and the vision of those who, for lack of a more definite term, we must call psychics or clairvoyants'.[166] Later in the text, she recalled an earlier dream or 'flash of vision' of a carved block of stone, a solid shape that appeared before her eyes 'before sleeping or just on wakening'.[167] 'Crossing the line', 'crossing the threshold', were H.D.'s signature phrases; they referred both to the blurred borderline between ordinary experience and 'psychic' life, and to the threshold between the states of sleeping and waking. In this indeterminate zone, films and dreams shared a reality.

For H.D., remembered scenes, recalled in the analytic session, 'are like transparencies, set before candles in a dark room', and the network of memories built up to become a surface, onto which 'there fell inevitably a shadow, a writing-on-the-wall, a curve like a reversed, unfinished S and a dot beneath it, a question mark, the shadow of a question—*is this it?*'[168]

Throughout *Tribute to Freud* (and its companion text, 'Advent') we are led around (as in a cinematic panning-shot) the space of Freud's consulting-room in Vienna, following the line of its walls, the fourth of which is a wall which is not a wall, its folding-doors opening onto a connecting room, the 'room beyond' which 'may appear very dark or there may be broken light and shadow'.[169] She linked this 'fourth wall', and the room beyond, which contained Freud's books and antiquities, to the 'fourth dimension', the dimension that for Sergei Eisenstein, writing in *Close Up*, was the dimension of the Kino. It was the 'fourth wall' and the 'room beyond' which both H.D. and Freud faced or looked towards, as she lay on the couch with Freud seated in the corner behind her, his cigar smoke rising in the air.

In 'Advent', the account of her analysis with Freud based most closely on the notes she made at the time, H.D. represented Freud as absorbed by particular aspects of her Corfu experience, the Writing on the Wall of her hotel room, including 'the lighting of the room, or possible reflections or shadows. I described the room again, the communicating door, the door out to the hall and the one window. He asked if it was a French window. I said, "No—one like that," indicating the one window in his room'.[170] The space of the hotel room, the scene of the Writing on the Wall, thus became increasingly identified with the space of Freud's consulting room, an identity to which his own insistent questioning would seem to point. If both spaces were the sites of projection, of picture-writing, of a Writing on the Wall, then psychoanalysis too was a cinematographic arena, with both analyst and analysand facing towards a surface—wall or screen—onto which memories and imaginings could be projected. Psychoanalysis was itself understood as cinematographic, the projection and play of sign, image, and scene upon a screen which, like H.D.'s representations of Freud's 'fourth wall', was simultaneously wall and not-wall, absence and presence, and, as in Dorothy Richardson's models of time and memory, at once past, present, and future.

Close Up Contributors, POOL Books and Film Aesthetics

In 1928, Ernest Betts, who began writing about the cinema in *Close Up*,[171] and, in 1930, became film critic of the *Week-end Review*, published a short book entitled *Heraclitus, or the Future of Films* for the publisher Routledge

Kegan Paul's 'To-Day and To-Morrow' series. It was to be, at least in part, he wrote, 'an aesthetic or "highbrow" study concerning films which are works of art'.[172] The study was built around the conceit of film's Heraclitean flux, and of the complexities entailed in constructing a history and a future for a medium whose first principles were movement and change: 'nothing should be shown which does not represent movement and flux, or the drama of its arrest or of its interruption or of its conflict. The film is unique among the visual arts in postulating a perpetual fluidity or becoming as the basis of the conception.'[173] 'It is not criticism we want', he argued:

> What we want is creation itself, the moving picture, character in action, rhythm, architecture and design in motion, the pattern of humanity, drawn out into lines, gathered into forms and shadows and hung out in splendour. Mankind moving about in order.[174]

There are strong echoes here of Vachel Lindsay's writings, as in the phrase 'architecture and design in motion', as well as of Thomas Edison's writings on the Kinematograph's powers to produce, in Noël Burch's phrase, 'an ersatz of Life itself', and, more broadly, of the cinema as a second Creation. Here, too, then, the history of film was written as a history of decline from an extraordinary origin, to which it should seek to return. Betts indeed asserted that film, in order to fulfill its power as a medium, would have to be uncreated: 'We must uncreate again and again—a process for which our Western civilization has very little relish and is not at all prepared.' If film were to become art, its industrial and financial basis—its Americanization—would need to be undone: 'Any vital change in this insubstantial pageant can only come about by the complete de-Americanization of the industry.'[175] The 'return to simplicity' would mean an undoing of 'the moving-picture-theatre habit', a 'romantic city-habit, cunningly jammed into the middle of our ugly industrial life ... it is hard to see how any general improvement in the quality of films is to occur until all the glitter and "high light" nonsense which encumbers them has been drawn off, and the clean body of the picture is left standing by itself'.[176]

Behind cinema's late nineteenth-century origin, Betts suggests, was its true history:

> If you go to the old city of Bisitun, in Persia (the film will probably take you there for ninepence) you will see a great piece of sculpture cut into the rock high up in a cleft of the Black Rock Mountains. It is of Darius receiving the

tributary kings. He stands with his handful of the conquered marching up to him, each cut in duplication of the next, and with such astonishing art that the figures appear to be moving. The Bisitun sculptures have stood in this cleft for twenty-five centuries and the mind which conceived them and other such works embodying strong stylistic rhythms was manifestly a cinematic mind... We are rediscovering now in a different medium the long-lost idea of the moving picture, of mankind cast not in stone, bronze, paint or print, but in fluid images. A tremendous and magical discovery which was launched like a toy for a suburban shop-window![177]

What had been lost over the centuries, Betts suggested, was '*the mind that moves*', and a single, creative purpose: 'Few minds of this type exist. They will have to be evolved'. Evolution, in this context, also implied a return to a form of long-lost creative power. As with so many discussions of cinema and aesthetics in this period, Betts insisted upon the single creative will of the director, which would lead to 'the unity and singleness of a work of art at the end'.[178] Although at points in his text he was prepared to allow that the commercial film had a certain value—its 'extravagant efficiency brings delight and rest and a sort of beauty to this grief-struck globe, and is a rich mantle to poor folk, now and for years uncounted'[179]—the assumption was always that such 'efficiency', and the industrial basis of film production, with its multiple and dispersed functions, was incompatible with the creation of a work of art.

For Betts, more meant less: 'The whole of my argument... is directed towards proving that the film can never be fully effective until it has learned to dispense with some of its materials instead of adding to them'.[180] This was particularly true for him of sound. 'I am convinced', Betts wrote, 'that films should be seen and not heard... There is something monstrous about a speaking film... The two effects, marching out of step, carry the mind and senses different ways, and leave the spectator in conflict with himself... The film of a hundred years hence, if it is true to itself, will still be silent, but it will be saying more than ever'.[181] At this point, a footnote, clearly inserted after the study had been completed, attested that speaking films had been launched. Betts called this a self-destruction that 'violates the film's proper function at its source. The soul of the film—its eloquent and vital silence—is destroyed. The film now returns to the circus whence it came, among the freaks and the fat ladies.' The footnote thus undoes the text's own images of film's futurity.

The clustering of books on the cinema in the years of the mid-late 1920s led to a situation in which retrospect and prospect were constructed at the very moment when the history of film was, with the coming of sound, about to take a radically different turn. Lejeune's 1931 study *Cinema*, as we have seen, had already performed the critical transition to sound; a relatively easy one for Lejeune to make, as her articles on the topic, first in the *Manchester Guardian* and then in the *Observer,* reveal. Rudolf Messel, writing in 1927, confined his comments on film sound to a chapter entitled 'Oh, Come and Listen to the Band', in which he discussed musical accompaniment and the possibilities for developing Edison's original ideas for the vitaphone—'a sort of visual gramophone, for it tenders the musician at once visible and audible'.[182] On the other hand, Messel argued, 'the idea of talking films was not even considered (1926), for a film that talked, in English, in French, or in Italian, would of necessity be limited to a certain audience, and it requires no undue penetration on the part of the reader to see that such a limitation would have been undesirable'. A footnote then reads: 'And now in 1928 talking films *are* being considered—why?'[183]

Paul Rotha, who went on to become one of the significant film critics and theorists, as well as a documentary film-maker, of the following decades, published *The Film Till Now: A Survey of the Cinema* in 1930. It presented a synoptic account of international cinema, with chapters on British, American, French, German, and Russian film in its first section, but it also contained very substantial discussion of film aesthetics and theoretical issues. Kristin Thompson has argued that *The Film Till Now* 'set a pattern for surveys of world film history that has to a considerable extent remained with us': Rotha played down the invention of the cinema (with which studies like Terry Ramsaye's were so occupied) and industrial practices, instead 'examining individual national cinemas and their artistic trends'.[184]

For Rotha, 'film is an independent form of expression, drawing inspiration with reservation from the other arts' and essentially *visual* in its appeal: 'light and movement are the two elements employed in the creation of these visual images'. By contrast with Iris Barry, Rotha presented 'the abstraction of the absolute film' as 'the nearest approach to the purest form of cinema'. His arguments, and his views on cinema, were, at this stage in his writing and film career, formalist and anti-realist. The 'modernism' of Rotha's film aesthetic emerged in his commitment to montage theories, his fascination with the machine aesthetic in cinema, with urban and industrial modernity ('cinematic inspiration' is to be found, in the case of the semi-fiction picture, 'in the street, in the trains, in the factories or in the air'),[185] and with psychoanalysis and 'the mind of the audience'.[186] His theoretical models were clearly strongly influenced by the writings of Eisenstein, Dziga-Vertov, and Pudovkin. They also appear to owe a debt to Balázs, in particular to his writings on 'microphysiognomy', the centrality of 'face' (of persons and objects) and the animation of the object in cinema, and to the synthesis of film and psychoanalytic theories in the articles, in particular those written by the psychoanalyst Hanns Sachs, that were appearing in the pages of *Close Up* during the writing of Rotha's text. Rotha's early work thus gives a strong indication of the impact *Close Up* was making on the formative film culture and theory of the late 1920s and early 1930s.

'The result on the mind produced by the abstract film', with its 'relations of geometric figures changing their proportions, dissolving and displacing each other, thereby making vivid abstract patterns', Rotha argued, 'may be compared with that produced by the word patterns of the post-war school of poets, to certain forms of literature such as the work of James Joyce, and to music without melodic interest ... The film with its cinematic properties of rapid movement, contrast, comparison, rhythm, expansion and contraction of form is admirably suited to present a series of abstract visual images to the eye, capable of causing strong emotional reactions.'[187] The relationship between 'eye' and 'mind', which was so central to the film theories of the 1910s and 20s, was taken up by Rotha in ways strongly inflected by Eisenstein's writings on cinema of this period (in particular his discussions of montage aesthetics and mental processes) and psychoanalytic models of film spectatorship, to whose exploration *Close Up*, in particular, was committed. Thus Rotha wrote of the 'dissolve' as a way of representing the passing of time:

> A dissolve is never harsh or exciting. Its mood is smooth and harmonious to the eye, involving a slow rhythm. It causes an instantaneous *mental* dissolve in the mind of the spectator. This has been very well described as the momentary condensation of a train of thought into another that has yet to serve its purpose. The aim of the dissolve is to associate the old with the new in the mind of the audience.[188]

'In actuality', Rotha wrote, 'the camera is the mind of the spectator':

> It is not unnatural then that the principles of psycho-analysis play a large part in the conveyance of dramatic content to the audience. It will be

shown later, for example, in dealing with pictorial composition, that the
smallest movement on the screen is immediately magnified in importance
and becomes at once a source of interest to the spectator. From this it
will be realised that the so-called symptomatic actions of Freud, the small,
almost unnoticed and insignificant actions of behaviour on the part of a
person, are highly indicative of the state of his mind, and are of the utmost
value, when magnified on the screen, for establishing an understanding of
the state of mind in the audience. For this reason alone, it will be seen how
essential it is for a film player to be his natural self, and how detrimental
theatrical acting is to film purposes … there is no limit to the depth of
cinematic introspection … Added to which, there is to be considered the
very important part played by the presence of objects and things in the
construction of a scene.[189]

Such models of projection and transmission, between actor and audience,
between one mind and another, were, as we have seen, at the heart of the
Close Up group's film aesthetics.

At the opening of the second part of *The Film Till Now*—'The Theoretical'—Rotha wrote:

> Analysis of the film is, perhaps, more difficult than that of any of the other
> arts. Since its beginning in the days of the Lumière brothers and Friese-Green,
> the film has grown, retraced its steps, sprung in different directions at the
> same time, been hampered and impeded on all sides, in the most remarkable
> way, without any real stock being taken of its properties and possessions. Its
> very nature of light revealed by moving form defies systematic cataloguing
> of its capabilities.[190]

Studies such as Rotha's could be understood as attempts to ameliorate
this situation, within the given limits of the verbal medium's encapsulation
of the mobile, visual world of the cinema, and Rotha's text was indeed a
'taking stock' and an attempt at 'systematic cataloguing'. To this extent, and
as I suggested in the case of Lejeune's *Cinema* study, the books on cinema
of this period were themselves attempts to give a degree of stability to the
flux and ephemerality of the film medium and, to attempt to encapsulate a
state of affairs during, to borrow Lejeune's phrase, a period of transition and
experiment. This was particularly charged during the period leading up to,
and immediately following, the transition to sound. Writing shortly after
the coming of sound, Rotha continued to deplore the arrival of dialogue
films, which he described (in terms that would be echoed in Rudolf
Arnheim's essay 'The New Laocoön') as 'simply reductions to absurdity of

the attempt to join two separate arts, which, by their essential nature, defy synchronisation'.[191]

Eric Elliott's *Anatomy of Motion Picture Art* was published in 1928 by POOL, which produced a small number of books, including Bryher's cinematographic war-novel *Civilians* and Macpherson's two early novels. The other film books in the series were Oswell Blakeston's *Through a Yellow Glass* (1928), which explored, in Blakeston's typically idiosyncratic style, the practical dimensions of film-making and life in the film studio, and Bryher's *Film Problems of Soviet Russia* (1929). Elliott's text was, like Betts's *Heraclitus*, primarily focused on an aesthetic of films. Along with other early studies, it used comparisons and contrasts between the established arts—including painting, theatre, and music—as a way of defining the cinematic aesthetic. The 'permanent library of film literature', C. A. Lejeune wrote in her review of Elliott's text, 'is still lightly enough stocked for each new volume to be deserving of the closest scrutiny and judgement and every new contributor of a fair hearing'. She approved the concept of an 'anatomy' of film, as, in her words, a 'compound of analysis and synthesis; a close investigation of existing film material for the sake of building up the film that should be':

> The kinema, finding in its technique the perfect machinery of mimicry, has been content to copy, without understanding, the effects of literature, painting, and the theatre, and to imitate, without appreciation, the few fine compositions that its own directors, either by art or luck, have achieved; it has never troubled to distinguish between the scopes and materials of the various arts nor to turn the eye of the camera inward upon itself and determine the possibilities and limitations at its command ... We have got to analyse before we construct, construct because we have fully analysed. We have got to find out what the kinema is before we can say what the kinema should do.[192]

The key-note of the book, Lejeune noted, was that, in Elliott's words: 'All the things that the kinematograph has so far actually demonstrated, and all its possibilities as we now foresee them, should have been theoretically obvious the moment it became practicable to project on a screen a series of animated images in scenes.' Elliott's study was also predicated on the view that the 'essence' of cinema resided in movement and in light:

> In a motion picture it is essential that nothing be static, not even colour because a film portrays life; and in life nothing rests, nothing is still and nothing is without animation. Colour is really a mood of Light—Light, that is ever changing and ever influencing the human mind.[193]

In many ways, Elliott's study was a reworking of texts from the 1910s and early 1920s, including those by Lindsay, Münsterberg, and Freeburg. D. W. Griffith was the director on whose films Elliott drew most extensively for his arguments, and he focused on the pictorial dimensions of 'the photoplay'. He detailed the significance of film techniques such as the close-up, cutback, and parallel action, and forms of camera motion, including the pan, rotary movement, and the 'Cabiria movement' (a shot developed in the epic Italian film *Cabiria* of 1914, in which the camera advances towards the subject, taking us 'toward the particular section [of the scene] that concerns us'). As in Münsterberg's discussion, there was thus a sense that camera movement both directed and was attentive to the spectator's own acts of attention. The camera was, in Elliott's account, an independent agent—'the camera observes', 'the camera watches'—and the study was indeed a defence of the 'mechanical' nature of film:

> The charge of mechanicalness is made against the cinema with mechanical regularity, as if the motion picture alone should stand natural and pure among the arts. Is not literature mechanical in its means and technique? And music, even music of the human voice, does it not flourish on mechanical development?
>
> So cannot the cinema art flourish on, among other things, the mechanical improvements of the camera and its employment? For the camera is the vital agent between the picture drama and our eyes; and so from the eyes to our mind.[194]

Elliott, like Lindsay and Freeburg, was mounting an argument for the essential visuality of film and for its training of the human eye: 'the primal importance of eye-appeal throughout the progress of the human race'.[195] He was, however, writing at a point where the talking film was about to become a reality. In fact, and perhaps surprisingly, Elliott did not argue against the coming of sound. He took up, briefly, the question of language difficulties, asserting that 'it should be comparatively easy to make different versions of the photoplay for different countries', and suggested that a form of dubbing—'arranging that lines are spoken by competent artistes not revealed in the picture'—would solve the problem of an actor's unsuitable voice.[196]

It would seem that Elliott was determined not to weaken his account of cinema's intrinsic visuality by taking the question of sound film too seriously or by treating it at length, and he gave a great deal more space to the question of the sub-title and intertitle, arguing for their visual nature.[197]

His account of cinema was essentially imagistic, and the focus in the text on camera movement and on detail, expressed in particular through the close-up, was intended to highlight the symbolist nature of film, in which, as in Nature, 'a story may be written in the air by one falling petal'. (This last image was also one that fascinated Virginia Woolf; a falling leaf opens a sequence in *A Room of One's Own*, while a falling flower, she wrote, could symbolize 'the semi-mystic, very profound' life of a woman which might all be told on one occasion.)[198] While the art of the cinema was held to inhere in movement, there was also a desire to articulate its fragmentations and metonymies, in substantial part as a way of defeating the attraction to narrative and story, and of making montage central, though the term itself was not deployed. 'Far from being too mechanical now', Elliott wrote, 'motion picture technique is not mechanical enough. Far from its scenes being broken up too much now, they are not broken up enough; for a scene means stagnancy, and the motion picture requires not scenes, but fluency'.[199]

While Elliott argued that 'the cinema medium depends upon a new "sense" in ourselves as well as in its artists,'[200] he closed his study with the claim that 'the nearest analogy to this new art seems to be in music', deploying the image of the symphony central to the early writings of Edison and the Dicksons (and subsequently taken up in French film criticism through the concept of *cinégraphie*). He concluded with these words:

> That design, ENSEMBLE—the concinnity of detail to detail, scene to scene, motif to motif—a symphony of images, weaving in Time, Space and Motion, and picture by Light.[201]

Camera Vision

Writing of 'Film Imagery: Pudovkin', Robert Herring had begun with the interest of all film viewing, 'in seeing how the screen, the square sheet, is filled ... One can never quite get over the thrill of the dark seats, with other people sitting there, and then one's self, and then light bringing all these other others moving, not actual at all, but because of their patterns and speeds, so oddly real, so much odder than the lady breathing through her nose on our left, so much realer than the hat underneath, which is ours, and the feet denting it, ours also'.[202] He pursued the conceit in 'A New Cinema,

Magic and the Avant-Garde', exploring the question of the 'magic' of the cinema as a relation to 'reality', and in particular, the realities of light and movement. Herring was critical of a self-proclaimed 'avant-garde' cinema whose experiments in distortion and abstraction disregarded the abstract nature of *all* cinematic representations. The most conventional of narrative films is *also*, Herring suggested, a patterning of light and shadow moving in time: 'and so there is a little magic everywhere you see a cinema'.[203]

For Herring, cinematic 'magic' inhered primarily in *projection*:

> There is the screen, and you know the projector is at the back of you. Overhead is the beam of light which links the two. Look up. See it spread out. It is wider and thinner. Its fingers twitch, they spread in blessing or they convulse in terror. They tap you lightly or they drag you in. Magic fingers writing on the wall, and able to become at will ... a sword or an acetylene drill, a plume or waterfall. But most of all they are an Aaron's rod flowering on the wall opposite, black glass and crystal flowers ... Only now and again the rod becomes a snake, and whose films are those we know. ...
>
> You need not be a chamber to be haunted, nor need you own the Roxy to let loose the spirit of cinema on yourself. You can hire or buy or get on the easy system, a projector. You then have, on the occasions on which it works, people walking on your own opposite wall. By moving your fingers before the beam, you interrupt them; by walking before it, your body absorbs them. You hold them, you can let them go.[204]

Herring's models of the destruction of the 'aura' (the distance between spectator and spectacle) and of the blurring of a body/world division as the spectator inserts him or herself into the spectacle are characteristic of modernized vision and its altered perceptions of subject/object relationships.

In the article, Herring moves from the passages quoted above to imagining a future for cinema, an 'avant-garde', in which images would be rendered visible without the mediation of the screen, bodies and beings becoming solid projections of themselves. There is 'no reason', Herring wrote, 'why [man] should not create himself in motion and speech, moving in the patterns of his creation', echoing both Bergson's model of 'creative evolution' and the passage, quoted earlier, from Betts's *Heraclitus, or the Future of Films*: 'What we want is creation itself, the moving picture, character in action, rhythm, architecture and design in motion, the pattern of humanity, drawn out into lines, gathered into forms and shadows and hung out in splendour. Mankind moving about in order.'

Herring reached his image of the future by way of a discussion of recorded voice, adding 'speech' to Betts's description of silent splendour:

Now. We know sound waves can be caught on wax. The human voice recorded. Up till now, it has only been possible to reproduce it. That is very thrilling of course, that the noise made by a person some time ago can be let out again later, it is doing things with time. But it remains reproduction. You can't get voice pure, but reproduced voice. But suppose there is a machine which really lets the living voice itself out into the room ... Could not the avant people, the real ones, do the same with the visual image? Can we not see people as we shall soon hear them? At present there is the screen and gramophone. But the gramophone will soon cease to insist itself any more than the person's presence detracts from the voice. If the voice can leave this machine, as I know it can, and be itself, why should not the visual image leave the screen, why should we not do without screens? They are giving stereoscopy to the image, giving them depth and solidity. They will be able to be brought into the room, as the voice is. It is after all, absurd to be tied down to a screen.

First what [man] did can survive, now what he is. First the work of his hands, work of brain, the effects of his hands and brain. But all still and mute. Then his voice could be kept, and his image could be kept. Moving. Now they will have to be detached, and instead of him contenting himself with making dolls and statues and music he could only hear as it was being played, he will have these images in which sound and sight meet, detached so to speak from their owners. Man making man, of a kind. ... There is logically ... no reason why he should not ultimately create himself in motion and speech, moving in the patterns of his creation.[205]

Herring's article thus moved from projection as the inscription of images, symbols, and hieroglyphics by 'magic fingers writing on the wall' to projection as the patterning of light which creates cinematic reality, by means of a lamp like that of Aladdin's, and to projection as a throwing-forth of the self first, by way of the insertion of the spectator's body into the spectacle ('You hold them, you can let them go') and, finally, by the construction of three-dimensional moving-image-beings. One striking aspect of early film criticism and theory, as I have noted throughout this study, is the extent to which paradigms of and fantasies about the new art of the cinema emerging from diverse contexts shared similar language and images. Herring's seemingly idiosyncratic model in his 'Magic' article echoed, for example, Faure's Bergsonian *The Art of Cineplastics,* describing a similar conceptual trajectory. In Faure's account, cinema history was imagined as a progression from the writing on the wall/screen as (thin) inscription, to the thickness of gesture and finally to the future creation of a visual symphony understood as the projection—a throwing out or forth—of a whole being, a 'whole nature'. Those beings who would project themselves forth were, perhaps, to be understood as the *Übermenschen* of a future society.

This is a question that could also be posed of Herring's article, which was itself anticipated in a letter he wrote to Bryher in early 1929:

> Well, Bryher, well. I feel like the whole of the world. Exceptional circumstances and I have just had a most extraordinary evening…Robeson and I…went after the show to-night to a man called Ogden. Writes 'The Meaning of Meaning'. I. A. Richards. 'Psyche'. That means something…We got to a house in Frith Street [and] went down to a cellar that was just a Fritz Lang laboratory. It was panelled in white linen-fold plaster, but one was bare, & was of two different kinds of wood, and a hair (?) curtain went across to absorb the echoes. We went there to hear a new gramophone. There were charts of circles of celophane mounted on cardboard, and charts of colour harmonies, and sound waves in red and white on grey board. There were (?) glass balls pinned on one wall, from Woolworths. On a grand piano in the centre 2 machines with leather horns 3 feet long, and a box of chocolates. There were records and records and a cabinet of records…Two odd square machines in opposite corners. Robeson was in a black suit and a black hat and a shirt of perfectly Spanish whiteness. He is 9 feet high: and the room was low and white. There were stacks of gramophone records in albums and some in envelopes. Ogden played a machine. It was the voice in the room. It was *not* a reproduction, but a release. Robeson was in the room; Robeson's voice was in the room. Robeson stood and listened. 'Why am I here, Ogy?', he said. I really must go to my bed: it is 3.15 and I must go to 'Dr Mabuse' to-morrow and a plumber is coming to see to my bath at 10. But before I go, my next article for *Close Up* will be on *Magic*, & will treat of the elimination of the screen from projection.[206]

Taking up his story again, Herring writes:

> Friday. I can't tell you what it was like, last night…The voice was a living thing, moving amongst you. We turned out the lights, and Robeson sang, and then the machine played the same song on a record. Do you see, the voice can be detached from the person, and kept, that is all, on the wax, and let out again…And it means to me this; if really and truly the voice can be kept like that, which is only a matter of dealing with time, I do not see why, as voice is sound waves, in time we could not do the same with light waves, and keep and bring the images of cinema, moving people into a room in the same way. Give them depth and all roundness. No screen. Before, the voice

has not come into the room, but from the machine. This is just the voice, heard in real purity, but after it was used to make those sounds. Now, a man makes with his voice the sounds he likes or can or is trained to. A director makes of people the images, for short, that he wants. He brings out of them what he wants. Can't this same principle apply in time to us? I mean, can't it? And there's man making man.

What do we make of the components here—C. K. Ogden, Paul Robeson, a new type of gramophone? Ogden—a mathematician, philosopher and psychologist—was also the inventor and chief exponent of Basic English, the pared-down version of English which he intended would serve as a 'universal language', and as part of a programme of 'Debabelization'. Founder of the Orthological Institute, he was also centrally involved in recorded sound—we have, for example, his recordings of Joyce reading passages from *Work-in-Progress* (*Finnegan's Wake*). In *The Meaning of Meaning* Ogden and I. A. Richards took as one of their many philosophical targets what they called Word-Magic—a 'primitive ... instinctive attitude to words as natural containers of power'.[207] It is a nice irony that magic should return so vividly—at least in Herring's account—in the realms of sound and the power of virtual presence.

A further aspect of Herring's narrative was its echo not only of Edison's and the Dicksons' imaginings of a 'total cinema' but of Villiers de L'Isle Adam's novel *L'Ève future* (1880), in which, we recall, Lord Ewald meets the female automaton/Android Hadaly in her subterranean chambers. The link is the way in which new technologies bring forward Frankensteinian fantasies of origins and of newly created, automatic or virtual beings; the difference lies in the fact that the New Woman, and the representation of technology as an (artificial) female, has given way to the New Man—nine feet high in the low white room. Robeson, a study in black and white, like a film, is doubly present, not least because his voice *is* his presence, and thus Herring is able to imagine newly created visible beings added to sonorous/aural presence. Here sight is added to sound, rather than sound to sight. The inversion (which is also a 'true' history, in that the phonograph preceded the kinetoscope and led from thence to the cinema) reminds us that this was a critical period in the transition from silent to sound cinema, taking place a year before the *Close Up* group made its *silent* film *Borderline*—in which Herring acted the part of a pianist and Robeson appeared as Pete (a Negro), shot as if he were indeed nine feet high but, of course, voiceless. Representations of 'the Negro' in *Borderline* as both the New Man of the cinema and the primitive Other of modernism also reveal the profound imbrication of fantasies, and fears, of origins and of the future with modernity's relationship to the technologies which both shape and are shaped by it.[208]

Stills and Photographs

For Herring, questions of the appropriate language for film criticism were central. 'Rhythm', he wrote, 'must be conspicuous in film-articles because one is writing of movement, and any satisfactory movement, or representation of it, must be rhythmical'. This statement was made in the context of a review, for the *London Mercury*, of Anthony Asquith's film *Underground*: 'We feel like a pulse the movement of the trains and the crowds they draw down and what it all means.'[209] His articles for the journal *Drawing and Design* in the same period were, however, like his editorial comments in *Films of the Year*, in the tradition of pictorial film criticism, with echoes of Victor Freeburg's work, and including commentary on the formal composition of selected stills. 'Drawing and Design', he wrote, 'is an art magazine, and I accordingly confine myself in it to pointing out the design of the lines and masses rather than the moral implications of the story; this seems to me to be the function of an art critic'.[210]

This suggests a pragmatic tailoring of critical discourse to the context and the occasion. Herring's articles for *Drawing and Design* ran along similar lines to those of 'Mercurius' for *The Architectural Review* in the late 1920s and early 1930s, though 'Mercurius' tended to point up the limited nature of the still by comparison with cinematic motion. 'Pictures in the "Pictures": *The Wonderful Deception of Nina Petrovna*', offered a pictorialist account of the formal and compositional aspects of films, showing how form and content were interrelated, and illustrating his argument with references to, and stills from, *The Wonderful Deception of Nina Petrovna*, a Gaumont-Ufa film.

The stills included in the article were captioned with citations from the text, and called attention to chiaroscuro effects and the patterns made by the disposition of objects and figures. They emerge as tableaux, complete in and of themselves. The final lines of the article, however, returned to the principle that 'the art of film is an art of movement. Static reproductions of film pictures cannot adequately present the pictorial element of cinematic art. The real art of pictorial composition in the film is the maintenance of a balanced and harmonious pictorial composition in a state of constant movement and in constant relation to the changing content of the scene'.[211] A page of stills from the film *Montparnasse* was accompanied by the caveat that 'the expression of the abstraction with which the film is primarily concerned, the artistic life of Montparnasse, is revealed only when these details are related, in deliberate sequence, by the essential change and movement of the cinematic medium'.[212] The strictures of 'Mercurius' on the film still's inability to represent adequately a medium whose essence is movement, like Herring's account of the still as an 'advertisement' for the film, were to some extent conventional conceptual gestures, which failed to pursue a significance both writers seemed to glimpse in the still, which would be defined by Roland Barthes as 'not a sample…but a quotation…the fragment of a second text *whose existence never exceeds the fragment*'.[213] Similar terms were used by Man Ray, in his introduction to a series of stills from his film *Emak Bakia*, reproduced in an early issue of *Close Up*. In Man Ray's words: 'A series of fragments, a cinepoem with a certain optical sequence make up a whole that still remains a fragment. Just as one can much better appreciate the abstract beauty in a fragment of a classic work than in its entirety so this film tries to indicate the essentials in contemporary cinematography.'[214]

Oswell Blakeston's article in the March 1931 issue of *Close Up*, entitled 'Stills and their Relation to Modern Cinema', was written in a fragmented form which, as he himself suggested, failed to cohere: 'Stills in newspapers; stills outside theatres. Trying to do the job. Trying to catalogue. Trying to order a review under their title, *Stills and their relation to Modern Cinema*.'[215] The question of the relationship of still to film, fragment to whole, and the dispersal of the film beyond its frame (in newspapers, outside theatres), was thus replicated in the form of the article itself. In his brief comment on 'Talking Stills', Blakeston wrote that: 'With talking pictures greater care must be exercised in judging stills. Will in future, all stills carry the words of spoken dialogue written under the picture?' as if, once sound had been added to vision, the film still could no longer be presented as a purely visual image.[216] Blakeston was in fact to write extensively on the art and technique of taking still photographs in film studios, a relationship of photograph to film which clearly differs from, while bearing a complex relationship to, the use of the still in its identity as film frame.

In her article on G. W. Pabst, 'An Appreciation', written during the making of *Pandora's Box*, H.D. wrote of a conversation with Pabst in a

Berlin restaurant, in which she had asked him about a still she had seen from *Joyless Street*: 'a still of a dead body, a very beautiful still of the figure of the mundane lady who, you will recall, is killed in the "house" she went to with her lover'. Pabst, she wrote, 'burst into a torrent of wailing and apology: "O, a dead body…a dead body …" there is no such thing as a dead body on the screen'. H.D. connected his response to his war experience in an internment camp, where a number of his companions had died or killed themselves *'after the armistice'*: the emphasis suggests a concern with the Freudian concept of deferred shock and the 'belatedness' of traumatic experience. She recalled herself, in her article, to the question of 'screen art simply … and with a particular still that did not match up with the cinema scene itself':

> 'I saw *Joyless Street* a second time. It was only last year. Then I did make a point of looking for the dead body and *did* see it. The first time I was so enchanted with light filtering through those shutters in that half-darkened room, I was so interested in the mass effect you got with the men's thick shoulders and blocked in shapes … is it possible that in the earlier version the shots showing the dead woman on the floor were for some reason deleted?'
>
> 'Ah,' interrupted Mr Pabst delightedly, 'I did not *mean* you to see the body of the murdered woman on the floor.'[217]

The passage is highly coded, but the connection of the 'still' with the second viewing of the film could be read through Barthes's concept of the 'still' as 'the fragment of a second text', as well as the deferred effects of trauma. The occlusion of the dead body by the effects of light, shadow, and shape, which H.D. had experienced on her first viewing of the film, and which Pabst claimed as a deliberate directorial strategy ('I did not *mean* you to see the body of the murdered woman on the floor'), could, in turn, be linked to the concept of the film still itself as a 'dead body', an association with death, as Raymond Bellour has written of the still photograph, usually concealed by the film's movement.[218] The dead and motionless body is film's secret stillness, which, as Garrett Stewart writes, is 'never shaken loose … but is merely lost to view'.[219]

The secret of cinema is its stillness, 'lost to view' in the illusion of its motion, and H.D. appears to have been suggesting that on her second viewing she had seen cinema's secret, the secret of its motionlessness, which Pabst did not mean her, or any spectator, to see. Yet, as H.D.'s film writing makes clear, she by no means perceived herself as any spectator, but as a reader of symbols and secrets, as well as a 'projector' of film images, from whom cinema's secret stillness, and the secret of its stillness, could not be concealed. This was also the knowledge possessed by the *Close Up* circle, who both made films (turning still images into moving ones) and, on the pages of their journal, transmuted the moving image into the still image.

Macpherson's penultimate 'As Is', which appeared in September 1931, the issue which also contained uncaptioned stills from Eisenstein's uncompleted film project *Qué Viva Mexico*, was a review of Helmar Lerski's book of photographs, *Köpfe des Alltags*. In Lerski's ultra-close-up pictures of faces, Macpherson wrote, there is 'a blending of visible and "invisible" ', remembered and 'unremembered', and 'inevitable appreciation of the slow unfolding, the exploration, the documentation and swift discovery—here is cinema at its best. There is for once, enough of life and of movement in the inferences here exposed'.[220] Photography had become, he thus suggested, 'cinema at its best', and 'movement' was now seen to inhere within the still image itself.[221] Lerski's work, for Macpherson as for other commentators, commanded comparison with the Russian film directors who avoided professional actors, finding their 'types' in the everyday world. In Curt Glaser's account of Lerski, in his introduction to *Köpfe des Alltags*—'believing as he does that everyone has a face, only one must make an effort to see it'—there were echoes of Balázs's physiognomic model of film, and his fascination with 'the face of things'.[222] 1931 was also the year of publication of Walter Benjamin's essay 'Little History of Photography', in which Benjamin described the photographer August Sander's compilation of 'a series of faces that is in no way inferior to the tremendous physiognomic gallery mounted by an Eisenstein or a Pudovkin'.[223]

It is certainly possible that Macpherson's celebration of photography represented a reaction to the coming of sound, which had undoubtedly affected the responses to his films, *Borderline* in particular, in adverse ways. On the other hand, photography was, from an early stage in *Close Up*'s publication, perceived as, in Blakeston's words, 'an art closely allied to cinematography',[224] and, as David Mellor has suggested, *Close Up* became 'a vital channel for the transmission of the new German photography'. Soviet films, seen in Berlin, 'multiplied and reinforced the new vision that was emerging in photography'.[225] The photographer Humphrey Spender, Mellor records, 'would spend time examining stills from German and Soviet films, printed in *Close Up*, trying "to decide which shots could be real and which posed" ',[226] and he was particularly drawn to the stills taken by Pabst's studio photographer Hans Casparius, many of which were published in the pages of *Close Up*, and on whom Macpherson wrote an appreciation. From these perspectives, we can trace a film-photography nexus which runs parallel to, or intersects with, the film-literature relationship in *Close Up*, and which places the journal, and Macpherson's interests, in the forefront of developments in the new German photography of the early 1930s.

Film Writing and Film-Making

The POOL group produced three short films — *Wing-Beat* (1927), *Foothills* (1929), and *Monkey's Moon* (1929) — before its most substantial film project, *Borderline* (1930).[227] *Wing-Beat*, 'a film sequence', in H.D.'s words,[228] was announced as 'a study in thought', 'a film of telepathy', attempting to approximate thought through the use of poetic association and, in particular, superimposition. It is not clear whether the film was ever publicly shown: a manuscript on the film written by H.D. referred to 'seeing the fragments [in] a private performance in a tiny way-side cinema', reinforcing her sense that it was 'made to the initiate [*sic*]'.

> [T]he art of Mr Kenneth Macpherson, still in the making, has a lyric quality, a formless pulse and beat of light and that is wholly of the air, of the hills, of the light un-charted areas where genius dwells and has its dwelling. The question is, how far can genius, so clarid, so lucid, succeed in this new medium? How far, succeeding in this new art medium, can it get its audience, can it find its status, and its contacts and its deserved appreciation? Mr Macpherson is one of the young pioneers of the cinema as an art, yes, the cinema as a high art and moreover the cinema as *the* art of today. The young, thank god, are *not* satisfied with stuffed birds in cages, will *not* (thank god) accept the worn out and outworn creed and tradition that sent their older brothers to infamous butchery of one another and of the arts and of all glamour and beauty … Their aim is with the living, and their concern is simply with the flight and beat and pulse of living creatures. The film is their one medium.[229]

Foothills echoed the plot of Murnau's *Sunrise* (1927) in its tale of a city woman (played by H.D.) who, bored with town life, visits the Swiss countryside and, observed by disapproving village gossips, has a flirtation with a young peasant, until interrupted by the arrival of her fiancé. It was, a synopsis declared, 'a four reel film experimentally made in a small studio arranged and equipped by the author of the scenario [Macpherson], who also directed, part photographed and part played in the production. Unlike most of the One-Man films made to date, it does not attempt abstractions, freak effects, or incoherency, but is a simple story simply told, of life in a small Swiss village. The locations are genuine beauty spots of Switzerland, none of the artistes are professionals, one of the roles is actually played by a Swiss peasant'.[230] Robert Herring and Marc Allégret came out for the making of the film, Herring playing the male lead and Allégret filming some of the footage. Bryher and Macpherson showed *Foothills* to Pabst in August 1929: H.D., Bryher wrote to her, 'took the laurels' in Pabst's opinion, though he was somewhat critical of the speed of her movements, as of Macpherson's camera work.

In the *Foothills* synopsis, the assertion that 'experimentalism' need not be equated with abstraction re-enforces the sense that the commitment of the *Close Up* group was to the 'avant-gardism' of the narrative cinema of Pabst and Eisenstein rather than that of abstract and Dadaist film, though existing sequences from the early POOL films suggest some influence from Germaine Dulac and other film-makers associated with surrealism. Macpherson's engagement with narrative—'a simple story simply told'—hints at the way in which the films became a form of 'working through' of the group's complex and often fraught interrelationships, a significant motivation in H.D.'s 'autobiographical' novella of this period, a number of them privately printed and circulated, as indeed of her fiction as a whole.[231] *Foothills*, like *Borderline*, played out questions of social inclusion and exclusion, of narrow provincial life and its hostility to the stranger, of desire crossing the boundaries of age, class, and, in the case of *Borderline*, normative sexualities and race, 'the reactions of "borderline" people who "don't fit" in this world'.[232] In *Borderline*, Bryher played a cigar-smoking café proprietress and Robert Herring, in the words of one critic of the time, 'a nance pianist'.

The films were made in a period in which amateur film-making flourished. *Close Up*'s Berlin correspondent, Andor Kraszna Kraus, was also the editor of the magazines *Film Technik* and of *Film für Alle*, the monthly publication of the League of Film Amateurs, a position from which he was removed in 1935, as a result of, as Bernhard Rieger has written, 'either his Jewish ancestry or his sympathies for progressive aesthetics such as the Bauhaus movement, or both'.[233] *Film für Alle* ran a lengthy article by Macpherson discussing the making of *Foothills*, in which he drew a contrast between his film-making and that of the 'the professionals', linking, moreover, film-making and film criticism: 'I was certain that my critical orientation towards cinematography would be deepened by a film in which I was myself electrician, cameraman, director and from time to time actor ... If every critic wanted to do the same thing, our film criticism would look quite different.'[234] He discussed the difficulties of finding appropriate studio space and of access to sufficiently powerful lighting (their correspondent Silka came from Paris to 'struggle' for the necessary amps). Bryher, he noted, worked as his assistant, helping with the filming in the scenes in which Macpherson was himself acting. External shots were taken from a camera mounted on a moving cart, and Macpherson represented the filming as a form of community event in their Swiss village. 'One can make films and will continue to make them', he wrote, concluding: 'Because one has the possibility of free unhindered experimentation with one's friends and other people who have never before stood in front of a camera, one has the opportunity to make the *best* films. The reason for this is that one can thereby create a work just as one wants and not as the production firm wants it, and this will result in something that is attractive to the public.'

In the first issue of *Close Up*, Macpherson had written that 'the hope of the cinema lies with the amateur'.[235] To some extent, however, he blurred the distinction between 'alternative' and 'amateur' cinema, from whose typical forms—the home movie, the film evoking the family circle or family memories—*Foothills* was differentiated, both by its fictional scenario and by the contributions of film professionals to its making. The next substantial step in film making for Macpherson was the more ambitious project of *Borderline*, described, in notes written, perhaps by H.D. or Macpherson, as 'the intellectual film of the future'.[236]

Borderline (which cost £800 to make) was story-boarded in nearly 1,000 sketches specifying camera angle and movement, described in the '*Borderline* pamphlet' (published anonymously but almost certainly written by H.D)[237] as 'a sort of dynamic picture writing', whose 'actual directions for each special picture read like captions'.[238] The film's story was told in a printed libretto which accompanied at least some of the screenings. In a 'small "borderline" town anywhere in Europe' Adah (Eslanda Robeson) has been involved in an affair with Thorne (Gavin Arthur) and staying in rooms with the white couple Thorne and Astrid (H.D.). Adah does not realize that her husband Pete (Paul Robeson) is in the same town working in a hotel-cafe whose manageress was played by Bryher. In a quarrel between Thorne and Astrid, Astrid is 'accidentally' killed, Adah is blamed and Pete ordered to leave town, 'a scapegoat for the unresolved problems, evasions and neuroses for which the racial "borderline" has served justification'.[239]

Figure 14. Greta Garbo as Grete Rumfort in *Die Freudlose Gasse* (*The Joyless Street*) (G. W. Pabst, Germany, 1925). It seems certain that H.D. and Bryher saw the two women as Mirror-Images of themselves.

Figure 15. Bryher, in *Borderline* (Kenneth Macpherson, GB, 1929).

Figure 16. H.D. in *Borderline*.

Paul and Eslanda Robeson's participation has underlain much of the interest (albeit, until recent years, limited) in the film. Robert Herring was instrumental in arranging for their involvement, having initially made contact with Robeson over the special issue of *Close Up* on 'negro cinema'. At the close of 1928, Herring had written to Bryher to tell her of receiving 'an unsolicited letter from a negro...Paul Robeson', after Herring had written an article on 'negro films' in the *Manchester Guardian*: 'Wrote a very interesting letter, and asked among other things the name of the paper that wanted a negro number. So I sent him, replying, *Close-Up*...his name carries weight as an educated and received negro. And I think it would be fun if such negroes *did* realise the cinema through *Close-Up*, & he is suffering from the "colour question" in films at the moment.'[240]

Peter Noble, in his study *The Negro in Films*, insisted that 'director Macpherson allowed no distinction to be drawn between the Negro and the white characters. In fact he was so deliberate about this that one film reviewer at the time [in fact H.D. writing in the *Borderline* pamphlet] remarked, "The white folk of necessity, in this film, take subsidiary value. Macpherson has decreed this with delicate irony and ferocity"'. Noble added: 'As a kind of defiant gesture, Kenneth Macpherson in 1930 decided to make this contribution to film art, which he considered had come to the end of its greatest phase with the advent of the sound film; in any study of the Negro on the screen his gesture, "Borderline," will not only *not* be forgotten but will always have a place of primary importance.'[241] Noble thus represented Macpherson's 'defiance' as directed both against commercial/sound cinema and racism. Thomas Cripps, in *Slow Fade to Black*, included *Borderline* in a chapter entitled 'Two Cheers', noting the ways in which Robeson became 'a many-layered symbol of blackness...The film was a visual experiment in lights and shadows, and a comment on racism...In the end it is the white world turned upside down, the Negro made whole, the European idiom reordered with black the symbol of virtue and white the incarnation of evil. Black purity stands against European decadence, "sordid decadence and unbridled jealousy".'[242] While expressing admiration for the film's ambitions, Cripps suggested that, within the framework of advances for black Americans, 'Robeson's presence happened in a vacuum'. He also argued that 'what passed for racial liberalism was often no more than a worship of presumed primitiveness'.

Figure 17. Robert Herring in *Borderline*.

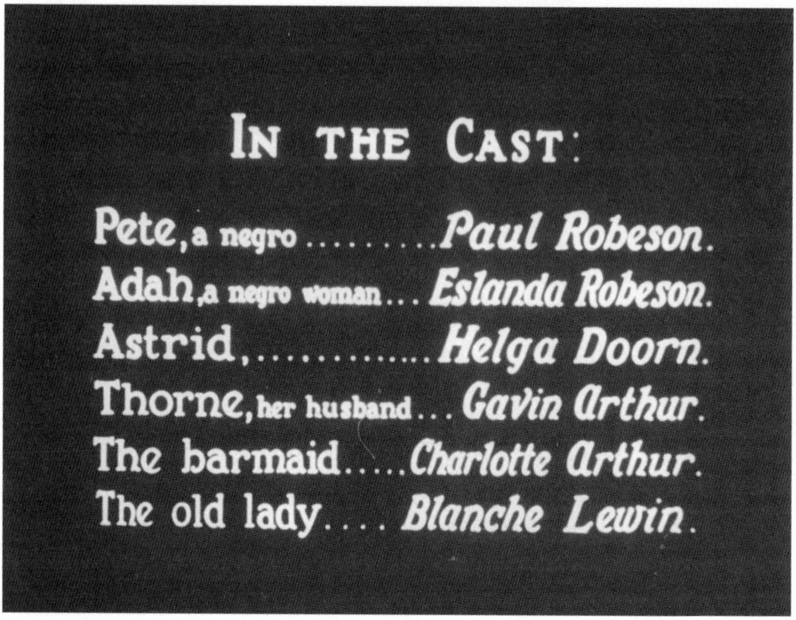

IN THE CAST:

Pete, a negro .... *Paul Robeson.*
Adah, a negro woman ... *Eslanda Robeson.*
Astrid, ... *Helga Doorn.*
Thorne, her husband ... *Gavin Arthur.*
The barmaid ..... *Charlotte Arthur.*
The old lady .... *Blanche Lewin.*

Figure 18. *Borderline* cast list.

The lengthy *Borderline* pamphlet opened with the question of 'black' and 'white'. Writing about the film in which she herself had played a central role (using the name 'Helga Doorn', whose Nordic resonances were presumably intended to echo the name of Greta Garbo), H.D. focused on the contrast between 'a flash of white hand' and 'the high lights across the knuckles of a black hand', 'a dark brow, that great head that bends forward, very earth giant' and 'a weathered woman-face ... That face beats through the film like the very swift progress of those wings, doomed it is evident, and already extinguished in this "borderline" existence'.[243] In *Borderline*, Astrid (H.D.') stares into the camera as if, in Morris's words, 'she were emptying her mind out onto the screen, or, even more uncomfortably, as if she were attempting a direct transfer of her psychic content into the mind of the viewer'.[244] In the pamphlet, H.D. suggested that Macpherson, as director, confounded racial 'borderlines': 'He says when is white not white and when is black white and when is white black?' In more troubling ways, it could be argued that the psychological excess of the 'civilized' white woman becomes a 'dark continent' which slides into association with the 'primitive', the racial Other.[245]

The *Borderline* pamphlet, written as a form of manifesto, made substantial claims both for 'cinema art' and for Macpherson's creative powers, comparing him to Leonardo. The Renaissance genius brought together art and the machine, while 'the film *per se* is a curious welding of mechanical and creative instincts' and Macpherson was, in H.D.'s words, 'machine man', at one with his camera: 'a hard-boiled mechanic, as if he were all camera, bone and sinew and steel-glint of rapacious grey eyes'.[246] The art of Leonardo, H.D. wrote, entailed both a cutting apart of the human body in order to understand its workings and the invention of a 'personal secret script'. Film, too, was to be defined through these images. The 'secret script' is the new language of the cinema, the film hieroglyphic, a 'dynamic picture writing'. The cutting and slicing encoded, as we have seen, the 'diagonal' vision of Macpherson's 'alternative' or 'counter' film-making in his film criticism, his cinemas of the mind, as well as montage aesthetics more broadly. The sequence in *Borderline* in which H.D.'s character, Astrid, slashes through the air with a knife (with its echoes of both Pabst's *Secrets of a Soul* and Hitchcock's *Blackmail*) used Eisenstein's montage techniques to make 'cutting' visible and palpable: this 'jagged lightening effect' was achieved, H.D. wrote, 'by the cutting and fitting of tiny strips of film, in very much the same manner that you would fit together a jig-saw puzzle'.[247]

Figure 19. *Borderline* collage, Kenneth Macpherson.

As *Borderline* was being planned, *Close Up*, as Anne Friedberg notes, began to publish essays by Eisenstein, whose theories of 'overtonal montage' (explored in 'The Fourth Dimension in the Kino' and 'Methods of Montage', published as parts one and two of 'The Fourth Dimension of the Kino' in *Close Up* for March and April 1930) seem to have been central to Macpherson's conception of the workings of association and the connections between shots in *Borderline*.[248] This was to be combined, as notes made at the time suggest, with a model of the 'undertonal', the 'appeal to the unconscious'. Nonetheless, and perhaps in response to criticisms that the film was overly derivative of German and Russian film practice and theory, Macpherson was to suggest that he had intuited the necessity of the 'overtonal' rather than working directly with the concept. The article by 'Mercurius' on *Borderline* in *The Architectural Review*, entitled 'Act, Fact, and Abstraction', used four stills from the film to explore 'pictorial suggestion' and ' "overtonal" mounting'. Thus a shot of the pianist in the film, played by Robert Herring, was described as 'a close-up taken from below and at a slant [which] suggests a world gone awry: the mental view of the pianist'. The 'pictorial suggestion' then leads, the article claimed, to the identification of the audience with the scene before them:

> In 'overtonal' mounting a powerful suggestion is made to the audience—in this case by the pictorial composition of shot (a)—who are then left to carry on the suggested scene by means of their imagination, whilst a different scene is enacted on the screen. The impression made by the second scene is co-existent with the train of thought arising from the first suggestion. In other words, the direct impression of the second scene receives what is known as an 'overtone' from the imaginary enactment started by the first suggestion.[249]

The concept of 'suggestion' was also a significant one, central to Freud's writings on the uses of hypnosis and 'psychotherapy' at the beginnings of psychoanalysis, and reformulated in his 'Introductory Lectures', in which he differentiated between 'suggestion' in hypnosis and in analysis—'the former acts like a cosmetic, the latter like surgery'—and called attention to the ways in which the psychoanalyst 'guides' the patient's 'suggestion' through the transference.[250] The conceptual framework of *Borderline* thus brought together Freud's theories, often channelled by and through Hanns Sachs, and those of Eisenstein, as did the pages of *Close Up* itself.

Macpherson's editorial, 'As Is', for November 1930 was given over to discussion of *Borderline*: 'This funny business about *Borderline*. The reviews have
been coming in, and there seem to be deductions worth making about film
criticism in general.'[251] Outlining his intentions for the film, Macpherson
wrote of his decision to make *Borderline* with a 'subjective use of inference'.

> By this I meant that instead of the method of externalised observation,
> dealing with objects, I was going to take my film into the minds of the
> people in it, making it not so much a film of 'mental processes' as to
> insist on a mental condition. To take the action, the observation, the
> deduction, the reference, into the labyrinth of the human mind, with
> its queer impulses and tricks, its unreliability, its stresses and obsessions,
> its half-formed deductions, its glibness, its occasional amnesia, its fantasy,
> suppressions, and desires.[252]

Alluding to the critical charge that the film was 'chaotic', Macpherson
brought in Eisenstein's concept of 'overtone': 'Over this chaos rings and
reverberates one pure, loud, sullen note. I had no specific name for it, but
now we know it is overtone ... Static forms have been used, certainly. And
very often. But solely to drive forward the mental impetus.'[253]

As Roland Cosandey noted, the succession of shots in the film was
'dictated by a subjective logic', with the appearance of 'places, faces and
landscapes ... correspond[ing] largely to a sort of interior call on the part of
one of the characters, summoning them there at that moment'. Cosandey
followed Macpherson in emphasizing *Borderline* as a 'mental condition', but
he also noted the film's 'extreme physical expressivity ... the body being
used as an unconscious indicator of emotions and at the same time the most
appropriate way of communicating them to us'.[254]

Macpherson, in his editorial, suggested that the negative responses to the
film in Britain were due to the emotional repression of the English—'The
Englishman's fear of "morbidity" and the neurotic is a race neurosis which
sets him at a disadvantage when it comes to emotional, or mental-emotional
experience'—as well as their anti-intellectualism. This latter charge was
more forcefully made by Bryher in an article on 'Danger in the Cinema'
in the same issue of *Close Up*. Linking the question of 'thought' in film,
and its avoidance, with her habitual preoccupation with the question of
education and its vicissitudes, she wrote:

> There seems to have developed a dangerous tradition in England that the
> cinema 'must be simple.' And if this statement be investigated it will be

found to mean, '*the cinema must not think.*' ... It is probable that the Chaplin films have the effect of hypnosis on some spectators because they were the first pictures that moved that these spectators saw, as children. This should be no barrier to their enjoyment, but it is a definite reason against making them the standard for film art... What is needed in the English cinema is psychological investigation and the stating of facts people would prefer not to know existed. Unless the intellect can dominate cinema, let us put films away with meccanos and picture blocks.[255]

Although Bryher did not specify the context, her article was, clearly, also written as a reaction to the critical responses to *Borderline* and, as I discuss in the next section, to C. A. Lejeune's in particular.

'The only really "avant-garde film" ever made'[256]

The exhibition of *Borderline* was confined to a small number of ciné-club and film society screenings, including the Birmingham Film Society, where it was screened in a 1931 season which also included Dovzenko's *Earth*. *Borderline*'s first screening, at which its 'silence' was highlighted by the absence of musical accompaniment, was at the Academy Cinema in London in October 1930: it generated significant response from film journals as well as from film critics writing for the mainstream press. It was subsequently shown at the Second International Congress of Independent Cinema in Brussels in November 1930 as, along with Francis Brugière and Oswell Blakeston's *Light Rhythms*, the English contribution. The status of the other avant-garde film-makers represented on this occasion—Ruttmann and Richter for Germany, Vertov and Dovzkenko for Russia, Henri de Chomette, Clair, and Man Ray for France—gives some sense of *Borderline*'s contemporary importance as a British avant-garde film, though a reviewer wrote (in a comment that suggests that neither the 'libretto' nor the pamphlet were distributed to the audience on this occasion): 'This English work was received rather coldly, despite its careful mise-en-scene, the admirable composition of its images, and the perfection of the principal actors' representation. It appeared long and unexplained. It would undoubtedly have benefited from some sort of exposition of its scenario.'[257] It was screened and well-received at a cine-club in Catalonia in January 1931—one reviewer called it a great film, 'perhaps the greatest that has as yet been produced in "pure cinema"'—before being shown in Berlin in April 1931.[258]

The invitations to the private showing of *Borderline* ('A POOL film, starring *Paul Robeson*') at 11.00, 13 October 1930 at the Academy Cinema in Oxford Street gave the following account of the film:

> '*Borderline*' has been directed, photographed and largely acted by British people, and it is an attempt to make an interesting film from an intellectual viewpoint rather than that of the 'entertainment angle' with its often rudimentary simplifications. It was made at nominal cost in a small studio, and is the first film in which Paul Robeson has appeared.
>
> We are told that such a film cannot possibly succeed in England.
>
> We have dared to think, however, that a discriminating English audience would respond just as interestedly to the experiment as the private foreign audience to whom '*Borderline*' was shown, resulting in an immediate offer of commercial showing.
>
> Before '*Borderline*' is shown abroad we want to know what English audiences think of it, for '*Borderline*' is a British film.

The *Close Up* group's desire for a positive 'English' response, and their situating of *Borderline* as 'a British film' contains some ironies, given the fairly unremitting attacks on British cinema in the pages of the journal. Despite the appeals to their national sympathies, the British reviewers were for the most part critical, though not, with the exception of the trade press, dismissive.[259] There was a shared sense that, in one reviewer's words, 'Mr Macpherson has still to find his technique; at the moment he seems too much under the influence of widely differentiated directors, including Pabst',[260] and more than one critic suggested that Macpherson would be well served by spending time in a commercial studio. *Cinema* called the film 'interesting even if it is often obscure', commending Macpherson's photography and admiring the daring of the experiment: '"Borderline" is indeed so advanced in subject and treatment as to be ahead even of the Russian and Pabst schools. Obviously Mr. Macpherson is a very modern psychologist and "Borderline" is psychology in excelsis'. The reviewer noted, however, the hopelessness of putting the film before the English trade, which 'cares little for such profundities'.[261]

The *Manchester Guardian* reviewer repeated the incorrect claim, made on the invitation, that *Borderline* was Robeson's first film (he had in fact appeared in Oscar Micheaux's 1924 *Body and Soul*) and observed, as did other critics, that it was misleading to describe him as 'starring' in the film: 'He is only part of a composition of moving images in which his powers as an actor and his box-office attractiveness as a personality are subordinated and sometimes obliterated by the director, Mr Kenneth Macpherson, who is obviously more interested in pictorial than in dramatic values.'[262]

C. A. Lejeune, by this point writing a regular column, 'The Pictures', for *The Observer*, devoted her weekly article to *Borderline*, heading it 'Critic as Creator', and it was this review in particular, with its reference to the 'chaos' of the film and demand for 'simplicity' in the cinema, to which Macpherson and Bryher appear to have been responding in their *Close Up* articles. Lejeune focused on the work of Macpherson, critic and creator, and treated *Borderline* and *Close Up* together, measuring the film against the high standards set by the journal, and finding it wanting: 'Here is a picture designed by the editor and staff of a periodical which claims to be "the only magazine devoted to films as an art" ... it will require a great deal of courage and clear-sightedness from the readers of "Close Up", amongst whom most of the intelligent film-goers in this country are numbered, to perceive "Borderline", in their own terms, "as is," and not as in the theories of its makers, should be':

> For the sake of every jot of real endeavour in the commercial studios, for every urgency of real achievement among the amateurs, we must be honest in our contact with an altogether warring picture in which fragments of every school, every thought, every symbolic language, strive and destroy one another. Finite it may be, in the mind of its makers, who have the written word and the drawn sketch as supplement and corollary, but to the public, facing it without pre-conception, the film is formless—urgent perhaps, but urgent in a chaos, lacking that single broad stream of creation, whether of theme, or mood, or simply rhythm, along which any work of art must travel towards its implicit end ... those of us who respect [Macpherson's] ideals will not compliment him. We could not do so without declaring his own standards peccant. For 'Borderline' is not the stuff to which the true Macpherson would extend patronage, and to congratulate him on it would only be to delay still further the achievement of that cinema-haven of intelligence which we must believe honestly to be his goal.[263]

While Lejeune's doctrine of 'simplicity' might seem a limiting and indeed conservative one ('what can be simpler than the pantomime of Chaplin, the movement of Mickey, the argument of Seldes, the logic of Clair? ... they carry their own testimonies, needing none'), her arguments raise significant questions about the extent to which *Borderline* as a film required the 'testimony' of its explanatory film writing (in the shape of the *Borderline* pamphlet, as well as the discussions of the film, as of *Wing Beat* and *Foothills*, in the pages of the journal). Other critics suggested that the film would have been incomprehensible without the accompanying booklet. E. A. Baughan called it 'an absurd high-brow pamphlet';[264] Lejeune suggested that Macpherson might be seen not as 'the artist-scientist of a new renaissance', as the *Borderline* pamphlet claimed, but as one of the renaissance princes, 'patrons in the most generous sense of all the arts; ready to warm, select, appreciate, defend; powerful to destroy; impotent only when they aim to create'. She had not a good word to say for the film—and it is striking that she made no mention of Robeson or of any of its actors—but her review took seriously the intellectual project of *Close Up* and did not belittle its mission. In his editorial, Macpherson returned repeatedly to the critique of *Borderline*'s 'chaos' and the critical demand for 'simplicity', and it would certainly seem that Lejeune's response was the one that had troubled Macpherson and Bryher most intensely. 'I say', wrote Macpherson, 'that the essence of film art is not and can never be so simple as "simplicity" ... the film, to me, and to anybody who bothers to think twice, is *life*, and life is not simple, and life cannot be kept within any shallow limits of form or formulae'.[265]

In a letter to H.D. and Macpherson, dated 26 April 1931, Bryher described the screening of *Borderline* at a Berlin *kino*, at the close of a day 'too comic and exciting'.[266] The day began at 4.30, with screenings at the Kamera of *Kain und Artem* ('fuller of flies and blood and horrors than ever') and Dovzenko's *Earth*, followed by a lecture delivered by the anthropologist and psychoanalyst Géza Róheim. She attended with Sachs, who before the lecture, and with no obvious referent, went 'trotting round to everyone and saying "ein ganz merkwürdisches sadistisches Phantasie [*sic*]"' [267] ('a quite remarkable sadistic phantasy'). Bryher described the lecture in some detail; it concerned initiation rites and the opening up of circumcision wounds among young Australian aboriginal men, and photographs were passed around: 'they were most extraordinary and rather gruesome'. The evening continued at Die Rote Mühle, 'a very elaborate large kino', where an audience of at least three hundred arrived (included the Metzners, Dr Eckhard, and Andor Kraszna-Kraus, Dr Koch, and Lotte Reiniger), and 'a man announced that *Borderline* by Macpherson, editor of *Close Up*, would be shown and that it showed states of the soul and was not an action film'. Before *Borderline*, there was a screening of part of Germaine Dulac's film *The Mussel*: 'it is called a psycho-analytical film':

> Then Border started. And then there was uproar. It hit their unconscious too badly. Turtle said it was not a typical Berlin audience, Metzner yelled

THE MOMENT OF CLOSE UP

furiously at them 'ruhe' and wanted to fight them. If I had been on my own, I too would have joined in. We had a real surrealist evening. Half of them yelled, whistled, not straight but in a kind of hysterical way, (I think one female did have hysterics)—then a block in the centre shouted 'ruhe', 'ruhe', and applauded. At the end of the show, there were almost three fights in the hall.

... What they couldn't stand was Gavan [*sic*]. Every time Thorne appeared they whistled and boo'd him. They howled with laughter when the cat appeared. They were absolutely quiet for all the bar room and Robeson stuff but they shrieked at the landscapes, every time Thorne appeared, and were divided about Astrid. The worst moment was in the hysteric scene and the row behind me of women burst into uncontrollable sadistic laughter. Suddenly the 'Augen' shot of Astrid, and there was a sudden hush like after an explosion in the whole kino and then somebody whispered 'Augen' like a small explosion. I got some whistles over the cigar.

It was really most extraordinary and I myself believe much more now in the film than ever before because it was quite obvious that it drove people beside themselves—as if Eisenstein's theory had been applied. I think without knowing it Kenneth must have played a little with his desire to torture because suddenly somebody would get up and rush out suddenly as if they could not bear to remain a moment longer in their seats.

... On the whole I should say that fifty per cent either left or were so angry that they wanted to fight somebody. The other fifty per cent, were as wildly enthusiastic.

Bryher did suggest that parts of the film might have been too long and too slow: 'the rhythm of Berlin is very swift'. She also took this question up in a note on the screening of *Borderline* in *Close Up*, justifying the slowness of the film on the grounds that 'the rhythm of life' was slower in England than in Berlin: '*Borderline* is an English film and should not be a copy of German or Russian methods'.[268] In her letter she noted that Koch, Lotte Reiniger *et. al.* 'came up and said it was magnificent but far too fine for an average public':

Rover's [Macpherson's] work is too deep or too modern for the mass. He is a worker or pioneer for the few and will be appreciated in another generation's time. My job on the other hand is mass work. And there's an enormous difference. I am not sure if I were 'managing' Rover that I would not have only tiny private shows at two guineas a ticket and a psychological examination beforehand. You see, Rover, you get too deeply on the corns encrusting the repressions of the average individual, particularly if there is any repressed homosexuality in them.

The letter ended with Bryher's mention of her analysis the following morning: 'Got a lot of interesting material up in my hour ... as a result of the Australian savages.'

In Bryher's account, the showing of *Borderline* became inextricably intertwined with the transgressive sexualities she found in Berlin, with psychoanalysis and anthropology, and with surrealism. The film began, in her account, to take on some of the lineaments of an Artaudian 'raw cinema' or a 'theatre of cruelty'. She also represented the screening of the film in ways that conjured up the avant-garde performances of the Dadaists and Surrealists, in which the uproar was an essential part of the event. A letter to H.D. written at this time noted 'a row' with the Film Liga, who were concerned about showing the film: 'I made tender enquiries as to why they showed avant garde films if they were not prepared for a row ... Apparently the *Kamera* fears the beautifully roccoco [*sic*] ceiling might be wrecked. I am hinting delicatedly that that is what the French avant garde cinemas hope for, as then they know they have a success'.[269]

The violent responses were, however, also represented as those of the 'mob' (Sachs explained to her that the crowd was 'communistic'), unfit for experimental cinema. She described *Borderline* as 'an onslaught' on the unconscious, and raised the question of its representations of homosexuality. Her invocations of audience hysteria (mirroring H.D.'s performance of 'hysteria' in *Borderline*) and of the women's 'uncontrollable sadistic laughter' (with its echoes of Macpherson's 'desire to torture') turned the film into a mirror-screen of the spectators' neuroses, individual and collective, and of repressed desires. The term 'hysteria', used in this context, may also have conjured up the overwrought responses to the screening of Pudovkin's *Storm over Asia*, including G. A. Atkinson's claim in *The Sunday Express* that the 'work of Russian film producers in general is mainly screen hysteria'.[270] Bryher indeed suggested that *Borderline* would be best reserved for a minority audience who had been psychologically tested beforehand; a subsequent letter described a plan to show it at the Film Liga with Pabst (who, Bryher reported to Macpherson, claimed *Borderline* was 'the only really avant garde film'[271]) 'lecturing in front of it', again recalling the association with *Secrets of a Soul* and Pabst's accompanying pamphlet.[272] She drew a clear distinction between Macpherson's 'minority', avant-garde film practice and her sense that her own job must be 'mass work', a perception that certainly shaped her commitment to psychoanalysis and film as widely diffused elements of 'education' and 'development' in society at large. It is also significant that her description of the screening followed from the account of the graphic discussion of initiation rights in Roheim's lecture, invoking a 'primitivism' which was never far from the film's representations of racialized identity. There was, her letter seemed to suggest, something fundamental, sexual, and bloody that both psychoanalysis and *Borderline* had opened up, and her reception of both arose in the context of a Berlin coming close to political terror and mass violence.

Writing from Berlin in mid-1931, Bryher reported the growing seriousness of the political situation, and Pabst's and Metzner's plans to leave Germany in order to continue film-making. Film and politics became increasingly intertwined for her, and she was excited by Brecht's film *Kuhle Wampe*, which she saw in June 1931; 'It is exactly the kind of film I would make.'[273] Letters from this period also reveal Bryher's encouragement to Macpherson to continue with his work in film, either independently or by joining a studio,[274] but he did not pursue any of the openings that Bryher, at least, believed were being held out to him, and appears to have had no more involvement with film direction or production until 1946, when he was listed as one of the producers (along with Peggy Guggenheim) of Hans Richter's film *Dreams that Money Can Buy*, for which a number of avant-garde directors produced dream sequences. In the early and mid-1930s there were plans for film projects, including a sound film with music by Eric Walter White,[275] none of which were realized, with Macpherson continuing to express his hatred of commercial cinema and English films: 'The ideal of art has been driven from the film, and dates along with surrealism, dadaism, cubism, etc. Film, in short, is now as much a trade and has the same purpose and ideology as the Stock Exchange.'[276]

Bryher continued to write for and to edit *Close Up*, doing the bulk of the work when Macpherson broke up their ménage by taking a male lover, and, after 1930 or so, losing much of his former passion for film and film-making.[277] Yet, she suggested later, psychoanalysis was from the start more of a pull for her than cinema, and her involvement with it grew. By 1931, both H.D. and Macpherson were in analysis with Mary Chadwick in London: H.D., apparently, to recover from the shock of Macpherson's desertion; Macpherson as the price he had to pay for Bryher's continued financial support. Bryher's analysis with Sachs in Berlin was, meanwhile, leading to her taking seriously the idea of a training analysis, though she expressed her boredom at listening to lectures at the Berlin Institute: 'I was bored most of the time. Passive again—don't want to listen to other people on P.A. but want to get on the job myself!'[278]

Of all the writers on film for *Close Up*, it was Bryher and Sachs who most fully acknowledged the growing political dangers of the early 1930s, the impact of politics on film, and the role of film in political culture. Her lengthy article in *Close Up*, 'Berlin April 1931', opened with the assertion that to be back to Berlin 'means always a reawakening of life'.

> For it is the most stimulating city, intellectually, in Europe, because the new buildings express outwardly modern thought. Other cities try to hide or stem the current of progress but here interest is expressed in visible terms; the city exterior has accepted thought in spite of the inner reaction which, friends tell me, is sweeping Germany back, particularly in education, towards old unprogressive methods.[279]

A year later, she opened an article entitled 'Notes on Some Films: Berlin, June 1932', with these lines:

> Berlin is too unsettled, too fearful of the coming winter to care much for cinema. The atmosphere in the streets is only to be compared with that of any large city in 1914–1918. After two or three days, the visitor wonders why revolution does not happen, not that there is any specific thing to provoke it apparent to the eyes, but outbreak against this odd insecure heaviness is to be preferred than waiting for a storm that has sometime got to burst.[280]

The piece was followed by Hanns Sachs's article 'Kitsch', in which he translated Freud's ideas about popular fiction into an account of popular film, and Freud's assertion that 'a happy person never phantasies, only an unsatisfied one' into the statement that 'Kitsch is the exploitation of daydreams by those who never had any'.[281] Producers, he argued, cynically manipulate fantasy, his words echoing Kracauer's assertion that 'the stupid and unreal fantasies are the *daydreams of society*, in which its actual reality comes to the fore and its otherwise repressed wishes take on form'.[282] Sachs's article also alluded to the political dangers of kitsch, with its refusal to recognize mental and ethical conflict, ambivalence, and choice. In 1932, he left Germany permanently for the United States, where he died in 1947.

Bryher's 'What Shall You do in the War?', published in the June 1933 issue, was her final article for *Close Up*, and it described the violence being perpetrated by the national socialists in Germany, and the increasing oppression of Jews and liberals. It was not until the very end of her article that she invoked film, arguing that peace could be fought for with cinema.

She advocated a refusal to see films 'that are merely propagandistic for any unjust system', a cooperation with America and a tolerance of its linguistic differences, and an awareness, when choosing films to see, of the directors, actors, and film architects 'who have been driven out of the German studios and scattered across Europe, because they believed in peace and intellectual liberty'.[283] Nonetheless, her reference to the film societies and 'small experiments [which] raised the general level of films considerably in five years', seemed to suggest that the energies that had gone into alternative cinema and cinema theory would now be needed to 'raise respect for intellectual liberty' if 'we' were not to plunge 'in every kind and color of uniform, towards a not to be imagined barbarism'. 'What Shall You Do in the War?' would be, as it transpired, a valediction, both for *Close Up*'s project and for its moment.

Coda: The Coming of Sound

There can scarcely fail to be an increase in the mind of the pictures when they find tongues.[1]

A complete boycott of 'talking films' should be the first duty of anyone who has achieved a moment's pleasure from the contemplation of any film.[2]

A lthough the demise of *Close Up* almost certainly resulted from the changing political situation in Europe, as well as Macpherson's loss of interest in the journal and in film-making and the death of Bryher's father, Bryher later represented it in her memoir *Heart to Artemis* as a direct result of 'the collapse of the silent film'. The period between the late 1920s and early 1930s was, Bryher writes, 'the golden age of what I call "the art that died" because sound ruined its development':

> I have written already that we had to get away from the nineteenth century if we were to survive. The film was new, it had no earlier associations and it offered occasionally, in an episode or a single shot, some framework for our dreams. We felt we could state our convictions honourably in the twentieth-century form of art and it appealed to the popular internationalism of those so few years because 'the silents' offered a single language across Europe.[3]

Later in the memoir Bryher added:

> [*Borderline*] was part of 'the art that died' because these small pictures were training the directors and cameramen of the future as the 'little reviews' had trained the writers but sound came in, nobody could continue on account of the expense and by 1934 *Close Up* and about sixty of these groups had ceased to exist.[4]

The identification between the 'small picture' and the 'little review', *Borderline* and *Close Up*, was thus made explicit.

In 1938, Bryher showed *Borderline* to the analysts Walter and Melitta Schmideberg (Melanie Klein's estranged daughter) at a private viewing arranged by Lotte Reiniger, at which Eric Walter White was also present. 'The rhythm is slow', Bryher wrote to Macpherson, by this time living in New York, 'but otherwise it might have been done to-day. I cant tell you how well the photography emerges. I do feel you ought to get the museum of modern art to buy a copy ... It makes one so sad that an art—that of the silent film—died. So much in the faces.'[5] This could be read, however, rather differently from the comment in her memoir, in which Bryher claimed that cinema was ruined by sound. In 1938 she seemed to have been suggesting that silent film could have survived alongside sound film as a separate art.[6]

In his November 1930 discussion of *Borderline*, Macpherson wrote:

> Eighteen months ago everybody was saying the silent film had reached perfection. It had no further to go. When in reality it had only reached the first stage in an intensive development. And oddly enough, it was not until after the talkies had swept the silent film out of existence, that *Borderline*, perhaps the only really 'avant-garde' film ever made, came about.[7]

From this perspective, *Borderline* was not outmoded or anachronistic as a silent film made in the sound era; its avant-gardism was predicated on its use of silence in the face of the possibility of sound. Macpherson's was a prescient comment, given that both silent and black and white film have survived almost exclusively in the context of avant-garde and experimental cinema.

Dorothy Richardson, in her *Continuous Performance* articles, articulated her mourning for the end of the silent period, arguing that the multiple auralities of 'the talkies'—music, synch sound/speech, 'dead' silences—fragmented the continuous stream provided by film music in silent cinema and its unifying aesthetic. The coming of sound brings: 'Apparatus rampant: the theatre, ourselves, the screen, the mechanisms, all fallen apart into competitive singleness.'[8] From this perspective, sound was a mechanical intrusion into the medium, and a mechanism too far, making apparent (though this was not always acknowledged) the human itself as, in Tom Conley's words, 'a function of the operation of an artificial apparatus or the illusion of habit'.[9] 'The talkies' arrived, moreover, at a point by which, as we have seen, critics and commentators had confidently announced the rebirth, or new birth, of cinema through a focus on *photogénie*, light and motion, often drawing it away, in discursive terms, from its mechanical origins (though there continued to be many theorists and practitioners celebrating the machine aesthetic) through the languages of organicism and vitalism. For 'Mercurius', in a column published in 1929: 'The "talkies" are not a reality, they are a substitute for reality. The silent film has ceased to be an illusion, it exists in its own right.'[10] Silent film had thus become 'reality' itself, and the 'talkies' a mere simulacrum. For Paul Rotha, writing in 1930: 'Immediately a voice begins to speak in a cinema, the sound apparatus takes precedence over the camera, thereby doing violence to natural instincts.'[11]

As I discussed in Chapter 1, H.D.'s critical response to the coming of the 'movietone' was to align silent film, dream-life, hieroglyphics (in which gesture and the 'hieroglyphics' of the performing body played a central role), and the mythic 'impersonality' of experimental (and more particularly mime and marionette) theatre. The 'movietone' was, by contrast, a 'mere example of mechanical inventiveness'. While H.D. acknowledged that sound might increase film's potential for communication and political 'understanding', she suggested that the price was a high one to pay for the loss of 'that half-world of lights and music and blurred perception ... into which the being floats as a moth into summer darkness'.[12]

Dorothy Richardson shared with many women writers and critics a perception that silent film had been an essentially female form. While the responses of critics and commentators during the transition period did not divide absolutely along gendered lines, and the representation of sound film was indeed ambivalently gendered (we recall the image of the mechanical, chattering, female speaking body) there was a quite marked hostility among women writers to sound technology, and a greater degree of regret for the loss of the silent film. In the first years of sound, film-makers often attempted to rejuvenate silent films by grafting dialogue scenes onto them: these became known as 'goat-gland movies', or 'goat-glanders', in a reference to a surgical procedure developed around 1920, in which goat testes were surgically implanted into human males as a cure for impotence.[13] Some resistance to these phallic prerogatives seems to enter into responses such as those of Richardson, who wrote: 'In becoming audible and particularly in becoming a medium of propaganda, [film] is doubtless fulfilling its destiny. But it is a masculine destiny.'[14] The silent screenplay writer, Lenore Coffee, remarked that 'A silent film was like writing a novel, and a script [for a talking picture] was like writing a play. That's why women dropped out. Women had been good novelists, but in talking pictures women were not predominant.'[15]

Richardson's hostility (not, ultimately, absolute), was, in the first instance, like that of many critics in the transition period, to dialogue and synchronized speech, which had become identified with America's hegemony, 'her vast scheme', as Paul Rotha put it in 1930, 'for capturing the entertainment market of the world. On these lines will the film retrace its steps, becoming a mechanical means of the theatrical presentation of spectacles superior commercially to the stage'.[16] Silent film, it was argued, had been a universal medium, developing, in Balázs's phrase, 'an international universal humanity', and operating in a kind of visual Esperanto, including, for Balázs, a 'comparative "gesturology"'.[17] Moreover, it was perceived to animate the object world, often in revelatory ways, rather than making the human face and voice its only measure. Sound film, it was argued, produced a destructive competition between eye and ear, and in the writings of many film aestheticians we find a hostility to so-called 'hybrid' forms and an insistence that the aesthetic of film was determined by its unity and its visual purity. There was also significant concern about the 'fall' into linguistic diversity, which it was felt American cinema would use to its own advantage. The coming of synchronized recorded sound to cinema not only completed the mechanization but also, it has been argued, the standardization, of the film medium.

While these are all undoubtedly significant dimensions of the response to the coming of sound, none seems to account fully for the experience of loss which was so strongly articulated at this time. As Stanley Cavell has written:

> The new emergence of the ideas of silence and fantasy and motion and separateness take us back, or forward to beginnings. For it isn't as if, long after our acceptance of the talkie, we know why the loss of silence was traumatic for so many who cared about film... What was given up in giving up the silence of film, in particular the silence of the voice? Why suppose that there will be some simple answer to that question?[18]

We might turn for the moment, then, from the necessarily partial attempt to explicate loss to the acknowledgement of recompense. From 1929, when Richardson began to focus on the silent/sound transition, she began to write about silent film as 'memory'. Although resigned, she wrote in a column entitled 'A Tear for Lycidas', to a 'filmless London' once 'speech-films' had taken over the cinemas:

> There was, there always is, one grand compensation: we came fully into our heritage of silent films. 'The Film,' all the films we had seen, massed together in the manner of a single experience … became for us treasure laid up. Done with in its character of current actuality, inevitably alloyed, and beginning its rich, cumulative life as memory. Again and again, in this strange 'memory' (which, however we may choose to define it, is, at the least, past, present and future powerfully combined) we should go to the pictures; we should revisit, each time with a difference, and, since we should bring to it increasing wealth of experience, each time more fully, certain films stored up within. But to the cinema we should go no more.[19]

Inscribing silent film as 'memory' (and deploying a model of 'untensed' time—past, present, and future combined—that had become central to early twentieth-century philosophies of time), Richardson also represented cinema in the narrative mode of her novel-sequence *Pilgrimage*. In 'A Tear for Lycidas', the film spectator becomes a *flâneur*, or *flâneuse*, wandering the London streets and finding 'in a central neglected backwater' the survival 'of something of London's former quietude'. In this backwater, the 'incredible' is discovered, on the facade of the 'converted Scala theatre: Silent Films. Continuous Performance. *Two Days. The Gold Rush*'.[20]

The lure of the silent films was not, Richardson suggested, merely nostalgic. The Scala was a 'converted' theatre, showing silent films in, and in spite of, the full awareness of sound, just as the writer-wanderer's entry into the silent London by-street was preceded by the experience of the 'rapids of a main thoroughfare', and the cinema spectator watched silent film in possession of 'all we had read and heard and imaginatively experienced of the new dimensions'. The silent/sound divide could be crossed in both directions, and silent films, now viewed not 'innocently', but in the knowledge of sound, became a way of 'seeing again'. Richardson, despite her writing and theorizing against the coming of sound (or, more precisely, speech) could thus also be seen as a 'convert' of a kind. The aesthetic of the silent film became the gift of the transition to sound, brought into (new) being by the forms that succeeded it, as, for Macpherson, *Borderline*, 'came about after the talkies had swept the silent film out of existence'.

The Jazz Singer

The Jazz Singer broke onto the scene in the first months of *Close Up*'s existence. While it is too simple to see it as the film which singlehandedly shattered the silents, it was undoubtedly a highly charged text and event. On 26 August Warner Bros. produced their first sound feature, *Don Juan*, and in October 1927, released *The Jazz Singer* which was, in fact, more of a 'singing' than 'talking' film, with nearly all the dialogue sections still conveyed by intertitles. It could most accurately be described as a silent film with Vitaphoned sequences, in line with Warner's strategy of producing Vitaphone shorts (primarily recordings of vaudeville and musical acts) as a way of introducing sound shorts into the distribution and exhibition networks while they built up sound film production. Al Jolson, the star of *The Jazz Singer*, also made the greatest number of sound shorts. *The Jazz Singer* as an event, as film historians have noted, takes much of its meaning from an exhibition context in which recorded acts directly replaced the live musical and vaudeville entertainment which, in the mid-1920s, would have been a central feature of first-run theatre performances, accompanying the feature film.[21]

The exhibition of sound technology, through the Vitaphone and Movietone shorts of the late 1920s, forms a strong connection between early sound film and early silent film as, in Tom Gunning's model, 'a cinema of attractions', which directly solicited the attention of the spectator, through visual spectacle and the direct address to the audience.[22] These dimensions of the early 'cinema of attractions' re-emerged with the coming of sound and the cinematic display of its technical possibilities. The early sound-movie shorts returned, however, to film origins (newsreel documentaries (Fox) and vaudeville performances (Warner Bros.)), in order to show, as Michael Rogin argued, 'how they could improve on silent pictures. The silent versions of these shorts had exposed the limitations of the stage; the sound versions revealed the shortcomings of the silents'.[23]

In the film, Jakie Rabinowitz wishes to be a jazz singer, a desire which brings him into conflict with his orthodox Jewish father, a cantor in a synagogue on New York's Lower East Side. Returning home a success, and having changed his name to Jack Robin, he is thrown out of the house. When Jack is about to open on Broadway, he learns that his father is dying. He abandons the show, and replaces his father for the synagogue service on

Figure 20. Publicity Poster, *The Jazz Singer*.

the Day of Atonement, chanting as his father dies. He is, however, back on the Broadway stage the following night, and in the film's final scene is singing 'My Mammy' in blackface to his Jewish mother, his Gentile girlfriend watching in the wings.

The film, as Michael Rogin and others have noted, presents the death of silent cinema as a form of parricide—the killing of the father—that is also a freedom from a stifling immigrant tradition. In Rogin's account, 'Vitaphone carries the generational conflict in its three revolutionary scenes—the first, character-embedded, singing voice; the first lip-synchronized singing and first lines of speech; and the first dialogue.'[24] It is to his mother that Jack sings and speaks in the centre of the film, a music-with-speech sequence interrupted by the father's cry 'Stop', the last spoken (as opposed to sung) word in the film. As the critic Robert Sherwood wrote in 1927: 'There is one moment in *The Jazz Singer* that is fraught with tremendous significance. Al sits down at the piano and sings "Blue Sky [Skies]" to his mother... His father enters the room, realizes that his house is being profaned with jazz and shouts "Stop!". At this point the Vitaphone withdraws... Such is the moment when... I for one realized that the end of the silent drama is in sight.'[25] The father, representing a superseded tradition (now linked to silent film) will not survive the conversion to the new, now identified with the talkies. Yet Jack both acknowledges his 'race' and achieves his freedom in blackface. The film simultaneously embraces and repudiates American cinema's origins, as a popular form, in blackface minstrelsy, both recognizing and occluding the centrality of race to culture.

During the transition period, and in the pages of *Close Up*, there was intense discussion of 'Negro cinema', with white directors making 'all-black' movies, such as Paul Sloane's *Hearts in Dixie* and King Vidor's *Hallelujah!*, and a growing debate about black cinema, fuelled in part by the cultural energies of the Harlem Renaissance in the late 1920s and early 1930s. Robert Herring had campaigned vigorously for a 'Negro number' of *Close Up*: it appeared as the August 1929 issue, though without several of the articles from 'Negro writers' that Herring had hoped to commission, who had included Countee Cullen, W. R. Dubois and (James Weldon) Johnson.[26] There were, however, substantial articles from the writers Geraldyn Dismond and Elmer Anderson Carter (the editor of *Opportunity Magazine: A Journal of Negro Life*), as well as letters from the black playwright Paul Green and the Secretary of the National Association for the Advancement of Colored People, Walter White. Contributions from Macpherson, Potamkin, Herring, and Blakeston on 'Negro cinema' made up the rest of the issue.

Virtually all the articles took up the question of the 'Negro voice' in relation to the coming of sound. Carter quoted the *New Yorker* drama critic Robert Benchley—'It may be that the talking-movies must be participated in wholly by Negroes, but, if so, then so be it. In the Negro the sound picture has found its ideal protagonist'[27]—while Dismond concluded: 'And the talkie which is being despised in certain artistic circles is giving [the Negro movie actor] the great opportunity to prove his right to a place on the screen.'[28] For Macpherson: 'Talking films took films from us but they have given us a glimpse of him [the negro].'[29] *Close Up's* increasing concern with 'the talkies' thus became intertwined with the question of black cinema. While the black writers in the special issue explored sound film and its cultural possibilities, Macpherson and Potamkin, in particular, focused on the question of vision in ways that indicated the complex and ambivalent nature of their perceptions of silence and sound, vision and aurality, in relation to the black actor, the 'Negro' film and the visibility of racial identity. Discussing *The Emperor Jones*, for example, Potamkin argued that the play offers 'the ideal scenario for the film of sound and speech ... paralleling of sound and sight and their alternation'. The way would seem to have been paved for the sound film. Yet, Potamkin insisted, it was the black body (rather than the voice) that would ground the filmic (as opposed to the theatrical) experience, defined through its ability, unavailable to the more distancing stage, to portray 'the increasing sheen of sweat on the bare body'. 'The negro', he argued, 'is plastically interesting when he is most negroid ... Jones should not be mulatto or napoleonic, however psychological requirements demand it. He should be black so that the sweat may glisten the more and the skin be apprehended more keenly.'[30]

The hostility to sound cinema also became closely linked to racialized responses to film. For Dorothy Richardson, writing of *Hearts in Dixiee*—'We were about to see the crude, the newly-born'—described the performance of 'a soloist, the simulacrum of a tall sad gentleman who ... gave us, on behalf of the Negro race, a verbose paraphrase of Shylock's specification of the claims of the Jew to be considered human'.[31] She found 'the noble acceptable twin of the silent film' in the non-verbal aspects of (Negro) sound film—singing and the 'lush chorus of Negro-laughter', but described the speech as 'annihilating'.[32] Aldous Huxley's 1929 article, 'Silence is Golden: Being the Misanthropic Reflections of an English Novelist on First Hearing

a Picture Talk', gave an account of a film of a jazz-band performing and of
the experience of watching *The Jazz Singer.*

> A beneficent providence has dimmed my powers of sight, so that, at a
> distance of more than four or five yards, I am blissfully unaware of the
> full horror of the average human countenance. At the cinema, however,
> there is no escape. Magnified up to Brobdingnagian proportions, the human
> countenance smiles its six-foot smile, opens and closes its thirty-two inch
> eyes, registers soulfulness or grief, libido or whimsicality with every square
> centimetre of its several roods of pallid mooniness… The jazzers were
> forced upon me; I regarded them with a fascinated horror. It was the
> first time, I suddenly realized, that I had ever clearly *seen* a jazz band.
> The spectacle was positively terrifying. The performers belonged to two
> contrasted races. There were the dark and polished young Hebrews, whose
> souls were in those mournfully sagging, sea-sickishly undulating melodies of
> mother-love and nostalgia and yammering amorousness and clotted sensuality
> which have been the characteristically Jewish contributions to modern
> popular music. And there were the chubby young Nordics, with faces
> transformed by the strange plastic powers of the American environment into
> the likeness of very large uncooked muffins, or the unveiled posteriors of
> babes.[33]

Huxley thus responded to the visual dimensions, and in particular, the
physiognomic aspects, of the sound film's use of close-ups, his critique
recalling the strictures of critics on the grotesquely enlarged faces of
silent film. *The Jazz Singer* itself, with its 'sodden words' and 'greasy
sagging melody', could, for Huxley, only exacerbate his sense (undoubtedly
exaggerated for effect) of the 'degeneration' and 'putrefaction' of a culture
given over 'to the life-hating devil of a machine'. The intrusion of sound
was represented not only in terms of mechanization and falsification (the
actor in the sound film had now become, for Richardson, 'a simulacrum')
but was consistently figured through racial 'others'. The technology of
sound had produced a new and disturbing image of difference as the
'unnatural' and as a form of negation, with the black body reduced to
a yawning, gaping void of a mouth. Film may have 'found its tongue'
(the title of a 1929 study on the coming of sound), but sound was
perceived to emanate from the abysses, and the adenoids, of the human
organism.[34]

Rudolf Messel described the vitaphone in *This Film Business* in terms
similar to those of Huxley, with the image of a 'gaping black mouth',
whose monstrous magnification becomes inseparable from 'the distorting

Figure 21. 'Stop'. *The Jazz Singer* (Alan Crosland, US, 1927).

influence of song'. Unlike Huxley, however, he saw this as a stage to be overcome in the history of sound film, rather than as a further decline into degeneration. As Messel wrote of his viewing of a filmed jazz-band:

> There is no thrill about the trombone player in close-up, no sex appeal, and certainly no beauty. It is only the hitherto novel combination of sight and sound, and as soon as that novelty has worn off we shall be able to progress.
>
> But this is by no means the full tale of what the vitaphone is doing: it has brought the orchestra into close-up and has now turned its attentions to the singer—who likewise appears in close-up ... A singer singing in close-up! A gaping hole of a black mouth, distended cheeks, and staring eyes. Heaving chest and a face which, even in the normal, would not be called beautiful, is magnified twenty or thirty times, and, under the distorting influence of song, photographed and thrown on the screen. The soft light of the theatre or the opera house, and, above all, the distance of the seats from the stage, transforms the gaping black mouth into a small dot in a vast expanse ... But the vitaphone, with the gay impetuosity of youth cares for none of these things ... It is the story of the kinetoscope all over again.
>
> But this cannot last; it is merely an instance of history repeating itself. The enlarged singer and the orchestra in close-up will, in a few year's time, follow

the performing dogs and the sneezing mechanics into the lumber-room of discarded novelties—and the vitaphone, freed from its trappings, will be ready to begin.[35]

The silent film, it was frequently suggested in writings from the first part of the century, had become a mature art, and audiences had evolved as highly attuned interpreters of its particular, visual modes of representation, when the coming of sound end-stopped this history and threw the film back into a clumsy, stumbling, and this time noisy, infancy. In the first years of *Close Up*, Macpherson, and many of his contributors, expressed unqualified hostility, within and outside its pages, towards sound. As Ernest Betts wrote in 1928 of the coming of 'talking films': 'Not the slightest attention seems to have been paid to the fact that the introduction of speech is a violation of the film's proper function—namely, the imitation of life by action,—and that the film as drama depends largely for its eloquence and power on the gift of silence.'[36] One of the reasons for the journal's promotion of Soviet cinema was that its emphasis on montage rather than theatrical narrative was seen as a defense of 'pure cinema'—that is, silent cinema. Supporters of montage cinema feared that it would be destroyed by the introduction of sound, in part because an all too audible dialogue would drown out 'inner speech': that interiorised ground on which the filmic was said to be figured and which, it was argued, allowed the spectator to make connections between separate shots and to make meaningful the essentially metaphoric nature of visual representation.

In fact, Eisenstein, like many of his European contemporaries, feared at this stage the dominance of synchronized dialogue, rather than sound per se. As he stated in 1930:

I think that a 100 per cent talking film is nonsense and I believe that everyone agrees with me.

But sound film is much more interesting and the future belongs to it. Particularly Mickey Mouse films. The interesting thing about these films is that sound is not used as a naturalistic element.[37]

The 1928 'Statement on Sound', written by Eisenstein, Pudovkin, and Alexandrov and published by *Close Up* in October 1928, developed an argument for sound used in *counterpoint to the image*. Recent film historians and theorists have argued about the nature of this prescription, and the extent to which it was ever carried out in Soviet films. The avant-garde cinema of the 1920s in the USSR was, in any case, severely curtailed by the new political order and the Socialist Realist tenets of the 1930s.

It seems clear that the 1928 Manifesto was a strategic document, a way of bringing montage principles into the era of sound technology and, as Eisenstein wrote nearly twenty years later, an advance counter-response to the coming of the talkies. In *Nonindifferent Nature* (much of which was written in the 1940s) he constructed a three-stage model of cinema, in which the first stage, that of silent film, is continued by the third stage, audiovisual cinema, employing 'vertical montage'—that is, 'the cinematography of the organic fusion of sound and representation as commensurate and equivalent elements composing the film as a whole'. The middle stage was that of 'sound film'—'the least cinematographic, consisting mainly of "dialogue", this is that same median stage for which (in order to achieve the correct movement toward what was needed) I as well as Pudovkin and Alexandrov, recommended in *Manifesto*, 1928, a *strong explosion, divergence,* and *counterpoint opposition* of the elements of sound and the elements of representation'. There was a 'hidden sound' of silent films, Eisenstein argued, which was later developed in audio-visual montage; in this account, there was an essential continuity between silent and audiovisual cinema, with sound or dialogue film as the discounted middle stage or term.[38]

Thus it was rarely synchronized sound as such which was perceived to be the problem, but the failure to explore ways of incorporating sound as an element of montage. Increasingly, the Soviet directors became interested in the aesthetic possibilities opened up by sound, and other contributors to *Close Up*, including Macpherson, followed them. As Macpherson wrote in an editorial, in which he discussed Hitchcock's *Blackmail*: 'Sound must never be thought of alone. It must now be inseparably and forever sight-sound. The construction of sight-sound aesthetic must be taken in hand.'[39]

Blackmail

Blackmail, released in June 1929, was hailed as 'the first British all-talkie film'. It is of significant critical interest for at least two reasons: it was made in a silent and a sound version, thus allowing for a comparison of the two aesthetics, and it was the occasion for Hitchcock to experiment with the new technological and aesthetic opportunities of sound. Macpherson, writing very appreciatively of the film in his *Close Up* editorial, referred to Hitchcock's use of 'acoustical montage' and thus explicitly linked the director's sound techniques to those proposed in the Soviet 'Statement on Sound'.[40] The film was also discussed in a *Close Up* article written by Hugh Castle (included in the 'Negro' issue), in which he described the film as 'perhaps the most intelligent mixture of sound and silence we have yet seen'.[41]

For 'Mercurius', *Blackmail* employed the 'indirect relation of sound and vision', 'visual and aural image', that the column had been discussing, in more abstract terms, for some time.[42] 'Mercurius' focused on Hitchcock's discernment in the selectivity of sound, and noted that sound and vision had 'been blended into a single expressive medium'. Nonetheless, at this stage, the critic asserted that silent and sound films would continue to 'exist side by side, since each is appropriate to its peculiar purpose. The standards of criticism by which the one is judged must be modified or altered for an assessment of the other'. The perception was thus that silent and sound films would require different forms of critical judgement. This view was endorsed by Robert Herring, writing in the *London Mercury* in 1929, in a column which, on this occasion, he divided into 'the movies' and 'the talkies', as if silent and sound film were radically distinct media:

> All that is visible from *The Jazz Singer* is that the film itself has receded about twenty years in technique and mentality. When talkies develop, they will develop so much away from the screen as we now know it that they will need critics as specialised as that technique they will then have. I do not know if I propose to become one of those critics. The silent movies must stay, because they are not exhausted, because they give us so much that nothing else can, and because we are only just beginning to show what can be done with them. Films and talkies will proceed hand, in hand, as drama and opera proceed ...
>
> [T]he real uses are not solely in the reproduction of dialogue. This is really too dull. Sound and sight of the same thing is tautological, and they do not blend. We are aware of pictures doing a thing, and of sound doing a thing, and they are the same thing, but all it seems is very odd. Two things happen at once, but the only result is that half a thing is duplicated. Suppose, however, that the pictures did one thing and the sound another, but related, thing. THEN we should get *one* idea in our mind.[43]

Rapid developments in sound technology were already disproving this vision of silent's films continued and autonomous development, and to

some extent, and for some critics, the perceived divide became not
silent/sound but sound film/'talkies'. Herring's concept of specialized
film criticisms (distinct for the movies and the talkies) was not to be
put to the test, but it nonetheless raises significant questions about
the different nature of writing about the cinema in the silent and the
sound eras or, at least, about the perception that new forms of criticism, and new and different dispositions of the critic, would be required.
Blackmail played a crucial role in persuading critics that their film commentaries could, to borrow Macpherson's phrase, 'be inseparably and
forever sound-sight', attuned as much to the ear as to the eye. Sound,
Macpherson wrote in his discussion of *Blackmail*, is multiple and has
multiple effects:

> The million sounds you hear have a special timbre, rhythm, sound-sight
> significance. What a complicated, vast, never-ending science the investigation
> and psychology of sound is going to present to us, and some of us already are
> beginning to say that talkies are an art ... Till then, gee, honey, ah'm jes *crazy*
> 'bout yu, and I don't mind telling the world I miss the sound now in a silent
> film and *you'll* be with me.[44]

Blackmail was initially set up and shot as a silent film, but with the
industry's conversion to sound, it was decided (by the British International
Pictures management) to add some dialogue, in order to make the film a
'part-talkie'. At this stage in sound's development, it was still undecided as
to how much dialogue there should be in any given sound film. Hitchcock
had in fact planned for the arrival of sound, so that it was possible to
produce a 'full talkie' version, with the dialogue scenes more or less spread
throughout the picture. The 'talkie' was released first, followed two months
later by the silent version, released to those suburban and provincial cinemas
not yet converted to sound.

There was substantial interchange between the two versions. The silent
version withheld its first intertitle, and the sound version its first line of
dialogue for around seven minutes. Up to this point, both versions used the
same footage, documenting the arrest of the suspect whose case does not
connect with the main story.[45] Like other early British talkies, *Blackmail*, as
Tom Ryall notes, withheld dialogue until well into the film to highlight the
moment of its arrival, and, it would seem, to represent and dramatize the
coming of sound to cinema.[46] The presentation in the opening sequence
was derived from key silent film traditions, and German silent cinema in

Figure 22. Publicity poster, *Blackmail* (Alfred Hitchcock, GB, 1929).

particular, using expressionist framing and lighting. This opening sequence was 'a résumé of silent film techniques',[47] 'a virtuoso farewell to the obsolescent medium incorporated as a preface to a pioneering exploitation of the new one'.[48] Hitchcock himself stated, in a comment made to Francois Truffaut about the scene in the film in which Crewe, the painter, lures

Alice up to his apartment 'with the intention of seducing her and which winds up with his being killed':

> I did a funny thing in that scene, a sort of farewell to silent pictures. On the silent screen the villain was generally a man with a moustache. Well, my villain was clean-shaven, but an ironwork chandelier in his studio cast a shadow on his upper lip that suggested an absolutely fierce-looking moustache.[49]

At the start of the second reel of the film, the sound version acquires a dialogue track, but the transition is carefully managed, avoiding lip-synchronization until the point at which Alice meets the two policemen, one of them her boyfriend Frank, at the door.[50] The doorman whispers a joke to Alice, which the film viewer cannot hear, although her responsive laughter is fully audible: the point is thus reinforced that a talking film does not have to let the audience hear everything that is said. The film also ends with laughter, but by this time it has become associated with Alice's guilt, and it is accompanied by the image of the painted Jester whose mocking presence punctuates and silently comments on the action of the film.

Overhearing and off-screen conversations are central to the construction of *Blackmail*, as in the scene in which the sponger, who will become the blackmailer, lurks outside the house in which Crewe lives and to which he takes Alice. The conversation between Crewe and the sponger is seen but not heard, so that the audience is excluded from full aural access, and sound becomes a form of withholding, used in the service of suspense. Crewe's attempted seduction, or rape, ends with his murder, as Alice struggles with him, finally killing him with a knife. Hitchcock used a variety of expressionist techniques and sound effects to represent her nightmare walk, as she wanders the London streets after the killing. The dead Crewe's outstretched hand is intercut with an image of a traffic policeman's hand, while the neon sign of an animated cocktail shaker is transformed into a stabbing knife. The words of the advertisement, illuminated against the night sky, announce the 'White Purity' of Gordon's Gin, providing an ironic commentary on the issues of purity and corruption in the film's plot. The shot of the dead hand is reinserted twice again, cut with the outstretched hand of a sleeping tramp. There is a scream on soundtrack and a shot of the landlady discovering Crewe's dead body; the scream, which seems to begin with Alice seeing the tramp, in fact emanates from the landlady. The use of sound here chimes interestingly

Figure 23. Anna Ondra in *Blackmail*.

with the claim of the theorist Michel Chion that cinema 'is a machine
made in order to deliver a cry from the female voice ... the film functions,
like those big animating machines, full of gears and connecting rods, of
chains of actions and reactions, here a machine made in order to deliver
a cry'.[51]

The most striking sound sequence in the film, and the one that has received most critical attention, is the 'knife' scene after Alice has stabbed Crewe (which was first worked out and shot entirely in silent terms). Alice has returned home, and is having breakfast with her parents, while a neighbour stands at the dining-room door gossiping about the murder the previous night. The talk becomes increasingly a confusion of noises, with the one repeated word 'knife' insistently audible. Then Alice hears her father's voice asking 'Alice, please pass me the bread-knife', and she has to pick up a knife similar to the one used for the killing, while the others go on talking about the murder. The knife flies out of her hand, and at this point the shop-bell rings.

The 'knife' scene could be said to counterpoint sound and image, in ways promoted in the Eistenstein, Pudovkin, and Alexandrov 'Statement on Sound', with the woman's dialogue from off-screen space matched to a large close-up of Alice. The construction of the scene in terms of Alice's subjective perceptions—the distortion of the dialogue—is accompanied, as Ryall notes, by a subjectivizing in the camera placement and movement. The return of 'objectivity' (with all the participants in view) occurs at the point at which she is jolted out of her nightmare reverie.[52]

Writing in the 1940s, the British film-maker Anthony Asquith asserted that: 'Just as in silent films we saw that we could identify the eye of the audience with that of one of the characters in the film, so in sound films we can identify the ear, and not only the physical ear, but the emotional ear, with the ear of the audience.'[53] In the knife scene Hitchcock was attempting to produce a word close-up (the close-up on the word 'knife'), equivalent to a close-up of a face or an object. In the silent version, the open surface of the bread on the dining-room table acted as a screen for the hand's shadowplay. By contrast, the sound version uses an uncut loaf that provides no such surface or screen: one of the techniques Hitchcock used to translate the visual into the aural was to remove the shadows cast by the hand on the knife and the bread. As Balázs wrote: 'Sounds throw no shadows ... sounds cannot produce shapes in space.'[54]

The scene, and the film as a whole, was of central importance in opening up the ways for sound experiments at this critical stage of the transition from silent to sound film; many sequences in the film reveal a film-maker resistant to the new and hastily established 'rules' of dialogue shooting. Hitchcock played with the coming and going of sound throughout the film, in particular in the use of the phone-booth in Alice's father's shop.

Figure 24. Still from the breakfast scene in the silent version of *Blackmail*.

Figure 25. Still from the breakfast scene in the sound version of *Blackmail*.

The technology of the telephone (which, as I suggested in the discussion of Woolf's *The Years*, produced a complex interplay between the realms of sound and sight in film) played a crucial role in Hitchcock's cinema, as in that of Fritz Lang. The phone-booth in *Blackmail* was also a reference to, or joke about, the sound-proofed glass-fronted booths in which cameras were often immured in the first years of the talkies. The fluctuations in sound, with the opening and closing of the door, also produces a constant interplay between aural presence and absence in the film, suggesting a strong awareness of the spectator-auditor's subjective and psychical investment in the aural as well as the visual sphere of cinema.

Eisenstein/Joyce

In a 1930 article on Alfred Döblin's *Berlin Alexanderplatz*, Walter Benjamin celebrated the use of montage in Döblin's novel, tracing its lineage from Dadaism (which 'used montage to turn daily life into its ally') to film and then to Döblin's epic of Berlin life. The narrator of *Berlin Alexanderplatz* 'speaks from within Berlin. It is his megaphone'. Defining Döblin's method, with 'its waves of incident and reflection' which sweep over the reader and its 'spray of actual spoken speech', Benjamin wrote: 'this does not mean that we must operate with technical terms, such as *dialogue interieur,* or refer the reader to James Joyce. In reality, something quite different is at work. The stylistic principle governing this book is that of montage'. Yet two years earlier, Döblin, in a 1928 review of *Ulysses*, the novel which profoundly shaped the writing of *Berlin Alexanderplatz*, had defined Joyce's novel precisely in the terms of cinematic montage: 'The cinema has penetrated the sphere of literature; newspapers must become the most important, most broadly disseminated form of written testimony, everybody's daily bread. To the experiential image of a person today also belongs the streets, the scenes changing by the second, the signboards, automobile traffic.'[55] He referred to 'the so-called crisis of today's novel' as one resulting from the inability of most authors 'to close ranks with the age', as Joyce had done. Benjamin's article was entitled 'The Crisis of the Novel', and applied to *Berlin Alexanderplatz* everything that Döblin found in *Ulysses*, while at the same time disallowing it to Joyce, who he placed in the tradition of the interiorized novel and the 'roman pur' (which is actually 'pure interiority'), on a Flaubert—Gide—Joyce axis.[56] The split here was between 'montage' and interior narration.

Eisenstein's response to Joyce (which took up Benjamin's terms, but with different resonances) bears in complex and interesting ways on the question of word and image, sound and silence, in the discourse of cinema. His comments on Joyce, and on *Ulysses* in particular, are scattered throughout his writings, often linked with his thoughts on Dreiser's *An American Tragedy*: 'the concept of "inner monologue" in cinema was formulated, an idea that I had been carrying around for years before the advent of sound made its practical realisation possible.' Here silent film is placed on the side of exterior show, sound on the side of interiority: 'the fever of inner debates as opposed to the stony mask of the face.'[57] The contrast itself contrasts with much contemporary writing about silence and sound as (and as we have seen) divided along the axis of interiority and exteriority. Eisenstein's distinctions were on the one hand between silence and sound, and on the other between 'dialogue' and 'inner monologue'. 'Montage' and interiority are aligned, not opposed.

> Knitted brows, rolling eyes, spasmodic breathing, contorted frame, a stony face, convulsive movements of the hands—all this emotional apparatus was inadequate to express the subtleties of the internal conflict in all its phases.
>
> We had to photograph what was going on inside Clyde's mind.
>
> We had to demonstrate audibly and visibly, the feverish torrent of thoughts, interspersed with external action, with the boat, with the girl sitting opposite, with his own actions
>
> The form of the internal monologue was evolved.
>
> These montage sheets were wonderful.[58]

In writing that 'the film alone has as its command the means of presenting adequately the hurrying thoughts of an agitated man',[59] Eisenstein made an exception for *Ulysses*, which he was elsewhere to call the most significant event in the history of *cinema*.[60] Recalling their meeting, Eisenstein wrote: 'And not in vain, when I met Joyce in Paris, did we eagerly discuss my plans in regard to the inward film monologue, which has far wider possibilities than the literary monologue.'[61]

In an autobiographical fragment, written around 1946, Eisenstein fleshed out the details of the encounter. He repeated earlier arguments about Joyce's significance for cinema, and his closeness to his own project ('de-anecdotalization', 'physiologism of detail/In close-up ... Cinema again'[62]),

stating: 'And this "a–synctacicism" of his writing, uncovered in the foun-
dations of discours interieur, which each of us speaks in his or her way,
and which only Joyce's genius thought of making the very basis of literary
writing.'[63] But the fragment also centred on Joyce's blindness, the extent
of which Eisenstein only realized when, after an afternoon discussing his
(silent) films with Joyce in the expectation that he would soon be seeing
them, Joyce pawed the air in the brightly-lit hall in search of Eisenstein's
overcoat. 'And it was only then that I realized how poor was the eyesight,
at least for the external world, of this man, in truth almost blind, whose
external blindness undoubtedly determined that particular penetration of
interior vision which marks the description of intimate life in *Ulysses* and
in *Portrait of the Artist* with the aid of the astonishing method of the interior
monologue.'[64]

Eisenstein's autobiographical fragment intertwined Joyce's blindness,
inscriptions, and the voice. He commented on the near illegible dedication
Joyce transcribed with difficulty on the flyleaf of *Ulysses*. The date was
30 November 1929, the year of Hitchcock's *Blackmail*, and one in which
sound film was still hovering on the brink of public and critical acceptance.
Joyce then 'reads' him a passage from Work in Progress. But how is this
possible, Eisenstein's imagined reader will ask, when Joyce is near-blind? 'I
said "the voice of Joyce" and not "Joyce", is the reply.' Eisenstein was in
fact listening to a gramophone recording of a section of 'Work in Progress':

> And I followed the text he was reading on an immense page a metre
> high covered with giant lines of gigantic letters. These are the considerably
> enlarged images of the miniature pages of the 'little book' [Anna Livia
> Plurabelle], by means of which Joyce with great difficulty strengthened his
> memory to record the disc. The exaggerated size of the dimensions of the
> miniature page of the miniature book-fragment.
>
> How that fits the character. How that is located in the structure of the
> magnifying glass which he moves over the microscopic circumvolutions
> of the mysteries of literary writing. How this symbolically expresses his
> peregrinations along the turns and detours of the intimate movements of the
> emotions and the intimate structure of the interior discourse![65]

A crucial context for Eisentein's celebration of Joyce's microscopic
method was the Congress of Soviet Writers conference of August 1934,
in which the party chairman Karl Radek described Joyce's writing as 'a
heap of dung, teeming with worms and photographed by a motion-picture
camera through a microscope'.[66] Three months later, in November 1934,

Eisenstein gave a lecture to the State Institute of Cinematography in which he argued explicitly against Radek and for the importance of Joyce's microscopy: 'For the first time you have a literary texture shown in that way, that is, a literary discovery of almost the same scope as the possibility of seeing the human texture under a microscope under the first time.'[67]

The 'giant lines of gigantic letters' recall Iris Barry's invocation of the cry which breaks out in the subtitle on the screen as 'an illumination, an amplification, a secret disgorged'—the auditory imaginary of the silent cinema. The movement between the microscopic and the gigantic is framed in the terms of a cinematic aesthetic which struck commentators from the beginnings of film: 'We can pass in an instant from the infinitely great to the infinitely little', as H. G. Wells put it. At the same time, Eisenstein constructed his meeting with Joyce in the terms of the coming of sound. Eisenstein and Joyce spend their afternoon constructing a symbiosis between cinema and literature: 'he asked me not to fail to show him my films, being interested in the experiments in cinematographic language which I conduct on the screens just as I am excited by similar attempts in literature.'[68] The cinema they created discursively was doubly interiorised in that it occurred in the absence both of projection and of Joyce's sight, and was followed by a reading (of 'Work in Progress') in which they listened to Joyce's voice, not Joyce, in a form of voice-over, or Joyce-over, to their film.

Writers and the Sound Cinema

Graham Greene discussed, in more general terms, the issue, raised by 'Mercurius' in his article on *Blackmail*, of the necessary selectivity of sound. In his 1958 'Memories of a film critic', Greene recalled that in the 1920s he had been 'a passionate reader of *Close-Up*', and 'horrified by the arrival of "talkies" (it seemed the end of film as an art form)...Curiously enough it was a detective story with Chester Morris which converted me to the talkies—for the first time in that picture I was aware of *selected* sounds; until then every shoe had squeaked and every door handle had creaked'.[69] Greene's critical 'conversion to sound', the phrase identical to that used to describe the film institution's and apparatus's own technological transformations in the late 1920s and 1930s, has as its context the radical impact of sound film on writers. As Greene recalls, with the emergence of 'a selectivity of sound which promised to become as formal as the warning shadow', the writer 'was no longer merely the spectator or the critic of the screen. Suddenly the cinema needed him: pictures required words as well as images'.[70]

Greene's involvement with cinema was perhaps the most extensive of any twentieth-century British writer. As a film critic in the 1920s and 1930s he wrote weekly reviews of an exceptionally wide range of films. The cinema, Greene wrote in 1937, 'has got to appeal to millions; we have got to accept its popularity as a virtue, not turn away from it as a vice'.[71] He was a prolific script-writer, whose work in this field included the scripts for five of his own stories. In his novels he experimented with cinematic techniques, most fully, perhaps, in *Stamboul Train* and *It's a Battlefield*, which Greene described as 'intentionally based on film technique'. In interview, Greene stated:

> When I describe a scene, I capture it with the moving eye of the cine-camera rather than with the photographer's eye—which leaves it frozen. In this precise domain I think the cinema has influenced me ... I work with a camera, following my characters and their movements.[72]

It's a Battlefield (1934) is structured around the interplay of sound and sight, the visual and the aural, including the forms of coming and going of sound explored in *Blackmail*. Of a character in a newspaper office Greene states: 'Conder opened one of the sound-proof boxes on the top floor and closed the door. Immediately all the typewriters in the room became silent, the keys dropped as softly as feathers.'[73] Sound can now be withheld, as it was in Hitchcock's *Blackmail*, and, as in Woolf's *The Years*, rendered separately from sight. 'A man was talking,' Greene writes. 'He could hear the voice before he could see the face. The window above was open.' *It's a Battlefield* extended the cinematographic dimensions of Eliot's *The Waste Land* and Woolf's *Mrs Dalloway*, texts which it echoes very directly, intertwining references to Woolf's novel (while refusing its epiphanic moments) with allusions to the filmic 'city symphonies' of the 1920s, Ruttmann's *Berlin* in particular:

> In the height of a pale-blue sky an aeroplane twisted and turned, leaving a trail of smoke which hung about for a time, then blew away. It was as if the pilot had begun an advertisement and then remembered it was Sunday. Men stood in their doorways and read the *News of the World* and spat ... Dogs barked and bit each other in a zoological shop across the way, and very

faintly, because the traffic was almost stilled, it was possible to hear the lions in Regent's Park roaring to be fed.[74]

The cinema also played a central role in Greene's 1938 novel *Brighton Rock*. Bernard Bergonzi has noted the ways in which Greene represented both popular music and film in this text, deploying an image of 'the crooner' which he had earlier used in a 1936 review of a Western entitled *Rose of the Rancho*.[75] In the review, Greene had expressed his dislike of the romantic music in the film and of the actor John Bowles:

> I find Mr Bowles, his air of confident carnality, the lick of black shiny hair across the plump white waste of face, peculiarly unsympathetic; and never more so than in this film as he directs his lick, his large assured eyes, towards Miss Swarthout and croons:
>
> > I call you a gift from the angels
> > For I feel in my heart you're divine.[76]

Greene's image of 'the crooner', with its focus on the grotesque moonscape of the singer's face in close-up, recalls those of both Huxley and Messel, though, like a photographic negative, the contrast between black and white is here reversed (with Greene's imaging of white face and the 'lick' of black hair). The same figure appears twice in *Brighton Rock*, indicating the extent to which Greene's film criticism became continuous with his fiction writing. Greene first introduces 'the crooner' at a dance-hall to which the fiercely virginal Pinkie, the teenage gangland killer ('the Boy') who is the novel's anti-hero, has taken the guileless and hapless Rose: 'A spotlight picked out a patch of floor, a crooner in a dinner jacket, a microphone on a long black musical stand. He held it tenderly as if it were a woman, swinging it gently this way and that, wooing it with his lips while from the loudspeaker under the gallery his whisper reverberated hoarsely over the hall, like a dictator announcing victory, like the official news following a long censorship. "It gets you," the Boy said, "it gets you," surrendering himself to the huge brazen suggestion.'[77] As in Woolf's *The Years*, the seductions of popular culture and the mass media (most negatively described by F. R. Leavis in his essay 'Mass Civilization, Minority Culture' as 'involv[ing] surrender, under conditions of hypnotic receptivity, to the cheapest emotional appeals'[78]) had become inextricably linked to mass culture, propaganda, and the words of 1930s dictators.

The crooner's second appearance is in a film to which Pinkie has taken Rose after he has married her (a wife could not in law give evidence against her husband):

> Slumped grimly in the three and sixpenny seats, in the half-dark, he asked himself crudely and bitterly what it was she was hoping for: beside the screen an illuminated clock marked the hour. It was a romantic film: magnificent features, thighs shot with studied care, esoteric beds shaped like winged coracles. A man was killed, but that didn't matter. What mattered was the game. The two main characters made their stately progress towards the bed-sheets: 'I loved you that first time in Santa Monica ...' A song under a window, a girl in a nightdress and the clock beside the screen moving on. He whispered furiously, to Rose, 'Like cats.' ... The actor with a lick of black hair across a white waste of face said, 'You're mine. All mine.' He sang again under the restless stars in a wash of incredible moonshine, and suddenly, inexplicably, the Boy began to weep ... He said at last, 'Let's go. We'd better go.'
>
> It was quite dark now: the coloured lights were on all down the Hove front. They walked slowly past Snow's, past the Cosmopolitan. An aeroplane flying low burred out to sea, a red light vanishing. In one of the glass shelters an old man struck a match to light his pipe and showed a man and a girl cramped together in the corner. A wail of music came off the sea. They turned up through Norfolk Square towards Montpellier Road: a blonde with Garbo cheeks paused to powder on the steps up to the Norfolk bar. A bell tolled somewhere for someone dead and a gramophone in a basement played a hymn. 'Maybe,' the Boy said, 'after tonight we'll find someplace to go.'[79]

As in Messel's representations of Hollywood cinema, the film is represented—and appears to Pinkie—as a machine whose sole function is to get a man and a woman into bed together, but it is also one, Greene suggests, whose sounds and sentiments have the power to make hard men weep. Leaving the cinema is, moreover, not a departure from a filmic world: Greene the novelist and/as film scenarist constructs a different film to the one Pinkie and Rose have been watching, composed of the coloured lights of the town, the flaring match and the couple it illuminates, and the 'blonde with Garbo cheeks' whose self-image is continuous with the film-world. The sequence also brings into further play the relationship between sight and sound—the sounds of the burring aeroplane, the wailing music, the tolling bell—in a novel in which the disembodied words recorded in a gramophone booth—Pinkie's message of hate to Rose—become, at its close and after his death, 'the worst horror of all'.

The cinema was also at the heart of Christopher Isherwood's writing of the period. His autobiographical novel *Prater Violet* (the working-title of which had been 'O.K. for Sound'), published in 1945, recalls his experiences in London in the early 1930s as a scriptwriter to an Austrian émigré film-director whom he calls Friedrich Bergmann, the fictional counterpart of the Weimar director Berthold Viertel. Viertel's credits included the street-film *The Adventures of a Ten-Mark Note* (1926), a film (now lost) set in Berlin in the years of inflation. Its techniques appear, to an extent, to be echoed in Isherwood's *Goodbye to Berlin*, the first section of which opens with his image of the narrative 'I' as a camera-eye recording a Berlin street scene, in which streets and houses are imaged as 'shabby monumental safes crammed with the tarnished valuables and second-hand furniture of a bankrupt middle class':

> I am a camera with its shutter open, quite passive, recording, not thinking. Recording the man shaving at the window opposite and the woman in the kimono washing her hair. Some day, all this will have to be developed, carefully printed, fixed.[80]

Isherwood's 'camera eye' laid claim to the documentarists' 'objectivity'—he is the 'camera' and not the photographer or the projectionist. Samuel Hynes suggests, however, that beneath the documentary surface, 'it is a personal testament; like Eliot, Isherwood recorded himself in recording his city'.[81] In fact, the absoluteness of the division between objectivity and subjectivity was breaking down in the work of 1930s 'observers', Isherwood included, producing more complex and self-reflexive approaches, as in Charles Madge and Tom Harrisson's account of the 'new method' of Mass-Observation in 1937: 'Ideally, it is the observation by everyone of everyone, including themselves.'[82]

In 1933, Berthold Viertel asked Isherwood to script Gaumont-British's film *Little Friend*, a family drama in the script of which Isherwood was able to suggest themes of repressed and illicit sexuality. In Isherwood's fictionalized account of his experiences, the film becomes *Prater Violet*, an 'unashamedly corny musical set in pre-1914 Vienna'. The shift served Isherwood's purpose, as Keith Williams has argued, of pointing to his own complicity and, by extension, that of other writers on the Left, with the political evasions and trivializations of the mass media with which he and they had become increasingly involved.[83] As *Prater Violet* is filmed, news comes of the crushing of the Social Democrats and the socialists' strongholds in Vienna by Dollfuss's Christian Socialist Party; the film, Bergmann states angrily, 'lies and declares that the pretty Danube is blue, when the water is red with blood'.[84]

The function of *Prater Violet* as a text is to reveal both the political events occluded by the historical costume drama and the workings of the film apparatus which must be hidden from the film spectator's view. 'On rare occasions', Isherwood writes, 'the microphone itself manages to get into the shot, without anybody noticing it. There is something sinister about it, like Poe's Raven. It is always there, silently listening.'[85] The shadow in the text of this microphone-shadow (a warning shadow, indeed, to recall Graham Greene's words) which Bergmann calls 'the Original Sin of the Talking Pictures', conjures up some of the more dystopian images in 1930s fiction and film of media surveillance. It may also recall Woolf's 'shadow on the screen' and its bodying forth of 'fear itself'. In the *Prater Violet* of 1930s Europe, film and fear are differently but no less fully imbricated, as if a trajectory 'from *Caligari* to Hitler' were indeed being charted:

> 'Do you know what the film is?' Bergman cupped his hands, lovingly, as if around an exquisite flower: 'The film is an infernal machine. Once it is ignited and set in motion it revolves with an enormous dynamism. It cannot pause. It cannot apologize. It cannot retract anything. It cannot explain itself. It simply ripens to its inevitable explosion.'[86]

Christopher reframes Bergmann's statement to his admiring mother and brother, but in doing so turns the account into one of film *speed*: 'There's the film, and you have to look at it as the director wants you to look at it ... He's started something and he has to go through with it.'[87] Yet the echoes in Bergmann's original formulations of the last lines of W. H. Auden's *Spain*—'We are left alone with our day, and the time is short and History to the defeated / May say Alas but cannot help or pardon'—is a reminder that the issue was no longer that of the innovation of cinematic time and movement, as it was for cinema's first viewers, but of film as a way of grasping the force and inexorability of history in a state of emergency.

The use of sound was the topic to which Charles Davy returned in his essay, 'The Film Marches On', for his edited collection of 1938, *Footnotes to the Film*. His teasing away at the issue of non-synchronous sound a decade after Pudovkin's talk and the Soviet directors' 'Statement on Sound' indicates something of the significance of this issue for those writers on film whose interests were also in literary representation. While Davy remained concerned that 'a disturbingly artificial effect will be created if you show a person talking without allowing his words to be heard', he believed that the Soviet statements on sound of the late 1920s contained 'valuable germs of truth capable of a development which as yet they have scarcely at all received'. At the heart of these, he argued, lay the 'separation of sound and visual content…film sounds and images are separable, and…the cinema will continue with tied hands until the possibilities of this separation are fully explored. Probably the most fruitful starting-point would be to assume that the essential function of sound and dialogue is to act as a commentary on the visual action'.[88] In this model, then, sound is secondary to the visual image, while at the same time acting as a commentary upon it; we hear echoes here of the function of the film explainer himself, now become part of the cinematic apparatus.

Writing on the sound apparatus in *Cinema Quarterly*, in an article entitled 'The G.P.O. Gets Sound', the documentary film-maker and theorist John Grierson described the screening of *6.30 Collection* at a London cinema and the responses to the use of 'natural noises' and 'overheard comments, orders, calls and conversations [which] created a new and curious relationship between the audience and the screen. The distance was broken down in a certain intimate delight—I presume—at seeing strangers so near. Eavesdropping, who knows, may yet be one of the pillars of our art.'[89] Grierson also described a new project for a film about the Savings Bank, and his desire to give a sense of the 'human cares and fears and hopes and responsibilities' which are 'tucked away in a myriad numbered slips', and to which visual images alone could no do justice: 'over the mechanical visuals we propose to put a chorus indicating—it may be in short snatches of confession, or in plain objective record, or in *vers libres*—the human reference behind the slips of the filing cabinets':

> What development there might be if the often beautiful formulae of sound and word which occur in life were to be given dramatic value! … And why not, at last, use the poet? The *vers librists* were made for cinema. The monologues of Joyce, covering as they do the subjective aspects of human action, are as important for the sound film as the dialogue of the dramatist. The masked changes in O'Neill between the word spoken and the word thought represent the simplest properties of any considered sound film. Eisenstein has possibly put the monologue too high in his account, by isolating it from chorus. It is only one species of choral effect, limited somewhat to personal story. The larger possibilities lie beyond monologue,

I believe, in the poetry which, in the case of streets, say, will arrange some essential story in the mumble of windows, pub counters and passers-by.

For Grierson, then, the 'poetry' of speech lay in the contingency, collectivity, and naturalness of sound, and, for all his commitment to montage cinema, his account was less insistent than that of Davy on the importance of contrapuntal and non-synchronized sound. It chimes with that of Cavell, who argued that with talkies 'we get back the clumsiness of speech, the dumbness and duplicities and concealments of assertion... Then the task is to rediscover the poetry in speech... The poetry of synchronized speech arises from the fact that just that creature, in just those surroundings, is saying just that just now'.[90] This poetry would not, Cavell suggests, be 'the poetry of poetry', although 'it seemed at first as if it ought to have been'.

This was perhaps the idealized way in which the association between poetry and film—'the poetry of poetry'—had appeared to Paul Rotha, whose *Documentary Film* explored the question of sound in some detail. While his 1930 study, *The Film Till Now*, was, as I discussed in the previous chapter, implacably opposed to sound film, in *Documentary Film* Rotha argued that 'sound and speech... have quickened the whole pace of a film's progress':

> Sound and picture working together permit more than one idea to be expressed at the same time. Imagistic and atmospheric sound allow quite new flights of imagination to govern the cutting of picture.[91]

Despite some significant experiments with sound, Rotha argued, 'the story-film has, on the whole, failed to make more interesting use of sound than for the mere reproduction of written dialogue and the sound of objects as performed in front of the camera and microphone.' His concerns were, in this context, rather with the uses of sound in documentary film, including 'commentary or narration', especially that in which 'the speaker becomes a part of the film rather than the detached "Voice of God", and with "the poet as narrator"'.

Rotha's call, in *Documentary Film*, for the introduction of poetry in film speech was accompanied by a reference to W. H. Auden's 'stimulating' use of chorus in the GPO Film Unit documentary *Coal Face* (1935). The film was made soon after the Unit, under Grierson's leadership, had acquired a sound studio, and was directed by Alberto Cavalcanti with Stuart Legg and Basil Wright. Cavalcanti, brought over from Paris as an expert on the use of sound in film, was largely responsible for directing Auden and

Benjamin Britten's collaborative contribution, in which commentary and music were composed together:[92] the film critic Roger Manvell described the film as 'an oratorio of mining'.[93] It was shown at the Film Society in London on 27 October 1935, along with Arthur Elton and Edgar Anstey's GPO documentary film *Housing Problems* and Dziga Vertov's 1934 film *Three Songs of Lenin*, for which Auden produced verse subtitles. The Film Society programme notes described *Coal Face* as the presentation of 'a new experiment in sound':

> A very simple visual band was taken and an attempt made to build up, by use of natural sound, music and chorus, a film oratorio. The usual method of speaking commentary to a background of music was avoided and commentary and music were composed together. The effect is to incorporate commentary more clearly in the body of the film. To this foreground of sound were added a recitative chorus of male voices and a choir of male and female voices. The recitative chorus was used to fill out, by suggestion, the direct statement of the commentary. The choir was used to create atmosphere. The poem sung by the female voices on the return of the miners to the surface was written for the film by W. H. Auden:
>
>> O lurcher loving collier black as night,
>> Follow your love across the smokeless hill.
>> Your lamp is out and all your cages still.
>> Course for her heart and do not miss
>> And Kate fly not so fast
>> For Sunday soon is past,
>> And Monday comes when none may kiss.
>> Be marble to his soot and to his black be white.[94]

Coal Face was followed by *Night Mail* (1936), directed by Harry Watt, which was the most successful of the GPO films, and the only one to receive wider public circulation. The idea for a verse commentary came quite late in the film's conception, apparently brought about by Grierson's sense that the early film assemblage of the mail train's journey from London to Scotland failed to 'say anything about the people who're going to get the letters'.[95]

In 1924, Grierson had travelled to America on a Rockefeller Foundation scholarship, studying in Chicago at the School of Political Science. 'I came for Carl Sandburg', Grierson was to say of his travels to the Mid-West, and he indeed met Sandburg in Chicago: the writings of Sherwood Anderson and Vachel Lindsay were further attractions. Sandburg's documentary, montage 'public poem' *The People, Yes*, would be published in the mid-1930s. In earlier poems, too, Sandburg performed the role of the 'exemplary watcher':[96] 'I am the people—the mob—the crowd—the mass / I am the audience that witnesses history.' Sandburg's poetic form (in poems such as 'Skyscraper' and 'Chicago') was, Grierson would later write, equivalent to the 'symphonic form' in documentary film, 'concerned with the orchestration of movement'.[97]

Lines from Sandburg's poem 'The Sins of Kalamazoo' (in his 1920 collection *Smoke and Steel*) seem to have stayed with Grierson up to the making of *Night Mail*:

> Sweethearts there in Kalamazoo
> Go to the general window of the post office
> And speak their names and ask for letters
> And ask again, 'Are you sure there is nothing for me?
> I wish you'd look again—there must be a letter for me.'

Grierson's first choice for a poet to write the verse for *Night Mail* was apparently Hugh McDiarmid, but it seems his contribution was found unsuitable, and Auden chosen instead. As he composed the verse, it was cut to fit the visuals. Those passages timed to the beat of the train's wheels were spoken by Stuart Legg, while Grierson spoke the slower-paced passages, including the final lines:

> And none will hear the postman's knock
> Without a quickening of the heart,
> For who can bear to feel himself forgotten.

Graham Greene, in his review of *Night Mail* for *The Spectator*, praised the final sequences of the film, 'set to the simple visual verse of Mr Auden', and attacked C. A. Lejeune's review of the film for *The Observer*. Lejeune's comments, Greene wrote, 'show an amazing lack of cinema *ear*. To criticize Mr Auden's words (timed selective commentary made to match the images on the screen) as if they were lyric poetry is absurd'.[98] In a later review, he further commented on what he called the 'seeable' nature of Auden's verses in *Night Mail*.[99]

Sound, Paul Rotha asserted, 'more than doubles the expressive capacities of the silent film and puts the whole method of interpretation on a higher and more influential basis than before … The future of sound, linked up with dramatic, symphonic and poetic elements, will be inherent in the future of documentary. Sound will be inseparable from sight.[100] His words were a direct echo of Kenneth Macpherson's in *Close Up*, written some six years earlier. Documentary cinema rose to exceptional importance in the early 1930s, and became the focus for those theoretical film journals, including *Film Art* and *Cinema Quarterly*, which extended the work of *Close Up*. It also raised crucial questions about the role of 'voice' in film, with documentary voice-over, as explanatory, interpolated, or ironic commentary, becoming a new form of 'talking in the cinema'. In the silent years, film critics and commentators, as well as those writers incorporating the cinematic into their fictional or poetic texts, had a very particular relationship to a medium whose words, if they appeared at all, were inscribed, as intertitles or 'leaders', on the screen. The coming of sound brought into being new debates over the relationship between sound and visual image, and between the 'poetry of poetry' (associated by the novelist and dramatist Margaret Kennedy, for example, with film exhibition and spectatorship in the private sphere[101]) and the poetry of speech and the street. The words of writers, and the discourses of the cinema, its 'third machine', began to take on new significance and new valencies.

Abbreviations Used in Notes and Bibliography

Abel, *French Film Theory*	Richard Abel (ed.), *French Film Theory and Criticism*, vol. 1, *1907–1929* (Princeton: Princeton University Press, 1988)
BFFS	British Federation of Film Societies
BFI	British Film Institute
Cinema and Modernism	James Donald, Anne Friedberg, and Laura Marcus (eds.), *Close Up 1927–1933: Cinema and Modernism* (London: Cassell, 1998)
Davy, *Footnotes*	Charles Davy (ed.), *Footnotes to the Film* (London: Lovat Dickson, 1938)
Deleuze, *Cinema 1*	*Cinema 1: The Movement Image*, trans. Hugh Tomlinson and Barbara Hammerjam (Minneapolis: University of Minnesota Press, 1991)
Deleuze, *Cinema 2*	Gilles Deleuze, *Cinema 2: The Time Image*, trans. Hugh Tomlinson and Robert Galeta (London: The Athlone Press, 1989)
Dukore, *Bernard Shaw*	*Bernard Shaw on Cinema*, ed. Bernard F. Dukore (Carbondale, Ill.: Southern Illinois University Press, 1997)
Eisenstein, *Selected Works*	*Selected Works*: vol. 1: *Writings, 1922–1934*, ed. and trans. Richard Taylor (London: BFI Publishing and Bloomington: Indiana University Press, 1988); vol. 2: *Towards a Theory of Montage*, ed. Michael Glenny and Richard Taylor (London: BFI Publishing and Bloomington: Indiana University Press, 1991)
Film Society Programmes	*The Film Society Programmes 1925–1939* (New York: Arno Press, 1972)

Majumdar &   Majumdar, Robin, and Allen McLaurin (eds.),
  McLaurin   *Virginia Woolf: The Critical Heritage* (London:
                    Routledge and Kegan Paul, 1975)
Münsterberg on   *Hugo Münsterberg on Film: The Photoplay: A*
  Film   *Psychological Study and Other Writings*, ed. Allan
                    Langdale (London: Routledge, 2002)
Woolf, *Diary*   *The Diary of Virginia Woolf*, vol. 1: *1915–1919*, vol. 2:
                    1920–24, vol. 3: *1925–1930*, ed. Anne Olivier Bell
                    (Harmondsworth: Penguin, 1979, 1981, 1982)
Woolf, *Essays*   *The Essays of Virginia Woolf*, vol. 2: *1912–1918*;
                    vol. 4: *1925–1928*, ed. Andrew McNeillie (London:
                    Hogarth Press, 1987, 1994)
Woolf, *Letters*   *The Letters of Virginia Woolf*, ed. Nigel Nicolson and
                    Joanne Trautmann, 6 vols. (London: Hogarth Press,
                    1975–80)

Notes

EPIGRAPHS

1 Myron Lounsbury, *The Origins of American Film Criticism 1909–1939* (New York: Arno Press, 1973), 117, quoting Robert Sherwood, 'The Tenth Muse', *Life* 77 (1921), 142.
2 Jean Epstein, 'The Senses 1', in Abel, *French Film Theory*, 241.
3 Eric Walter White, *Parnassus to Let: An Essay about Rhythm in the Films* (London: Hogarth Press, 1928), 42.
4 Sergei Yutkevich and Sergei Eisenstein, 'The Eighth Art. On Expressionism, America and, of course, Chaplin' (1922); *Selected Works*, vol. 1, 29.
5 Margaret Kennedy, *The Mechanized Muse* (London: George Allen & Unwin, 1942), 52.
6 Herbert Read, 'Towards a Film Aesthetic', *Cinema Quarterly* 1: 1 (Autumn 1932), 8.
7 Hanns Sachs, 'The Mission of the Movies', *Life and Letters To-Day* 26 (July 1940), 268.

INTRODUCTION

1 Kenneth Macpherson, 'As Is', *Close Up* ii: 2 (February 1928), 8.
2 There is of course a vast literature on this topic. For bibliographies of material on film and literature, see Harris Ross, *Film as Literature, Literature as Film: An Introduction to and Bibliography of Film's Relationship to Literature* (Westport, Conn.: Greenwood Press, 1987) and Jeffrey Egan Welch, *Literature and Film: An Annotated Bibliography, 1909–1977* (New York: Garland Publishing, 1981). Recent studies of film and literature by authors including Susan McCabe, Michael North, David Trotter, and Keith Williams are listed in the Bibliography.
3 Arthur Symons, 'The Decadent Movement in Literature', *Harper's New Monthly Magazine* (November 1893), quoted in Holbrook Jackson, *The Eighteen Nineties: A Review of Art and Ideas at the Close of the Nineteenth Century* (London: Grant Richards, 1913).
4 Ricciotto Canudo, 'Reflections on the Seventh Art', trans. Claudia Gorbman, in Abel, *French Film Theory*, vol. 1, 296.

5 Jean Epstein, *La Poésie d'aujourd'hui un nouvel état d'intelligence: lettres de Blaise Cendrars* (Paris: Éditions de la Sirène, 1921), 179–80. (My translation.) Epstein was also enjoying a joke at the expense of the Italian Futurists, and their celebrations of speed and modernity. The slowness of Italian films, he argued, was a result of the slowness of thought of the Italian brain, which he contrasted with the rapidity of the French brain: 'What is still a mystery which interests and fools the Italian spectator is grasped in flight by us French and for fifteen seconds we don't know what to do with ourselves. It is for this and other reason that there will never be, for the élite, an international cinema' (174). Rimbaud, Epstein argued, produced 'one image a second' in his poetry, while Marinetti managed 'hardly one image for five seconds', and the same difference, in his view, pertained between French and Italian films.

6 See Canudo, 'Reflections on the Seventh Art', 296.

7 Henri Bergson, *The Creative Mind*, trans. Mabelle L. Andison (New York: Greenwood Press, 1968), 18.

8 Ibid. 21.

9 Significant discussions of Bergson, cinema and aesthetics include essays in Gregory Flaxman (ed.), *The Brain is the Screen: Deleuze and the Cinema* (Minneapolis: University of Minnesota Press, 2000); Paul Douglass, 'Bergson and Cinema: Friends or Foes', in John Mullarkey (ed.), *The New Bergson* (Manchester: Manchester University Press, 1999), 209–27; Mark Antliff, *Inventing Bergson: Cultural Politics and the Parisian Avant-Garde* (Princeton: Princeton University Press, 1993).

10 Huntly Carter, *The New Spirit in the Cinema* (London: Harold Shaylor, 1930). Carter also commended the 'sociological value' of animated films and cartoons: 'They exhibit man in society caught in a network of events undergoing or trying to escape the consequences. They are in fact a comment, a very witty instructive and biting comment on the absurdities of Man and other living things seen in the light of materialism. At the same time they are human, tragic and comic' (30). Carter, whose work was strongly influenced by turn of the century sociological thought, had also had early engagements with theosophy. In the early 1910s he wrote extensively on art and theatre for Orage's *The New Age*. His strong interest in Soviet theatre and film found expression in his 1924 study *The New Theatre and Cinema of Soviet Russia*, the greater part of which was given over to Carter's accounts of his travels through war-torn Europe and, in particular, Eastern Europe and the Soviet Union, in which he described how cinemas became the only refuge in devastated and war-torn communities. War-consciousness was indeed at the heart of Carter's study, the nodal point around which his conceptual models of progress and decline or 'regression' were gathered. In *The New Spirit in the Cinema*, Carter combined his 'utopian' representations of the role of cinema in modern culture with a great deal of research

into the reception of cinema, an internationalist perspective, and a strong awareness of the British film culture of the 1920s. He discussed *Close Up* magazine, the Film Society, the Avenue Pavilion ('House of Silent Shadow' cinema, committed to 'the silent film campaign' (387)) and the Federation of Workers' Film Societies, noting the ways in which they had become united (despite the divide between 'aesthetic' and political approaches to the cinema) in the war against censorship. See my Chs. 4 and 5 for discussion of these topics.

11 For an interesting discussion of this aspect of Epstein's film writings, see Mikhail Iampolski, 'The Logic of Illusion: Notes on the Genealogy of Intellectual Cinema', in Richard Allen and Malcolm Turvey (eds.), *Camera Obscura, Camera Lucida: Essays in Honour of Annette Michelson* (Amsterdam: Amsterdam University Press, 2003), 35–50.

12 For excellent discussion of these issues see Giuliana Bruno's *Atlas of Emotion: Journeys in Art, Architecture and Film* (London: Verso, 2002). Bruno discusses the 'haptic' dimensions of cinema, defining the term through its Greek etymology, 'able to come into contact with', and exploring both the ways in which the haptic—the sense of touch—'constitutes the reciprocal con*tact* between us and the environment, both housing and extending communicative interface'. But the haptic, she adds, 'is also related to kinesthesis, the ability of our bodies to sense their own movement in space' (6). Vivian Sobchack's *The Address of the Eye: A Phenomenology of Film Experience* (Princeton: Princeton University Press, 1992) provides an invaluable account of phenomenological approaches to cinema.

13 A. J. Walkley, *Pastiche and Prejudice* (London: Heinemann, 1921), 226.

14 William Morgan Hannon, 'The Photodrama: Its Place Among the Fine Arts' (1915), repr. in *Screen Monographs II* (New York: Arno Press and the *New York Times*, 1970), 32.

15 *The Journal of Gamaliel Bradford, 1883–1932*, ed. Van Wyck Brooks (Boston and New York: Houghton Mifflin, 1933), 233, 269.

16 See e.g. Noël Carroll, *Theorizing the Moving Image* (Cambridge: Cambridge University Press, 1996); Murray Smith, *Engaging Characters: Fiction, Emotion and the Cinema* (Oxford: Oxford University Press, 1995); Carl Plantinga and Greg M. Smith (eds.), *Passionate Views: Film, Cognition and Emotion* (Baltimore: Johns Hopkins University Press, 1999); Ed. S. Tan, *Emotion and the Structure of Narrative Film: Film as an Emotion Machine*, trans. Barbara Fasting (Mahwah, NJ: Lawrence Erlbaum Associates, 1996).

17 Hugo Münsterberg, *Hugo Münsterberg on Film: The Photoplay: A Psychological Study and Other Writings*, ed. Allan Langdale (London: Routledge, 2002), 99. The complex question of acting styles in early film is beyond the scope of my study. For excellent discussions of this topic, see Tom Gunning, *D. W. Griffith and the Origins of American Narrative Film* (Urbana: University of Illinois Press, 1991) and Roberta E. Pearson, *Eloquent Gestures: The*

Transformation of Performance Style in the Griffith Biograph Films (Berkeley and Los Angeles: University of California Press, 1992).

18 Münsterberg, *Hugo Münsterberg on film*, 99.

19 Robert Musil, 'Toward a New Aesthetic: Observations on a Dramaturgy of Film' (1925), in *Precision and Soul: Essays and Addresses*, ed. and trans. Burton Pike and David Luft (Chicago: Chicago University Press, 1990), 200.

20 Balázs, *Der Sichbare Mensch*, quoted by Musil in 'Toward a New Aesthetic', 197.

21 David Platt, 'The New Cinema', *Experimental Cinema* 1: 1 (February 1930), 1–2.

22 Michael North, *Camera Works: Photography and the Twentieth-Century Word* (Oxford: Oxford University Press, 2005), 4. The phrase 'Words of Light' was used by the 19th-cent. pioneer of photography, Frederick Fox Talbot.

23 Ibid. 11.

24 Ibid. 11–12.

25 Canudo, 'Reflections on the Seventh Art', 296.

26 Ibid. 297.

27 John Gould Fletcher, *The Crisis of the Film* (Seattle: University of Washington Book Store, 1929), 31.

28 Tom Conley, 'The Talkie: Early Cinematic Conversations', in S. I. Salamensky (ed.), *Talk, Talk, Talk: The Cultural Life of Everyday Conversation* (New York and London: Routledge, 2001), 83–93. Conley also makes the interesting suggestion in this article that there was a connection between intertitles and 'parentheses as they are found in modern literature, whose form refers to an inner speech or a third voice that is pondered in writing without being said to represent "speech itself"'.

29 Shelley Stamp, *Movie-Struck Girls: Women and Motion Picture Culture after the Nickolodeon* (Princeton: Princeton University Press, 2000), 27–8. See also Miriam Hansen's discussion in *Babel and Babylon: Spectatorship in American Silent Film* (Cambridge, Mass: Harvard University Press, 1991), 95.

30 Deleuze, *Cinema 1*, 241.

31 Walter S. Bloem, *The Soul of the Moving Picture*, trans. Allen W. Porterfield (New York: E. P. Dutton, 1924), 54.

32 John Rodker, 'The Theatre', *The Egoist* (2 November 1914), 414.

33 The Kino-Debatte is documented in a volume edited by Anton Kaes, *Kino-Debatte. Texte zum Verhältnis von Literatur und Film 1909–1929* (Tübingen: Niemeyer, 1978); see also a revised version in English of Kaes's 'Introduction' in Anton Kaes, 'The Debate about Cinema: Charting a Controversy (1909–29)', *New German Critique* 40 (Winter 1987), 7–33.

34 See Stuart Liebman, 'French Film Theory, 1910–1921', *Quarterly Review of Film Studies* 7 (Winter 1983), 1–23; Richard Abel (ed.), *French Film Theory and Criticism 1907–1939* 2 vols. (Princeton: Princeton University Press, 1988). There is a very full discussion of the context of film clubs and specialist

cinemas by Christophe Gauthier in *La Passion du cinéma. Cinéphiles, ciné-clubs et salles spécialisées à Paris de 1920 à 1929* (Paris: Association Française de Recherche sur l'Histoire du Cinéma, 1999).

35 See esp. Yuri Tsivian, *Early Cinema in Russia and its Cultural Reception*, trans. Alan Bodger, ed. Richard Taylor with introd. by Tom Gunning (University of Chicago Press, 1998).

36 Georg Lukács, 'Gedanken zu einer Aesthetik des Kinos' in Kaes, *Kino-Debatte*, 112–17. Quoted in Sabine Hake, *The Cinema's Third Machine: Writing on Film in Germany 1907–1933* (Lincoln, Neb., and London: University of Nebraska Press, 1993), 77.

37 Kaes, *Kino-Debatte*, 18–19.

38 Ibid. 82–3.

39 Hake, *The Cinema's Third Machine*, x.

40 Cited by Liebman, 'French Film Theory', 1.

41 Ibid. 4.

42 Hake, *The Cinema's Third Machine*, xi.

I. THE THINGS THAT MOVE: EARLY FILM AND LITERATURE

1 Erwin Panofsky, 'Style and Medium in the Motion Pictures', *Bulletin of the Department of Art and Archaeology* (1934). Repr. in Daniel Talbot (ed.), *Film: An Anthology* (Berkeley and Los Angeles: University of California Press, 1959), 15–32.

2 Alexander Bakshy, 'The New Art of the Moving Picture', *Theatre Arts Monthly* xi (April 1927), 280–1.

3 Arnold Hauser, *The Social History of Art*, vol. 4 (1962). (London: Routledge, reprinted 1989), 243.

4 Alexander Bakshy, 'The Road to Art in the Motion Picture', *Theatre Arts Monthly* xi (June 1927), 456.

5 Ian Christie, *The Last Machine: Early Cinema and the Birth of the Modern World* (London: British Film Institute, 1994), 27.

6 Sergei Eisenstein, 'Dickens, Griffiths and the Film Today', in *Film Form: Essays in Film Theory*, ed. and trans. Jay Leyda (New York: Harcourt, Brace, Jovanovich, 1949), 232–3.

7 Stephen Kern, *The Culture of Time and Space, 1880–1918* (Cambridge, Mass.: Harvard University Press, 1983), 1.

8 Ibid. 117.

9 Ibid. 40.

10 See Lynne Kirby, *Parallel Tracks: The Railroad and Silent Cinema* (Exeter: University of Exeter Press, 1997); Sara Danius, *The Senses of Modernism: Technology, Perception and Aesthetics* (Ithaca, NY, and London: Cornell University Press, 2002); Tim Armstrong, *Modernism: Technology and the Body: A Cultural Study* (Cambridge: Cambridge University Press, 1998); Leo Charney, *Empty*

Moments: Cinema, Modernity and Drift (Durham, NC, and London: Duke University Press, 1998).

11 Danius, *The Senses of Modernism*, 2.

12 W. K. L. Dickson and Antonia Dickson, *History of the Kinetograph, Kinetoscope and Kineto-Phonograph* (1895). (Facsimile edition, The Museum of Modern Art, New York, 2000), 14.

13 *The Times*, Thursday 18 October 1894, 4. Quoted in John Barnes, *The Beginnings of the Cinema in England 1894–1901:* (New York: Barnes and Noble, 1976), 14.

14 Dickson and Dickson, *History of the Kinetograph,* 12.

15 Ibid. 16–17.

16 Ibid. 24.

17 Ibid. 30.

18 For an excellent discussion of the trope of 'first contact' and the primitive in film theory, see Rachel O. Moore, *Savage Theory: Cinema as Modern Magic* (Durham, NC, and London: Duke University Press, 2000).

19 Dickson and Dickson, *History of the Kinetograph*, 33.

20 Ibid. 34.

21 Ibid. 37.

22 Ibid. 43.

23 Ibid. 50.

24 Ibid. 52.

25 Ibid. 51.

26 Ibid. 52.

27 Ibid. Preface.

28 Ibid. 50.

29 'In order', Metz wrote, 'to understand the film (at all), I must perceive the photographed object as absent, its photograph as present, and the presence of this absence as signifying'. Christian Metz, *The Imaginary Signifier: Psychoanalysis and Cinema*, trans. Celia Britton, Annwyl Williams, Ben Brewster and Alfred Guzzetti (Bloomington: Indiana University Press, 1982), 57.

30 Noël Burch, *Life to those Shadows*, trans. and ed. Ben Brewster (London: British Film Institute, 1990), 7. As Gaby Wood notes, 'Death seemed to be on everyone's mind, observing Edison's invention' (*Living Dolls: A Magical History of the Quest for Mechanical Life* (London: Faber and Faber, 2002), 123). Contemporary commentators noted the strange and startling powers of a machine that would be able to reproduce the voices of the dead. Edison himself explained to a *New York Post* reporter:

Your words are preserved in the tin foil, and will come back upon the application of the instrument years after you are dead in exactly the tone of voice you spoke them in ... This tongueless, toothless instrument, without larynx or pharynx, dumb, voiceless matter, nevertheless mimics your tones, speaks with your voice, utters your words, and centuries after you have crumbled into dust will repeat again and again, to a generation that could never know you, every idle thought, every fond fancy, every vain word that you choose to whisper against this thin iron diaphragm. (Quoted in Wood, *Living Dolls*, 123–4.)

31 William K. L. Dickson, *The Life and Inventions of Thomas Edison* (London: Chatto & Windus, 1894), 121.

32 Ibid. 128.

33 Wood, *Living Dolls*, 118.

34 Dickson, *The Life and Inventions of Thomas Edison,* 302–3

35 Ibid. 312.

36 See Charles Musser, ~~*Thomas A. Edison and his Kinetographic Motion Pictures*~~ (New Brunswick, NJ: Rutgers University Press, 1995), 20.

37 Raymond Bellour, 'Ideal Hadaly', *Camera Obscura* 15 (Fall 1986), 126.

38 Villiers de l'Isle-Adam, *Tomorrow's Eve*, trans. Robert Martin Adams (Chicago: University of Illinois Press, 1982), 9–10.

39 Francette Pacteau, *The Symptom of Beauty* (London: Reaktion Books, 1994), 47.

40 de l'Isle-Adam, *Tomorrow's Eve*, 131.

41 Ibid. 190.

42 Annette Michelson, 'On the Eve of the Future: The Reasonable Facsimile and the Philosophical Toy', *October* 29 (Summer 1984), 3–21.

43 Bellour, 'Ideal Hadaly', 130–1.

44 Quoted in Felicia Miller Frank, *The Mechanical Song: Women, Voice and the Artificial in Nineteenth-Century French Narrative* (Stanford: California University Press, 1995), 148.

45 Ibid. 163.

46 de l'Isle-Adam, *Tomorrow's Eve*, 132.

47 Iwan Bloch, *The Sexual Life of Our Time: In its Relation to Modern Civilization*, trans. from the 6th German edn. by M. Eden Paul (London: Rebman Ltd., 1908) 647.

48 Ibid. 648.

49 Madame B., *La Femme Endormie*, (Paris 1899). Reference in Bloch, *The Sexual Life of our Time*, 648.

50 de l'Isle-Adam, *Tomorrow's Eve*, 117.

51 Ibid. 118.

52 Ibid. 122.

53 Huntly Carter, *The New Spirit in the Cinema* (London: Harold Shaylor, 1930), 138.

54 Peter Wollen, 'Modern Times: Cinema/Americanism/The Robot', in (id.), *Raiding the Icebox: Reflections on Twentieth-Century Culture* (Bloomington and Indianapolis: Indiana University Press, 1993), 35–71.

55 Thomas Mann, *The Magic Mountain*, trans. H. T. Lowe-Porter (Harmondsworth: Penguin, 1960), 316–18

56 George Bernard Shaw, 'Shaw Finds Talkies Opening New Field', *New York Times*, 19 May 1929, in Dukore, *Bernard Shaw*, 59.

57 H.D., 'The Mask and the Movietone', *Close Up* 1: 5 (November 1927), 19–21; *Cinema and Modernism*, 114–15.

58 Ibid. 23.

59 Jean Epstein, 'On Certain Characteristics of Photogénie' (1924); Abel, *French Film Theory*, vol. 1, 317.

60 Carter, *The New Spirit in the Cinema*, 176.

61 Rudolf Messel, *This Film Business* (London: Ernest Benn, 1928).

62 Huntly Carter, 'Art and Drama: The Impersonal Note of England, Russia and Japan', *The Egoist* 1: 24 (15 December 1914), 462.

63 Huntly Carter, 'Spontaneics', *The Egoist* 3: 2 (1 Feb. 1916), 29.

64 Edward Gordon Craig, 'The Actor and the Über-Marionette', *The Mask* 1: 2 (April 1908), 5.

65 Ibid. 13.

66 Ibid. 8.

67 Ibid. 14–15.

68 H.D., 'The Mask and the Movietone', 23; *Cinema and Modernism*, 116.

69 John Rodker, 'The Theatre', *The Egoist* 1: 21 (2 November 1914), 414.

70 Ibid. 414.

71 H.D., 'The Mask and the Movietone', 30; *Cinema and Modernism*, 119.

72 See Laura Mulvey, *Death 24 [Times] a Second: Stillness and the Moving Image* (London: Reaktion Books, 2006), 51. As Stephen Heath notes, Freud, in refusing to collaborate on the making of the 'Freudian film', G. W. Pabst's *Secrets of a Soul*, with its accompanying pamphlet written by Hanns Sachs (discussed in Ch. 5), said: 'There can be no avoiding the film, any more than one can avoid the fashion for bobbed hair [*Bubikopf*]; I however will not let my hair be cut and will personally have nothing to do with this film' (Heath, 'Cinema and Psychoanalysis: Parallel Histories', in Janet Bergstrom (ed.), *Endless Night: Cinema and Psychoanalysis, Parallel Histories* (Los Angeles: University of California Press, 1999), 27). See also Laura Marcus, 'Dreaming and Cinematographic Consciousness', *Psychoanalysis and History* 3: 1 (2001), 51–68, for discussion of Freud's relationship to the cinema.

73 Portia Dadley, 'The Garden of Edison: Invention and the American Imagination', in Francis Spufford and Jenny Uglow (eds.), *Cultural Babbage: Technology, Time and Invention* (London: Faber and Faber, 1996), 95.

74 Wood, *Living Dolls*, 125.

75 Abel Gance, 'A Sixth Art' (1912), in Abel, *French Film Theory*, vol. 1, 67.

76 *The Times*, 10 January 1914.

77 Edison's Kinetoscope appeared in prototype form in 1892, followed by the Mutascope, a peepshow device patented in 1894, which was adapted with a mirror device to become the Biograph of 1895. Edison's Vitascope, a variant on the Kinetoscope (and initially named the Phantoscope) was first exhibited in 1896. The Lumières' Cinématographe was patented in 1895.

78 H. G. Wells, *The King who was a King: The Book of a Film* (London: Benn, 1929), 10.

79 Raymond Fielding, 'Hale's Tours: Ultrarealism in the Pre-1910 Motion Picture', in John F. Fell (ed.), *Film Before Griffith* (Berkeley and Los Angeles, University of California Press, 1983), 117. Fielding finds no evidence that Hale knew of the Wells/Paul design.

80 *The English Mechanic*, 21 February 1896 (quoted in Barnes, *The Beginnings of the Cinema in England,* 41.) Soon after the English debut of the Kinetoscope on 17 October 1894, Robert Paul was commissioned to make replicas. The drawback was the lack of films: those that were available were restricted to the users of original Edison machines. Paul had no alternative but to make his own. He invented a camera and by the end of March 1895 had succeeded in making films, having joined forces with Birt Acres, a professional photographer (See Barnes, *The Beginnings of the Cinema in England*, 8). The Cinématographe-Lumière was the first successful film projector to appear: it also served as camera and printer. Its first public screen performance was an immediate success: the days of the Kinetoscope peepshow device were numbered. Paul set about inventing a projection apparatus of his own:

The Cinématographe-Lumière was brought to London, and when it began its triumphant run at the famous Empire Theatre of Varieties in Leicester Square, all London flocked to see the so-called living photographs. The other London music-halls, not to be outdone, immediate clamoured for the new invention. The Lumière machine was exclusive to the Empire Theatre and the only other apparatus available in England at that time was Paul's, which had just been put into commercial production. For several months, Paul had almost a monopoly in London and was very soon penetrating the provinces as well as the foreign market. So successful an enterprise could not long remain the preserve of one man, and others started to enter the field. A steady trickle of new machines and films from home and abroad began to appear, so that before the year ended the cinema had established a temporary home in practically every major music-hall in the country' (Barnes, *The Beginnings of the Cinema in England*, 9).

81 *British Journal of Photography*, 28 Feb. 1895 (quoted in Barnes, *The Beginnings of the Cinema in England*, 42).

82 Terry Ramsaye, *A Million and One Nights* (1926; London: Frank Cass, 1954), 154–5.

83 Quoted in Barnes, *The Beginnings of the Cinema in England*, 38–9.

84 Quoted in Barnes, *The Beginnings of the Cinema in England,* 37.

85 H. G. Wells, *The Time Machine* (1895) (London: Everyman, 1995), 16.

86 Ibid. 77.

87 Ramsaye, *A Million and One Nights*, 154.

88 H. G. Wells, *The Invisible Man* (1897) (London: Everyman, 1995), 81.

89 Ibid. 27.

90 *The Invisible Fluid* (1908), American Mutoscope and Biograph Company, directed by Wallace McCutcheon, cinematography by G. W. ('Billy') Bitzer; *L'Homme invisible* (1909), Pathé, France, directed by Ferdinand Zecca.

91 Ivor Montagu, *Film World* (Harmondsworth: Penguin, 1964), 84.

92 R. E. C. Swann, 'Art and the Cinema: A Chance for the British Producer', *The Nineteenth Century and After*, 100 (August 1926), 223.

93 Ibid. 227.

94 Yuri Tsivian, *Early Cinema in Russia and its Cultural Reception,* trans. Alan Bodger (Chicago and London: University of Chicago Press, 1998), 202.

95 H. G. Wells, *The Complete Short Stories of H. G. Wells*, ed. John Hammond (London: J. M. Dent, 1998), 488.

96 Ibid. 489.

97 Ibid. 493–4.

98 Ibid. 495.

99 Walter Benjamin, 'The Work of Art in the Age of Mechanical Reproduction', *Illuminations: Essays and Reflections*, ed. Hannah Arendt, trans. Harry Zohn (New York: Shocken Books, 1969) 237.

100 Annette Michelson, 'Dr Crase and Mr Clair', *October* 11 (1979), 30–53.

101 R. D. Charques, 'The Technique of the Films', *Fortnightly Review* 124 (July–December 1928). See also the anonymous review from 1914:

This world of ours is a moving world and no static art can adequately represent it. There is no such thing as still life, or still anything else in the whole universe. Everywhere and always there is motion and only motion and any representation of reality at rest is a barefaced humbug … Bergson has shown us what a paralyzing influence static conceptions of reality have had upon the history of philosophy and how futile have been all attempts to represent movement by rest. The scientist of today thinks in terms of motion. All modern thought is assuming kinetic forms and we are coming to see the absurdity of the old ideas of immutability and immobility. A similar revolution is impending in art … What will our posterity, familiar with moving portraiture, think of our admiration of Mona Lisa's smile, frozen on her lips for four centuries? A smile is essentially a fleeting thing, an evanescent expression. A fixed smile is not a smile at all but a grimace. It is only by the most violent effort of the imagination that we can ignore the inherent artificiality and limitations of paintings sufficiently to get from them the illusion of reality (*The Independent*, 6 April 1914. Repr. in Lewis Jacobs, *Introduction to the Art of the Movies*, 44–7, at 45).

102 H. G. Wells, *Experiment in Autobiography: Discoveries and Conclusions of a Very Ordinary Brain (Since 1866)*, vol. 2 (London: Victor Gollancz and The Cresset Press, 1934), 515.

103 Wells, 'The Crystal Egg', in *The Complete Short Stories of H. G. Wells*, 273.

104 Such as the two Greeks, Georgiades and Trajedes, who, arriving in London with their Kinetoscopes purchased in New York, visited Robert Paul with the request that he duplicate them. It was at this time, the story runs, that Paul realized that Edison had failed to patent his machine in England, leaving the field open. See Ramsaye, *A Million and One Nights*, 147–8.

105 H. G. Wells, *Anticipations: Of the Reaction of Mechanical and Scientific Progress Upon Human Life and Thought* (London: Chapman and Hall, 1902), 4.

106 Ibid. 11.

107 Ibid. 29.

108 H. G. Wells, *When the Sleeper Wakes* (1899) (London: Phoenix, 2004), 35–6.

109 Ibid. 30.

110 Ibid. 48–9.

111 Ibid. 49.

112 Ibid. 50.

113 Ibid. 51.

114 Ibid. 49.

115 Ibid. 102.

116 Ibid. 106.

117 Paul, patent application, cited in Barnes, *The Beginnings of the Cinema*, 39.

118 Charlie Chaplin, 'Foreword', in L'Estrange Fawcett, *Films: Facts and Forecasts* (London: Geoffrey Bles, 1927), v–vi.

119 Paul Rotha, *The Film Till Now: A Survey of the Cinema* (London: Jonathan Cape, 1930), 57.

120 Wells, *The King who was a King: The Book of a Film*, 21.

121 See also Kenneth Macpherson, 'The Novelist who was a Scenarist', *Close Up* IV: 3 (March 1929), 79.

122 Ibid. 8.

123 Ibid. 10.

124 Ibid. 13.

125 Ibid. 14–15.

126 Ibid. 15–17.

127 Ibid. 18.

128 Carter, *The New Spirit of the Cinema*, 190.

129 Dorothy Richardson, 'Continuous Performance: Almost Persuaded', *Close Up* IV: 6 (June 1929), 35; *Cinema and Modernism*, 192.

130 Wells, *The King who was a King*, 227.

131 Ibid. 70.

132 Macpherson, 'The Novelist who was a Scenarist', 79–80.

133 Robert Herring, 'Storm over London', *Close Up* iv: 3 (March 1929), 43.

134 In 1928 H. G. Wells scripted three short comic films, *Bluebottles, The Tonic,* and *Daydreams*. These were directed by Ivor Montagu, with Frank Wells as Art Director: actors included Elsa Lanchester and Charles Laughton.

135 Wells, *When the Sleeper Wakes*, 4.

136 H. G. Wells, 'The Silliest Film: Will Machinery Make Robots of Men?', in *The Way the World is Going* (London: Ernest Benn, 1928), 179–189.

137 Ibid. 184.

138 Ibid. 187.

139 Ibid. 186.

140 Ibid. 180.

141 Margaret Atwood, 'Introduction' to H. G. Wells, *The Island of Dr Moreau* (London: Penguin, 2005), xxiii.

142 H. G. Wells, *Things to Come* (London: The Cresset Press, 1935), 13. Rudolf Messel's *This Film Business* (1928) has a chapter on '*Metropolis* or Film Criticism', in which Messel examines H. G. Wells' highly critical review of Lang's film in the context of a discussion of the state of film criticism at the time at which he writes. The film, he argues, 'is an entirely new form of artistic expression, demanding therefore an entirely novel form of artistic criticism':

The film art is young, and film criticism is even younger: so young in fact that there are as yet no supposedly absolute standards to which other films can be related. Everyone has his own views about the cinema ... With the solitary exception of 'Greed' there is no common ground on which film critics can meet, and from which they can sally forth on their excursions of destruction. The situation is remarkable; it is unique ... In truth a Babel ... In another twenty years things may be different (they are sure to be different) but for the moment they are just as I have sketched them, an irrational and distracting welter of conflicting opinions. (148–9)

Messel used Wells's review of *Metropolis* to show 'that of which the art of the film does not consist'; Wells, he argued, criticised the film 'from the standpoint of an economist and a politician', failing to see 'that a film is a film'. For Messel, the purpose of a film 'is firstly to express an idea in terms of motion, light and shade, and secondly to express the said idea beautifully'. The subject may have been futile, but its technique was perfect:

There was nothing of the photographed play about 'Metropolis'; from beginning to end it was a film. One lovely picture after another ... And furthermore, it did things which only the film could do—the creation of the mechanical woman, the building of Babel, and the shots of Metropolis itself. All these were beautiful, and not one of them could have been achieved through any medium other than that of the cinema...

Just as transcendental questions admit only of transcendental answers, so things cinematographic must be treated in a way that is cinematographic. In other words, cinematographic questions admit only of cinematographic answers. (153)

143 Messel, *This Film Business*, 14.
144 Ibid. 14–15.
145 In the event, Léger's drawings were not used and Le Corbusier proved unimpressed by Wells's versions of the future. The sequences designed by Moholy-Nagy, with their interiors influenced by Russian Constructivist sculpture, were filmed, but substantially cut in the final version of the film, so that only ninety or so seconds survive, intercut with other designs and found footage of machines. See Frayling, *Things to Come* (London: BFI, 1995), 72–3.
146 Wells, *Things to Come*, 9.
147 J. P. Delotte, *A Distant Technology: Science Fiction Film and the Machine Age* (Hanover and London: Wesleyan University Press, 1999), 150–61.
148 Wells, *The King who was a King*, 15.
149 Delotte, *A Distant Technology*, 158.
150 G. K. Chesterton, 'On the Movies', from *Generally Speaking* (London: Watt and Son, 1929). Repr. in Harry Geduld (ed.), *Authors on Film* (Bloomington and Indiana: Indiana University Press, 1972), 111–12.
151 C. A. Lejeune, 'The Week on the Screen', *Manchester Guardian*, 14 November 1925.
152 Kirby, *Parallel Tracks*, 9.
153 Ibid. 2.
154 Ibid. 7.
155 *La Vie en chemin de fer* (1861), quoted in Wolfgang Schivelbusch, *The Railway Journey: Trains and Travel in the Nineteenth Century*, trans. Anselm Hollo (Oxford: Blackwell, 1980), 63.
156 Stephen Bottomore, 'The Panicking Audience? Early Cinema and the "Train Effect"', *Historical Journal of Film, Radio and Television* 19: 2 (1999), 177.
157 Christian Metz, *The Imaginary Signifier: Psychoanalysis and Cinema*, trans. Celia Britton, Annwyl Williams, Ben Brewster, and Alfred Guzzetti (Bloomington: Indiana University Press, 1982), 73.
158 Walter Benjamin, 'Kriminalromane, auf Reisen' ['Detective Novels, on Journeys'] (1930). In *Gesammelte Schriften*, Werkausgabe, vol. 10, 381–2. See Laura Marcus, 'Oedipus Express: Trains, Trauma and Detective Fiction', in Warren Chernaik, Martin Swales and Robert Vilain (eds.), *The Art of Detective Fiction* (London: Macmillan, 2000), 201–21. Repr. in *New Formations* 41 (Autumn 2000), 173–88.
159 Rudolf Arnheim, *Film* (London: Faber and Faber, 1933), 72.

160 Bottomore, 'The Panicking Audience', 202.

161 Tom Gunning, 'The Cinema of Attractions: Early Film, its Spectator and the Avant-Garde', in Thomas Elsaesser (ed.), *Early Film: Space, Frame, Narrative* (London: British Film Institute, 1990), 58.

162 Tom Gunning, 'An Aesthetic of Astonishment: Early Film and the (In)credulous Spectator', repr. in Leo Braudy and Marshall Cohen (eds.), *Film Theory and Criticism: Introductory Readings* (Oxford: Oxford University Press, 1999), 820–25.

163 Maxim Gorki, 'The Kingdom of Shadows', in Gilbert Adair (ed.), *Movies*, (Harmondsworth: Penguin, 1999), 10–11.

164 Gunning, 'An Aesthetics of Astonishments', 822–3.

165 Tsivian, *Early Cinema in Russia*, 6.

166 Gorki, 'The Kingdom of Shadows', 11.

167 Ibid, 11.

168 Scott McQuire, *Visions of Modernity: Representation, Memory, Time and Space in the Age of the Camera* (London: Sage, 1998) 68.

169 Gorki, 'The Kingdom of Shadows', 12.

170 Ibid. 12–13.

171 Erwin Panofsky extended this motif in his 1934 essay 'Style and Medium in the Motion Pictures': 'While it is true that commercial art is always in danger of ending up as a prostitute, it is equally true that noncommercial art is always in danger of ending up as an old maid' (30).

172 Gorki, 'The Kingdom of Shadows', 13.

173 Tsivian, *Early Cinema in Russia*, 5.

174 Sigmund Freud, 'The Uncanny', in *The Standard Edition of the Complete Psychological Works of Sigmund Freud,* vol. 17: *1917–1919* (London: Hogarth Press, 1955), 244.

175 Deleuze, *Cinema 2*, 263.

176 O. Winter, *New Review* (February 1896), quoted in Colin Harding and Simon Popple, *In the Kingdom of Shadows: A Companion to Early Cinema* (London: Cygnus Arts, 1996), 13.

177 Ibid. 14.

178 Ibid.

179 G. R. Baker, in *The British Journal of Photography* 43, Supplement (6 March 1896), 17–18. Quoted in Barnes, *The Beginnings of the Cinema*, 87.

180 Anna de Bremont, 'Living Photography', review of Lumière-Cinématographe in *St Paul's Magazine* (20 February 1896), 436. Quoted in Barnes, *The Beginnings of the Cinema*, 85.

181 'The Prince's Derby: Shown by Lightning Photograph', *The Strand Magazine* XII (July–December 1896).

182 In a further early response, the critic appears to divide the Lumières' film into a number of separate scenes: 'In one instance', he writes, 'a busy railway station is shown, a train is seen approaching, it draws up at the platform, the

carriage doors open, the passengers alight and talk to one another, and the guard steps forward and signals the engine-driver to proceed on his journey' ('The Month: Science and Art', *Chamber's Journal* (25 April 1896). Quoted in Harding and Popple, *In the Kingdom of Shadows*, 9).

183 Films of breaking waves were also frequently discussed in relation to their effects on the spectator. During Paul's Animatographe tour of 1896, the most popular picture was *A Sea Cave Near Lisbon*, which was still listed in the Robert Paul catalogues in 1903. The catologue for June read: 'This famous film has never been equalled as a portrayal of fine wave effects. It is taken from the interior of a great cave, looking over the ocean. Big waves break into the mouth of the cave and rush towards the spectator with the finest and most enthralling effect' (quoted in Barnes, *The Beginnings of the Cinema*, 114). *Rough Sea at Dover* was exhibited at Coster and Bial's Music Hall, New York, when the Vitascope received its Broadway debut on 23 April, and was described by Thomas Armat (the designer of the Edison-made machine) in these terms: 'This scene was of storm-tossed waves breaking over a pier on the beach at Dover, England—a scene that was totally unlike anything an audience had ever before seen in a theater. When it was thrown upon the screen the house went wild; there were calls from all over the house for "Edison", "Edison", "speech", "speech".' (*Journal of the Society of Motion Picture Engineers* 24 (March 1935). Repr. in Raymond Fielding, *A Technical History of Motion Pictures and Television* (Berkeley and Los Angeles: University of California Press, 1967), 17).

184 Quoted in Barnes, *The Beginnings of the Cinema*, 84–5.

185 *Punch* (6 August 1898), quoted in Harding and Popple, *In the Kingdom of Shadows*, 10.

186 See Tsivian's discussion of Gorki's short story 'Revenge', 'the spiritual drama of the prostitute who takes a new look at her life as a result of the impression the Lumières' picture made on her' (Tsivian, *Early Cinema in Russia*, 36–7).

187 Rudyard Kipling, 'Mrs Bathurst', in *Short Stories: Volume 1* (Harmondsworth: Penguin, 1971), 82.

188 Ibid. 83–4.

189 Ibid. 85.

190 Ibid. 92.

191 D. H. Lawrence, *The Lost Girl* (Cambridge: Cambridge University Press, 2002), 107.

192 Ibid. 110.

193 Ibid. 186.

194 D. H. Lawrence, 'Pornography and Obscenity', in *Phoenix: The Posthumous Papers of D. H. Lawrence*, ed. Edward D. McDonald (London: Heinemann, 1936), 87. For discussion of Lawrence, film, and sexuality, see Linda R. Williams, *Sex in the Head: Visions of Femininity and Film in D. H. Lawrence* (Hemel Hempstead: Harvester Wheatsheaf, 1993).

195 Kipling, 'Mrs Bathurst', 91.

196 Heath, 'Cinema and Psychoanalysis', 31.

197 Nicholas Daly, *Literature, Technology, and Modernity, 1860–2000* (Cambridge: Cambridge University Press, 2004), 60.

198 Ibid. 74.

199 Ibid. 75. In *Something of Myself*, Kipling wrote: 'In the late summer, I think, of 1913, I was invited to Manueouvres round Frensham Ponds at Aldershot...When the sham fight was developing, the day turned blue-hazy, the sky lowered, and the heat struck like the Karroo, as one scuttled among the heaths listening to the uncontrolled clang of the musketry fire. It came over me that anything might be afoot in such weather, pom-poms for instance, half-heard on a flank, or the glint of a helio[graph] through a cloud-drift. In short I conceived of the whole pressure of the dead of the Boer War flickering and re-forming as the horizon flickered in the heat.' (Rudyard Kipling, *Something of Myself* (1936; London: Penguin, 1988), 159–60.)

200 Mary Anne Doane, *The Emergence of Cinematic Time: Modernity, Contingency and the Archive* (Cambridge, Mass.: Harvard University Press, 2002), 195.

201 Elliot Gilbert, *The Good Kipling: Studies in the Short Story* (Oberlin: Ohio University Press, 1970), 98.

202 Doane, *The Emergence of Cinematic Time*, 179.

203 Kipling habitually brought together new technologies and supernaturalism, as in his short story 'Wireless'.

204 John Rodker, *Poems and Adolphe 1920*, ed. and introd. by Andrew Crozier (Manchester: Carcanet, 1996), xx.

205 Rokder, *Adolphe 1920*, 137.

206 Robert Musil, 'Toward a New Aesthetic: Observations on a Dramaturgy of Film' [1925 review of Balázs *Der sichtbare Mensch*], in *Precision and Soul: Essays and Addresses*, ed. and trans. Burton Pike and David Luft (Chicago: University of Chicago Press, 1990), 194.

207 Rokder, *Adolphe 1920*, 153–4.

208 Quoted in Geduld, *Authors on Film*, 93–4.

209 Jean Epstein, 'Magnification' (1921), trans. Stuart Liebman and Richard Abel, in Abel (ed.), *French Film Theory and Criticism*, 235–6.

210 Danius, *The Senses of Modernism*, 151.

211 Joyce, *Letters*, vol. 2, ed. Richard Ellmann (London: Faber and Faber, 1966), 217.

212 For discussion of this episode, see Richard Ellmann, *James Joyce* (Oxford: Oxford University Press, 1959), 310–24.

213 H. G. Wells, *The New Republic* (10 March 1917).

214 Christopher Butler, quoted in Derek Attridge, *The Cambridge Companion to James Joyce* (Cambridge: Cambridge University Press, 1990), 265–6.

215   In Robert H. Deming (ed.), *James Joyce: The Critical Heritage*, 2 vols. (London: Routledge, 1970), vol. 1, 192.

216   Harry Levin, *James Joyce: A Critical Introduction* (London: Faber and Faber, 1960), 82.

217   S. M. Eisenstein, 'Help Yourself', *Selected Works*, vol. 1, 219–37. See also 'Literature and Cinema', ibid. 95–9.

218   Sergei Eisenstein, 'Sur Joyce', *Change* (May 1972), 51. (My translation.)

219   See Marie Seton, *Sergei M. Eisenstein: A Biography* (London: Bodley Head, 1952), 149: 'Joyce told his friend Jolas, the editor of *transition*, that if *Ulysses* were ever made into a film, he thought that the only men who could direct it would be either Walter Ruttman the German, or Sergei Eisenstein the Russian.'

220   Ezra Pound, *The Dial*, January 1922.

221   Levin, *James Joyce*, 113.

222   Keith Williams, 'Ulysses in Toontown: "vision animated to bursting point" in Joyce's "Circe"', in Julian Murphet and Lydia Rainford (eds.), *Literature and Visual Technologies: Writing after Cinema* (Basingstoke: Palgrave Macmillan, 2003), 107. See also Austin Briggs, '"Roll Away the Reel World, the Reel World": "Circe" and the Cinema', in Morris Beja and Shari Benstock (eds.), *Coping with Joyce: Essays from the Copenhagen Symposium* (Columbus: Ohio State University Press, 1989), 145–56.

223   See Briggs, '"Roll Away the Reel World, the Reel World"', 149.

224   David Robinson, *Georges Méliès: Father of Film Fantasy* (London: BFI, 1993), 55.

225   Ibid. 102.

226   Fernand Léger, 'A New Realism: The Object', *Little Review* (Winter 1926), 7.

227   James Joyce, *Ulysses* (Harmondsworth: Penguin, 1969), 73.

228   Sara Danius, *The Senses of Modernism*, 162.

229   John McCourt, *The Years of Bloom: James Joyce in Trieste 1904–1920* (Madison: University of Wisconsin Press, 2000), 147.

230   Thomas L. Burkdall, 'Cinema Fakes: Film and Joycean Fantasy', in Morris Beja and David Norris (eds.), *Joyce in the Hibernian Metropolis* (Columbus, Ohio State University Press, 1996), 264.

231   Joyce, *Ulysses*, 601.

232   'Another Scope', *New York Herald*, 7 February 1897. (Quoted in Charles Musser, *History of the American Cinema*, vol 1: *The Emergence of Cinema: The American Screen to 1907* (Berkeley and Los Angeles: University of California Press, 1990), 176).

233   Joyce, *Ulysses*, 363–4.

234 Ibid. 366.

235 See George Pratt, *Spellbound in Darkness: Readings in the History and Criticism of the Silent Film* (University of Rochester, 1966), 16, and Charles Musser, *The Emergence of American Cinema*, 187.

236 Musser, *The Emergence of Cinema*, 187.

237 See Brian Coe, *The History of Movie Photography* (Westfield, NJ: Eastview Editions, 1981), 81. Cited in Philip Sicker, ' "Alone in the Hiding Twilight": Bloom's Cinematic Gaze in "Nausicaa" ', *James Joyce Quarterly* 36: 4 (Summer 1999), 827.

238 Kemp R. Niver, *Early Motion Pictures: The Paper Print Collection in the Library of Congress* (Washington, DC: Library of Congress, 1895), 367. Quoted in Briggs, ' "Roll Away the Reel World, the Reel World" ', 148.

239 Joyce, *Ulysses*, 357.

240 Katherine Mullin, *James Joyce, Sexuality and Social Purity* (Cambridge: Cambridge University Press, 2003), 156.

241 Joyce, *Ulysses*, 76.

242 Ibid. 348.

243 Ibid. 363.

244 Sicker, ' "Alone in the Hiding Twilight" ', 832.

245 Mullin, *James Joyce, Sexuality and Social Purity*, 151.

246 Ibid. 152.

247 Joyce, *Ulysses*, 462.

2. THE SHADOW ON THE SCREEN: VIRGINIA WOOLF AND THE CINEMA

1 Clive Bell, 'Art and the Cinema', *Vanity Fair* (November 1922), 40, and 'Cinema Aesthetics: A Critic of the Arts Assesses the Movies', *Theatre Guild Magazine* 7: 39 (October 1929), 62–3.

2 Roger Fry, *Vision and Design* (1920; Oxford: Oxford University Press, 1981) and 'The Artist and Psycho-Analysis', in Christopher Reed (ed.), *A Roger Fry Reader* (Chicago: University of Chicago Press, 1996), 359.

3 The films Virginia Woolf is known to have seen in the late 1920s and early 1930s were René Clair's *Le Million,* and in Berlin in 1929, Pudovkin's *Storm over Asia.* In her diary entry for 25 January 1915, Woolf wrote: 'My birthday ... I was then taken up to town, free of charge, & given a treat, first at a Picture Palace and then at Buzzards ... The Picture Palace was a little disappointing—as we never got to the War pictures, after waiting 1 hour & a half' (Woolf, *Diary*, vol. 1, 28).

4 See Leslie Kathleen Hankins, 'Across the Screen of My Brain: Virginia Woolf's "The Cinema" and Film Forums of the 1920s', in Diane Gillespie

(ed.), *The Multiple Muses of Virginia Woolf* (Columbia, Missouri: University of Missouri Press, 1993), 148–79 and 'A Splice of Reel Life in Virginia Woolf's "Time Passes": Censorship, Cinema, and "the usual battlefield of emotions"', *Criticism* (Winter 1993). Hankins notes that Leonard Woolf recorded, in his role as literary editor of the *Nation and Athenaeum*, receipt of a review copy of the special issue on Cinema of *Les Cahiers du Mois* (Paris: Editions Emile-Paul Freres, 1925/6), which included Philippe Soupault's 'Quelques poèmes cinématiques', and suggests that this volume might have been an important inspiration for Virginia Woolf's absorption of film aesthetics into her writing.

5 Simon Watney, *The Art of Duncan Grant* (London: John Murray, 1990), 39.

6 See Richard Shone, *The Art of Bloomsbury* (London: Tate Gallery, 1999), 154–5.

7 Ian Christie, 'Before the Avant-Gardes: Artists and Cinema, 1910–1914', in *La decima musa: il cinema e le altre arts* (Proceedings of the VI Domitor Conference/VII International Film Studies Conference, Udine, 2000), 373.

8 Duncan Grant papers, quoted in Francis Spalding, *Duncan Grant: A Biography* (London: Pimlico, 1998), 155.

9 Letter to Lady Ottoline Morell, January 1915. Quoted in Shone, *The Art of Bloomsbury*, 155.

10 Woolf, *Letters*, vol. 1, 497.

11 Leonard Woolf, *Beginning Again*, vol. 2: *1911–1916* (Oxford: Oxford University Press, 1980), 22. For discussion of Bloomsbury and the Russian Ballet, see Evelyn Haller, 'Her Quill Drawn from the Firebird: Virginia Woolf and the Russian Dancers', in Gillespie (ed.), *The Multiple Muses of Virginia Woolf*, 180–226.

12 See e.g. Walter Shaw Hanks, 'Cinema and Ballet in Paris', *Criterion* IV: 1 (June 1926), 178–84.

13 Virginia Woolf, '"Anon" and "The Reader": Virginia Woolf's Last Essays', ed. Brenda R. Silver, *Twentieth-Century Literature* 25 (1979), 395.

14 Virginia Woolf, 'The Movie Novel' (1918); *Essays*, vol. 2, 290–1.

15 See Hankins, 'A Splice of Reel Life in Virginia Woolf's "Time Passes"', for discussion of the significance of the interplay between 'motion' and 'emotion' for Virginia Woolf.

16 Eric Walter White, *Parnassus to Let: An Essay about Rhythm in the Films* (London: Hogarth Press, 1928), 37–8.

17 Letter dated 24 January 1930. Quoted in Huntly Carter, *The New Spirit in the Cinema* (London: Harold Shaylor, 1930), 378.

18 There is an interesting contrast between Woolf's comments and those of Thomas Mann. Mann asked:

But now tell me: why is it people weep so, at the cinema? Or, rather, why do they fairly howl, like a maidservant on her afternoon out? ... The atmosphere of art is cool ... you control yourself. But take a pair of lovers on the screen, two young folks as pretty as a picture, bidding each other an eternal farewell in a real garden, with the grass waving in the wind—to the accompaniment of the meltingest of music; and who could resist them, who would not blissfully let flow the tear that wells to the eye? For it is all raw material, it has not been transmuted, it is life at first hand; it is warm and heartfelt, it affects one like onions or sneezewort. I feel a tear trickling down in the darkness, and in silence, with dignity, I rub it into my cheekbone with my finger tip.

(Thomas Mann, 'On the Film' (1933), reprinted in Harry M. Geduld (ed.), *Authors on Film* (Bloomington and Indiana: Indiana University Press, 1972), 130–1).

19 Woolf, 'Life and the Novelist' (1926); *Essays*, vol. 4, 402–3.

20 Ibid. 404.

21 O. Winter in Harding and Popple (eds.), *In the Kingdom of Shadows*, 15.

22 W. T. Stead, 'The Church's Picture Galleries: A Plea for Special Sunday Cinemas', *The Review of Reviews* (November 1912), in Harding and Popple (eds.), *In the Kingdom of Shadows*, 86–7.

23 Woolf, 'Life and the Novelist', 405.

24 Ibid. 400.

25 Woolf, 'The Cinema'; *Essays*, vol. 4, 352.

26 Ibid. 348.

27 Ibid. 348–9.

28 David Trotter, 'Virginia Woolf and Cinema', *Film Studies* 6 (Summer 2005), 3–18. This material is now incorporated into Trotter's excellent study *Cinema and Modernism* (Oxford: Blackwell, 2007), which came out after this book had gone into production.

29 René Clair, *Reflections on the Cinema*, trans. Vera Traill (London: William Kimber, 1953), 59.

30 Gerald Buckle, *The Mind and the Film: A Treatise on the Psychological Factors in the Film* (London: Routledge, 1926), 14.

31 Ibid. 24.

32 Ibid. 13.

33 Ibid. 14.

34 *Münsterberg, Hugo Münsterberg on Film*, 137.

35 Fry, *Vision and Design*, 14–15.

36 Woolf, 'The Movies and Reality', *New Republic* (4 August 1926); *Essays*, vol. 4, 595. This is the conclusion to the version of the essay 'The Cinema', published in *Arts* (New York), June 1926 and in the *Nation and Atheneum*, 3 July 1926, and repr. in *Essays*, vol. 4, 348–53.

37 See André Bazin, *What is Cinema?*. Essays selected and trans. Hugh Gray, 2 vols. (Berkeley and Los Angeles: University of California Press, 1967, 1971), and Siegfried Kracauer, *Theory of Film: The Redemption of Physical Reality*, (New York: Oxford University Press, 1965).

38 Stanley Cavell, *The World Viewed: Reflections on the Ontology of Film*, enlarged edn. (Cambridge, Mass.: Harvard University Press, 1979), 23, 41.

39 Garrett Stewart, *Between Film and Screen: Modernism's Photo Synthesis* (Chicago: Chicago University Press, 1999), 127.

40 Cavell, *The World Viewed*, 226.

41 Ibid. 166.

42 'All these things shoulder each other out across the screen of my brain. At intervals I begin to think (I note this, as I am going to watch for the advent of a book) of a solitary women musing a book of ideas about life. This has intruded only once or twice, & very vaguely: it is a dramatisation of my mood at Rodmell. It is to be an endeavour at something mystic, spiritual; the thing that exists when we aren't there' (Woolf, *Diary*, vol. 3 (30 October 1926), 114).

43 Claire Colebrook, *Deleuze: A Guide for the Perplexed* (London: Continuum, 2006), 43.

44 Gilles Deleuze and Félix Guattari, *What is Philosophy?*, trans. Graham Burchell and Hugh Tomlinson (London: Verso, 1994), 169.

45 Alexander Bakshy, 'The Road to Art in the Motion Picture', *Theatre Arts Monthly* XI (June 1927), 455.

46 Woolf, 'The Cinema', *Essays*, vol. 4, 351.

47 Fernand Léger, 'The Spectacle: Light, Color, Moving Image, Object-Spectacle' (1924), in *Functions of Painting*, trans. Alexandra Anderson (London: Thames and Hudson, 1973), 42.

48 Woolf, 'The Cinema', *Essays*, vol. 4, 350.

49 Winter, in Harding and Popple (eds.), *In the Kingdom of Shadows*, 16.

50 Ibid. 350–1.

51 Béla Balázs wrote: 'The film can evoke thoughts in the spectator, but must not project on to the screen ready-made thought-symbols, ideograms which have definite, known conventional meanings, like a question mark or exclamation point, a cross or swastika, for these would be merely a primitive picture-writing, hieroglyphs, that would be less convenient than an alphabet and certainly not art'. (*Theory of the Film: Character and Growth of a New Art*, trans. Edith Bone (London: Denis Dobson, 1951), 129).

52 Gilbert Seldes, 'The Abstract Movie', *The New Republic* (Sept.–November 1926), 95.

53 Ibid.

54 Ibid.

55 Milton Waldman 'The Movies', *London Mercury* XIV: 81 (May–October 1926).

56 Seldes, 'The Abstract Movie', 96.

57 Woolf, 'The Cinema', *Essays*, vol. 4, 351–2. The image of women with 'shingled' or 'bobbed' hair recalls Freud's strictures on the film, and the image of 'the flapper' more generally.

58 Woolf, 'The Movies and Reality', *Essays*, vol. 4, 595.

59 Woolf, 'The Cinema', *Essays*, vol. 4, 352.

60 Ibid. 352–3.

61 Ernest Betts, *Heraclitus, or the Future of Films* (London: Kegan Paul, Trench, Trubner & Co., 1928), 12.

62 Eric Elliott, *Anatomy of Motion Picture Art* (Territet, Switzerland: POOL Books, 1928), 142.

63 Elizabeth Bowen, 'Why I Go to the Cinema', in Charles Davy (ed.), *Footnotes to the Film* (London: Reader's Union, 1938), 219–20.

64 Betts, *Heraclitus*, 23.

65 In her essay on Walter Sickert, to take a central example, an imaginary conversation on colour in painting moves to an account of 'those insects, still said to be found in the primeval forests of South America, in whom the eye is so developed that they are all eye, the body a tuft of feather, serving merely to connect the two great chambers of vision'. Entering a picture gallery, likened to 'the primeval forest', the viewer, it is suggested, becomes 'completely and solely an insect—all eye' (Virginia Woolf, 'Walter Sickert: A Conversation' (London: Bloomsbury Workshop, 1992), 13).

66 Woolf, 'The Cinema', *Essays*, vol. 4, 352.

67 Ibid. 350.

68 Quoted in Richard Murphy, *Theorizing the Avant-Garde* (Cambridge: Cambridge University Press, 1998), 223. Hankins ('A Splice of Reel Life in Virginia Woolf's "Time Passes"') also notes the possible influence of Philippe Soupault's 'Quelques poemes cinématiques', which linked cinema with emotional expression: 'Rage', 'Force', 'Adieu', 'Gloire', and 'Regret'.

69 Balázs, *Theory of the Film*, 105–6

70 See Sara Danius, *The Senses of Modernism: Technology, Perception and Aesthetics* (Ithaca, NY: Cornell University Press, 2002).

71 Stephen Heath, 'Cinema and Psychoanalysis: Parallel Histories', in Janet Bergstrom (ed.), *Endless Night: Cinema and Psychoanalysis, Parallel Histories* (Berkeley: University of California Press, 1999), 31.

72 Deleuze, *Cinema 1*, 100.

73 Ibid. 51.

74 William Hunter, *Scrutiny of Cinema* (London: Wishart and Co., 1932), 13.

75 Gilbert Seldes, *The 7 Lively Arts* (New York: Sagamore Press, 1957), 18.

76 Clive Bell, 'Art and the Cinema: A Prophecy that the Motion Pictures, in Exploiting Imitation Art, will Leave Real Art to the Artist', *Vanity Fair* (November 1922), 39.

77 Ibid. 40.

78 Clair, *Reflections on the Cinema*, 15.

79 Mike Budd (ed.), *The Cabinet of Dr. Caligari: Texts, Contexts, Histories* (New Brunswick, NJ: Rutgers University Press.1990), 89.

80 Deleuze, *Cinema 1*, 50−1.

81 Beinecke, Bryher papers. Box 7, Folder 1357. 9 May 1921.

82 Peter Conrad, *Modern Times, Modern Places: Life and Art in the Twentieth Century* (London: Thames and Hudson, 1998), 466.

83 Ibid. 466.

84 George Bernard Shaw, 'The Cinema as a Modern Leveler', *New Statesman* (27 June 1914); Dukore, *Bernard Shaw*, 9.

85 Rebecca West, 'Review of *Jacob's Room*', *New Statesman* (4 November 1922), 142; Majumdar and McLaurin, 101.

86 Clive Bell, *Dial* (December 1924), 451−65; Majumdar and McLaurin, 139.

87 Unsigned review, 'Dissolving Views', *Yorkshire Post* (29 November 1922), 4; Majumdar and McLaurin, 107.

88 Unsigned review, 'A Novelist's Experiment', *Times Literary Supplement* (21 May 1925); Majumdar and McLaurin, 162.

89 When Woolf read *South Riding,* the novel for which Holtby is best known, Woolf wrote: 'I think (so far) she has a photographic mind, a Royal Academician's mind. Its as bright as paint, but how obvious, how little she's got beneath the skin. That's why it rattles on so, I think. One's never pulled up by a single original idea. She's seen nothing for the first time, for herself' (*Letters*, 6, 382).

90 Winifred Holtby, *Virginia Woolf: A Critical Memoir* (Chicago: Academy Press, 1978), 111.

91 Balázs, *Theory of the Film*, 54−5.

92 H. G. Wells, *The King who was a King*, 15−16.

93 Holtby, *Virginia Woolf*, 101.

94 Virginia Woolf, *Jacob's Room* (1922; Harmondsworth: Penguin, 1992), 7.

95 Holtby, *Virginia Woolf*, 117−18.

96 Bryher, '*Dawn's Left Hand*, by Dorothy Richardson', *Close Up* VIII: 4 (December 1933); *Cinema and Modernism*, 210.

97 Dorothy Richardson, Letter to Bryher (22 December 1931), in *Windows on Modernism: Selected Letters of Dorothy Richardson*, ed. Gloria Fromm (Athens, Ga.: University of Georgia Press, 1995), 231.

98 Dorothy Brewster, *Virginia Woolf* (London: George Allen & Unwin Ltd., 1963), 101.

99 Other commentators suggested continuities with related forms of perception, as in the writer Hugo von Hoffmansthal's claim (in the early 1920s) that

spectators knew how to watch films because they were also dreamers, and
that the relations of space and time in dreams were closely linked to those of
film). Hugo von Hoffmansthal 'A Substitute for Dreams', *The London Mercury*
IX (November 1923–April 1924), 177–9.

100 This might also provide some explanation for the intense but sporadic critical
    fascination with the film–literature relationship and the cinematic text, as if
    cinema's presence within literature, and in the novel in particular, is cyclically
    illuminated and obscured.

101 Woolf, *Jacob's Room*, 5.

102 Ibid. 9.

103 Ibid. 81.

104 Danius, *The Senses of Modernism*, 162.

105 Joyce, *Ulysses* (Harmondsworth: Penguin, 1969), 76.

106 Holtby, *Virginia Woolf*, 136.

107 Woolf, *Jacob's Room*, 134.

108 Holtby, *Virginia Woolf*, 140.

109 Quoted by Virginia Woolf, *Diary*, vol. 2, 186.

110 Holtby's own interests in cinema were revealed in the regular column she
    wrote for the journal *The Schoolmistress* in the early 1930s, during the period
    in which she was working on her study of Woolf. The editor of *The
    Schoolmistress*, Evelyne White, who wrote a memoir of Holtby after her
    early death in 1935, commented on her knowledge of films—'there were
    few pictures of note she did not see'—and her interest in the personality
    of the actor, as a far more significant dimension of film than 'the wonders
    of photography, sequence, pattern or rhythm'. Thus Holtby wrote: 'The
    moments when a flat shadow on a screen becomes a symbol for some truth
    about human character, about physical or spiritual beauty, love or hatred,
    power or passion, or wonder, or revenge, so long as life endures we have
    one endless source of interest—the diversities and similarities of the human
    heart' (Evelyne White, *Winifred Holtby: As I Knew Her* (London: Collins,
    1938), 120–1).

111 This was interestingly commented on in the *Times Literary Supplement*
    review, entitled 'The Enchantment of a Mirror', in which the reviewer
    (A. S. McDowell) wrote, in a discussion of the 'delicious moments of reality
    and light' in the novel, of 'the clear and yet enchanted glass which she
    [Woolf] holds up to things…each of those moments has caught a gleam of
    wit from the surface of the mirror, or a musing thought from the reflective
    depths in it'. (Repr. in Majumdar and McLaurin, 162).

112 Noël Burch, *Life to those Shadows*, 184.

113 Woolf, *Jacob's Room*, 96.

114 Stewart, *Between Film and Screen*, 132.

115 Woolf, *Letters*, vol. 2, 573, 581, 591.

116 Woolf, *Diary*, vol. 2, 214.

117 Woolf, *Letters*, vol. 2, 597–8.
118 Woolf, *Jacob's Room*, 136.
119 Ibid. 132.
120 Woolf, *Diary*, vol. 2, 158.
121 Woolf, *Jacob's Room*, 136.
122 There is in fact no actual evidence that Woolf read Bergson at all, though one of the early books on the philosopher was written by her sister-in-law, Karin Stephen. See Karin Stephen, *The Misuse of Mind* (London: Kegan Paul, Trench, Trubner, 1922). For discussion of Woolf and Bergson, see Shiv Kumar, *Bergson and the Stream of Consciousness Novel* (London: Blackie, 1962).
123 Henri Bergson, *L'Évolution créatrice* (1907), trans. Arthur Mitchell as *Creative Evolution* (London: Macmillan, 1911), 323.
124 Ibid. 324–5.
125 Edward Murray, *The Cinematic Imagination: Writers and the Motion Pictures* (New York: Frederick Ungar, 1972), 149–150. Keith Cohen argued, in his study *Film and Fiction*, that 'simultaneity', 'the artistic expression of the "space-time continuum"', had a crucial role to play in the development of film: 'the cinema seems to have arrived at narrativity *through* the concept of simultaneity' (Keith Cohen, *Film and Fiction: The Dynamics of Exchange* (New Haven and London: Yale University Press, 1979), 86). In Cohen's account, fiction's remaking of its forms in the early twentieth century led to the transferring of 'simultaneity' (and related cinematic techniques, including the standardization of mimetic objects, temporal distortion, shifting point of view, and discontinuous continuity) from film to the novel.
126 Paul Ricoeur, *Time and Narrative*, trans. K. McLaughlin and D. Pellauer (Chicago: University of Chicago Press, 1984), vol. 2, 112.
127 Woolf, *Diary*, vol. 2, 47.
128 Ibid. 301.
129 Dorothy Richardson, 'Continuous Performance: Narcissus', *Close Up* VIII: 3, (September 1931); *Cinema and Modernism*, 203.
130 See Keith Williams, 'Symphonies of the Big City: Modernism, Cinema and Urban Modernity', in Paul Edwards (ed.), *The Great London Vortex: Modernist Literature and Art* (Bath: Sulis Press, 2003), 31–50.
131 James Donald, *Imagining the Modern City* (Minneapolis: University of Minnesota Press, 1999), 132.
132 Virginia Woolf, *Mrs Dalloway* (1925; Harmondsworth: Penguin, 1964), 181.
133 Ibid. 179.
134 Ibid. 182.
135 Raymond Williams, *The Country and the City* (1973; London: The Hogarth Press, 1993), 242.
136 Raymond Williams, *The Politics of Modernism: Against the New Conformists*, ed. Tony Pinkney (London: Verso, 1989), 11.

137 Woolf, *Diary*, vol. 3, 102.

138 Virginia Woolf, *Orlando* (1928; Harmondsworth: Penguin, 1993), 82.

139 Ibid. 98.

140 Suzanne Raitt, *Virginia Woolf's To the Lighthouse* (Hemel Hempstead: Harvester Wheatsheaf, 1990), 61.

141 Virginia Woolf, *To the Lighthouse* (1927; Harmondsworth: Penguin, 1992), 214.

142 Alexander Bakshy, 'The Road to Art in the Motion Picture', *Theatre Arts Monthly* XI (1927), 456.

143 V. I. Pudovkin, *Film Technique and Film Acting*, trans. Ivor Montagu (London: Vision Press, 1954), 77.

144 Woolf, *To the Lighthouse*, 177.

145 Woolf, *Diary*, vol. 3, 106.

146 Woolf, *To the Lighthouse*, 171.

147 Balázs, *Theory of the Film*, 55.

148 Woolf, *To the Lighthouse*, 204.

149 Vernon Lee, *The Beautiful: An Introduction to Psychological Aesthetics* (Cambridge: Cambridge University Press, 1913).

150 Woolf, *To the Lighthouse*, 139.

151 Ibid. 210.

152 Ibid. 171.

153 Ibid. 141.

154 See Emily Dalgarno, *Virginia Woolf and the Visible World* (Cambridge: Cambridge University Press, 2001), for a complex and suggestive account of Woolf's relationships to classical thought and theories of vision and beauty.

155 Francis Cornford (ed.), *The Republic of Plato* (Oxford: Oxford University Press, 1941), 223 n. 1.

156 See Gillian Beer, 'Hume, Stephen and Elegy in *To the Lighthouse*', in *Virginia Woolf: The Common Ground* (Edinburgh: Edinburgh University Press, 1996), for discussion of the novel's relationship to the 18th-cent. philosophy of mind, and to questions of 'absence' and human perception in these contexts.

157 Woolf, *To the Lighthouse*, 149.

158 Virginia Woolf, 'Julia Margaret Cameron', in Tristram Powell (ed.), *Victorian Photographs of Famous Men & Fair Women*, with introduction by Virginia Woolf and Roger Fry, 1926 (expanded edn., London: Chatto and Windus) 1992.

159 Ibid. 23.

160 Frances Spalding, *Duncan Grant: A Biography* (London: Pimlico, 1998), 136.

161 Powell (ed.), *Victorian Photographs*, 26.

162 Perry Meisel, *The Absent Father: Virginia Woolf and Walter Pater* (New Haven: Yale University Press, 1980), 47.

163 Woolf, *To the Lighthouse*, 141.

164 Ibid. 204, 207.

165 Ibid. 175.

166 Maggie Humm, *Modernist Women and Visual Cultures: Virginia Woolf, Vanessa Bell, Photography and Cinema* (Edinburgh: Edinburgh University Press, 2002), 38. Humm looks in detail at Bell's and Woolf's photo-albums in this study, and in her *Snapshots of Bloomsbury: The Private Lives of Virginia Woolf and Vanessa Bell* (London: Tate Publishing, 2006). There is now a fairly extensive literature on Woolf and photography. See e.g. Diane Gillespie, '"Her Kodak Pointing at his Head": Virginia Woolf and Photography', in *The Multiple Muses of Virginia Woolf*, 113–47; Elena Gualtieri, '*Three Guineas* and the Photograph: The Art of Propaganda', in Mary Joannou (ed.), *Women Writers of the 1930s* (Edinburgh: Edinburgh University Press, 1999), 165–78; Nicola Luckhurst, 'Photoportraits: Gisèle Freund and Virginia Woolf', in Nicola Luckhurst and M. Ravache, *Virginia Woolf in Camera* (London: Cecil Woolf, 2001).

167 Powell (ed.), *Victorian Photographs*, 9.

168 Ibid. 18.

169 Quoted in Powell's 'Preface' to *Victorian Photographs*, 9–10.

170 Woolf, *To the Lighthouse*, 193.

171 Leslie Stephen, *Sir Leslie Stephen's Mausoleum Book* (Oxford: Clarendon Press, 1977), 32–3.

172 Powell (ed.), *Victorian Photographs*, 25.

173 Virginia Woolf, 'Sketch of the Past', in *Moments of Being* (London: Pimlico, 2002), 97–8.

174 Woolf, *To the Lighthouse*, 215.

175 Woolf, 'The Movies and Reality', *Essays*, vol. 4, 595.

176 Woolf, *To the Lighthouse*, 121.

177 Siegfried Kracauer, 'Photography' (1927), in *The Mass Ornament: Weimar Essays*, ed. Thomas Y. Levin (Cambridge, Mass.: Harvard University Press, 1995), 50.

178 Kracauer, *The Mass Ornament*, 56.

179 Theodora Bosanquet, Review of *The Years*, *Time and Tide*, 13 March 1937, 352–3; Majumdar and McLaurin, 367.

180 Woolf, *Diary*, vol. 4, 332.

181 Virginia Woolf, *The Waves* (Harmondsworth: Penguin, 1992), 82.

182 Virginia Woolf, *The Years* (Harmondsworth: Penguin, 1968), 107.

183 Eric Walter White, *Parnassus to Let: An Essay about Rhythm in the Films* (London: Hogarth Press, 1928), 18. White had started to plan 'An Essay on cinematographic rhythm' while still a student at Oxford. On 8 December 1927, he wrote in a letter to Thorold Dickinson, a friend from school and university who was seeking to forge a career in films, and who read and commented on the essay for him: 'It may interest you to know that Leonard Woolf wrote "The subject interests us & we think it might be worked up into a suitable essay for our series. We shd be glad to see it again in its final

form".' White concluded to Dickinson: 'I'm sure you are right when you say that a new book on the cinema is badly needed in England at the moment' (Thorold Dickinson papers, Special Collections, British Film Institute). In late 1928, White sent his study of Stravinsky, *Sacrifice to Apollo*, to the Hogarth Press, hoping, as he wrote to Dickinson, that it would appear 'early next summer in time for the next London season of Russian Ballet' (30 October 1928). It was in fact published in 1930, and was followed by *Walking Shadows*, White's study of Lotte Reiniger's silhouette films. White became close to Reiniger and her husband, Hans Koch, while living in Berlin in the late 1920s, and it is certainly possible that his image of the new Muse in *Parnassus to Let* inspired Lotte Reiniger's image 'The Tenth Muse'.

184 Graham Greene, 'A Film Technique: Rhythms of Time and Space' (*The Times*, 12 June 1928). Repr. in *Mornings in the Dark: A Graham Greene Film Reader*, ed. David Parkinson (Harmondsworth: Penguin, 1995), 392.

185 Siegfried Kracauer, *Theory of Film: The Redemption of Physical Reality* (Oxford: Oxford University Press, 1960), 54.

186 Woolf, *The Years*, 243.

187 Woolf, *Letters*, vol. 4, 331–2. See also the editorial note in Woolf, *Diary*, vol. 4, 147, which states that Leonard Woolf's engagement diary for the period between 17 February and 25 March records their viewing of a René Clair film.

188 C. A. Lejeune, *Cinema: A Review of Thirty Years' Achievement* (London: Alexander Maclehose, 1931), 164–5.

189 Woolf, *The Years*, 107.

190 Ibid. 118–19.

191 Repr. in Majumdar and McLaurin, 390.

192 Woolf, *The Years*, 104.

193 Vachel Lindsay, *The Art of the Moving Picture* (1922; New York: Modern Library, 2000), 40.

194 Balázs, *Theory of the Film*, 55.

195 See the excellent essays by Melba Cuddy-Keane, Bonnie Kime Scott, and Michael Tratner in Pamela L. Caughie (ed.), *Virginia Woolf in the Age of Mechanical Reproduction* (New York: Garland Publishing, 2000) for fuller discussion of this topic. See also ch. 6, 'Spectacles of Violence, Stages of Art: Walter Benjamin and Virginia Woolf's Dialectic', in Karen Jacob, *The Eye's Mind: Literary Modernism and Visual Culture* (Ithaca, NY: Cornell University Press, 2001).

196 Woolf, *The Years*, 250–1.

197 Ibid. 260–1.

198 Ibid. 295.

199 Ibid. 301.

200 Ibid. 292.

201 Ibid. 309–10.

202 Elliott, *Anatomy of Motion Picture Art*, 58.

203 Woolf, *The Years*, 299.

204 Ibid. 325.

205 Virginia Woolf, 'The Leaning Tower', *Collected Essays*, vol. 2 (London: The Hogarth Press, 1966), 164.

206 Ibid. 232.

207 Quoted in Tsivian, *Early Cinema in Russia*, 46.

208 Woolf, *The Years*, 268–70.

209 Siegfried Kracauer, *Schriften: Aufsätze 1927–1931* (Frankfurt am Main: Suhrkamp Verlag, 1990), 19. (My translation.)

210 Woolf, *The Years*, 312.

211 Ibid. 366.

212 Ibid. 395.

213 Woolf, *Mrs Dalloway*, 59.

214 Woolf, *The Years*, 37.

215 In Woolf's final fragmentary works, 'Anon' and 'The Reader', she wrote:

1. Anon.

2. [*The audience*] The ear & the eye.

3. The individual. 3. The audience.

4. Words?
   [*The eye & the*]
   The ear & the eye.
   'The Reader'
   The reader then comes into existence some time at the end of the sixteenth century, and his life history could we discover it would be worth writing, for the effect it had upon literature. At some point his ear must have lost its acuteness; at another his eye must have become dull...And the curious faculty—the power to make places and houses, men and women and their thoughts and emotions visible on the printed page is always changing. The cinema is now developing his eyes; the Broadcast is developing his ear. His importance can be gauged by the fact that when his attention is distracted, in times of public crisis, the writer exclaims: I can write no more. (Virginia Woolf, ' "Anon" and "The Reader" ', ed. Silver, 376, 428.)

216 Davy, *Footnotes*, 281–2.

217 Ibid. 283.

218 Ibid. 286–7.

219 As G. W. Stonier wrote in 'The Movie', published in his 1933 collection of essays *Gog Magog*: 'One of the most important technical discoveries of the movies was the close-up and, developing from that, the substitution of part of an image for the whole of it. I mean: the picture of feet crossing on a pavement; a seagull and a masthead; a hat floating among drift-weed; cigarette-smoke

spiralling up a window. Such devices (by mean of words) have always been part of the technique of novelist and poet. Tchekov to a young writer: "You must make them feel the moonlight as it glints from a fragment of bottle in the garden." The exploitation, continuous and varied, of such devices in films has brought home their value afresh to the writer: he sees now their particular *visual* property' (G. W. Stonier, *Gog Magog and Other Critical Essays* (London: J. M. Dent, 1933), 187–8).

220 Davy, *Footnotes*, 287.

221 Elie Faure, 'The Art of Cineplastics', trans. Walter Pach (Boston: The Four Seas Company, 1923), 32.

222 Herbert Read, 'Towards a Film Aesthetic', *Cinema Quarterly* 1: 1 (Summer 1932), 11.

223 Herbert Read, 'The Poet and the Film', *Cinema Quarterly* 1: 4 (Summer 1933), 204.

224 Erwin Panofsky, 'Style and Medium in the Motion Picture' (1934), in Daniel Talbot (ed.), *Film: An Anthology* (Berkeley: University of California Press, 1959), 18.

225 Hauser, *The Film Age*, 228.

226 Ibid. 251.

227 Ibid. 254.

228 Ibid. 259.

229 Ibid. 242.

3. 'A NEW FORM OF TRUE BEAUTY': AESTHETICS AND EARLY FILM CRITICISM

1 Gert Hoffmann, *The Film Explainer*, trans. Michael Hoffmann (London: Minerva, 1996), 53.

2 Ibid. 82–3.

3 Ibid.

4 Ibid. 179.

5 Ibid. 226.

6 Ibid. 250.

7 Christian Metz, *The Imaginary Signifier*, trans. Celia Britton, Annwyl Williams, Ben Brewster, and Alfred Guzzetti (Bloomington: Indiana University Press, 1982), 9.

8 Vachel Lindsay, *The Art of the Moving Picture* (1922; New York: Modern Library, 2000), 15–16.

9 See e.g. Dorothy Richardson's article 'Animal impudens', *Close Up* II: 3 (March 1928); *Cinema and Modernism*, 174–6.

10 See Tom Gunning, *D. W. Griffith and the Origins of American Narrative Film: The Early Years at Biograph* (Urbana and Chicago: Illinois University Press, 1994),

91–4 and Rick Altman, *Silent Film Sound* (New York: Columbia University Press, 2004), 55–72, 133–55.

11 Epes Winthrop Sargent, 'Advertising for Exhibitors—Using the Lecture', *Moving Picture World* (2 July 1912), 39. Cited in Altman, *Silent Film Sound*, 144.

12 Altman, *Silent Film Sound*, 71–2.

13 Woolf, 'The Cinema' (1926), *Essays*, vol. 4, 349.

14 Jean Epstein, 'Magnification', trans. Stuart Liebman and Richard Abel, in Abel, *French Film Theory*, vol. 1, 236.

15 Jean Epstein, 'Art of Incidence' (1927), trans. Tom Milne, in Abel, *French Film Theory*, vol. 1, 413.

16 Louis Delluc, 'Beauty in the Cinema' (1917), in Abel, *French Film Theory*, vol. 1, 137.

17 Elie Faure, *The Art of Cineplastics*, trans. Walter Pach (Boston, Mass.: The Four Seas Company, 1923), 25.

18 Johann Wolfgang von Goethe, *Theory of Colours* (1810), trans. Charles Lock Eastlake (Cambridge, Mass: MIT Press, 1980), 22.

19 Mary Ann Doane, *The Emergence of Cinematic Time: Modernity, Contingency and the Archive* (Cambridge, Mass.: Harvard University Press, 2002), 73.

20 Robert Herring, *Films of the Year 1927–1928* (London: The Studio Ltd., 1928), 1.

21 Ibid. 1.

22 Eric Elliott, *Anatomy of Motion Picture Art* (Territet, Switzerland: POOL, 1928), 15.

23 Herring, *Films of the Year 1927–1928*, 1.

24 Elliott, *Anatomy of Motion Picture Art*, 49

25 Herring, *Films of the Year 1927–1928*, 4.

26 Ibid. 1

27 Elliott, *Anatomy of Motion Picture Art*, 16.

28 Herring, *Films of the Year 1927–1928*, 3.

29 Charles Davy, 'Between Painting and Writing', *The Bookman* LXXXVII: 517 (October 1934), p 40.

30 See Max Saunders, 'Literary Impressionism', in David Bradshaw and Kevin J. H. Dettmar (eds.), *A Companion to Modernist Literature and Culture* (Oxford: Blackwell, 2006), 204–11, and Jessie Matz, *Literary Impressionism and Modernist Aesthetics* (Cambridge: Cambridge University Press, 2001).

31 Steven Connor, 'The Modern Auditory I', in Roy Porter (ed.), *Rewriting the Self: Histories from the Renaissance to the Present* (London: Routledge, 1997), 211.

32 Leo Charney, *Empty Moments: Cinema, Modernity and Drift* (Durham, NC: Duke University Press, 1998), 52.

33 Charles Baudelaire, 'The Painter of Modern Life', in *The Painter of Modern Life and Other Essays*, trans. and ed. Jonathan Mayne (London: Phaidon, 1964), 13.

34 Martha Kinross, 'The Screen—From this Side', *Fortnightly Review* 130 (July–Dec 1931), 511.

35 Charney, *Empty Moments*, 70.

36 Walter Pater, *The Renaissance* (Oxford: Oxford University Press, 1998), 152.

37 'For the cinephile', Paul Willeman has written, 'there is a moment in a film (and it happens more often in certain kinds of films) when cinema, in showing you one thing, allows you to glimpse something else that you are not meant to see': the film allows you to think or to fantasise a 'beyond' of cinema, a world beyond representation which only shimmers through in certain moments of the film. Where you see it shimmering is largely, but not exclusively, up to you. The cinephiliac claim is that cinema can do this' (Paul Willeman, *Looks and Frictions: Essays in Cultural Studies and Film Theory* (London: British Film Institute, 1994), 241).

38 Important studies of Vachel Lindsay include Lawrence Goldstein, 'An American Millenium: Vachel Lindsay and the Poetics of Stargazing', in *The American Poet at the Movies: A Critical History* (Ann Arbor: University of Michigan Press, 1995), 19–38; Michael Pressler, 'Poet and Professor on the Movies', *Gettysburg Review* 4: 1 (Winter 1991), 157–65; Glenn Joseph Wolfe, *Vachel Lindsay: The Poet as Film Theorist* (New York: Arno Press, 1973); Ann Massa, *Vachel Lindsay: Fieldworker for the American Dream* (Bloomington: Indiana University Press, 1970); Myron Lounsbury, *The Origins of American Film Criticism 1909–1939* (New York: Arno Press, 1973) and (id.), 'Introduction' to Vachel Lindsay, *The Progress and Poetry of the Movies: A Second Book of Film Criticism* (Lanham, Md: Scarecrow Press, 1995).

39 This and the following quotations are from Lindsay, *The Art of the Moving Picture*, 157–8

40 Edgar Holt, 'Vachel Lindsay: Poet and Pioneer of the Cinema', *The Bookman* LXXXI (October 1931–March 1932), 244.

41 George Eggers, 'A Word from the Director of the Denver Art Association', Lindsay, *The Art of the Moving Picture*, xxii.

42 Ibid. 149.

43 Marc Chénetier (ed.), *Letters of Vachel Lindsay* (New York: Burt Franklin, 1979), 120–1.

44 Walter P. Eaton, 'Class-Consciousness and the Movies', *Atlantic Monthly* CXV (1915), 54–5.

45 Lindsay, *The Art of the Moving Picture*, 57.

46 Ibid. 95.

47 Critics who have discussed this aspect of Lindsay's work include Rachel O. Moore and Nick Browne. Moore's study, *Savage Theory: Cinema as Modern Magic* (Durham, NC: Duke University Press, 2000) looks at the 'primitivism' inherent in Lindsay's film writings; Browne's article, 'American Film Theory in the Silent Period: Orientalism as an Ideological Form', *Wide Angle* 11: 4

(n.d. 1989), 23–31, notes the complexity of the 'universal language' myth of cinema at a time of mass working-class immigration and a substantially immigrant and working-class audience for the cinema. (On this latter point see also Miriam Hansen, *Babel and Babylon: Spectatorship in American Silent Film* (Cambridge, Mass.: Harvard University Press, 1991)). For important discussions of Egyptology and early cinema, see Antonia Lant, 'The Curse of the Pharaoh, or How Cinema Contracted Egyptomania', *October* 59 (Winter 1992), 86–112 and 'Haptical Cinema', *October* 74 (Fall 1995), 45–73.

48 Lindsay, *The Progress and Poetry of the Movies*.

49 Lindsay, *The Art of the Moving Picture*, 12.

50 Ibid. 121. In an unpublished MS, Lindsay wrote: 'The photoplay art should be literature, and a sacred book, not a smutty scrawl on an alley fence. It has the possible dignity of Egyptian hieroglyphics and Egyptian temples, and the possible splendor of the paintings of Michaelangelo and Titian, the possible epic grace of the Russian Dancers, it should have the apocalyptic gleam that will be the glory in the future, the prophetic fire already [] our state papers that point towards the future, The declaration of Independence, and Lincoln's Gettysburg address. And with all these possibilities we are treated to floods of unutterable stupidity. To go to the films is like trying to read the literature of a great nation with nothing left but the inscriptions scrawled at Pompiaa [*sic*]' (Lindsay, 'A Special Delivery Letter', *c.*1922, University of Virginia, Special Collections, Vachel Lindsay papers, Box 16).

51 Michael North, *Camera Works: Photography and the Twentieth-Century Word* (Oxford: Oxford University Press, 2005), 37.

52 Lindsay, *The Art of the Moving Picture*, 5.

53 Lindsay, *The Progress and Poetry of the Movies*, 172.

54 Lindsay, 'Photoplay Progress', *The New Republic* (17 February 1917), 76.

55 Lindsay, *The Art of the Moving Picture*, 110.

56 Myron Lounsbury's lengthy 'Introduction' to *The Progress and Poetry of the Movies* provides a vivid account of Lindsay's lectures and performances (1–149, *passim*).

57 Ibid. 25.

58 Ibid. 29.

59 Ibid. 42.

60 Ibid. 43

61 Ibid. 121.

62 As Ann Massa notes, Lindsay 'worked in and around Springfield for the Anti-Saloon League from 1909–1911, a time when the League's aim was not national Prohibition, but the abolition of the saloon' (Massa, *Vachel Lindsay*, 195).

63 Lindsay, *The Art of the Moving Picture*, 139.

64 Ibid. 140.

65 Ibid. 140.

66 Ibid. 140–1.
67 Ibid. 143–4.
68 Ibid. 130.
69 Ibid. 131.
70 Ibid. 132.
71 Ibid.
72 Ibid. 131–2.
73 Ibid. 133
74 Ibid. 135
75 Ibid. 122. In 1929, the Imagist poet John Gould Fletcher took up Lindsay's analogies, arguing that 'a good film is really an art-gallery in miniature. It differs from an art-gallery only in this: it first limits the range of colors to black-and-white, but as compensation, gives us what no art gallery can ever give: one picture linked to another, one picture growing out of another ... Instead of a series of arrested bits of reality isolated by gilt frames from each other, it can give us the whole of a single reality flowing from a given beginning to a given end, and held in a single focus' (*The Crisis of the Film* (Seattle: University of Washington Book Store, 1929), 31). Fletcher was making his arguments about the essentially visual nature of film at the point at which sound film was making an increasing impact. In his pamphlet, Fletcher also argued for the establishment of a 'film university somewhere in America', which would produce trained spectators, and in which the curriculum would include 'the study of drama, of pictorial art, and of musical rhythm simultaneously' (33).
76 Lindsay, *The Art of the Moving Picture*, 124.
77 Ibid. 21.
78 Ibid. 73–4.
79 Ibid. 27.
80 Massa, *Vachel Lindsay*, 92.
81 Lindsay, *The Art of the Moving Picture*, 4.
82 Ibid. 36.
83 Woolf, 'The Movies and Reality', *Essays* vol. 4, 595.
84 Lindsay, *The Progress and Poetry of the Movies*, 187–8.
85 Ibid. 271.
86 Paul Virilio, *The Aesthetics of Disappearance*, trans. Philip Beitchman (New York: Semiotext[e], 1991), 104.
87 Hans Richter, *The Struggle for the Film*, trans. Ben Brewster (Aldershot, Hampshire: Wildwood Press, 1986), 44–6.
88 Lindsay, *The Progress and Poetry of the Movies*, 317, 326.
89 Münsterberg, *Hugo Münsterberg on Film*, 160.
90 'Photoplay Progress', *The New Republic* 17 (February 1917).
91 Margaret Münsterberg, *Hugo Münsterberg: His Life and Work* (New York: D. Appleton and Company, 1922), 281.

92 In Münsterberg, *Hugo Münsterberg on Film*, 172.

93 The fullest existing study of Hugo Münsterberg's film theory is Donald Laurence Frederickson's *The Aesthetic of Isolation in Film Theory: Hugo Münsterberg* (New York: Arno Press, 1977). Frederickson suggests that 'film was very much on [Münsterberg's] mind several years before 1915, when he discovered Annette Kellerman in *Neptune's Daughter*,' and that Münsterberg may well have been involved with film in his psychological and scientific work, including his development of a prototype for a driving skill machine (22–3).

94 Münsterberg, *Hugo Münsterberg on Film*, 63.

95 Ibid. 58.

96 Ibid.

97 Ibid. 59.

98 Ibid. 99.

99 Ibid. 60.

100 Ibid. 61. Münsterberg was much taken with the film *Neptune's Daughter*, now lost, in which the Australian swimming-star Annette Kellerman played a mermaid.

101 Ibid. 61.

102 Ibid. 62.

103 Ibid. 64.

104 Münsterberg, 'The Problem of Beauty', *The Philosophical Review*, 18: no. 2 (March 1909), 135.

105 Ibid. 133.

106 Ibid.136.

107 Münsterberg, *Hugo Münsterberg on Film*, 59.

108 Münsterberg. 'The Problem of Beauty', 136.

109 Münsterberg, *Hugo Münsterberg on Film* 65

110 Ibid. 78

111 Ibid. 65

112 Ibid. 71.

113 Ibid.

114 Ibid. 77.

115 Ibid. 71

116 Joseph and Barbara Anderson, 'Motion Perception in Motion Pictures', in Teresa de Lauretis and Stephen Heath (eds.), *The Cinematic Apparatus* (Basingstoke: Macmillan, 1980), 83–4.

117 Münsterberg, *Hugo Münsterberg on Film,* 98.

118 Ibid. 129.

119 Ibid. 78.

120 Tom Gunning, 'Introduction' to Lawrence Mannoni, *The Great Art of Light and Shadow: Archaeology of the Cinema*, trans. and ed. Richard Crangle (Exeter: Exeter University Press, 2000), xxvi.

121 Robert Sklar, *Movie-Made America: A Cultural History of American Movies* (New York: Vintage, 1994), 17.

122 Münsterberg, *Hugo Münsterberg on Film*, 79.

123 Ibid. 80.

124 Ibid. 87–8.

125 Ibid. 90.

126 Ibid. 129

127 Ibid.107.

128 For an interesting discussion of this aspect of Münsterberg's study, see Giuliano Bruno, *Atlas of Emotion: Journeys in Art, Architecture and Film* (London: Verso, 2002), 259–62.

129 Michael Pressler, 'Poet and Professor on the Movies', *Gettysburg Review* 4: 1 (Winter 1991), 161.

130 Münsterberg, *Hugo Münsterberg on Film*, 117.

131 Ibid. 137.

132 See Elaine Mancini, 'Theory and Practice: Hugo Münsterberg and the Early Films of D. W. Griffith', *New Orleans Review* 10: 2–3 (Summer–Fall, 1983), 154–60.

133 Münsterberg, *Hugo Münsterberg on Film* 103.

134 Lindsay, *The Progress and Poetry of the Movies*, 201.

135 Münsterberg, *Hugo Münsterberg on Film*, 153.

136 Ibid. 127.

137 See Henri Bergson, *Creative Evolution*, trans. Arthur Mitchell (London: Macmillan, 1911), 287–391. I have not been able to take on, in the space of this chapter, the very substantial critical and theoretical material arising out of Bergson's comments on time and the cinema, developed in particular in the work of Gilles Deleuze.

138 Münsterberg, *Hugo Münsterberg on Film*, 160.

139 Münsterberg, *Psychology and Industrial Efficiency* (London: Constable, 1913), 54–5.

140 Ibid. 66.

141 Münsterberg, *Hugo Münsterberg on Film*, 86.

142 Jonathan Crary, *Suspensions of Perception: Attention, Spectacle and Modern Culture* (Cambridge: Mass.: MIT Press, 1999).

143 Münsterberg, *Hugo Münsterberg on Film*, 204–5.

144 Münsterberg, *Psychology and Industrial Efficiency*, 68.

145 Ibid. 272.

146 Victor Oscar Freeburg, *The Art of Photoplay Making* (New York: The Macmillan Company, 1918), 'Foreword'.

147 Victor Oscar Freeburg, *Pictorial Beauty on the Screen* (New York: Macmillan Company, 1923). References in this article are to the Arno Press reprint (New York: Arno Press and the *New York Times*, 1970). The quotation appears in the author's preface, ix.

148 Freeburg, *The Art of Photoplay Making*, 5.
149 Ibid. 18.
150 Ibid. 25.
151 Freeburg, *Pictorial Beauty on the Screen*, 44.
152 Ibid. 6.
153 Ibid. 154.
154 Ibid. 7.
155 Freeburg, *The Art of Photoplay Making*, 62.
156 Ibid.
157 Ibid. 63.
158 Ibid. 67.
159 William James, *Principles of Psychology* (New York: Holt, 1890), 680.
160 Michael Levenson, 'The Time-Mind of the Twenties', in Laura Marcus and Peter Nicholls (eds.), *The Cambridge History of Twentieth-Century English Literature* (Cambridge: Cambridge University Press, 2004), 211.
161 Ethel D. Puffer, *The Psychology of Beauty* (1907) (Kessinger Publishing repr., n.d.), 30.
162 C. W. Valentine, *An Introduction to the Experimental Psychology of Beauty* (London: T. C. and E. C. Jack, n.d.), 46.
163 Freeburg, *Pictorial Beauty on the Screen*, 124.
164 Vernon Lee, *The Beautiful: An Introduction to Psychological Aesthetics* (Cambridge: Cambridge University Press, 1913), 13.
165 Ibid. 109.
166 John Ruskin had described mountains as Nature in motion, and plains as Nature at rest.
167 Lee, *The Beautiful*, 65.
168 Ibid. 80−1
169 Ibid. 79.
170 Freeburg, *The Art of Photoplay Making*, 27.
171 Lee, *The Beautiful*, 53.
172 Gottfried Ephraim Lessing, *Laocoön: An Essay on the Limits of Painting and Poetry*, trans. Edward Allen McCormick (Baltimore: Johns Hopkins University Press, 1984), 19.
173 Freeburg, *Pictorial Beauty on the Screen*, 107.
174 Lindsay, *The Art of the Moving Picture*, 111.
175 Freeburg, *Pictorial Beauty on the Screen*, 188.
176 Ibid. 189−90.
177 Ibid. 153.
178 Ibid. 38.
179 Ibid. 36.
180 Ibid. 51
181 Ibid.

182 Ibid. 125.

183 Ibid. 124.

184 Freeburg, *The Art of Photoplay Making*, 31.

185 Kaveh Askari has explored the pre-play 'picture play' tradition as exemplified by Alexander Black, and its impact on the pictorial tradition in early film criticism, including the writings of Lindsay and Freeburg. See his articles 'From "The Horse in Motion" to "Man in Motion": Alexander Black's Detective Lectures', *Early Popular Visual Culture*, 3: 1 (May 2005), 59–76 and 'Photographed Tableaux and Motion Picture Aesthetics: Alexander Black's Picture Plays', in J. Plunkett and J. Lyons (eds.), *Optical to Digital: Excavating Multimedia History* (Exeter: University of Exeter Press, forthcoming). For discussion of film pictorialism and the tableau, see also Ben Brewster and Lea Jacobs, *Theatre to Cinema: Stage Pictorialism and the Early Feature Film* (Oxford: Oxford University Press, 1997), *passim*.

186 See my discussion of 'movement' as pertaining to both 'motion' and 'emotion' in the Introduction.

187 Freeburg, *Pictorial Art in the Movies*, 4–5.

188 Ibid. 200.

189 Ibid. 201.

190 Balázs, *Theory of the Film*, 114–15.

191 John Hutchens, 'L'Enfant Terrible: The Little Cinema Movement', *Theatre Arts Monthly* 13 (1929), 694.

192 Gilbert Seldes, *The Encyclopaedia Britannica*, quoted Harry A. Potamkin, *Close Up* v: 5, 389. Potamkin comments on Seldes's claim: 'This is not altogether true … What Mr. Seldes may mean is that it made movie criticism for Mr Seldes'.

193 *Pictorial Beauty on the Screen*, 166.

194 Ibid. 180.

195 Lindsay, *The Art of the Moving Picture*, 6.

196 Ibid. 8.

197 Ibid. 7.

198 Ibid. 8.

199 Faure, *The Art of Cineplastics*, 20.

200 Ibid. 23.

201 Ibid. 26.

202 Ibid. 26–7.

203 Bergson, *Creative Evolution*, 108.

204 Faure, *The Art of Cineplastics*, 28.

205 Ibid. 32–3

206 Rudolph Messel, *This Film Business* (London: Ernest Benn, 1928).

207 Faure, *The Art of Cineplastics*, 48.

208 Ibid. 50.

209 Eisenstein, 'The Montage of Attractions' (1923), repr. in Richard Taylor and Ian Christie (eds.), *The Film Factory: Russian and Soviet Cinema in Documents 1896–1939* (London: Routledge, 1988), 88.

210 Gilbert Seldes, *An Hour with the Movies and the Talkies* (London: John Lippincott, 1929), 65–6.

211 Quoted in Esther Leslie, *Hollywood Flatlands* (London, Verso, 2002), 17.

212 Emmy Veronica Sanders, 'America Invades Europe', *Broom: An International Magazine of the Arts* 1: 1 (November 1921), 92.

213 Matthew Josephson, 'Made in America.', *Broom*, 269.

214 Ibid. 268.

215 Ibid. 270.

216 Soupault, 'The "U.S.A." Cinema', *Broom* 5: 2 (September 1923), 68.

217 Ibid. 69.

218 Blaise Cendrars, *Broom* 2 (July 1922), 351; trans. Stuart Liebman in Abel, *French Film Theory*, vol. 1, 271.

219 Ibid. 351; 271.

220 Seldes, *The 7 Lively Arts*, 18.

221 Quoted in Peter Conrad, *Modern Times, Modern Places: Life and Art in the Twentieth Century* (London: Thames and Hudson, 1998), 429.

222 Ibid. 436.

223 Michael Kammen, *The Lively Arts: Gilbert Seldes and the Transformation of Cultural Criticism in the United States* (New York: Oxford University Press, 1996), 84.

224 In his foreword to the 1957 edn. of *The 7 Lively Arts*, and commenting on his views in 1924, Seldes wrote: 'The distinction I tried to make between the great arts and those I called the *faux bon* is not sharp enough, perhaps because I couldn't find an exact name for them in English' (5).

225 As Seldes wrote: 'The sacred 7 came from the classics, from "the seven arts" (which was also the name of a magazine recently defunct) and I never tried to categorize the contents of the book to conform to the figure. If you tried you could make seven, counting feature movies and Keystone comedies as one you could make ten if you counted all the forms of music separately. I never took a position in the matter' (*The 7 Lively Arts*, 8).

226 Ibid. 20.

227 Ibid. 21

228 Ibid. 35.

229 Ibid. 36–7.

230 Ibid. 298.

231 Ibid. 41.

232 Bakshy, 'The New Art of the Moving Picture', *Theatre Arts Monthly* xi (April 1927), 281.

233 Seldes, *The 7 Lively Arts*, 289.

4. THE CINEMA MIND: FILM CRITICISM AND FILM CULTURE IN 1920S BRITAIN

1 Alistair Cooke, 'The Critic in Film History', in Davy (ed.), *Footnotes*, 238.

2 Ibid. 51–2.

3 Ibid. 261.

4 Gilbert Seldes, *Movies for the Millions: An Account of Motion Pictures, Principally in America* (London: Batsford, 1937), 3, 8.

5 Cooke, in Davy (ed.), *Footnotes*, 251.

6 Rachael Low, *The History of the British Film: 1918–1929* (London: George Allen and Unwin, 1971), 20.

7 D. L. LeMahieu, *A Culture for Democracy: Mass Communication and the Cultivated Mind in Britain Between the Wars* (Oxford: Clarendon Press, 1988), 47.

8 Ibid. 47.

9 Iris Barry's film writings, as well as her unparalleled contribution to the film archive movement, have recently received significant critical attention. A memorial volume, *Remembering Iris Barry,* ed. M. Akermak was published in 1980 (New York: Museum of Modern Art). See also Bruce Henson, 'Iris Barry: American Film Archive Pioneer', *The Katherine Sharp Review* 4 (Winter 1997); Leslie Kathleen Hankins, 'Iris Barry, Writer and Cineaste, Forming Film Culture in London 1924–26: The *Adelphi*, the *Spectator*, the Film Society and the British *Vogue*', *Modernism/Modernity* 11: 3 (2004), 488–515; Haidee Wasson, 'Writing the Cinema into Daily Life: Iris Barry and the Emergence of British Film Criticism', in Andrew Higson (ed.), *Young and Innocent? British Silent Cinema* (Exeter: Exeter University Press, 2001), 321–37; Wasson, 'The Woman Film Critic: Newspapers, Cinema and Iris Barry', *Film History: An International Journal*; Wasson, 'Women and the Silent Screen', ed. Amelie Hastie and Shelley Stamp, 18: 2 (2006) and Wasson, *Museum Movies: The Museum of Modern Art and the Birth of Art Cinema* (Berkeley and Los Angeles: University of California Press, 2005). In *Museum Movies*, Wasson examines the creation of the Film Library of the Museum in Modern Art in 1935, in which Barry played a central role. This topic is also explored in Peter DeCherney's study *Hollywood and the Culture Elite: How the Movies Became American* (New York: Columbia University Press, 1995).

10 Kurt von Stutterheim, *The Press in England* (London: George Allen and Unwin, 1934), 157.

11 See Jeffrey Richards, *The Age of the Dream Palace: Cinema and Society in Britain 1930–1939* (London: Routledge, 1984), 3–5.

12 C. A. Lejeune, *Cinema: A Review of Thirty Years' Achievement* (London: Alexander Maclehose, 1931), 20–1.

13 Rudolf Arnheim, *Film Essays and Criticism*, trans. Brenda Benthien (Madison: University of Wisconsin Press, 1997), 13.

14 Iris Barry, *Let's Go to the Pictures* (London: Chatto and Windus, 1926), ix.

15 St John Ervine, 'The Alleged Art of the Cinema', University College Union Society, University of London. (The Oration Delivered by St John Ervine, Esq., during the 38th Foundation Week, on Thursday 15 March 1934).

16 Bertram Higgins, 'The Cinema: An Outburst', *The Spectator* 130 (12 May 1923), 801.

17 St John Ervine, 'The Alleged Art of the Cinema', 5.

18 Ibid. 28.

19 Walter Benjamin, 'The Work of Art in the Age of Mechanical Reproduction', in *Illuminations*, ed. Hannah Arendt, trans. Harry Zohn (New York: Shocken Books, 1969), 238.

20 Quoted in Ervine, 'The Alleged Art of the Cinema', 13.

21 Ibid. 15.

22 Ibid. 3.

23 Robert Richardson, *Literature and Film* (Bloomington: Indiana University Press, 1969), 37.

24 Brewster and Jacobs, *Theatre to Cinema*, 213.

25 See E. A. Baughan, 'The Art of Moving Pictures', *Fortnightly Review* 106 (July–Dec. 1919), 449.

26 Stanley Rowland, 'The Future of the Cinema', *The Quarterly Review* (January 1932), 511.

27 Alfred Barge, 'Gesture and the Cinema Play', *Drama* 1 (1919), 86–7.

28 Bertram Clayton, 'The Cinema', *Quarterly Review* 234 (July–October 1920), 186.

29 Bertram Clayton, 'The Cinema and its Censor', *Fortnightly Review* 109 (February 1921), 228.

30 Betty Balfour, 'The Art of the Cinema', *English Review* 37 (1923), 388.

31 Bryher, *Film Problems of Soviet Russia* (Territet, Swizerland: POOL, 1929), 131.

32 Brewster and Jacobs, *Theatre and Cinema*, 5.

33 Christopher Innes, *Avant-Garde Theatre 1892–1992* (London: Routledge, 1993), 79.

34 Ibid. 60.

35 Baughan, 'The Art of Moving Pictures', 448.

36 Gerald Maxwell, 'The Fascination of the Film', *Fortnightly Review* 114 (July–December 1923), 114.

37 Baughan, 'The Art of Moving Pictures', 456.

38 Ibid. 449.

39 Ibid. 452.

40 Ibid.

41 Ibid. 452–3.

42 Ibid. 452.

43 Ibid. 456.

44 George Bernard Shaw to Mrs Patrick Campbell (19 August 1912); Dukore, *Bernard Shaw*, 5.

45 'The Cinema as a Modern Leveler', *New Statesman* (27 June 1914); Dukore, *Bernard Shaw*, 12.

46 George Bernard Shaw, 'What the Films May Do to the Drama', *Metropolitan Magazine* (May 1915); Dukore, *Bernard Shaw*, 15.

47 Duhore, *Bernard Shaw*, 19.

48 George Bernard Shaw, 'Stage Theatres and Cinema Theatres'; Dukore, *Bernard Shaw*, 36.

49 George Bernard Shaw, 'What I Think of the Cinema', *Picture Plays* (13 March 1920); Dukore, *Bernard Shaw*, 25.

50 Shaw, 'What the Films May Do to the Drama', 13.

51 Ibid. 17.

52 George Bernard Shaw, 'The Art of Talking for the Talkies', *World Film News* (November 1936); Dukore, *Bernard Shaw*, 121.

53 Anthony Asquith, 'The Play's the Thing', *Films and Filming* 5 (February 1959), 13.

54 George Bernard Shaw, 'Relation of the Cinema to the Theatre', Responses to questions from Huntly Carter (9 May 1932); Dukore, *Bernard Shaw*, 79.

55 George Bernard Shaw, 'The Drama, the Theatre, and the Films', *Fortnightly Review* (1 September 1924), 293–4.

56 Shaw, 'A Question to Many', 99.

57 'No one who frequents moving-pictures even rarely can fail to be struck by the extraordinary disparity between the quality of the picture, as a piece of mechanics, and its quality as a piece of entertainment. A magnificent apparatus is employed for the production of puerile stories. There can scarcely fail to be an increase in the mind of the pictures when they find tongues. Things that are too silly to be said can be sung, but things which are silly enough to be pantomimed are too silly to be spoken … The "talkie" offers nothing but great opportunities to English players who have hitherto had less place in the moving-picture world than they would seem to deserve. If they fail to seize them, they will have none but themselves to blame. In any event, though great results may not follow from the development of the "talkie," I can see no harm coming from it. I can see much good' (St John Ervine, *The Spectator* (4 May 1929), 682).

58 George Bernard Shaw, 'Education and the Cinematograph', *The Bioscope, Educational Supplement* (18 June 1914), in Dukore (ed.), *Bernard Shaw on Cinema*, 7.

59 George Bernard Shaw, 'The Cinema as a Moral Leveler', *New Statesman* (27 June 1914), *Special Supplement on the Modern Theatre*; Dukore, *Bernard Shaw*, 9.

60 Ibid. 10-11.

61 Writing in on 'Movies and Morals', Carleton Kemp Allen referred to enquiries
into the effects of film-viewing, in particular on children and young adults,
and notes the unprecedented growth of cinema attendance. He also connected
questions of 'bad' morality with 'bad' art, in ways that might suggest that
the call for aesthetic definition was not always separable from the demand for
moral control; both were attempts at the constraint and containment of this
monstrous, and monstrously expanding, creation. The article argued for a need
to support British cinema and to limit American supremacy, with the suggestion
that the British commercial defeat had a 'very serious imperial aspect'. The
tone is reminiscent of degenerationist arguments of the turn of the century, not
least in its account of the deleterious influence of cinema on 'the boyhood and
girlhood of the nation' (*The Quarterly Review* 486 (October 1925), 325).
62 Alec Waugh, 'The Film and the Future', *Fortnightly Review* 116 (July–
December 1924), 524–5.
63 J. Ecclestone, 'The Cinema', *The Nineteenth Century* (October 1923), 634–5.
64 Ibid. 635–6.
65 Sergei Eisenstein, *Laocoön; Selected Works*, vol. 2, 109–202.
66 Ecclestone, 'The Cinema', 637.
67 Ibid. 638.
68 Anthony Vidler has argued that film acts as both test and limit case for the
opposition of the static and poetic arts that he sees as lying at the heart of
modernist debates about aesthetic form more generally:

On the one hand, it is obvious that film has been the site of envy and even
imitition for those more static arts concerned to produce effects or techniques
of movement and space-time interpenetration. Painting, from Duchamp's *Nude
Descending a Staircase*; literature, from Virginia Woolf's *Mrs Dalloway*; poetry, from
Marinetti's *Parole in libertà*; architecture, from Sant'Elia to Le Corbusier, have all
sought to reproduce movement and the collapse of time in space; and montage,
or its equivalent, has been a preoccupation in all the arts since its appearance, in
primitive form, with rapid-sequence photography. On the other hand, it is equally
true that the Enlightenment roots of modernism ensured that film, as well as all
the other arts, were bound, à la Lessing, to draw precise theoretical boundaries
around the centers of their conceptually different practices—practices understood
as distinct precisely because of their distinct media; each one, like Lessing's own
poetry and painting, more or less appropriate to the representation of time *or* space.
Thus, despite the aspirations of avant-garde groups, from Dada to Esprit Nouveau,
to syncretism and synesthesia, the relations of the arts still could not be conceived
without their particular essences being defined: as if the arts were so many nations,
romantically rooted in soil and race, each with characteristics of their own to be
asserted before any treaties might be negotiated. Thus, since the late nineteenth
century, film has provided a test case for the definition of modernism in theory
and technique. It has also served as a point of departure for the redefinition of the

other arts, a paradigm by which the different practices of theater, photography, literature, and painting might be distinguished from each other.

(Anthony Vidler, *Warped Space: Art, Architecture, and Anxiety Modern Culture* (Cambridge, Mass.: MIT Press, 2000), 100)

69 Ibid. 636.

70 Johann Wolfgang von Goethe, 'Observations on the Laocoön' (1798), in John Gage (ed.) *Goethe on Art* (London: Scolar Press, 1980), 82.

71 Kinross, 'The Screen—From this Side', 511.

72 Bakshy, 'The New Art of the Moving Picture', 281.

73 Ibid. 281.

74 Bakshy, 'The Road to Art in the Motion Picture', 456.

75 Renato Poggioli, *The Theory of The Avant-Garde* (Cambridge, Mass.: Harvard University Press, 1965), 201.

76 Evelyn Gerstein, 'Four Films of New Types', *Theatre Arts Monthly* XI (April 1927), 295.

77 Ibid. 458.

78 Ibid. 459.

79 Ibid. 459–60.

80 Abel, *French Film Theory*, vol. 1, 215.

81 Bakshy, 'The Road to Art in the Motion Picture', 462.

82 Bakshy, 'The New Art of the Moving Picture', 279.

83 R. E. C. Swann, 'Art and the Cinema: A Chance for the British Producer', *The Nineteenth Century* 100 (August 1926), 227.

84 Ivor Brown, 'An Art in Search of its Youth', *The Saturday Review* (19 January 1924), 56–7.

85 Swann, 'Art and the Cinema', 221.

86 Swann writes: 'Although, then, the laws that should govern film production are quite distinct from the laws that govern play production, the film producer can make good use of the experience of the stage in his search for film settings. Here the circus can be of little help to him. The bourgeois theatre of bedroom plays and the fourth-wall-missing theory can be of little help to him. But among stage craftsmen as opposed to stage carpenters and decorators there are several whose work definitely clamours to be used in the development of the cinema. Take for instance one of Mr. Gordon Craig's designs for *King Lear*. Picture it on the screen—immense billowy clouds, beating shafts of hail, and three tiny struggling puppets of men—and compare it with anything the screen has yet given us. Producers may plead that they are busy giving the public what it wants, but if the cinema is ever to be regarded seriously as an art there should be among them a steadily increasing number who will make their directors consider the screen as Mr. Craig considers his stage and every artist his canvas—as a space to be filled with light and shade and, above all, movement in exact balance' ('Art and the Cinema', 225–6).

87 Ibid. 227. Comte de Beaumont, who introduced the film on that occasion, noted the film's absence of plot, and the ways in which 'its interest centres in the values, rhythms and speed of the perspectives'. Faces (those of famous French aristocratic 'beauties') 'fuse little by little into landscapes, crystal sparks, frolicking lights in the night. Suddenly one bursts out of the dark to rush full speed round Paris, first by land and then on the water. Vision becomes obscure, and finally the dream vanishes in a dazzling light'. Programme note for The Film Society's 3rd performance, 20 December 1925. Repr. in *The Film Society Programmes 1925–1939* (New York: Arno Press, 1972), 11.

88 Comte de Beaumont, 'Of What are the Young Films Dreaming?', *The Little Review* (Winter 1926), 73.

89 See Christophe Gauthier, *Le Passion du cinéma: cinéphiles, ciné-clubs et salles spécialisées à Paris de 1920 à 1929* (Paris: Association Française de Recherche sur L'Histoire du Cinéma, 1999), 103–23.

90 Ibid. 139 (my translation).

91 Ibid. 142–3.

92 Walter Shaw Hanks, 'Cinema and Ballet in Paris', *Criterion* IV (1 June 1926), 178.

93 Ibid. 157 (my translation).

94 Ivor Montague [*sic*], 'The New Film Society', *The Isis* (10 June 1925), 19–20.

95 Don Macpherson, 'The Film Society', in (ed.), *British Cinema: Traditions of Independence* (London: BFI Publishing, 1980), 103.

96 Montagu, 'The New Film Society', 19.

97 Ibid. 20.

98 Ivor Montagu, *Youngest Son: Autobiographical Sketches* (London: Lawrence and Wishart, 1970), 273.

99 Montagu, 'The New Film Society', 20.

100 The Film Society Collection, British Film Institute, Item 9 (Membership information and leaflets to members, 1925).

101 In 1959, the film critic and historian David Robinson (recommended by Ernest Lindgren) was commissioned to write a history of the Film Society, but it has not been published. The manuscript, 'The Career and Times of the Film Society', is held in The Film Society Collection, British Film Institute Special Collections (Item 45b). Correspondence from Iris Barry, written in 1963, shows that she disliked Robinson's account, which devoted less than a quarter of its pages to discussion of the Film Society *per se*, focusing instead more broadly on the film culture of the period. She also took exception to Robinson's focus on the press attacks on the Film Society in the late 1920s for its showing of Soviet films, which 'gives a quite unfair impression that the F.S. was largely some sort of organ of Soviet propaganda and its members a horde of rough-necks'. (Item 45a). There have subsequently been articles on the Film Society, including Jen Samson, 'The Film Society', in Charles Barr (ed.), *All Our Yesterdays: 90 Years of British Cinema* (London: British Film Institute, 1992), 306–13 and Jamie

Sexton, 'The Film Society and the Creation of an Alternative Film Culture in Britain in the 1920s', in Higson (ed.) *Young and Innocent?*, 291–305. See also the interview with Ivor Montagu, conducted by Peter Wollen, Alan Lowell, and Sam Rohdie, published in *Screen* 13:3 (Autumn 1972), 71–113.

102 Montagu, *The Youngest Son*, 273.

103 Ivor Montagu collection, British Film Institute, Item 16 'The Film Society: 50th Anniversary. Correspondence with Lord Bernstein' (meeting with Sidney Bernstein, Ivor Montagu and Anne Simor: 11.6.75).

104 Iris Barry, 'The Cinema: Progress is Being Made', *The Spectator* (14 February 1925), 236.

105 'We did become a focus for the kinds of intellectual snobs who were active in and created the literary and artistic and intellectual life of the day and at the time had not been hitherto interested in cinema. It was they whom we wished to interest in cinema. They joined and showed their presence by quarrelling sometimes loudly and all that kind of thing and so making remarks in the gossip columns and we knew they were there but really the purpose of it was that we wanted to see the films. We couldn't get people to send them over unless we agreed to show them and we wanted to see them with an orchestra and we couldn't pay for an orchestra unless we had a Society of members to pay the subs and that's all we were interested in' (Sidney Bernstein, article on the Film Society for *FILM* (BFFS house mgazine), 25 September 1975). Ivor Montagu Collection, Item 16.

106 Film Society Collection, British Film Institute. Item 4a: Council of the Film Society Meeting notices and agendas 1926–31.

107 Jamie Sexton, 'The Film Society', 295.

108 Programme note for the first performance (25 October 1925). Repr. in *Film Society Programmes*, 3.

109 Jerry Turvey, 'Ivor Montagu and British Film Culture in the 1920s', in *Young and Innocent?*, 313–14.

110 A note at the end of the programme for the 9th performance (24 October 1926) of the Film Society stated: 'It is impossible ... to show as requested films from the earliest programmes ever commercially screened, for these would require special primitive projection apparatus, unsuited to the New Gallery Kinema.' In 1931, however, the Film Society was able to show films from around 1900 from the collection of 'Primitives of the Film', assembled by the Institut für Kulturforschung in Berlin, at the Tivoli Palace, Strand.

111 The Film Society Programme, 1st performance, Sunday 25 October 1925; *Film Society Progammes*, 4.

112 Ibid. 23.

113 Ibid. 39.

114 Ibid. 106.

115 Ibid. 98.

116 Ivor Montagu, *The Political Censorship of Films* (London: Victor Gollancz, 1929).

117 The Film Society Collection, Item (6c) (Pamphlet: Study Groups, Season 1929–30). Eisenstein gave six lectures in the second half of November 1929 on 'Filmic Representation'.

118 'Eisenstein's Lectures in London: A Reconstruction by Basil Wright and J. Isaacs', Saturday 17 December 1949, Third Programme 10.05–10.45 p.m. Transcript in Film Society Collection.

119 *Film Society Programmes*, 131.

120 John Grierson, in *Grierson on Documentary*, ed. Forsyth Hardy (London: Faber and Faber, 1966), 20.

121 See *British Cinema: Traditions of Independence*, ed. Don Macpherson (London: BFI Publishing, 1980), 105.

122 See *The Film Society Collection*, Item 37. The film made as part of the Film Society study group, *Everyday*, is thought to have been lost.

123 *Film Society Programmes*, 117.

124 V. I. Pudovkin, *Film Technique*, trans. Ivor Montagu (London: George Newnes, 1933), 143.

125 Ibid. 143–4.

126 *Film Society Programmes*, 114.

127 Robert Herring, 'Storm over London', *Close Up* IV: 3 March 1929, 38.

128 Charles Davy, *Yorkshire Post*, 29 October 1929.

129 Ivor Montagu Collection. Item 34: 'The Future of the Sound Film', *c*.1930. The archive also contains a draft from 1936 (Item 54) on the inadequacies of the 'talkies', entitled 'Lament of a diehard'. Montagu's objections to sound film were made on formal, aesthetic and psychological grounds, but it was also the case that it was the coming of sound that made it particularly difficult for him to find work in the transition period and into the 1930s.

130 Ivor Montagu, *Cinema Quarterly* 1:1 (Winter 1932–3).

131 The film, described by Picabia (in a phrase which Montagu's account echoes) as respecting nothing except 'the desire to burst out laughing', is in fact an extraordinary play with cutting and motion, parodying avant-garde motifs while at the same time extending them, sending up high art forms (a ballerina shot from below becomes a bearded man with a marked resemblance to Lytton Strachey) and (in line with the 'archival' dimensions of the film culture of the period) celebrating and reinscribing early cinematic forms, including chase sequences.

132 In Richard Abel's version of the event: 'The performance opened with a short film prologue that featured Picabia and the ballet's composer, Erik Satie, descending from the sky in slow motion to load a cannon. The cannon shot signalled the beginning of the ballet on stage. At the entr'acte, the rest of Clair's film was projected—to a rising storm of boos, whistles, howls of disgust, and scattered applause. In the end, a character breaks through the "End" title (in slow motion), and Rolf de Maré, the Théâtre de Champs-Elysées manager, kicks him back through—to signal the beginning of the ballet's second act'

(380–1). A year later, the two parts were combined into a 22-minute film for the opening of the Studio des Ursulines.

133 Peter Wollen, 'The Two Avant-Gardes', in his *Readings and Writings: Semiotic Counter-Strategies* (London: Verso, 1982), 92–104.

134 Annette Michelson, *New Forms in Film* (Exhibition catalogue), Montreux (1974), 10. Quoted in Deke Dusinberre, 'The Avant-Garde Attitude in the Thirties', in *British Cinema: Traditions of Independence*, ed. Don Macpherson (London: BFI Publishing, 1980), 35.

135 'From Alpha to Omega', *Nation & Atheneum* (31 October 1925), 182.

136 'From Alpha to Omega', *Nation & Atheneum* (26 December 1925), 469.

137 'From Alpha to Omega', *Nation & Atheneum* (20 February 1926).

138 'From Alpha to Omega', *Nation & Atheneum* (20 March 1926).

139 Bonamy Dobrée, 'Seen on the Stage', *Vogue* 66: 12 (Late December 1925), 82.

140 Bonamy Dobrée, 'Seen on the Stage', *Vogue* 68: 11 (Early December 1926), 116, 118.

141 Bonamy Dobrée, 'Seen on the Stage', *Vogue* 66: 12 (Late December, 1926), 66.

142 Bonamy Dobrée, 'Seen on the Stage', *Vogue* 67: 8 (Late April 1926), 94.

143 Iris Barry, 'The Scope of Cinema', *Vogue* 66: 4 (Late August 1924), 76.

144 Ibid. 76.

145 Iris Barry, 'The Cinema in Three Moods', *Vogue* 64: 7 (Early October 1924), 104.

146 Iris Barry, 'Paris Screens and Footlights', *Vogue* 65: 1 (Early January 1925), 37.

147 Iris Barry, 'Paris Screens and Footlights', *Vogue* 65: 3 (Early February 1925), 82–3.

148 Iris Barry,'The Future of Cinema', *Vogue*, 67: 5 (Early March 1926), 69.

149 Barry, 'The Cinema: Progress is Being Made', 235.

150 Iris Barry, *Let's Go to the Pictures* (London: Chatto and Windus, 1926), viii.

151 Ibid. 16.

152 In an article on 'Phonofilm'—'It Talks and Moves'—written in 1924, Barry argued that talking films opened up new possibilities, particularly in the filming of opera and stage plays, though at this stage she continued to uphold the specific and independent 'aesthetic' of the silent film (*Spectator* (7 June 1924), 915–16). She also suggested 'a use for these new sound-films which might well be half-reproduction and half art: that is as a Phonofilmed opera. It would be already something to broadcast both moving pictures and music as they actually are seen and heard in the opera house, but it might be much better to photograph only the voices and the orchestra and to juxtapose an original film, composed on the vast and impressive lines of *The Niebelungs*, neatly synchronized with the music: a dream-picture to tell the story of the opera imposingly. The advantage of having slender Isoldes and Brunhildas to look at as well as heavenly voices to listen to would be enormous'. The relationship between sound and sight, we might note, continues to be conceptualised in

terms of the female body. This article also compares interestingly with that of
H.D. on 'The Mask and the Movietone', discussed in Chapter 1.

153 Ibid. 13.

154 Ibid. viii.

155 Ibid. 25–6.

156 In his obituary of Barry, 'Birmingham Sparrow', Ivor Montagu described her as
'co-founder of the world's first "Film Society"' (*Sight and Sound* 39:2 (Spring
1970), 106).

157 In addition to the studies by Akermak, Henson, Wasson, and DeCherney, cited
above, see Mary Lea Bandy, 'Nothing Sacred: "Jock Whitney Snares Antiques
for Museum": The Founding of the Museum of Modern Art Film Library',
Studies in Modern Art (New York: MOMA, December 1995), 3–38 for this
period in Barry's career.

158 *Poetry: A Magazine of Verse* VIII (April–September 1916), 187–90.

159 A clutch of letters from Pound to Iris Barry from the Spring of 1916 onwards
reveal him giving detailed criticism of poems which she has sent him. He found
much of it indistinguishable 'from a lot of neo-imagists and there are too many
d'd neo-imagists just at present', but helped her get published. He also offered
advice on a play she was writing, which seems to have been a fantasy about
the death of elderly female relatives: 'I should give the old lady a very short
death', Pound recommended: 'Either she can stagger to door, or bed can be
visible and make-up can do the rest. Let jaw drop. Give her a line or two
if necessary. Not a long drawn agony, a la cinema. Sic: OLD FEMALE: "I
am dying of boredom." Obit'. (96). Above all, Pound sent her reading lists
which grew longer by the letter, a guide to 'KOMPLETE CULTURE': 'If you
can't escape your Birmingham, you had better get Karl Appel's Provenzalische
Chrestomatic out of the university library … (There is a university in B. isn't
there?) … Perhaps you should read all of [Voltaire's] Dictionaire Philosophique.
Presumably no other living woman will have done so.' He also gave advice
on finding lodgings in London ['WITH BAWTH'] and directions for life in
the capital: 'I believe being a bar maid would be no obstacle, BUT one would
be obliged to conceal the fact.' In 1917, Barry moved to London, and there
were no more letters from Pound, though he wrote in September of that year
to Margaret Anderson of *The Little Review* about her work: 'The Iris Barry
and Rodker stuff is not a compromise but a bet. I stake my critical position,
or some part of it, on a belief that both of them will do something. I am not
risking much, because I have seen a lot of their mss. Barry has done the draft of
a novel, and it has the chance of being literature. Rokder has convinced me,
at last, that he "has it in him". And one must have les jeunes.' See *The Selected
Letters of Ezra Pound: 1907–1941*, ed. D. D. Paige (London: Faber and Faber,
1950), 76–122.

160 Paul O'Keefe's biography of Wyndham Lewis, *Some Sort of Genius: A Life
of Wyndham Lewis* (London: Jonathan Cape, 2000), provides brief glimpses of

Barry in this period through her letters. In the summer of 1920, she wrote to Lewis, 'I have led a singular kind of life all the last year to try and fit in with your life; I have no friends and no acquaintances and nothing at all either hobby or career or what not to "live" for except to "get on" with you.' A year earlier she had had a child, possibly fathered by Lewis. This son, Robin, stayed with his maternal grandmother until he was three, and was then placed in a private children's home. At the time of the letter quoted above (August 1920), Barry was in a nursing home waiting to give birth to their second child—which she was having as a gesture of 'goodwill'—Lewis having entertained doubts about the paternity of the first. She passed the time in hospital, O'Keefe notes, knitting brown woollen socks for Lewis which gave her ideas for a business—'I should begin in a very unambitious way by employing only one or two cheap cripples or people like that and…lay in a stock of sample work for people to order from—specially for Christmas. I should…teach knitting; and try to arrange with some firm of manufacturers making woollen underwear to be an agent for them, selling women's and children's vests etc. on commission. As I got more orders, I should employ more knitters, and aim eventually at doing nothing but sell.' The business could be run from home, 'if we had two furnished rooms near wherever you have your next studio'. Barry also wrote to Lewis about the problem of what to do with the new baby. 'There is a Home in the London suburbs ("for the Infants and Children of Gentle People").' It would cost 27 shillings a week to look after the baby, 'which is a lot but then you don't have to buy a pram'. 'Some place has to be found for it when I leave here, and I don't suppose you want to try and find anywhere even if you had time. What shall I do?' Lewis was in fact having a holiday in France with T. S. Eliot when this letter was sent, and his reply is not recorded. A baby girl was born on 1st September: her birth certificate records her name as 'Maisie Wyndham', daughter of Percy Wyndham Lewis (journalist) and Iris Crump of 'no occupation'. At some point Maisie went into the children's home, and Lewis and Barry separated sometime in 1921. Barry found a job working at a couturier in Bond Street—which specialized in silk and the ubiquitous wool—and correspondence between Lewis and Barry consisted only in arguments over money for Maisie's upkeep which Lewis was ever-reluctant to come up with: 'You must absolutely cease to regard me as a portion of Providence', he wrote to Barry at this time.

These episodes express extremely complex negotiations with, and repudiations of, domesticity and the norms of femininity on Barry's part: acting as unpaid housekeeper for Lewis (there is a telegram in the archives in which he instructs Barry to have dinner ready for him at 8.00); having at least one child, and possibly two, by him without any suggestion, it would seem, that either of them would be much involved in their upbringing; knitting socks for him (one of Lewis's finest drawings of the period is of Barry knitting in a chair) but imagining the turning of the knitting of 'women's and children's vests' into profit. A significant act of self-making must, moreover, have been involved in passing from the Iris Crump of 'no occupation' at the beginning of the 20s to the Iris Barry who became central to British film culture a very few years later in the same decade. In the mid and late 1920s, Barry was married to the poet and literary critic Alan Porter, but their relationship appears not to have survived the move to the US. In the States, she married John E. Abbott, who was Director of the Museum of Modern Art's Film Library from 1935 to 1946.

161 Iris Barry, 'The Ezra Pound Period', *Bookman* (New York), (October 1931), 165.

162 Peter Brooker, *Modernity and Metropolis: Writing, Film and Urban Formations* (London: Palgrave, 2002), 45.

163 One of Barry's poems, 'A City Song', was published in *The Spectator* (14 July 1923), 51, before she began to write film criticism for the journal; her first film review appeared on 2 February 1924.

164 Five poems by Barry appeared in *Poetry* xx (April–September 1922): 'Virgin Moon', 'Silence', 'Shadows', 'Shadow-boughs', and 'Dreams'.

165 Barry, *Let's Go to the Pictures*, viii–ix.

166 Ibid. 82.

167 Herbert Read, 'The Poet and the Film', *Cinema Quarterly*, 1:4 (Summer 1933), 202. Read's article included a lengthy discussion of Jean Cocteau's surrealist film *Le Sang d'un Poète*, in which a statue comes to life.

168 Iris Barry, 'The Cinema', *Spectator* (3 May 1924), 707.

169 Iris Barry, 'The Cinema', *Spectator* (15 November 1924), 734.

170 Wyndham Lewis, *Filibusters in Barbary* (New York: Haskell House Publishers, 1973), 112.

171 Ibid. 120.

172 Wyndham Lewis, *Time and Western Man* (California: Black Sparrow Press, 1993), 65.

173 Barry, *Let's Go to the Pictures*, vii, 42–3.

174 Joyce, *Ulysses*, 176.

175 Barry, *Let's Go to the Pictures*, 30.

176 Ibid. 40.

177 Jessie Dismorr, 'Matinee', *The Little Review* IV: 2 (March 1918), 31.

178 Barry, *Let's Go to the Pictures*, 244–5.

179 Bryher, 'More-About-Films', *The Outlook* (22 January 1927), 90.

180 T. E. Hulme, who had written extensively on Henri Bergson, and translated Bergson's *Introduction to Metaphysics* (1913), heard Worringer lecture in Berlin in 1912–13, and became absorbed by his thought. *Abstraktion und Einfühlung* (*Abstraction and Empathy*) was published in 1908, and played a significant role in the conceptualisation of the first Post-Impressionist exhibition (1910) to which Roger Fry was central. See the discussion in William C. Wees, *Vorticism*

and the English Avant-Garde (Manchester: Manchester University Press, 1972), 78–80.

181 Barry, 'The Cinema', *Spectator* (14 June 1924), 955.

182 Barry, 'The Cinema', *Spectator* (28 March 1925), 497.

183 Barry, *Let's Go to the Pictures*, 78–9.

184 Barry, 'The Cinema', *Spectator* (17 May 1924), 788.

185 Barry, 'The Cinema', *Spectator* (2 August 1924), 158.

186 Barry, 'The Cinema', *Spectator* (14 November 1925), 870.

187 Barry, 'The Cinema', *Spectator* (7 August 1926), 208.

188 Barry, *Let's Go to the Pictures*, 163.

189 Ibid. 176–7.

190 Writing to Ivor Montagu from Beverley Hills in 1927, Barry noted of the Hollywood film scene: 'Pommer's influence I think has been enormous and the fact that the magnates have so lately been found wanting in business sense and shown up by Wall Street has put new pep into the hands of those among the film makers here who do know their job. It is astonishing how almost ingenuously keen on making films as well as they can, they are—even celebrated directors. Of course there are masses of fools, masses of idiot actors. But there is a corps of serious people too, keen as we are'. (Iris Barry, letter to Ivor Montagu (27 September 1927), in Ivor Montagu Collection, British Film Institute Special Collections, Item 311, Correspondence 1925/1970).

191 'How Twelve Famous Women Scenario Writers Succeeded in this Profession of Unlimited Opportunity and Reward', *Photoplay* (August 1923).

192 Lizzie Francke, *Script Girls: Women Screenwriters in Hollywood* (London: British Film Institute, 1994), 26.

193 Iris Barry, *Let's Go to the Pictures*, 59.

194 Ibid. 5–6.

195 Ibid. 59.

196 Ibid. 66.

197 Ibid. 73.

198 Ibid. 13.

199 Ervine, 'The Alleged Art of the Cinema', 4.

200 C. A. Lejeune, *Thank You for Having Me* (London: Hutchinson, 1964), 68–9.

201 Ibid. 78.

202 Lejeune, *Cinema*, 247.

203 Montagu, *The Youngest Son*, 280.

204 Lejeune, 'The Week on the Screen: Single-Star Weakness: A Film From Sweden', *Manchester Guardian* (7 January 1922).

205 Christine Gledhill, *Reframing British Cinema 1918–1928: Between Restraint and Passion* (London: BFI, 2003), 77.

206 Lejeune, 'The Week on the Screen: Thrills, Contests, and Conflicts', *Manchester Guardian* (14 January 1922).

207 Dorothy Richardson, 'Continuous Performance VI: The Increasing Congrega-
    tion', *Close Up* I: 6 (December 1927), 65; *Cinema and Modernism*, 171.
208 H.D., 'The Cinema and the Classics, I: Beauty', *Close Up* I: 1 (July 1927), 23;
    Cinema and Modernism, 105.
209 Lejeune, 'The Week on the Screen: Monochrome and Colour', *Manchester
    Guardian* (21 January 1922).
210 Lejeune, *Cinema*, 246.
211 Lejeune, 'The Week on the Screen', *Manchester Guardian* (4 February 1922).
212 Lejeune, 'The Week on the Screen', *Manchester Guardian* (12 August 1922).
213 Lejeune, 'The Week on the Screen', *Manchester Guardian* (4 November 1922).
214 Lejeune, 'The Week on the Screen', *Manchester Guardian* (30 December 1922).
215 Lejeune, 'The Week on the Screen', *Manchester Guardian* (2 September 1922).
216 Lejeune, 'The Week on the Screen', *Manchester Guardian* (18 November 1922).
217 Lejeune, 'The Week on the Screen', *Manchester Guardian*, (5 March 1927).
218 Lejeune, 'The Week on the Screen', *Manchester Guardian* (17 October 1925).
219 Lejeune, 'The Week on the Screen', *Manchester Guardian* (15 January 1926).
220 Ibid.
221 Bowen, 'Why I Go to the Cinema', in Davy (ed.), *Footnotes*, 207.
222 Ibid. 208.
223 Lejeune, 'The Week on the Screen', *Manchester Guardian* (2 January 1926).
224 Dorothy Richardson, 'Continuous Performance', *Close Up* I: 1 (July 1927),
    35–6; *Cinema and Modernism*, 160–1.
225 Repr. in *The C. A. Lejeune Film Reader*, ed. Anthony Lejeune (Manchester:
    Carcanet, 1991), 70. Anthony Lejeune's anthology has an excellent introduction
    to his mother's work. The Reader is substantially made up of the reviews C. A.
    Lejeune wrote for *The Observer*, and includes only a few of her writings from
    the 1920s, on which I have focused in this chapter. See also C. A. Lejeune's
    Chestnuts in her Lap: 1936–1946 (London: Phoenix House, 1947), a selection of
    her reviews from *The Observer*.
226 Ivor Montagu, Review of *Stella Dallas*, *Observer* (7 February 1926).
227 Lejeune, 'The Week on the Screen', *Manchester Guardian* (2 January 1926).
228 Lejeune, *Cinema*, 191.
229 Ibid. 193.
230 Carter, *The New Spirit in the Cinema*, 27.
231 Lejeune, *Cinema*, 205.
232 Ibid. 206.
233 Lejeune, 'The Week on the Screen', *Manchester Guardian* (14 November 1925).
234 Lejeune, *Cinema*, 187.
235 Ibid. 245–6.
236 Lejeune, 'The Week on the Screen', *Manchester Guardian* (10 April 1926).
237 Lejeune, *Cinema*, 185–6.
238 Lejeune, 'The Week on the Screen', *Manchester Guardian* (30 January 1926).

239 Lejeune, 'The Week on the Screen', *Manchester Guardian* (27 January 1927). Ivor Brown also called attention to film posters, 'which continue to attain the very depths of pictorial degradation, while the art of the poster is elsewhere so markedly approving. The craft of advertisement has been in many trades refined by some taste and moderation of style, but to read the usual puff supplied by the film companies' press-agents is still like stumbling upon a trough of verbal hog-wash. Caliban remains the totem of the trade' ('An Art in Search of its Youth', *Saturday Review* (19 January 1924), 56).

240 Edgar Allan Poe, 'The Purloined Letter', in *The Works of Edgar Allan Poe* (Harmondsworth, Penguin, 1982), 219.

241 Terry Ramsaye, *A Million and One Nights*, vii.

242 Barry, 'Work and Progress', *The Museum of Modern Art Film Library* (January 1937), 1. Film archive. Cited in Bandy, 'Nothing Sacred', 10.

243 Cited in Bandy 'Nothing Sacred', 14.

244 Lejeune, 'Week on the Screen', *Manchester Guardian* (25 February 1922).

245 Lejeune, *Cinema*, 115.

246 Ibid. 111.

247 Ibid. 115.

248 Gilbert Seldes, 'A Letter to the International Film Art Guild', *New Republic* 44: 333 (1925). Quoted in Lounsbury, *The Origins of American Film Criticism 1909–1939* (New York: Arno Press, 1973), 172

249 Robert Herring, 'Twenty Years Ago', *Manchester Guardian* (8 September 1928), 10.

250 Rudolf Messel, *This Film Business*, 119–20.

5. THE MOMENT OF CLOSE UP

1 Herman Weinberg—Letter to Bryher (Beinecke Rare Book and Manuscript Library, Yale University [hereafter Beinecke], n.d.)

2 'Mercurius', 'Film Structure and the Work of *Close Up*', *Architectural Review* 68 (November 1930), 221.

3 The essay appeared in two parts, in *Close Up* VI: 3 (March 1930) and VI: 4 (April 1930).

4 Some mystery hangs over this. The film historian Roland Cosandey claimed 'Mercurius' to be the pseudonym of James Burford, whose brother Roger Burford wrote occasionally for *Close Up*, and whose name appeared as joint author with Oswell Blakeston of a film article in the *Architectural Review* in 1932 and in *Close Up* (x: 3 (September 1933), 258–9), and this attribution was supported by Deke Dusinberre, who interviewed Oswell Blakeston towards the end of his life. (See Roland Cosandey, 'On *Borderline*', in Michael O'Pray (ed.), *Avant-Garde Film: 1926–1995* (Luton, Bedfordshire: University of Luton Press, 1996), 79, and Deke Dusinberre, 'The Avant-Garde Attitude in the Thirties',

in *Traditions of Independence* (London: BFI, 1980), 47.) When I contacted the *Architectural Review*, I was told that no archive existed, but a note was found which referred to 'Mercurius' as the pseudonym of Oswell Blakeston, itself the pseudonym of Henry Hasslacher. It is, however, true that the style of the 'Mercurius' articles does not seem to tally with that of Blakeston.

Writing on Dreyer's *Joan of Arc*, 'Mercurius' stated (*Architectural Review* 68 (November 1930), 221): 'When Dreyer made *The Passion of Joan of Arc* he was obsessed with his units. His pre-plan must have been unprecedented, and yet he had overlooked something. His insistence on emotional transcendentalism (achieved through sonorous rhythm and sliced images) insisted finally on emotional stagnation. The failure was in some non-recognition of the cumulative power of units, in themselves cramped and uncomfortable. Relief from this kind of tension would have caused, no matter how momentary, the emotional "pins and needles" which he was striving to impart, instead of an increasing numbness.'

The terms are very close to those used by H.D. in her critical review of the film. 'We are numb and beaten' was her account of the film's impact on the spectator. She also took up the question of motion and emotion in the film. (See H.D., 'Joan of Arc', in *Close Up* III: 1 (July 1928); *Cinema and Modernism*, 130–3.)

5 See North, *Camera Works*, ch. 2: 'Transition: The Movies, the Readies, and the Revolution of the Word', 61–82.
6 *Transition* (4 July 1927).
7 *The Nation* (13 August 1927). There were, by the late 1920s, numerous French-language film journals, including *Le Film* (1914–19); Pierre Henri's *Ciné pour tous* (1919–23), *Cinemagazine* (1921–), Jean Delluc's *Cinea* (1921–3).
8 Kenneth Macpherson, 'As Is', *Close Up* I: 1 (July 1927), 11. Such attitudes have put *Close Up* beyond the pale for many contemporary British film historians, but it should be noted that critics such as C. A. Lejeune, who wrote extensively and often favourably of British films in her columns, felt that she could not include discussion of the British film in *Cinema: A Review of Thirty Years, Achievement*. As Lejeune wrote in her Preface ('Retrospect'): 'It may seem a little paradoxical that a book, which attempts a survey of the cinema from a point above a British centre, should omit any discussion of the British industry or the British craftsmen from its text. I am aware of the paradox, but I stand fast to the omission. Before everything else I have attempted to keep my subject proportional, and it would be doing no service to the British movie to pretend that its achievements, even the best of its achievements, are distinguishable in feature to any observer taking a bird's-eye survey of the world's screen' (8–9).

Recent historians of British cinema have written emphatically against such judgements. Significant studies include Charles Barr, *The English Hitchcock*

(Moffat: Cameron and Hollis, 1999) and, as editor, *All Our Yesterdays: 90 Years of British Cinema* (London: BFI, 1986); Christine Gledhill, *Reframing British Cinema: 1918–1928: Between Passion and Restraint* (London: BFI, 2003); Andrew Higson, *Waving the Flag* (Oxford: Clarendon, 1995) and, as editor, *Dissolving Views: Key Writings on British Cinema* (London: Cassell, 1996), and *Young and Innocent? The Cinema in Britain 1896–1930* (Exeter: Exeter University Press, 2002); Jeffrey Richards (ed.), *The Unknown 1930s: An Alternative History of the British Cinema 1929–1939* (London: I. B. Tauris, 1998); Amy Sargeant, *British Cinema: A Critical History* (London: BFI, 2005).

9 Marianne Moore, 'Fiction or Nature', *Close Up* x: 3 (September 1933), 260–5 and 'Lot in Sodom', *Close Up* x: 4 (December 1933), 318–19.

10 Marianne Moore, *The Dial* 83 (November 1927), 449–50.

11 Dorothy Richardson, Letter to Bryher, in Gloria Fromm (ed.), *Windows on Modernism: Selected Letters of Dorothy Richardson* (Athens, Ga.: University of Georgia Press, 1995), 135.

12 Copies of the first issue of *Close Up* were sent to a number of writers and critics, including Ivor Montagu, May Sinclair, Virginia Woolf, Walter White, Gertrude Stein, Langston Hughes, Carl Van Vechten, Anita Loos, John Dos Passos, and E. E. Cummings; the presence among these names of figures associated with the Harlem Renaissance is particularly striking.

13 See Anne Friedberg, 'Writing about Cinema: Close Up 1927–1933' (Ph.D.: New York University, 1983) and 'Reading *Close Up*, 1927–1933', in *Cinema and Modernism*, 1–27; Susan Gevirtz, *Narrative's Journey: The Fiction and Film Writing of Dorothy Richardson* (New York: Peter Lang, 1996).

14 Blakeston's *I Do Like to be Beside the Seaside?* (1927) has been described as 'something of a spoof on the pretentiousness of "intellectual" film criticism' (Dusinberre, 'The Avant-Garde Attitude in the Thirties', in Don Macpherson, *British Cinema*, 36). The only print of the film was, apparently, destroyed by fire in the Second World War, though stills from the film survive in the Blakeston archive at the Harry Ransom Institute, University of Texas at Austin. Blakeston also made an abstract film, *Light Rhythms*, with the photographer Francis Bruguière, in 1930, and, in general terms, introduced significant discussion of abstract film and of still photography into the pages of *Close Up*.

15 See North, *Camera Works*, ch. 3, '*Close Up*: International Modernism's Struggle with Sound', 83–105.

16 Ivor Montagu, '*Film Society*: Notes on the 17th Programme', *Close Up* i: 6 (December 1927), 80–2.

17 Letter from Oswell Blakeston to Kenneth Macpherson (Beinecke Gen MSS 97 1, Box 3, Folder no. 118, 1928–9: 6 January 1929): 'I thought you would be as angry as I was about the Film Society note. They mocked the Metzner all through with heaving music, doing all kinds of cheap serial tricks. After

reading "burlesque" on the programme everyone took it as a huge joke and a poor film ... I feel rather strongly, it is, to my mind, such a definite attack on *Close Up*.'

18 Kenneth Macpherson, 'As Is', *Close Up* VI: 2 (February 1930), 88.

19 Beinecke, Bryher papers, Box 149, Folder 5064, Diary (1924–47). In a letter to H.D. (1 May 1931), Bryher wrote: 'I love Berlin so much, like a person I think. It is so peaceful here and at the same time so quick so exciting. AND I have discovered what one does—all the old dames in Berlin pile into the kinos with their market bags and one or two schoolboys at five o'clock, you sit anywhere you like for 90 pfennigs. It's wonderful, I went last afternoon again to the Drei groschen Oper on my own. A magnificent achievement of Pabst. I cannot bear the thought of having to buy my railway ticket.'

20 See Jayne E. Marek, *Women Editing Modernism: 'Little' Magazines and Literary History* (Lexington, Ky.: University of Kentucky Press, 1995), esp. ch. 4, 'Towards International Cooperation: The Literary Editing of H.D. and Bryher', 101–37. For discussion of H.D.'s involvement with modernist magazines, see also Georgina Taylor, *H.D. and the Sphere of Modernist Women Writers* (Oxford: Oxford University Press, 2001).

21 Friedberg, 'Writing about Cinema', 242.

22 'Dope or Stimulus,' *Close Up* III: 3 (September, 1928), 61.

23 P.J.M., 'New Novels: Adventurous Writers,' *Manchester Guardian* (8 January 1928).

24 Born in Vienna in 1881, Sachs was trained as a lawyer. In 1904, he was introduced to psychoanalysis through his reading of Freud's *The Interpretation of Dreams* (1900). He abandoned his law career in its early stages and followed Freud into psychoanalytic work, initially through writing and editing and, from 1920 onwards, through the training of analysts, when he was asked by the newly founded Berlin Psychoanalytic Institute to develop the new field of training analysis, including analysing psychoanalysts who were already practicing. Sachs, one of Freud's most trusted colleagues, became one of the group of seven—the Secret Committee—around Freud. Sachs remained in Berlin until 1932, when he was invited by the Harvard School of Medicine to become a training analyst in Boston, a function he continued until his death in 1947. His publications were substantially contributions to applied psychoanalysis. Freud's 'dream book' remained a key text for him, as did the essay of 1908, 'Creative Writers and Daydreaming'. Fascinated by the applications of psychoanalysis to the creative process and to the reception of works of art, and by the concept of the work of art as a 'collective day-dream', Sachs explored the idea of 'day-dreams in common'. In 1912 Freud entrusted to Sachs and Otto Rank the editing of the newly founded journal *Imago*, intended to develop the application of psychoanalytic knowledge to broader cultural and human-scientific spheres:

Sachs continued this publication as *The American Imago* after his move to the US.

25 H. C. Abraham and E. L. Freud (eds.), *A Psychoanalytic Dialogue: The Letters of Sigmund Freud and Karl Abraham 1907–1926* (New York: Basic Books, 1964), 80. For fuller discussion of Freud's relationship to cinema, see Laura Marcus, 'Dreaming and Cinematographic Consciousness', *Psychoanalysis and History* 3:1 (2001), 51–68.

26 Hanns Sachs, *Psycho-Analyse: Rätsel des Unbewussten* (Berlin: Lichtbild Buhner, 1926). For discussion of Pabst's *Secrets of a Soul*, see Anne Friedberg, 'An *Unheimlich* Maneuver between Psychoanalysis and the Cinema: *Secrets of a Soul* (1926)', in Eric Rentschler (ed.), *The Films of G. W. Pabst: An Extraterritorial Cinema* (New Brunswick, NJ: Rutgers University Press, 1990), 41–51.

27 Kenneth Macpherson, 'As Is', *Close Up* VII: 5 (November 1930); *Cinema and Modernism*, 237.

28 Kenneth Macpherson, 'As Is', *Close Up* III: 4, (October 1928), 8.

29 Hugo von Hoffmannsthal, 'A Substitute for Dreams', *The London Mercury* IX (November 1923–April 1924), 179. Trans. of '*Der Ersatz für die Traume*' (1921).

30 Hanns Sachs, 'Film Psychology', *Close Up* III: 5 (November 1928); *Cinema and Modernism*, 250–4.

31 Bryher, Letter to H.D. 24 April 1931 (Beinecke).

32 Bryher, Beinecke, Box 72, 2855, Berlin, 2-page typescript.

33 Isherwood wrote that 'To Christopher, Berlin meant Boys' in *Christopher and his Kind 1929–1939* (London: Methuen, 1978), a memoir that gives a very detailed account of his years in Berlin. See also Norman Page, *Auden and Isherwood: The Berlin Years* (London: Macmillan, 2000), which contains an interesting chapter on Weimar cinema.

34 Stephen Spender, *World within World: The Autobiography of Stephen Spender* (London: Hamish Hamilton, 1951), 132–3.

35 Ibid. 111. Spender had included this scene in his autobiographical novel *The Temple*, written in 1930, and rewritten for publication in 1988:

Colours, sounds, scents, the taste of absinthe, wisps of remembered conversation, wove patterns in his brain, as he sat there in the dark, waiting for the film to begin.

The picture leaped out of the darkness, a new sequence of images in his head. Boys and girls skiing jerkily down a snowy slope. The sky black against the snow. When they reached a bump at the bottom of the slope they lifted their sticks in order to propel themselves forward. A girl looked up into the camera. She seemed to be greeting someone in this room. Joachim. They all laughed and clapped and called out 'Joachim'. Now the scene was on board ship, under a hot sky. Iron shadows drew straight and curved lines across a deck. Joachim leaned on railings, staring out to sea. His face was motionless. He turned—and laughed at his friends in this room—skin wrinkling in the sun. Now he was playing deck tennis, laughing and gesticulating from that deck towards his friends in this room. Paul was his friend. Now on the screen there was a party held in this very studio, with boys and girls dancing. Some of them were there then, some of them here now—dancing. The camera sauntered among twisting and turning figures, taking in the interior of the studio, the tubular furniture, the cube-shaped lamps, occasionally singling out a pretty face, a stripped torso, a thigh, a bare foot. Suddenly they all fell on top of each other on the floor, some of them now present in this room. Looking up with flashing eyes into the light, Willy lay stroking the head of Irmi, on the ground beside him, beside Paul. Willy turned, his face thrust up into the light, and kissed the top of her head, then his head seen from above with its thick curls, covered the light on her lips. Everyone laughed. Paul heard Willy, lying beside him on the floor, laugh. Paul laughed.

The studio lights were turned on again. They all stood up, for a moment speechless, vibrant. Two or three couples started dancing softly, to no music. One couple stopped dancing, frozen in a tableau embrace. (Stephen Spender, *The Temple* (London: Faber and Faber, 1988), 44–5)

36 Benjamin, 'The Work of Art in the Age of Mechanical Reproduction', in *Illuminations*, 235–7.
37 Béla Balázs, *Schriften zum Film II* (1926–1931), ed. Wolfgang Gergsh (Berlin: Henschel, 1984), 60.
38 Sachs, 'Film Psychology,' 252.
39 Bryher, letter to H.D. (23 October 1927), Beinecke, H.D. Papers YCAL MSS 24 I Box 3, Folder 83.
40 Ibid.
41 Bryher became a close friend of Bergner's, and supported her when she came to England. Bryher described her as 'the Colette of the screen' in a letter to H.D. (22 April 1931) and wrote in 'Berlin April 1931' (*Close Up* VIII: 2 (June 1931), 131) of *Ariane*: 'The film depends entirely upon the reaction of the audience to Elizabeth Bergner. And this again depends upon the person being either very simple or an experienced psychological observer. For each of her gestures can be interpreted two ways; simply or as the reflex of an involved psychological process not to be understood unless the key to the language is known. She is the Colette of the screen'.
42 Bryher, letter to H.D. (27 October 1927), Beinecke, H.D. Papers YCAL MSS 24 I Box 3, Folder 83.
43 Bryher to H.D. (28 October 1927), Beinecke.
44 H.D., 'The Cinema and the Classics 1: Beauty', *Close Up* I: 1 (July 1927), 26–7; *Cinema and Modernism*, 106–7
45 H.D., 'An Appreciation', *Close Up* IV: 3 (March 1929), 64; *Cinema and Modernism*, 144.
46 H.D., 'Joan of Arc', in *Close Up* III: 1 (July 1928), 19; *Cinema and Modernism*, 132.

47 Ibid. 133.

48 H.D., 'The Cinema and the Classics I: Beauty', 107, 109

49 Bryher reported Pabst as saying: 'War was the mixture of hunger and erotic feelings' (Bryher, letter to H.D. (28 October 1927), Beinecke). In notes on this period made many years later, Bryher wrote:

> As Pabst said, 'real life is so romantic and so ghostly.'
> Joyless Street. The horrors of war had fallen chiefly upon those who neither accepted it nor understood it.
> We shall always remember Garbo as she crossed that street (Freudlose Gasse).
> Anyone can photograph a beautiful woman, Pabst said, it is to get the value behind the beauty that is rare.
> We could accept the images of a new art.
> (Beinecke, Bryher, Autobiographical notes: Berlin Box 72, Folder 2856)

50 Lotte H. Eisner, *The Haunted Screen*, trans. Roger Greaves (Berkeley: University of California Press, 1973), 256.

51 Kenneth Macpherson, 'As Is' *Close Up* I: 6 (December 1927), 24.

52 H.D. 'Russian Films', *Close Up*, III: 3 (September 1928), 28; *Cinema and Modernism,* 138.

53 In an otherwise appreciative review of C. A. Lejeune's *Cinema*, Macpherson wrote: 'My complaint is disappointment in the first chapter that Chaplin is again approached as a minor deity, as the great panjandrum of the whimsical. Chaplin is played out now, spoilt really by what has been written about him. Little has survived the wreckage' (*Close Up* VIII: 4 (December 1931), 332).

54 Bryher, 'War from More Angles', *Close Up* I: 4 (October 1927), 45.

55 Paul Rotha, *The Film Till Now: A Survey of the Cinema* (London: Jonathan Cape, 1930), 124.

56 Kenneth Macpherson, 'As Is', *Close Up* III: 3 (September 1928), 10.

57 H.D., 'Russian Films', 135.

58 Paul Virilio, *War and Cinema: The Logistics of Perception*, trans. Patrick Camiller (London: Verso, 1989), 20.

59 Macpherson, *Close Up* III: 3, 12.

60 Macpherson, *Close Up* I: 6, 26.

61 Kenneth Macpherson wrote of Edith Jehanne in *Die Liebe der Jeanne Ney*: 'Here she goes through the film like an arrow, unblurred and definite and admirable. Her power is in her eyes which give the dual impression of defencelessness and courage. Pabst moves her through his film bringing out both these qualities until the power of it is almost stunning' (*Close Up* I: 6 (December 1927), 22).

62 Macpherson, *Close Up*, III: 3 (September 1928), 5.

63 Ibid. 8.

64 Ibid. 13.

65 Jean Lenauer's article on Dziga-Vertov appeared in *Close Up* V: 6 (December 1929), 464.

66 Kenneth Macpherson, *Close Up*, III: 3 (September 1928), 25.

67 Bryher, *Film Problems of Soviet Russia*, 26.

68 Ibid. 56.

69 Ibid. 116.

70 Ibid. 132.

71 Ibid. 24.

72 H.D., 'Expiation', *Close Up* II: 5 (May 1928), 42; *Cinema and Modernism*, 126.

73 Bryher, *Film Problems of Soviet Russia*, 38.

74 Ibid. 76.

75 Leo Mur, in a conversation on *The Battleship Potemkin* at one of the Association for Revolutionary Cinema's Thursday discussions (14 January 1926). Quoted in Anne Nesbet, *Savage Junctures: Sergei Eisenstein and the Shape of Thinking* (London: I. B. Tauris, 2003), 6.

76 S. M. Eisenstein, 'The New Language of Cinematography', in *Close Up* IV: 5 (May 1929), 12.

77 Anthony Gishford, *Isis* (14 January 1930).

78 Robert Herring, 'The Week on the Screen', *Manchester Guardian* (13 April 1929).

79 *Workers' Life* (17 May 1929).

80 Ralph Bond, Review of *Film Problems*, *Film Weekly* (8 September 1929).

81 Henry Dobb, Review of *Film Problems*, *Sunday Worker* (23 June 1929).

82 Harry Alan Potamkin, Review of *Film Problems*, *Experimental Cinema: A Monthly Projecting Important International Film Manifestations*, 1: 1 (February 1930), 3.

83 'Storm over Asia', *Daily Express* (15 January 1929).

84 In May 1930, Eisenstein and the cinematographer Tisse sailed to New York, followed soon after by Alexandrov. They then joined Montagu in Hollywood. Eisenstein worked on scenarios for two films—*Sutter's Gold* (based on Blaise Cendrars' novel *L'or*) and Dreiser's *An American Tragedy*. Neither project came to fruition in the forms planned by Eisenstein; Paramount turned to Josef von Sternberg to film the Dreiser novel. Eisenstein then travelled to Mexico, with the sponsorship of the writer Upton Sinclair, to make a film about the country, to be called *Qué Viva Mexico*: financial and practical difficulties arose which led to the withdrawal of the support of the Soviet authorities for Eisenstein's work abroad. Eisenstein's film footage was used to make other films, including *Thunder over Mexico*. Eisenstein returned to the USSR, deeply disappointed by the experience, in 1932. See Ronald Bergan, *Eisenstein: A Life in Conflict* (London: Little, Brown, 1997), 190–240, and Ivor Montagu, *With Eisenstein in Hollywood* (Berlin: Seven Seas, 1968). Montagu's book contains the scenarios of *Sutter's Gold* and *An American Tragedy*.

85 Macpherson responded with some coolness to Montagu's offer of an article on 'what the Russian Cinema is doing', illustrated with stills, and Montagu and the *Close Up* group remained distanced, though in later years Montagu would speak very positively of their activities and of *Film Problems of Soviet Cinema*:

'Bryher's book made people interested [in Russian cinema]. Bryher and *Close Up* made the films known before we showed them' (Montagu, interview in *Sight and Sound*, 13: 3 (Autumn 1972), 94).

86 Conservative Party Memorandum, held in The Film Society Collection, BFI, Item 16. Henry Dobb, film critic of *Cinema*, appears to have leaked a copy of the Memorandum ('Memorandum on Revolutionary Film Propaganda, carried out in England by direction of the Soviet Government, 1927–May 1930') to Sidney Bernstein. The entry for 1930 reads: 'The first five months of 1930 have shown striking results of the co-ordinated work of the *Film Society* (Ivor Montagu), the *London Workers' Film Society* (Ivor Montagu, Emile Burns, R. Bond), "*Close-Up*", a Film Magazine published by *Pool* (containing articles by R. Bond, S. M. Eisenstein, Bryher, etc.), and the Communist Party of Great Britain supported by the *Komintern.*'

87 *Close Up*, February 1930, page 14 is given as the source for this quote, but it does not appear there.

88 G. A. Atkinson, film critic for the *Daily Express*, launched a public attack on the Film Society in a column published on 22 October 1930, entitled 'Propaganda by Banned Films: How the Censors are defied. Private Societies'. He wrote that the private film societies, founded 'with the ostensible object of showing films of an "unusual" or "cultural" nature', had in fact as their real object the serving 'as a channel for the exploitation of subversive and undesirable film, chiefly of Moscow origin, the entrance of which, by other means, had been stopped.' By this date the private societies included not only the Film Society, but also the workers' film societies which, Atkinson asserted, 'are linked up with an international organisation of workers' film societies, which takes its orders direct from Moscow, via an organisation called the "Komintern". The method on which the workers' film societies operate is to appoint an organiser in each factory, whose duty it is to recruit attendance for these exhibitions of subversive films'. An Editorial in the same paper, entitled 'What is the Film Society?' stated: 'This society started by being an innocent diversion of the intellectuals, for whom Sunday afternoon is always a trying time. But the films it is now in the habit of presenting suggest that, knowingly or unknowingly, it is engaged in furthering the subversive propaganda of the Bolsheviks—an extremely undesirable form of activity for a British society.'

Defending the Film Society in a letter to the editor, Edmund Dulac wrote: 'The sole criterion of the Council in selecting programmes has been artistic and technical merit, and it is unreasonable to expect a Society formed for the express purpose of studying the evolution of film art and technique, to discriminate against any one country, particularly when that country has, by universal consent, produced by greatest living master of film technique [Eisenstein].' (Both MSS held in The Film Society Collection, BFI, Item 16.)

89 Robert Herring to H.D., Beinecke, Box 10, Folder 353.

90 Robert Herring, *Films of the Year 1927–1928* (London: The Studio Ltd., 1928),
    5. Herring wrote: 'The cinema alone can answer our growing need to be fully
    articulate—to have one sense no longer left out in the cold, taken no notice
    of, told to be good and repress itself. But this sense of movement cannot be
    repressed because our life is more and more influenced by it. Our reactions are
    being more and more caused by it, our feelings, as we drive down a busy street
    or fly over it are more and more stirred by the fact of driving and flying. Three
    dimensional painting and stream of consciousness writing are but misdirected
    attempts to achieve in a static what can be done in a fluid medium. That is why
    the cinema is an art—because it expresses a part of us that can be expressed
    no other way' (5–6). The use of a form of 'stream of consciousness' in writing
    about the cinema, was, however, an attempt by Herring, and the *Close Up*
    writers more generally, to achieve a sense of the fluidity of film in a discursive
    medium.

91 Kenneth Macpherson, 'As Is', *Close Up* I: 2 (August 1927), 5.

92 Anne Friedberg's *Writing about Cinema* discusses this aspect of *Close Up* in very
    interesting ways.

93 Macpherson, *Close Up* III: 3 (September 1927), 5.

94 Dorothy Richardson, 'Continuous Performance', *Close Up*, I: 1 (July 1927), 34;
    Cinema and Modernism, 160.

95 Robert Herring, 'Jannings in *The Way of All Flesh*', *Close Up* I: 5 (November
    1927), 33.

96 Ibid. 35.

97 'Comment and Review', *Close Up* I: 2 (August 1927), 63–4.

98 Kenneth Macpherson, 'As Is', *Close Up* I: 4 (October 1927), 8.

99 Ibid. 10.

100 This concept of film's appeal to, and engagement of, eye and mind was, as we
    have seen, a central trope in early film criticism. It lay at the heart of Gerald
    Buckle's *The Mind and the Film* (1926) (reviewed critically by Bryher ('More-
    About-Films', *The Outlook* (22 January 1927), 90) especially in his chapter on
    'Photographic Aids to the Mind'. Rachael Low wrote of his account: 'Here
    [Buckle] discussed the techniques of cinematography as if a retinal impression
    was the only consequence of the image. Again and again it was assumed that the
    spectator's mind would be doing what the film image was doing: if the picture
    faded the mind would experience "complete loss of the thought movement",
    slow motion cinematography would cause slow thought, overuse of leisurely
    fading would even produce "a state of coma". In fact, of course, what the
    mind would be doing was to observe that fading or slow movement was being
    presented before it, and interpreting its significance. It was as a corollary to
    Buckle's mechanistic view that despite his good intentions he undervalued the
    very aspect of film in which he claimed to be most interested, the part played
    by the mind. What both he and [Vachel] Lindsay ignored was that besides

being visual, the film occupied time. Because of this it was necessary to provide the mind with something to think about at the risk, quite simply, of being a bore. Leisurely fading produces not a coma, but a spectator who is thinking about something else. But their complete lack of interest in film content, and therefore in film structure, made it unlikely that either of them would discover the truth.' (Rachael Low, *The History of the British Film: 1918–1929* (London: George Allen and Unwin, 1971) 24–5).

101 Kenneth Macpherson, 'As Is', *Close Up* I: 4 (October 1927), 15–16.

102 Dorothy Richardson, 'Captions', 'Continuous Performance,' *Close Up* I: 3 (September 1927), 54–5; *Cinema and Modernism*, 165.

103 Harry A. Potamkin, 'The Compound Cinema', *Close Up*, IV: 1 (January 1929), 32–7.

104 Kenneth Macpherson, 'Matinee', *Close Up* I: 5 (November 1927), 55.

105 Ibid. 55.

106 Ibid. 60–1.

107 Kenneth Macpherson, 'As Is', *Close Up* V: 6 (December 1929), 454.

108 H.D., Letter (23 September 1927), Beinecke, Box 13 Folder 545.

109 Deleuze, *Cinema 1*, 110.

110 Balázs, *Theory of the Film*, 176.

111 Robert Herring, *London Mercury* vol. XVII (November 1927–April 1928), 702.

112 Ibid. 702–3.

113 For further discussion of this relationship, see Susan Gevirtz, *Narrative's Journey: The Fiction and Film Writing of Dorothy Richardson* (New York: Peter Lang, 1996); Laura Marcus, 'Continuous Performance: Dorothy Richardson', in *Cinema and Modernism*, 150–9; Carol Watts, *Dorothy Richardson: Writers and their Work* (Plymouth, Devon: Northcote House, 1995).

114 Gevirtz, *Narrative's Journey*, 47.

115 Dorothy Richardson, *Dawn's Left Hand*, in *Pilgrimage*, vol. 4 (London: Virago, 1979), 141.

116 May Sinclair, 'The Novels of Dorothy Richardson', *Egoist* 5 (April 1918), 57–9. Repr. in Bonnie Kime Scott (ed.), *The Gender of Modernism* (Bloomington: Indiana University Press, 1990), 444.

117 Dorothy Richardson, letter to Bryher, spring 1927, *Selected Letters of Dorothy Richardson*, ed. Fromm, 134.

118 Dorothy Richardson, 'Continuous Performance', *Close Up* I: 1 (July 1927), 35–6; *Cinema and Modernism*, 160–1.

119 *New York Herald*, 24th April, 1896. Quoted in E. W. and M. M. Robson, *The Film Answers Back* (London: Bodley Head, 1939), 27–8.

120 Dorothy Richardson, 'Continuous Performance: A Tear for Lycidas', *Close Up* VII: 3 (September 1930), 200; *Cinema and Modernism*, 200.

121 Dorothy Richardson, 'Continuous Performance: There's no Place like Home', *Close Up* I: 5 (November 1927), 44; *Cinema and Modernism*, 168.

122 Ibid. 168.

123 Dorothy Richardson, 'Continuous Performance: Narcissus', *Close Up* VIII: 3 (September 1931) 185; *Cinema and Modernism*, 203.

124 See Giuliana Bruno, *Atlas of Emotion*, 7.

125 Dorothy Richardson, 'Continuous Performance XI: Slow Motion', *Close Up* II: 6 (June 1928), 55; *Cinema and Modernism*, 182.

126 Dorothy Richardson, 'Continuous Performance: A Tear for Lycidas', 196.

127 Dorothy Richardson, 'Continuous Performance: Captions', *Close Up* I: 3, (September 1927), 52–3; *Cinema and Modernism*, 164.

128 Ibid. 165.

129 Dorothy Richardson, 'Continuous Performance: Dialogue in Dixie', *Close Up* V: 3 (September 1929), 217; *Cinema and Modernism*, 196.

130 Sergei Eisenstein, *Film Form: Essays in Film Theory*, ed. and trans. Jay Leyda (New York: Harcourt Brace Jovanovich, 1949), 130.

131 Boris Eikhenbaum, 'Problems of Film Stylistics' (1927), in *Screen* 15: 4 (Winter 1974/5), 7–34.

132 Lev Vygotsky, *Thought and Language* (1936; Cambridge, Mass.: MIT Press, 1962), 2.

133 Eikhenbaum, 'Problems of Film Stylistics', 14–15.

134 Dorothy Richardson, 'Continuous Performance II: Musical Accompaniment', *Close Up* I: 2 (August 1927), 59–60; *Cinema and Modernism*, 162.

135 Ibid. 163.

136 Erwin Panofsky, 'Style and Medium in the Motion Picture'. Repr. in Talbot (ed.), *Film*, 20.

137 Thomas Y. Levin, 'Introduction', Siegfried Kracauer, *The Mass Ornament: Weimar Essays*, trans. and ed. by Thomas Y. Levin (Cambridge, Mass.: Harvard University Press, 1995), 25.

138 Ibid. 326.

139 In the articles for his column, written in French, Prévost discussed in detail the parts of the face and the ways in which emotion was expressed through their movements, devoting articles to 'Le Front' (forehead), 'Les Joues' (cheeks), 'Yeux, Nez, Bouche' (eyes, nose, mouth), etc. There are connections here with Jean Epstein's writings on the close up, including his article 'Magnification', though Prévost's is a more 'scientific', even anatomical discourse. The column bears in interesting ways on a number of the tropes of film writing in the period: the interplay between motion, here the muscular movements of the face, and emotion; the identification between the human face and the cinema screen, both surfaces on which motion and emotion would be played out; the relationship between proximity and distance in the aesthetics and politics of *Close Up* as a whole.

140 Dorothy Richardson, 'Continuous Performance: Narcissus', 201–2.

141 Walter Benjamin, 'Little History of Photography', *Selected Writings Volume 2: 1927–1934*, trans. Rodney Livingstone (Cambridge, Mass.: Harvard University Press, 1999), 518.

142 Dorothy Richardson, 'Continuous Performance VII: The Front Rows', *Close Up* II: 1 (January 1928), 60–1; *Cinema and Modernism*, 172–3.

143 Ibid. 63–4; 173–4.

144 Dorothy Richardson, 'Continuous Performance VIII', *Close Up* II: 3 (March 1928), 55; *Cinema and Modernism*, 176.

145 H.D., response to 'Questionnaire', *The Little Review* (12 May 1929), 38–9.

146 H.D., 4 May 1931, Beinecke, Box 14 Folder 551 (May–July 1931).

147 H.D., Beinecke, Folder 546 (31 August 1928).

148 Adalaide Morris, 'The Concept of Projection', in Susan Stanford Friedman and Rachel Blau DuPlessis (eds.), *Signets: Reading H.D.* (Madison: University of Wisconsin Press, 1990), 274–5.

149 Rachel Connor's *H.D. and the Image* (Manchester: Manchester University Press, 2004), is a detailed exploration of the relationship between H.D.'s involvement with film and her fiction and poetry. See also Diana Collecott, 'Images at the Crossroads: The H.D. Scrapbook', in Friedman and DuPlessis (eds.), *Signets*, 155–181; Susan Edmunds, *Out of Line: History, Psychoanalysis and Montage in H.D.'s Long Poems* (Stanford, Calif.: Stanford University Press, 1994); Charlotte Mandel, 'Garbo/Helen: The Self-Projection of Beauty by H.D.', *Women's Studies: An Interdisciplinary Journal* 7: 1–2 (1980), 127–35 and 'The Redirected Image: Cinematic Dynamics in the Style of H.D.', *Literature/Film Quarterly* 11 (1983), 36–45; Susan McCabe, *Cinematic Modernism: Modernist Poetry and Film* (Cambridge: Cambridge University Press, 2005).

150 H.D., *Bid Me to Live: A Madrigal* (New York: Grove Press, 1960), 125.

151 H.D., 'The Cinema and the Classics II: Restraint', *Close Up* I: 2 (August 1927), 30; *Cinema and Modernism*, 110

152 Roger Fry, 'Mr. Gordon Craig's Stage Designs', *The Nation* (16 September 1911), 871.

153 Ibid. 112.

154 H.D., 'The Cinema and the Classics II: Restraint', *Close Up* I: 2, 36; *Cinema and Modernism*, 112–13.

155 H.D., 'Borderline', pamphlet; *Cinema and Modernism*, 232.

156 Sigmund Freud, 'A Metapsychological Supplement to the Theory of Dreams' (1917), *The Standard Edition of the Complete Psychological Works of Sigmund Freud*, trans. James Strachey (London: The Hogarth Press and the Institute of Psychoanalysis, 1957), vol. 14, 225.

157 H.D., 'Expiation', *Close Up* II: 5 (May 1928), 38; *Cinema and Modernism*, 125.

158 Ibid. 39–40; 125.

159 H.D., 'Conrad Veidt: *The Student of Prague*', *Close Up* I: 3 (September 1927), 44; *Cinema and Modernism*, 124.

160 See Laura Marcus, 'The Contribution of H.D.', *Cinema and Modernism*, 102.

161 Eisenstein, 'The Cinematographic Principle and the Ideogram', *Film Form*, 30.

162 H.D., *Tribute to Freud* (Manchester: Carcanet, 1985), 93.

163 Freud, *The Interpretation of Dreams*, Standard Edition (1953), vol. 5, 500.

164 H.D., *Tribute to Freud*, 92.

165 Balázs, *Theory of the Film,* 183.

166 H. D., *Tribute to Freud,* 41.

167 Ibid. 64.

168 Ibid. 30.

169 Ibid. 23.

170 Ibid. 170.

171 Betts's contributions included an article on 'Criticism and the Film Critic' (*Close Up* v: 5 (November 1927), 39–43) in which he argued that: 'In this country, at any rate, film criticism is in a state of chronic muddle … The qualities of permanence must be established.'

172 Ernest Betts, *Heraclitus or the Future of Films* (London: Kegan Paul, Trench, Trubner & Co., 1928), 7.

173 Ibid. 16.

174 Ibid. 14.

175 Ibid. 48.

176 Ibid. 55.

177 Ibid. 32. If the rock-sculpture (like the Theban wall pictures or the Archer Frieze at Susa) was in fact cinema *avant la lettre*, it was, in the modern age, most likely to be seen on the cinema screen, in a context in which films were themselves turning to more and more elaborate representations of early civilizations, whether of Egypt, Greece, Babylon, or Rome.

178 Ibid. 31.

179 Ibid. 30

180 Ibid. 65.

181 Ibid. 85–8.

182 Messel, *This Film Business*, 247.

183 Ibid. 247.

184 Kristin Thompson, '*Dr. Caligari* at the Folies-Bergère', in Mike Budd (ed.), *The Cabinet of Dr. Caligari: Texts, Contexts, Histories* (Brunswick, New Jersey: Rutgers University Press, 1990), 122. See also Duncan Petrie, 'Paul Rotha and Film Theory', in Duncan Petrie and Robert Kruger (eds.), *A Paul Rotha Reader* (Exeter: Exeter University Press, 1999).

185 Rotha, *The Film Till Now,* 249.

186 Ibid. 44.

187 Ibid. 59.

188 Ibid. 263.

189 Ibid. 270–1.

190 Ibid. 241.

191 Ibid. 11.

192 C. A. Lejeune, 'The Week on the Screen', *Manchester Guardian* (12 May 1928).

193 Eric Elliott, *Anatomy of Motion Picture Art* (Territet, Switzerland: POOL, 1928), 38.

194 Ibid. 73.

195 Ibid. 144.

196 Ibid. 139.

197 Ibid. 81.

198 In her diaries, Virginia Woolf wrote, as she revised *To the Lighthouse*: 'I am now & then haunted by some semi mystic very profound life of a woman, which shall all be told on one occasion; & time shall be utterly obliterated; future shall somehow blossom out of the past. One incident—say the fall of a flower—might contain it'. (*Diary*, vol. 3, 118).

199 Elliott, *Anatomy of Motion Picture Art*, 150.

200 Ibid. 142.

201 Ibid. 151.

202 Robert Herring, 'Film Imagery: Pudovkin', *Close Up* III: 4 (October 1928), 32.

203 Robert Herring, 'A New Cinema, Magic and the Avant Garde', *Close Up* IV: 4 (April 1929), 49–50; *Cinema and Modernism*, 51.

204 Ibid. 51–2; 54.

205 Ibid. 54–6.

206 Herring correspondence with Bryher, Beinecke, Gen MSS 97, Box 18.

207 C. K. Ogden and I. A. Richards, *The Meaning of Meaning* (London: Kegan Paul, 1930), 225.

208 While both Macpherson and Herring would almost certainly have seen themselves as 'negrophilic', their attitudes and judgements now seem naive and ignorant. In one letter, Herring wrote to Bryher (17 Feb. 1929): 'What I can't get clear is the African background. It is awfully odd for us to have these Negroes like us in America and then across in Africa Negroes still uncivilised, isn't it? As if the Stone Age was happening simultaneously in Ireland.'

209 Robert Herring, 'The Movies', *London Mercury* 19: 111 (January 1929), 316.

210 Robert Herring, 'The Films', *Drawing and Design* IV: 23 (May 1928), 118.

211 'Mercurius', 'Pictures in the "Pictures": The Wonderful Deception of Nina Petrovna', *Architectural Review* (July 1929), 41.

212 'Mercurius', 'Abstractions', *Architectural Review* (September 1929), 140.

213 Roland Barthes, 'The Third Meaning: Research Notes on Some Eisenstein Stills', in *Image, Music, Text*, essays selected and trans. by Stephen Heath. (London: Fontana, 1977), 67.

214 Man Ray, 'Emak Bakia', *Close Up* I: 2 (August 1927), 40.

215 Oswell Blakeston, 'Stills and their Relation to Cinema', *Close Up* VIII: 1 (March 1931), 26.

216 Oswell Blakeston, 'Talking Stills', *Close Up* v: 5 (November 1929), 425.

217 H.D., 'An Appreciation', *Close Up* IV: 3 (March 1929), 66–7; *Cinema and Modernism*, 147. Ibid. 58, 147–8.

218 See Raymond Bellour, 'The Pensive Spectator', *Wide Angle* IX: 1 (1987) 6–7. Bellour's argument is discussed in Laura Mulvey, *Death 24 [Times] a Second*, 185–6, in which Mulvey explores the relationship between the still and the moving image, linking this to the ways in which new visual technologies have enabled a slowing and pausing of the moving image, and exploring the temporal and subjective implications of this stilling of the film.

219 Garrett Stewart, *Between Film and Screen: Modernism's Photosynthesis* (Chicago: Chicago University Press, 1999), 39.

220 Kenneth Macpherson, 'As Is', *Close Up* VIII: 3 (September 1931), 225.

221 In the same issue a photocollage of Macpherson's appeared and, as Anne Friedberg has suggested, 'his excitement about the still photograph at precisely the moment when the sound cinema seemed inevitable and the restraints of film censorship seemed most pronounced was not accidental'. (*Writing about Cinema: "Close Up" 1927–1933*, 232). The photocollage was, in fact, captioned as 'A photo-montage by Kenneth Macpherson of stills from the new "Philips Radio Film" of Joris Ivens'. Ivens's sound film (entitled *Symphonie Industrielle* in France) was an industrial documentary, commissioned by Philips as a publicity film but in fact showing, in the director Léon Moussinac's words, 'the spectre of the physical and moral ruin' of the Eindhoven factory workers employed in producing electric lamps and radio receivers. (Léon Moussinac, *L'Humanité*, 1931. Quoted in Rosalind Delmar, *Joris Ivens: 50 Years of Film-Making* [London: British Film Institute, 1979], 23–4.) Macpherson's photo-montage emphasised the physical labour involved in the making of neon-bulbs through glass-blowing, but the political import of his constructed image remains opaque.

222 Curt Glaser, 'Introduction to Helmar Lerski, *Köpfe des Alltags*. Repr. in David Mellor (ed.), *Germany—The New Photography 1927–33* (London: Arts Council of Great Britain, 1978), 63.

223 Walter Benjamin, 'Little History of Photography', 520.

224 Oswell Blakeston, 'Two Exhibitions', *Close Up* v: 4 (October 1929), 322.

225 Mellor, *Germany—The New Photography*, 115–16.

226 Ibid. 117.

227 Anne Friedberg reassembled the fragments of *Foothills* and *Wing Beat*; they are held in the film collection of the Museum of Modern Art, New York. See also Friedberg, 'Fragments de Films "POOL": 1927–1929', *Travelling*, 56–7, Documents Cinémathèque Suisse (Spring 1980), 60–2.

228 H.D. Autobiographical Notes, Beinecke, Y CAL 24 III Box 47, 1182.

229 H.D. Beinecke. Unpublished 'Wing-Beat' manuscript.

230 Bryher Papers, Beinecke, Gen MSS 97 VIII, Box no 170, Folder no 5674.

231 See, e.g. H.D.'s story 'Narthex', in Alfred Kreymborg, Lewis Mumford and Paul Rosenfeld (eds.), *The Second American Caravan* (New York: Macaulay,

1928); *Kora and Ka* ['Kora and Ka'; 'Mira-Mare'], (Dijon: Darantière, 1935); *The Usual Star* ['The Usual Star', 'Two Americans'], (Dijon: Darantière, 1934); *Nights*, by John Helforth (pseudonym of H.D.), (Dijon: Darantière, 1935.)

232 'Mercurius', 'Act, Fact, and Abstraction', *The Architectural Review* LXVIII (October 1930), 258.

233 Bernhard Rieger, *Technology and the Culture of Modernity in Britain and Germany 1890–1945* (Cambridge: Cambridge University Press, 2005), 218. Rieger's study contains a very interesting account of amateur film-making in Germany in the 1920s and early 1930s: see 193–223.

234 Kenneth Macpherson, 'Wie ein Meisterstück enstand', *Film für Alle* 12 (1929). (My translation).

235 Kenneth Macpherson, *Close Up* i: 1 (July 1927), 14.

236 Beinecke. *Borderline* scrapbook, 23.

237 The *Borderline* pamphlet was first published by Mercury Press in 1930. It is reprinted in *Cinema and Modernism*, 221–36.

238 *Borderline*; *Cinema and Modernism*, 234.

239 Beinecke. *Borderline* programme note.

240 Herring, letter to Bryher, 21 December 1928, Beinecke. Racial representations in Bryher's letters are particularly troubling. Letters from Bryher to H.D. *c.*1933–4 chart her visit to Harlem, Kenneth Macpherson's plans for a book on 'Negro culture', and Nancy Cunard's 'Negro' anthology, combined with this remark: 'Nancy has one new black illiterate gorilla and one small but even blacker negro from Oxford' (? 1933). 'Negroes' are frequently described as monkeys and gorillas. A letter from Bryher to H.D. discussed Kenneth's black boyfriend: 'I shouldn't worry about Rvr (Macpherson). I think he has zoophilia probably and is really looking for a gorilla ... It's sheer vanity because the dark woolliness sets off the Kelt.'

241 Peter Noble, *The Negro in Films* (London: Skelton Robinson, n.d.), 145.

242 Thomas Cripps, *Slow Fade to Black: The Negro in American Film 1900–1942* (Oxford: Oxford University Press, 1977), 209–10.

243 *Borderline*; *Cinema and Modernism*, 223.

244 Adalaide Morris, 'The Concept of Projection', 284.

245 H.D.'s story 'Two Americans', a barely fictionalized account of the time spent by the Robesons in Switzerland with Macpherson, Bryher, Herring, and herself, was written in 1930, at around the same time as the *Borderline* pamphlet. It opens with a description of faces (those of Saul Howard (Paul Robeson) and Raymonde Ransome (H.D.)) become 'static symbols ... mask on contrasting mask, the one white, the other, as it happened, black'. The image strongly recalls not only the masked theatre and poetic drama (discussed in Ch. 1) which seems to have so strongly underlain H.D.'s models of film, but also Man Ray's photographic series of 1926, *Noire et blanche*, and, in particular, his photographs of the model Kiki, the perfect white oval of her face adjacent to an African mask. The title poem of H.D.'s collection 'Red Roses for Bronze' (London:

Chatto and Windus, 1931), was an impassioned address to Robeson, in which she represented him as a bronze statue.

246 *Borderline*; *Cinema and Modernism*, 226.

247 *Borderline*; *Cinema and Modernism*, 230.

248 See Anne Friedberg, 'Introduction' to *Borderline*; *Cinema and Modernism*, 219–20.

249 'Mercurius', 'Act, Fact and Abstraction', *Architectural Review* LXVIII (October 1930), 258.

250 Freud, 'Introductory Lectures', *Standard Edition*, vol. 16, (1963) 450.

251 Kenneth Macpherson, 'As Is', *Close Up* VII: 5 (November 1930), 294; *Cinema and Modernism*, 236.

252 Ibid. 293–4; 236–7.

253 Ibid. 296; 237–8

254 Roland Cosandey, 'On *Borderline*', 54.

255 Bryher, 'Danger in the Cinema', *Close Up* VII: 5 (November 1930), 302–3.

256 Kenneth Macpherson, 'As Is', *Close Up* VII: 5 (November 1930), 294

257 Carl Vincent (5 December 1930), *Indépendence Belge*, Beinecke, *Borderline* Scrapbook, 5.

258 The film was impounded at customs in America in October 1931, and refused entry, presumably because of its representations of 'interracial' sexualities.

259 *The Daily Film Renter* wrote: 'If you want to be relieved of the necessity of counting your takings I suggest you get a date on this film' (14 October 1930).

260 David Ockham, Beinecke, cutting in *Borderline* Scrapbook, 11.

261 *Cinema*, 14.10.30.

262 J.S., *Manchester Guardian* (14 October 1930).

263 C. A. Lejeune, 'The Pictures: Critic as Creator', *Observer* (19 October 1930).

264 E. A. Baughan, 'Robeson as Film Player: A High-Brow Amateur Picture', *News Chronicle* (4 October 1930)

265 Macpherson, *Close Up* VII: 5 (November 1930), 295–6; *Cinema and Modernism*, 237.

266 Correspondence Bryher–Kenneth Macpherson, 1931–2, Beinecke, uncat. Ms vault Pearson/Bryher.

267 The phrase should read: 'eine ganz merkwürdige sadistiche Phantasie'.

268 Bryher, 'Berlin April 1931', *Close Up* VIII: 2 (June 1931), 132–3.

269 Bryher, letter to H.D., Beinecke, 29 April 1931.

270 Quoted in 'Sense of Strangulation', *Film Weekly*, 11.2.1929. Clipping in Beinecke, Gen Mss 97, Bryher Papers, Box 178, Folder 5750. Scrapbook: Cinema 1927–9).

271 Bryher, letter to Macpherson, Beinecke, May 1931.

272 Bryher also saw *Das Lied des Lebens* at this time, which included the filming of a Caesarian operation: 'I really wonder though if these kind of films are good for the general public. Far be it from me to be narrow minded and it may be good to show them but they certainly are a psychic shock and I don't know how far good if one is not analysed or some way sure of one's reactions.

Henselmann alternately squirmed and gloated and I think it may not be good for one's sadistic instincts' (Beinecke. Letter to H.D., 30 April 1931).

273 Bryher, letter to Kenneth Macpherson, Beinecke, 23 June 1932, MS Vault Uncat. Pearson–Macpherson, Bryher to KM, 1931–2.

274 Bryher, letter to Macpherson, Beinecke, 7 August 1932.

275 Oswell Blakeson, letter to Kenneth Macpherson, Beinecke, 19 September 1932.

276 Macpherson, letter to Bryher, Beinecke, 26 September 1936.

277 On 30 August 1934, Macpherson wrote to Bryher: 'I ceased making films when it was useless making any more films without sound, and ... I have always said that the commercial film does not interest me ... after the sound film, Switzerland was no place for films any more—and there were no films and no developments to give vitality to something checked and maybe finished as an art.' In the late 1930s, Macpherson began work on a 'History of the Negro', his art and culture. This project was first offered to Bryher by the publisher Cobden Sanderson: in 1938 she passed it on to Macpherson (who had contributed to Nancy Cunard's *Negro* anthology), but the book never materialized.

278 Bryher, letter to H.D., Beinecke, 25 April 1931.

279 Bryher, 'Berlin April 1931', 126.

280 Bryher, 'Notes on Some Films: Berlin, June 1932'. *Close Up* IX: 3 (September 1932), 196.

281 Hanns Sachs, 'Kitsch', *Close Up* IX: 3 (September 1932), 202; *Cinema and Modernism*, 264.

282 Siegfried Kracauer, 'The Little Shopgirls Go to the Movies', in *The Mass Ornament*, 292.

283 Bryher, 'What Shall You Do in the War?', *Close Up* X: 2 (June 1933), 192; *Cinema and Modernism*, 309.

CODA: THE COMING OF SOUND

1 St John Ervine, *Spectator* (4 May 1929), 682.

2 John Gould Fletcher, *The Crisis of the Film* (Seattle: University of Washington Book Store, 1929), 28.

3 Bryher, *The Heart to Artemis: A Writer's Memoirs* (London: Collins, 1963), 247–8. Bryher, in fact, continued to see and to write about films after the demise of *Close Up*. The magazine *Life and Letters To-Day*, which Bryher bought in 1935, and which was edited by Robert Herring, included a substantial amount of writing on the cinema. In a letter, Herring wrote to Bryher: 'as a great many of our readers may not at first take to the idea of an enlarged cinema section, would it not be a good idea to explain what cinema stands for? I thought of writing to numbers of people, asking them to say what they get from film, or think film, might do, or what it doesn't do. Make of their replies a sort of symposium which would give readers who may not have followed film, some realisation' (29 June 1935, Beinecke, Box 18, Robert Herring Folder 705). In

1939, Bryher also bought the *London Mercury* (which had 3,000 suscribers) for £800 (2 April 1939: Beinecke Folder 2579).

4 Bryher, *Heart to Artemis*, 265.

5 Bryher, letter to Macpherson, Beinecke, Correspondence 1938 (Gen MSS 97 1, Box 67, Folder 2575), 12 April 1938.

6 It is certainly the case that in 1931, Bryher was struck by Metzner's suggestion that *Borderline* could have been made as a sound film in Berlin for less money than they had paid 'and that if we could get about five hundred pounds together we could easily make a sound film here and even perhaps tie up with a company to produce it' (Letter to H.D., Beinecke, 3 May 1931).

7 Kenneth Macpherson, 'As Is', *Close Up* VII: 5 (November 1930), 294; *Cinema and Modernism*, 237.

8 Dorothy Richardson, 'Continuous Performance: Dialogue in Dixie', *Close Up* V: 3 (September 1929), 214; *Cinema and Modernism*, 194.

9 Tom Conley, 'The Talkie: Early Cinematic Conversation', in S. I. Salamensky (ed.), *Talk, Talk, Talk: The Cultural Life of Everyday Conversation* (New York and London: Routledge, 2001), 86.

10 'Mercurius', 'Sound Film and the "Talkies" ', *The Architectural Review* LXV (June 1929), 301.

11 Rotha, *The Film Till Now*, 306.

12 H.D., 'The Mask and the Movietone', *Close Up* I: 5 (November 1927), 31; *Cinema and Modernism*, 119.

13 See Scott Eyman, *The Speed of Sound: Hollywood and the Talkie Revolution, 1926–1930* (New York: Simon and Schuster, 1997), 208 and Tim Armstrong, *Modernism, Technology and the Body: A Cultural Study* (Cambridge: Cambridge University Press, 1998), 222–6.

14 Dorothy Richardson, 'Continuous Performance: The Film Gone Male', *Close Up* IX: 1 (May 1932), 206.

15 Quoted in Eyman, *The Speed of Sound,* 278.

16 Rotha, *The Film Till Now*, 300.

17 Balázs, *Theory of the Film*, 44–5. For Balázs, gesture was intertwined with the expression and comprehension of emotion. Michael North, in his chapter on *Close Up* in *Camera Work*, points out that there was a contradiction between the claim for the universality of silent film's appeal and the idea that spectators had to be 'trained' into spectatorship. In fact, a number of critics in the early decades of the century suggested that both the medium and its spectators had to learn the new languages of universalism and of internationalism (Esperanto, after all, had to be acquired like any other second language) and of visual representation. Thus the novelist and dramatist Margaret Kennedy wrote, in her pamphlet *The Mechanized Muse* (1942):

For twenty years the silent film, developing inside its inherent limitations, had been making progress towards its own kind of form and shape. Sound was denied to it; therefore its tendency was to make sound irrelevant. Obliged to rely upon the eye alone, it was exploring the field of visual experience, and learning how to reject all material which could not be treated visually. Captions were disappearing. The picture was less and less liable to be interrupted by printed placards, telling the audience what was happening and what the characters were saying to one another. A technique had been evolved which could largely dispense with them. Actors emerged who felt no need of speech. Charlie Chaplin, for instance, felt the need of it so little that, when the sound film was invented, he refused the new tool and continued, for many years, to act silently. For him, as for all great artists, the limitation had become the inspiration: the impossible was also the superfluous. Truth, for him, was not to be found in speech.

(Margaret Kennedy, *The Mechanized Muse*
(London: George Allen & Unwin, 1942), 14.)

18 Cavell, *The World Viewed*, 147.

19 Dorothy Richardson, 'Continuous Performance: A Tear for Lycidas', *Close Up* VII: 3 (September, 1930), 197; *Cinema and Modernism*, 196.

20 Ibid. 200.

21 There is a vast literature on early sound film and sound technology. Early book-length discussions included Fitzhugh Green, *The Film Finds its Tongue* (New York: G. B. Putnam, 1929) and John Scotland, *The Talkies* (London: Crosby Lockwood and Son, 1930). Rudolf Arnheim and Béla Balázs produced some of the most interesting theoretical discussions of the aesthetics of sound in its early years. More recent studies include Richard Abel and Rick Altman (eds.), *The Sounds of Early Cinema* (Bloomington: Indiana University Press, 2001); Rick Altman (ed.), *Sound Theory, Sound Practice* (New York and London: Routledge 1992); Rick Altman, *Silent Film Sound* (New York: Columbia University Press, 2004); Pascal Bonitzer, *Le Regard et la voix* (Paris: Union Général d'Editions, 1976); Michel Chion, *La Voix au cinéma* (Paris: Cahiers du *Cinéma*, 1982); Harry M. Geduld, *The Birth of the Talkies: From Edison to Jolson* (Indiana: Indiana University Press, 1975); Douglas Gomery, *The Coming of Sound* (New York, Routledge: 2005); Steve Neale, *Cinema and Technology: Image, Sound, Colour* (London/Basingstoke: Macmillan/British Film Institute, 1985); Kaja Silverman, *The Acoustic Mirror: The Female Voice in Psychoanalysis and Cinema* (Bloomington: Indiana University Press, 1988); Elisabeth Weis and John Belton, *Film Sound: Theory and Practice* (New York: Columbia University Press, 1985). See also the *Yale French Studies* special issue on film sound, vol. 60, (1980), 269–86.

22 Tom Gunning, 'The Cinema of Attractions: Early Film, its Spectator and the Avant-Garde', in Joanne Hollows, Peter Hutchings, and Mark Jancovich (eds.), *The Film Studies Reader* (London: Arnold, 2000), 163.

23 Michael Rogin, *Blackface, White Noise: Jewish Immigrants in the Hollywood Melting Pot* (Berkeley and Los Angeles: Universiy of California Press, 1996), 91.

24 Ibid. 82–3.

25 Quoted ibid. 83.

26 Herring had written to Bryher: 'Do get Fisher, White, Hughes, Cullen, W. R. Dubois, Johnson. Write the stars of "Hallelujah"—Honey Brown and Daniel Haynes—for their views, and James B. Low of "Uncle Tom" (Universal) and King Vidor wrote once for you, he ought to again, on "Hallelujah's" making. But as few whites as possible ... Forgive, forgive, forgive, but I'll do ANYthing, & I'm so afraid a Negro number will fall through, and I'm sure it shouldn't' (Herring to Bryher, Beinecke, 1 February 1929).

27 Elmer Anderson Carter, 'Of Negro Motion Pictures', *Close Up* v: 2 (August 1929), 119.

28 Geraldyn Dismond, 'The Negro Actor and the American Movies', *Close Up* v: 2 (August 1929), 97.

29 Kenneth Macpherson, 'As Is', *Close Up* v: 2 (August 1929), 90.

30 Harry A. Potamkin, 'The AfraAmerican Cinema', *Close Up* v: 2 (August 1929), 114; *Cinema and Modernism*, 70.

31 Richardson, 'Dialogue in Dixie', *Close Up* v: 3 (September 1929), 213; *Cinema and Modernism*, 193–4.

32 Ibid. 194. See also Rebecca Egger, 'Deaf Ears and Dark Continents: Dorothy Richardson's Cinematic Epistemology', *Camera Obscura* 30 (May 1992), 5–33.

33 Aldous Huxley, 'Silence is Golden: Being the Misanthropic Reflections of an English Novelist on First Hearing a Picture Talk', *Vanity Fair* (July 1929), 72.

34 Green, *Film Finds a Tongue*. These issues are discussed in very interesting ways by Tim Armstrong in *Modernism, Technology and the Body*.

35 Messel, *This Film Business*, 252–3.

36 Ernest Betts, 'Talking Films', *Manchester Guardian* (1 September 1928).

37 Eisenstein, 'The Principles of the New Russian Cinema' (1930), in *Selected Works*, vol. 1, 200.

38 Sergei Eisenstein, *Nonindifferent Nature: Film and the Structure of Things*, trans. Herbert Marshall (Cambridge: Cambridge University Press, 1987), 226.

39 Kenneth Macpherson, 'As Is', *Close Up* v: 4 (October 1929), 262; *Cinema and Modernism*, 92.

40 Ibid. 90.

41 Hugh Castle, 'Elstree's First "Talkie"' *Close Up*, v: 2, (August 1929), 133.

42 'Mercurius', 'Blackmail', *Architectural Review* LXVI (August 1929), 87.

43 Robert Herring, *London Mercury* XIX (November 1928–April 1929), 201–2.

44 Macpherson, *Close Up* v: 4, (October 1929), 263; *Cinema and Modernism*, 93.

45 The connection would, in fact, have been made if Hitchcock had been allowed to produce the ending he had planned, in which, as he put it, 'After the chase and the death of the blackmailer, the girl would have been arrested and the young man would have had to do the same things to her that we saw at the beginning: handcuffs, booking at the police station, and so on ... But the producers claimed it was too depressing' (François Truffaut, *Hitchcock* (London: Paladin, 1978), 70–1).

46 Tom Ryall, *Blackmail* (London: British Film Institute, 1993), 36.

47 Ibid. 39.

48 Barr, *English Hitchcock*, 83.

49 Truffaut, *Hitchcock*, 74.

50 Alice was played by the actress Anny Ondra, whose heavy Czech accent was unsuitable for the sound track; Joan Barry spoke the lines from just off camera while Ondra mimed to the camera. Dubbing was not a possibility for Hitchcock at this stage of sound technology.

51 Michel Chion, *La Voix au Cinema*, quoted in Kaja Silverman, *The Acoustic Mirror: The Female Voice in Psychoanalysis and Cinema* (Bloomington: Indiana University Press, 1988), 77.

52 Ryall, *Blackmail*, 53.

53 Anthony Asquith, *The Penguin Film Review*, no. 1, (1946) 23. Quoted in Ryall, *Blackmail*, 33.

54 Balázs, *Theory of the Film*, 213.

55 Alfred Döblin, '*Ulysses* by Joyce', in Anton Kaes, Martin Jay, and Edward Dimendberg (eds.), *The Weimar Republic Sourcebook* (Berkeley and Los Angeles: University of California Press, 1994), 514.

56 Walter Benjamin, 'The Crisis of the Novel' (1930), in *Walter Benjamin: Selected Writing*, vol. 2: *1927–1934* (Cambridge, Mass.: Harvard, 1999), 301.

57 Eisenstein, 'Help Yourself', in *Selected Works*, vol. 1, 234–6. See also 'Literature and Cinema', ibid. 95–9.

58 Eisenstein, 'An American Tragedy', *Close Up* X: 2 (June 1933), 120.

59 Ibid.

60 Eisenstein, 'Literature and Cinema', *Selected Works*, vol. 1, 96.

61 Eisenstein, *An American Tragedy*, 121.

62 Eisenstein, 'Literature and Cinema', *Selected Works*, vol. 1, 96.

63 Eisenstein, 'Sur Joyce', *Change* (May 1972) 51. My translation.

64 Ibid. Joyce told Harriet Shaw Weaver about the 'prolonged cinema nights' he had experienced when his eyes were bandaged after a cataract operation. He explained this further in a letter: 'Whenever I am obliged to lie with my eyes closed I see a cinematograph going on and on and it brings back to my memory things I had almost forgotten' (Letter to Signora Schmitz, cited in James Joyce, *Letters*, vol. 3, ed. Richard Ellmann (New York: Viking, 1966), 216).

65 Eisenstein, 'Sur Joyce', 52–3.

66 Quoted in Gleb Struve, *Russian Literature Under Lenin and Stalin 1917–1953* (Norman: University of Oklahoma Press, 1971), 273–5. Cited in Emily Tall, 'Eisenstein on Joyce: Sergei Eisenstein's Lecture on James Joyce at the State Institute of Cinematography, November 1, 1934', *James Joyce Quarterly*, 24:2 (1987), 133–42.

67 Transcript of Eisenstein's lecture in Tall, 'Eisenstein on Joyce', 137.

68 Eisenstein, 'Sur Joyce', 51.

69 Graham Greene, *Mornings in the Dark: The Graham Greene Reader*, ed. David Parkinson (Harmondsworth: Penguin, 1993), 447–8.

70 Ibid. 444.

71 Ibid. 414.

72 Ibid. xxxii.

73 Graham Greene, *It's a Battlefield* (1934) (London: Vintage, 2002), 24.

74 Ibid. 136–7.

75 Bernard Bergonzi, *Reading the Thirties* (London: Macmillan, 1938), 120–2.

76 Greene, *Mornings in the Dark*, 80.

77 Graham Greene, *Brighton Rock* (London: Vintage, 2004), 52

78 F. R. Leavis, 'Mass Civilization, Minority Culture', in *Education and the University* (London: Chatto and Windus, 1948), 149. The 'emotional appeals' of film, Leavis writes, are 'the more insidious because they are associated with a compellingly vivid illusion of actual life'.

79 Greene, *Brighton Rock*, 195–6.

80 Christopher Isherwood, *Goodbye to Berlin* (London: The Hogarth Press, 1939), 13.

81 Samuel Hynes, *The Auden Generation: Literature and Politics in England in the 1930s* (London: Faber and Faber, 1979), 356.

82 Charles Madge and Tom Harrisson, *Mass-Observation* (London: Frederick Muller, 1937), 10.

83 Keith Williams, *British Writers and the Media 1930–45* (Basingstoke, Macmillan, 1996), 174. For discussion of *Prater Violet*, see also Michael Wood, 'Modernism and Film', in Michael Levenson (ed.), *The Cambridge Companion to Modernism* (Cambridge: Cambridge University Press, 1999), 218–19.

84 Christopher Isherwood, *Prater Violet* (London: Minerva, 1997), 77.

85 Ibid. 64.

86 Ibid. 23.

87 Ibid. 25.

88 Davy, *Footnotes*, 290–1.

89 John Grierson, 'The G.P.O. Gets Sound', in *Cinema* (Summer 1934), 217.

90 Cavell, *The World Viewed,* 150.

91 Paul Rotha, *Documentary Film* (London: Faber and Faber, 1936), 199.

92 For discussion of Auden and Britten's collaborations, see Donald Mitchell, *Britten and Auden in the Thirties: The Year 1936* (Woodbridge, Boydell, 2000). Auden worked for the GPO Film Unit for six months in 1935–6. The experience appears not to have been an altogether satisfactory one, and he used the writing of a review of Rotha's *Documentary Film* as an occasion for criticizing the British documentary film movement more generally. He argued that the creative and political freedoms of film-makers within government outfits such as the EMB and the GPO Film Units were severely compromised: 'A documentary film is a film that tells the truth, and truth rarely has advertisement value.' He criticized the schedules of film-making, which required directors to 'turn out a film in a ridiculously short period': 'Inanimate objects, like machines, or facts of organisation, can be understood in a few weeks, but not human beings,

and if documentary films have hitherto concentrated on the former, it is not entirely the fault of the directors.' He also referred to the obstacle of class: 'It is doubtful whether an artist can ever deal more than superficially (and cinema is not a superficial art) with characters outside his own class, and most British documentary directors are upper middle.' Above all, he took issue with the documentary film's concentration on the public as opposed to the private life, insisted upon by Grierson, among others, when he wrote (in an article entitled 'The Story of the Documentary Film'): 'in making films of man in his modern environment, one would be articulating the corporate character of that environment and finding again, after a long period of sloppy romanticism and the person in private, an aesthetic of the person in public.' For Auden, by contrast, 'the private life and the emotions are facts like any others, and one cannot understand the public life of action without them ... A story is the device by which the public and private life are related to each other for the purposes of presentation, and no film which ignores either completely can be good'.

93 Roger Manvell, *Film* (Harmondsworth: Penguin, 1946), 362.

94 Programme notes for 81st Film Society performance, 27 October 1935, repr. in *The Film Society Programmes*, 330.

95 Grierson, quoted by Forsyth Hardy, *John Grierson: A Documentary Biography* (London: Faber and Faber, 1979).

96 Lawrence Goldstein, *The American Poet at the Movies: A Critical History* (Michigan: University of Michigan Press, 1994), 72.

97 *Grierson on Documentary*, ed. Forsyth Hardy (London: Faber and Faber, 1979), 43.

98 Greene, review of *Night Mail*, *The Spectator* (20 March 1936), in *Mornings in the Dark*, 85.

99 Greene, *The Spectator* (11 September 1936), in *Mornings in the Dark*, 138.

100 Rotha, *Documentary Film*, 223.

101 In *The Mechanized Muse*, Kennedy suggested a move from the novel to poetry in film's relationship to literature. She wrote that 'the greatest advantage of the screen medium is a power which it shares with poetry to fuse humanity with its setting, to charge even inanimate objects with emotional significance ... In this way does a poet achieve that touch of universality which is essential if pathos is to be raised to tragedy ... Very little screen poetry has been made as yet. Fifty years of experiment have not lifted this new art much beyond the level of prose. But it is possible to hope that, at the end of another fifty years, poets may have taken to making pictures. And when they do, then at last full use will be made of the medium, with its suggestive subtlety, its rhythm, its deliberate variation of pace, its complete exclusion of anything outside the pattern' (46–7).

If this potential were to be realized, Kennedy suggested, the author would be able to claim the status currently afforded the director: 'It may be that in time screen composers will have fought their way into such a position that they can insist on their own signature'. Kennedy linked this reclamation of authorship to a model of exhibition and spectatorship in the private sphere: 'Films intended for a small audience, a family, possibly only one person, in a dwelling-room, would have to be different from those intended for a crowd in a hall. Anyone who has seen a popular film run through in a small room, for one or two spectators, must have noticed how wrong the pitch seems to be. It is directed at something in him which he should share with several hundred people who are not there. But if films for the home are ever produced there will not be this need to seek for, and satisfy, a great common denominator. There will not be one film public but dozens—as many publics as there are for novels or gramophone records. And among these publics the screen-Keats may get his chance' (51).

Bibliography

Abel, Richard and Rick Altman (eds.), *The Sounds of Early Cinema* (Bloomington Indiana University Press, 2001).

Adair, Gilbert (ed.), *Movies* (Harmondsworth: Penguin, 1999)

Allen, Carleton Kemp, 'Movies and Morals', *The Quarterly Review* 486 (October 1925), 313–30.

Allen, Richard and Malcolm Turvey (eds.), *Camera Obscura, Camera Lucida: Essays in Honour of Annette Michelson* (Amsterdam: Amsterdam University Press, 2003).

Altman, Rick, *Silent Film Sound* (New York: Columbia University Press, 2004).

——(ed.), *Sound Theory, Sound Practice* (New York and London: Routledge 1992).

Akermak, M., *Remembering Iris Barry* (New York: Museum of Modern Art, 1980).

Anderson, Joseph and Barbara, 'Motion Perception in Motion Pictures', in Teresa de Lauretis and Stephen Heath (eds.), *The Cinematic Apparatus* (Basingstoke: Macmillan, 1980), 76–95.

Antliff, Mark, *Inventing Bergson: Cultural Politics and the Parisian Avant-Garde* (Princeton: Princeton University Press, 1993).

Armstrong, Tim, *Modernism, Technology and the Body: A Cultural Study* (Cambridge: Cambridge University Press, 1998).

Arnheim, Rudolf, *Film* (London: Faber and Faber, 1933).

——*Film Essays and Criticism*, trans. Brenda Benthien (Madison: University of Wisconsin Press, 1997).

Askari, Kaveh. 'From "The Horse in Motion" to "Man in Motion": Alexander Black's Detective Lectures', *Early Popular Visual Culture*, 3:1 (May 2005), 59–76.

——'Photographed Tableaux and Motion Picture Aesthetics: Alexander Black's Picture Plays', in J. Plunkett and J. Lyons (eds.), *Optical to Digital: Excavating Multimedia History* (Exeter: University of Exeter Press, forthcoming).

Asquith, Anthony, 'The Play's the Thing', *Films and Filming* 5 (February 1959), 13.

Atkinson, G. A., 'Propaganda by Banned Films: How the Censors are Defied: Private Societies', *Daily Express* (22 October 1930).

Attridge, Derek, *The Cambridge Companion to James Joyce* (Cambridge: Cambridge University Press, 1990).

Atwood, Margaret, Introduction to H. G. Wells, *The Island of Dr Moreau* (London: Penguin, 2005).

Madame B., *La Femme Endormie* (Paris 1899).

Bakshy, Alexander, 'The New Art of the Moving Picture', *Theatre Arts Monthly* XI (April 1927), 280–1.

—— 'The Road to Art in the Motion Picture', *Theatre Arts Monthly* XI (June 1927), 456.

Balázs, Béla, *Schriften zum Film II (1926–1931)*, ed. Wolfgang Gergsh (Berlin: Henschel, 1984), 60.

—— *Theory of the Film*, trans. Edith Bone (London: Dennis Dobson, 1951).

Bandy, Mary Lea, 'Nothing Sacred: "Jock Whitney Snares Antiques for Museum": The Founding of the Museum of Modern Art Film Library', *Studies in Modern Art* (New York: MOMA, December 1995), 3–38.

Barge, Alfred, 'Gesture and the Cinema Play', *Drama* 1 (1919), 86–7.

Barnes, John, *The Beginnings of the Cinema in England 1894–1901*, vol. 1: *1895* (New York: Barnes and Noble, 1976).

Barr, Charles (ed.), *All Our Yesterdays: 90 Years of British Cinema* (London: British Film Institute, 1986).

—— *The English Hitchcock* (Moffat: Cameron and Hollis, 1999).

Barry, Iris, 'The Ezra Pound Period', *Bookman* (New York), (October 1931), 159–71.

—— *Let's Go to the Pictures* (London: Chatto and Windus, 1926).

Barthes, Roland, 'The Third Meaning: Research Notes on Some Eisenstein Stills', *Image, Music, Text,* essays selected and trans. Stephen Heath (London: Fontana, 1977).

Baudelaire, Charles, 'The Painter of Modern Life', in *The Painter of Modern Life and Other Essays*, trans. and ed. Jonathan Mayne (London: Phaidon, 1964).

Baughan, E. A., 'The Art of Moving Pictures', *Fortnightly Review* 106 (July–December 1919), 448–56.

—— 'Robeson as Film Player: A High-Brow Amateur Picture', *News Chronicle* (14 October 1930).

Bazin, André, *What is Cinema?* Essays selected and trans. Hugh Gray. 2 vols. (Berkeley and Los Angeles: University of California Press, 1967, 1971).

Beaumont, Comte de, 'Programme note for The Film Society's 3rd Performance, 20 December 1925', *Film Society Programmes*, 11.

—— 'Of What are the Young Films Dreaming?', *The Little Review* (Winter 1926), 73.

Beer, Gillian, *Virginia Woolf: The Common Ground* (Edinburgh: Edinburgh University Press, 1996).

Bell, Clive, 'Art and the Cinema: A Prophecy…', *Vanity Fair* (November 1922), 40.

—— 'Cinema Aesthetics: A Critic of the Arts Assesses the Movies', *Theatre Guild Magazine* 7: 39, (October 1929), 62–3.

Bellour, Raymond, 'Ideal Hadaly', *Camera Obscura* 15 (Fall 1986), 111–34.

—— 'The Pensive Spectator', *Wide Angle* IX:1 (1987), 6–10.

Benjamin, Walter, 'The Work of Art in the Age of Mechanical Reproduction', *Illuminations: Essays and Reflections*, ed. Hannah Arendt, trans. Harry Zohn (New York: Schocken Books, 1969), 217–52.

Benjamin, Walter, 'The Crisis of the Novel' (1930), *Walter Benjamin: Selected Writing*, vol. 2: *1927–1934* (Cambridge, Mass: Harvard, 1999), 301.

—— 'Kriminalromane, auf Reisen' ['Detective Novels, on Journeys'](1930), *Gesammelte Schriften*, Werkausgabe, vol. 10, 381–2.

—— 'Little History of Photography', *Selected Writings Volume 2: 1927–1934*, trans. Rodney Livingstone (Cambridge, Mass.: Harvard University Press, 1999), 518.

Bergan, Ronald, *Eisenstein: a Life in Conflict* (London: Little, Brown, 1997), 190–240.

Bergson, Henri, *L'Évolution créatrice*, trans. Arthur Mitchell as *Creative Evolution* (London: Macmillan, 1911).

Bergonzi, Bernard, *Reading the Thirties* (London: Macmillan, 1938).

Betts, Ernest, 'Criticism and the Film Critic,' *Close Up* v: 5 (November 1927), 39–43.

—— *Heraclitus or the Future of Films* (London: Kegan Paul, Trench, Trubner & Co., 1928).

—— 'Talking Films', *Manchester Guardian* (1 September 1928).

Blakeston, Oswell, 'Two Exhibitions', *Close Up* v: 4 (October 1929), 321–3.

—— 'Stills and their Relation to Modern Cinema', *Close Up* viii: 1 (March 1931), 20–6.

—— 'Talking Stills', *Close Up* v: 5 (November 1929), 425.

Bloch, Iwan, *The Sexual Life of Our Time: In its Relations to Modern Civilization*, trans. from the 6th German edn. by M. Eden Paul (London: Rebman Ltd., 1908).

Bloem, Walter S., *The Soul of the Moving Picture*, trans. Allen W. Porterfield (New York: E. P. Dutton, 1924).

Bond, Ralph, Review of *Film Problems*, *Film Weekly* (8 September 1929).

Bonitzer, Pascal, *Le regard et la voix* (Paris: Union Général d'Editions, 1976).

'*Borderline* Scrapbook', Beinecke Rare Book and Manuscript Library, Yale University.

Bottomore, Stephen, 'The Panicking Audience? Early Cinema and the "Train Effect", *Historical Journal of Film, Radio and Television* 19: 2 (1999), 177–216.

Bowen, Elizabeth, 'Why I Go to the Cinema', in Charles Davy (ed.), *Footnotes to the Films* (London: Lovat Dickson, 1938), 205–220.

Bradford, Gamaliel, *The Journal of Gamaliel Bradford 1883–1932*, ed. Van Wyck Brooks (Boston and New York: Houghton Mifflin, 1933).

Brewster, Dorothy, *Virginia Woolf* (London: George Allen & Unwin, 1963).

Brewster, Ben, and Lea Jacobs, *Theatre to Cinema: Stage Pictorialism and the Early Feature Film* (Oxford: Oxford University Press, 1997).

Briggs, Austin, ' "Roll Away the Reel World, the Reel World": "Circe" and the Cinema', in Morris Beja and Shari Benstock (eds.), *Coping with Joyce: Essays from the Copenhagen Symposium* (Columbus: Ohio State University Press, 1989), 145–56.

Brooker, Peter, *Modernity and Metropolis: Writing, Film and Urban Formations* (London: Palgrave, 2002).

Brown, Ivor, 'An Art in Search of its Youth', *The Saturday Review* (19 January 1924), 56–7.

Browne, Nick, 'American Film Theory in the Silent Period: Orientalism as an Ideological Form', *Wide Angle* 11:4 (1989), 23–31.

Bruno, Giuliano, *Atlas of Emotion: Journeys in Art, Architecture and Film* (London: Verso, 2002)

Bryher, 'Berlin April 1931', *Close Up* VIII: 2 (June 1931), 126–33.

—— 'Danger in the Cinema', *Close Up* VII: 5 (November 1930), 299–304.

—— 'Dope or Stimulus', *Close Up* III: 3 (September 1928), 61.

—— *Film Problems of Soviet Russia* (Territet, Swizerland: POOL, 1929).

—— *The Heart to Artemis: A Writer's Memoirs* (London: Collins, 1963).

—— 'More-About-Films', *The Outlook* (22 January 1927), 90.

—— 'Notes on Some Films: Berlin, June 1932', *Close Up* IX: 3 (September 1932), 196–9.

—— 'The War from More Angles', *Close Up* I: 4 (October 1927), 44–8.

—— 'What Shall You Do in the War?', *Close Up* X: 2 (June 1933), 192.

Buckle, Gerald, *The Mind and the Film: A Treatise on the Psychological Factors in the Film* (London: Routledge, 1926).

Budd, Mike (ed.), *The Cabinet of Dr. Caligari: Texts, Contexts, Histories* (New Brunswick, NJ: Rutgers University Press, 1990).

Burch, Noël, *Life to those Shadows*, trans. and ed. Ben Brewster (London: British Film Institute, 1990).

Burkdall, Thomas L., 'Cinema Fakes: Film and Joycean Fantasy', in Morris Beja and David Norris (eds.), *Joyce in the Hibernian Metropolis* (Columbus: Ohio State University Press, 1996), 260–9.

—— *Joycean Frames: Film and the Fiction of James Joyce* (New York and London: Routledge, 2001).

Canudo, Ricciotto, 'Reflections on the Seventh Art', trans. Claudia Gorbman, in Abel, *French Film Theory*, 291–303.

Noël Carroll, *Theorizing the Moving Image* (Cambridge: Cambridge University Press, 1996).

Carter, Huntly, 'Art and Drama: The Impersonal Note of England, Russia and Japan', *The Egoist* 1: 24 (15 December, 1914), 461–2.

Carter, Elmer Anderson, 'Of Negro Motion Pictures', *Close Up* V: 2 (August 1929), 119.

—— *The New Spirit in the Cinema* (London: Harold Shaylor, 1930).

—— 'Spontaneics', *The Egoist* 3: 2 (1 February 1916).

Castle, Hugh, 'Elstree's First "Talkie"', *Close Up* V: 2 (August 1929), 131–5.

Caughie, Pamela L. (ed.), *Virginia Woolf in the Age of Mechanical Reproduction* (New York: Garland Publishing, 2000).

Cavell, Stanley, *The World Viewed: Reflections on the Ontology of Film*, enlarged edn. (Cambridge, Mass.: Harvard University Press, 1979).

Chaplin, Charlie, 'Foreword', in L'Estrange Fawcett, *Films: Facts and Forecasts* (London: Geoffrey Bles, 1927), v–vi.

Charney, Leo, *Empty Moments: Cinema, Modernity and Drift* (Durham, NC: Duke University Press, 1998).

Charques, R. D., 'The Technique of the Films,' *Fortnightly Review* 124 (July–December 1928), 504–11.

Chénetier, Marc (ed.), *Letters of Vachel Lindsay* (New York: Burt Franklin, 1979).

Chesterton, G. K., 'On the Movies', *Generally Speaking* (London: Watt and Son, 1929). Repr. in Harry Geduld (ed.), *Authors on Film* (Bloomington and Indiana: Indiana University Press, 1972), 111–12.

Chion, Michel, *La Voix au cinéma* (Paris: Cahiers du Cinéma, 1982).

Christie, Ian, 'Before the Avant-Gardes: Artists and Cinema, 1910–1914', in *La decima musa: il cinema e le altre arts*. Proceedings of the VI Domitor Conference/VII International Film Studies Conference (Udine, 2000), 367–84.

——— *The Last Machine: Early Cinema and the Birth of the Modern World* (London: British Film Institute, 1994).

Clair, René, *Reflections on the Cinema*, trans. Vera Traill (London: William Kimber, 1953).

Clayton, Bertram, 'The Cinema', *Quarterly Review* 234 (July–October 1920), 177–87.

——— 'The Cinema and its Censor', *Fortnightly Review* 109 (February 1921), 222–8.

Cohen, Keith, *Film and Fiction: The Dynamics of Exchange* (New Haven and London: Yale University Press, 1979).

Colebrook, Claire, *Deleuze: A Guide for the Perplexed* (London: Continuum, 2006).

Collecott, Diana, 'Images at the Crossroads: The H. D. Scrapbook', in Susan Friedman and Rachel Blau du Plessix (eds.), *Signets: Reading H. D.* (Wisconsin: University of Wisconsin Press, 1990), 155–81.

Conley, Tom, 'The Talkie: Early Cinematic Conversation', in S. I. Salamensky (ed.), *Talk, Talk, Talk: The Cultural Life of Everyday Conversation* (New York and London: Routledge, 2001), 83–93.

Connor, Steven, 'The Modern Auditory I', in Roy Porter (ed.), *Rewriting the Self: Histories from the Renaissance to the Present* (London: Routledge, 1997).

Connor, Rachel, *H.D. and the Image* (Manchester: Manchester University Press, 2004).

Conrad, Peter, *Modern Times, Modern Places: Life and Art in the Twentieth Century* (London: Thames and Hudson, 1998).

Cooke, Alistair, 'The Critic in Film History', in Charles Davy (ed.), *Footnotes to the Film* (London: Lovat Dickson, 1938), 238–63.

——— (ed.), *Garbo and the Night Watchmen: A Selection from the Writings of British and American Film Critics* (London: Jonathan Cape, 1937).

Cornford, Francis (ed.), *The Republic of Plato* (Oxford: Oxford University Press, 1941).

Cosandey, Roland, 'On *Borderline*', in Michael O'Pray (ed.), *Avant-Garde Film: 1926–1995* (Luton, Bedfordshire: University of Luton Press, 1996).

Craig, Edward Gordon, 'The Actor and the Über-Marionette', *The Mask* 1: 2 (April 1908), 3–15.

Crary, Jonathan, *Suspensions of Perception: Attention, Spectacle and Modern Culture* (Cambridge: Mass.: MIT Press, 1999).

Cripps, Thomas, *Slow Fade to Black: The Negro in American Film 1900–1942* (Oxford: Oxford University Press, 1977).

Dadley, Portia, 'The Garden of Edison: Invention and the American Imagination', in Francis Spufford and Jenny Uglow (eds.), *Cultural Babbage: Technology, Time and Invention* (London: Faber and Faber, 1996), 81–98.

Dalgarno, Emily, *Virginia Woolf and the Visible World* (Cambridge: Cambridge University Press, 2001),

Daly, Nicholas, *Literature, Technology, and Modernity, 1860–2000* (Cambridge: Cambridge University Press, 2004).

Danius, Sara, *The Senses of Modernism: Technology, Perception and Aesthetics* (Ithaca, NY, and London: Cornell University Press, 2002).

Davy, Charles, 'Between Painting and Writing', *The Bookman* LXXXVII: 517 (October 1934).

—— (ed.), *Footnotes to the Film* (London: Lovat Dickson, 1938).

—— *Yorkshire Post* (29 October 1929).

DeCherney, Peter, *Hollywood and the Culture Elite: How the Movies Became American* (New York: Columbia University Press, 1995).

Deleuze, Gilles, and Félix Guattari, *What is Philosophy?*, trans. Graham Burchell and Hugh Tomlinson (London: Verso, 1994).

Delotte, J. P., *A Distant Technology: Science Fiction Film and the Machine Age* (Hanover and London: Wesleyan University Press, 1999).

Delluc, Louis, 'Beauty in the Cinema' (1917), in Richard Abel (ed.), *French Film Theory and Criticism*, vol. 1, *1907–1929* (Princeton: Princeton University Press, 1988), 137–9.

Delmar, Rosalind, *Joris Ivens: 50 Years of Film-Making* (London: British Film Institute, 1979).

Deming, Robert H. (ed.), *James Joyce: The Critical Heritage*, 2 vols. (London: Routledge, 1970).

Dickson, W. K. L. *The Life and Inventions of Thomas Edison* (London: Chatto & Windus, 1894).

Dickson, W. K. L. and Antonia Dickson, *History of the Kinetograph, Kinetoscope and Kineto-Phonograph* (1895), facsimile edn. (New York: The Museum of Modern Art, 2000).

Dismond, Geraldyn, 'The Negro Actor and the American Movies,' *Close Up* V: 2 (August 1929), 90–7.

Dismorr, Jessie, 'Matinee', *The Little Review* IV: 2 (March 1918), 31.

Doane, Mary Ann, *The Emergence of Cinematic Time: Modernity, Contingency and the Archive* (Cambridge, Mass.: Harvard University Press, 2002).

Dobb, Henry, Review of Bryher, *Film Problems of Soviet Russia* in *Sunday Worker* (23 June 1929).

Döblin, Alfred, 'Ulysses by Joyce', in Anton Kaes, Martin Jay, and Edward Dimendberg (eds.), The Weimar Republic Sourcebook (Berkeley and Los Angeles: University of California Press, 1994), 514.

Dobrée, Bonamy, 'Seen on the Stage', Vogue 66: 12 (Late December 1925), 82.

—— 'Seen on the Stage', Vogue 67: 8 (Late April 1926), 94.

—— 'Seen on the Stage', Vogue 68: 11 (Early December 1926), 116, 118.

—— 'Seen on the Stage', Vogue 68: 12 (Late December, 1926), 66.

Donald, James, Imagining the Modern City (London: Athlone, and Minneapolis: University of Minnesota Press, 1999).

Douglass, Paul, 'Bergson and Cinema: Friends or Foes', in John Mullarkey (ed.), The New Bergson (Manchester: Manchester University Press, 1999), 209–227.

Dusinberre, Deke, 'The Avant-Garde Attitude in the Thirties', in Traditions of Independence (London: BFI, 1980), 34–50.

Eaton, Walter P. 'Class-Consciousness and the Movies', Atlantic Monthly CXV (1915), 48–56.

Ecclestone, J., 'The Cinema', The Nineteenth Century (October 1923), 634–9.

Edmunds, Susan, Out of Line: History, Psychoanalysis and Montage in H.D.'s Long Poems (Stanford, Calif.: Stanford University Press, 1994).

Egger, Rebecca, 'Deaf Ears and Dark Continents: Dorothy Richardson's Cinematic Epistemology', Camera Obscura 30 (May 1992), 5–33.

Eikhenbaum, Boris, 'Problems of Film Stylistics' (1927), Screen 15: 4 (Winter 1974/5), 7–34.

Eisenstein, Sergei, 'An American Tragedy', Close Up X: 2 (June 1933), 120.

—— 'The Cinematographic Principle and the Ideogram', Film Form: Essays in Film Theory, ed. and trans. Jay Leyda (New York: Harcourt, Brace, Jovanovich, 1949), 28–44.

—— 'Dickens, Griffiths and the Film Today', in Film Form: Essays in Film Theory, ed. and trans, Jay Leyda (New York: Harcourt, Brace, Jovanovich, 1949), 195–255.

—— 'Fourth Dimension in the Kino', Close Up VI: 3 (March 1930), 184–94 and VI: 4 (April 1930), 253–68.

—— 'Help Yourself', Selected Works, vol. 1, 219–37.

—— Laocoön, Selected Works, vol. 2, 109–202.

—— 'Literature and Cinema', Selected Works, vol. 1, 95–9.

—— 'The New Language of Cinematography', Close Up IV: 5 (May 1929), 10–13.

—— Nonindifferent Nature: Film and the Structure of Things, trans. Herbert Marshall (Cambridge: University of Cambridge Press, 1987).

—— 'The Principles of the New Russian Cinema' (1930), Selected Works, vol. 1, 195–202.

—— 'Sur Joyce', Change (May 1972), 48–53.

Eisner, Lotte H., The Haunted Screen, trans. Roger Greaves (Berkeley: University of California Press, 1973).

Elliot, Eric, Anatomy of Motion Picture Art (Territet, Switzerland: POOL, 1928).

Ellmann, Richard, *James Joyce* (Oxford: Oxford University Press, 1959).

Elsaesser, Thomas (ed.), *Early Film: Space, Frame, Narrative* (London: British Film Institute, 1990).

Epstein, Jean, 'Art of Incidence' (1927), trans. Tom Milne, in Abel, *French Film Theory*, vol. 1, 412–14.

—— 'Magnification' (1921), trans. Stuart Liebman and Richard Abel, in Abel, *French Film Theory*, vol. 1, 235–41.

—— *La Poésie d'aujourd'hui un nouvel état d'intelligence: lettres de Blaise Cendrars* (Paris: Éditions de la Sirène, 1921).

—— 'On Certain Characteristics of Photogénie' (1924), in Abel, *French Film Theory*, vol. 1, 314–18.

Ervine, St John, 'The Alleged Art of the Cinema', University College Union Society, University of London. (The Oration Delivered by St. John Ervine, Esq., during the 38th Foundation Week on Thursday 15 March 1934).

—— *Spectator* (4 May 1929), 682.

Eyman, Scott, *The Speed of Sound: Hollywood and the Talkie Revolution, 1926–1930* (New York: Simon and Schuster, 1997).

Faure, Elie, *The Art of Cineplastics*, trans. Walter Pach (Boston: The Four Seas Company, 1923).

Fell, John L. (ed.), *Film Before Griffith* (Berkeley and Los Angeles: California University Press, 1983).

Fielding, Raymond, 'Hale's Tours: Ultrarealism in the Pre-1910 Motion Picture', in John F. Fell (ed.), *Film Before Griffith* (Berkeley and Los Angeles: University of California Press, 1983), 117.

—— *A Technical History of Motion Pictures and Television* (Berkeley and Los Angeles: University of California Press, 1967).

The Film Society Collection, British Film Institute. Item 4a: Council of the Film Society Meeting notices and agendas 1926–1931.

—— Item 6c: (Pamphlet: Study Groups, Season 1929–30), 'Eisenstein's Lectures in London: A Reconstruction by Basil Wright and J. Isaacs', Saturday 17 December 1949, Third Programme 10.05–10.45 p.m. Transcript in Film Society Collection, BFI.

—— Item 9: (Membership information and leaflets to members, 1935).

Flaxman, Gregory (ed.), *The Brain is the Screen: Deleuze and the Cinema* (Minneapolis: University of Minnesota Press, 2000).

Fletcher, John Gould, *The Crisis of the Film* (Seattle: University of Washington Book Store, 1929).

Francke, Lizzie, *Script Girls: Women Screenwriters in Hollywood* (London: British Film Institute, 1994).

Frank, Felicia Miller, *The Mechanical Song: Women, Voice and the Artificial in Nineteenth-Century French Narrative* (Stanford: California University Press, 1995).

Frayling, Christopher, *Things to Come* (London: BFI, 1995).

Frederickson, Donald Laurence, *The Aesthetic of Isolation in Film Theory: Hugo Münsterberg* (New York: Arno Press, 1977).

Freeburg, Victor Oscar, *The Art of Photoplay Making* (New York: The Macmillan Company, 1918).

—— *Pictorial Beauty on the Screen* (New York: Macmillan Company, 1923). Repr. New York: Arno Press and the *New York Times*, 1970.

Freud, Sigmund, *The Interpretation of Dreams: The Standard Edition of the Complete Psychological Works of Sigmund Freud*, vol. 5 (London: Hogarth Press, 1955), 500.

—— 'Introductory Lectures', *Standard Edition*, vol. 16, 450.

—— 'A Metapsychological Supplement to the Theory of Dreams' (1917), *Standard Edition*, vol. 14, 225.

—— *A Psychoanalytic Dialogue: The Letters of Sigmund Freud and Karl Abraham 1907–1926*, ed. H. C. Abraham and E. L. Freud (New York: Basic Books, 1964).

—— 'The Uncanny,' *Standard Edition*, vol. 17.

Friedberg, Anne, 'Fragments de Films "POOL": 1927–1929', *Travelling*, 56–7, Documents Cinémathèque Suisse (spring 1980), 60–2.

—— 'Writing about Cinema: *Close Up* 1927–1933' (Ph.D.: New York University, 1983).

—— 'Reading *Close Up*, 1927–1933', in *Cinema and Modernism*, 1–27.

—— 'An *Unheimlich* Maneuver between Psychoanalysis and the Cinema: *Secrets of a Soul* (1926)', in Eric Rentschler (ed.), *The Films of G. W. Pabst: An Extraterritorial Cinema* (New Brunswick, NJ: Rutgers University Press, 1990), 41–51.

Fry, Roger, 'The Artist and Psycho-Analysis', in Christopher Reed (ed.), *A Roger Fry Reader* (Chicago: University of Chicago Press, 1996), 359.

—— 'Mr. Gordon Craig's Stage Designs', *The Nation* (16 September, 1911), 871.

—— *Vision and Design* (1920) (Oxford: Oxford University Press, 1981).

Gance, Abel, 'A Sixth Art' (1912), in Abel (ed.), *French Film Theory and Criticism*, vol. 1, 67.

Gauthier, Christophe, *Le Passion du Cinéma: Cinéphiles, ciné-clubs et salles spécialisées à Paris de 1920 à 1929* (Paris: Association Française de Recherche Sur L'Histoire du Cinéma, 1999).

Geduld, Harry M. (ed.), *Authors on Film* (Bloomington and Indiana: Indiana University Press, 1972).

—— *The Birth of the Talkies: From Edison to Jolson* (Indiana: Indiana University Press, 1975).

Gerstein, Evelyn, 'Four Films of New Types', *Theatre Arts Monthly* XI (1927), 295–298.

Gevirtz, Susan, *Narrative's Journey: The Fiction and Film Writing of Dorothy Richardson* (New York: Peter Lang, 1996).

Gilbert, Elliot, *The Good Kipling: Studies in the Short Story* (Oberlin: Ohio University Press, 1970).

Gillespie, Diane (ed.), *The Multiple Muses of Virginia Woolf* (Columbia, Mo.: University of Missouri Press, 1993).

—— ' "Her Kodak Pointing at his Head": Virginia Woolf and Photography', in Gillespie (ed.), *The Multiple Muses of Virginia Woolf*, 113–47

Gishford, Anthony, *Isis* (14 January 1930).

Glaser, Curt, Introduction to Helmar Lerski, *Köpfe des Alltags*, repr. in David Mellor (ed.), *Germany—The New Photography 1927–33* (London: Arts Council of Great Britain, 1978).

Gledhill, Christine, *Reframing British Cinema 1918–1928: Between Restraint and Passion* (London: BFI, 2003).

Goethe, Johann Wolfgang von, 'Observations on the Laocoön' (1798), in John Gage (ed.), *Goethe on Art* (London: Scolar Press, 1980).

—— *Theory of Colours* (1810), trans. Charles Lock Eastlake (Cambridge, Mass.: MIT Press, 1980).

Goldstein, Lawrence, *The American Poet at the Movies: A Critical History* (Ann Arbor: University of Michigan Press, 1995).

Gomery, Douglas, *The Coming of Sound* (New York, Routledge: 2005).

Gorki, Maxim, 'The Kingdom of Shadows', in Gilbert Adair (ed.) *Movies* (Harmondsworth: Penguin, 1999), 10–13.

Green, Fitzhugh, *The Film Finds its Tongue* (New York: G. B. Putnam, 1929).

Green, Graham, *Brighton Rock* (1938) (London: Vintage, 2004).

—— *It's a Battlefield* (1934) (London: Vintage, 2002).

—— *Mornings in the Dark: The Graham Greene Film Reader*, ed. David Parkinson (Harmondsworth: Penguin, 1993).

Grierson, John, 'The G.P.O. Gets Sound', *Cinema* (Summer 1934).

—— *Grierson on Documentary*, ed. Forsyth Hardy. (London: Faber and Faber, 1966).

—— 'Making a Film of the Actual: A Problem in Film Construction', *Close Up* v: 5 (November 1929), 402–9.

Gualtieri, Elena, '*Three Guineas* and the Photograph: The Art of Propaganda', in Mary Joannou (ed.), *Women Writers of the 1930s* (Edinburgh: Edinburgh University Press, 1999), 165–78.

Gunning, Tom, 'An Aesthetic of Astonishment: Early Film and the (In)credulous Spectator', in Leo Braudy and Marshall Cohen (eds.), *Film Theory and Criticism: Introductory Readings* (Oxford: Oxford University Press, 1999).

—— 'The Cinema of Attractions: Early Film, its Spectator and the Avant-Garde', in Thomas Elsaesser (ed.), *Early Film: Space, Frame, Narrative* (London: British Film Institute, 1990), 56–62.

—— *D. W. Griffith and the Origins of American Narrative Film: The Early Years at Biograph* (Urbana and Chicago: Illinois University Press, 1991).

—— 'Introduction' to Lawrence Mannoni, *The Great Art of Light and Shadow: Archaeology of the Cinema*, trans. and ed. Richard Crangle (Exeter: Exeter University Press, 2000), xix–xxx.

Hake, Sabine, *The Cinema's Third Machine. Writing on Film in Germany 1907–1933* (Lincoln and London: University of Nebraska Press, 1993).

Haller, Evelyn, 'Her Quill Drawn from the Firebird: Virginia Woolf and the Russian Dancers', in Gillespie (ed.), *The Multiple Muses of Virginia Woolf*, 180–226.

Hankins, Leslie Kathleen, 'Across the Screen of My Brain: Virginia Woolf's "The Cinema" and Film Forums of the 1920s', in Gillespie (ed.), *The Multiple Muses of Virginia Woolf*, 148–79.

—— 'A Splice of Reel Life in Virginia Woolf's "Time Passes": Censorship, Cinema, and "the usual battlefield of emotions"', *Criticism* (Winter 1993).

—— 'Iris Barry, Writer and Cineaste, Forming Film Culture in London 1924–26: The *Adelphi*, the *Spectator*, the Film Society and the British *Vogue*', *Modernism/Modernity* 11:3 (2004) 488–515.

Hanks, Walter Shaw, 'Cinema and Ballet in Paris', *Criterion* IV: 1 (June 1926), 178–84.

Hannon, William Morgan, 'The Photodrama: Its Place Among the Fine Arts' (1915), repr. in *Screen Monographs II* (New York: Arno Press and the *New York Times*, 1970).

Hansen, Miriam, *Babel and Babylon: Spectatorship in American Silent Film* (Cambridge, Mass.: Harvard University Press, 1991).

Harding, Colin, and Simon Popple (eds.), *In the Kingdom of Shadows: A Companion to Early Cinema* (London: Cygnus Arts, 1996).

Hardy, Forsyth, *John Grierson: A Documentary Biography* (London: Faber and Faber, 1979).

Hauser, Arnold, *The Social History of Art*, vol. 4: *Naturalism, Impressionism, The Film Age* (London: Routledge, 1962), 1st edn. 2 vols. 1951; 2nd edn. 4 vols. 1962 (repr. 1989).

H. D., Autobiographical Notes, H. D. Papers, Beinecke Rare Book and Manuscript Library, Yale University.

—— *Bid Me to Live: A Madrigal* (New York: Grove Press, 1960).

—— '*Borderline* pamphlet', (London: Mercury Press, 1930), repr. in *Cinema and Modernism*, 221–36.

—— *Kora and Ka* ['Kora and Ka'; 'Mira-Mare'], (Dijon: Darantière, 1935).

—— 'Narthex', in Alfred Kreymborg, Lewis Mumford, and Paul Rosenfeld (eds.), *The Second American Caravan* (New York: Macaulay, 1928).

—— Response to 'Questionnaire', *The Little Review* 12 (May 1929), 38–9.

—— *Tribute to Freud* (Manchester: Carcanet, 1985).

—— 'Two Americans', in *The Usual Star* ['The Usual Star', 'Two Americans'], (Dijon: Darantière, 1934).

—— Unpublished MS 'Wing-Beat', H. D. papers, Beinecke Rare Book and Manuscript Library, Yale University.

Heath, Stephen, 'Cinema and Psychoanalysis: Parallel Histories', Janet Bergstrom in (ed.), *Endless Night: Cinema and Psychoanalysis, Parallel Histories* (Los Angeles: University of California Press, 1999).

Henson, Bruce, 'Iris Barry: American Film Archive Pioneer', *The Katherine Sharp Review* 4 (Winter 1997).

Herring, Robert, 'Film Imagery: Pudoukin', *Close Up* III: 4 (October 1928), 31–9.

—— 'The Films', *Drawing and Design* IV: 23 (May 1928), 118.

—— *Films of the Year 1927–1928* (London: The Studio Ltd., 1928).

—— 'Jannings in *The Way of All Flesh*', *Close Up* I: 5 (November 1927), 31–8.

—— *London Mercury* XIX (November 1928–April 1929), 201–2.

—— 'The Movies', *London Mercury* XVII, November 1927–April 1928, 702–3.

—— 'The Movies', *London Mercury* XIX: 111 (January 1929), 316.

—— 'A New Cinema, Magic and the Avant Garde', *Close Up* IV: 4 (April 1929), 47–57.

—— 'Storm over London', *Close Up* IV: 3 (March 1929), 34–44.

—— 'Twenty Years Ago', *Manchester Guardian* (8 September 1928), 10.

—— 'The Week on the Screen', *Manchester Guardian* (13 April 1929).

Higgins, Bertram, 'The Cinema: An Outburst', *The Spectator* 130 (12 May 1923), 801.

Higson, Andrew (ed.), *Dissolving Views: Key Writings on British Cinema* (London: Cassell, 1996).

—— *Waving the Flag* (Oxford: Clarendon, 1995).

—— (ed.), *Young and Innocent? The Cinema in Britain 1896–1930* (Exeter: Exeter University Press, 2002).

Hoffman, Gert, *The Film Explainer*, trans. Michael Hoffmann (London: Minerva, 1996).

von Hoffmannsthal, Hugo, 'A Substitute for Dreams', *The London Mercury* IX (November 1923–April 1924), 177–9.

Holtby, Winifred, *Virginia Woolf: A Critical Memoir* (Chicago: Academy Press, 1978).

'How Twelve Famous Women Scenario Writers Succeeded in this Profession of Unlimited Opportunity and Reward', *Photoplay* (August 1923).

Hutchens, John, 'L'Enfant Terrible: The Little Cinema Movement', *Theatre Arts Monthly* 13 (1929), 694.

Humm, Maggie, *Modernist Women and Visual Cultures: Virginia Woolf, Vanessa Bell, Photography and Cinema* (Edinburgh: Edinburgh University Press, 2002).

—— *Snapshots of Bloomsbury: The Private Lives of Virginia Woof and Vanessa Bell* (London: Tate Publishing, 2006).

Hunter, William, *Scrutiny of Cinema* (London: Wishart and Co., 1932)

Huxley, Aldous, 'Silence is Golden: Being the Misanthropic Reflections of an English Novelist on First Hearing a Picture Talk', *Vanity Fair* (July 1929), 72.

Hynes, Samuel, *The Auden Generation: Literature and Politics in England in the 1930s* (London: Faber and Faber, 1979).

Iampolski, Mikhail, 'The Logic of Illusion: Notes on the Genealogy of Intellectual Cinema', in Richard Allen and Malcolm Turvey (eds.), *Camera Obscura, Camera*

Lucida: Essays in Honour of Annette Michelson (Amsterdam: Amsterdam University Press, 2003), 35–50.

Isherwood, Christopher, *Christopher and his Kind 1929–1939* (London: Methuen, 1978).

—— *Goodbye to Berlin* (London: The Hogarth Press, 1939).

—— *Prater Violet* (London: Minerva, 1997).

Jackson, Holbrook, *The Eighteen Nineties: A Review of Art and Ideas at the Close of the Nineteenth Century* (London: Grant Richards, 1913).

Jacob, Karen, *The Eye's Mind: Literary Modernism and Visual Culture* (Ithaca, NY: Cornell University Press, 2001).

James, William, *Principles of Psychology* (New York: Holt, 1890).

Josephson, Matthew, 'Made in America', *Broom* 2: 3 (June 1922), 266–70.

Joyce, James. *Letters*, ed. Stuart Gilbert (vol. 1) and Richard Ellmann (vols. 2 and 3) (New York: Viking; London: Faber and Faber, 1957, 1966).

—— *Ulysses* (Harmondsworth: Penguin, 1969).

Kaes, Anton *Kino-Debatte. Texte zum Verhältnis von Literatur und Film 1909–1929* (Tübingen: Niemeyer 1978).

—— 'The Debate about Cinema: Charting a Controversy (1909–29)', *New German Critique* 40 (Winter 1987), 7–33.

Kammen, Michael, *The Lively Arts: Gilbert Seldes and the Transformation of Cultural Criticism in the United States* (New York: Oxford University Press, 1996).

Kennedy, Margaret, *The Mechanized Muse* (London: George Allen & Unwin, 1942).

Kern, Stephen, *The Culture of Time and Space, 1880–1918* (Cambridge, Mass.: Harvard University Press, 1983).

Kinross, Martha, 'The Screen—From this Side', *Fortnightly Review* 130 (July–December 1931), 497–512.

Kipling, Rudyard, 'Mrs Bathurst', *Short Stories: Volume 1* (Harmondsworth: Penguin, 1971).

—— *Something of Myself* (London: Penguin, 1988).

Kirby, Lynne, *Parallel Tracks: The Railroad and Silent Cinema* (Exeter: University of Exeter Press, 1997).

Kracauer, Siegfried, *The Mass Ornament: Weimar Essays*, ed. and trans. Thomas Y. Levin (Cambridge, Mass.: Harvard University Press, 1995).

—— *Schriften: Aufsätze 1927–1931* (Frankfurt am Main: Suhrkamp Verlag, 1990).

—— *Theory of Film: The Redemption of Physical Reality* (Oxford: Oxford University Press, 1960)

Kumar, Shiv, *Bergson and the Stream of Consciousness Novel* (London: Blackie, 1962).

Lant, Antonia, 'The Curse of the Pharaoh, or How Cinema Contracted Egyptomania', *October* 59 (Winter 1992), 86–112.

—— 'Haptical Cinema', *October* 74 (Fall 1995), 45–73.

Lauretis, Teresa De and Stephen Heath (eds.), *The Cinematic Apparatus* (Basingstoke: Macmillan, 1980), 76–95.

Lawrence, D. H., *The Lost Girl* (Cambridge: Cambridge University Press, 2002).

—— 'Pornography and Obscenity', *Phoenix: The Posthumous Papers of D. H. Lawrence*, ed. Edward D. McDonald (London: Heinemann, 1936).

Leavis, F. R., 'Mass Civilization, Minority Culture', in *Education and the University* (London: Chatto and Windus, 1948).

Lee, Vernon, *The Beautiful: An Introduction to Psychological Aesthetics* (Cambridge: Cambridge University Press, 1913).

Léger, Fernand 'The Spectacle: Light, Color, Moving Image, Object-Spectacle' (1924), in *Functions of Painting*, trans. Alexandra Anderson (London: Thames and Hudson, 1973), 42.

Lejeune, C. A., *Chestnuts in her Lap: 1936–1946* (London: Phoenix House, 1947).

Lejeune, Anthony (ed.), *The C. A. Lejeune Film Reader* (Manchester: Carcanet, 1991).

—— *Cinema: A Review of Thirty Years' Achievement* (London: Alexander Maclehose, 1931).

—— *Thank You for Having Me* (London: Hutchinson, 1964).

LeMahieu, D. L., *A Culture for Democracy: Mass Communication and the Cultivated Mind in Britain Between the Wars* (Oxford: Clarendon Press, 1988).

Lenauer, Jean, *Close Up* v: 6 (December 1929), 464–8.

Lessing, Gottfried Ephraim, *Laocoön: An Essay on the Limits of Painting and Poetry*, trans. Edward Allen McCormick (Baltimore: Johns Hopkins University Press, 1984).

Leslie, Esther, *Hollywood Flatlands* (London, Verso, 2002).

Levenson, Michael, 'The time-mind of the twenties', in Laura Marcus and Peter Nicholls (eds.), *The Cambridge History of Twentieth-Century English Literature* (Cambridge: Cambridge University Press, 2004), 197–217.

Levin, Harry, *James Joyce: A Critical Introduction* (London: Faber and Faber, 1960).

Levin, Thomas Y., 'Introduction', in Siegfried Kracauer, *The Mass Ornament: Weimar Essays*, trans. and ed. Thomas Y. Levin (Cambridge, Mass.: Harvard University Press, 1995).

Lewis, Wyndham, *Filibusters in Barbary* (New York: Haskell House Publishers, 1973).

—— *Time and Western Man* (California: Black Sparrow Press, 1993).

Liebman, Stuart, 'French Film Theory, 1910–1921', *Quarterly Review of Film Studies* 7 (Winter 1983), 1–23.

Lindsay, Vachel, *The Art of the Moving Picture* (1922; New York: Modern Library, 2000).

—— *Letters of Vachel Lindsay*, ed. Marc Chénetier (New York: Burt Franklin, 1979).

—— 'Photoplay Progress', *The New Republic* (17 February 1917).

—— *The Progress and Poetry of the Movies: A Second Book of Film Criticism*, ed. and with commentary by Myron Lounsbury (Lanham, Md.: Scarecrow Press, 1995).

—— 'A Special Delivery Letter', *c.*1922. Vachel Lindsay papers. Special Collections, University of Virginia.

de l'Isle-Adam, Villiers, *Tomorrow's Eve*, trans. Robert Martin Adams (Chicago: University of Illinois Press, 1982).

Lounsbury, Myron, *The Origins of American Film Criticism 1909–1939* (New York: Arno Press, 1973).

——Introduction to Vachel Lindsay, *The Progress and Poetry of the Movies: A Second Book of Film Criticism* (Lanham, Md.: Scarecrow Press, 1995).

Low, Rachael, *The History of the British Film: 1918–1929* (London: George Allen and Unwin, 1971).

Luckhurst, Nicola, 'Photoportraits: Gisèle Freund and Virginia Woolf', in Nicola Luckhurst and M. Ravache, *Virginia Woolf in Camera* (London: Cecil Woolf, 2001).

McCabe, Susan, *Cinematic Modernism: Modernist Poetry and Film* (Cambridge: Cambridge University Press, 2005).

McCourt, John, *The Years of Bloom: James Joyce in Trieste 1904–1920* (Madison: University of Wisconsin Press, 2000).

Macpherson, Kenneth, 'Matinee', *Close Up* I: 5 (November 1927), 54–63.

Macpherson, Don, 'The Film Society', in *British Cinema: Traditions of Independence*, ed. Don Macpherson (London: BFI Publishing, 1980), 103–5.

——'The Novelist who was a Scenarist', *Close Up* IV: 3 (March 1929).

——Review of C. A. Lejeune's *The Cinema*, *Close Up* VIII: 4 (December 1931), 332–335.

——'Wie ein Meisterstuck enstand', *Film für Alle* 12 (1929).

McQuire, Scott, *Visions of Modernity: Representation, Memory, Time and Space in the Age of the Camera* (London: Sage, 1998).

Madge, Charles, and Tom Harrisson, *Mass-Observation* (London: Frederick Muller, 1937).

Majumdar, Robin, and Allen McLaurin (eds.), *Virginia Woolf: The Critical Heritage* (London: Routledge and Kegan Paul, 1975).

Man Ray, 'Emak Bakia', *Close Up* I: 2 (August 1927), 40.

Mancini, Elaine, 'Theory and Practice: Hugo Münsterberg and the Early Films of D. W. Griffith', *New Orleans Review* 10: 2–3 (Summer–Fall, 1983), 154–160.

Mandel, Charlotte, 'Garbo/Helen: The Self-Projection of Beauty by H.D.', *Women's Studies: An Interdisciplinary Journal* 7: 1–2 (1980), 127–35.

——'The Redirected Image: Cinematic Dynamics in the Style of H.D.', *Literature/Film Quarterly* 11 (1983), 36–45.

Mann, Thomas, *The Magic Mountain*, trans. H. T. Lowe-Porter (Harmondsworth: Penguin, 1960).

——'On the Film', repr. in Harry Geduld (ed.), *Authors on Film* (Bloomington and Indiana: Indiana University Press, 1972), 130–1.

Mannoni, Lawrence, *The Great Art of Light and Shadow: Archaeology of the Cinema*, trans. and ed. Richard Crangle (Exeter: Exeter University Press, 2000).

Manvell, Roger, *Film* (Harmondsworth: Penguin, 1946).

Marcus, Laura, 'Dreaming and Cinematographic Consciousness', *Psychoanalysis and History* 3: 1 (2001), 51–68.

—— 'Oedipus Express: Trains, Trauma and Detective Fiction', in Warren Chernaik, Martin Swales and Robert Vilain (eds.), *The Art of Detective Fiction* (London: Macmillan, 2000), 201–221. Repr. in *New Formations* 41 (Autumn 2000), 173–188.

Marcus, Laura and Peter Nicholls (eds.), *The Cambridge History of Twentieth-Century English Literature* (Cambridge: Cambridge University Press, 2004).

Marek, Jayne E., *Women Editing Modernism: 'Little' Magazines and Literary History* (Lexington, Ky.: University of Kentucky Press, 1995).

Massa, Ann, *Vachel Lindsay: Fieldworker for the American Dream* (Bloomington: Indiana University Press, 1970).

Matz, Jessie, *Literary Impressionism and Modernist Aesthetics* (Cambridge: Cambridge University Press, 2001).

Maxwell, Gerald, 'The Fascination of the Film', *Fortnightly Review* 114 (July–December 1923), 453–459.

Meisel, Perry, *The Absent Father: Virginia Woolf and Walter Pater* (New Haven: Yale University Press, 1980), 47.

Mellor, David (ed.), *Germany—The New Photography 1927–33* (London: Arts Council of Great Britain, 1978).

'Mercurius', 'Abstractions', *Architectural Review* LXVI (September 1929), 140–1.

—— 'Act, Fact and Abstraction', *Architectural Review* LXVIII (October 1930), 258.

—— 'Blackmail', *Architectural Review* LXVI (August 1929), 87.

—— 'Film Structure and the Work of *Close Up*', *Architectural Review* LXVIII (November 1930), 221.

—— 'Pictures in the "Pictures": The Wonderful Deception of Nina Petrovna', *Architectural Review* LXVI (July 1929), 41.

—— Review of *Joan of Arc*, *Architectural Review* 68 (November 1930), 221.

—— 'Sound Film and the "Talkies" ', *Architectural Review* LXV (June 1929), 301.

Messel, Rudolph, *This Film Business* (London: Ernest Benn, 1928).

Metz, Christian, *The Imaginary Signifier: Psychoanalysis and Cinema*, trans. Celia Britton, Annwyl Williams, Ben Brewster, and Alfred Guzzetti (Bloomington: Indiana University Press, 1982).

Michelson, Annette, 'Dr Crase and Mr Clair', *October* 11 (1979), 30–53.

—— 'On the Eve of the Future: The Reasonable Facsimile and the Philosophical Toy', *October* 29 (Summer 1984), 3–21.

—— *New Forms in Film* (exhibition catalogue), Montreux (1974), 10.

Mitchell, Donald, *Britten and Auden in the Thirties: The Year 1936* (Woodbridge: Boydell, 2000).

Montagu, Ivor, 'Birmingham Sparrow', *Sight and Sound* 39 (Spring 1970).

—— 'The Film Society: London', *Cinema Quarterly* I: 1 (Winter 1932–33).

—— '*Film Society*: Notes on the 17th Programme', *Close Up* I: 6 (December 1927), 80–82.

—— *Film World* (Harmondsworth: Penguin, 1964).

—— 'The Future of the Sound Film', *c.*1930. Ivor Montagu Collection, British Film Institute.

Montagu, Ivor, Interview with Ivor Montagu, *Screen* 13:3 (Autumn 1972), 71–113.

—— 'Lament of a Diehard', (1936). Ivor Montagu Collection, British Film Institute.

—— 'The New Film Society', *The Isis* (10 June 1925), 19–20.

—— *The Political Censorship of Films* (London: Victor Gollancz, 1929).

—— Review of *Stella Dallas*, *Observer* (7 February 1926).

—— *With Eisenstein in Hollywood* (Berlin: Seven Seas, 1968).

—— *The Youngest Son: Autobiographical Chapters* (London: Lawrence and Wishart, 1970).

Moore, Marianne, *The Dial* 83 (November 1927), 449–50.

—— 'Fiction or Nature', *Close Up* x: 3 (September 1933), 260–5.

—— 'Lot in Sodom', *Close Up* x: 4 (December 1933), 318–19.

Moore, Rachel O., *Savage Theory: Cinema as Modern Magic* (Durham, NC: Duke University Press, 2000).

Morris, Adalaide, 'The Concept of Projection', in Susan Stanford Friedman and Rachel Blau du Plessis (eds.), *Signets: Reading H.D.* (Madison: University of Wisconsin Press, 1990), 273–96.

Katherine Mullin, *James Joyce, Sexuality and Social Purity* (Cambridge: Cambridge University Press, 2003),

Mulvey, Laura, *Death 24 [Times] a Second: Stillness and the Moving Image* (London: Reaktion Books, 2006).

Münsterberg, Hugo, *Hugo Münsterberg on Film: The Photoplay: A Psychological Study and Other Writings*, ed. Allan Langdale (London: Routledge, 2002).

—— *Psychology General and Applied* (New York and London: D. Appleton and Company, 1914).

—— *Psychology and Industrial Efficiency* (London: Constable, 1913).

—— 'The Problem of Beauty', *The Philosophical Review* 18: 2 (March 1909), 121–46.

Münsterberg, Margaret, *Hugo Münsterberg: His Life and Work* (New York: D. Appleton and Company, 1922).

Murphy, Richard, *Theorizing the Avant-Garde* (Cambridge: Cambridge University Press), 1999.

Edward Murray, *The Cinematic Imagination: Writers and the Motion Pictures* (New York: Frederick Ungar, 1972).

Musil, Robert, 'Toward a New Aesthetic: Observations on a Dramaturgy of Film' (1925), in *Precision and Soul: Essays and Addresses*, ed. and trans. Burton Pike and David Luft (Chicago: Chicago University Press, 1990), 193–208.

Musser, Charles, *History of the American Cinema*, vol. 1: *The Emergence of Cinema: The American Screen to 1907* (Berkeley and Los Angeles: University of California Press, 1990).

—— *Thomas A. Edison and his Kinetographic Motion Pictures* (New Brunswick, NJ: Rutgers University Press, 1995).

Neale, Steve, *Cinema and Technology: Image, Sound, Colour* (London/Basingstoke: Macmillan/British Film Institute, 1985).

Nesbet, Anne, *Savage Junctures: Sergei Eisenstein and the Shape of Thinking* (London: I. B. Tauris, 2003), 6.

Noble, Peter, *The Negro in Films* (London: Skelton Robinson, n.d.).

North, Michael, *Camera Works: Photography and the Twentieth-Century Word* (Oxford: Oxford University Press, 2005).

Ogden, C. K. and I. A. Richards, *The Meaning of Meaning* (London: Kegan Paul, 1930).

O'Keefe, Paul, *Some Sort of Genius: A Life of Wyndham Lewis* (London: Jonathan Cape, 2000).

O'Pray, Michael (ed.), *The British Avant-Garde Film 1926–1995: An Anthology of Writings* (Luton, Bedfordshire: University of Luton Press/Arts Council of England, 1996).

Pacteau, Francette, *The Symptom of Beauty* (London: Reaktion Books, 1994).

Page, Norman, *Auden and Isherwood: The Berlin Years* (London: Macmillan, 2000).

Panofsky, Erwin, 'Style and Medium in the Motion Pictures' (1934), repr. in Daniel Talbot (ed.), *Film: An Anthology* (Berkeley and Los Angeles: University of California Press, 1959), 15–32.

Pater, Walter, *The Renaissance* (Oxford: Oxford University Press, 1998).

Pearson, Roberta E., *Eloquent Gestures: The Transformation of Performance Style in the Griffith Biograph Films* (Berkeley and Los Angeles: University of California Press, 1992).

Petrie, Duncan and Robert Kruger (eds.), *A Paul Rotha Reader* (Exeter: Exeter University Press, 1999).

P.J.M., 'New Novels: Adventurous Writers', *Manchester Guardian* (8 January 1928).

Plantinga, Carl, and Greg M. Smith (eds.), *Passionate Views: Film, Cognition and Emotion* (Baltimore: Johns Hopkins University Press, 1999).

Platt, David, 'The New Cinema', *Experimental Cinema* i: 1 (February 1930), 1–2.

Poe, Edgar Allan, 'The Purloined Letter', *The Works of Edgar Allan Poe* (Harmondsworth, Penguin, 1982).

Poggioli, Renato, *The Theory of the Avant-Garde* (Cambridge, Mass.: Harvard University Press, 1965).

Potamkin, Harry A., 'The AfraAmerican Cinema', *Close Up* v: 2 (August 1929), 107–17.

—— 'Kino and Lichtspiel', *Close Up* v: 5 (November 1929), 387–98.

—— 'The Compound Cinema', *Close Up* iv: 1 (January 1929), 32–7.

—— Review of *Film Problems*, *Experimental Cinema: A Monthly Projecting Important International Film Manifestations* i: 1 (February 1930), 3.

Pound, Ezra, *The Selected Letters of Ezra Pound: 1907–1941*, ed. D. D. Paige (London: Faber and Faber, 1950).

Powell, Tristram (ed.), *Victorian Photographs of Famous Men & Fair Women*, with introduction by Virginia Woolf and Roger Fry, 1926. (Expanded edn., London: Chatto and Windus, 1992).

Pratt, George, *Spellbound in Darkness: Readings in the History and Criticism of the Silent Film* (University of Rochester, 1966).

Pressler, Michael, 'Poet and Professor on the Movies', *Gettysburg Review* 4:1 (Winter 1991), 157–65.

'The Prince's Derby: Shown by Lightning Photograph', *The Strand Magazine* XII (July–December, 1896)

Pudovkin, V. I., *Film Technique*, trans. Ivor Montagu (London: George Newnes, 1933).

——*Film Technique and Film Acting*, trans. Ivor Montagu (London: Vision Press, 1954).

Puffer, Ethel D., *The Psychology of Beauty* (1907) (Kessinger Publishing repr., n.d.).

Raitt, Suzanne, *Virginia Woolf's To the Lighthouse* (Hemel Hempstead: Harvester Wheatsheaf, 1990).

Ramsaye, Terry, *A Million and One Nights* (1926) (London: Frank Cass & Co. Ltd, 1954).

Read, Herbert, 'Experiments in Counterpoint', *Cinema Quarterly* 3 (Autumn 1934), 17–21.

——'The Poet and the Film', *Cinema Quarterly* 1: 4 (Summer 1933), 197–202.

——'Towards a Film Aesthetic', *Cinema Quarterly*, 1: 1 (Summer 1932), 7–11.

Richards, Jeffrey, *The Age of the Dream Palace: Cinema and Society in Britan 1930–1939* (London: Routledge, 1984).

——(ed.), *The Unknown 1930s: An Alternative History of the British Cinema 1929–1939* (London: I. B. Tauris, 1998).

Richardson, Dorothy, *Dawn's Left Hand, Pilgrimage*, vol. 4 (London: Virago, 1979).

——*Windows on Modernism: Selected Letters of Dorothy Richardson*, ed. Gloria Fromm (Athens, Ga.: University of Georgia Press, 1995).

Richardson, Robert, *Literature and Film* (Bloomington: Indiana University Press, 1969).

Richter, Hans, *The Struggle for the Film*, trans. Ben Brewster (Aldershot, Hampshire: Wildwood Press, 1986).

Paul Ricoeur, *Time and Narrative* (3 vols.) trans. K. McLaughlin and D. Pellauer (Chicago: University of Chicago Press, 1984).

Rieger, Bernhard, *Technology and the Culture of Modernity in Britain and Germany 1890–1945* (Cambridge: Cambridge University Press, 2005).

Robinson, David, *Georges Méliès: Father of Film Fantasy* (London: British Film Industry, 1993).

Robson, E. W., and M. M. Robson, *The Film Answers Back* (London: Bodley Head, 1939).

Rodker, John, *Poems and Adolphe 1920*, ed. and introd. Andrew Crozier (Manchester: Carcanet, 1996).

——'The Theatre', *The Egoist* (2 November 1914), 414–15.

Rogin, Michael, *Blackface, White Noise: Jewish Immigrants in the Hollywood Melting Pot* (Berkeley and Los Angeles: Universiy of California Press, 1996).

Ross, Harris, *Film as Literature, Literature as Film: An Introduction to and Bibliography of Film's Relationship to Literature* (Westport, Conn.: Greenwood Press, 1987).

Rotha, Paul, *Documentary Film* (London: Faber and Faber, 1936).

—— *The Film Till Now: A Survey of the Cinema* (London: Jonathan Cape, 1930).

Rowland, Stanley, 'The Future of the Cinema', *The Quarterly Review* (January 1932), 511.

Ryall, Tom, *Blackmail* (London: British Film Institute, 1993).

Sachs, Hanns, 'Film Psychology', *Close Up* III: 5 (November 1928), 8–15.

—— 'Kitsch', *Close Up* IX: 3 (September 1932), 202,

—— 'The Mission of the Movies', *Life and Letters To-Day* 26 (July 1940), 261–8.

—— *Psycho-Analyse: Rätsel des Unbewussten* (Berlin: Lichtbild Buhner, 1926).

Samson, Jen, 'The Film Society', in Charles Barr (ed.), *All Our Yesterdays: 90 Years of British Cinema* (London: British Film Institute, 1992), 306–313.

Sanders, Emmy Veronica, 'America Invades Europe,' *Broom: An International Magazine of the Arts* 1: 1 (November 1921), 92.

Sargeant, Amy, *British Cinema: A Critical History* (London: British Film Institute, 2005).

Sargent, Epes Winthrop, 'Advertising for Exhibitors—Using the Lecture', *Moving Picture World* (2 July 1912).

Saunders, Max, 'Literary Impressionism', in David Bradshaw and Kevin J. H. Dettmar (eds.), *A Companion to Modernist Literature and Culture* (Oxford: Blackwell, 2006), 204–12.

Schivelbusch Wolfgang, *The Railway Journey: Trains and Travel in the Nineteenth Century*, trans. Anselm Hollo (Oxford: Blackwell, 1980).

Scotland, John, *The Talkies* (London: Crosby Lockwood and Son, 1930).

Seldes, Gilbert, *The 7 Lively Arts* (New York: Sagamore Press, 1957).

—— *An Hour with the Movies and the Talkies* (London: John Lippincott, 1929).

—— *Movies for the Millions: An Account of Motion Pictures, Principally in America* (London: Batsford, 1937).

Seton, Marie, *Sergei M. Eisenstein: A Biography* (London: Bodley Head, 1952).

Sexton, Jamie, 'The Film Society and the Creation of an Alternative Film Culture in Britain in the 1920s', in Andrew Higson (ed.), *Young and Innocent: The Cinema in Britain, 1896–1930* (Exeter: Exeter University Press, 2002), 291–305.

—— 'The Drama, the Theatre, and the Films', *Fortnightly Review* (1 September 1924), 288–302.

—— *Bernard Shaw on Cinema*, ed. Bernard F. Dukore (Carboudale: Southern Illinois University Press, 1997).

Shone, Richard, *The Art of Bloomsbury* (London: Tate Gallery, 1999).

Silverman, Kaja, *The Acoustic Mirror: The Female Voice in Psychoanalysis and Cinema* (Bloomington: Indiana University Press, 1988).

Sinclair, May, 'The Novels of Dorothy Richardson', *Egoist* 5 (April 1918), 57–9, repr. in Bonnie Kime Scott (ed.), *The Gender of Modernism* (Bloomington: Indiana University Press, 1990), 444.

Sitney, P. Adams, *Modernist Montage: The Obscurity of Vision in Cinema and Literature* (New York: Columbia, 1990).

Sklar, Robert, *Movie-Made America: A Cultural History of American Movies* (New York: Vintage, 1994).

Smith, Murray, *Engaging Characters: Fiction, Emotion and the Cinema* (Oxford: Oxford University Press, 1995).

Sobchack, Vivian, *The Address of the Eye: A Phenomenology of Film Experience* (Princeton: Princeton University Press, 1992).

Soupault, Philippe, 'The "U.S.A." Cinema', *Broom* 5: 2 (September 1923), 65–9.

'The American Influence in France' (1930), trans. Babette and Glenn Hughes (Seattle: University of Washington Bookstore, 1930). Repr. in *The Literature of Cinema: Screen Monographs II* (New York: Arno Press, 1970).

Spalding, Francis, *Duncan Grant: A Biography* (London: Pimlico, 1998).

Spender, Stephen, *The Temple* (London: Faber and Faber, 1988).

—— *World within World: The Autobiography of Stephen Spender* (London: Hamish Hamilton, 1951).

Spiegel, Alan, *Fiction and the Camera Eye: Visual Consciousness in Film and the Modern Novel* (Charlottesville: University of Virginia Press, 1976).

Stamp, Shelley, *Movie-Struck Girls: Women and Motion Picture Culture after the Nickolodeon* (Princeton: Princeton University Press, 2000).

Stephen, Karin, *The Misuse of Mind* (London: Kegan Paul, Trench, Trubner, 1922).

Stephen, Leslie, *Sir Leslie Stephen's Mausoleum Book* (Oxford: Clarendon Press, 1977).

Stewart, Garrett, *Between Film and Screen: Modernism's Photosynthesis* (Chicago: Chicago University Press, 1999).

Stonier, G.W., *Gog Magog and Other Critical Essays* (London: J. M. Dent, 1933)

Struve, Gleb, *Russian Literature Under Lenin and Stalin 1917–1953* (Norman: University of Oklahoma Press, 1971).

von Stutterheim, Kurt, *The Press in England* (London: George Allen and Unwin, 1934).

Swann, R. E. C., 'Art and the Cinema: A Chance for the British Producer', *The Nineteenth Century and After* 100 (August 1926), 221–8.

Talbot, Frederick A., *Moving Pictures: How they are Made and Worked* (London: William Heinemann, 1912).

Talbot, Daniel (ed.), *Film: An Anthology* (Berkeley and Los Angeles: University of California Press, 1959).

Tall, Emily, 'Eisenstein on Joyce: Sergei Eisenstein's Lecture on James Joyce at the State Institute of Cinematography, November 1, 1934', *James Joyce Quarterly* 24:2 (1987), 133–42.

Tan, Ed. S., *Emotion and the Structure of Narrative Film: Film as an Emotion Machine*, trans. Barbara Fasting (Mahwah, NJ: Lawrence Erlbaum Associates, 1996).

Taylor, Richard and Ian Christie (eds.), *The Film Factory: Russian and Soviet Cinema in Documents 1896–1939* (London: Routledge, 1988).

Taylor, Georgina, *H.D. and the Sphere of Modernist Women Writers* (Oxford: Oxford University Press, 2001).

Thompson, Kristin, 'Dr. Caligari at the Folies-Bergère', in Mike Budd (ed.), *The Cabinet of Dr. Caligari: Texts, Contexts, Histories* (Brunswick, NJ: Rutgers University Press, 1990).

Trotter, David. 'Virginia Woolf and Cinema', *Film Studies* 6 (Summer 2005), 3–18.

—— *Cinema and Modernism* (Oxford: Blackwell, 2007).

Truffaut, François, *Hitchcock* (London: Paladin, 1978).

Tsivian, Yuri, *Early Cinema in Russia and its Cultural Reception*, trans. Alan Bodger (Chicago and London: University of Chicago Press, 1998).

Turvey, Jerry, 'Ivor Montagu and British Film Culture in the 1920s', in Higson (ed.), *Young and Innocent?*, 313–14.

Valentine, C. W., *An Introduction to the Experimental Psychology of Beauty* (London: T. C. and E. C. Jack, n.d.)

Vidler, Anthony, *Warped Space: Art, Architecture, and Anxiety in Modern Culture* (Cambridge, Mass.: MIT Press, 2000).

Vincent, Carl, *Independence Belge* (5 December 1930), *Borderline* Scrapbook, Beinecke Rare Book and Manuscript Library, Yale University.

Virilio, Paul, *The Aesthetics of Disappearance*, trans. Philip Beitchman (New York: Semiotext[e], 1991).

—— *War and Cinema: The Logistics of Perception*, trans. Patrick Camiller (London: Verso, 1989).

Vygotsky, Lev, *Thought and Language* (1936) (Cambridge, Mass.: MIT Press, 1962).

Walkley, A. J., *Pastiche and Prejudice* (London: Heinemann, 1921)

Wasson, Haidee, *Museum Movies: The Museum of Modern Art and the Birth of Art Cinema* (Berkeley and Los Angeles: University of California Press, 2005).

—— 'Women and the Silent Screen', ed. Amelie Hastie and Shelley Stamp, *Film History: An International Journal* 18: 2, (2006).

—— 'Writing the Cinema into Daily Life: Iris Barry and the Emergence of British Film Criticism', in Higson (ed.), *Young and Innocent?*, 321–37.

Watney, Simon, *The Art of Duncan Grant* (London: John Murray, 1990).

Watts, Carol, *Dorothy Richardson: Writers and their Work* (Plymouth, Devon: Northcote House, 1995).

Waugh, Alec, 'The Film and the Future', *Fortnightly Review* 116 (July–December 1924), 524–31.

Wees, William C., *Vorticism and the English Avant-Garde* (Manchester: Manchester University Press, 1972).

Weis, Elisabeth and John Belton, *Film Sound: Theory and Practice* (New York: Columbia University Press, 1985).

Welch, Jeffrey Egan, *Literature and Film: An Annotated Bibliography, 1909–1977* (New York: Garland Publishing, 1981).

Wells H. G., *Anticipations: Of the Reaction of Mechanical and Scientific Progress Upon Human Life and Thought* (London: Chapman and Hall, 1902).

Wells H. G., 'The Crystal Egg', *The Complete Short Stories of H. G. Wells*, ed. John Hammond (London: J. M. Dent, 1998).

—— *Experiment in Autobiography: Discoveries and Conclusions of a Very Ordinary Brain since 1866*, 2 vols. (London: Gollancz, 1934).

—— *The Invisible Man* (1897) (London: Everyman, 1995).

—— *The King who was a King: The Book of a Film* (London: Benn, 1929).

—— 'The New Accelerator' (1901), *The Complete Short Stories of H. G. Wells*, ed. John Hammond (London: J. M. Dent, 1998).

—— Review of Joyce's *Portrait of the Artist as a Young Man*, *The New Republic* (10 March 1917).

—— 'The Silliest Film: Will Machinery Make Robots of Men?', in *The Way the World is Going* (London: Ernest Benn, 1928), 179–89.

—— *Things to Come* (London: The Cresset Press, 1935).

—— *The Time Machine* (1895) (London: Everyman, 1995).

—— *When the Sleeper Wakes* (1899) (London: Phoenix, 2004).

White, Eric Walter, *Parnassus to Let: An Essay about Rhythm in the Films* (London: Hogarth Press, 1928).

—— *Walking Shadows* (London: Hogarth Press, 1931)

White, Evelyne, *Winifred Holtby: As I Knew Her* (London: Collins, 1938).

Willeman, Paul, *Looks and Frictions: Essays in Cultural Studies and Film Theory* (London: British Film Institute, 1994).

Williams, Keith, *British Writers and the Media 1930–45* (Basingstoke, Macmillan, 1996).

—— 'Symphonies of the Big City: Modernism, Cinema and Urban Modernity', in Paul Edwards (ed.), *The Great London Vortex: Modernist Literature and Art* (Bath: Sulis Press, 2003), 31–50.

—— 'Ulysses in Toontown: "vision animated to bursting point" in Joyce's "Circe"', in Julian Murphet and Lydia Rainford (eds.), *Literature and Visual Technologies: Writing after Cinema* (Basingstoke: Palgrave Macmillan, 2003).

Williams, Linda R., *Sex in the Head: Visions of Femininity and Film in D. H. Lawrence* (Hemel Hempstead: Harvester Wheatsheaf, 1993).

Raymond Williams, *The Country and the City* (1973) (London: The Hogarth Press, 1993).

—— *The Politics of Modernism: Against the New Conformists*, ed. Tony Pinkney (London: Verso, 1989).

Wolfe, Glenn Joseph, *Vachel Lindsay: The Poet as Film Theorist* (New York: Arno Press, 1973).

Wollen, Peter, Alan Lowell, and Sam Rohdie, 'Interview with Ivor Montagu', *Screen* 13:3 (Autumn 1972), 71–113.

—— 'Modern Times: Cinema/Americanism/The Robot'), in *Raiding the Icebox: Reflections on Twentieth-Century Culture* (Bloomington and Indianapolis: Indiana University Press, 1993), 35–71.

—— 'The Two Avant-Gardes', in *Readings and Writings: Semiotic Counter-Strategies* (London: Verso, 1982), 92–104.

Wood, Michael, 'Modernism and Film', in *The Cambridge Companion to Modernism*, ed. Michael Levenson (Cambridge: Cambridge University Press, 1999), 218–19.

Wood, Gaby, *Living Dolls: A Magical History of the Quest for Mechanical Life* (London: Faber and Faber, 2002).

Woolf, Virginia, ' "Anon" and "The Reader": Virginia Woolf's Last Essays', ed. Brenda R. Silver, *Twentieth-Century Literature* 25 (1979).

Woolf, Leonard, *Beginning Again*, vol. 2: *1911–1916* (Oxford: Oxford University Press, 1980).

—— 'The Leaning Tower', *Collected Essays*, vol. 2 (London: The Hogarth Press, 1966).

—— *Moments of Being* (London: Pimlico, 2002).

—— *Mrs Dalloway* (1925) (Harmondsworth, Penguin, 1964).

—— *Orlando* (1928; Harmondsworth: Penguin, 1993).

—— *To the Lighthouse* (1927; Harmondsworth: Penguin, 1992).

—— 'Walter Sickert: A Conversation' (London: Bloomsbury Workshop, 1992).

—— *The Waves* (Harmondsworth: Penguin, 1992).

—— *The Years* (Harmondsworth: Penguin, 1968).

Yale French Studies, special issue on film sound, vol. 60 (1980), 269–86.

Index